The Battle for Moscow

In November 1941 Hitler ordered German forces to complete the final drive on the Soviet capital, then less than 100 km away. Army Group Centre was pressed into the attack for one last attempt to break Soviet resistance before the onset of winter. From the German perspective, the final drive on Moscow had all the ingredients of a dramatic final battle in the east, which, according to previous accounts, only failed at the gates of Moscow. David Stahel now challenges this well-established narrative by demonstrating that the last German offensive of 1941 was a forlorn effort, undermined by operational weakness, poor logistics, and driven forward by what he identifies as National Socialist military thinking. With unparalleled research from previously undocumented army files and soldiers' letters, Stahel takes a fresh look at the battle for Moscow, which, even before the Soviet winter offensive, threatened disaster for Germany's war in the east.

David Stahel is a lecturer at the University of New South Wales in Canberra. His previous publications include *Operation Barbarossa and Germany's Defeat in the East* (2009), *Kiev 1941* (2011), *Nazi Policy on the Eastern Front, 1941* (2012) and *Operation Typhoon* (2013).

The Battle for Moscow

David Stahel

CAMBRIDGE
UNIVERSITY PRESS

University Printing House, Cambridge CB2 8BS, United Kingdom

One Liberty Plaza, 20th Floor, New York, NY 10006, USA

477 Williamstown Road, Port Melbourne, VIC 3207, Australia

314-321, 3rd Floor, Plot 3, Splendor Forum, Jasola District Centre, New Delhi - 110025, India

79 Anson Road, #06-04/06, Singapore 079906

Cambridge University Press is part of the University of Cambridge.

It furthers the University's mission by disseminating knowledge in the pursuit of education, learning and research at the highest international levels of excellence.

www.cambridge.org
Information on this title: www.cambridge.org/9781107457454

First published 2015
Reprinted 2015
Paperback edition first published 2017

A catalogue record for this publication is available from the British Library

Library of Congress Cataloging in Publication data
Stahel, David, 1975–
The Battle for Moscow / David Stahel.
pages cm
ISBN 978-1-107-08760-6
1. Moscow, Battle of, Moscow, Russia, 1941–1942. I. Title.
D764.3.M6S819 2014
940.54´21731–dc23

2014023806

ISBN 978-1-107-08760-6 Hardback
ISBN 978-1-107-45745-4 Paperback

CONTENTS

ILLUSTRATIONS

MAPS

TABLE

ACKNOWLEDGEMENTS

In *Foucault's Pendulum* Umberto Eco wrote: 'I believe that what we become depends on what our fathers teach us at odd moments, when they aren't trying to teach us. We are formed by little scraps of wisdom.' The day I was born I had an infant older brother and a mother who had been diagnosed with multiple sclerosis during her pregnancy with me. In the months leading to my birth my mother had lost the use of her legs and eyes. Two years before my father had been a single young man with next to no responsibility and then, in 1975, he found himself with two infant sons and a severely disabled wife. Of course, growing up I hardly gave any of this much thought. My father just had a lot to do to take care of us all – and he never wavered in that commitment. Recalling those days and recounting the moments from which I might have gleaned little scraps of wisdom would probably fill a book in itself, but, since I am an historian and not a memoirist, this book will have to do. Happy dedication dad.

In the first instance, I wish to extend my gratitude to my long-standing mentor, colleague and friend, Eleanor Hancock. As with my past work, her support and ideas have left their mark on this study. I also owe a debt of thanks to the history department at UNSW Canberra, in particular Jeffrey Grey, who ensured that I had the time needed to complete this project. In Germany, Alex Kay has filled a number of holes in my source material as well as providing his usual insightfulness into all matters of Nazi German history. Likewise, assistance from a host of historians must be acknowledged, including David Glantz, Dennis

Showalter, Robert Citino, Jacob Kipp, Jack Radey, Charles Sharp, Mark Edele and Jeff Rutherford. Thanks also to Chrisie Rotter for her artwork and Jakob Graichen for proofing some of my more complex translations. Last, but not least, thanks to my editor Michael Watson and all the staff at Cambridge University Press for their consistently professional support.

GLOSSARY

BA-MA	Bundesarchiv-Militärarchiv (German Military Archive)
Das Reich	2nd SS Division
Einsatzgruppen	'action groups' of the SD and Security Police, used mainly for mass killings
Endsieg	final victory
Erhaltungsegedanken	conservation of strength and preparation for winter
Grossdeutschland	'Greater Germany' Infantry Regiment (later division)
Grosstransportraum	'large transport area'. Referring to the transport regiment responsible for bridging the gap between front-line divisions and railheads
KTB	Kriegstagebuch (war diary)
Landser	German infantry man
Lebensraum	living space
Leibstandarte Adolf Hitler	SS Regiment (later division)
Luftwaffe	German Air Force
OKH	*Oberkommando des Heeres* (High Command of the Army)
OKW	*Oberkommando der Wehrmacht* (High Command of the Armed Forces)
Ostheer	Eastern Army
Pz. Div.	Panzer Division

rasputitsa	'quagmire season'; refers to the biannual difficulties caused by heavy rains or melting snow in Russia, Belarus and Ukraine
Reichsbahn	German railways
SD	*Sicherheitsdienst* (Security Service)
Sondermeldungen	special news bulletins
SS	*Schutzstaffel* (Protection Echelon)
Stavka	Soviet High Command
Vernichtungskrieg	War of annihilation
Wehrmacht	German Armed Forces
Wirkungsgedanken	exploitation of all resources to achieve maximum effect

TABLES OF MILITARY RANKS AND ARMY STRUCTURES

Table of equivalent ranks

German army/ Luftwaffe	Translation used in this study	Equivalent US army rank
Officer ranks		
Generalfeldmarschall	Field Marshal	General of the Army
Generaloberst	Colonel-General	General
General	General	Lieutenant General
der Infanterie	of Infantry	
der Artillerie	of Artillery	
der Flakartillerie	of Flak Artillery	
der Flieger	of Aviation	
der Kavallerie	of Cavalry	
der Luftwaffe	of the Luftwaffe	
der Panzertruppe	of Panzer Troops	
der Pioniere	of Engineers	
Generalleutnant	Lieutenant-General	Major General
Generalmajor	Major-General	Brigadier General
Oberst	Colonel	Colonel
Oberstleutnant	Lieutenant-Colonel	Lieutenant Colonel
Major	Major	Major
Hauptmann	Captain	Captain
Oberleutnant	1st Lieutenant	1st Lieutenant
Leutnant	Lieutenant	2nd Lieutenant
Enlisted ranks		
Stabsfeldwebel	Master Sergeant	Master Sergeant
Oberfeldwebel	Technical Sergeant	Technical Sergeant

(cont.)

German army/ Luftwaffe	Translation used in this study	Equivalent US army rank
Feldwebel	Staff Sergeant	Staff Sergeant
Unterfeldwebel	Sergeant	Sergeant
Unteroffizier	Corporal	Corporal
Gefreiter	Private	Private 1st Class
Soldat	Private	Private 2nd Class

Source: Karl-Heinz Frieser, *The Blitzkrieg Legend. The 1940 Campaign in the West* (Annapolis, 2005) p. 355.

Structure and size of the German army

Germany army formation	English translation	Number of subordinate units	Average number of personnel[a]
Heeresgruppe	Army Group	Two or more armies	100,000 to more than a million
Armee	Army	Two or more corps	60,000–250,000
Korps	Corps	Two or more divisions	40,000–70,000
Division	Division	Two or more brigades	12,000–18,000
Brigade	Brigade	Two or more regiments	5,000–7,000
Regiment	Regiment	Two or more battalions	2,000–6,000
Bataillon	Battalion	Two or more companies	500–1,000
Kompanie	Company	Two or more platoons	100–200
Zug	Platoon		30–40

Note: [a] Wide variations of these figures occurred, especially after 1941.
Source: Author's own records.

INTRODUCTION

The battle of Moscow involved 2.5 million men on both sides of the eastern front, making it one of the largest and, without question, one of the most important battles of the Second World War. According to Andrew Roberts, Hitler's offensive towards the Soviet capital was nothing less than decisive: 'It is no exaggeration to state that the outcome of the Second World War hung in the balance during this massive attack'.[1] For both sides, the battle for Moscow was an epic of endurance and sacrifice, while its sheer magnitude concentrated the world's attention as never before.

There can be no debate that Nazi Germany's drive on Moscow was a human calamity with few precedents in history. The battle began at the start of October 1941 with Operation Typhoon and, with a two-week pause at the start of November, continued to the very gates of Moscow by early December 1941. As one German soldier wrote: 'Burning villages, the bodies of dead Russian soldiers, the carcasses of dead horses, burned-out tanks, and abandoned equipment were the signposts of our march.'[2] Magnifying this level of destruction across a front nearly 700 km wide, Army Group Centre, the German force charged with seizing the Soviet capital, left a torrent of devastation through central Russia.

The offensive towards Moscow was only the latest in an unbroken series of battles that Army Group Centre had fought since June 1941. The trail of destruction began with a two-week battle at Minsk, followed by a two-month battle at Smolensk, and then a month of fighting down into Ukraine for the battle of Kiev. Even before the battle of Moscow, the number of dead, wounded and missing in the Nazi–Soviet war counted in the millions. It was warfare on a colossal scale, which was not lost on the participants of the time. Kurt Vogeler wrote home in December 1941 shortly before his own death:

> The world has seen many great, even grand wars. But there has probably never been a war in its history, which can measure up to the present in Eastern Europe. This is true both of its size, which stretches for many hundreds of kilometers of active front, the vast spaces that host battles with million-man armies of opposing nations, but also by the method and manner of the fighting itself.[3]

Truly comprehending warfare on this scale is especially difficult. Reviewing the wartime records of armies, corps and divisions, checking supply timetables and production graphs, reading the accounts of the leading generals all goes a long way towards capturing the overall picture of events, but it only paints, in the broadest of brush strokes, how the war was actually experienced by the men who fought it. Even first-hand accounts only tell us the stories of those who survived and had the opportunity to publish their experiences or otherwise commit them to a public record. There is no doubt there are some very valuable soldiers' memoirs (notwithstanding the problems post-war accounts present), as well as some outstanding publications of letters and diaries, but these are still relatively few in number given the millions of men that took part.

Visiting the battlefields on the approaches to Moscow one can hardly avoid the imposing number of Soviet memorials. These testify to the fact that however much we may have learned about this chapter of history there is far more that must be left unrecorded, which died with its participants. In that sense it is even more important not to lose sight of the human dimension of this battle, because it is apparent just how much has already been lost. Yet the old Soviet battlefields serve as much more than just sites for passive reflection about the past. These battlefields are very much active sites for historical inquiry, as well as dangerous work-sites for the discovery, identification and reburial of countless lost soldiers still listed as 'missing in action'.

In September 2012, I visited some of these battlefields together with government-approved 'searchers', Russian volunteers who work every summer looking for artefacts, clearing away ordinance and seeking to lay to rest as many remaining war dead as possible. At first glance, the vast tracts of undisturbed forest appear like any other in northern Europe; only the odd mangled and rusted vehicle, often obscured by undergrowth and trees, are traces of the events that once took place here. For the most part, the forest appears like any other; its historical importance is deceptively inconspicuous. Yet once the metal detectors were turned on a vast battlefield was revealed to lie just below the surface of the forest floor. Literally every few steps yield new discoveries. Most of these objects are harmless – parts of weapons, gas masks, helmets, bayonets or shell fragments – but not infrequently unexploded grenades and other ordinance are dug up, making it easy to see why searchers die every year in Russia. Indeed, the fact that Hitler's war in the east is still today claiming Russian victims is one reason why the Nazi–Soviet war remains so very much a part of the contemporary Russian national identity.

For my part, the piles of artefacts coming out of the ground were a stark reminder of the scale of this battle, but it was all still somewhat detached from its human dimension. Only the occasional personal effect from an unknown man gave any sense of the human tragedy that the site also represented. The searchers told me that very few bodies are recovered, on average their team discovers just one or two each summer and even then it is extremely unlikely that the soldier will ever be formally identified. Soviet soldiers in 1941 did not carry 'dog tags',[4] but rather capsules in which their personal details were recorded on a small piece of rolled paper. Yet the seepage of moisture often ensured that the identity of the owner could never be determined even if the capsule was recovered. Another common problem was a wartime superstition among Soviet soldiers that stipulated a man would not be killed if he had not filled out the identification paper, meaning that countless capsules are recovered with blank papers or none at all.

After many hours in the forest we were preparing to leave with a load of artefacts destined for the local museum in Vaz'ma. We had already started the long walk back to our 4WDs when word came that a body had been found and was carefully being dug out of the ground, one bone at a time. We arrived to find the soldier's leg arranged on a dirty blanket next to his wartime grave. Over the next hour the rest of the skeleton, along with gas mask and personal effects were removed from the ground. His lower jaw still had its full set of teeth. The work proceeded in a heavy silence; a mixture of quiet disbelief and unspoken reverence at what we were all witnessing. Eventually, even his capsule

Figure I.1 The excavated equipment from Sergei's gravesite in a forest near Vaz'ma (September 2012)

was recovered, and that night in a controlled room (to protect whatever remained of its contents) the capsule was opened for the first time since 1941. There was a paper, it was still intact and the name legible. Without the family's permission I shall not record the full details here, other than to say the man's first name was Sergei. His younger sister was still alive, and within days was informed that her brother's body had been found seventy-one years after he went missing. A month later, Sergei was reburied with his family present and full military honours.[5] His fate reminds us that behind the faceless enormity of the battle for Moscow there are countless family tragedies as well as innumerable untold stories.

Indeed, the battle of Moscow itself, while hardly an untold story, often lacks an appropriate strategic context. The picture commonly portrayed centres overwhelmingly on the proximity of German forces to Moscow, and the close-run race between German offensive strength and Soviet defensive power. The fact that German forces reached the outermost parts of the city is often accepted as evidence for just how close the city came to capture. Indeed, many in the postwar generation remained firmly convinced that if only Army Group Centre could have pressed on a few more kilometres and seized Moscow, Germany's 1941 campaign in the east would have been capped by a resounding success. At the same time, failure at Moscow granted the Red Army its first real victory of the war, allowing a glimmer of hope for the Soviet people and shattering the German army's myth of invincibility. In these accounts the battle for Moscow assumes tremendous importance as an all or nothing, knife-edge encounter worthy of all the drama and suspense histories have hitherto attributed to it. Edgar Snow, a well-known American author and journalist of the period, helped to establish the myth of a close-run battle when he wrote that Moscow's defenders 'went to certain death, but the few hours they held the panzers back enabled the Siberian troops to reach the city and win the critical battle'.[6] Such a thrilling account flowed seamlessly into the postwar narratives as one of Nazi Germany's great 'lost opportunities' of the Second World War.[7]

More contemporary accounts have not always disagreed. In his first-rate history of Hitler's and Stalin's dictatorships, the eminent Second World War scholar Richard Overy presents the Soviet line at Moscow as being 'held by the finest of margins'.[8] Indeed, it is only with the launch of the Soviet winter offensive on 5 December that Overy sees the character of the war changing and a shift away from Blitzkrieg 'finally creating the conditions for a long war of attrition and averting a rapid German victory'.[9] I have previously argued that this shift occurred much earlier in the Nazi–Soviet war and that a campaign running into the autumn of 1941 had long since precluded a rapid German victory, yet it is how we understand the battle of Moscow that most concerns this study. Part of the problem is that Overy's characterisation of events, as with other contemporary acounts, is not incorrect – there was indeed a bitter struggle, desperately fought on the roads leading to Moscow. Yet that is only one aspect of the battle.

The strategic context in which the battle of Moscow was fought casts the events at the front in a different light, and shows the Soviet Union far from defeat in November and December 1941. Indeed, Moscow's fall was never seriously in question. It was Army Group Centre that was tempting fate by continuing with an offensive that had already ground itself to a halt at the end of October, and was now expending the last of its desperately short reserves of men and supplies just to reach the Soviet capital (to say nothing of conquering the city). The weather and conditions precluded a repeat of the rapid warfare that had typified Army Group Centre's earlier successes and, consequently, the November fighting took the form of frontal assaults with the panzer forces acting largely as battering rams. One German officer explained the transformation of operations in 1941: 'We gradually lost the ability to manoeuvre. War became one of linear movement. We did not bother about creating a "*Schwerpunkt*" [a concentration of forces]. We were no longer instructed to surprise, outflank and annihilate the enemy. We were told: "You will hold the front from such a point to such and such a point, you will advance to such a line".'[10] The success of these German operations may have brought them to the very outskirts of the Soviet capital, but only at the cost of seriously depleting, and utterly exhausting, their forces. What is more, the German offensive never came close to encircling Moscow (as German plans stipulated), nor did they have the strength to launch even a single assault against the city (which Hitler had in any case prohibited).[11]

Determining the course of the battle is as much about understanding German weakness as it is about appreciating Soviet strength. An essential element of the battle for Moscow was the careful build-up of Soviet reserves throughout the November fighting. No less than five Soviet reserve armies were withheld from the Moscow front as the Germans fought their way towards the city and Marshal Georgi Zhukov, commanding the Soviet Western Front, emphatically told Stalin in mid-November: 'We will, without fail, hold Moscow.'[12] Zhukov's confidence was not mere bravado. There was a conscious Soviet decision to absorb the German offensive, committing as few of their reserves to this task as possible before assuming a more offensive posture. Had the German offensive enjoyed greater success more Soviet reserves would simply have been released earlier. Zhukov's reports during the latter half of November informed Stalin that Army Group Centre was being 'bled white' and had no further reserves to call upon. The German attack maintained its slow grinding progress through sheer grit and strength of will. Soviet forces at the front were equally exhausted, but also equally determined. The difference was the *Stavka*'s (Soviet High Command) careful husbanding of reserves for a counteroffensive, which Zhukov noted, 'had been prepared all through the defensive actions'.[13] Thus, one must be careful not to equate German proximity to Moscow in November and December 1941 as some kind of harbinger of victory. Even without the presence of Soviet reserves, the likelihood that German forces could have forcibly seized the heavily fortified Soviet capital in costly urban combat must be considered remote. Thus, Zhukov's offensive on 5 December did not somehow snatch victory from the very jaws of defeat. The reality of the battle for Moscow is less sensational, but no less important. The strategic circumstances governing the course of the battle did not suddenly change from one day to the next, Army Group Centre was in grave difficulties even before the new Soviet offensive was launched and its progress was never favourable. Indeed, for a range of reasons that this study will explore (logistics, reserves, weather, mobility, equipment, communications and infrastructure) Army Group Centre's November plans were wildly optimistic.

While the fall of Moscow was never a realistic possibility in November 1941, accounting for this requires much more than just an understanding of material factors. As my past studies of German campaigns in 1941 have shown, the German *Ostheer* (Eastern Army) had been seriously eroded in strength, but its men were also suffering from the mental fatigue of constant campaigning. Doubts about ending the war in the east were openly being discussed in the autumn months, and fears for the coming winter only added to the trepidation. Yet the same concerns also convinced many soldiers of the absolute necessity of the task at hand. A final assault on Moscow could, many hoped, decide the war in Germany's favour, as well as provide winter quarters for the men and perhaps even allow some to return home for Christmas. The hope this engendered and the resolution with which it fired German resolve should not be underestimated. For those same reasons the implications of Army Group Centre's ultimate failure at Moscow were all the more destructive.

For all the fortitude that the men of Army Group Centre could muster in November 1941 this was paralleled or even surpassed by Soviet determination. The brutal German occupation practices as well as the Wehrmacht's murderous treatment of Red Army captives were well publicised by the Soviet information bureau, uniting soldiers and civilians, often to the bitter end, in their cause to defend Moscow. Cyrus Sulzberger, an American journalist based in Moscow at the start of the German offensive, recalled of the Soviet population:

> Moscow didn't present the aspect of a sorely threatened city whose outer limits were not too far from the raging battlefront. Its population gave the impression of going about its work with unusual seriousness, called on to perform special tasks necessitating extraordinary effort and attention. The prevailing calm reflected something fundamental in Muscovite temperament, perhaps based on the old Russian proverb: 'The maggot gnaws the cabbage but it dies before it's done.' There seems increasing confidence that the old cabbage would surfeit yet another maggot.[14]

While postwar Soviet accounts of the November period cited the people's courage and enthusiasm as well as the superior strategic planning of the *Stavka*, early western accounts tended to dismiss such explanations as communist propaganda. Of course, there were exaggerations in the writing of these Soviet histories, which certainly enhanced their propaganda value, but much of it had at least a basis in truth. Cold War suspicions, however, allowed little room for objective assessment of these claims and instead there was a much less critical embrace of German generals' memoirs, which uniformly dismissed Soviet explanations. Instead, the German failure before Moscow took on an entirely new explanation, one which would expunge the German army of any blame. As with so many events, the German generals found it convenient to blame Hitler, citing his diversion of Army Group Centre into Ukraine in August/September 1941. Through this decision, they argued, vital time was lost for the all-important drive on Moscow, leading to what they also characterised as a narrow failure.[15] The chief-of-staff of the Fourth Army, Major-General Günther Blumentritt, wrote after the war that the failure to take Moscow was a key turning point of the war in the east; 'our hopes of knocking Russia out of the war in 1941 had been dashed, at the very last minute. It was essential now that Germany's political leaders should realize that the days of the Blitzkrieg were over.'[16] In fact, as this study will reflect, it was the military commanders themselves that needed convincing. What is more, there was ample evidence available at the time (and presented to Halder at the Orsha conference) that the wide-ranging offensives and crushing, one-sided battles were no longer to be expected. Yet the tendency of later histories to represent the battle of Moscow as a near-run contest gave an air of plausibility to the accounts of the generals, which also served to play down their own culpability for the failure of the operations around Moscow. Indeed, the most conspicuous absence from the generals' memoirs in this period is any personal responsibility for the critical decisions of November and early December 1941, in which the failure before Moscow saw the generals playing the leading role with only Hitler's tacit approval.

This study will revisit Army Group Centre's battle for Moscow in November and early December 1941, providing a fresh perspective on the landmark events that ended Hitler's five-and-half-month series of rolling offensives in the east. The aim will be to provide a detailed account of Army Group Centre's inner workings – its command structure, its decisions, its resources, its men and its strategic environment. This book may be seen as a continuation of my larger body of work on Germany in the east in 1941[17] or a stand-alone study detailing Germany's fortunes in the pivotal weeks of the battle for Moscow. As with my past studies, the best method of assessing Germany's offensive strength is through its panzer divisions, corps, groups and armies. Archival evidence at all these levels has been consulted, but the study also makes significant use of first-person accounts in the form of soldier's letters, war diaries and memoirs. The book will proceed chronologically beginning from Chapter 2. The first chapter, as in my past studies, will seek to further contextualise Hitler's war in the east through the exploration of thematic topics that impacted on the development of the military campaign. In this study, Chapter 1 will examine Hitler's war of annihilation (*Vernichtungskrieg*), which ultimately proved even more deadly than the conventional fighting,[18] and already by 1941 had seen the murder of hundreds of thousands of innocent civilians, both Jews and non-Jews. Assessing this vital aspect of the war is important both intrinsically and for the fact that it informed the manner in which the Wehrmacht conceived of its enemy in the east. It also formed the principal frame of reference for how the people of the Soviet Union were to understand the war that was being waged against them. Beyond the war of annihilation, I have also assessed the parallels and differences between Germany's eastern front in 1914 and 1941. This discussion further highlights German conceptions – and misconceptions – about warfare in the east in 1941, particularly the hubris associated with military planning. Yet a comparison of the two wars also reflects just how much they differed and thereby the unique undertaking that Hitler's commitment in Operation Barbarossa represented.

On 29 November, Joseph Goebbels, Hitler's propaganda minister, reflected back on the preceding months of Germany's offensive in the east and wrote in his diary: 'There are good days and bad ... From such a heavy fight one does not emerge without scars. It does not matter who comes out of such a fight with a black eye or bloody nose, it matters who is still standing firm in the ring; and that without doubt will be us.'[19] Clearly, even before Zhukov's famous winter counteroffensive the Red Army had dealt the Wehrmacht a few hard blows, which even Goebbels could not ignore. By comparison, Lieutenant-General Vassily Sokolovsky described to foreign journalists in Moscow that the Wehrmacht had sustained far more than a black eye or bloody nose. 'The Blitzkrieg, in its essentials, has been transformed into blitz-destruction of German men and materials. This began at [the battle of] Smolensk. The Blitzkrieg has developed into a continuous grinding of the German war machine. The process resembles [the battle of] Verdun, but in terms of ten or one hundred times the destruction'.[20] While Goebbels routinely understated the extent of the Wehrmacht's problems in the east, there can be no doubt that Soviet wartime propaganda also overstated them. This study will attempt to identify a middle road, charting the battle for Moscow from a strategic perspective, but hopefully without losing sight of the countless men like Sergei who died before it was over.

1 PARALLEL WARS

Degrees of separation: the eastern front, 1914 and 1941

While Germany's eastern front in the Second World War is known for its enormous scale and unprecedented bloodletting, it is also significant that the conflict was prefaced only a generation before by another war, which accounted for millions more German, Austrian and Russian casualties. Indeed, no two countries have killed more of their opposing citizens than Germany and Russia. On the eastern front in the First World War, the combined number of German and Russian dead and missing (excluding all other nationalities) amounted to some 2.75 million men (750,000 Germans and 2 million Russians).[1] In spite of this imposing figure, in December 1940 Hitler set Germany on course to attack the Soviet Union, but not out of fear of the power of his rival in the east; it was precisely because he believed it could be carried through easily in one swift campaign.[2] Hitler's eye was on the plentiful mineral and oil riches, the vast fields of fertile earth and the abundant access to human labour, which could free him forever from Britain's continental blockade and provide the building blocks to a new autarkic German economy destined for world power status. Hitler had long prophesied the acquisition of *Lebensraum* (living space) in the east, and it was the short-lived German victory over Russia in the First World War that provided the precedent. In 1918, the newly created Soviet Union ceded 1.4 million km^2 of land, including the Baltic states, parts of Belorussia and Ukraine, to Germany in the Treaty of Brest-Litovsk.[3] Yet, while Hitler and his generals were inclined to focus on the ultimate defeat of the Russians in the First World War, they ignored the fact that Russia had fought tenaciously for over three years against Germany and its allies, the Austro-Hungarian and Ottoman empires. Indeed, the German High Command of 1940–1 was influenced by a so-called 'Tannenberg myth', which contrasted a natural German military superiority with barbaric Russian hordes.[4] This not only reflected racial and cultural prejudices that impacted upon German behaviour in the east, but also pervaded their military plans and led to baseless assumptions that the war could be won in the initial border battles.[5] Indeed, the German victory at Tannenberg in August 1914 cast a long and imposing shadow, becoming the single most decisive, and accordingly best known, German battlefield victory of the First World War.[6] For Hitler and his generals the power of the 'Tannenberg myth' was reinforced by the fact that a single German army (the Eighth Army under Colonel-General Paul von Hindenburg)[7] managed to defeat superior Russian forces, while at the following battle of the Masurian Lakes it also turned back the Russian invasion of East Prussia.[8] Tannenberg was also unique for the manner in which it was won. Foreshadowing German successes with more mobile forms of warfare from 1939 to 1941, the German Eighth Army achieved a rare encirclement, destroying the Russian Second Army and capturing some 92,000 Russian prisoners of war with a further 50,000 killed and wounded.[9] For an outnumbered German army fighting initially on the defensive the result was easily exploited for propaganda purposes.[10]

Such perceptions flowed directly into the German planning for Operation Barbarossa in 1941. The Russian invasion of East Prussia in 1914 reflected the danger of a large-scale invasion from the east, which nearly doomed Germany in the earliest phase of the war as the bulk of the army was deployed in the west to carry out the invasion of Belgium and France (the Schlieffen Plan). The idea of an aggressive enemy in the east was immediately seized upon by Hitler to justify his invasion on 22 June 1941. He erroneously played on the notion of a belligerent Soviet Union and stated that in the weeks preceding the German attack, 'a renewed reinforcement of the Russian troop concentration along the eastern border of Germany took place. Armoured units and parachute troops were moved in increasing numbers alarmingly close to the German border.'[11] At the same time, Hitler suggested that German intentions in the east had been entirely peaceful:

> The German Wehrmacht and the German homeland know that, only a few weeks ago, not a single German panzer or motorized division was on our eastern border ... The victory of the Axis powers in the Balkans alone prevented the plan to engage Germany in the battle in the southeast for months on end this summer, while, in the meantime, the concentration of Soviet armies would be completed, their readiness for battle reinforced, and then, together with England and supported by the expected American deliveries, Russia would suffocate and crush the German Reich and Italy.[12]

This was the Nazi myth of Operation Barbarossa as a preventative war, which played on the notion of a treacherous and hostile adversary in the east.[13] It also gave rise to frightful stories, exploited by Nazi propaganda, of Russian war crimes during their brief occupation of East Prussian lands in 1914.[14] Hoth, the commander of Panzer Group 3 in Army Group Centre's invasion of the Soviet Union, described the 'bestial cruelty' of the Russians in this period, while the commander of the XXXXIII Army Corps in Operation Barbarossa, General of Infantry Gotthard Heinrici, wrote that the Russians had perpetrated acts of 'blind destruction and mindless annihilation of a kind we would never have thought possible'.[15] It all acted to depict Hitler's attack as a defensive action, a pre-emptive war to save Germany and Europe from communist domination and untold cruelties.[16] However, this view of the Russians as both antagonistic towards Germany and remorseless in their behaviour was only one half of the Nazi *Feindbild*, or enemy image.

While 1914 supported the view that Russia posed a credible threat to Germany, it also provided a contrasting view of military weakness.[17] Tannenberg may have been the best known battle of the eastern campaign in the First World War, but it was also one of the least representative, assuming a disproportionate weight in the popular imagination. This, and the ultimate defeat of Russia in 1917, created a perception that Russia was militarily weak. The later Soviet setbacks in the Spanish Civil War and the Winter War against Finland further diminished the Red Army's image, allowing the Soviet Union to be cast in the opposing roles of an aggressive colossus looking to expand, while at the same time being portrayed as a weak state reliant more on the size of its armed forces than any military proficiency. By all accounts in 1941, against Hitler's Wehrmacht, Stalin's state would be unable to resist a German attack.[18] Vejas Liulevicius suggested that the experience of

German warfare and occupation in the east during the First World War accounted for many of the later perceptions and policies the Nazis adopted in the Second World War.[19] Even Germany's so-called *Ostforscher* (academic 'experts' on the east) were profoundly influenced by entrenched anti-Slavic and anti-Bolshevik beliefs and stereotypes.[20] With such plentiful historical and intellectual 'proof' for Nazi conceptions of the east, the parallel notions of attacking both a weak Soviet state and a threatening communist enemy provided convincing arguments for the pursuit of Hitler's *Lebensraum*.[21]

With German conviction in the veracity of their *Feindbild* little attention was paid to the reliability of its underlying assumptions. Some of the most senior German commanders in Operation Barbarossa had served for various periods on the eastern front in the First World War (Colonel-Generals Franz Halder and Ewald von Kleist, Field Marshals Erich von Manstein and Albrecht Kesselring), and they displayed a dismissive first-hand knowledge of the enemy. Field Marshal, Rundstedt, the commander of Army Group South, served on the eastern front from 1915 to 1918, but ascribed little combat value to the enemy in the east.[22] Bidding a final farewell to his counterpart from Army Group North, Field Marshal Wilhelm Ritter von Leeb, Rundstedt remarked in May 1941: 'Well then, see you again in Siberia.'[23] Such confidence was no doubt part of the Wehrmacht's resolute determination to carry out orders and meet whatever objectives it was set, but it was also a result of what German officers did not know about their enemy as opposed to what they did. Tannenberg may have instilled a confidence in the superiority of the German soldier over and above that of the Russian, but the campaigns in the east in 1914 were not simply defined by that one single battle. In 1914, as in 1941, a battle was not an end in itself and the failed Russian offensive in East Prussia was hardly the measure by which the tsar's armies should have been evaluated. As Holger Herwig concluded, 'The battles of Tannenberg and the Masurian Lakes, while freeing East Prussia of Russian forces and soothing the nervous national psyche, were peripheral to the outcome of the war.'[24]

While two Russian armies invaded East Prussia in August 1914, the majority of Russian forces upon mobilisation were directed towards the enormous front running from the border of neutral Romania to Cracow in Austrian Poland. Here four Russian armies (Third, Fourth, Fifth and Eighth) faced Germany's ally the Austro-Hungarian Empire, which deployed its strength to meet the Russian army as well as Serbia in the south. The Russian–Austrian frontier was to be the main theatre for most of the fighting in the east in 1914. The August/September battles in Galicia were confused and bloody affairs, but ultimately the Russian armies, after initial setbacks, gained the upper hand and advanced over 200 km into Austro-Hungarian territory. Losses for the Austro-Hungarian army numbered some 400,000 men, almost three times the Russian losses at Tannenberg.[25] Yet the German victory in East Prussia came to form the dominant picture of war against Russia for Germany. Nor was it accurate or fair to explain Russian successes in Galicia as caused by Austro-Hungarian weaknesses.[26] Although many Germans subscribed to this view at the time, the Austrians had in fact committed many of their best formations to the Galician campaign, while the mass of the army was at this point still riding high on patriotic fervour and was not yet gripped by internal ethnic divisions or war weariness.[27] What is more, the Russians at Tannenberg and in the early setbacks in Galicia reflected a remarkable ability to bounce back from their defeats, as would also be seen in 1941.

Believing in the infallibility of the German Wehrmacht and buttressed by the scornful assessment such notions as the Tannenberg myth and Nazi racial ideology provided, Hitler's *Ostheer* surged across the German–Soviet border in June 1941 intent on fighting a short, victorious campaign. It was anticipated that the initial border battles, the encirclement of the Red Army's first strategic echelon set within the first 300 km of the Soviet border, would largely decide the war. Thereafter, the German advance would face little serious opposition and could proceed towards its distant objectives in something akin to a 'railway advance', a concept derived from the German experiences in Russia during 1918 when the absence of resistance enabled German soldiers simply to ride the Russian railways from one station to the next capturing towns and soldiers.[28] To the German command in 1941 the initial weeks were to prove the most decisive, and already by the second day of the offensive Halder proclaimed operations at Army Group Centre to be proceeding 'according to plan' and talked of soon achieving 'full operational freedom' behind the shattered Soviet front.[29] On the same day, in response to an assessment by Lieutenant-General Friedrich Paulus, the Senior Quartermaster I at the *Oberkommando des Heeres* (Army High Command – OKH), that the campaign would be of short duration, Field Marshal Walter von Brauchitsch is said to have responded: 'Yes, Paulus, you may be right, we shall probably need six to eight weeks for finishing Russia.'[30] Indeed, in the first ten days of the campaign Army

Group Centre won what it viewed as a crushing victory over the Red Army in the battle of Minsk. The number of troops encircled was double that of Tannenberg and Army Group Centre's panzer and motorised divisions were already pressing ahead towards Smolensk. By 19 July 1941, Hitler was sufficiently confident to issue War Directive 33, the tone of which pointed to a war already won on the central front. 'The second series of battles in the East has ended', it proclaimed, with 'mopping up' operations in Army Group Centre required to eliminate the remaining resistance. Thereafter, the next phase of the campaign would have to 'prevent any further sizable enemy forces from withdrawing into the depths of Russia, and to wipe them out'.[31] The Red Army, however, had no intention of withdrawing into the depths of Russia, and the battle of Smolensk was in fact only just getting underway with weeks of bitter and costly fighting to come.[32] Nor was the Soviet response unprecedented. In 1914, in the aftermath of the annihilation of the Russian Second Army at Tannenberg, the accompanying Russian First Army steadfastly refused to retreat from East Prussia and had to be forced out in the September fighting at the Masurian Lakes. Even then a renewed Russian invasion of East Prussia followed a few weeks later when the Russian Tenth Army attempted to reopen the campaign at the battle of Augustow (29 September–5 October 1914).[33]

In the immediate aftermath of the encirclement at Smolensk in 1941 the Germans once again proclaimed a crushing victory.[34] Army Group Centre had advanced another 300 km to the east and captured another 300,000 Soviet POWs. A German victory seemed beyond dispute, but the six- to eight-week timeframe for finishing the Soviet Union, which Brauchitsch had so confidently forecast, had almost elapsed and there was no indication that the war was nearing its end. A solid Soviet front was still holding in the east, more Soviet armies were assembling, and it was the Red Army that took to the offensive against Army Group Centre from early August until the second week of September. Field Marshal Fedor von Bock's army group was in no way prepared for such an eventuality and the defensive front repeatedly threatened to buckle wherever motorised reserves could not be found to plug local Soviet breakthroughs. As Halder noted on 15 August:

> The front of the army group, with its 40 divisions over 730 kilometres is so strained that moving to a determined defence entails far-reaching considerations, which have not been thought through in detail. The present deposition and line organisation is in no way suited for a sustained defence.[35]

On 25 August, General of Infantry Hermann Geyer, commanding the defending IX Army Corps, reported to Army Group Centre that Soviet attacks against the 263rd Infantry Division had resulted in roughly 2,100 casualties in August alone, and that such losses 'cannot be borne much longer'.[36] He also stated that the fighting resembled the trench warfare and artillery duels of the western front in the First World War. Geyer noted that the same routine repeated itself over and over again; an immense Soviet bombardment followed by a massed ground assault into the German defences, and concluded by local German counterattacks to repel the frequent penetrations.[37] Not surprisingly in such conditions the exhaustion of the German infantry divisions reached dangerous levels; towards the end of August the 161st Infantry Division, for example, was estimated to possess just 25 per cent of its combat strength and in eight days of heavy fighting had lost roughly 2,000 men and 57 officers.[38] At Army Group Centre, Bock was frantic. He had been warning since the middle of the month about the weakening of his front and the inability to hold sustained defensive positions, but now it appeared that a disintegration of the front was at hand. Speaking on the phone, Bock told Halder on the morning of 28 August: 'I must report to you that the situation on the defensive front of Ninth Army is very serious. It is such that an end to the resistance is foreseeable if the Russians remain on the offensive.' Finally, Bock asked the decisive question: 'What should I do then if as a result the front collapses?'[39]

Of course, the enormous pressure exerted against Bock's front also came at a tremendous cost to the Red Army, which decisively weakened the Soviet fronts defending Moscow in the lead-up to the renewal of Bock's October offensive.[40] Yet by mid-September, after almost three months of warfare, Operation Barbarossa had clearly failed to bring about its single most important objective. The Soviets had doggedly survived the German offensive, but unlike 1914, when the failure of the Schlieffen Plan led to the replacement of the Chief of the Great General Staff (General Erich von Falkenhayn replaced General Helmuth Johann Ludwig von Moltke), there were no such repercussions for Barbarossa's failure. This is perhaps even more surprising given that during the summer of 1941 Hitler had engaged in a long and bitter dispute with his generals over German strategy in the east and the opposition was led by Halder, the Chief of the Army General Staff.[41] Unlike Kaiser Wilhelm II, Hitler asserted himself over his generals and dominated the direction of the military campaign in the east. Indeed, while Army Group Centre's infantry were holding the line throughout August and September most of Bock's mobile divisions were dispatched south on Hitler's orders to cut off and encircle the Soviet Southwestern Front in Ukraine.[42] Indeed, on 14 September, when the lead panzer division from Bock's army group finally made contact with the forces of Army Group South coming up from Kremenchug, Lieutenant-General Walther Model instructed that the password for his forces be 'Tannenberg'.[43] By the same token, Colonel-General Maximilian Freiherr von Weichs, the commander of the Second Army who participated in the battle of Kiev, later wrote: 'One may think about the significance of the battle for the overall conduct of war as one will, in any case, military historians will compare the operational implementation of the battle by the commander of Army Group South as worthy of comparisons to battles such as Cannae and Tannenberg.'[44] Without disputing the decisiveness of such battles, the German generals nevertheless missed the fundamental point that in 1914 and 1941 even their greatest battles did not necessarily determine the outcome of their campaigns or wars. At Tannenberg, Cannae and Kiev the victor ultimately lost.

Even before the conclusion to the battle of Kiev Hitler accepted the OKH's view that a drive on Moscow should follow the fighting in Ukraine, and the dictator ordered planning to begin immediately. The drive into Ukraine was not even two weeks old, but on 6 September Hitler signed War Directive 35 ordering yet another major offensive to the east by Army Group Centre due to commence at the end of September (but subsequently delayed until 2 October). Without a word of mention about the staggering losses of the campaign or the run-down condition of the motorised and panzer divisions, Hitler imposed a tremendous new undertaking on the hard-pressed *Ostheer*. War Directive 35 commanded that the Soviet forces defending Moscow be 'annihilated in the limited time which remains before the onset of winter'.[45] It then went on to insist that an advance on Moscow should follow, which at the time was still another 300 km to the east. Such ambitious operations so late in the year were not only folly given the conditions of the *Ostheer* and the fact that a victory at Kiev was still far from assured, but they took no account of the Red Army's remarkable resilience, which as much as any other factor had derailed Operation Barbarossa. There was also the ominous precedent of the German offensive towards Warsaw in 1914.

At the end of September 1914 the new German Ninth Army, consisting of most of the German forces in the east, launched an offensive from Silesia to threaten Russia's control of Poland, supported three days later by their Austrian-Hungarian allies from the south. Initially, the armies of the Central Powers made progress (as well as taking thousands of Russian POWs) in spite of the appalling weather conditions and deep mud.[46] Russian forces were purposefully falling back and carefully concentrating forces for a massive counterblow from across the Vistula. The German Ninth Army missed the danger and believed they were simply exploiting the weakness of the Russian positions north of Warsaw. The Ninth Army's Chief of the Staff, General Erich Ludendorff, openly proclaimed victory and pressed on to seize Warsaw.[47] Yet the timely detection of well-placed Russian dispositions quickly convinced Ludendorff and Hindenburg[48] of the perilous danger to their left flank, and a retreat was quickly undertaken on 18 October that took them all the way back to their starting positions near Breslau.[49] According to General Erich von Falkenhayn, the new Chief of the Army General Staff, this operation had nevertheless resulted in 'very serious losses',[50] while Russian forces were only 320 km from Berlin. At the same time, Grand Duke Nikolai Nikolaevich, the commander of the Russian front, wrote to the French commander Joseph Joffre of 'the greatest victory since the beginning of the war'.[51]

While the Germans opted for retreat, the Austrian-Hungarians were less prudent and their First Army lost 40,000 men after being caught in the flank by a Russian counterattack. Additionally, in the subsequent retreat the fortress of Przemysl was cut off with some 150,000 soldiers inside (and destined to fall to the Russians in the coming winter).[52] The events of October 1914 were certainly of a smaller scale than October 1941, but just as Ludendorff and Hindenburg courted peril in their quest for Warsaw, Hitler, with even less caution, risked everything on his march to Moscow. Initial successes in each operation only tempted the attackers into greater risk-taking, all the while dismissive of Russian/Soviet countermeasures. Indeed, the willingness of the Russians to concede ground, bide their time and await the opportune moment to strike an oncoming enemy featured in October 1914 and at the end of Bock's autumn offensive in early December 1941.[53] Moreover, the underestimation of Russian/Soviet forces in the aftermath of German success is characteristic of both 1914 and 1941. As Hew Strachan noted of German operations in October 1914: 'Excessive German ambition in

Figure 1.1 German troops on the eastern front in Poland (1914–15)

relation to numerical strength ... explain the unravelling of the Hindenburg–Ludendorff master-plan.'[54] The same is true of 1941 with Hitler, Halder and Bock bearing the weight of responsibility.

Hitler and Halder viewed their drive on Moscow, codenamed Operation Typhoon, as the last great offensive of 1941, which would finally strike down the Soviet colossus. They still believed that a winter campaign could be avoided and the Red Army decisively defeated before operations came to a halt. Indeed, when the bulk of the Soviet armies defending Moscow were encircled in early October, the Reich Press Chief, Dr Otto Dietrich, was told by Hitler on 9 October that the Soviet Union was stricken and would never rise again.[55] Accordingly, Dietrich proclaimed to the international press: 'The campaign in the east has been decided by the smashing of Army Group Timoshenko.'[56] The following day (10 October) the *Völkischer Beobachte*, a Nazi daily newspaper, carried banner headlines extolling the news: 'The Great Hour has Struck!'; 'Campaign in the East Decided!'; 'The Military End of the Bolsheviks'.[57] The hubris of the Nazi state was soon laid bare when events on the ground did not match German predictions. Operation Typhoon was slowed first by the elimination of the large Soviet pockets at Viaz'ma[58] and Briansk and then, as the advance attempted to resume, by the biannual Russian difficulties caused by heavy rains and melting snow known as the *rasputitsa*. Bock's panzer and motorised divisions were restricted to the few available roads, which allowed the Soviets to concentrate their meagre resources to slow them. At the same time, Soviet defensive efforts focused on preparing the Mozhaisk Defensive Line, which sought to block the main approaches to Moscow at the four main approaches to the Soviet capital: Volokolamsk, Mozhaisk, Maloiaroslavets and Kaluga. Throughout the remainder of October Bock's forces assaulted and took each of the four defensive bastions on the road to Moscow, but the fighting exhausted the combat formations and depleted their ranks. The autumn conditions had also hindered the forward movement of supplies to such an extent that German forces were frequently cut off from resupply. Some men did not eat for days, horses starved or collapsed, vehicles had no fuel, guns no munitions and in many units there was also no sign of the long promised winter clothing. At its nearest point Army Group Centre was still 80 km short of Moscow and Soviet resistance was stiffening. The mud and rain denied the German motorised divisions their speed and rapid manoeuvreability, making every attack a costly frontal assault, while the success of any renewed push forward only extended the distance supplies had to travel. The army group's files reveal that many middle-ranking officers were pleading with the higher authorities for an operational pause in order to allow supplies and men to reach the front (many of the divisions were badly strung out as 'light' combat formations were sent forward to keep the advance moving). Moreover, the huge effort exerted throughout the second half of October to maintain the advance through the *rasputitsa* convinced many officers that the army group would do better to await the arrival of the first winter frosts when the ground would again harden and allow movement to resume. Hitler, Halder and Bock, however, had been convinced by their successes at Viaz'ma and Briansk, and were determined to exploit the enormous breach in the Soviet front. Yet no set of orders from above could change the conditions on the ground, and by the last week of October the army group's advance had slowed to a crawl. At the end of the month Bock at last called a halt to Typhoon, but planning began almost at once for a renewed offensive towards Moscow in November.[59]

It was at this period in the campaign that memories of 1914 did in fact play a profound part in the motivations and thinking of the German high command. To contemporary observers, the question often asked is why the German command did not adopt winter quarters once it became clear that Operation Typhoon had ground to a halt and the dreaded Russian winter beckoned. Yet few of the principal German commanders entertained any such notion of assuming winter positions while still short of Moscow. Understanding this has a lot to do with the Wehrmacht's own offensive ethos, which itself has long roots in German military culture,[60] but was sharpened by the adoption of new tactics and technology in the aftermath of the First World War.[61] The Wehrmacht's leadership was also accepting of the Nazi concept, personified by Hitler, of individual 'will', which denoted leadership qualities capable of bending events to serve any objective. Failure to do so was a reflection on the individual not the circumstances. The requisite 'will' to carry out an order or achieve an objective was therefore accorded decisive importance.[62] In early November 1941 suggesting the advance on Moscow should be abandoned or that the conditions had become too difficult for another offensive flew in the face of the Wehrmacht's prevailing military culture as well as its proven modus operandi for success. Yet if the battle of Tannenberg provided the ideal model for what the Germans wanted to achieve in the east in 1941, there was another dominant memory from 1914 that they wanted to avoid at all costs. In September 1914, the western allies proclaimed the so-called 'Miracle of the Marne', the battle that finally stopped the German offensive sweeping through northern France and denying them outright victory. As the western front quickly transformed into the stalemate of trench warfare many later German commanders viewed the failure not as a reflection of an overly ambitious campaign objective or the prevailing battlefield conditions, rather it was a result of excessive caution and a failure to press the attack on Paris with every means possible in the hope of clinching the decisive success. Now Moscow was the objective and too much caution or a failure to press the attack were the lessons of 1914 that should not be forgotten. A new cult of the offensive, which had already pushed the German armies well beyond their limits in Operation Barbarossa, was still alive and well in Operation Typhoon. Weichs claimed after the war that he had suggested adopting winter positions before the ground hardened and prevented the digging of defensive fieldworks, but, as he recalled, 'I was accused of not supporting the offensive'. As a veteran of the eastern front in the First World War, Weichs claimed: 'I know from experiences in the First World War how quickly winter falls here – and it is far more extreme than in central Europe. I doubted whether the operation against Moscow was still feasible this year.'[63]

It is important to acknowledge that in 1914 and 1941 each of the states that went to war were fundamentally different; Wilhelm II's Imperial Germany was not analogous to Hitler's Nazi regime any more than Nicholas II's Russian Empire was to be equated with Stalin's Soviet Union. Yet the experience of war in 1914 impacted upon the peoples who fought them and left legacies that affected the perception of events in 1941, even if some of these were rooted in exaggeration or even outright falsehood. While the Wehrmacht's commanders indulged a Tannenberg-inspired myth of superiority, this was just as ignorant of their experiences against the Russians in 1914 as it was of the more recent performance of the Red Army in its brief war against Japan in 1939. These diverged sharply from the common perception of a bungling Soviet Union in the Winter War with Finland.

There was an even greater distortion of the Soviet enemy based on Nazi racial ideas, which exploited the brief Russian occupation of East Prussia in 1914 to give rise to the most virulent depictions of savage easterners. According to one sensationalised account from 1914: 'The Russian army resembled migrating rats who, in times of great destruction, forsake their hiding places in the Siberian tundra in order to eat bare the settled lands. Ever fresh hordes come forth in a brown milling mass from the seething steppe.'[64] With a foundation in such hostile propaganda, it is hardly surprising that notions of the Soviet communist state as a threatening godless enemy of 'cultured' Europe found fertile ground in 1941, and it goes some distance towards explaining why so many ordinary German men, including the entire command of the *Ostheer*, embraced Hitler's war of annihilation.[65] Moreover, the First World War record of German conduct in the occupied lands of the east, while by no means analogous to the extremes of the Wehrmacht, nevertheless included plundering and exploitation.[66]

Although clear differences existed, the events of 1941 were not always distinct from those of 1914. Separated by only a generation, the parallel wars in Germany's east provide many insights into how and why Barbarossa and Typhoon were conducted in the way they were. Certainly, the Wehrmacht's generals sought answers from 1914, but only tended to heed the lessons that bolstered their preconceived ideas about the enemy they faced and the victorious war they intended to fight. A more objective assessment showed the Russian army to be a far more formidable foe, posing a very real threat to German war plans in both 1914 and 1941.

Nazi Germany's war of annihilation

A fundamental aspect of the battle for Moscow was that it took place in a period after German plans had anticipated final victory. This had grave implications for the development of German operations during the battle (which will be explored in detail in subsequent chapters), however, it also had a profound effect on the way in which the war was being fought by November 1941. The radicalisation of Nazi policy in the east had already begun in the planning phase of Operation Barbarossa, but the full horror of Nazi Germany's conception of warfare was revealed only as the campaign developed. By the battle for Moscow thousands of innocent Soviet civilians or defenceless POWs were dying every day. This in turn radicalised Soviet responses to the war and helped to galvanise support for Stalin's regime. Hitler's war of annihilation therefore provides another important strategic context for the battle of Moscow in which the operations at the front were directly impacted by the killings at the rear – killings that, by November 1941, were already unprecedented in the modern era.

On the morning of 30 March 1941 Hitler spoke to an assembly of around 100 senior Wehrmacht officers for two and half hours on the upcoming war against the Soviet Union. Hitler made it clear that the war he intended to fight in the east was to be very different from the one he had ordered in the west.[67] As the Chief of the Army General Staff,

Halder, noted in his diary Operation Barbarossa was to be a 'Clash of two ideologies.' Hitler then took aim at the nature of the Soviet state. 'Crushing denunciation of Bolshevism, identified with social criminality. Communism is an enormous danger for our future. We must forget the concept of comradeship between soldiers. A communist is no comrade before or after the battle. This is a war of annihilation . . . We do not wage war to preserve the enemy.' Halder then recorded how Hitler foresaw the role of the army in his new 'war of annihilation'. In order to achieve the 'extermination of the Bolshevist commissars and of the communist foe', Hitler made clear that there would be 'no job for military courts. The individual troop commander must know the issues at stake. They must be the leaders in this fight . . . Commissars and GUP men are criminals and must be treated as such.' There could be no doubt about the methods to which Hitler was referring. In fact, Halder's account concludes with Hitler insisting: 'Commanders must make the sacrifice of overcoming their personal scruples.'[68] Hitler need not have worried. Not only was the army leadership prepared to back such policies, but they in fact took the initiative in drafting the so-called 'criminal orders' that would instigate important aspects of the killing process.[69] Days before Hitler made his speech, Brauchitsch, the Commander-in-Chief of the Army, had told senior commanders of the *Ostheer* on 27 March that: 'The troops have to realise that this struggle is being waged by one race against the other, and proceed with the necessary harshness.'[70] That harshness was embodied by the two most notorious criminal orders, which the army issued on 13 May and 6 June 1941. The first was known as the *Erlaß über die Ausübung der Kriegsgerichtsbarkeit im Gebiet 'Barbarossa' und über besondere Maßnahmen der Truppe* ('Decree on the Exercise of Martial Jurisdiction in the Area "Barbarossa" and Special Measures of the Troops').[71] The order freed German soldiers from the possibility of any form of prosecution for war crimes committed in the Soviet Union (except for sexual misdeeds with what were judged to be racially inferior Slavs),[72] while at the same time opening the way to collective reprisals of 'suspects' deemed to have engaged in 'criminal action'. The second criminal order was titled the *Richtlinien für die Behandlung politischer Kommissare* ('Guidelines for the Treatment of Political Commissars'),[73] and required that upon capture these men be separated from other prisoners of war and promptly shot.[74] Importantly, these orders were specifically directed towards the officers of the Wehrmacht, who were then required to carry out the executions independently of the *Schutzstaffel* (SS) or *Sicherheitsdienst* (SD).

In contrast to the flood of postwar claims from German generals proclaiming their opposition to such orders, at the time there was hardly a murmur of disagreement. Following Hitler's morning address on 30 March, Major-General Walter Warlimont attended a lunch hosted by Hitler for all the army commanders of the upcoming eastern campaign, yet, according to Warlimont, 'none of those present availed themselves of the opportunity even to mention the demands made by Hitler during the morning'.[75] Not only was there no active resistance from the generals, but many of them independently decided to issue orders to their troops explaining the necessity for harsh measures in the east. On 2 May, Colonel-General Erich Hoepner, commander of Panzer Group 4, instructed his men:

> the war against Russia is an important chapter in the struggle for the existence of the German nation. It is the old battle of the Germanic against the Slavic peoples, of the defence of European culture against the Moscovite-Asiatic inundation, and the repulse of Jewish Bolshevism. The objective of this battle must be the destruction of present-day Russia and it must therefore be conducted with unprecedented severity. Every military action must be guided in planning and execution by an iron resolution to exterminate the enemy remorselessly and totally. In particular, no adherents of the contemporary Russian Bolshevik system are to be spared.[76]

Colonel-General Eugen Ritter von Schobert, who commanded the Eleventh Army, not only pledged to kill all captured political officers of the Red Army, but also ordered 'political commissars of the civil administration to be shot without further ado'.[77] Such a blatant extension of the killing process was in no way required by the army guidelines, showing the scope for radicalisation from below.

While the Wehrmacht maintained a far closer adherence to the Geneva Convention during the western campaign in 1940,[78] the Commissar Order and the Barbarossa Jurisdiction Decree effectively granted *carte blanche* for war crimes against the Soviet political establishment and civilian population.[79] Even more revealing, these new orders were greeted with hardly any dissent. On 4 June, Bock complained that the Barbarossa Jurisdiction Decree 'was not compatible with discipline',[80] and requested changes from the OKH. When these were not forthcoming, Bock contacted Brauchitsch and was told that the order 'was intended as I wished to interpret it'.[81] This was precisely the problem. Officers may insist upon 'discipline' or allow their men to engage in all manner of excesses. Significantly, Bock's opposition was not based on any moral outrage or concern for the Soviet populace, but rather his strict adherence to preserving the essential military ethos of order and discipline within the ranks. German officers were much more opposed to a 'wild', indiscriminate killing by their troops than they were to a measured and orderly execution. It was the process that mattered more than any moral quibbles about the outcome. Indeed, for the more questioning elements within the Wehrmacht's officer corps the murder of suspect elements was still an acceptable instrument of policy if administered correctly and determined by an officer rather than a private. Four days into the war General of Panzer Troops Joachim Lemelsen, the commander of the XXXXVII Panzer Corps, protested against the 'senseless shootings' being carried out by his men. 'This is murder!' He proclaimed with indignation. Yet while Lemelsen complained that such killings were being conducted 'in an irresponsible, senseless and criminal manner', he nevertheless went on to express support for Hitler's order that commissars and partisans 'should be taken aside and shot'.[82] Lemelsen was clearly prepared to embrace the killing process, as long as it was authorised from above and conducted in a 'responsible' manner. Similarly, Lieutenant-General John Ansat, the commander of the 102nd Infantry Division, stated that his soldiers were 'no hangman's assistants' and refused to carry out the order to kill commissars. At the same time, however, Ansat ensured that captured political officers were separated from other POWs and delivered into the hands of 'other units' (presumably the Field Gendarmerie or the SS) who could assume responsibility for the executions.[83]

Notwithstanding the grumblings of a select minority of generals, there was certainly no outcry of resistance to the criminal orders within the *Ostheer*. After the war men such as Colonel-General Heinz Guderian and Manstein, who emerged as the public faces of the Wehrmacht through their best-selling memoirs, categorically denied any involvement in the dissemination or implementation of the criminal orders.[84] In fact, however, the orders were distributed and carried out by both men. At his postwar trial, Manstein was found guilty of multiple counts of compliance with the Commissar Order during his command of the Eleventh

Army,[85] while evidence from Guderian's Panzer Group 2 shows that 183 commissars were shot up until the end of October 1941.[86] Colonel-General Hermann Hoth, who commanded the neighbouring Panzer Group 3 until early October 1941, also wrote a memoir centred solely on his panzer group's operations in the east during the summer of 1941. Yet in this account discussion of the criminal orders is conspicuously absent.[87] Hoth was another of the generals to have issued an order of the day proclaiming the German 'superiority of race' over 'Asiatic barbarism', and then concluding: 'This fight can be ended only by the destruction of one or the other of us. There is no room for compromise.'[88] It is therefore hardly surprising that an intelligence officer in Hoth's Panzer Group 3 reported at the beginning of August 1941 that the Commissar Order was implemented without 'any problem for the troops', and that 170 commissars had already been executed.[89] The unparalleled research of Felix Römer, who investigated the implementation of the Commissar Order in all the German divisions on the eastern front, confirms just how extensive its application in fact was. Römer found evidence that Soviet political officers were executed in all thirteen armies, all forty-four army corps, and more than 80 per cent of the almost 150 German front-line divisions. Moreover, if one includes cases that are more suggestive than explicit in their mention of carrying out the order, the number of divisions rises to over 90 per cent.[90]

The Barbarossa Jurisdiction Decree, exempting German soldiers from prosecution for war crimes, produced its own victims but without defining the target group. In short, Soviet citizens could be killed at any time and for almost any reason. Nowhere was the Wehrmacht more deeply implicated in the killing process than in anti-partisan warfare.[91] Stalin's famous radio appeal of 3 July 1941, extolling the formation of partisan detachments throughout the occupied areas was seen by Hitler as an opportunity 'to eliminate anything that opposes us' and 'to shoot dead anyone who even looks at us askance'.[92] The military leadership soon acted to ensure that there was no ambiguity in what was expected. War Directive 33a, issued on 23 July 1941, stipulated that resistance in the rear areas should be quelled, 'not by legal punishment of the guilty, but by striking such terror into the population that it loses all will to resist. The commanders concerned are to be held responsible, together with the troops at their disposal, for quiet conditions in their areas. They will contrive to maintain order, not by requesting reinforcements, but by employing suitably draconian methods.'[93] Needless to say, there was no outcry from the Wehrmacht's security divisions, which had already instigated bloody pacification measures, and, assisted by elements of the Order Police and SS detachments, quickly transformed anti-partisan warfare into a reign of terror and mass murder. During the month of October, the three security divisions of Bock's Army Group Centre reported vast disparities in the body counts resulting from their engagements with 'partisans', indicating that the great majority of their victims were defenceless non-combatants. Lieutenant-General Kurt Müller's 286th Security Division listed killing 714 'partisans' for the loss of just eight men. During the same period, Lieutenant-General Wolfgang von Ditfurth's 403rd Security Division reported shooting 1,093 'partisans' for 'no significant loss'. Finally, during a ten-week period starting in the middle of September, Lieutenant-General Johann Pflugbeil's 221st Security Division killed 1,746 'partisans' for the loss of just eighteen men.[94] Clearly, anti-partisan operations had taken on another meaning, which, like a number of other German euphemisms used in the Second World War, was often only a guise for mass murder. Leo Mattowitz, an eighteen-year-old recruit in 1941, recalled his first battle in the east in which his unit had to attack an enemy village: 'I hadn't slept at all the night before the attack, I was shaking so much.' Mattowitz then stated that the battle was not what he had expected: 'I'd never taken part in an attack before. Then, just after three in the morning, we got the order to fire. But there was something wrong. By the time the attack was over, there were only dead civilians in the villages, dead women, burning houses, and not one single soldier. We'd been killing civilians.'[95] In 1941, the Soviet partisan movement may still have been in its infancy, but it could nevertheless provoke a harsh response from the German security forces. Hans Becker described a typical German response:

> If a single hostile act against the German army took place in any Russian village the place was immediately branded as partisan and marked down for punishment. Retribution was usually meted out according to a standard procedure. On the very same evening that the 'crime' had been committed the village would be surrounded by troops and no one allowed out on any pretext whatever ... The village was set on fire and the entire population systematically slaughtered. To the west this process of mass obliteration became notorious from the particular instance of Lidice;[96] but it was a common, almost daily occurrence on the eastern front.[97]

Following exactly this procedure, Matthias Jung described how his unit burned and shot all the inhabitants of a town after a partisan attack in which eighteen German soldiers were killed.[98] Similarly, Helmut Pabst recorded watching Russians fleeing from the village of Leshenko, which German gunfire had set alight. Pabst then witnessed events that went beyond his previous experience of soldiering: 'I now know the meaning of the word "frightfulness".'[99] Others were more explicit. Private Heydenreich's diary recorded taking part in an anti-partisan operation on 23 September 1941 in which he wrote: 'The village and the woods were surrounded and fine combed. All suspicious characters were shot. We also settled those who tried to run away. Then we set fire to the village'. Two days later Heydenreich noted that some 300 people were found hiding about 24 km from the village. 'We decided that these must be the ones who were constantly keeping us on the jump. All were shot.'[100] What the German commanders did not anticipate was the extent to which this embittered the population against them as well as ending the illusions of some older Soviet people who had experienced a more benevolent form of German occupation in the First World War and hoped for a degree of liberation from communist rule. The implication for the battle for Moscow was that the vast

Figure 1.2 The shooting of suspected Soviet partisans in the area of Army Group Centre (December 1941)

expanse of occupied territory in Army Group Centre's rear area offered no tangible benefit to the invaders and instead necessitated a major drain on military resources.

After the war the International Military Tribunal at Nuremberg had *Obergruppenführer*[101] Erich von dem Bach-Zelewski, the former Higher SS and Police Chief as well as head of anti-partisan operations on the central sector of the eastern front, act as a witness for the prosecution. In spite of orchestrating some of the bloodiest atrocities of the Second World War,[102] Bach-Zelewski was never charged with war crimes.[103] His written testimony did, however, reflect the lengths to which 'anti-partisan' warfare extended in the east. According to Bach-Zelewski:

> There is no question but that reprisals both by the Wehrmacht and by SS and Police overshot the mark by a long way. This fact was repeatedly established at conferences with generals held by [General of Infantry Max von] Schenkendorf.[104] Moreover the fight against partisans was gradually used as an excuse to carry out other measures, such as the extermination of Jews and gypsies . . . The commanders in chief with whom I came in contact and with whom I collaborated (for instance Field Marshals von Weichs, [Georg] von Küchler, von Bock and [Günther] von Kluge,[105] Colonel-General [Georg-Hans] Reinhardt[106] and [Lieutenant-]General [Karl] Kitzinger) were as well aware as I of the purposes and methods of anti-partisan warfare.[107]

In a study of Army Group Centre by Timothy Mulligan, the number of partisans killed between July 1941 and March 1942 was put at 63,257 as against 1,993 Germans. The low number of Germans killed again tends to support the conclusion that many included in the total figure of 'partisans' were more often than not innocent civilians.[108] Targeted studies by Theo Schulte and Omer Bartov have further strengthened this view. Throughout 1941 the records kept by Major Graf Yrsch record 627 partisans killed for the loss of just two men.[109] Likewise, Colonel-General Ernst Busch's Sixteenth Army recorded killing 387 partisans in a week-long operation for the loss of just ten Germans.[110] Perhaps most conclusive is the recent evidence of Sönke Neitzel and Harald Welzer, who reviewed thousands of secretly recorded conversations between everyday German soldiers during their time as POWs. These offer an insight into what the average soldier thought with a degree of veracity and candour unmatched by any other source. As they concluded: 'German soldiers considered executing partisans as nothing short of a dictate of common sense, beyond question, since partisans did not enjoy the status of combatants.'[111]

As countless German orders attest, any and all resistance was to be ruthlessly crushed by the most severe methods. Erich Kern, a German soldier in Ukraine, recounted the story of a woman who was found berating two Soviet soldiers for surrendering to the Germans. She was therefore brought in for questioning and, as Kern notes: 'She guessed what she was in for and became insolent, and that finally settled her fate. The execution squad was to be formed.'[112] In another example of the arbitrary nature of German rule in the east, Private Max Landowski recorded: 'I saw a woman hanging there ... It was a Russian woman, and the *Oberst* [Colonel] had ordered her to bake bread ... Now it may be that she had replied, "no bread" ... But in spite of her having done nothing else, she was just hanged.'[113] A German doctor at the front, Heinrich Haape, wrote a postwar memoir in which he openly told of how he dealt with civilians working for him: 'so that none of them would shirk his job ... I would have anyone shot who failed to carry out my instructions'.[114] The brutality and sadism even extended to children. An order from the 12th Infantry Division in October 1941 advised its troops that 'information is usually carried by youngsters aged 11 to 14', and recommended 'flogging [as] the most advisable measure for interrogation'.[115] Since execution often followed interrogation, special measures had to be adopted for children. 'In cases where children are included among the hostages [aiming at the normal height] such persons may escape execution altogether ... and have to be despatched by hand of the officer in charge of the burial party.'[116]

Not all soldiers in the Wehrmacht engaged in the killing process, but while war crimes are a feature of all conflicts, the German war against the Soviet Union was by no means an ordinary war. The line between legal and illegal killing was blurred systematically right from the outset, and Nazi racial propaganda as well as the orders of the Wehrmacht commanders further discouraged the view that Slavs were in any way equal.[117] Indeed, the view was commonly shared that Germany's problems in the rear area could be solved only by the harshest possible countermeasures. As Corporal Hans Efferbergen wrote in his diary on 29 August: 'We are too easy-going, too open-hearted, too human. Only when we come down on the enemy like an avalanche of fury will the fate of this war be in our hands.'[118] Rudolf Lange agreed: 'That confounded

German humanity is out of place here. I have to spread this idea throughout the platoon.'[119]

Yet precisely because the indoctrination was so intense and the dangers of insubordination so profound, the few German soldiers who did actively risk themselves for the well-being of Soviet citizens, and especially Jews, are all the more noteworthy. Solomon Perel, a sixteen-year-old Jewish boy who had fled Germany to escape the Nazis, was captured during Operation Barbarossa by elements of the 12th Panzer Division. Insisting he was an orphan of Baltic German heritage, Solomon began working for the Germans as a translator until his secret Jewish identity was discovered by the unit's medical officer, Heinz Kelzenberg. 'Don't cry', Kelzenberg told Solomon when he made the discovery, 'they mustn't hear you outside. I won't hurt you and I won't betray your secret.'[120] Another German, known only as Corporal Bormann, who worked in a camp for Soviet POWs helped to conceal Jewish inmates during inspections and assisted escape attempts by providing passes and even weapons.[121] Evgenij Mordukhovich, a Russian Jew who lived with his family in Rostov and had to accommodate a German soldier in his apartment, was subsequently warned that a sweep for Jews was about to take place. The unknown German soldier not only warned them, but helped them escape the city.[122]

Beyond those who risked their lives for Jews there were others who were willing to face execution rather than participate in Nazi Germany's war in the east. Heinz Drossel told of one young soldier from Vienna who refused to fight even after being threatened with the death penalty. Drossel pressed the man to concede to the military authorities and 'just shoot in the air' at the front. Yet the young man steadfastly refused, all the while knowing that in the German Wehrmacht his 'offence' carried with it a death sentence. He was subsequently shot by firing squad. As Drossel later stated; 'He was the only hero that I ever met in my life.'[123] While the actions of such men are exceptions to an ideologically imbued Wehrmacht, they do not alter the fact that the great majority of the men in the German army fought determinedly for the Nazi regime and not against it.[124] Indeed, the examples of Heinz Kelzenberg, Corporal Bormann and the nameless German soldier in Rostov suggest that opportunities did in fact exist for individuals to resist Nazi policy in the east.[125]

On the more difficult question, which in the past twenty years has produced unceasing debate in Germany, of just how many 'everyday' men in the Wehrmacht took part in war crimes in the east, one can only say that the figure represents a far higher number of 'average' men than any other war of the modern era.[126] Attempting any more comprehensive answer depends in the first instance on how broadly one interprets 'war crimes' within the Wehrmacht. The distinction between 'good' and 'bad' German soldiers on the eastern front is not simply a matter of separating murderers from respectable soldiers, as though a clear distinction exists. War provides many grey areas where the moral impetus of right and wrong becomes distorted.[127] The brutality of German anti-partisan warfare is a good example. Combating partisans was seen as a necessary and wholly justified objective for the Wehrmacht. Accordingly, executions of those branded 'bandits', 'saboteurs' or 'suspect elements' were by no means secret. Indeed, many executions were conducted in public, watched and photographed by large crowds of German soldiers and Soviet civilians both as a warning and as a public spectacle.[128] From the letters and diaries of the German soldiers witnessing these events, there appears to have been little sense of injustice, to say nothing of disgust, with these methods. Indeed, many soldiers sympathised with such actions, seeing them as necessary to ensure their own continued safety and survival. Executions and reprisals were thus rationalised on pragmatic grounds and defended as a 'necessary' element of 'defence' against illegal *francs-tireurs*.[129] The fact that the Soviet Union had not signed the Geneva Convention and Stalin had called upon his people to conduct internationally outlawed irregular warfare, only further served, in the eyes of many Germans, to justify the Wehrmacht's harsh response. Thus, however many German soldiers were directly engaged in the killing process, it was the remainder of the *Ostheer* that condoned these perpetrators and helped to legitimise their actions by their 'understanding'. Critics may wish to point out that whatever the thoughts and opinions of those within the *Ostheer*, these cannot possibly be equated with those who directly perpetrated war crimes. Such attitudes, however, certainly helped to establish the *Ostheer*'s modus operandi, offering rationalisation and support for the perpetrators' deeds. This, in turn, made their tasks appear much more 'normal' and therefore easier to perform. While by no means an assertion of equal guilt implicating the entire Wehrmacht, an understanding of the culture of violence sustained and propagated within the German army goes a long way to understanding how so many 'ordinary men' became complicit in so much violence.[130]

While anti-partisan warfare was only just beginning in 1941 and in subsequent years would lead to many of the most horrific crimes perpetrated against non-Jews, there was another element to the partisan struggle in 1941 which attempted to disguise an even more sinister Nazi objective. Because partisan warfare had been openly declared by Stalin, justifying in the Nazi view operations against civilian targets, there existed the possibility for the Germans of large-scale 'actions' against Jews under the pretext of combating partisans. Soon after the start of Operation Barbarossa Hitler himself made this connection and Jews quickly became synonymous with partisan activity.[131] Indeed, in many orders Jews were equated with partisans and were to be dealt with in the same way.[132] As one order to a police battalion operating in the east read: 'Where there is a partisan there is a Jew and where there is a Jew there is a partisan.'[133] Himmler himself said on 9 July during an inspection tour at Grodno that 'all Jews are to be regarded as partisans, without exception'.[134] Similarly, the SS Cavalry Brigade reported on 3 September: 'Communication between the various partisan units is maintained above all by the Jews.'[135] Another formation reported on 10 September: 'The Jewish class, which forms the largest section of the population in the towns, is the driving force behind the growing resistance movement in some areas.'[136] With Soviet Jews now marked as hostile elements and indistinguishable from partisans, German 'actions' against Jewish settlements needed no evidence to justify their elimination. While such wholesale campaigns of murder against all Jews were by no means absent from the early weeks of the campaign, these were part of the radicalisation from below – in which local SS commanders ordered such 'actions' on their own authority. The planned murder of all Soviet Jews was not part of the original plan, but quickly developed over the summer of 1941.[137]

In addition to his instructions to the army which led to the criminal orders, on 17 March 1941 Hitler also instructed: 'The intelligentsia installed by Stalin must be destroyed. The leadership machine of the Russian empire must be defeated. In the Greater Russian area the use of the most brutal force is necessary.'[138] This translated into the elimination of all communist functionaries (not just Red Army commissars), Jews in party and state posts, and 'radical elements' defined as saboteurs, assassins, propagandists and agitators.[139] These tasks were entrusted to *Reichsführer-SS*[140] Heinrich Himmler, who in turn charged his deputy *Obergruppenführer* Reinhard Heydrich, the Chief of the Reich Security

Main Office (RSHA, *Reichssicherheitshauptamt*), with organising mobile killing squads known as the *Einsatzgruppen* (action groups).[141] The total strength of the *Einsatzgruppen* came to only about 3,000 men organised into four battalion-sized groups, designated A, B, C and D. *Einsatzgruppe* A was to operate behind Army Group North; *Einsatzgruppe* B was to follow Bock's Army Group Centre; *Einsatzgruppe* C was assigned to the northern elements of Army Group South; and *Einsatzgruppe* D was to operate in the extreme south of Ukraine with the German Eleventh Army.[142] Given the vast size of the operational areas the individual *Einsatzgruppe* operated in smaller company-sized groups known as *Einsatzkommandos* or *Sonderkommandos*, which fanned out over the newly occupied territories in search of victims.[143] In addition to their mandated targets, the *Einsatzgruppen* were also instructed to incite *Selbstreinigungsbestrebungen* ('self-cleansing efforts') against Jews by the local non-Jewish population, which effectively meant instigating pogroms. These were often ruthless killing sprees targeting any and all Jews irrespective of age or occupation.

One of the first such actions took place in Kaunas (also known as Kovno) in central Lithuania, where *Einsatzgruppe* A took violent criminals from a local prison and armed them with iron bars. They then waited in a town square as others brought in captured male Jews. SS officers were present, but they did not give instructions in order to make the action appear spontaneous. Members of the Wehrmacht also crowded the square and one of the soldiers later recorded what he witnessed:

> When I reached the square there were about fifteen to twenty bodies lying there ... I saw the Lithuanians take hold of the bodies by their hands and legs and drag them away. Afterwards another group of offenders was herded and pushed into the square and without further ado simply beaten to death by civilians armed with iron bars. I ... then had to look away because I could not watch any longer. These actions seemed extremely cruel and brutal ... The Lithuanian civilians could be heard shouting out their approval and goading the men on.[144]

Such horrific eye-witness accounts reflect the brutality of the process, but not the scale. A report from the head of *Einsatzgruppe* A, *Brigadeführer*[145] Dr Franz Walther Stahlecker, stated that on the night of 25/26 June more than 1,500 Jews were killed, and on the following nights a further 2,600 Jews were 'rendered harmless'. Stahlecker also commented on how the actions of his men were received within the *Ostheer*.[146] 'I am able to say that from the outset cooperation with the Wehrmacht was generally good, and in certain cases, as for example with Panzer Group 4 under the command of General Hoepner, extremely close, one might even say warm.'[147] There are even instances of direct participation by members of the Wehrmacht,[148] as one member of the *Einsatzgruppen* stated after the war, 'on some occasions members of the Wehrmacht took the carbines out of our hands and took our place in the firing squad'.[149] Clearly, the Wehrmacht was proving itself willing to go along with all aspects of the Nazi agenda in the east.[150] Indeed, as the battle for Moscow reached its apex there were even plans afoot for a special 'Advance Commando Moscow' to follow German troops into the city and conduct mass shootings.[151]

As the German advance thrust forward in the opening days and weeks of the campaign, the occupied areas expanded tremendously. At the same time in much of the newly won territories, especially in the heavily forested areas of Belarus, Lithuania and Latvia, the shattered fragments of large Soviet armies remained at large and frequently attacked vulnerable German targets. Given the vast size of the rear area, the inadequacies of the *Ostheer*'s nine security divisions were soon made all too clear and the perceived association between partisan resistance and the Jews called for stronger measures. As *Einsatzgruppe* A reported: 'Spontaneous cleansing actions were insufficient to stabilize the rear army area, especially as the eagerness of the local population [to kill Jews] was quickly waning.'[152] In the area of *Einsatzgruppe* B such operations had failed to gain an indigenous backing from the outset, and it was soon clear that pogroms were an inadequate means of aiding the work of the *Einsatzgruppen*. In spite of the SS quickly shifting towards a more total anti-Jewish policy in the early weeks of the war, the opening period of the campaign was by no means devoid of large-scale massacres conducted entirely by Germans. One soldier wrote in a letter on 24 June about the fictitious Allied atrocity propaganda that appeared during the First World War. 'And now this!' The soldier complained. 'The reality [in this war] is worse, more dreadful and brutish than any fantasy.'[153] On 27 June, after the capture of Belostok, more than 700 Jews were forced into the Great Synagogue and burned alive, which, in addition to the people killed in the city itself, resulted in over 2,000 deaths.[154] Indeed, in the first six weeks of the war the murderous

German occupation policies had already led to Jewish deaths in the tens of thousands.[155] With such a large and expanding rear area as well as the bitter resistance by encircled Soviet troops in many areas behind the front, German security forces were clearly inadequate. Accordingly, in July Himmler dispatched substantial reinforcements to the east, including an SS Cavalry Brigade, a volunteer regiment and several brigades of motorised *Waffen-SS*. Additionally, there were orders for the transfer of eleven battalions of Kurt Daluege's Order Police,[156] and the rapid formation of auxiliary police units[157] 'from reliable non-communist elements among Ukrainians, Estonians, Latvians, Lithuanians and Belarusians'.[158] These forces not only substantially boosted the security forces, but also provided the means for a dramatic increase in the killing of Jews.

Determining when exactly the order came from Hitler to commence the wholesale extermination of all Soviet Jews is impossible to ascertain with certainty because no written order has ever been found.[159] Almost certainly such implicit instructions were never committed to paper, but rather passed verbally first to Himmler and then to his SS chiefs in the field. It is possible that the order came in mid-August when Hitler, who had been uncharacteristically indecisive in strategic military matters, finally regained his composure and decided on a new course in the war.[160] At the same time, on 19 August, Goebbels recorded in his diary after a private meeting with Hitler:

> We talked about the Jewish problem. The Führer is convinced that his earlier prophecy in the Reichstag is proving correct, that if the Jews succeed again in provoking another world war it would end with the annihilation of the Jews. This is being proved in these weeks and months with an apparently eerie certainty. In the east the Jews must pay for this . . .[161]

Whereas the *Einsatzgruppen*, Order Police and local auxiliary units killed approximately 63,000 Jews by mid-August, the numbers of victims then spiked dramatically and within the next four months 500,000 Jews would be shot in the Soviet Union.[162] Long before the death camps industrialised the process, the Holocaust was underway in the east using much cruder means. *Standartenführer*[163] Karl Jäger, who commanded an *Einsatzkommando* in Lithuania, reported in detail on the killing process (Table 1.1). Jäger's tally for the second

Table 1.1 *The murder of Jews in the second half of August by* Einsatzkommando *3*

Date	Place	Jewish victims			
		Male	Female	Children	Total
18–22 August 1941	Kreis Rasainiai	466	440	1,020	1,926
23 August 1941	Panevezys	1,312	4,602	1,609	7,523
25 August 1941	Obeliai	112	627	421	1,160
25–26 August 1941	Seduva	230	275	159	664
26 August 1941	Zarasai	767	1,113	687	2,569
26 August 1941	Kaisiadorys	no detailed data recorded			1,911
27 August 1941	Prienai	no detailed data recorded			1,078
28 August 1941	Pasvalys	402	738	209	1,349
28 August 1941	Kedainiai	710	767	599	2,076
29 August 1941	Rumsiskis and Ziezmariai	20	567	197	784
29 August 1941	Utena and Moletai	582	1,731	1,469	3,782

half of August 1941, excluding smaller massacres, amounts to almost 25,000 murdered Jews, and this was the result of just one *Einsatzkommando* (together with local auxiliaries) operating in one region. What Lucy Dawidowicz referred to as 'the war against the Jews'[164] was now underway in the east, and the result was an unprecedented level of murder. In just two days at the end of September elements of *Standartenführer* Paul Blobel's *Sonderkommando* 4a, together with two commandos of Police Regiment South, Ukrainian militia and the Kiev city commandant Major-General Kurt Eberhard, shot over 33,000 Jews at Babi Yar.[165]

Nor were the Germans alone in their racial war.[166] The Romanian head of state, General Ion Antonescu, was not only a fervent anti-communist, but also shared Hitler's extreme anti-Semitism. During his campaign to reoccupy northern Bukovina and Bessarabia,[167] Antonescu's forces, acting in unison with *Gruppenführer*[168] Otto Ohlendorf's *Einsatzgruppe* D, killed 12,000 to 20,000 Jews over the summer of 1941.[169] Later during their occupation of Odessa Romanian forces alone killed a further 19,000 Jews.[170] While the Romanians were the most active collaborators in the mass murder, the Hungarian government knowingly expelled thousands of Jews into the zones where German forces were conducting the killings. There were also pogroms organised by Hungarian forces in western Ukraine and even direct Hungarian participation in mass shootings at Kamianets Podolsk.[171]

Figure 1.3 In December 1941 around 1,000 Jewish women and children were murdered in Liepāja by a German police unit

While the killing of the Jews proceeded with such ruthlessness and force the method of implementation was quickly adapted from pogroms and isolated mass burnings to a systemised procedure for mass shootings developed by the *Einsatzgruppen*.[172] Lieutenant-General Heinrich Kittel observed one such mass shooting and described the events to a fellow prisoner after his capture by the Americans in 1944. Kittel was interned along with many of the highest ranking German officers at Trent Park, a mansion north of London. Not knowing that British intelligence was secretly recording their private conversations for any important disclosures, in a conversation on 28 December 1944 Kittel described to Major-General Paul von Felbert what he had seen in the east:

Felbert: Have you also known places from which the Jews have been removed?
Kittel: Yes
Felbert: Was that carried out quite systematically?
Kittel: Yes
Felbert: Women and Children – everybody?
Kittel: Everybody. Horrible!
Felbert: Were they loaded onto trains?
Kittel: If only they had been loaded onto trains! The things I've experienced! . . . I was lying in bed early one Sunday

morning when I kept on hearing two salvoes followed by small arms fire. I got up and went out and asked: 'What's all this shooting?' . . . men, women and children – they were counted off and stripped naked; the executioners first laid all the clothes in one pile. Then twenty women had to take up their position – naked – on the edge of the trench, they were shot and fell down into it.

Felbert: How was it done?

Kittel: They faced the trench and then twenty Latvians came up behind and simply fired once through the back of their heads. There was a sort of step in the trench, so that they stood rather lower than the Latvians, who stood up on the edge and simply shot them through the head, and they fell down forwards into the trench. After that came twenty men and they were killed by a salvo in just the same way.[173]

Kittel then told of his disgust at what he had witnessed and his resolve to do something about it. Yet, as was often the case with the army commanders, Kittel's concern was not for the Jewish victims, but rather his own men. As Kittel recounted his complaint to the ranking SD officer. 'If you shoot people in the wood or somewhere no one can see, that's your own affair. But I absolutely forbid another day's shooting there. We draw our drinking water from deep springs; we're getting nothing but corpse water there.' Finally, Felbert asked what had happened to the Jewish children, at which point the record noted Kittel became 'very excited'. 'They seized three-year-old children by their hair, held them up and shot them with a pistol and then threw them in. I saw that for myself.'[174]

It is a testament to the horrifying dimensions of Hitler's war of annihilation in the east that the murder of Soviet Jews in 1941 could, during the same period, be surpassed by another policy of mass murder. During the course of 1941, 3.3 million Soviet POWs were captured by the *Ostheer*, yet by February 1942 over 60 per cent, roughly 2 million soldiers, were already dead.[175] It was less the result of an active policy of execution, as in the case of the Jews, than an active policy of neglect by the German army, which resulted in the same outcome. Captured Soviet soldiers died en masse in POW camps from epidemics of dysentery and typhus, exposure to the freezing conditions and wholesale starvation. Even before their internment, it was not uncommon for surrendering Soviet soldiers to be killed and, if taken prisoner, their journey to the POW camps typically took the form of death marches in which those who could not keep up were shot at the back of the column. One German soldier's letter described shooting a Soviet soldier in cold blood after he had surrendered and then continued: 'The first Russian. Since then I have shot hundreds. I have such a rage. Since then, I took only one Russian prisoner, a German.'[176]

There are no reliable figures for the extent of such immediate killings, but according to Christian Streit, a five-, or possibly even a six-, figure number are thought to have been shot by the Wehrmacht en route to the camps.[177] Such outright murder was not a cause for alarm because it was condoned at the highest levels. During one of his late-night diatribes in mid-September Hitler told his inner circle that maniacs and sadists had undermined the German state before continuing: 'I make no distinction between them and the brutes who populate our Russian POW camps.'[178] With such a contemptuous view, it is hardly surprising that conditions in the camps were appalling and in direct contravention of all international law.[179] Many were little more than open fields surrounded by barbed-wire with the prisoners living in their own crude shelters, which were typically just dugouts or sod houses offering little protection from the elements.[180] Overcrowding in the camps was endemic, which, in addition to the wanton violence of the German guards, soon led to excessive brutality among the prisoners themselves as they competed for the meagre quantities of food that the Germans did supply. As one German inspection tour noted in its report; 'When the water carrier brings the water for the kitchen, a ferocious brawl always breaks out, which can only be ended by shooting. Hunger revolts with incessant shooting are also the order of the day.'[181] According to a directive from the OKH, the army was supposed to supply POWs who worked with 15,400 calories per week, while those who did not work were to get 10,407 calories.[182] In practice, however, even such minimum requirements were not met, and in many instances nothing at all was given to the prisoners.[183] At one camp in Hola, Poland, 100,000 Soviet POWs were herded together, but given no food. By the end of 1941 they were all dead.[184] Not surprisingly such dire circumstances led to the most frightful spectacles. Hans Becker, a German soldier who entered a Soviet POW camp to collect a working party, recalled his first observations upon entering a hut:

> A whirling mass of bodies staggered through the gloom, grunting, biting and tearing at each other. A figure was hurled on to a plank

> bed, and I realized that they were all attacking one man. They were gouging his eyes out, twisting his arms right off and tearing the flesh from his bones with their nails. He was knocked down and literally torn apart.
>
> Dumbfounded, I shouted to them to stop, but without any effect. Not daring to move further into the room I stood mesmerized by the horror of what was happening. The murderers were now cramming the flesh down their throats, I caught glimpses of the bare skull and ribs of the man on the bed, while on the other side of the room two men were fighting over his arm and cracking the fingers off in their tug-of-war.[185]

When Becker rushed to a nearby guard and told him what he had witnessed the man was unmoved. 'This Happens every day.' Becker was told. 'We stopped worrying about it a long time ago.'[186]

Neglect typified the German approach to the plight of Soviet POWs, which is not surprising given that they created the conditions that led to so many deaths in the first place. Certainly, there were already food shortages in the east, which has led to attempts to explain, and thereby exculpate, the culpable role of the German army.[187] Yet death from starvation resulted far more from the army's conscious decisions than any extenuating circumstances. As the army's senior Quartermaster-General, Major-General Eduard Wagner, explained in November 1941: 'Non-working prisoners of war ... have to starve to death.'[188] It was a sentiment shared by many in the armed forces, who felt no pity, much less responsibility, for the soldiers of the Red Army. On 17 September, one German soldier noted in a letter to his wife: 'Henning writes that the number of Russians dying daily from starvation in the camp for the war prisoners now runs into three figures. That's how it should be! As it is we have to make superhuman efforts to supply our soldiers. We can't provide food for the prisoners too.'[189] Another wrote home: 'We'll take no prisoners but shoot them all. That's the best thing. Besides they'd eat us bare in Germany.'[190] Other German soldiers were moved by the plight of Soviet prisoners, but hardened their hearts just as German propaganda insisted they must. Karl Fuchs wrote: 'Sometimes I'm tempted to feel sorry for them because many of the soldiers are young boys, hardly sixteen or seventeen years old. But you can't afford to have pity on them.'[191] One person who did pity them was the Jewish boy Solomon Perel who, while working as a translator for the Wehrmacht, visited a temporary POW camp. He recalled thousands of prisoners guarded by armed German soldiers and crowded together:

> Their heads had been shaved, and they were sitting crossed legged in the searing sun without water or food ... I noticed a wounded man lying on the ground dressed only in a Russian military jacket. The lower half of his body was naked; there was a deep wound where his genitals should have been. He was groaning and pleading for water.[192]

While the POW camps in the east became death camps for many of the Soviet men interned, it was not until 1942 that the German authorities began to see a possible economic use for so much manpower and conditions began to improve. In 1941, Soviet POWs were viewed almost exclusively as economic burdens, which could not be tolerated. The more fortunate ones were kept to build roads or construct bunkers for the troops near the front, but their expendability was demonstrated by their use in other tasks such as clearing minefields,[193] or acting as the first test victims for trials of Zyklon B gas at Auschwitz in September 1941.[194] To the German authorities the lives of Soviet POWs were worthless, and even after the death of roughly 2 million in the first seven months of the war some German generals later concluded that they had not gone far enough. Lieutenant-General Maximilian Siry, who commanded the 246th Infantry Division from 1941 to 1943,[195] observed, while himself a POW of the British at Trent Park:

> One mustn't admit it openly, but we were far too soft. All these horrors have landed us in the soup now. But if we'd carried them through to the hilt, made the people disappear *completely* – no one would say a thing. These *half* measures are always wrong.
>
> In the east I suggested once to the 'Korps' – thousands of PW [prisoners of war] were coming back, without anyone guarding them, because there were no people there to do it ... [I]n Russia there was a space of 50–80 km, that is to say a 2 to 3 days' march, between the armoured spear-heads and the following close formations. No Russians went to the rear; they lagged behind and then took to the woods left and right, where they could live all right. So I said: 'That's no good, we must simply cut off one of their legs, or break a leg, or the right forearm, so that they won't be able to fight in the next four weeks and so that we can round them up.' ... We've seen that we

cannot conduct a war because we're not *hard* enough, not barbaric enough.[196]

Siry's statement makes clear that despite all the horrors Hitler's state perpetrated in the east there were some who were quite prepared to go even further. According to pre-invasion planning for the Soviet Union even the mass murder of Soviet Jews and POWs was to be surpassed.[197] If there was any doubt about Nazi Germany's resolve to implement the harshest measures in pursuit of Hitler's goals, *Generalplan Ost* (General Plan East)[198] offers a frightening vision of Nazi plans for the east. In his 1925 publication of *Mein Kampf* Hitler spoke of Russia as Germany's future *Lebensraum*,[199] and within days of his accession to power Hitler declared to his generals on 3 February 1933 that the purpose of the new Wehrmacht was for: 'Conquering new *Lebensraum* in the East and ruthlessly Germanizing it.'[200] *Generalplan Ost* foresaw this ruthless Germanisation. By 1941, subsequent drafts of *Generalplan Ost* spoke of a replacement of Slavs by some 4.5 million German settlers. The eastern *lands* were to be Germanised, but not the inhabitants, and this entailed a programme of ethnic cleansing of unprecedented proportions. The RSHA estimated that some 31 million people would have to be expelled to Siberia, with those that remained either being reduced to servitude under German overlords or being killed under a parallel plan known simply as the Hunger Plan.[201]

Worked out in the first half of 1941, the Hunger Plan sought to make good occupied Europe's grain shortfall by redirecting the distribution of Ukrainian and southern Russian grain stocks to the west. The aim was to prevent the kind of domestic food shortages that had plagued Germany during the First World War, and to this end no moral quibbles were expressed about starvation in any other parts of Europe.[202] The chief architect of the plan was the Permanent Secretary in the Agricultural Ministry, Herbert Backe, who worked closely with General of Infantry Georg Thomas, the Chief of the War Economy and Armaments Department at the *Oberkommando der Wehrmacht* (OKW – High Command of the Armed Forces).[203] The plan was as straightforward in its objectives as it was cold-blooded in its consequences. The eastern territories were to be divided into 'surplus regions', which produced more food than their inhabitants needed, and 'deficit regions', which were dependent on outside food imports. Under the Soviet model the surplus regions had supplied the deficit regions, but under the new German plan deficit regions would receive nothing, thus leading to mass starvation in Belarus and northern Russia.[204] At the critical meeting of the *Staatssekretäre* on 2 May 1941,[205] the plan was agreed with its murderous conclusions set down in writing.

1. The war can only continue to be waged if the entire Wehrmacht is fed from Russia during the third year of the war.
2. As a result, if what is necessary for us is extracted from the land, tens of millions of people will doubtlessly starve to death.[206]

With predicted Soviet deaths so high German planners anticipated 'a most serious distress from famine', but at the same time warned against 'false humanitarianism', which would 'reduce Germany's staying power' in the war.[207] The most senior Nazi administrative official in Ukraine, *Reichskommissar* Erich Koch, a man selected for the post because of his well-known ruthlessness,[208] made clear the purpose of German rule in Ukraine: 'The attitude of the Germans ... must be governed by the fact that we deal with a people which is inferior in every respect.' Koch then stated that the German occupation was not intended 'to bring blessings on Ukraine but to secure for Germany the necessary living space and a source of food.'[209] While official plans for the calculated mass starvation of whole Soviet regions was to take effect after victory had been won over the Soviet Union, during the campaign the Wehrmacht's wholesale expropriation of foodstuffs (to reduce the strains on their overburdened logistical apparatus) caused widespread hunger, sickness and death.[210] The 18th Panzer Division, for example, ordered its troops before the invasion to undertake 'full exploitation of the land', which later resulted in instances where whole villages were looted with anyone who resisted being shot.[211] One SS report denounced such practices of the army, complaining;

> The positive attitude towards the Germans is being jeopardised by the indiscriminate requisitions by the troops, which become generally known, further by individual instances of rape, and by the way the army treats the civilian population, which feel handled as an enemy people.[212]

The diaries and correspondence of German soldiers suggest many viewed the plight of the Soviet civilians as a result of their looting with attitudes ranging from ambivalence to outright contempt. Werner Bergholz's diary for 5 July 1941 bluntly observed that 'we're now on enemy territory and can grab whatever we like'.[213] Helmut Pabst wrote about how he and his comrades looted onions and turnips from people's gardens and took milk from their churns. 'Most of them part with it amiably', he wrote home in a letter, but he also made clear his indifference: 'Willingly or unwillingly, the country feeds us.'[214] Erich Petschan's letter was even more direct when it came to the matter of suffering civilians: 'I don't lack bread here as I managed to scrounge a centner and a half [equivalent to 75 kg] of rye from the Russians. One thing I can assure you: I'll see ten Russians croak before I do any starving.'[215] Indeed, the excessive looting by the soldiers led to orders from many high-ranking commanders attempting to limit the troops' level of destruction and plunder. Such orders were less inspired by the plight of the Soviet civilians than by the damage done to the *planned* economic exploitation of the Soviet Union. As the commander of Army Group North, Field Marshal Wilhelm Ritter von Leeb, stated in an order on 16 August 1941: 'the start-up work of the economic authorities is being rendered impossible by the senseless "organisations" of the troops'.[216]

Whether robbed by the soldiers themselves or by the new German administrators, it was clear that the needs of the Soviet civilians were the lowest priority. For troops newly arrived from Germany the scenes of dire poverty and utter desperation within the Soviet population created a disturbing spectacle. Henry Metelmann recounted what he witnessed during his journey to the front in the autumn of 1941:

> Real poverty was evident everywhere ... the harassed-looking people were starving *en masse* ... Hollow-eyed children, often in rags, came begging for bread. Not having any on us, we were of course in no position to give them any ... we had been told in special little lectures before we were let out of our train that they were enemy children, dangerous breeds.[217]

With Germany's war of annihilation committed to such blatant policies of exploitation, abuse and outright murder the consequences of what was taking place in the east were without precedent. The sheer scale of war crimes was impossible to conceal, causing some German soldiers to wonder where it all might lead and what might result if Hitler's long prophesised victory did not materialise. One solider commented after burning a Soviet village: 'If what we do here ever comes back to us then God have mercy. This is terrible.'[218] After witnessing a mass shooting of Jews at Paneriai, another German soldier remarked: 'May God grant us victory because if they get their revenge, we're in for a hard time.'[219] Even soldiers like Konrad Jarausch, who had no direct involvement in the mass murder of Jews, knew enough to fear for the future. As Jarausch wrote in a letter on 13 September 1941:

> I'm often worried by the thought that all these peoples, who we had to hit hard and humiliate, will one day band together for revenge. My comrades mostly agree that once the Jews have been slaughtered there will be new forces in place everywhere. But history, including the Russian with which I have concerned myself, shows something else.[220]

Three days later (16 September), Jarausch returned to these thoughts and revealed himself to be surprisingly well informed as to Nazi Germany's strategic circumstances:

> We have lived until now because we have always managed to tap new sources [of materials]: first 1940 Western Europe, then now 1941 the Ukraine. We are living at the expense of these peoples and draining them to the last. What should be the result other than bitterness and the wish to be free from this foreign rule? That is the great moral chance that England, and above all America, have.[221]

The bitterness of foreign peoples and the challenge Jarausch accurately foresaw that they would constitute to Nazi rule could only lead to further cycles of radicalising violence. Far from standing aloof in Hitler's war of annihilation, the Wehrmacht was an instrumental component of Nazi rule. When Kesselring, the commander of Air Fleet 2 covering Army Group Centre, was questioned after the war about the conduct of German forces and whether or not a soldier should refuse any order violating human rights he answered: 'A soldier's first duty is to obey, otherwise you might as well do away with soldiering ... Things which come up against human rights and had bad consequences, however, couldn't necessarily be called crimes.'[222] As

Kesselring's reply suggests, and his wartime record in Italy confirms,[223] human rights were not a concern for many senior Wehrmacht commanders. At Trent Park near London the secretly recorded conversations of captured German generals confirm both their knowledge of war crimes as well as their deep-rooted collusion with the Nazi state and its ideas. In October 1944, General of Infantry Dietrich von Choltitz stated: 'We are also to blame. We have cooperated and have almost taken the Nazis seriously ... I've persuaded my men to believe in this nonsense and caused those people who still regarded the Officer Corps as something worth respecting, to take part, without due consideration. I feel thoroughly ashamed.'[224] Similarly, Lieutenant-General Hans Schaefer stated at the end of December 1944: 'I mean in our hearts; when one goes over all the crimes that have been committed, it makes one's hair stand on end ... One can only say that if Germany is destroyed it is justice and nothing else.'[225] Yet such private admissions, by a minority of officers and after the fact, did not form the popular picture of the Wehrmacht's role at the end of the war. Publicly the generals vigorously maintained their innocence, which endured largely intact in the west until the late 1970s, and maintained that the Wehrmacht's virtuous good conduct at the front had been betrayed by SS crimes in the rear.[226] Even the 1947–1948 High Command Trial (officially known as *The United States of America* v. *Wilhelm von Leeb et al.*), which acquitted only two of the fourteen generals indicted, did not suffice to implicate the Wehrmacht, in the popular mind, to equal status with other Nazi criminals.[227] The myth of the Wehrmacht's 'clean hands' not only helped to clear many former soldiers and officers of any association with Nazi crimes, but even allowed them a degree of victimhood and heroism, having supposedly struggled and sacrificed at the front while Hitler's regime secretly orchestrated mass murder.[228] The contrasting perceptions of the German armed forces in the Second World War have had a polarising effect, which is reflected in many of the works published about the Wehrmacht. Until relatively recently books have tended to fall into one of two categories: either popular operational accounts focusing exclusively on the Wehrmacht's campaigns and battles or more scholarly works dealing with the Wehrmacht's criminal activities.[229]

On the Soviet side research by G. F. Krivosheev estimates that the total war dead between June 1941 and May 1945 came to almost 27 million people.[230] Of these, David Glantz suggests that only about 10 million constituted the losses of the Red Army.[231] It may therefore be estimated that Germany's war of annihilation in the east left somewhere in the order of 17 million Soviet civilians (i.e., non-combatants) dead. Many were murdered as a result of the deliberate extermination polices under discussion in this chapter, but even more died as a result of the conditions created by the Germans in the east. Malnutrition, overwork, disease, sickness, exposure, or a combination of these, killed incalculable numbers of Soviet civilians.[232] In the course of the Second World War some 17 million men served in the Wehrmacht,[233] and from June 1941 most of these served exclusively, or for a significant period of time, on the eastern front. While many Germans who served as soldiers on the eastern front later maintained their innocence, denied any involvement in war crimes and fiercely rejected the blanket condemnation of the Wehrmacht as a criminal organisation, many of their denials avoided inconvenient truths. Far from acting against the wanton destruction of human life in the east, the Wehrmacht was the very backbone of Hitler's drive for *Lebensraum*. Even beyond the direct role a significant percentage of German soldiers played in the war of annihilation it is not too much to say that the whole *Ostheer* contributed to the final Soviet non-combatant death toll. The men of the Wehrmacht lived from food and livestock stolen from impoverished villages, benefited from civilians forced into exhausting labour details, requisitioned beds and medicines at occupied hospitals, seized vital farming equipment for the army's use, burned whole settlements thought useful to partisans or the Red Army, and typically showed little or no regard for the well-being of civilians caught up in the fighting. In winter, they routinely stripped local inhabitants of their warmest clothing, and on cold nights occupied houses at the expense of whole families. Such actions may not have immediately resulted in the deaths of the victims, nor might their deaths have even been the intention of the instigators, but the resulting deaths nevertheless stemmed from the actions of the Wehrmacht. Indeed, war crimes in the east were so ubiquitous and the number of victims so extraordinarily high that the idea that the soldiers within the *Ostheer* served their country like any others, with a simple duty-bound mandate to follow orders, is impossible to accept.[234] A photograph found on the body of a German soldier showed a group of company commanders sitting behind a large sign which read: 'The Russians Must Die, So That We Can Live.'[235] While each and every member of the *Ostheer* cannot be condemned as a war criminal, at the same time, very few could claim to be entirely innocent.

Set against the background of the German war of annihilation the fighting around Moscow was much more than a movement of armies vying for control of the Soviet capital. By November 1941, Germany aimed to strike a final decisive blow in the east and force an end to the war. Yet for the Soviet population the stakes were even higher – avoiding defeat in 1941 was quite simply a matter of life or death.

2 THE IDLE TYPHOON

Killing time before Moscow: Army Group Centre's stagnant offensive

At the start of November Bock's Army Group Centre occupied a great arching position in the centre of the eastern front, which measured some 800 km in length (linear distance). Weichs' Second Army held the southernmost reaches of the army group, and was poised to seize Kursk after a long and exhausting advance hindered more by the roads and conditions than by enemy resistance. To his north was Guderian's Second Panzer Army, which had just completed a month-long drive from Orel to Tula and was now looking to threaten Moscow from the south. Counting on this support was Kluge's Fourth Army, which had been fought to a standstill on the approaches to Moscow from Tarusa to Volokolamsk. This was in spite of the fact that Kluge retained command over Hoepner's Panzer Group 4, which in numerical strength was the most powerful German panzer group on the eastern front. Holding the northern flank of the army group was Colonel-General Adolf Strauss' Ninth Army, which, together with elements of General of Panzer Troops Georg-Hans Reinhardt's Panzer Group 3,[1] maintained control of Kalinin in spite of intense enemy counterattacks.[2]

The size of the operational area and the difficulties under which the army group had to labour to sustain itself in the field given the paucity of supplies taxed its strength tremendously. It was hoped that the operational pause would replenish enough of the army group's stockpiles to support another offensive, but the Wehrmacht objectives were never made conditional to the requirements of the Quartermaster-General and over-extension resulted from every major offensive in 1941. As Hans Jürgen Hartmann noted at the start of the month, November promised to be no different:

> Even if no one speaks of it, all of us are feeling a heavy weight that presses down on the soul, as time and time again we think about the advance on Moscow. We know from the Wehrmacht news bulletins roughly where our troops are and where the *Schwerpunkt* [point of concentration] will be . . . All in all, as I look eastwards, and see the grey, forbidding November clouds which sweep towards us, I fear we have become dangerously overstretched.[3]

Illustrating the point futher was Helmut Günther's observation that his division (the 2nd SS Division *Das Reich*) often only had a few rounds of ammunition per rifle and a single belt of bullets for the machine gun.[4] Likewise, the elite Infantry Regiment *Grossdeutschland* reported that it could not afford to stockpile even the smallest amount of its supplies for a future operation as everything was needed just to maintain itself in the field.[5] Typically, the SS and panzer groups were the best supplied formations in the *Ostheer*, but by November even they were grossly under-resourced. On 2 November, Bock noted that auxiliary detachments from field units were being subordinated to railway construction engineers in order to bring the railheads closer to the front. The wider Soviet gauge had to be narrowed to accommodate the smaller European trains, but, while the work was simple enough in theory, the retreating Red Army made a point of tearing up tracks and bending rails, transforming a conversion job into a total reconstruction. Army Group Centre lived from the railway connections with Germany and, as Bock noted in his diary, 'everything depends' upon their extension.[6] Yet the railways were not everything. The state of the roads was equally important, as the supplies had to be transported from the railheads to the front lines. Most of the vehicles Germany used in the east had been requisitioned from civilian stocks and did not have high ground clearance or four-wheel drive. During October they were bogged down by the thousands and had to be pulled through the worst stretches by tracked vehicles or tractors. Even when they could drive the conditions took a huge toll, particularly as shell craters and large holes were filled with water that masked their depth. As one soldier noted accidents and

Figure 2.1 The commander of Army Group Centre, Field Marshal Fedor von Bock

breakdowns 'repeated a hundred times a day with monotonous regularity ... Every few hundred yards is a broken-down vehicle; or a dead horse with swollen belly; or a corpse.'[7]

Indeed, in early November as the panzer corps focused on rebuilding their strength for what they knew would be the inevitable resumption of the advance, the state of the roads and lack of supplies became the dominant concern. On 1 November, Reinhardt's Panzer Group 3 noted that that the main fuel depot at Smolensk was empty and that as a result the fuel trucks would have to drive another day and half to reach supplies at Orsha, some 430 km from Kalinin (linear distance).[8] It was at Kalinin that Lieutenant-General Friedrich Kirchner's XXXXI Panzer Corps,[9] together with infantry divisions from the Ninth Army, had been fighting a bitter battle to keep the city from being cut off and encircled by Colonel-General I. S. Konev's Kalinin

Front. The only consolation for the declining access to fuel supplies was the corresponding reduction in the number of vehicles available to Reinhardt's panzer group. On 4 November, Major-General Walter Krüger's 1st Panzer Division could muster only fifteen of the obsolete Mark II tanks, along with a further seven Mark IIs with flame-throwers as a main armament. The backbone of the 1st Panzer Division's strength rested upon its remaining twenty-two Mark III and four Mark IV tanks; however, since Krüger's division was the only panzer division available to Kirchner's XXXXI Panzer Corps such figures were disappointing.[10] Reinhardt's other panzer corps was General of Panzer Troops Ferdinand Schaal's LVI Panzer Corps with two panzer divisions (the 6th and 7th). Although these divisions had seen much less fighting in October and remained some of Army Group Centre's numerically strongest panzer divisions, their size only made them harder to supply and move. There were also bottlenecks to their mobility. In the worst areas trucks could move forward only with the help of tracked vehicles or tractors, and Major-General Hans Freiherr von Funck's 7th Panzer Division reported on 4 November that half of all the division's towing vehicles were out of operation.[11] The next day (5 November), the same division reported that of the sixty-three remaining towing vehicles no less than twenty-three had broken down or had to be removed from service for repair.[12] Major-General Erhard Raus, a brigade commander in the 6th Panzer Division, wrote that in the sunken conditions even whole columns could be effectively written off by the mud. After a sudden frost, Raus wrote that one column was 'cemented' into the ground and reduced to 'a state of complete uselessness'. He then continued: 'Because we could not reach it any other way, gasoline, towropes, and food supplies had to be air-dropped along this line of stranded armour, but all attempts to move proved futile.' He concluded that 'it never moved again' and that such losses 'proved serious since no replacements were being received'.[13] The logistic crisis at Panzer Group 3 did not arise because of the need to stockpile supplies for the next offensive; there was hardly enough to maintain a hand-to-month existence. The panzer group lived in this way as it desperately fought to retain control of Kalinin. As Reinhardt wrote of his panzer group's supply status by the start of November:

> As a result of the weather it was almost impossible to supply the troops in and around Kalinin even with the most basic battle and food requirements. He who has not experienced it cannot imagine

> what kind of experience every movement by road demands from mid October to the beginning of November, even on the so-called good roads. What was achieved in this time, especially by the drivers, to bring up supplies for hundreds of kilometres through the mud and snow sludge was astonishing. In the end only the panje [Russian horse] columns, and sometimes boats on the Volga, remained to bring up the most important goods.[14]

Not only was Reinhardt struggling to supply his existing operations, the OKH would also soon be seeking a renewal of the offensive to the east, ensuring that what was already over-extension would quickly threaten to tear Panzer Group 3 apart.

The situation was no more promising at Hoepner's Panzer Group 4, where transportation and supply issues dominated the war diaries of the panzer corps. General of Panzer Troops Adolf Kuntzen's LVII Panzer Corps noted that the heavy artillery of one division remained some 100 km from the front, while its light artillery was being brought forward at the greatest effort to man and beast. One divisional report noted that no less than twenty-two horses were needed to move a single gun in the conditions, while some of the men had not changed their socks or shirts in weeks. At the same time, the motorised divisions had to be converted from vehicles to panje columns in order to move weapons and supplies to the front.[15] General of Panzer Troops Georg Stumme's XXXX Panzer Corps reported great difficulties in the area of Yel'nya, where so-called 'mud-holes', concealed pot-holes in the road, reached 1.5–2 metres in depth. Yet the roads were in any case impassable because of an estimated 50–75 cm of viscous mud, which topped almost all the roads in the area. This not only consumed the vehicles up to their axles, but even extended up over the chassis frame, rendering some too heavy even for towing. Those that could be towed faced new problems, as the corps' war diary noted: 'most of these vehicles will be damaged because of the resistance due to the depth of the mud'. The report went on to state that the radiators would typically be forced up and the oil pan torn open. 'From the vehicles committed in the past few days ninety-five per cent have come back with more or less heavy damage so that before being serviceable again repairs requiring several days are necessary. Furthermore, the situation with regard to spare parts is extremely critical.'[16]

General of Panzer Troops Heinrich Freiherr von Vietinghoff's XXXXVI Panzer Corps wrote a long report on 1 November openly

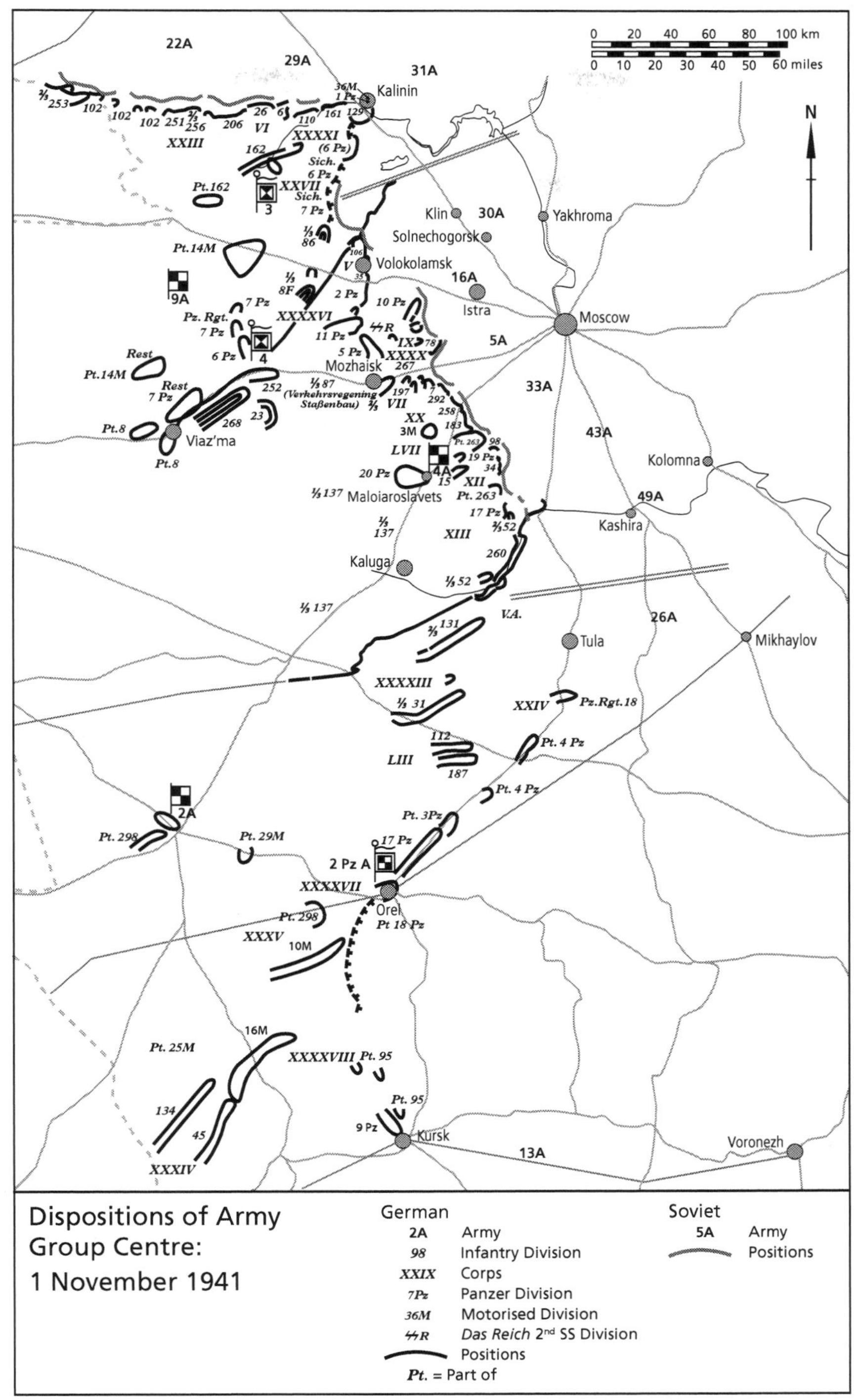

Map 2.1 Dispositions of Army Group Centre, 1 November 1941

questioning the use of his corps in any further offensive operations. The men were living on one-third of their typical rations and even this could not be maintained for long. The roads were just too poor to ensure a meaningful supply and Vietinghoff noted that without an improvement in the weather it would soon not be possible to provide the troops with even 'the most essential food, fuel and munitions'.[17] On the following day (2 November 1941), the corps' war diary projected that, as a result of the continuing rains and worsening conditions, the highway between Gzhatsk and Mozhaisk, on the corps' main supply route, had become impassable even to towing vehicles. The implications for the corps were projected to entail a 'grave worsening' of its logistic crisis.[18] In such circumstances Vietinghoff's doubts about the future of the offensive were simply a statement of the obvious, and yet Hoepner, the panzer group commander, remained convinced that offensive operations could continue once the ground froze.[19] Thus, while Panzer Group 4 paralleled its counterpart to the north in being over-extended and utterly ill-equipped, men like Hoepner still sought a solution by attacking further to the east. The folly of the German army's over-estimations preceded even the launch of Operation Barbarossa, but by November 1941, having learned nothing from their past mistakes, the *Ostheer*'s optimism bordered on the absurd.

Guderian, at Second Panzer Army, was another case in point. He had directed a successful drive on Tula at the end of October, which seemingly disproved the idea that the conditions rendered offensive action impossible. Yet the conditions were only half of the problem. The Red Army was still very much in evidence on the road to Moscow, but rather than contesting every metre of ground Marshal Georgi Zhukov was concentrating his limited resources in defensive bastions like Tula. Thus, while Guderian's drive on Tula was an achievement in itself, the enemy still remained to be defeated and the panzer army's spearhead was now harder than ever to supply and reinforce. What is more, Tula was a heavily defended urban centre and a major armament production site, which threatened a repeat of the deadly urban fighting that had proved so costly to the ill-trained panzer troops at Dnepropetrovsk in August and September.[20] With his forces stalled at Tula, Guderian, like Hoepner, looked forward to the early winter frosts to restore his movement.[21] Yet a long report in Second Panzer Army's war diary on 4 November drew attention to the possibility that heavy snow falls either before or accompanying the frosts could render any movement on the roads impossible.[22] Even in the absence of such an eventuality Guderian noted that once a prolonged frost took hold it would only be possible 'to gain ground very slowly and at the cost of great wear and tear to the motorized equipment'.[23] It was hardly the recipe for success that the rapid movement of the *Panzertruppe* was founded on and, given that Tula was another 170 km from Moscow, Guderian's task looked extremely unlikely.

Like Panzer Groups 3 and 4, the actions of the Second Panzer Army would be dictated more by the state of the roads and its access to supplies than by the defiant orders of its commanding officer. On 1 November, the panzer army's war diary stated that there was not a single road in its vast area of operations that allowed for the smooth operation of its vehicles supplying major formations. At the same time, it noted that vehicles that had attempted overland routes must now be regarded as 'completely lost'. More worryingly for any renewed offensive by the Second Panzer Army, the main rail supply line extending over Gomel–Briansk–Orel could meet the most basic requirements of fuel and munitions, however, that was the very limit of its capacity. As the war diary recorded: 'A refilling of the completely exhausted stocks for the troops or the formation of absolutely necessary stockpiles for the army, to see us through any unforeseen difficulties, is for the time being out of the question.'[24] Guderian also needed to extend his railway line to Tula or his long road to Moscow would place impossible demands on the *Grosstransportraum* (the truck-based transport fleets bridging the railheads with the armies). Yet as Guderian noted: 'Despite consistent exhortations to hurry, the repair work was making only slow progress. The lack of locomotives made me look around for alternative transport and I suggested the use of railway lorries, but none were sent to me.'[25]

The spearhead of the Second Panzer Army was made up of General of Panzer Troops Leo Freiherr Geyr von Schweppenberg's XXIV Panzer Corps, which by early November commanded all of Guderian's major tank units. Schweppenberg commanded the 3rd, 4th and 17th Panzer Divisions, as well as the panzer regiment from the 18th Panzer Division and the Infantry Regiment *Grossdeutschland*. Supplies were being flown to a forward airbase and then taken the rest of the way to Tula by truck. Yet the state of the roads placed heavy demands on the towing vehicles, and between Mtsensk and Tschern (two towns on the road from Orel to Tula) the panzer corps reported a fall-out rate of twenty from twenty-four prime movers.[26] Many of these towing vehicles came from the divisional artillery units, which since the halt in Army Group Centre's operations were directed to helping the traffic on the roads. Major-General Willibald Freiherr von Langermann-Erlancamp's 4th Panzer Division had freed its artillery's prime movers for service in the rear on 27 October, but reported at the start of November that this kind of constant heavy work seriously endangered its future mobility.[27] By the same token, the war diary of Major-General Walter Nehring's 18th Panzer Division noted that since the start of Barbarossa its remaining tanks had travelled a distance of 4,000 km with the resulting consequences.[28]

General of Panzer Troops Joachim Lemelsen's XXXXVII Panzer Corps commanded the 10th, 25th and 29th Motorised Infantry Divisions as well as the 18th Panzer Division (minus its panzer regiment). The corps was generally well supplied, but it was also deep in the rear area near Orel after regrouping from the fighting around the Briansk pocket in October. Lieutenant-General Friedrich-Wilhelm von Loeper's 10th Motorised Infantry Division was not, however, on the main supply route and was able to be supplied only by air drops and towing vehicles.[29] Yet the XXXXVII Panzer Corps was now looking beyond wheeled transport, and instructed its divisions on 4 November that it would soon be necessary to set up sled units 'for patrol, reconnaissance and fighting'.[30] In addition to Guderian's two panzer corps, the Second Panzer Army also commanded two army corps, Heinrici's XXXXVIII and General of Infantry Karl Weisenberger's LIII Army Corps. Weisenberger's corps was closer to the main supply route and received limited supplies through official channels, but Heinrici's two divisions were too far north and reported to be 'without noteworthy supply and living from the land'. In such a sparsely populated region and at a time of the year when mobility was so limited, it was not surprising that the men and the horses were going hungry.[31] At the same time, such circumstances typically spelled much worse for the local Soviet population, who were left to starve.

While Reinhardt, Hoepner and Guderian controlled the vast bulk of Army Group Centre's tanks, there was one more panzer corps' assigned to Weichs' Second Army on Bock's southernmost flank. Weichs had been pushing towards Kursk for the best part of October, and by 1 November had at last reached the city gates and was making preparations for an assault. Ironically, the famous German offensive at Kursk in July 1943 did not involve the city itself in any of the fighting, but in early

November 1941 the city was the objective of the attack and was taken in bitter house-to-house fighting. A report in Second Army's war diary detailed just how desperate was the state of Lieutenant-General Werner Kempf's XXXXVIII Panzer Corps before the attack. The corps' sole panzer division, Lieutenant-General Alfred Ritter von Hubicki's 9th Panzer Division, retained just seven tanks for the attack on Kursk and noted that its units and men were spread over no less than 260 km of its advance route. Similarly, the accompanying 95th Infantry Division, commanded by Lieutenant-General Hans-Heinrich Sixt von Armin, was also spread thin and, owing to the miserable state of its horses, had no artillery to support its attack. As the report concluded: 'In the assault on Kursk both divisions will give their last, so that after carrying out the attack a rest period will be absolutely necessary.'[32] On 1 November, the assault began with one German soldier writing in his diary: 'the orders to attack Kursk came through. At last a real city ... Under cover of ... heavy weapons, our men from the company move forward towards the Russians a jump at a time; and in one swoop they are on them, yelling "Hurrah". Those who don't surrender ... are mowed down by an MG. It's a bloody business.'[33] On the following day (2 November), the Germans pressed the attack into the city centre and the diary continues:

> At 9:00 we start to take over the city. Civilians inform us that the streets are full of barricades and that a lot of mines have been laid to hinder our progress. The Red Army has cleared out, but armed a lot of partisans beforehand ... Of the 120,000 inhabitants, 30,000 are said to have fled to Voronezh ... Every second a bullet wings past us. You never know where it comes from. Pressed flat against the house walls, bent down, your gun ready to shoot, your grenade in the other hand, you creep along ... Some civilians, who despite our order don't stand still, are shot down ... Armed civilians and suspicious characters on the one hand, wounded on the other – who can wonder if we mow down everything in our path ... We do find a nice place, though – real furniture, large windows and best of all a bed.[34]

It took another two days before the city was cleared of its last pockets of resistance,[35] but, as at Kiev, it took much longer to clear the city of hidden explosives in the houses and buildings.[36] While clandestine bombings at Kiev were the justification for the mass murder of Jews at Babi Yar, Kursk did not have a large Jewish population; however, this did not prevent German atrocities. On the second day of the German occupation fifteen communist activists were made to dig their own graves near the central square before each one was shot. At the same time rumours circulated that some 700 women had been rounded up and sent off to work as prostitutes for the German troops. As one Soviet intelligence report noted: 'The shops have been looted. There is no mains water and no electricity. Kursk has collapsed. Life there has frozen.'[37]

Having achieved his objective after an arduous campaign, which began at the end of September,[38] Kempf's supposedly 'absolutely necessary' rest period was quickly disregarded by the OKH who now set their sights on Voronezh, over 200 km further east. In spite of the fact that Army Group Centre's offensive was temporarily suspended, and notwithstanding the dreadful state of Kempf's forces, the OKH remained convinced that Soviet resistance on this part of the front had been broken. Even so, Halder acknowledged that marching on Voronezh was 'however, theory. Practically speaking the troops are stuck in the mud and can be happy if enough towing vehicles can be made operational to move provisions forward.'[39]

Of course, after issuing such orders to the exhausted troops there was nothing theoretical about it. The Wehrmacht did not consider orders on the basis of what was realistic or unrealistic, the troops would simply be ordered out of Kursk and sent on the long road to another distant objective, but there would be nothing theoretical about their sufferings and deprivations. Paradoxically, the frequent accusations levelled at Hitler by his generals after the war that the dictator showed a callous indifference to the suffering and lives of his soldiers were all too often duplicated in the orders of the army high command. On 3 November, the Second Army reported that east of Kursk there were no hard roads and that a further advance was 'not possible'.[40] Instead, Weichs wanted to use the time to concentrate on winter positions, however, this provoked a quick response from the Chief of the Operations Department in the Army General Staff, Colonel Adolf Heusinger. He argued that the troops should 'not gain the impression of a winter base' as otherwise 'they will not understand the order to set out again'.[41] Realistically, of course, from the standpoint of the troops, it would hardly matter what the officers said, the order to resume the advance over establishing winter quarters in a city offering shelter and warmth would never be 'understood'. As Wilhelm Prüller wrote after being told the news at an assembly:

> We almost fell over. We innocent angels thought we had in front of us some pleasant weeks which we would spend next to nice warm stoves; we hadn't a clue what our superiors had in store for us. All those dire prophesies had something to them. Now they've caught up with us: we are to advance in the direction of Voronezh! But now comes the most interesting part: we are to go *on foot*! We've become infantry! How fatuous! ... And all you can do the whole time you serve is to marvel. So I laughed, and laughed heartily, out of malicious joy at my own misfortune.[42]

While Kempf's XXXXVIII Panzer Corps, along with other elements from Weichs' army, was being ordered to resume the advance east, the OKH was also keen to remind Army Group Centre that a general renewal of the advance was only a matter of time. The logistic difficulties would just have to be overcome and according to the army's senior Quartermaster-General, Wagner, preparations for the upcoming winter were well in hand. After hearing a lecture from Wagner on 1 November, Goebbels evinced supreme optimism that the *Ostheer* would be adequately supplied. 'Everything has been thought of and nothing forgotten. If the enemy places his hopes in General Winter and believes that our troops in the east will freeze or go hungry he is completely mistaken.'[43] Goebbels then praised Wagner as 'a man with excellent nerves, who knows what he wants and does not let anything get him down'.[44] Brauchitsch was similarly optimistic and foresaw, with the advent of frosts, operations continuing to Moscow and all the way to Stalingrad in the south.[45]

At the front, of course, the situation could not have been more different and even Bock, who was desperate not to relinquish his claim on Moscow, could not ignore the warning signs. On 3 November, he wrote in his diary: 'The condition of the roads is becoming ever worse; even the highway has given way in various places, so that supplying the units is becoming increasingly difficult. Only in a few places can the superiors reach the front lines. The units are strained to the utmost.'[46] Halder was determined not to allow transport or supply issues to give any cause for second thoughts about a resumption of the offensive. On 1 November, Army Group Centre's war diary recorded Halder's discussion with Bock's chief-of-staff, Major-General Hans von Greiffenberg: 'He [Halder] is completely convinced that the army group has done everything possible to overcome the great difficulties and to prepare for

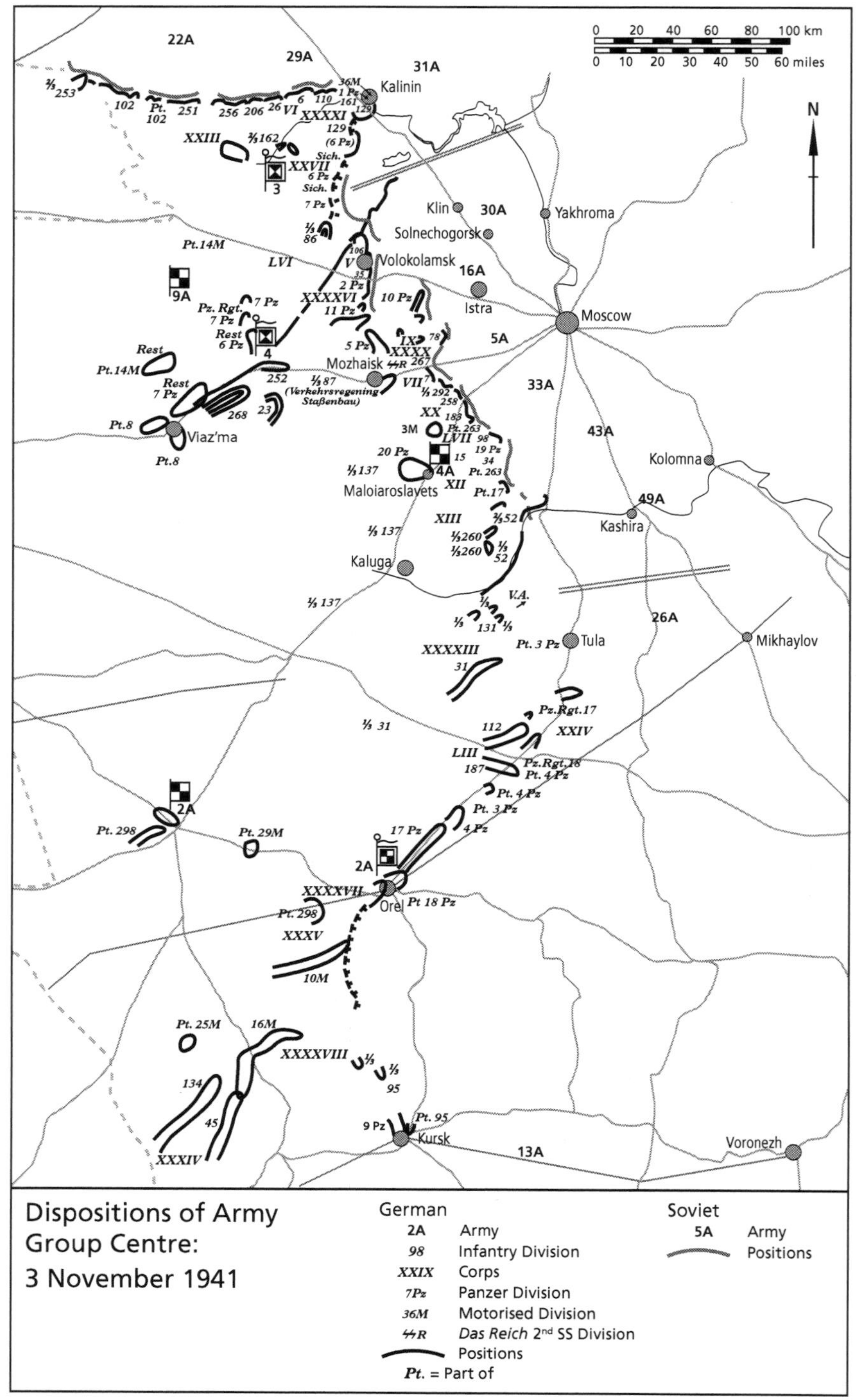

Map 2.2 Dispositions of Army Group Centre, 3 November 1941

the later attack and further advance.'[47] Three days later, on 4 November, the message was repeated: 'In conclusion Colonel-General Halder noted that he was of the opinion that the army group would gradually overcome the supply difficulties.'[48] Halder's intention was not merely to express his confidence, but to make it clear that supply and transport difficulties were surmountable obstacles and, as a result, were not cause to question plans for the continued march on Moscow. As dead as Operation Typhoon may have looked from the viewpoint of many of the haggard panzer corps at the front, the OKH was determined to take the fight to Moscow.

While Army Group Centre's logistics boded ill for any continuation of the advance to Moscow, many of the men at least welcomed the chance for rest and recreation (aside from those in the Second Army). Erich Hager, who served in the 17th Panzer Division, wrote in his diary on 2 November that he and his comrades had nothing to do; 'things are easier for us' he noted and the time was spent playing skat (a German card game) until late in the evening.[49] For many men, however, the halt in operations gave them little real rest, with the time spent reinforcing positions and constructing new dugouts. Free time was often devoted to long-neglected essentials like shaving, washing clothes, cleaning weapons and engaging in the tedious ritual of hunting body lice. There was also much time and energy spent searching for food and warm clothing. Too much idle time was also a potential danger to morale as thoughts turned to home and the long absence many of the men had already endured. Some units opted for a return to barracks life with daily exercises, inspections and cleaning details.[50] The condition of the troops was in some cases extremely poor and bore little comparison with the order and regulation of barracks life. As Helmut Pabst alluded in letter:

> Then there are jokes, because the motorised boys call us the Hunger Division, always on the spot, without a supply echelon, waifs and strays . . . We get no new boots or shirts when our old ones wear out: we wear Russian trousers and Russian shirts. And when our boots have had it, we wear shoes and Russian puttees – or else make the puttees into ear muffs. But we have our rifles and a bare minimum of ammunition.[51]

Even Wagner, the fervently upbeat army Quartermaster-General, had to concede in a letter on 2 November: 'How the troops look no one can imagine', yet he then went on to declare, 'But the mood is good everywhere, only the how-long and, above all, the winter concern people.'[52] Of course, these were hardly minor considerations and many of the individual soldiers expressing such concerns did not have any idea how extensive the crisis confronting the *Ostheer* really was. At the same time, the OKH was showcasing for Hitler an exhibition of new winter uniforms. According to Nicolaus von Below, Hitler's Luftwaffe adjutant: 'The army Quartermaster-General, General Wagner, stated that work on winter clothing was in hand and that sufficient quantities would be made available to men in the field. Hitler took note of the report and appeared satisfied.'[53] In fact, according to Colonel Wilhelm von Rücker, attached to the planning staff of the Quartermaster-General's office, 'a few hundred additional trains would have to have been sent' to meet the needs of the troops for the coming winter.[54] Not only was there not the transport capacity for winter equipment, but other higher priority materials, such as fuel and ammunition, were also decidedly under-resourced by the Quartermaster-General.[55] Army Group Centre's coming winter crisis was as much the result of appalling German planning as anything which might be said in favour of Soviet plans and operations.

Incredibly, even at this late stage in the campaign, the yawning credibility gap between the high command and the events at the front still endured. The delusion of an impending German victory had become the operative discourse within the OKH even before Barbarossa began, but its resilience was quite remarkable. Not only was the army command able to ignore the appalling road conditions, the state of the *Ostheer*'s supplies and the near total absence of winter clothing for the men, but even the Red Army was now seemingly disappearing. On 4 November, Halder told Greiffenberg that he believed the Red Army would abandon the entire area between Moscow and the Caucasus as it was 'not important to the Russians either from an industrial or strategic point of view'. The remaining Soviet forces, Halder stated, would therefore be committed to defending southern Russia and around Moscow.[56]

Nor was this just the view – or the fault – of the OKH. At the front some senior commanders also failed to judge the limitations of their forces, and some even admitted their ignorance in their postwar writings. Field Marshal Kesselring, the commander of the Luftwaffe within Army Group Centre, wrote how he was convinced at the time that it 'would have been no great feat ... for Hoepner and Guderian to drive their Panzer forces straight through to Moscow and even beyond'.[57] Other commanders were similarly deluded, and even with the benefit of hindsight appeared to have learned little. Blumentritt, the chief-of-staff of the Fourth Army, wrote after the war: 'With amazement and disappointment we discovered in late October and early November that the beaten Russians seemed quite unaware that as a military force they had almost ceased to exist.'[58] Such statements were a reflection of just how little German officers knew about the Red Army rather than how much. Indeed, the reverse was true; it was Fourth Army's offensive strength that had almost ceased to exist. On 5 November, Kluge, who commanded the army, visited one of his infantry divisions (the 98th) and spoke for half an hour with one of its regimental commanders, who told the field marshal: 'Four weeks without real rest and replenishment for the men and material and without the supply of winter clothing and equipment have led to the troops being "consumed" so to speak and unable to participate with a chance of success in an attack.'[59] As an indication of just how exhausted the division was, over the three-month period from the start of August to the end of October the 98th Infantry Division had sustained almost 6,000 casualties.[60] That same day (5 November), while Kluge was visiting his men at the front, Army Group Centre's war diary included a report from German agents who reported Moscow to be to 'overcrowded' with Soviet troops.[61] Clearly, there would be no German blitzkrieg to Moscow and, much to the surprise of some of the German commanders, Soviet resistance would be formidable.

Riders of the storm: the German command keep faith with Operation Typhoon

While the bulk of Army Group Centre had halted the offensive, there were still attempts at forward movement on some parts of the front. Fourth Army's VII Army Corps, under the command of General of Artillery Wilhelm Fahrmbacher, was continuing its offensive just south of the main highway between Mozhaisk and Moscow. The fighting here had been bitter, and in just three days at the end October one of Fahrmbacher's divisions (the 267th Infantry Division) had lost 900 men, while another (the 7th Infantry Division) had suffered a further 400 casualties.[62] Now, in spite of the general halt in operations, Fahrmbacher pushed his men on, winning some ground against fierce resistance on 2 November. The following day the attack resumed, but after further heavy fighting Fahrmbacher was unable to make any progress in spite of his attack being aided by tanks. On 4 November, Fahrmbacher reported that his divisions were exhausted and retained only one-third to half of their established combat strengths.[63] The VII Army Corps' offensive was a local operation, but it was also further evidence suggesting that a larger-scale offensive would quickly flounder.

Fearing that consequence was Vietinghoff, the commander of the XXXXVI Panzer Corps. While he was much too junior to decide German strategy, Vietinghoff remained unconvinced by his orders and unwilling to place the lives of his men ahead of his professional judgement. As a result, he wrote a damning report openly questioning the plans of the whole German command, and sent it to Hoepner, his commanding officer.[64] Vietinghoff was careful to couch many of his concerns in the context of his own panzer corps, but at times the report read more generally and referred only to the weaknesses of 'the operation', which may be taken to mean Operation Typhoon. He cited four reasons why the planned offensive to seize the Moscow–Volga canal, the main objective of the thrust north of Moscow, would experience major difficulties. First, Vietinghoff believed the intervening swamplands would not be sufficiently affected by a frost to allow wheeled vehicles free movement. Secondly, according to all forms of intelligence (Vietinghoff cited pilots' reports, captured maps, Russian inhabitants and military geographic studies) there was 'not one single road with <u>real</u> load-bearing substructures' from Volokolamsk, where the offensive would begin, to Klin, Istra or points further south. Thirdly, Vietinghoff stated that the hitherto periods of frost offered only limited improvement in the road conditions, while also introducing new problems. The sub-zero temperatures resulted in 'very high fallout of vehicles' because they 'literally get torn apart in the frozen wheel ruts' with damage to the springs, differential and steering. Fourthly, Vietinghoff stressed the dire shortage of winter equipment, especially studs and snow chains, which he stated 'could not be emphasized too strongly'.[65] It was a comprehensive and prophetic assessment, yet it was in the conclusion to his report that Vietinghoff set out the 'painful' truth of Operation Typhoon's failure:

> The following conclusions can be drawn: The success of an operation in the present season, where at any time serious traffic problems can arise from frosts, heavy snowfalls or snow drifts, is only guaranteed if

> (a) the organisation of the mot[orised] division is eased and for each panzer division one viable road is available.
> (b) full replenishment of these divisions with fuel, special provisions and food prior to commencement (5 daily rations) is achieved.
>
> After careful evaluation of all experiences of the past weeks I am forced to conclude – although painful for the corps – that no benefits are to be expected from the deployment of the panzer corps under present and expected weather and road conditions. The wear on the troops, equipment and fuel bears no relationship to the possible success. The massing of mot[orised] troops is only a hindrance and not of any use.[66]

Vietinghoff was effectively stating that his corps could not, and should not, be committed to an operation that promised no chance of success. Yet he was also calling into question the whole basis for an offensive by Army Group Centre; an assessment that did not enjoy a sympathetic reception at the higher echelons of the German command. Hoepner read the report and then sent it up the chain of command to Kluge, but not before pouring a little scorn on the conclusions. In spite of acknowledging Vietinghoff as a veteran commander with 'clear judgement' whose comments gave 'a good picture of what should be expected of motorised forces under the circumstances and where their limits lie', Hoepner nevertheless remained adamant that Vietinghoff was overstating the problems. In an attached covering letter to Kluge, Hoepner dismissed the idea that no benefit could be expected from the forthcoming resumption of the offensive. He then continued: 'I consider a success with the onset of frost, especially snow-free frost, still possible. Also, there could perhaps be a sudden slackening in the resistance of the Russians that would allow, and demand, rapid exploitation.'[67]

There is no record of a response by Kluge to the report, but it is clear that the commander of the Fourth Army was far from impressed by the state of his forces, including Hoepner's numerically powerful Panzer Group 4. Indeed, Kluge was the most sceptical within Army Group Centre about a resumption of the advance, but, importantly, he was not opposed to it. Not surprisingly, Hoepner felt constrained by Kluge's more cautious view and the antipathy between them, which had arisen during the previous month's advance, was set to deepen. Hoepner longed for the kind of operational freedom that Guderian enjoyed as an

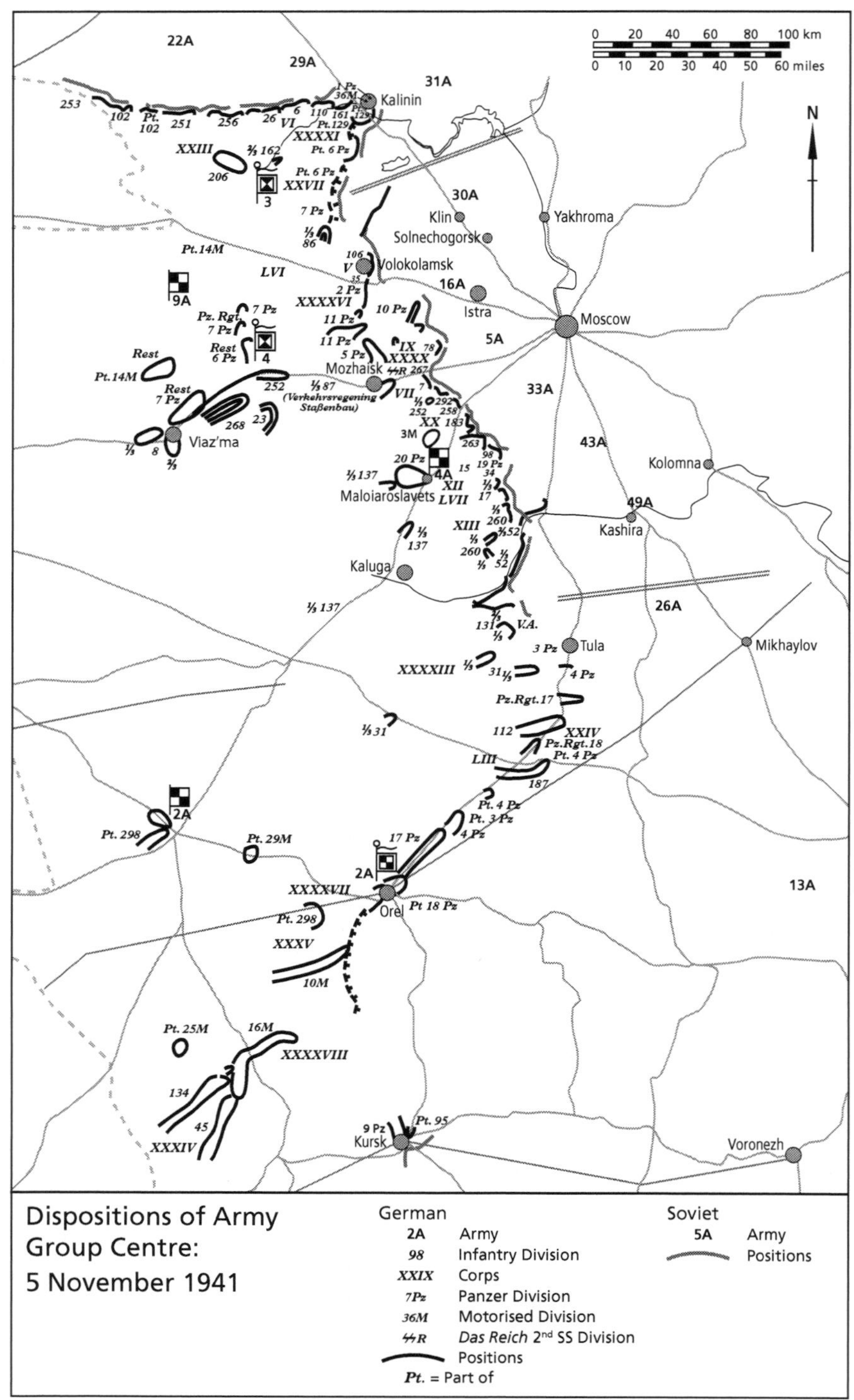

Map 2.3 Dispositions of Army Group Centre, 5 November 1941

independent army commander answering only to Bock and unbound by what many senior panzer commanders regarded as the overly cautious conservatism of the infantry generals. Hoepner was, after all, the commander of the single most powerful panzer group on the eastern front and he was in many respects blinded by this fact. He believed he possessed the strength to drive on Moscow and that it was only the absence of an enduring frost that prevented his forces from achieving that end. Yet, on 5 November, Hoepner's luck appeared to be changing when a lasting frost seemed to have taken hold. Hellmuth Stieff, a staff officer at the Fourth Army, noted on 5 November:

> Since yesterday we have had frost and – thank God – the worst of the mud is over. Before this happened, it was impossible to think about continuing the attack. Now we must retrieve our vehicles, which are scattered everywhere, and sort out our supply situation. It has been so frustrating to become stuck so close to our goal – scarcely 60 kilometres from Moscow.[68]

Yet the relief was short-lived as temperatures rose again and the roads returned to their liquid state. For the impatient Hoepner, his frustration was clearly evident from a personal letter on 5 November:

> I'm in a bad mood because it is not going forward. One is powerless. Yesterday and today we finally had frost. From tomorrow on the temperature should rise again. Thus the hopes of moving again are shot down. Even now I do not know how I am supposed to ensure the supply just of foodstuffs. For the new attack a preparation in the supply of at least 10 days is required.[69]

On the same day (5 November) that Hoepner was lamenting his stalled offensive he also took steps to ensure that when the time did come his commanders knew what would be expected of them. Accordingly, Hoepner visited Vietinghoff's panzer corps and made clear that the operational plan for an encirclement of Moscow 'will absolutely be maintained'. Hoepner also stated that the projected date for the new offensive was 19 November 'in the hope that until then sufficient supply of the corps has been carried out'.[70] In the meantime, the panzer troops had to concern themselves with the not inconsiderable problem of meeting day-to-day needs, which, as Hoepner's letter stated, was a serious challenge because Panzer Group 4 was still so poorly resourced.

Figure 2.2 The commander of Panzer Group 4, Colonel-General Erich Hoepner

Two of Hoepner's four panzer divisions only joined the war in the east at the start of October, so their casualties were much lower than the veteran panzer divisions. The average company strength of motorised infantry within Major-General Gustav Fehn's 5th Panzer Division and Lieutenant-General Rudolf Veiel's 2nd Panzer Division were set at 125 and 91 men, respectively. This compares with just a thirty-seven-man average for Major-General Walter Scheller's 11th Panzer Division and a sixty-one-man average for Major-General Wolfgang Fischer's 10th Panzer Division.[71] Yet it was in tanks that Panzer Group 4 derived its real strength. On 4 November, Veiel's 2nd Panzer Division commanded 134 combat-ready tanks with another thirty-six under repair. Although no figures are available for Fehn's 5th Panzer Division, the indications are strong (because it appears to have seen less fighting) that it had at least as many tanks as Veiel's division and probably more. Even Hoepner's two veteran panzer divisions were well stocked considering the time they had spent in the east, although both had had long periods of inactivity, relative to other panzer divisions, before Typhoon began in October. Fischer's 10th Panzer Division had ninety-two serviceable tanks and another sixty in the workshop, while Scheller's 11th Panzer Division had eighty-seven combat ready tanks and a further forty-eight awaiting repair. In total, therefore, Panzer Group 4 commanded some

450 combat-ready tanks (assuming a rough parity in tank numbers between the 5th and 2nd Panzer Divisions), although more than a hundred of these tanks consisted of the hopelessly obsolete Mark I (twenty-four) and Mark II (eighty-two) tanks.[72] Hoepner certainly had the raw firepower for a renewed offensive against Moscow, especially with the support of Reinhardt's Panzer Group 3, but it was everything else that he lacked and it must be recognised that tanks do not attack in a strategic vacuum.

A local attack by Fehn's 5th Panzer Division on 3 November demonstrated just how vulnerable tanks operating alone could be. Here Fehn's tanks drove forward unsupported by German infantry, who refused to leave their forest bunkers to aid the attack. Accordingly, the tanks were left unprotected against enemy anti-tank troops who hit many panzers with Molotov cocktails, causing a total loss of twenty-one German tanks (damaged as well as total losses). The attack floundered without any significant gain and, as the war diary of the 5th Panzer Division noted, left serious questions about the *Angriffsgeist* ('attacking spirit') of the infantry.[73] Such an episode would have been unthinkable in the German Wehrmacht only a few months before, but incidences of serious mistrust between the ranks and even outright disobedience were on the rise throughout the *Ostheer*. On the same day that the infantry had failed to attack (3 November), Scheller's 11th Panzer Division recorded rising tensions between the division and corps command. The corps accused Scheller's division of submitting 'obviously exaggerated' reports and complained that fuel lying 600 km in the rear had not been picked up by the allotted date.[74] If the officers were experiencing heightened tension over disputed reports and administrative timetables, it is easy to understand why freezing soldiers might no longer be inclined to listen to their superiors when ordered out of warm bunkers to risk their lives so that they could then dig themselves new bunkers a few kilometres further east. As Franz Frisch wrote after the war:

> No soldier could understand the idea of a winter offensive under such miserable conditions. The spirit of the troops was also below zero. We suffered terribly ... The wind blew almost all the time. We never officially received winter clothes and could not understand why they were not given to us. Our men received pieces from home in the mail, mostly socks. We improvised by wearing newspapers inside shoes and all our shirts and underwear at the same time, and

> tried making straw and rope boots to cover the shoes. Our clothes became infested with lice which added to the cold misery. Our skin was greasy and itchy. We dared not sweat too much, if that was possible, because it gave us a nasty chill in the wind.[75]

Clearly Frisch and his comrades wanted to remain in their makeshift winter quarters, but there were also many men in Army Group Centre who wanted the attack to continue in the belief that only the seizure of Moscow would end major operations on the eastern front and allow the winter to be spent in the warm houses of Muscovites. On 6 November, Karl Fuchs, a tank gunner in the 7th Panzer Division, proudly wrote to his father that his unit was moving out again 'in the direction of Moscow'. His letter noted the 'terrible cold and snow', but concluded emphatically: 'On to new deeds and victories!'[76] Another soldier wrote home of his doubts that Moscow would fall anytime soon – 'the resistance of the Bolsheviks is in different places still very striking' – yet he too maintained faith in the eventual outcome: 'Despite everything the war in the east is slowly but surely ending!'[77] Yet faith in outright victory was increasingly a reflection of German propaganda, trust in the higher officer corps and the steadfast power of the Hitler myth over any tangible reality.

The enduring optimism in Operation Typhoon's potential was not only shared at the highest levels of the army command, it was also stimulated from that quarter. The Chief of the Operations Department at the Army General Staff, Colonel Adolf Heusinger, noted in a letter on 5 November that just three weeks of light frost would see Germany 'at the end of our goal'.[78] By the same token, Halder expressed the opinion on 3 November that the Red Army was 'no longer in a position to defend a cohesive front' in Ukraine, while further north, he observed, the Soviets were stripping their front in order to raise reserves to defend Moscow.[79]

The delusion of an impending Soviet collapse was, however, punctuated by a bleak realism, which other more junior officers had no trouble recognising. Hans Meier-Welcker, a general staff officer in the 251st Infantry Division, wrote home on 7 November:

> The fallacy in the war against Russia is that it was believed that the Soviet Union would collapse internally after the first German military successes. Even in the present stage of the war, there are no signs of this. Since the idea of a rapid internal collapse of the Soviet

> Union was a misjudgement, we now find ourselves in a situation not foreseen, which none of us really know how to master.
>
> A second fallacy was the view that the great German offensive of Army Group Centre ... in October would end in success deciding the entire campaign. Before the war against Russia, and continuously during the campaign, the military strength of Russia was underestimated. So it was believed much too soon in mid-October that all battle-worthy elements of the Russian army were smashed. Yet it is astounding how fast and how numerous the Russians establish new forces ...[80]

In spite of the fact that Army Group Centre's losses were only a small percentage of those suffered by the opposing Soviet fronts, the available reserves of the Replacement Army in Germany were, nevertheless, insufficient to fill the gaps in the ranks. As one regimental commander of the battered 98th Infantry Division wrote to its commanding officer (Lieutenant-General Erich Schroeck) on 2 November: 'Without a complete replacement of the missing officers, non-commissioned officers and weapons specialists, without reordering and replacement of clothing, equipment, weapons, vehicles and horses ... the troops have no more combat value!'[81] Even Brauchitsch had to admit to Hitler on 7 November that the war in the east would not be ended in 1941,[82] a conclusion that others had reached back in August.[83] Clearly, opinions surrounding Germany's predicament in early November were heavily polarised.

On the same day that Brauchitsch was meeting with Hitler (7 November), Halder informed Army Group Centre that he was planning a meeting in the town of Orsha in about a week's time to discuss the forthcoming offensive. He also sent a map with two boundaries drawn on it reflecting 'minimum' and 'maximum' lines of advance that the renewed offensive would be expected to achieve. The minimum line began east of Leningrad and stretched southeast to a point 250 km east of Moscow, and then down to Rostov on the Don River.[84] Even in the first offensive of Operation Typhoon Army Group Centre had advanced only about 220 km east, and for this it was much better resourced and had begun its advance in far more favourable weather conditions. Now its forces were dispersed, badly equipped, extremely poorly resourced, and the weather and ground conditions were abysmal. Not only that, Halder's objective required first advancing the 80 km to Moscow (from the nearest point) and seizing the city. Not to be deterred, Halder's map also included a maximum line of advance, which included the capture of Murmansk on the Barents Sea and even further advances in the northern and central sections of the eastern front. These extended between 120 and 145 km further east than the projections of the minimum line and included the capture of Vologda and Gorky.[85] In the south, Halder's maximum line extended 50 km to the east of Stalingrad (some 480 km from the current German line) and some 350 km down into the Caucasus to Maykop.[86] The hubris reflected in such planning was staggering, and for the first time many of the senior officers within Army Group Centre were beginning to recognise the folly of the OKH's plans.

Throughout the planning phase for Operation Barbarossa as well as the summer campaign Field Marshal Bock had always been a consistent advocate of an advance on Moscow, and in this regard the single most important supporter of Halder's plans. Bock fervently believed that the Soviet capital was the surest road to victory in the east and bitterly regretted Hitler's decision to divert Guderian's panzer group into Ukraine and give Kiev precedence over Moscow. Operation Typhoon was supposed to ensure Moscow was also taken before the winter and now that plan too was under threat by the reckless desire to again attempt too much. On 11 November, Bock contacted Halder and told him:

> In my opinion, the objectives you marked on the recently-delivered map as worthwhile surely cannot be reached before winter, because we no longer have the required forces and because it is impossible to supply these forces after reaching these objectives on account of the inadequate potential for supply by rail. Furthermore, I no longer consider the objectives designated 'worthwhile' by me in the army group order for the encirclement of Moscow, specifically the line Ryazan [185 km southeast of Moscow] – Vladimir [180 km east of Moscow] – Kalyazin [165 km north of Moscow], to be attainable. All that remains, therefore, is to strive for a screening front in the general line Kolomna [100 km southeast of Moscow] – Orekhovo [85 km east of Moscow] – Zagorsk [70 km northeast of Moscow] – Dmitrov [70 km north of Moscow], which is absolutely vital to the encirclement of Moscow. I will be happy if our forces are sufficient to obtain this line.[87]

While not giving up on the idea of capturing Moscow, Bock at least recognised the utter impracticality of the OKH's expectations and took steps to correct them. The reckless optimism within the OKH was in stark contrast to the dire warnings emerging from the lower ranks, which spoke of deplorable conditions for the men and declining combat readiness. Yet the position of the OKH was bolstered by the steadfast determination, and often excessive confidence, of men like Hoepner, Reinhardt, Guderian and Kesselring, which fed Bock's hopes that Moscow could still fall. Unlike some of Hitler's other field marshals, such as Brauchitsch or Wilhelm Keitel, Bock was a man of stronger character and sharper intellect, who was not so easily overawed by dominating personalities. Accordingly, Bock listened to the council of all his subordinates and superiors, but ultimately made up his own mind. His decision to press on with the attack to Moscow was a reflection of his belief that the objective was still obtainable, but he was also driven in this conclusion by a fervent ambition to be the conqueror of Moscow, a blow, he believed, that would prove fatal to the Soviet Union.

While Bock is arguably the single most important figure in the east during the first year of the Nazi–Soviet war, a lot of what was written about him in the early postwar era reflects the erroneous views of the period and holds little credence today. Bock was not a courtly Prussian gentleman thrust into Hitler's undignified war against the Soviet Union, later to be replaced by a more 'Nazi' breed of general better equipped for the special tasks of the east. Bock in fact conducted himself with vigour and displayed unqualified loyalty to Hitler's new war, and offered no opposition to either the army's criminal orders or the mass murder being conducted by the *Einsatzgruppen* in his army group's rear area.[88] Nor is the postwar characterisation of Bock's method of command as old-fashioned or 'passive' accurate just because he earned his reputation as an infantry officer in the First World War.[89] Indeed, the fact that Bock spent both world wars as a largely successful commander reflects his accomplished understanding of warfare in each era. Bock even had the experience of fighting against Russia in the First World War, serving with the 200th Infantry Division in the Carpathian Mountains and repelling the 1916 Brusilov offensive. By the end of that war, Bock had earned an outstanding reputation for staff work and command, while having learned very good Russian (which was comparable to his English, but surpassed by his fluent French). During the First World War he had also been awarded the Iron Cross First and Second Class, the Order of the House of Hohenzollern and, in April 1918, the *Pour le Mérite*.[90] Yet, unlike some other successful officers of the First World War, Bock had little trouble adapting to a new war of rapid movement, and by 1941 he had proved himself to be an aggressive, highly adaptable and remarkably modern general. Yet if Bock shared these traits with his younger panzer commanders, he also shared their failure to grasp the weaknesses of such operations in logistics as well as the inherent dangers of over-extension. More than anyone else, Bock was responsible for the mauling of the unsupported panzer groups at Smolensk in late July and early August, a decision that allowed his army group to eliminate another major Soviet pocket, but at profound cost to his future striking power.[91] In the battle of Kiev, Bock fed Guderian's panzer group a steady supply of reinforcements to keep the offensive moving south, in spite of the desperate Soviet counterattacks threatening to collapse the defences of the army group's endangered Ninth Army.[92] Now, as Operation Typhoon threatened to stagnate under the weight of its difficulties, Bock remained insistent that the offensive be renewed and the single most important objective, Moscow, be maintained. In reaching his decision, Bock took little account of the suffering and hardships his men had endured over the long months of the campaign, and simply expected them to conduct yet another major offensive. His aim was still the elusive victory over the Soviet Union, and Operation Typhoon, having failed in that regard in October, would finally have to deliver.

While Bock sought only to restrain Halder's enthusiasm for conquest, his counterpart at Army Group South was even less convinced. Field Marshal Rundstedt, whose army group possessed the only other panzer group on the eastern front, immediately protested when hearing of Halder's minimum and maximum objectives. Rundstedt knew that even the minimum proposed line was well beyond the strength of his forces and, unlike at Army Group Centre, there was a far more credible sense of the extent, and the danger, of the yawning credibility gap between the OKH and the front.[93] Even at the end of October Rundstedt's chief-of-staff, General of the Infantry Georg von Sodenstern, noted:

> It is no longer possible to mitigate the situation by saying: 'It will be all right, it has always been alright up to now despite frequent reports that the troops cannot go on any longer.' There comes a time when – physically – they really cannot go on any longer, and, having examined the situation thoroughly, I believe that this point has now ... been reached.[94]

Halder was not to be dissuaded and, against their better judgement, the command staff at Army Group South were compelled to drive Kleist's First Panzer Army to the very limit of its capabilities. As Siegfried Roemer wrote home to his family on 4 November: 'We have been driven to areas, which we never could have dreamed that we would ever see. Now we have conquered them. The Donets region is firmly in our hands; the Caucasus, the Volga and Caspian come to the fore.'[95] Sodenstern was adamant that such distant objectives should not be attempted and informed Heusinger at the OKH: 'To be perfectly honest ... under the present circumstances both the operation [to] the Maykop oilfields and the advance on the Don will not be possible before the spring'.[96] The warning would prove prophetic and provided the first exchange in an increasingly acrimonious dispute between the staff of Army Group South and the German high command.

In the north, too, Field Marshal Leeb was under pressure to maintain his army group's advance towards Tikhvin (almost 200 km southeast of Leningrad), which was only the first objective in linking up with the Finnish Army and cutting the Red Army off from Leningrad via Lake Ladoga. The offensive had been underway since mid-October and was driven forward by the only two panzer divisions left in Army Group North (Major-General Josef Harpe's 12th Panzer Division and Major-General Erich Brandenberger's 8th Panzer Division). It was a painfully slow advance hindered by a combination of bad weather, awful terrain, a single road for the advance (flanked on both sides by swamps) and the familiar Soviet resistance.[97] Alexander Stahlberg, who participated in the advance, wrote after the war: 'Heavy losses, though not a single tank had appeared against us – what could panzers do here? ... The Russians certainly knew where to find the islands in the marshes from which they could fire on us – feeling as we did like targets set up for hunting practice along the causeway from Chudovo to Tikhvin.'[98] In spite of their hardships, by 8 November Tikhvin had fallen to the Germans, while Soviet losses included some 20,000 POWs and ninety-six tanks destroyed or captured. However, the seizure of Tikhvin would prove to be the high-water mark of Leeb's autumn offensive, and was followed by a month-long battle just to hold the town until a retreat was finally authorised.[99] Once again the projections of the OKH proved to be well beyond the capacity of the men at the front, and resulted in an abortive offensive that came nowhere near its lofty objectives.

While Leeb and Rundstedt held well-founded doubts over the continuation of their smaller-scale offensives, Bock remained committed to continuing with Operation Typhoon. He not only had the support of Hitler and Halder, but was backed by Greiffenberg, his chief-of-staff, as well as his three panzer commanders who were all impatient to resume the advance. At the end of October, Reinhardt unsuccessfully pleaded with Strauss and Bock to allow his panzer group to launch an offensive towards Yaroslavl-Rybinsk (250 km northeast of Kalinin) as early as 4 November.[100] At the same time, Hoepner was proudly proclaiming in a letter home that just fourteen days of frost would suffice for his panzer group to surround Moscow.[101] Finally, Guderian's Second Panzer Army had recently completed a remarkable 120-km drive from Mtsensk to Tula and was now preparing to strike out towards Moscow from the south. There was a real sense of urgency to beat the onset of extreme winter weather as well as heavy snowfalls, which, it was recognised, would paralyse the advance just as effectively as the mud and rain. Thus, in Army Group Centre's race to Moscow Bock would have to achieve everything in the narrow window provided by frosts freezing the roads, but before the onset of severe winter conditions. Yet, in their fixation with weather and road conditions, the German command was paying scant attention to the growing discrepancy between German offensive strength and Soviet staying power. Indeed, the Red Army would prove to be the single greatest obstacle to reaching Moscow and, even if it was not apparent to the principal German commanders, a Rubicon had been crossed and the success of Operation Typhoon was at exceptionally long odds. Kesselring, the commander of Army Group Centre's air fleet and another of Bock's supporters in advocating a continued offensive, later admitted the error of his judgement. He explained that the German defeat was due in part to the seasonal difficulties, but above all to the Red Army's resistance: 'Jupiter Pluvius[102] disposed otherwise; the Russians were given the chance to build up a thin front west of Moscow and to man it with their last reserves ... They fought heroically and stopped the assault of our almost immobilised forces.' As Kesselring then concluded: 'This was the turning-point of the great sequence of battles in the east.'[103]

3 PREPARING THE FINAL SHOWDOWN

Heading for victory: Hitler and Stalin see success

On the eve of the twenty-fourth anniversary of the October Revolution on 6 November members of the Moscow Soviet gathered in the Mayakovski Metro Station on Gorky Street. The station was the most grandiose of Moscow's famous metro architectural projects, but, more importantly, it was also the deepest, ensuring the best possible protection in the event of a German air attack. The contingency proved well founded as a German air raid attacked the city in the early evening. Yet events deep underground proceeded undisturbed as Stalin arrived, to rapturous applause, on a special train at seven o'clock. His speech to the party faithful was broadcast across the Soviet Union and reported throughout the world; it was to become one of the defining speeches of Stalin's wartime leadership.[1] To begin with Stalin was not inclined to hide the danger his country faced:

> I already stated in one of my speeches at the beginning of the war that the war had created a serious danger for our country ... Today, as a result of four months of war, I must emphasize that this danger – far from diminishing – has on the contrary increased. The enemy has captured the greater part of the Ukraine, Belorussia, Moldavia and Estonia, and a number of other regions, has penetrated the Donbas, is looming like a black cloud over Leningrad, and is menacing our glorious capital, Moscow.[2]

Having sounded this warning, Stalin insisted that the war had already turned in his favour and that it was Germany that faced the dire consequences of a long, drawn out war: 'There can be no doubt that as a result of four months of war, Germany, whose manpower reserves are already becoming exhausted, has been considerably more weakened by the war than the Soviet Union, whose reserves are only now unfolding to their full extent.'[3] Indeed, Stalin's resolve to prosecute the war against Germany with all necessary vigour alluded to Germany's own parallel war of extermination:

> The Hitlerite party and Hitlerite command ... call for the annihilation of the great Russian nation, the nation of Plekhanov and Lenin, Belinskii and Chernishevskii, Pushkin and Tolstoi, Glinka and Tschaikovskii, Gorki and Chekhov, Sechenov and Pavlov, Repin and Surikov, Suvorov and Kutuzov!
>
> The German invaders want a war of extermination against the peoples of the USSR. Well, if the Germans want a war of extermination, they shall have it.[4]

Such rhetoric should not be taken to mean that Stalin or the Soviet state was planning to conduct a war of extermination on a par with Hitler's and, importantly, the well-known Soviet excesses that were to become a feature of their 1944/5 campaign through eastern Germany were not condoned or directed from above. Rather, the Soviet dictator was alluding to the iron resolve and relentless fortitude with which the Soviet people were to oppose their German invaders. Referring to a war of extermination, Stalin left no doubt as to the stakes inherent in a war with Nazi Germany and provided the answer as to who would be annihilated if that was the war that Germany chose to fight.[5]

Stalin's speech on 6 November was only the prelude to an even greater statement of Soviet resolve in the face of the Nazi threat. Every year on the anniversary of the 7 November Revolution Moscow's Red Square hosted an elaborate military parade observed by the top Soviet leadership, including Stalin himself. With the Soviet front torn open in October and German armies rolling towards Moscow there were, understandably, no plans afoot for any such parade in 1941. Yet towards the end of October Stalin approached a number of his generals in the air force and asked if a parade could in fact be held. The suggestion was met with wonderment and a host of objections. Such an auspicious date in the

Soviet calendar seemed likely to attract a major German air raid and, in any case, the Red Army was scraping the bottom of the barrel just to provide a bare minimum of troops to patch up the front.[6] Zhukov, however, was supportive. He correctly judged that Bock's army group was attempting to rebuild its strength and, for the time being at least, was no longer actively seeking to advance its front.[7] Zhukov cautioned that Moscow's air defences should be reinforced, but otherwise gave his consent.[8]

Zhukov's confidence that Moscow had been granted a temporary respite is reflected in documents from the operations staff of his western front. These make clear that the Soviet command had a remarkably clear picture of Army Group Centre's force strengths and capabilities. A report from 1 November concluded: 'Having suffered great losses in previous battles and not having the strength to further advance on Moscow, [the] enemy has switched to the defence, regrouping his forces and bringing up reserves'. Later the document continued:

> It is unlikely that the opponent in the next 2–3 days will be able to advance on Moscow. To build up operational reserves, provide food and ammunition as well as tanks and other equipment, the enemy will need at least half a month, to provide everything needed for a new offensive prepared in advance in the area of Smolensk–Viaz'ma.[9]

Such predictions proved to be highly accurate, which speaks both to the success of Soviet intelligence and the somewhat overstated gamble that Stalin's decision to host a parade represents.[10]

Frantic efforts were then taken to train the latest batch of raw recruits in parade-ground marching, but none of these men were told the true significance of such drills. Leonid Shevelev recalled: 'For us it was incredible: the enemy was near Moscow and we were practising our marching!' Yet early on the morning of 7 November when Shevelev and his comrades were told that they were to march through Red Square under the watchful eye of Stalin himself the boost to morale was enormous. 'We had heard that Stalin had left the capital. It was very important for us to see that our leader chose to stay with us in Moscow. This made us march with the kind of determination as if we were nailing down the coffins of the advancing Nazis.'[11] In total some 28,000 men took part in the parade, including cadets and veterans of the

Figure 3.1 Red Army troops parade through Red Square on the twenty-fourth anniversary of the October Revolution

revolution.[12] Stalin again gave a speech (which had to be re-recorded the following day owing to a technical fault with the sound) telling the assembled soldiers: 'The whole world is looking at you, for it is you who can destroy the marauding armies of the German invader. The enslaved peoples of Europe look upon you as their liberators ... Be worthy of your mission!'[13]

Many of the soldiers then began their march directly from Red Square outside the city to the front lines, where the mystique of such a parade and its boost to morale proved to be a triumph of propaganda, reaffirming the Soviet leadership's commitment to defending Moscow and providing an appearance of strength that was somewhat fabricated.[14] Yevgeny Teleguyev recounted that when his unit reached the front, the soldiers they met were abuzz with the rumour of a parade and he was able to confirm: 'There was [a parade] and we even participated in it.'[15] As Zhukov later noted: 'The domestic, political and international significance of this November parade was undoubtedly great.'[16] Internally this was reflected by the Moscow military censors who checked 2,626,507 pieces of correspondence between 1 and 15 November, and discovered a rise in 'positive sentiments' as well as a near absence of defeatism and political dissatisfaction (although this may simply have been because of such censorship).[17] The real significance of the November parade is highlighted by recent research into the motivations of the Soviet people in which resistance to the Soviet cause by ordinary citizens was judged most likely to occur when the state was perceived to be weak.[18] If Stalin had a sense of this his decision to hold the parade even with the German soldiers closer than ever to Moscow reflected once again an astute political instinct.

While the defence of Moscow was partly a question of hearts and minds, pragmatic considerations were also fundamental to the defence of the city. By the beginning of November a system of new defensive lines was rapidly taking shape; an outer 'main' defensive line running in a semi-circle around Moscow for a radius of 16 km. This was then augmented by three separate 'urban' lines inside the city itself, which were designated 'circular railway line', 'urban ring A' and 'urban ring B'.[19] Moscow City Council directed construction, and each district was issued detailed instructions of what to build and where. Roads were heavily barricaded with steel 'hedgehogs',[20] barbed-wire entanglements, reinforced concrete pillboxes and fortified gun emplacements. Narrow gaps allowed vehicles to pass, while all movement was observed from the surrounding buildings, which had been transformed into strong points with bricked-up windows, fortified balconies and narrow firing slits hiding machine-gun nests and anti-tank detachments.[21] Irina Bogolyubskaya recalled soldiers coming into her family's apartment and setting up a machine-gun emplacement at one of their windows overlooking the street. 'They were preparing for street fighting,' she noted.[22] The American war correspondent Ralph Ingersoll wrote that Moscow's population 'gave me the impression of being determined to defend their city – and resigned to the hardships they knew that defence entailed'. He then added: 'I had not been in Moscow long before I concluded that the Germans had little chance of taking the city by frontal attack ... Preparations to meet them were too thorough.'[23]

The city transportation had been commandeered for military purposes, with Moscow's bus service ferrying troops and supplies to the front, while convoys of trams, travelling nose to tail with white painted stripes on the rear of each alerting the following driver to his proximity in the dark, travelled as far outside the city as their lines extended.[24] Moscow was now both the political and military focal point of the Soviet Union's total war effort and commanded the attention of the world, a fact that the celebrated Soviet writer Ilya Ehrenburg recorded in an article for *Red Star* on 7 November:

> Today the whole world looks towards Moscow. People are talking of Moscow in Narvik and Melbourne. The telegraph wires of the world keep repeating the word Moscow, Moscow isn't just a city, it has become the hope of the world ... Yet Moscow has remained a Russian city. Each one of its streets holds a memory for us. All our life and history is in its jumbled plan, in the mingling of old houses with new skyscrapers. By day, Moscow lives an ordinary industrious life. Only the crunch of glass and the stern look in people's eyes are reminders of this terrible autumn. By night Moscow is blacked out. Yet this dark night-wedded Moscow remains a beacon for tortured humanity ... Moscow is fighting for itself, for Russia, and for you, distant friends, for humanity and for the whole world.[25]

Even while the Soviets were desperately preparing for the defence of Moscow there was no let up in their often ill-fated offensive mentality, which in the past had seriously weakened already under-strength divisions and fatally undermined large sections of the front. In the first half of November, Soviet offensives were again resumed in an attempt to exploit weaknesses in the German line and disrupt their preparations for the anticipated resumption of Typhoon. Such local attacks usually proved to be much more costly than their gains, if any, justified, but they certainly denied many of Army Group Centre's divisions the rest they so badly needed. On 3 November, Bock noted in his diary that minor penetrations of the Fourth Army's right wing had been reported, while on the same day the Ninth Army suffered a break-through, which temporarily cut the vitally important road to Kalinin.[26] Further south, an intelligence report from *Fremde Heere Ost* (Foreign Armies East) for 6 November noted the 'considerable reinforcement' of enemy forces near the Second Panzer Army at Tula.[27] As Guderian acknowledged, 'it was plain that the enemy was planning an attack both to the east and the west of Tula'. He also drew attention to the weakness of his overstretched forces: 'As an example of how critical the situation in the Tula area was at this time, four weak rifle battalions of the 4th Panzer Division were responsible for a front of 20 miles [32 km] to the west of Dedilovo with the additional task of maintaining contact between LIII Army Corps and the 3rd Panzer Division fighting outside

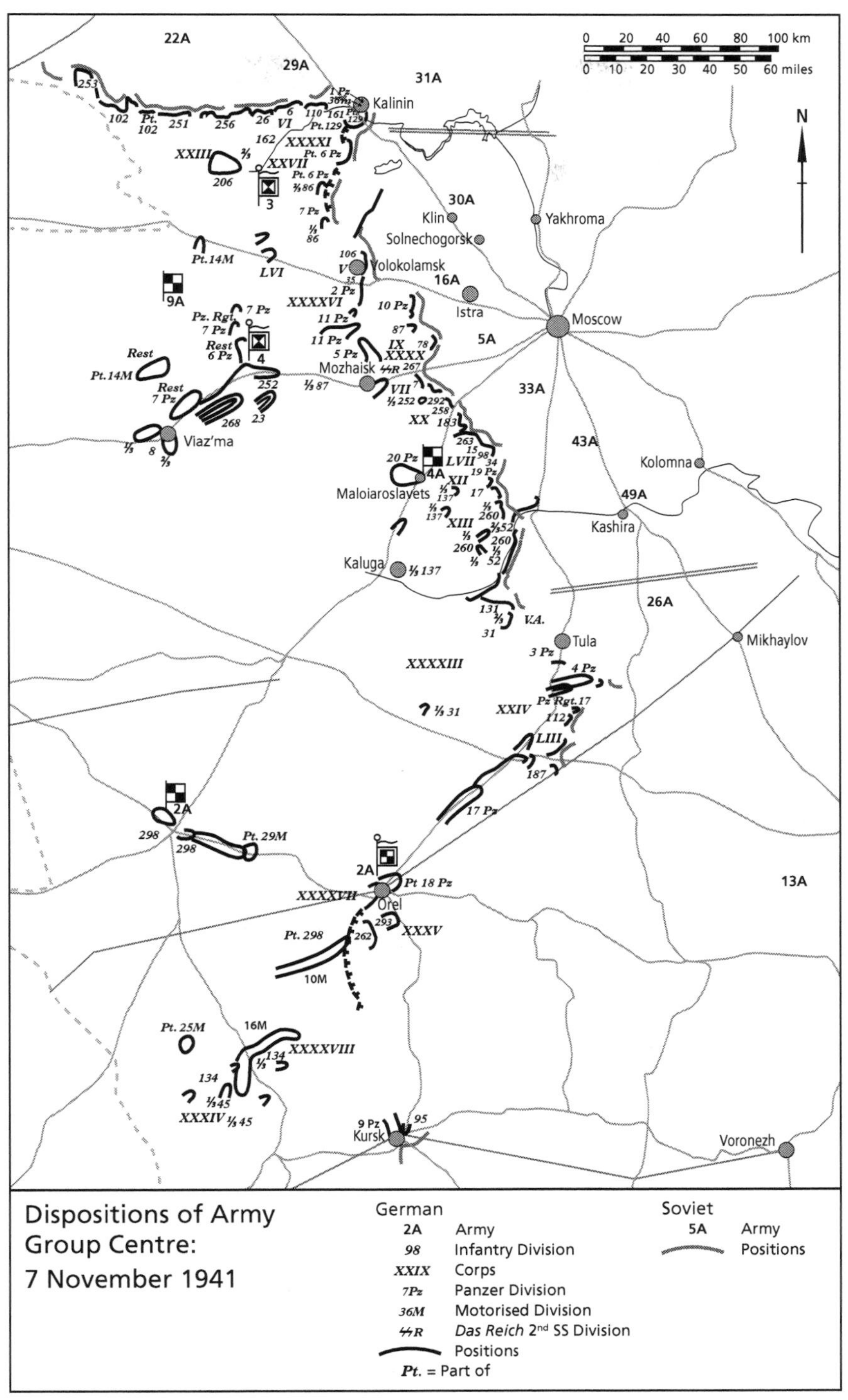

Map 3.1 Dispositions of Army Group Centre, 7 November 1941

Tula.'[28] Foreign Armies East also predicted continued attacks against the Fourth and Ninth Armies, which were not long in coming.[29] On 7 November, Bock reported local attacks against Kluge's front, while Strauss' army suffered 'a more serious attack against VI Corps'.[30] While the Soviet attacks were not particularly threatening at the strategic level, they were still bitterly contested battles for the men who had to repel them. On 6 November, Major Hans Riederer wrote in his diary about the strength of one Soviet attack, the weakness of his forces and the refusal of his divisional command to provide any more reserves. At the front, in the most dangerous sector, one of his officers was leading a stand with his last twenty men.[31] Another solider, Kurt Miethke, wrote to his wife on 9 November how his unit had 'again' come under attack by 1,500 Soviet soldiers.[32]

While a sizable number of Soviet commanders even in 1941 exhibited a thoroughly professional understanding of modern tactics and weaponry there was also another group, which eschewed such thinking and advocated a return to the tactics of the civil war.[33] These were officers who had typically earned rapid promotion in the era of the purges, when the innovative ideas of Mikhail Tukhachevsky's 'deep operations'[34] were shunned and loyalty to the party line and an outdated doctrine were the prerequisites to promotion and higher office.[35] Some of the Soviet offensives in November bore the hallmark of this naivety and ineptitude, leading to senseless losses on the battlefield. One of the more remarkable was the charge of the newly arrived 44th Mongolian Cavalry Division directly into the defensive fire of the German 106th Infantry Division. In a matter of minutes some 2,000 Soviet cavalrymen were cut to pieces without a single German loss.[36] One German witness to the attack later described the scene:

> We could not believe that the enemy intended to attack us across this broad field, which lay open like a parade ground before us. But then three ranks of cavalry started moving towards us. Across the sunlit field the horsemen rode into the attack bent over their horses' necks, their sabres shining. The first shells exploded in their midst and soon a thick black cloud hung over them. Torn scraps of men and horses flew into the air. It was difficult to distinguish one from the other. In this hell the maddened horses were running about wildly. The handful of survivors was finished off by artillery and machine gun. And then out of the wood a second wave of horsemen

> rode to the attack. It was impossible to imagine that after the annihilation of the first squadrons the nightmare sight would be repeated. But our guns were now zeroed in on the target, and the destruction of the second wave of cavalry took place even more quickly than the first.[37]

Nor was this an isolated example of such futile and excessive wastage. It was not just the inexperience of the Soviet commanders that made such carnage possible. Their obstinate refusal to accept the consequences of failure and take responsibility for the flawed method of attack convinced them to go on ordering fresh waves of men to surge forward, thereby escalating the scale of the disaster. The effect was calamitous, but it did have one unintended consequence. The fact that the men of the Red Army would still advance even after having witnessed the fate of their comrades convinced many German soldiers of their enemy's unflappable bravery and devotion. After one German soldier endured countless Soviet massed assaults over a three-day period he later wrote:

> The number, duration and fury of those attacks had exhausted and numbed us completely. Not to hide the truth they had frightened us ... I think that on that autumn day 1941 some of us began to realize for the first time that the war against the Soviet Union was going to be bigger than we had thought it would be and a sense of depression, brought about by a fear of the unknown, settled upon us.[38]

With so many Red Army troops killed in senseless frontal attacks numerous German battlefield accounts give an impression of Soviet soldiers that tend to reflect the dehumanising depictions of Nazi propaganda. However, such accounts may also be a result of the trauma associated with these memories and the desire to distance one's self from involvement in bloody and barbarous actions. In that sense Nazi propaganda not only offered 'explanations' for Soviet actions, but also provided coping strategies for the wholesale killing that was often demanded on the battlefield. As one young soldier in the SS noted as he advanced through the bloody aftermath of Soviet battlefields:

> Everywhere lie tens of thousands of Russian corpses. They have fallen on the hillsides, on the banks of the rivers, on both sides of the

> bridges, in the open country. They have been scythed down as they fought, by division, by battalions, by regiments, by sections. Often the piles of interlaced bodies are a yard or more high, as though a machine gun has mown them down, wave after wave of them. One has to see this monstrous mass of decomposing corpses to realise fully what war is like ... Wherever we camp we first have to spray all the carrion in the vicinity with quicklime or gasoline.[39]

While the Red Army was capable of inflicting some of its bloodiest battlefield defeats on itself, the common depiction of an inept peasant army in the early months of the war is quite inaccurate. The Red Army's mastery of combined arms warfare in the latter half of the war was not a sudden occurrence, nor was it simply attributable to lessons learned from the Germans. It was built on the back of countless earlier defeats, as well as a fair share of localised victories, where surviving junior commanders with their own innovative ideas to refine tactical and operational concepts slowly gained in recognition.

While the carnage the Red Army endured in 1941 was the dominant theme to many postwar historians of Operations Barbarossa and Typhoon, it was by no means the whole story. In the course of achieving its unprecedented string of battlefield victories the *Ostheer* was being bled white and, unlike the Soviet Union, Germany did not have the manpower resources to stem the flow as well as meet its increasing economic needs. A report produced by the army high command on 6 November told of just how weak the *Ostheer* had become. Seventeen German panzer divisions had invaded the Soviet Union on 22 June, but it was estimated that their combined strength now equalled just six panzer divisions or an average 35 per cent of their former strength. Likewise, the thirteen motorised infantry divisions were judged to have a combined strength of just eight divisions, which amounted to 60 per cent of their former number. From a starting point of 101 infantry divisions (without any motorisation), it was estimated that they together represented a force of only sixty-five divisions having shed a third of their former strength. In total, of the 136 major formations assessed in the east[40] it was determined that together they possessed a combined strength of just eighty-three full strength formations.[41] This was barely enough to hold the eastern front, especially given the approach of winter and the *Ostheer*'s continual decline in strength, but the OKH was in no way dissuaded from launching another wide-ranging offensive. Indeed, the extent of the ambivalence was further illustrated when on the same day (6 November) Halder recorded the updated casualty figures for the *Ostheer* since the start of Operation Barbarossa. In total no less than 20 per cent, or one in five men of the *Ostheer* (686,108 men from 3.4 million),[42] had become casualties in the four and a half months of the war and there was still no end in sight.[43] The great majority of German soldiers could name at least a comrade or two who had been killed in action, and many could recite a long list. One soldier, whose unit was just 80 km from Moscow, wrote home in a letter on 5 November: 'Until now we have forty-nine dead and ninety-one wounded in the company. I think one can see that we certainly were in battle.'[44] The next day (6 November), Karl Knoblauch, who served in Weichs' Second Army, wrote: 'The losses have increased significantly in recent weeks. The [Soviet] defence has become much stronger – the rest is due to the unusual weather conditions.'[45]

Indeed, Army Group Centre had lost some 90,000 men since the start of Operation Typhoon with some 40,000 of these having been sustained in the period between 16 October and 15 November, indicating that the period of the *rasputitsa* and the pause in operations were by no means devoid of serious casualties.[46] Hans Pichler noted the heavy losses by observing the presence of many new officers in his battalion headquarters, almost none of whom he recognised from the start of the campaign.[47] In an article published in the *Berliner Lokalanzeiger* on 6 August, the war correspondent Fritz Lucke noted the words of a young soldier who gave a eulogy at a collective funeral for the fallen men of his battalion: 'If one of us should die, the other stands for two. For God has given every fighter a comrade!'[48] By mid-November losses meant that one man was now standing for three or four. Of course, such heavy losses not only had a tangible effect on the fighting strength of the combat units; they also had a profound psychological impact on the remaining men. Günter von Scheven wrote home in a letter on 6 November: 'Of joy in this world I do not expect much. I have distanced myself to a great extent from what otherwise fulfils people. It is not yet time to speak about it. Horror and death are still too close. I must first get out of the gloomy atmosphere.'[49] On the same day Alois Scheuer wrote a letter with a similar sentiment:

> The war here in Russia in all its forms is terrible, all human thought and feeling you have to turn off. In addition to the enemy, with whom we have a life and death struggle, there is now also cold and

> hunger. But we have to endure as hard as it may be. Blessed be the man who survives this happy and healthy. I would like to do my duty as best I can, though it is often unspeakably difficult.[50]

While heavy losses had dogged the *Ostheer* from the start of the campaign until September, a constant stream of men from the reserve Replacement Army in Germany had at least covered the most immediate needs of the army groups.[51] Now, as the autumn advanced, the supply of men dried up and replacements were dependent on new recruits exiting the training grounds, whose numbers were woefully inadequate to meet the needs of the *Ostheer*. At the very least, Army Group Centre's pause in operations allowed a measure of reorganisation as units were amalgamated and basic training given to many men promoted to non-commissioned officers as a result of the dire shortfall in junior officers. The early November pause also dramatically cut the rate of loss within the combat units. Lieutenant-General Franz Landgraf's 6th Panzer Division recorded daily losses in its war diary, allowing a comparison between the first days of October when Operation Typhoon began and the first days of November when the offensive had ceased. Between 2 and 6 October the panzer division suffered sixty-six dead, 228 wounded and eighteen missing, while in the same period for November the rate of loss was just one dead, fourteen wounded and one man missing.[52] In many instances, however, the damage had already been done. Major-General Heinrich Recke's 161st Infantry Division alone had, in the defence of Kalinin (a two-week period), suffered some 2,000 casualties.[53] Stumme's XXXX Panzer Corps reported on 5 November that company strengths averaged just sixty-five men and noted the 'loss of physical and psychological strength'.[54] Even Lieutenant-General Rudolf Veiel's 2nd Panzer Division, which had arrived at full strength in the east for Operation Typhoon, had already suffered almost 1,000 casualties by November.[55] Nor were the losses all a result of combat. The harsh weather was already taking a heavy toll on the more exposed and poorly equipped units of Army Group Centre. Already on 7 November a battalion of Langermann-Erlancamp's 4th Panzer Division had reported the loss of seventy-five men from frostbite on their hands and feet and another 192 with severe influenza (of which 100 also had fever).[56] It was another stark warning of things to come as the full force of winter loomed, which, together with the resumption of the offensive, threatened another flood of German casualties.

While Stalin addressed the Soviet nation on 7 November to mark the anniversary of the revolution, the following day (8 November) was a similarly auspicious occasion for the Nazi state and Hitler also sought to mark it with a major speech. The German dictator had hardly left his secluded East Prussian headquarters since the war in the east had begun, but since seizing power he had never missed the opportunity to mark the occasion of the Nazi Putsch of 1923 at the Löwenbräukeller in Munich. Always politically astute when it came to public opinion, Hitler was no doubt aware by early November that his regime faced a credibility crisis after the bombastic claims of mid-October when the German people had been told that the war in the east had been decided. It was no time to break with tradition and ignore a major public event, which could only further fuel speculation that something was amiss in the east. On 3 November, the secret SD reports gauging German public opinion revealed a growing impatience for new *Sondermeldungen* (special news bulletins) concerning Leningrad and Moscow.[57] Three days later (on 6 November), the new SD report reflected disappointment and confusion about how the war in the east could be ended. As the report stated:

> There are still large sections of the population who are somewhat disappointed that Bolshevism has not been crushed as quickly as might have been hoped and that the end of the eastern campaign is not in sight. In discussions among our fellow countrymen about the military situation in the east the question continually posed is how an end to the war against Russia is even possible. On the one hand, the impossibility of a peace or ceasefire with Stalin is recognized; on the other, they also consider it impossible to occupy all of Russia with German troops, since there would not be enough ... The absence of more reports of success in the Moscow theatre is also giving the population more reason to wonder, all the more so since it was already reported fourteen days ago that German troops were 60 km from Moscow.[58]

Clearly, the German population was worried.[59] Goebbels fumed in his diary at the disastrous effect Otto Dietrich, the Reich's Press Chief who publicly announced that the war in the east had been decided, had had in raising false expectations.[60] Dietrich claimed that his statements had been dictated to him by Hitler.[61] However, Goebbels was himself in no small measure to blame for the overblown expectations of the German population. He had directed the fanfare of victory announcements, again at Hitler's behest, which for weeks had acted to sow the seeds of hope of an impending end to the war. Now Hitler had to explain the apparent dichotomy between Nazi propaganda and the achievements – or lack thereof – of the *Ostheer*. His 8 November speech in Munich was therefore an attempt to sell the message of a successful war and justify the hyperbole of recent announcements:

> The materiel we took in this period [of advance through the Soviet Union] is immense. Right now, we have over fifteen thousand planes, over twenty-two thousand tanks, twenty-seven thousand guns. It is truly an enormous amount of materiel. The entire industry of the world, including German industry, could only replace such amounts slowly. In any event, our democrats' industries will not replace it in the next few years! . . . We defeated France in around six weeks; the occupied area is only a fraction of what we conquered in the east. Now somebody comes and says that we had expected this to be done in the east in a month and a half. With all due respect to lightning warfare – you still have to march! . . . If you walk all the way from the German border to Rostov or the Crimea, or Leningrad, then we are talking real distances, especially considering the roads in the 'paradise of workers and peasants'.[62]

After Hitler had assured his listeners that the war in the east was an unqualified success, he then made the extraordinary claim that the Soviet Union was defeated:

> Never before has a gigantic empire been shattered and defeated in a shorter time than the Soviet Union has been this time. This could occur and succeed only thanks to the unheard-of, unique bravery and willingness to sacrifice of our German Wehrmacht, which takes upon itself unimaginable strains. What all the German arms have accomplished here cannot be expressed by words. We can only bow deeply before our heroes.[63]

That Hitler continued referring to the Soviet Union as 'shattered and defeated' speaks to his concern for public opinion as well as maintaining the idea that the war was still headed for a definitive conclusion.[64] It also reveals his determination to forecast victory consistently in spite of the strategic circumstances. He was supported in this by his inner circle of generals at the OKW (who in any case allowed their judgements to be shaped by Hitler) and Halder at the OKH. Halder by this point at least foresaw operations continuing into 1942, but only against the last remnants of a largely defeated Red Army. Indeed, on 8 November his diary noted enemy defensive works being built near Voronezh, which he concluded, 'speaks for the fact that the enemy were, for the time being, not yet giving up the area between Moscow and the Caucasus'. He soon expected to see similar enemy withdrawals north of Kalinin,[65] while the renewal of Operation Typhoon, he believed, would clear the remaining Soviet forces around Moscow and lead to the capture of the Soviet capital. For the German high command it was not a question of *if* the Soviet Union could be defeated, only how much longer it would take. Bock was somewhat more realistic believing all his resources would be necessary to seize Moscow, with none of the long easterly advances advocated by Halder's minimum and maximum lines, but he at least believed that this grandiose objective was possible and still hoped that it would prove the decisive blow (just as he believed the fall of Paris had caused French resistance to collapse the year before).[66]

Interestingly, the one man in Hitler's inner circle who sensed the dangers represented by the progress of the war in the east was Goebbels. Throughout September and October he had repeatedly confided in his diary his fears for the progress of the war, but characteristically Goebbels never questioned Hitler's desire for a more celebratory reporting of the war and, in fact, carried out his instructions with great gusto. Even before the SD reports confirmed it, however, Goebbels knew that the German people would become confused by the apparent disparity between the Nazi message and the course of events in the east. Thus, on 8 November he was moved to write an article in *Reich* entitled 'How and When', which subtly aimed to prepare the German people for a longer war than they might have expected:

> We must continue marching according to the law by which we started. Not one of us can escape ... Fate is leading us on severely and mercilessly, but with good intentions ... The question *how* the war will end is more important than *when* it will end. If we win, then we have won everything ... if we lose, then we have lost all that, and

> more ... The Axis powers are literally fighting for their existence, and the worry and hardship affecting us all in the war is but a pale reflection of the inferno that awaits us if we lose ... Can fate be blamed for putting us to the test just once more before the final triumph? ... Let us not ask when it [victory] will come, let us rather make sure it comes.[67]

Paul Schmidt, the chief foreign ministry interpreter, observed the radical transformation in the messages being broadcast by Nazi propaganda during the final months of 1941. As Schmidt recalled: 'Instead of "We have won the war", foreigners now heard "We shall win the war", and finally "We cannot lose the war".' In Schmidt's words: 'The gramophone records were being changed.'[68]

Heading for defeat: Army Group Centre's panzer forces

As Halder contemplated the renewal of the offensive he was keen to instil in the armies fighting in the east 'the thinking of the general staff'.[69] Speaking to Heusinger on 5 November, Halder explained that the army required some concept of how to close out the current campaign. As Halder saw it there were two competing alternatives for how the army should proceed: the first he termed *Erhaltungsgedanken* in which the conservation of strength and preparation for winter would determine German strategy; the other he dubbed *Wirkungsgedanken*, which aimed for the exploitation of all available resources to achieve maximum effect in the time remaining for the offensive. The two options would have to be weighed and balanced against each other and the results communicated to the eastern commanders so that they shared, understood and acted on the thinking of the general staff.[70] To achieve this, Halder planned a major conference in the east with all the chiefs-of-staff of the armies and army groups. Thus, the conference, which was to take place at Orsha in the rear area of Army Group Centre on 13 November, was less an exchange of ideas than an opportunity for the OKH to instruct its subordinate army groups and armies on the accepted strategic option.[71] That option was quickly determined by Halder, who, just two days after his discussion with Heusinger, sent each army group and army chief-of-staff an eleven-page document detailing his proposed offensive intentions, which confirmed that Halder had dismissed any further thoughts of *Erhaltungsgedanken* and was determined to instruct his commanders in the notion of *Wirkungsgedanken*. Nor was there any pressure from Hitler in reaching this conclusion. Indeed, the reverse was true; Halder looked to Hitler for acceptance of his operational goals.[72] The document that Halder sent also included his map with the minimum and maximum lines of advance. Moscow was portrayed as the 'bridgehead of Asia', and its fall would facilitate wide-ranging advances aided by the fact that the Red Army was said to be no longer capable of maintaining a continuous line from Lake Ladoga to the Black Sea.[73] Far from revealing the true depths to which the *Ostheer* had sunk, the agenda of the Orsha conference was already preordained to be a rubber stamp of the OKH's ill-considered offensive.

While the army high command demonstrated an unflappable support for the renewed offensive, the reports coming up from the divisions and corps of the panzer and motorised formations told an unmistakeable story of exhaustion and unprecedented weakness. Reinhardt, the commander of Panzer Group 3, who had himself relentlessly campaigned for an outlandish offensive 250 km northeast towards Yaroslavl-Rybinsk,[74] claimed after the war to have been shocked at the time by the extent of the proposals emanating from the high command. Their perceived success, Reinhardt contended, 'was built on the basis of an image of the enemy who was at the end of his strength, an image which we at the front viewed with doubt due to the enemy behaviour in the fighting around Kalinin'.[75] There is no record that Reinhardt's thinking was quite so critical at the time, but the area around Kalinin was undoubtedly one of the most active – and troublesome – in Army Group Centre. On 6 November, Kirchner's XXXXI Panzer Corps complained that it did not have the strength to free the vital southern supply road from enemy fire and therefore trucks and supplies were continually being lost. The Red Army controlled the heights around Petruschino from which they would have to be dislodged, but, according to its war diary, Kirchner's corps had neither the manpower nor the fuel for such an operation and munitions were only available, in the best case, for two to three days of defensive fighting.[76] To solve the problem on the following day (7 November), Strauss' Ninth Army outlined a plan to order the XXVII Army Corps to attack and push back the Soviet line, with Kirchner's corps playing only a minor support role. Yet Bock, upon hearing the plan, feared it lacked sufficient strength and ordered Kirchner's corps to commit stronger forces on foot. Bock saw no reason for its lack of mobility to be a hindrance to great success and even emphasised the point in his diary:

> a letter from the panzer group which arrived today held forth in great detail and in generally negative terms about the use of motorized troops as foot soldiers. In my reply I made reference to Panzer Army Guderian,[77] which is providing daily proof that motorized forces fighting on foot are capable of outstanding feats – they just have to want to![78]

Certainly, Guderian's thrust to reach Tula at the end of October was not achieved on foot, and his forces had since made very little headway using any form of movement. Yet disregarding material factors and explaining success, or lack thereof, as a question of motivation – the requisite 'will' to achieve – was a distinctly Nazi conception of which Bock was also at times a proponent.

If the panzer group was appalled by such thinking, the rank and file, while not privy to all the details, knew enough to hold deep reservations about the public boastings of their high command. One of the more insightful commentaries comes from Ludwig Freiherr von Heyl, a lieutenant in the 36th Motorised Infantry Division, who wrote on 12 November:

> When we talk about the war we are all of the same opinion: that the official army communiqués are largely exaggeration, that the Russians are in many respects an equal opponent to us and an opponent from whom we can learn something. For despite our series of victories, they are in no way broken, they continue to resist strongly against the whole German army, and an end to the campaign may not be reached before the winter. In a larger sense, the war has reached a critical stage.
>
> Further major attacks are no longer possible because of the difficulties we are having with our supplies. I personally believe that by December we will no longer be able to conduct large-scale military operations at all, and – although much remains unpredictable – we will then have to switch to a protracted defence. But no preparations are being made for such an eventuality.
>
> We have not lost our courage or our resolve, but a little realism from time to time would do no harm here.[79]

Realism, however, like so many things in the German army, was in short supply, and it seemed no end of reports from the lower echelons could disabuse Bock and Halder of their overblown expectations. Private Gerhard vom Bruch, who was quartered in a poor village east of Kalinin, asked perhaps the most fundamental question of his commanders: 'Do we really know for certain that only a few enemy divisions are left facing us and after that the road is clear to Moscow – and who knows what other cities?'[80] The experience of almost five months of fighting against the relentlessness of the Red Army had cultivated a healthy scepticism among the troops, and seizing Moscow, it was generally recognised, would be anything but easy.

While the high command proceeded with their fanciful notions of what could be achieved, in practice the battered instruments of operational success were irredeemable. On 8 November, Krüger's 1st Panzer Division, which had been fighting at Kalinin since it seized the city in mid-October, reported to Kirchner's XXXXI Panzer Corps that its tanks had driven an average of 8,000 km since the start of Barbarossa and very few had had a change or reconditioning of their engines. Of those remaining in service only about a company (between fifteen and twenty tanks) could be considered fully combat-ready, with the others only provisionally so.[81] Wheeled transport had also suffered terribly since the start of the campaign, and the difficulties of repair were also a problem of standardisation. One report from a motorised artillery unit included the usual list of repairs as well as the individual vehicle makes. Of six tractors there were five different makes, of five cars there were five different models and of seven trucks there were six different makes. The unit had captured Soviet equipment as well as a host of various vehicle firms including Ford, Chevrolet, Opel, Henschel, BMW, Tatra, Horch, Henschel, Magirus and Wanderer. In total the unit had eighteen vehicles in need of repair and no less than sixteen of these were of different makes and models.[82] Irrespective of makes and designs, some essential spare parts, such as replacement springs, were simply not to be found anywhere in the east and these constituted a major bottleneck to maintaining mobility. Springs taken from Soviet vehicles were a stop-gap solution, but it was soon noticed that they could not support as great a load.[83] Beyond the absence of spare parts, of which springs were only the top of the long list of shortages, the road conditions and general lack of maintenance meant that the previous average of 100 km per fuel supply ration now sufficed for just 15–25 km.[84] As Reinhardt noted prior to the

Figure 3.2 The commander of Panzer Group 3, General Georg-Hans Reinhardt

resumption of the November offensive: 'Many essential pieces of military equipment, including numerous important vehicles such as prime movers, were missing. The whole fleet of vehicles was only provisionally restored. Even in the panzer divisions one saw columns of harnessed horses, which had to help out.'[85] Panzer Group 3 may have looked unfavourably upon Bock's insistence that the panzer troops fight on as foot soldiers, but for many units there was little more that could be expected.

This is not to suggest that Reinhardt's panzer group was uniformly affected. While Kirchner's XXXXI Panzer Corps was reeling from the gruelling fighting at Kalinin, Schaal's LVI Panzer Corps (6th and 7th

Panzer Divisions) had been rested after the fighting at Viaz'ma and therefore was able to raise its complement of combat-ready tanks. Yet moving these closer to the front from the area around Viaz'ma entailed material losses as a result of movement through the Russian *rasputitsa*. Indeed, one brigade commander in the 6th Panzer Division reported that by the end of October his division's tanks had already travelled an average distance of 11,500 km in the eastern campaign.[86] The divisional war diary did not report a figure, but, while the panzer regiment would certainly have suffered from the redeployment east, its strength in mid-November would still have stood at around 100 tanks. Funck's 7th Panzer Division was even stronger. With the exception of some bitter fighting in the battle of Viaz'ma, the division had seen little action since early September, and by 14 November it recorded fielding an impressive 120 operational tanks. Even the battered 1st Panzer Division of Kirchner's XXXXI Panzer Corps benefited somewhat from the pause in operations by raising its panzer force from a mere twenty-four tanks on 21 October[87] to forty-eight tanks by 4 November, although almost half of these consisted of the small and long-since obsolete Mark II tanks.[88] Of course, the German preoccupation with raising panzer strengths was a flawed concept until they recognised that tanks do not exist and fight in a vacuum. Without supporting vehicles for motorised infantry, artillery, engineers etc., not to mention transporting the necessary fuel and munitions, the tanks would soon grind to a halt. It was precisely this point that Krüger's panzer division addressed when it proposed that any new march of 200–300 km would mean so few vehicles arriving at the objective that 'an operation by a detachment or even a company would be practically impossible'.[89] Such improvements in German armoured strength must also be seen against the parallel rise in the Red Army's tank numbers as well as the myriad of anti-tank ditches, mines and hidden road-side guns emplacements which the Soviets were frantically building. Beyond Bock's race with Zhukov to prepare their army groups for the coming encounter, on 4 November an intelligence report from Foreign Armies East ominously noted that some 100 British tanks had been unloaded and transported south from Archangel. They were to be the first of many, and as the report concluded: 'Their appearance [at the front] must be expected.'[90]

While Reinhardt's panzer group struggled to cope with the competing demands of defending at Kalinin and preparing for an offensive towards Moscow, Hoepner's better resourced Panzer Group 4 would clearly have to shoulder the bulk of the load in the offensive north of Moscow. Yet Hoepner's large number of panzer divisions (2nd, 5th, 11th, 19th and 20th), all working similarly hard to put as many tanks in the field as possible, only exacerbated the problem of a 'tank-heavy' force. The grossly inadequate support of wheeled motorisation rendered Hoepner's force, operating in conjunction with Panzer Group 3 to the north, effectively a spearhead without the spear's shaft. It was therefore impossible effectively to supply as well as augment the panzer groups with combined arms. Thus, while Major-General Wilhelm Ritter von Thoma's 20th Panzer Division had raised its complement of tanks from a mere thirty-four panzers on 16 October[91] to seventy-five by 6 November,[92] the impressive jump was a deceptive indication of strength. The tanks were only provisionally serviceable, while their increased numbers only made them harder to supply and support.

While the panzer regiments were the focus of the maintenance crews, to the extent of having essential supplies flown in,[93] the dire shortage of parts for the motorised columns within the divisions reached such proportions that Lieutenant-General Otto von Knobelsdorff's 19th Panzer Division resorted to dispatching trucks all the way back to Germany to secure special steel for the replacement of springs.[94] Such practices were not unheard of in the early period of Barbarossa, but by November with the depth of the German advance and the state of the roads such undertakings were a reflection of how desperate the situation had become. The precise demands placed on the vehicles of a panzer division were also set out in Knobelsdorff's divisional war diary. Since the start of Operation Barbarossa, the 19th Panzer Division had travelled an estimated 3,500 km through the Soviet Union; however, munitions had had to be transported over 6,000–7,000 km and fuel trucks had covered between 9,000 and 10,000 km.[95] Given the heavy loads, notoriously bad roads, generally poor servicing and the fact that the trucks were mainly civilian makes (most dating from the 1930s) it is little wonder that the attrition rate was as high as it was. From a starting total of 600,000 vehicles[96] at the beginning of Operation Barbarossa, the *Ostheer* was down to just 75,000 serviceable vehicles by mid-November 1941.[97] Compounding the problem was Germany's small manufacturing base for the motor-vehicle industry. In 1939, Germany had just twenty-five motor vehicles per 1,000 head of population, while Britain had double this, its dominions had from four to six times Germany's total (Australia 113, Canada 124 and New Zealand 164) and the United States had 227 vehicles per 1,000 people.[98]

Beyond the vehicles themselves, the conditions were also placing an exorbitant demand on Germany's single most important, and limited, economic resource – oil. Knobelsdorff's division kept detailed records on all categories of oil and fuel consumption, and the totals were well above the usual rates for the distances covered. Between 16 June 1941 and 31 October, the panzer division used 4,222,680 litres of gasoline, 1,013,110 litres of diesel and 200,060 litres of oil.[99] When one considers that there were seventeen panzer divisions operating on the eastern front from June (and nineteen from the start of October), the combined consumption, especially if one includes in this calculation the fuel used by the motorised, SS and infantry divisions, was enough to influence the German strategic direction in 1942.[100]

While Hoepner's 'tank-heavy' panzer group struggled to be ready for Typhoon's resumption, the problems associated with the upcoming offensive were not going unnoticed. Indeed, one of the changes most evident in the November period is the emerging tone of critical thinking within the army officer corps. One could justifiably suggest that this was a long time coming, but the semblance of battlefield success had prevented such thoughts until the contrast between the OKH's proposals and the state of the panzer forces finally became untenable. Hoepner, like Bock, was still impatient to get to Moscow and stubbornly rejected the doubters, but men like Kluge (Hoepner's nominal superior) were hesitant about the course upon which things were set and showed less enthusiasm for yet another major offensive.[101] Throughout the divisional and corps levels, officers were now drawing attention to the over-extension of the *Ostheer* and the dangerous lack of supplies both to sustain the new offensive and to survive the winter. Accordingly, victory pronouncements over the radio and the OKH's unrealistic estimates for how far the next offensive would extend the German lines provided the catalyst for shaking up the long-standing complacency of the officer corps. Hellmuth Stieff, a staff officer with the Fourth Army, wrote on 11 November:

> Our high command continues to issue wholly unrealistic orders, and we have not yet been properly resupplied with ammunition and fuel . . . For us, their attitude is utterly incomprehensible. They devise their objectives in the map room, as if the Russian winter did not exist, and our troops' strength is still the same as when the campaign

> started in June. However, winter is now on our doorstep, and our units are so burnt out that one's heart bleeds for them. Soon we will be unable to attack anything at all – the men desperately need rest.[102]

Exactly why the men in Fourth Army were so exhausted after what one might imagine to be a period of rest is illustrated by an account written on 10 November, which told of tank crews from Hoepner's panzer group living in pits dug into the ground under their armoured vehicles. 'Here they are relatively safe from constant enemy artillery fire, but icicles hang from the oil tubs, their ceiling, into their "rooms" and the icy wind whistles through the tracks in spite of the straw and wooden boards.'[103] If the vaunted panzer crews were reduced to such conditions, Army Group Centre's long front, manned by under-strength infantry divisions, exposed many of the ordinary troops to worse conditions. Hans-Heinrich Ludwig gave a sense of his circumstances in a letter written between 10 and 12 November: 'Deep snow. Many vehicle losses ... We are done. There are constant slogans about relief, but it goes on. The mood is indescribably low. Russian bombers by day, no accommodation by night. Frozen bread, sausage and butter.'[104] Not surprisingly many of the soldiers who heard the triumphalism of German propaganda were inclined to disagree. Harald Henry wrote to his family and informed them that he alone would tell the truth about Germany's war in the east, 'not the newsreel, which certainly *cannot*'. Henry concluded his letter: 'Who speaks of victories? Getting by is enough.'[105]

Not all reports from the area of Panzer Group 4 were negative and resentful. Some of the soldiers in fact took comfort from the positive reporting, perhaps in the hope that things really were not as bad as they seemed or maybe just to shield their loved ones from the harsh reality of life at the front. Stumme, the commander of XXXX Panzer Corps, stated that morale was generally still good in spite of the many demands and difficulties his men confronted. Yet he ominously concluded: 'Nevertheless, after the breakthrough of the enemy's current positions before Moscow we can expect that he will push back. Preconditions are; strong artillery, stuka and possibly panzer support. Alone the infantry cannot cope anymore, they are too weak.'[106] Stumme's hope for strong artillery and air support underlines the importance of rebuilding the panzer groups to fight as a combined arms force, something that time,

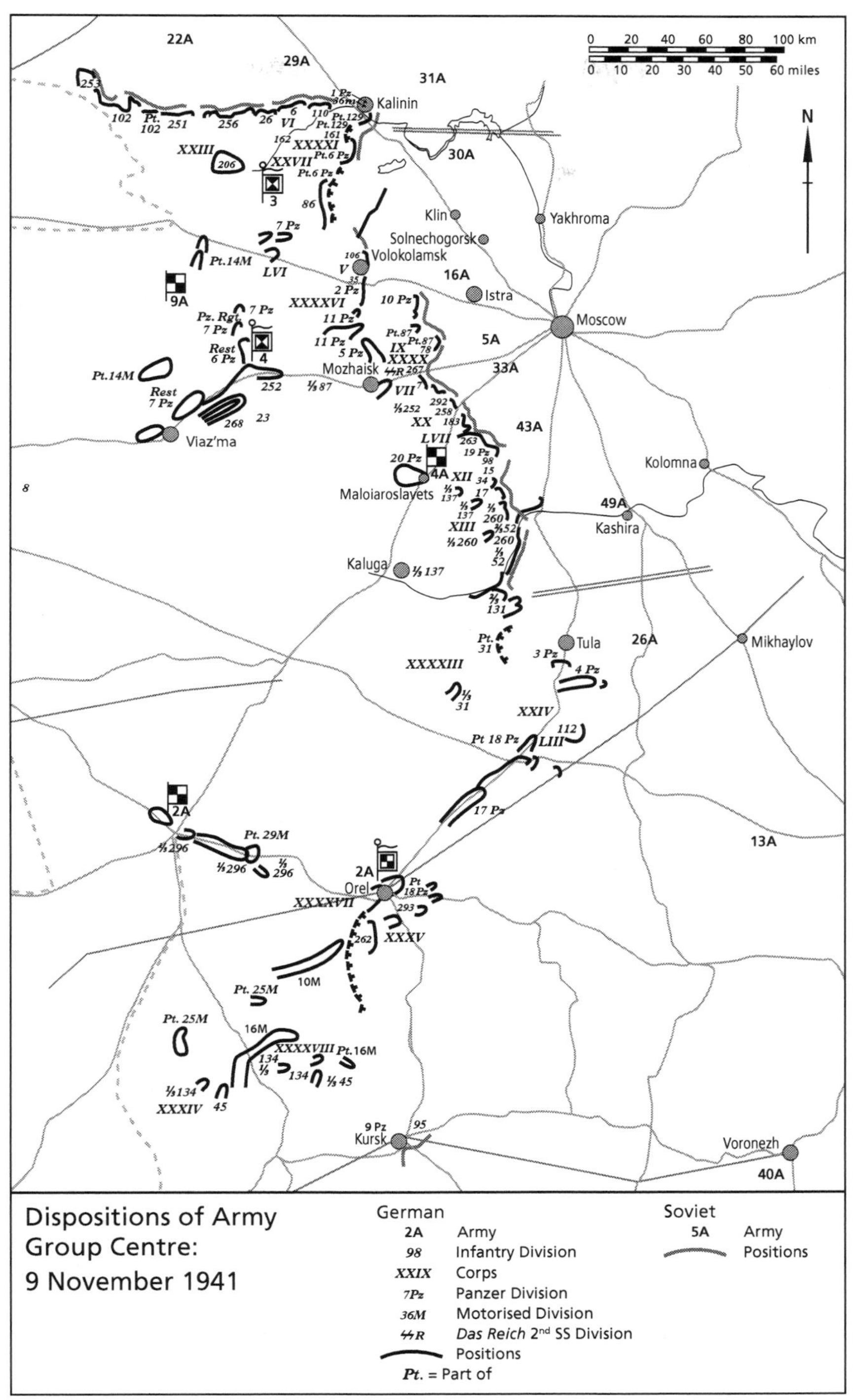

Map 3.2 Dispositions of Army Group Centre, 9 November 1941

the autumn conditions and material weakness largely precluded. As for the true state of German morale, one may wonder how many soldiers adopted Helmut Pabst's attitude: 'Of course we're depressed sometimes, but it's not worth talking about.'[107]

Beyond the intrinsic weaknesses of the Fourth Army and Hoepner's panzer group there was extrinsic pressure exerted by the Red Army, which discounts the idea that early November was a period of rest for much of Army Group Centre. Just as Konev's Kalinin Front periodically attacked Strauss' Ninth Army and Reinhardt's panzer group in the north, the Soviet Western Front, much to Zhukov's dismay, was under orders from Stalin to do the same against Kluge's front.[108] On 6 November, there were limited attacks against Major-General Paul Völcker's 78th Infantry Division and Fischer's 10th Panzer Division. These were followed the next day (7 November) by a more general set of offensives in battalion strength against Fahrmbacher's VII Army Corps, Geyer's IX Army Corps and the right wing of Stumme's XXXX Panzer Corps.[109] Five days later another Soviet attack, this time in regimental strength and reinforced by numerous Soviet medium and heavy tanks as well as rocket launchers, struck Stumme's corps causing 'heavy losses in personnel and material'.[110] The Germans were also pushed out of Szkirminowa and Marjino, and in the course of the fighting lost more tanks than their attackers (twenty German to fifteen Soviet).[111] Costly battles continued on 14 November, this time striking General of Infantry Hans-Gustav Felber's XIII Army Corps and General of Infantry Walter Schroth's XII Army Corps. Small territorial losses were again suffered, but beyond any material or terrain lost the real effect of the Soviet offensive was psychological. Kluge was clearly shaken by the force of the Soviet attacks, which heightened his concerns about the general attack and led him to suggest 'that the army's attack preparations would probably be delayed as a result'. He also now sought a more limited objective in the initial attack (cutting the road to Istra and capturing the high ground at Teryayevo).[112] The following day the situation worsened, with Felber's front broken in several places and Soviet attacks continuing right up to divisional headquarters, requiring more withdrawals. Kluge told Bock that his corps could no longer attack and that he would be pleased if it could even hold its front. The question was how to proceed. Hoepner's panzer group and General of Infantry Richard Ruoff's V Army Corps were committed to attack on the Fourth Army's left wing, but Kluge now questioned whether VII, XII and General of Infantry Friedrich Materna's XX Army Corps should support the attack. Bock was in favour, but left the decision with Kluge: 'I repeatedly told Kluge that only the army could oversee the details of this question and that his decision depended on it.'[113] It was a fateful delegation, which allowed Kluge a measure of freedom to support the forthcoming offensive. His reluctance to do so would become a major point of contention between himself and Hoepner and has generated debate ever since.

To the south of the Fourth Army Guderian's Second Panzer Army was holding a large bulging salient centred on Tula. Guderian, however, did not look on his position favourably. His forces were thinly spread, poorly resourced and weakened from their long advance to Tula at the end of October. Writing a letter on 6 November, Guderian lamented the pause in operations and time that was being lost:

> It is miserable for the troops and great pity for our cause that the enemy should thus gain time while our plans are postponed until the winter is more and more advanced. It all makes me very sad. With the best will in the world there is nothing you can do about the elements. The unique chance to strike a single blow is fading more and more, and I do not know if it will ever recur. How things will turn out, God alone knows. We can only go on hoping and keep our courage up, but this is a hard time . . . I don't enjoy complaining. But for the moment it is difficult to keep one's spirits up.[114]

Not only was Guderian upset at the pause in operations, but the high command's expectation of a general Soviet withdrawal towards the east appeared to the panzer general every bit as absurd as it was.[115] Indeed, on 8 November, Soviet forces attacked his southern flank and by the following day Bock was forced to acknowledge: 'Guderian's position doesn't look exactly rosy.'[116] His strung-out forces were hard pressed and the sunken roads still prevented the support of mobile forces from reaching weak points. Thus, local battles rumbled on, unable to impact the strategic picture, but contributing to the general attrition which the resumption of Typhoon could ill-afford. As an example from 10 to 13 November Heinrici's XXXXIII Army Corps suffered 706 casualties with another 180 men lost to frostbite.[117] Shortly thereafter another Soviet attack against Lieutenant-General Friedrich Mieth's 112th Infantry Division induced panic when the machine guns froze and T-34s simply drove over the German lines. As Guderian remarked after the war: 'it was a warning that the combat ability of our infantry was at an end and that they should no longer be expected to perform difficult tasks'.[118]

While little could be expected of the infantry in Guderian's army his panzer forces were an even greater cause for concern. The Second Panzer Army had seen action in the major battles fought at Minsk, Smolensk, Kiev and Briansk, and had advanced significantly further than any of the other panzer groups operating in the east. Heavy fighting and long advances were the shortest roads to exhaustion, and Guderian's tank fleet, unlike Panzer Groups 3 and 4, was almost decimated by mid-November. On 9 November, Langermann-Erlancamp's 4th Panzer Division was down to twenty tanks,[119] while Nehring's 18th Panzer Division had just nine.[120] A special flame-throwing tank detachment within Lemelsen's XXXXVII Panzer Corps had 720 people assigned to it and only five tanks.[121] A special battle group formed under Colonel Heinrich Eberbach, which had led the charge to Tula in late October and included three of Second Panzer Army's four panzer divisions, had a total strength of just fifty tanks by mid-November. As Guderian noted: 'The establishment for the three divisions should have been 600 [tanks].'[122] A report in the Second Panzer Army's war diary for 11 November reflected just how dire the situation had become: 'The available operational tanks and vehicles in the area of the Second Panzer Army are so limited in proportion to their allotted establishment that an amalgamation must take place over the winter in order to have a single combat ready mobile formation for spring.'[123] The panzer army suggested that they retain Lieutenant-General Hans-Jürgen von Arnim's 17th Panzer Division in the east over the winter and strengthen it with the remaining equipment from the other three panzer divisions. The personnel from the 3rd, 4th and 18th Panzer Divisions, it was recommended, should be transported back to Germany for rebuilding with new material.[124] It was not hard to see why Guderian was finding it hard to keep his spirits up and, although the panzer army's plan made sense, Hitler was against 'losing' any panzer forces that might detract from Typhoon's revival.

While Second Panzer Army was certainly not 'tank-heavy', it did, however, share the weaknesses in motorisation of the other panzer groups. On the main supply road from Orel to Tula the panzer army allocated enough trucks to transport 2,800 tons of supplies, but of this

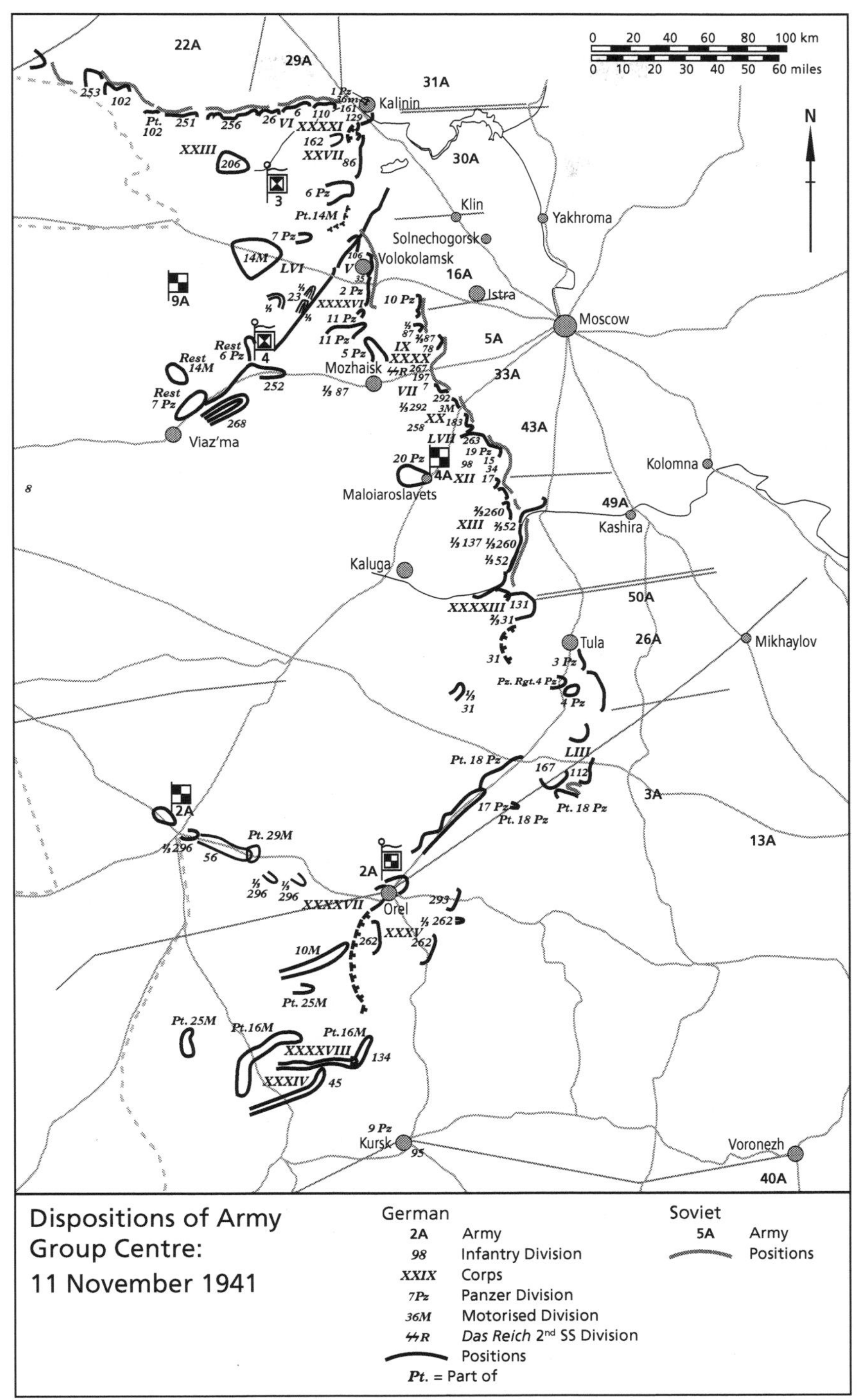

Map 3.3 Dispositions of Army Group Centre, 11 November 1941

only enough trucks remained operational to move 200 tons. There were another 600 tons of operational transport capacity available, but these were bogged down along the route and it was estimated that it would be two weeks before they could be pulled out.[125] At the front Lemelsen's XXXXVII Panzer Corps opted to follow the lead of the army and look at combining formations to maximise the use of its remaining trucks.[126] In the case of Nehring's 18th Panzer Division, it was estimated that truck losses reduced its former strength as a mobile formation by 50 per cent.[127] The war diary of Lieutenant-General Friedrich-Wilhelm von Loeper's 10th Motorised Infantry Division did not concern itself with combat strength, but expressed 'great worry' that there would be too little transport capacity to collect the winter clothing when it arrived in Orel.[128] Not surprisingly, on 10 November, the panzer army concluded: 'Units cannot go further away from the railheads than can be reached by horse and sled.'[129] Explaining the most common problem one soldier recalled after the war:

> Because of the extremely cold temperatures . . . many trucks, some of our guns and other vehicles developed 'cold breaks' in the leaf springs. Thirty percent of the leaf springs in our truck broke. If one broke in the rear, the truck lost braking capacity. [The army] started in a hurry to put together truck repair shops for springs, but we didn't have enough materials or the right quality steel to make reliable springs. It meant we started the offensive on Moscow with dilapidated equipment, and lost a lot of it.[130]

Overall Guderian expected nothing of his infantry, possessed the offensive strength equivalent to a single panzer division and had extremely limited motorisation with which to support any further attack. It was a depressing tally and, given the related problems of having no supplies to spare, the winter closing in and Tula (which was still firmly in Soviet hands) being 170 km from Moscow, the odds against Guderian reaching the Soviet capital were incredibly long.

One young infantryman, whose hard-pressed division had been in almost constant combat, held up the mystique of Guderian's panzer army and saw in it a salvation from the many trials and dangers of the war. In a letter home he wrote assuredly: 'Guderian will soon be in our neighbourhood. He is already rolling over Tula. He keeps our hopes up.'[131] Like so many things in the *Ostheer* by November 1941,

Guderian's reputation was a considerably more potent weapon than his panzer army's tangible reality. Indeed, a colossal state of delusion sustained the German high command, many of its soldiers and the great bulk of the German population. For those officers and men who knew, or suspected, a much darker truth, the resumption of Operation Typhoon was less a drive for outright victory than a hope that the myth of an invincible German army would not be shattered. One of those who was aware of Germany's weakness was the former diplomat and anti-Hitler conspirator, Ulrich von Hassell, who noted 'how vulnerable our situation is' as early as the middle of September, 'and how every chance for a reasonable peace goes to the devil as soon as the other side sees victory ahead'.[132] The 1941 eastern campaign had gutted the German army and, far from finishing off the Soviet Union, the Red Army was growing in size, strength and skill from month to month. The Nazi assurance of an eventual victory in the east was not so much incorrect as misguided as to whose victory it would be.

4 THE ORSHA CONFERENCE

A cold reception: Halder's offensive plans

Undeterred by the state of Army Group Centre, the OKH remained adamant that Bock could continue his attack towards Moscow and even achieve a resounding success. The feeling was that doubts within the command staff of the major formations in the east had to be countered with 'the thinking of the general staff',[1] and to do this Halder himself would travel to the east and meet with the chiefs-of-staff of the three army groups as well as most of the armies to fire the new offensive with the requisite vigour and resolve.

On 12 November, Halder left the army high command compound at Angerburg in East Prussia to board a special train to take him, and a number of his top branch chiefs, to Orsha in eastern Belarus. There he would meet with the three chiefs-of-staff of the army groups, Lieutenants-General Kurt Brennecke (north), Greiffenberg (centre) and General of the Infantry Georg von Sodenstern (south), as well as the chiefs-of-staff from seven of the ten armies operating in the east (from north to south, the Eighteenth, Sixteenth, Ninth, Fourth, Second Panzer, Sixth and Seventeenth).[2] The meeting took place in Halder's special train and began promptly at ten o'clock on the morning of 13 November. Halder commenced proceedings giving a speech that attempted to recast the history of the eastern campaign to fit his agenda for the *Ostheer*'s impending success. As Halder explained the 'fundamental idea' of the campaign had been to 'wrest a decision', but that this was no longer '100 percent attainable'. Indeed, without the slightest hint of irony,

Halder then made the contrasting admission that the Soviet Union had been weakened 'by at least fifty percent' and that therefore it could not simply be 'kept under observation'. The east, he said, would therefore have to remain an active theatre of war and the army now had to 'strive to maximise damage to the enemy' before the end of the year. Halder assured his officers that the situation was still favourable. 'Although weak in the knees, we are still, for practical purposes, in the pursuit. The enemy presently is worse off than we; he is on the verge of collapse. Therefore we are justified and obligated to exert full effort once more so that the troops will not have to pay in blood next year for what is neglected now.'[3] If, by Halder's own admission, the sum of Operations Barbarossa and Typhoon had succeeded only in weakening the Soviet Union 'by at least fifty percent', it is hard to imagine how that equated with being on the verge of collapse. Moreover, after nineteen weeks of intensive warfare in a campaign that the OKH projected would last for between six and ten weeks, claiming that the *Ostheer* was 'obligated to exert full effort once more' shows little comprehension of all that had gone wrong in the campaign. Indeed, framing the forthcoming offensive as a 'pursuit' could only have added insult to injury to many of the men present who knew far better than Halder with what determined resolve and weight of material their forces would be opposed.

If Halder had sought to charm and inspire the chiefs-of-staff by his upbeat vision and steadfast confidence, the following presentation by the head of Foreign Armies East, Colonel Eberhard Kinzel, could only have reinforced doubts that the Red Army was at a point of collapse.[4] Kinzel began by admitting that the prewar estimates of the Red Army had not proved to be very accurate – an understatement of astonishing proportions – but he claimed that estimates did not mean the same in the Soviet context because of their ability to generate new forces at an unheard of rate. Thus, while the Red Army was said to have had 140 divisions in June 1941 and lost most of these in the ensuing summer battles they still managed to field an estimated 190 divisions before the start of Operation Typhoon in October. Even after the victories at Viaz'ma, Briansk and the Sea of Azov in October, Kinzel now estimated that the Red Army numbered 160 divisions (in Europe). Thus, Halder's claim that the Soviet state had been weakened by at least 50 per cent could be disputed on the grounds that there were now, after a campaign of four and a half months, twenty more Soviet divisions than the OKH's starting assumption. Kinzel correctly explained that half of the current

Red Army consisted of men with only the most rudimentary training and officers promoted above their level of professional competence or experience. However, his soothing conclusion that this therefore relegated the 160 Soviet divisions to an effective strength of just seventy-five divisions[5] took no account of the parallel fact that the *Ostheer*'s 136 divisions were, by the OKW's own reporting, reduced to a combined strength of just eighty-three full-strength formations.[6] Moreover, in what should have raised the eyebrows of many of the general staff officers, Kinzel stated that the Red Army had forty tank brigades, which, in spite of being recently converted from cavalry divisions and therefore inexperienced in armoured warfare, were often well equipped. Similarly, in what could be construed as an exposé of Foreign Armies East's failings, Kinzel admitted that before the war his department anticipated the Red Army to possess 19,000 artillery pieces, but that so far some 24,000 guns had been captured. Additionally, the Soviets had not said 'a single word' about acquiring more artillery from the western allies in their recent Lend-Lease negotiations, which Kinzel suggested could only indicate a plentiful domestic supply.[7] On this basis, Kinzel projected the Red Army to be supplying 150 divisions by spring 1942, a somewhat frightening conclusion, which forced Halder to interject that Soviet force generation was 'opaque' even if substantial.[8]

If Kinzel's briefing dampened the mood of optimism that Halder had sought to instil, the two following lectures by Major-General Walter Buhle, the chief of the OKH's Organisation Branch, and Wagner, the army's Quartermaster-General, positively destroyed it. Buhle stated matter-of-factly that the large-scale expansion of the army in 1940 had never been intended for more than a year, enough, it was thought, to deal with the Soviet Union, but now there was no possibility of demobilisation and no replacements for the *Ostheer*. The only solution was to disband fifteen divisions in the east to create new reserves for those remaining. Buhle then alluded to the problem of 'tank-heavy' or unbalanced panzer divisions by declaring that the *Ostheer* would not be getting any more motor vehicles just tanks. Indeed, the panzer divisions would have their established allotment of vehicles cut by 500, infantry divisions were to be completely de-motorised and the *Grosstransportraum* were to become one-third horse-drawn. There were simply too few trucks rolling off the production lines to sustain the *Ostheer* and the domestic economy had already been ruthlessly exploited for Operation Barbarossa in the hope that many of the vehicles would be returned after the summer campaign.

Thus, the failure to end the war in the summer of 1941 profoundly intensified Germany's manpower and material crisis.[9]

Wagner's presentation compounded the bleak picture by informing the chiefs-of-staff that the *Ostheer* would experience an ammunition shortfall in early 1942, owing to the redirection of armament policy in July 1941 away from the army.[10] Priorities had since reverted back towards supporting the army, but the time lost in re-tooling had cut many weeks, even months, from production quotas.[11] More importantly, Wagner stated the obvious by pointing out that the most immediate problem was less the production of ammunition, but transporting it to the front. There were not enough trains reaching Army Groups Centre and South and only a 'bearable' number for Army Group North. Indeed, Wagner stated that the urgently requested winter clothing could be transported to the front only at the expense of other supplies and in any case would not arrive until February.[12]

The afternoon session was devoted to the chiefs-of-staff, allowing them to present their views. Brennecke, the chief-of-staff at Army Group North, bluntly told Halder that he had no more forces to spare for an extended drive to the east. The only place he could free up reserves would be from the Oranienbaum pocket west of Leningrad, where a Soviet army was still holding out, but achieving this would itself require extra men and materiel. Having made his case, Brennecke noted that, at the very least, Halder no longer made mention of his army group driving on Vologda. Halder, however, still hoped that Leeb would succeed in linking up with the Finns east of Lake Ladoga.[13] Greiffenberg, the chief-of-staff at Army Group Centre, was the most amenable to Halder's views given that his own immediate superior (Bock) was fully committed to renewing the offensive. Greiffenberg, however, did not appear very enthusiastic and recognised that the continuation of Typhoon would still leave much to be achieved in 1942.[14] His post-Orsha report, written on 15 November, made this quite clear:

> As far as the tasks ahead are concerned, we must proceed on the basis that we shall not have succeeded in destroying the Russian army and Russian industry in 1941, so that, as we had hoped, once the winter set in it would only have been necessary to watch over the captured territories for their protection ... large forces are pinned down in the east and will have to spend the winter here and resume the attack in the spring of 1942, if the political leadership agrees.[15]

Sodenstern, the chief-of-staff at Army Group South, was the most outspoken opponent of continued operations in 1941, which reflected the opposition of his commander at Army Group South. Indeed, Rundstedt had earlier described the proposed advance by his First Panzer Army all the way to Maykop as the best way to put it totally out of commission for 1942.[16]

As an indication of just how forthright was the rejection of Halder's proposals, the chief-of-staff of Guderian's Second Panzer Army, Colonel Kurt Freiherr von Liebenstein, dismissed a suggestion that his army should try for Gorky (400 km east of Moscow) by exclaiming that this was not the month of May and operations were not being conducted in France.[17] The chief-of-staff of Panzer Group 3 was not present because his formation had not been elevated to the status of an army, but he had sent a letter to the army high command arguing against a continuation of the offensive on the grounds that heavy snowfall could paralyse all movement and potentially cut off the advanced tanks from the rest of the panzer group. The infantry, he suggested, could be made to move under any weather conditions, but 'motors and machines do not take orders'.[18] After the war a critical tone was also taken by Colonel Walter Chales de Beaulieu, the chief-of-staff for Panzer Group 4, who claimed: 'What do initial successes mean if one arrives at Moscow exhausted and bled white only to be even more defenceless against enemy attacks!'[19] Whether he did in fact hold such a view at the time, especially in dealing with an imposing figure like Hoepner who was anxious to continue the attack, is unknown, but the point itself was valid.

After dinner that evening Halder collected his thoughts and opted to rescind his outlandish proposals from 7 November. He still, however, anticipated major operations being able to continue for about another month before the winter weather arrived, and he suggested that 'as much as humanly possible' would have to be extracted from the troops. Army Group Centre, he noted, would have not have gained 'substantial' ground beyond Moscow, but it was clear that Halder expected, at a minimum, that the city would be encircled. The more distant objectives of Vologda, Gorky, Stalingrad and Maykop would have to wait until the following summer when, as Halder put it, 'the Russians will have a plus in strength and we a minus'. His ultimate conclusion presented Germany's strategic position in remarkably upbeat terms. The Soviet Union, in spite of its 'enormous' military potential, was no longer considered by Halder a serious threat and could be discounted as a 'power factor'. Indeed, England was seen to be more of a concern to Halder because it had no 'handle by which it could be seized'.[20] The irony was that this same lack of a handle would shortly be providing Germany with protection from western invasion, while the Soviets proved themselves to be very much a power factor. Indeed, Orsha was a case in point of all that was wrong with the German general staff under Halder. The input of general staff officers in open dialogue to inform strategic options and achieve a certain balance of opinion had never been good in the German army (even long before the Second World War), but was positively absent under Halder. The chief of the general staff did not come to Orsha enquiring as to whether the virtues of *Erhaltungsgedanken* should take precedence over a more aggressive *Wirkungsgedanken* that he favoured. Rather, the OKH's strategy was determined in advance by Halder, subsequently backed by Hitler, and Orsha only served to determine what form of offensive the *Ostheer* should pursue. Establishing an objective and then engaging in the staff work to achieve it repeated the same basic flaws that preceded Operation Barbarossa and flew in the face of having staff work determine what objective was possible.

The perversion of the OKH did not start with the self-appointment of Hitler to Commander-in-Chief in December 1941. Halder had been the driving force guiding the army's direction since his appointment and more than any other officer bears responsibility for the litany of errors, oversights and downright blunders associated with the eastern campaign.[21] Indeed, since 10 November, when Brauchitsch suffered a severe heart attack,[22] Halder had served as a surrogate Commander-in-Chief of the army as well as Chief of the General Staff. More than any other man in Nazi Germany the resumption of Operation Typhoon, in spite of all the words of warning, depended upon Franz Halder.

The reaction to the Orsha conference was equally revealing. At the OKW Warlimont wrote in his memoir that after the middle of the November, once the *rasputitsa* had passed, 'people generally began to get optimistic once more'.[23] At the same time, however, Kesselring recalled that when the operational order arrived for the continuation of the offensive towards Moscow: 'The order was received with little enthusiasm, particularly by the commander primarily concerned, Field-Marshal von Kluge.'[24] The contrast between the front and the high command speaks to the gulf in understanding – or misunderstanding – of what was to be attempted. For Hans Meier-Welcker, a general staff officer, there was little such ambiguity and the day after the Orsha conference he noted in a letter that Germany was now in a 'long and uncertain war'. He then continued: 'May all thinking Germans *finally* become conscious of this realization. Unfortunately, so far everything has been done to prevent recognition of this.'[25] In fact, as the armies and panzer groups now turned their attention to the orders at hand all doubts and reservations had to be set aside, while new orders were drafted to the lower ranks that only reinforced the views of 'unthinking' Germans. In one such case Geyer, the commander of the IX Army Corps, wrote to his officers and impressed upon them the need to *not* to think, but rather to assume everything was possible from the outset:

> The positive aspects of every situation must first and foremost be recognized and emphasized. It is well known that the enemy invariably has problems too. It is also well known that all is not lost if all is not given up for lost. It is precisely in difficult situations that a soldier can do more than his best, even if it seems to be more than is humanly possible. Success often only comes at the last minute and hangs upon a single thread. Often one only realizes later that, given a little push, the enemy would have fallen over.[26]

Geyer's order speaks to the extremist culture, and indeed fanaticism, of the German Wehrmacht, especially in the east. That a senior officer might expect the men to achieve 'more than is humanly possible' seems so obviously contradictory and, even if this uncompromising attitude might explain some of the Wehrmacht's past successes, it begs the pertinent question that other officers were asking; even if men can be made to obey, 'motors and machines do not take orders'.[27]

That German soldiers were not always coping with the rigours of daily life at the front, even without the demands of a major new offensive, was seen from the many reports of depression and ill-discipline arising in the first half of November. Hellmuth Stieff, a staff officer at the Fourth Army, noted in early November that many men were 'becoming listless and apathetic'.[28] It was a condition that soon accounted for the indifferent behaviour of many men and even officers. The war diary of Second Panzer Army included a long list of transgressions that Guderian had compiled to prevent the men from undermining the work of the army's economic organisation who were seeking to exploit and manage the resources of the occupied area. The men were noted to be chopping up and burning anything that they could get their hands on, including useful items like sleds, snow fences, wooden floors in houses and even houses or tents themselves. Additionally, Guderian rebuked his men for the widespread practice, in spite of previous orders, of simply seizing livestock and other agricultural products without paying for them or issuing appropriate army certificates.[29] It was not concern for the well-being of the Soviet civilians that drove such policies, but the inability of the army to acquire sufficient resources for its own use. In fact, while the advance was in full swing, it was the encouraged practice of the panzer forces to have the troops live off the land as completely as possible, yet now that the advance had stagnated so too had the abundance of extorted local supplies. Moreover, if Guderian was upset that the army's economic organisation was having to scrape the bottom of the barrel for supplies, one should spare a thought for the Russian civilians in the forward areas of the German front, many of whom would not survive the coming winter because of German occupation practices. In any case, it was an ironic turn of events that Guderian was now being harmed by the same destructive practices that he had helped to unleash. Concluding his order to halt the damaging practices, Guderian complained: 'It is an unfortunate sign of the lack of discipline and the lack of intervention by officers, who stand idly by and observe these matters.'[30]

Rather than simply issuing persistent orders the German command might also have considered why their troops were engaged in such purposefully self-destructive practices. One anti-tank unit was so cold that they cut down all the telegraph poles carrying their own telephone lines (as well as to some other units) and burned them. Later an officer whose tank became tangled in the cable simply cut the line at the front and rear of the vehicle rather than carefully remove it. The report referred to the 'lack of camaraderie' and 'stupidity' of such actions,[31] but one might suspect that the men involved were motivated by a more basic rationale given the wintry conditions and lack of shelter. Indeed, until a permanent frost came the muddy conditions and driving rain of the *rasputitsa* did a lot more than just hinder movement and slow the delivery of supplies, it took a huge physical and mental toll on the men. Léon Degrelle, a newly arrived Belgian volunteer in the *Waffen-SS*, recalled after the war what his unit experienced in crossing vast stretches of the sunken steppe on foot:

> Crossing the belt of mud ... was a devilish ordeal; every metre of mud was an obstacle, exacting effort and suffering ... We fell in mud holes, dropping our weapons, then groping for them. The water rose to mid-thigh level. The holes were so dangerous that we had to tie ourselves together in groups of three so that we could quickly pull out anyone who stumbled in ... So it was that hundreds of thousands of soldiers struggled, like human frogs, along a 3,000 mile front of muck and slime ... The mud squelched our spirits. Our weakest broke down, exhausted. During this phase of combat, one of our men collapsed in the mire, his head blown open. His courage at an end, he had shot himself in the mouth with his rifle.[32]

In such circumstances cold, wet, exhausted and, in extreme cases, even suicidal, who could wonder if some soldiers cut down a telegraph pole to have a few hours of warmth? The war and its privations drove the men to the limits of their endurance, so it was no surprise that their behaviour radicalised accordingly. With such little understanding of their own army, its condition and capabilities, it is small wonder that the true strength of the Red Army so utterly escaped the German leadership.

Figure 4.1 German infantry pulling a car through the mud (November 1941)

While the *Ostheer* shivered and froze, it was another bitter irony that the German high command saw salvation in even colder temperatures, which, it was hoped, would enable their forces to regain mobility and again conduct major operations. The frozen ground would at last allow wheeled transport to support the attack and restore movement, but even Halder and Bock recognised that rapid, operational manoeuvre was a thing of the past. Their upcoming attack would have to be frontal rather than concentric, which could only mean greater losses and a slower rate of advance. As Halder noted on 11 November: 'Operational artworks are no longer possible. Troops are no longer able to be moved. Only expedient, tactical actions possible.'[33] Likewise, Bock noted that the resumption of Operation Typhoon would be very different from its original incarnation: 'The attack cannot become a great strategic masterpiece, because troop movements have so far largely been impossible and later will become impossible on account of the snow. The only thing that can matter, therefore, is to conduct the thrust in concentration at the tactically most favourable points.'[34] Everything now depended on a permanent frost, which finally came towards the middle of November when a cold spell sent temperatures plummeting and gave the *Ostheer* its first real taste of a Russian winter.

Light frosts had been a periodic feature of the *rasputitsa* as temperatures dropped in the night and small pools of water froze, but they were never enough to do more than coagulate the vast stretches of viscous mud, which in the daytime returned to its sodden state. Yet on 10 November the temperature reached -5°C on the central part of Bock's front and in the following days continued to drop; -8°C on 11 November and -12°C by 13 November.[35] These temperatures rose again during the daylight hours, but seldom above zero and therefore the ground was hardening each day. For the men of Army Group Centre already struggling to cope, the intense freeze was an ominous foretaste of things to come. Indeed, the writings of some German soldiers from different positions along Bock's long front refer to temperatures considerably colder than those cited above (which were recorded in Knobelsdorff's 19th Panzer Division's war diary belonging to Panzer Group 4). Erich Hager, who served in the 17th Panzer Division (part of Second Panzer Army), wrote in his diary on 13 November that the temperature had reached -20°C. 'That's quite something!' He concluded: 'If I go out then I run. How will things go on? In this cold?'[36] Similarly, Ernst Guicking serving in the nearby 52nd Infantry Division, noted the same temperature on 12 November with the comment: 'I don't

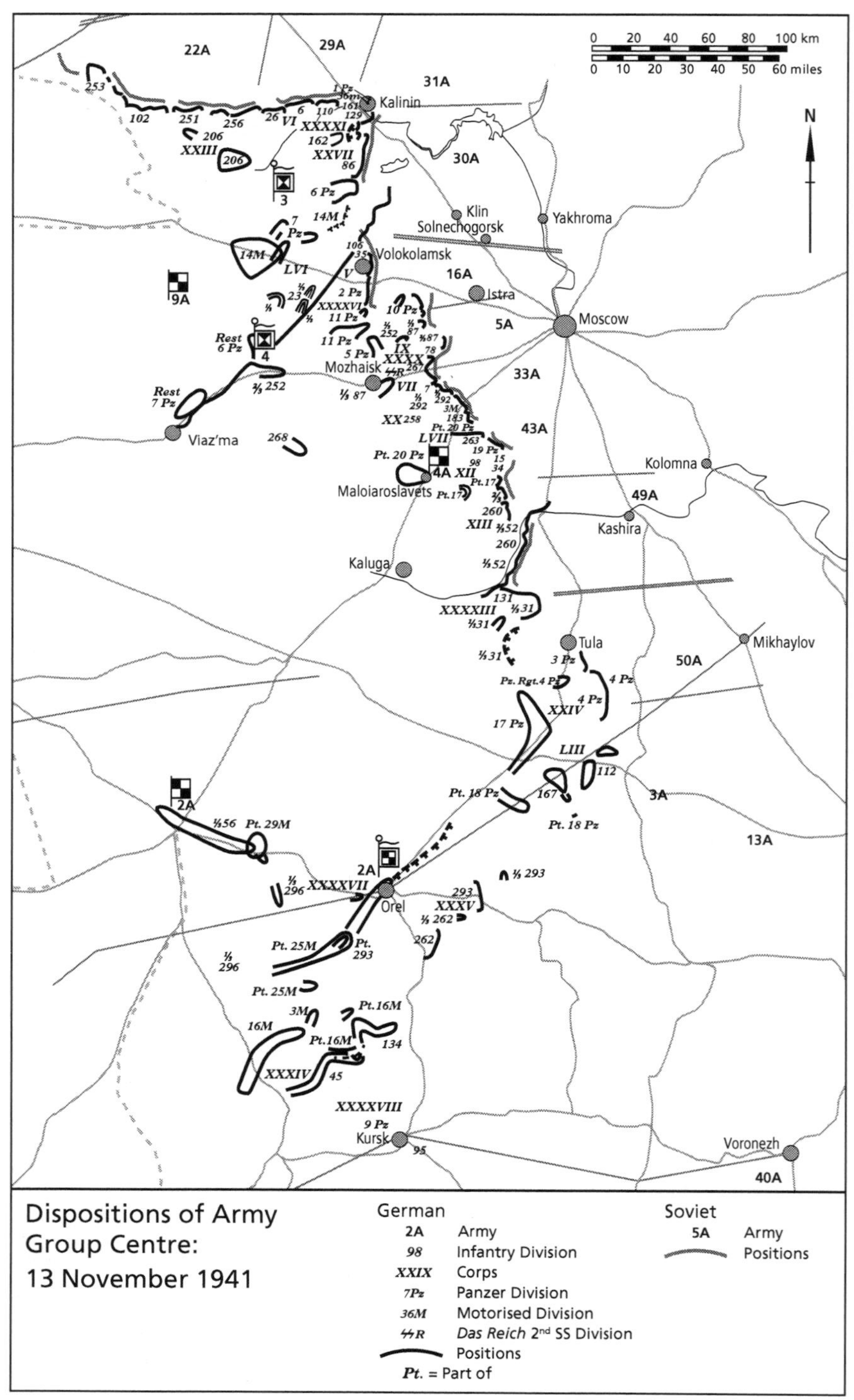

Map 4.1 Dispositions of Army Group Centre, 13 November 1941

go near the door unless it is absolutely necessary.'[37] At the same time in the north, in the area of Panzer Group 3, Ludwig Freiherr von Heyl, a lieutenant in the 36th Motorised Infantry Division, recorded temperature ranges between -5° and -20°C. 'The thought that the real winter is yet to come is a sobering one.'[38] For the men who had to serve outdoors the experience was an even more harrowing one. Siegfried Knappe noted that his unit was on the march on 12 November and looked anxiously for villages so that they could warm themselves up in the peasant houses.[39] Ernst Kern was ordered to the rear of his unit to bring up mess kits for the troops, but the food and tea, which was hot when it was served, had frozen solid by the time it was distributed to the men. 'It had to be splintered with bayonets and then sucked piece by piece, while bottles had to be defrosted by body heat in order to liquefy the tea.'[40] Even after the war Heinrich Haape remembered the day the winter weather commenced in earnest: 'On 13 November we awoke and shivered. An icy blast from the north-east knifed across the snowy countryside. The sky was cloudless and dark blue, but the sun seemed to have lost its strength and instead of becoming warmer towards noon as on previous days, the thermometer kept falling and by sundown had reached minus twelve degrees Centigrade.'[41]

Figure 4.2 Army Group Centre's troops inadequately dressed for the winter conditions (November 1941)

At Kalinin, on 13 November, the Volga River froze over with an ice sheet 12–15 cm thick.[42] At the same time, Kirchner's XXXXI Panzer Corps compiled a detailed report on the influence of the winter season on the conduct of operations. Already in November there was the expectation that the Red Army would be 'superior in coping and using the winter weather'. It was believed from this point on that enemy ski formations and infiltration units were to be expected 'by day and night'. The vulnerability of German vehicles to air attack was also cited now that the landscape was transforming from water and mud to frost and snow. German maps for the Soviet Union, already known to be unreliable, were almost useless in winter as the roads and landscape could often no longer be distinguished. The shortening hours of daylight, estimated at between six to eight hours, forced more limited daily attack objectives and therefore the difficulty of finding shelter for the heavy weapons (nothing at all was said of the fate of the men). Finally, the report cited the fundamental importance of logistics with the warning: 'In winter all operations are in many respects only partially achievable and in the broadest sense dependent upon their supply.'[43] While the problems of a winter campaign were varied and profound, it is not the case that the German army went into its ordeal blind. Yet identifying the problems did not necessarily make them any easier to solve, especially given the serious lack of planning and preparation on the part of the high command.

As an indication of the extent of these shortcomings Panzer Group 3 cited the rising health danger as a result of the absence of soap. The filthy conditions and limited bathing opportunities created the problem, but the lack of soap, like numerous other personal hygiene items, raised the spectre of disease.[44] One soldier's letter included a wish-list of items he needed or wanted, which reflected just how little the army was able to supply to its men as well as the fact that there were almost no 'luxury items' to be bought or acquired within the Soviet Union. Among the items listed were toothpaste, shoe polish, tobacco, a pipe, envelopes, chocolate, vitamin B and C supplements, meat stock, shaving gear and a number of other food products.[45] There was also a critical shortage of lighting material, especially cylinders for oil lamps and carbide. As a result the panzer group's war diary noted: 'it is currently not possible to light a great number of dwellings',[46] which, according to the 1st Panzer Division, left many of the troops sitting in darkness as of 4 pm.[47] Johannes Hamm's letter home on 16 November also included a long list of urgently needed items, at the top of which came torch batteries, matches and *Hindenburglichte* (an improvised form of candle first used by German troops in the First World War).[48]

The effects of the heavy frost on the tanks of Panzer Group 4 were specifically addressed in a report from the 19th Panzer Division written on 13 November. It was noted that motors, battery leads and transmission oil all freeze at -15°C. At the same time, it was discovered that the fuel contained droplets of water, which froze into a crystallised form, clogging the supply lines to the fuel pump and carburettor. The only way to avoid this was to run the motors, depending on the cold, up to three times a night. Additionally, it was recommended that the tanks be driven for a time to ensure the gear oil in the transmission, steering and brakes did not freeze. The process added substantially to the fuel consumption of each panzer regiment, while to protect the batteries they had to be taken out and reinserted before every usage – a task requiring about one hour of work. The report also noted that the newly hardened ground was cause for increased wear on the tracks, which revealed their worn state and their lack of maintenance in the preceding months. Splint pins were breaking and bolts that had become loose started popping out. Indeed, it was noted that the overall manoeuvrability of the main armament, mounting and turret were all limited in the extreme temperatures.[49] Clearly, maintaining Army Group Centre's tank fleet in such conditions, without the aid of adequate workshops, spare parts or antifreeze, would be an enormous task. After the war Lieutenant-General Fritz Bayerlein, who had been Guderian's operations officer at the start of Barbarossa, noted:

> Every four hours the motors [of the tanks] were run for 10–15 minutes until they reached a temperature of 140°Fahrenheit [60°Celsius]. These periods commenced for all tanks at exactly the same second in order to minimize interference with the forward listening posts . . . We discovered that the transmission must also be operated while the tank is idling, otherwise by a sudden start the metal parts of the power train from the engine to the drive sprockets would be damaged [because of the low viscosity of the oil at those temperatures].[50]

To cope with the new conditions many of the officers reached for their army training manuals and began issuing instructions to the men on how to survive and adapt in the wintery environment. The problem was that many of these instructions assumed certain pre-conditions that could seldom be met in the east.[51] As the war diary of the LVII Panzer Corps noted:

> Since early November there has been a constant stream of regulations, leaflets, advice etc., on measures to be taken for the winter, including relevant statements provided by captured Russian officers . . . The bulk of the troop leaders are no longer able to read these masses of paper in their shelters or foxholes or to monitor the implementation of the required measures. Many of the things require a longer period of preparation and with the temperature already at -15° to -20° these leaflets come too late. Furthermore, the implementation would often not be possible without the timely appearance of the necessary material (roofing felt and corrugated iron), which is not available and will not be delivered. On the subject of clothing and food the statements of the Russian officers are best not passed on to the troops because of their impracticability.[52]

There was a good deal, however, which escaped the ban on impractical directives being sent to the men. Gottlob Bidermann noted an army-issued pamphlet to the troops attempting to provide practical tips for managing in the cold weather. It advised that an extra pair of army socks could be cut to provide holes for the thumb and index finger allowing the discharge of a weapon. As one soldier bitterly commented; 'Someone was obviously not aware that our boots have been almost worn to scrap and that our socks were little more than rags, already with so many holes in them that we would have no difficulty in finding enough to poke all five fingers through.'[53]

If the war diaries of Panzer Groups 3 and 4 showed just how unprepared the panzer forces were for the winter conditions, the Second Panzer Army took a longer perspective and on 11 November questioned whether the mobile divisions could even be made ready for major operations in the spring of 1942. Even before calculating the effects of another major German offensive (to say nothing of a Soviet winter offensive) their conclusion was an unequivocal rejection. The report highlighted the lack of almost everything that such an achievement would require: repair stations, trained mechanics, support staff, spare parts, new motors, shelter for the vehicles, etc. As the war diary ominously concluded: 'The experience of the 1939–1940 winter in the Eifel showed that the use of German tanks in temperatures less than -15°Celsius is not possible.'[54] Two days later, on 13 November,

Bock noted in his diary: 'The engines of the tanks are beginning to fail as a result of the drop in temperatures to 15 to 20 degrees below freezing.'[55]

Troublesome equations: the logistics of continuing Typhoon

Speaking to the inner circle of OKW generals at his *Wolfschanze* ('Wolf's Lair') headquarters on 12 November, Hitler announced: 'It's a huge relief for our Party to know that the myth of the Workers' Paradise to the East is now destroyed. It was the destiny of all civilised States to be exposed to the assault of Asia at the moment when their vital strength was weakening.'[56] The irony was Germany had never been militarily weaker, nor more exposed to a defeat than it was now. Certainly, the *Ostheer* still retained the initiative for the time being, but the *Ostheer* was in an unmistakeable decline and the winter could only accelerate the process. The Red Army was without doubt the principal cause of the *Ostheer*'s deterioration, but the sheer scale of maintaining 3 million men at such depth in the east was well beyond Germany's prewar plans and improvised logistic capacity. A significant part of the *Ostheer*'s strength was lost, not through enemy activity, but by the slow exhaustion of resources and stockpiles that were not being replaced. In a sense, once supplies failed to meet the minimum requirements of the army groups, the *Ostheer* was consuming itself. That point had been reached in October when a combination of bad weather, poor infrastructure and another 200-km increase in the depth of operations placed the supply system, already overburdened, beyond even the minimum requirements of Army Group Centre. Thus, even with the pause in operations from the end of October, from a material point of view, some of Bock's forces (particularly Panzer Group 3 and the Second Panzer Army), far from regaining strength, were consuming more supplies than they were being delivered.[57] As one soldier phrased it: 'There are weeks in which no supplies reach us. Then the war must feed off itself.'[58] This was a worrying enough prospect given the time of year, but made much worse by the heedless determination of Bock and Halder to engage in a resource-intensive offensive, which would only extend supply lines still further.

At Orsha Halder was pointedly confronted over the issue to which he conceded there was no solution, while also agreeing that the problem was destined to worsen with the coming attack. When Major Otto Eckstein, the chief supply officer for Army Group Centre, pointed out the contradiction between the offensive's lofty aims and skeleton resources, the army chief-of-staff replied: 'You are certainly right to be anxious based on your calculations; but we don't want to hold Bock up, if he thinks he can do the thing; indeed it takes a little luck, too, to conduct a war.'[59] That luck was now invoked to cover for material deficiency was in itself a sign of desperation, but Halder's claim that Bock was pushing for the offensive in spite of the supply situation was not the whole truth.

On 11 November, the day before Halder's train left for Orsha, Bock telephoned him and objected to the plans as they currently stood on the basis of the number of trains arriving each day to supply his army group. Referring to the minimum line of advance to encircle Moscow Bock told Halder: 'I will be happy if our forces are sufficient to obtain this line. The attack can be supplied to this point if the previous number of trains running to the army group is authorized.'[60] Halder could not meet this requirement, but suggested to Bock that the attack be postponed until the end of the month to gather the necessary supplies. Halder probably knew that he was forcing Bock's hand at this point as there had been no serious consideration for a December offensive when, as Bock pointed out in his reply, deep snowfall would forestall major operations.[61] Thus, Bock was effectively being forced either to abandon the offensive altogether or to accept that the operational objectives could not be covered logistically. What Halder told Eckstein was therefore correct, but Halder also knew that Bock did not know how to supply the operation and, given Eckstein's concerns, nor did his top officials within Army Group Centre. Halder and Bock simply could not bring themselves to call off the offensive and therefore, in the face of an increasingly hopeless logistical equation, a little luck was all there was left to hope for.

The same afternoon that Bock spoke with Halder (11 November) the commander of Army Group Centre met with his top supply officials and learned that the situation was even worse than he had been led to believe. Army Group Centre needed at least thirty trains a day to continue stockpiling for the coming offensive, but only twenty-three were promised, and as Bock well knew promises from the army Quartermaster-General were not always kept. This lower figure caused Bock to consider calling the offensive off. As the commander of Army Group Centre dolefully noted in his diary; 'it turned out if the number of trains is kept at the reduced level of 23, stockpiling of the front, even for an attack with limited objectives, cannot be completed before

Figure 4.3 A destroyed German hospital train on the line between Vitebsk and Orsha (November 1941)

11 December; that means that in my opinion the attack will not take place!'[62] Bock then approached Brauchitsch and repeated his concerns: 'If a rapid stockpiling by maintaining the higher number of trains is not feasible, I will have to give the order to dig in for the winter. It is impossible to let the units lie around for another four weeks, for this evening the temperature dropped to ten degrees below freezing.'[63] Brauchitsch suggested the alternative of having Bock's front attack in different 'sectors' as the supply situation permitted. Bock agreed to the idea and announced that the first 'sector' would be Panzer Group 3 with the objective of securing the northern wing of the advance along the line of the Moskva River and Moscow canal.[64] That evening Strauss' Ninth Army was instructed to begin its attack on 15 November (codenamed *Wolgastaubecken* – Operation Volga reservoir), while it was assumed that Kluge's Fourth Army would be unable to attack until at least 18 November.[65]

The following day (12 November) Bock received word that several trains were transporting Jews from Germany into the rear area of his army group. Bock was incredulous and immediately lodged a protest with Halder – not for the sake of the Jews, to whose fate Bock was indifferent, but 'because these Jew trains must result in an equal loss of essential [supply] trains'.[66] On 14 November, with the commencement date for the offensive now pending, the lack of supplies throughout Army Group Centre caused some measure of consternation. As Bock noted in his diary: 'The armies are all complaining about serious supply difficulties in all areas – rations, munitions, fuel and winter clothing. With the limited number of trains in use it is impossible to do anything about it. Naturally this has significantly complicated the attack preparations.'[67] By 15 November, the date of Panzer Group 3's attack, Bock was in despair. The OKH had guaranteed him a minimum of twenty-three trains a day with an increase to thirty-one trains, but for the past two days the number of trains had failed to meet even the minimum figure.[68] The shortfall continued on 16 November when just twelve trains reached Army Group Centre.[69] At Second Army, on Bock's southern flank, trains arrived only intermittently between 12 November and 2 December, and sometimes not for days on end. Strauss' Ninth Army received only one fuel train between 9 and 23 November, and its contents hardly reached the front because the trucks bridging the railhead with the forward positions required most of the consignment.[70] Hoepner's Panzer Group 4 did not receive a single fuel train for the offensive after 17 November.[71] Guderian's Second Panzer Army stated that ten trains a day were required to meet its needs, but only five daily were planned to arrive before 15 November.[72] Given the promises made to Bock, one sees just how far ignorance of the problems, or outright incompetence in organisation, extended within the German army. On 19 November, after the whole army group had gone over to the offensive, Halder noted that of the necessary thirty-one trains a day, Army Group Centre was receiving just sixteen.[73]

Trains were the weakest link in the *Ostheer*'s logistics apparatus, which says a great deal given that motor vehicle haulage was estimated at being just 15 per cent of its total on 22 June.[74] The problem of the German railways was in part due to seasonal factors – German locomotives had their water pipes affixed external to their boilers meaning that 70–80 per cent of them burst when the water froze – yet there were also systemic failures in the organisation and management of the railways.[75] German prewar planning assumed the widespread capture of broad-gauge Soviet trains and only insignificant damage to the Soviet rail network.[76] The general disappointment of this optimistic expectation forced heavy reliance on the immediate eastward extension of the standard-gauge rail lines, while the deficit in locomotives and rolling stock had to be borne by the already over-strained *Reichsbahn* (German railways).[77] The *Eisenbahntruppe* (railway troops) charged with carrying out the conversion were faced with critical shortages of both manpower and materials, making rapid progress impossible. Indeed, a total of only 1,000 motor vehicles (mostly inferior French and British models) was allocated to the *Eisenbahntruppe* across the whole of the eastern front. As the distances grew, emphasis was placed on the speed of the conversion rate rather than on the quality of the work and consequently train speeds had to remain very low. Meanwhile, the coexistence of Soviet and German railways, although constantly being pushed forward, was never entirely eliminated and the transfer points became bottlenecks. Even in occupied Poland the Governor-General, Hans Frank, proved decidedly uncooperative and was only finally forced to accept absolute priority for military trains in the course of November. Still, traffic control on the railways was poor and trains were sometimes 'hijacked' by competing authorities or simply disappeared altogether.[78] Halder acknowledged that the personnel dispatched from the *Reichsbahn* to administer the new network in the east did not understand military requirements and were probably not the best people to begin with.[79] Security along the lines was also extremely poor as Army Group Centre's four security divisions proved totally inadequate to prevent even the nascent Soviet partisan movement from sabotaging tracks and sometimes derailing trains.[80]

The implications of the supply crisis were not always fully appreciated at the front because, on the one hand, the front had bogged down as of mid to late October (depending on the sector) and, on the other, because the temperature had not dipped below zero for extended periods. Up to this point German soldiers had certainly suffered from the cold, but it was from the middle of November that stories emerged of whole companies with frostbite and individual soldiers freezing to death on sentry duty.[81] It was also at this time that the utter inadequacy of the German summer uniforms became fully apparent. As Siegfried Knappe noted, the advent of the much anticipated frost came at a cost: 'We could move again, but now we were freezing because we still did not have winter clothing. We had the same field uniforms we had worn during the summer, plus a light overcoat ... We tried to spend the nights in villages so we could get out of the weather.'[82] Assuming new positions was also an ordeal in the frozen ground, especially since many German soldiers still had to sleep outside. Helmut Günther noted:

> The companies were on the high ground and had dug in. That was miserable work in the cold and with the frozen ground [we] stomped around listlessly looking for a spot of ground where we could bed down. Here we made a start, there we poked around – it just wasn't working . . . Finally, with a great deal of trouble, we came up with a meagre little hole and squatted together, freezing and with chattering teeth.[83]

Helmut Pabst was lucky enough to have a hut to share with his comrades, but there was a palpable dread of moving up to the line. 'Since five this morning it's been snowing again . . . We put our noses outside and fly back to the stove. Pity the poor rifle companies out there in their dugouts and foxholes. This isn't proper positional warfare. We're not equipped for it and we have no proper dugouts, although we've been stuck here for some time.'[84]

In Russia they have a saying that there is no such thing as cold weather, just the wrong kind of clothing.[85] Indeed, in the aftermath of the Winter War Stalin claimed that it was not true that an army's fighting strength decreased in winter. All the Russian army's major victories were won in winter, Stalin insisted, before citing: 'Aleksandr Nevskii against the Swedes, Peter I against the Swedes in Finland, Alexander I's victory over Napoleon. We are a northern country.'[86] This may have been a somewhat self-evident truth, but in the postwar world the German generals deflected the embarrassment of their unpreparedness by repeating the same claim Napoleon's apologists had made in the nineteenth century:[87] that the 1941 winter came early and was particularly severe.[88] As one former officer in the OKH noted after the war: 'That it is cold in Russia at this time belongs to the ABC of an eastern campaign.'[89] Among the rank and file there was indignation that their commanders had miscalculated so badly. After the war Heinrich Haape recalled the absurdity of the supplies that were distributed at the time. 'Four sets of winter clothing for each company! Sixteen greatcoats and sixteen pairs of winter boots to be shared among a battalion of eight hundred men!'[90] Helmut Günther was equally scathing:

> One hardly needed to be a general staff officer to know that it gets cold in winter! . . . We read in letters that warm clothing was being collected at home and that everyone, rich and poor alike, were donating great quantities. For us, however, all that was too late. By the time the first shipments arrived in early January, tens of thousands of *Landser* already had frozen limbs.[91]

It is difficult to reconstruct exactly how much winter equipment was stockpiled in Germany and occupied Poland, but it was certainly a great deal more than the train system could transport. Colonel Wilhelm von Rücker, a group leader in the supply division of the OKH, blamed the shortage of trains for the lack of winter supplies,[92] and there can be no doubt that great efforts were made on the home front to gather all manner of domestic clothing and winter paraphernalia.[93] After the war, Rundstedt insisted 'it is not entirely true that preparations for a winter campaign were not made. The famous winter clothing was there, but it didn't arrive, owing to rail difficulties and road transport.' In fact, because Rundstedt maintained the army had provided everything for the troops he remarked that Goebbels' public drive for winter clothing was nothing but 'revolting propaganda'.[94] While railways were the obvious bottleneck, singling these out may well have disguised a serious shortfall in what the army could provide the *Ostheer* in the autumn of 1941. However, this was still secondary to the primary problem of transferring what did exist to the front.[95]

On 7 November, Second Panzer Army recorded in detail exactly how much of its winter requirements had been delivered. The most common item was winter overcoats with an impressive 60 per cent delivered, then came hand mittens (40–50 per cent supplied), head warmers and gloves (30–40 per cent) and winter trousers (20 per cent). At the lower end of the spectrum there were just 10 per cent of the required woollen blankets and no felt boots.[96] If these figures are any indication the absence of winter uniforms should not be generalised across the board, but, clearly, there were still critical shortages. One soldier wrote home on 11 November:

> One just cannot understand why we have not received winter things. If it goes on like this it will be Napoleonic and untold numbers will freeze. I think in 1812 they were better equipped than we are. Almost everyone has ruined socks and no ear muffs (only those who owned them privately). This is the same in other units too. This is how little they provide for us! In the year 1941![97]

Yet not everyone took such a pessimistic view. Elmar Lieb wrote to his wife that the German army had survived a winter in northern Norway (1939–40) and four years of winters in the east during the First World War.[98] Winter uniforms were also not an end in themselves to solving the looming crisis. Erich Hager, for example, had just received a winter uniform, but even his diary speaks with foreboding about what was to come: 'Last night was dreadful, real Russian winter. A snowstorm like I've never seen before, and a dry cold. If it goes on like this it will be bad for us.'[99]

A sobering indication of what exactly improperly clothed troops on the offensive endured was provided on 13 November by General of Panzer Troops Rudolf Schmidt, who had just handed over command of the XXXIX Panzer Corps fighting at Tikhvin in the area of Army Group North. Writing to Paulus at the OKH, Schmidt painted a depressing picture:

> Boots are torn to shreds and are a disgrace. Many of the men are going about with their feet wrapped in paper, and there is a great dearth of gloves. As far as winter clothing is concerned, the Quartermaster-General deserves every curse that can be hurled at him ... This total lack of foresight and care makes even these splendid fellows of ours dispirited and rebellious ... Then in the newspapers they read wonderful speeches – 'come what may, this winter our brave soldiers need not fear the cold'.[100]

Blumentritt at Fourth Army repeated the same point after the war: 'The troops not unnaturally now resented the bombastic utterances of our propaganda in October. One began to hear sarcastic references to the military leaders far away in Germany. The troops felt that it was high time our political leaders came and had a look at the front. Our soldiers were overtired now, our units under strength.'[101]

The dearth of manpower throughout Army Group Centre was further exacerbated by the loss of a number of major formations during the course of late October and November. Major-General Kurt Feldt's 1st Cavalry Division was withdrawn from the front on 25 October (to be reorganised as the new 24th Panzer Division), while in November Lieutenant-General Johann Sinnhuber's badly depleted 28th Infantry Division and most of Major-General Gustav Höhne's 8th Infantry Division were sent to France for rebuilding. At the same time, Bock's only reinforcement was, in fact, a formation of French volunteers known as the *Légion des volontaires français contre le bolchevisme* (LVF) (Legion of French Volunteers against Bolshevism), but this only numbered some 3,000 men.[102] Much more worryingly, from early November

Bock would begin to lose Kesselring, the command staff of Air Fleet 2 and General of Aviation Bruno Loerzer's II Air Corps (with thirteen air groups), which were being reassigned to deal with supply problems across the Mediterranean in support of General of Panzer Troops Erwin Rommel's *Afrikakorps*.[103] This would leave Army Group Centre just Colonel-General Wolfram von Richthofen's VIII Air Corps, effectively halving Bock's air support at a time when the Soviet air force was proving to be remarkably resurgent and effective.[104]

Though the frost had arrived to restart the motorised columns and facilitate the advance, the hardening roads, while solving old problems, were at the same time creating new ones. The thousands of trucks, tractors, tanks, wagons and horses had left the roads churned and uneven, which was exactly their shape when the cold set in to freeze them. Léon Degrelle gave a vivid depiction of what this meant:

> The river of mud was now a river of bumpy lava. The mud had solidified ... It had hardened like stone into a network of rocky ridges, a half metre high, like black marble, which, fifty or a hundred feet wide, dipped and heaved, gashed by long ruts.
>
> It was useless to try and send ordinary autos into those ruts. A passenger car's gas tank would be smashed after the first few kilometres. Only heavy trucks and cross-country vehicles, with particularly high axles, could take a chance on that glazed frost. They alone could straddle the crevasses.[105]

Horst Lange watched as a truck nearly tipped over on the frozen ruts,[106] while Army Group Centre's war diary noted that this new phenomenon placed an even greater strain on the already brittle, and scarcely replaceable, truck springs and suspension.[107] Max Kuhnert suggested that the summer conditions had been difficult enough, but what Army Group Centre now confronted was 'sheer murder. The first hard frost came, and what that did to the mud, worse still the churned-up mud, you can imagine.'[108] Yet it was not just that the mud had frozen in its churned state, there was also a vast backlog of bogged down, half sunken vehicles that had to be retrieved from the powerful grip of the indissoluble ground. Watching a number of artillery pieces being towed out of their half-buried state, Blumentritt observed that a number of them 'were literally torn to pieces'.[109] At the same time, Ernst Kern observed how Soviet artillery became more dangerous as the shells were more likely to explode on the hard ground (as opposed to falling as duds in the mud) and there was more shrapnel than before.[110]

Since the summer months rampant, and often unsubstantiated, rumours circulated through every major German formation in the east. Despite their notorious unreliability many of the men placed more stock in the latest gossip than in almost any source of official information, which, given the overblown nature of German propaganda, was hardly surprising. No topic was more fervently speculated upon than the length of time their division would have to remain in the east, and men engaged in heated debates about the veracity of such information. Optimists offered the hope of salvation from the frightful conditions of the war, and many of the men naturally wanted to believe in a reassignment to France or even a return to Germany. Pessimists, on the other hand, could always point to the still undefeated Red Army and, as time went on, how many false promises had proven the virtue of their scepticism. Yet by November, with a number of major formations being transferred to the west, speculation was again rife about which division might be next to escape the menacing winter. As Ernst Kern recalled: 'We were still naive enough to believe that since the division had no winter uniforms, it would withdraw from Russia when winter came. Every kind of rumour was spread, but *everyone* was sure that we would be home by Christmas.'[111] One of those who remained steadfastly convinced was Wilhelm Prüller, who wrote in his diary: 'Who brings the rumours, and who thinks them up, you never know. All at once everyone's saying: winter quarters in Russia. If it weren't so ridiculous, one might believe it . . . Impossible is all I have to say to that.'[112] Many men, of course, took the middle ground and, while hoping for the best, they no longer dared to believe in it. Ernst Guicking explained in a letter to his wife on 5 November: 'I do not believe anything of it anymore ... [the pubic announcements and rumours] made us happy and yet greatly disappointed us. I do not want to be disappointed afterwards.'[113] Likewise, Wolf Dose suggested: 'They say the campaign will end before the onset of real winter, but I do not see much sign of this happening. It is best not to set one's hopes on miracles.'[114]

The generals of the OKH and OKW certainly did not believe that any divine intervention was necessary for their new war plans to be another resounding success. They were impervious to many of the problems and complaints of the field commanders, which, to their minds, only revisited many of the same issues that the same men had raised before

Operation Typhoon was launched in early October. The victories at Viaz'ma and Briansk seemed to convince the generals in East Prussia that there was more smoke than fire in the dire warnings they were now receiving. It was also the case that important figures within Army Group Centre were still backing the offensive, although not always because they believed in it, rather because it was a *fait accompli* and opposing it could only harm their career and standing. Bock genuinely believed there was still a success to be won and he was largely supported by Reinhardt and Hoepner, albeit with somewhat less enthusiasm by mid-November. Guderian, on the other hand, was torn. His hard-won reputation as the firebrand panzer general who was not to be denied his objective (according to Goebbels' propaganda), now clashed with the colossal disparity between his greatly diminished panzer army and the enormous task of encircling Moscow from the south. Guderian may have been a man of unbridled ambition and self-belief, remarkable even among the extravagant personalities of the *panzertruppe*, but he was also present at the front and knew the state of his men and machines. The charge that Guderian was head-strong and obnoxious is certainly valid, but he was also no fool, especially in operational matters. For all these reasons he could not bring himself to be the first German army commander to claim his orders were beyond him, particularly for a man with a well-deserved reputation for berating subordinates who baulked at carrying out his orders. Reinhardt and Hoepner were much closer to their objective, could materially support each other and had far stronger panzer divisions. Guderian, on the other hand, would have to contend with a much longer advance, a major fortress in his rear (Tula) and no extra troops to cover a growing right flank on his long journey north.

The infantry generals too had a sense of foreboding about the orders at hand and the perceived inability of their exposed and ill-equipped men to support another major attack so late in the year. According to Richthofen, Strauss at Ninth Army was 'unduly passive' and he observed that 'his inertia is quite unbelievable'.[115] Kluge too dithered and demurred, but stopped short of voicing any outright objection. With Hitler, Halder and Bock all supporting the attack, the army commanders were caught between the hammer and the anvil. While Kluge was clearly not prepared to oppose the attack, he did try to influence Bock in that direction. In a telephone discussion on 15 November, Kluge emphasised how battered and bloodied his right wing was from Soviet attacks. The XII and XIII Army Corps, he reported,

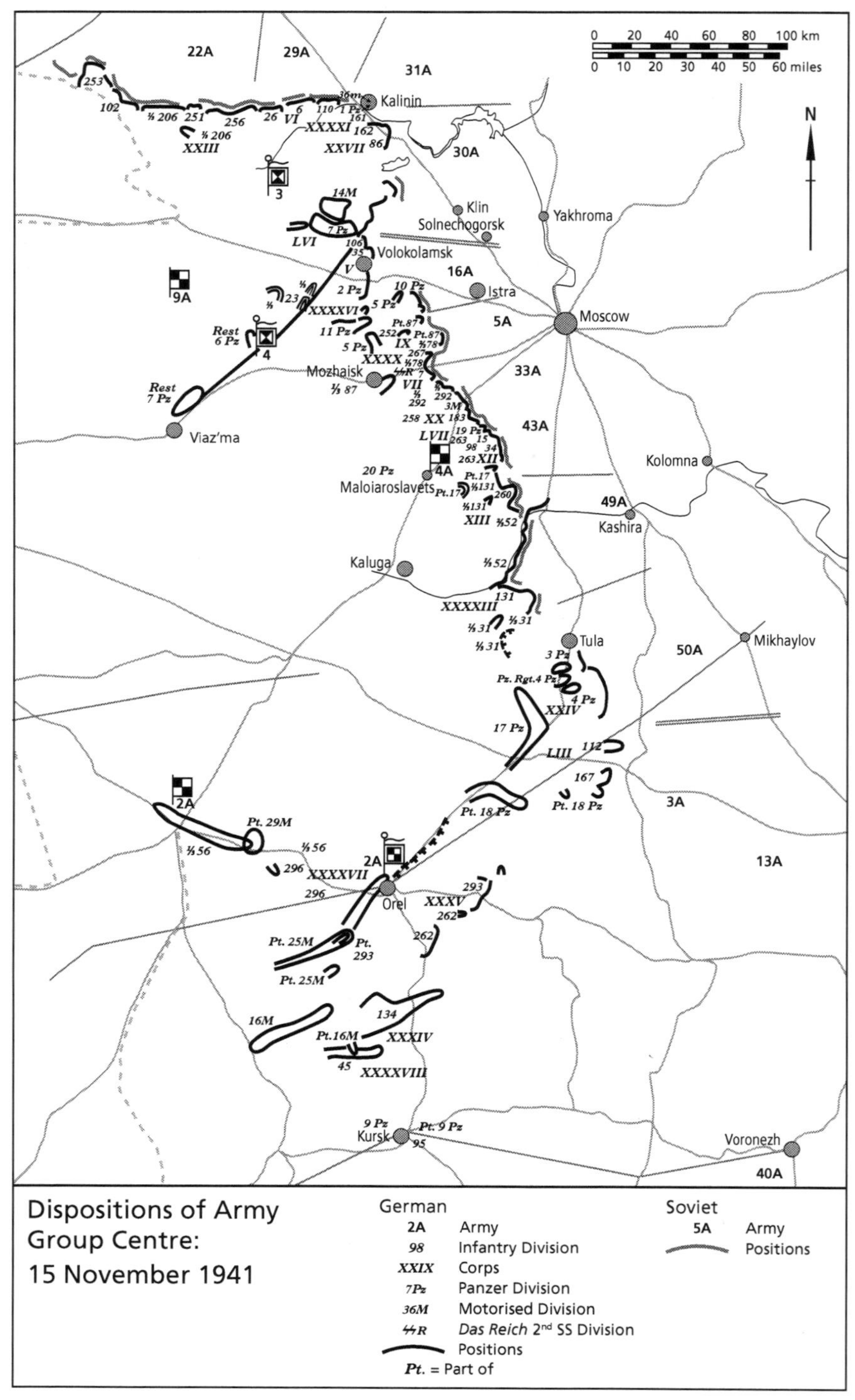

Map 4.2 Dispositions of Army Group Centre, 15 November 1941

could no longer attack, but then continued: 'In addition, the reduced combat strength of all other divisions and the shortage of reserves means that the planned attack poses a great risk if the enemy is strong enough to lead counterattacks.'[116] In the south, Weichs, the commander of the Second Army, had to be replaced as of 11 November on account of serious illness (he was flown directly back to Germany) and one might speculate this was at least in part brought on by the intractable demands of his position.[117] Certainly his replacement, Schmidt, who had just left his panzer corps at Tikhvin, did not mince words when he asserted, after assuming command, that the Second Army was at the most 'critical point on the whole front'.[118] The Second Army also had a panzer corps (Kempf's XXXXVIII) and, unlike the rest of Army Group Centre, it had already been ordered back onto the offensive towards Voronezh after the capture of Kursk. The attack, however, soon floundered owing to a lack of rest and resupply. Indeed, the weakness of Kempf's forces made a mockery of its designation as a panzer corps. His only panzer division (Hubicki's 9th) had just seven tanks remaining on 1 November,[119] and his exhausted forces had to be reorganised to advance as small 'expeditions'.[120] The resentment and sense of helplessness this engendered at the middle level of command is seen in an entry in the war diary of the 9th Panzer Division on 11 November: 'Among the troops one has the feeling that the higher bodies often lack an understanding for the peculiarities of a panzer division. Even for the other parts of the division [beyond the panzer regiment] the vehicle and spare parts situation is hopeless. Every relevant report from the division remains without any help.'[121] The disparity between the generals of the high command and the generals at the division and corps level was extraordinary, while those caught between them at the panzer group and army level were being influenced in opposite directions. Ultimately, however, the attack had been ordered and none of the senior commanders in Army Group Centre was prepared to risk ire or disdain by appearing to be hesitant, doubtful or uncertain. Typhoon would continue, but in the minds of many it was now a *coup de collier* (an action born of desperation).

Army Group Centre's operational plan for the resumption of Typhoon was set in stages, with the first to begin on 15 November. The Ninth Army, followed a day later by Panzer Group 3, was to breach Soviet positions on the Lama River and Volga reservoir, then they would press on to the Moscow–Volga canal. At Selizharovo, the Ninth Army's left wing would have to go over to the defensive and guard the northern

Figure 4.4 German troops in improvised camouflage moving out to resume the attack towards Moscow (17 November 1941)

flank of the developing offensive, while the remaining forces continued attacking towards the southeast to envelop Moscow.[122] As Gerhard vom Bruch of the 6th Panzer Division noted on 14 November: 'We are now awaiting instructions to move against the Volga reservoir and the Moscow canal. We are reassured, again and again, that these will be our last orders before winter. Our task will be to secure a bridgehead south of the reservoir and dam.'[123] On 17 November, Ruoff's v Army Corps (operating on the left wing of Kluge's Fourth Army) would begin its attack towards Teryayevo to capture the high ground and secure contact with the Ninth Army's southern flank. Elements of Panzer Group 4 were to support this attack. It was still unresolved if and when the rest of Kluge's Fourth Army would join the attack. In the south, Guderian's attack was set for 18 November when the Second Panzer Army would head northeast towards Kolomna, which was some 125 km from Tula, but still well short of Moscow (another 100 km away).[124]

While Army Group Centre suffered from chronic internal weakness and the increasing ferocity of the Russian winter, the final factor Bock had to consider was the Red Army. The scattered and beaten remnants of the Soviet Western Front in the first half of October were rapidly reformed, reorganised and resupplied – enough to stop Bock's offensive in the second half of the month (in tandem with the *rasputitsa*). However, Zhukov's forces were still far from adequate and, owing to Stalin's demand for offensive action in the first half of November, weakened to a perilous extent. Yet, close to transportation and supply networks, the strength of the Western Front was rising, while Bock was, at best, maintaining his strength in some sectors and losing it in most others. Dismissive, as so often before, of the strength of the Red Army, German commanders assumed that however bad things may seem for the *Ostheer*, the Red Army simply had to be much worse off. It was another fallacious assumption that would be repeated time and again in the coming weeks to counter sound arguments pointing to Army Group Centre's exhaustion. Yet in mid-November the commanders of Army Group Centre were largely oblivious to the resurgent power of the Western Front, and expressed surprise at what they subsequently encountered. Writing after the war Blumentritt wrote:

> Skilfully camouflaged strong points, wire entanglements and thick minefields now filled the forests which covered the western approach to Moscow. Strong armies had been formed from the remnants of those which had been defeated farther west and from fresh formations. The Moscow workers had been called out. New army corps were arriving from Siberia ... All this came as a surprise to us, nor could we believe that the situation would change dramatically after all our exertions and when the prize seemed almost within our grasp.[125]

Despite past experience, which suggested the dangerous potential of resurgent Soviet power, the files of Foreign Armies East also shed light on what might be expected before Moscow. Agent reports described the Soviet capital as 'overcrowded' with troops, while aerial intelligence pointed to 'heavy train traffic' in and out of the Moscow area.[126]

The rank and file in Army Group Centre, of course, had no strategic insight into the *Ostheer* or the campaign in which they were involved, but many nevertheless voiced comments on the events as they understood them. Albert Neuhaus sarcastically observed on 11 November that the 'last battle' in the east (according to Hitler's early October proclamation) had already been in progress for five weeks and there was no end in sight.[127] A divisional doctor from the 35th Infantry

Division noted on 13 November that the spirits of the men were 'apathetic ... mixed with gallows humour'.[128] Indeed, while numerous letters observed that the advent of frost had at last restored movement, doubts were still expressed about winning the war soon.[129] Others were less worried about the length of the war than the more immediate concern of leaving warm billets for a new objective that almost everyone agreed would be fiercely defended. Writing on 15 November, Alois Scheuer observed: 'The last few days we have been in a quiet village about eighty km from Moscow and have at least had warm quarters. In the next days things will continue forward (objective Moscow). I would much rather it if I never saw this city of horrors.'[130] However, orders were orders and, ready or not, Army Group Centre was destined to attack again. As Hans Roth concluded: 'It is finally here; the ground is frozen solid. We can start.'[131]

5 TYPHOON RE-LAUNCHED

Hanging by a thread in the north: Hoepner and Reinhardt march on Moscow

With the exception of the Second Army's slow advance in the south, Operation Typhoon resumed its active operations on 15 November, but the contrast with 2 October could not have been more apparent. The staggered offensive timetable meant that on 15 November only the XXVII Army Corps (from the Ninth Army) was able to commence the attack. Bock noted its 'good progress',[1] and Halder rejoiced at the news that the enemy was pulling back, to which he observed: 'That is something new in this campaign.'[2] The Soviet proclivity to defend every metre of ground had helped to facilitate the large-scale encirclements of the past, and if local commanders were adapting their methods to fixing defences on natural boundaries it was hardly a positive development. Reinhardt in fact described the attack as a punch into thin air (*Luftstoß*) and claimed that the enemy had already re-established its defences behind the Volga, with only screening troops in the forward positions. Moreover, the bridges that the XXVII Army Corps was supposed to capture had been blown.[3] On the following day (16 November) Schaal's LVI Panzer Corps joined the attack to the south of Wäger's corps. Unlike the shock effect of previous offensives, Funck's 7th Panzer Division, supported by concentrated artillery and rocket fire, made only slow progress.[4] Losses for the division on this first day came to eleven officers and some 120 men. The accompanying 14th Motorised Infantry Division was more successful, seizing two bridgeheads across the Lama River at Gribanowo and Kussowa.[5]

Further south, on 16 November, there was a preliminary attack by Veiel's 2nd Panzer Division (a day before the scheduled attack of Hoepner's panzer group) aimed at securing good starting positions for Ruoff's v Army Corps, which was also ordered to attack on the following day.[6] Opposing Veiel's advance was the Soviet 316th Rifle Division, and it was on this day that the legend of Panfilov's twenty-eight heroes originated. This was a well-crafted myth of Soviet propaganda in which twenty-eight men fought to the death to destroy dozens of German tanks. In spite of having no basis in truth, Commissar Vasily Klochkov's immortalised battle cry: 'Russia is vast, but there is nowhere to retreat – we have our backs to Moscow!' was no less inspiring as a result.[7] While Panfilov's twenty-eight remained an invention of Soviet propaganda, it inspired countless actual examples of Soviet valour and bravery.[8] As Dmitry Vonlyarsky noted: 'In mid-November, when the German offensive resumed, and our forces were suffering terrible losses, iron discipline alone would not have kept our soldiers going. It was a desperate patriotism, a love of our Motherland, that held us together. The resolve to defend Moscow to the last man sprang from that.'[9] Likewise, Lieutenant-General K. K. Rokossovsky, whose Sixteenth Army was in the direct path of the German advance on Moscow, noted after the war the gallantry with which Soviet soldiers acted upon the call to defend Moscow and that this was 'taken up by the whole army and nation'.[10]

As Typhoon again assumed the proportions of a major offensive, Kluge abruptly informed Bock on 16 November that he was postponing the planned attack by Hoepner's panzer group for another day until 18 November. As it was, only two regiments of v Army Corps would attack on 17 November to ensure contact with the Ninth Army's southern wing. When asked why the postponement was necessary, Kluge replied that he had again had to repel ongoing heavy enemy attacks against the vii and xx Army Corps.[11] On 17 November, Bock sent Greiffenberg to the Fourth Army to investigate and he reported that Kluge saw his position as especially difficult, in part because of Guderian's alleged failure to advance. Bock, however, remained unconvinced and sent a long reply to the Fourth Army conveying both his disappointment and increasing exasperation: 'As far as the number of divisions in relation to width of front is concerned, the Fourth Army is better off than all the other armies of the army group. In spite of the extraordinary drop in strength, on the whole the state of its forces is in no

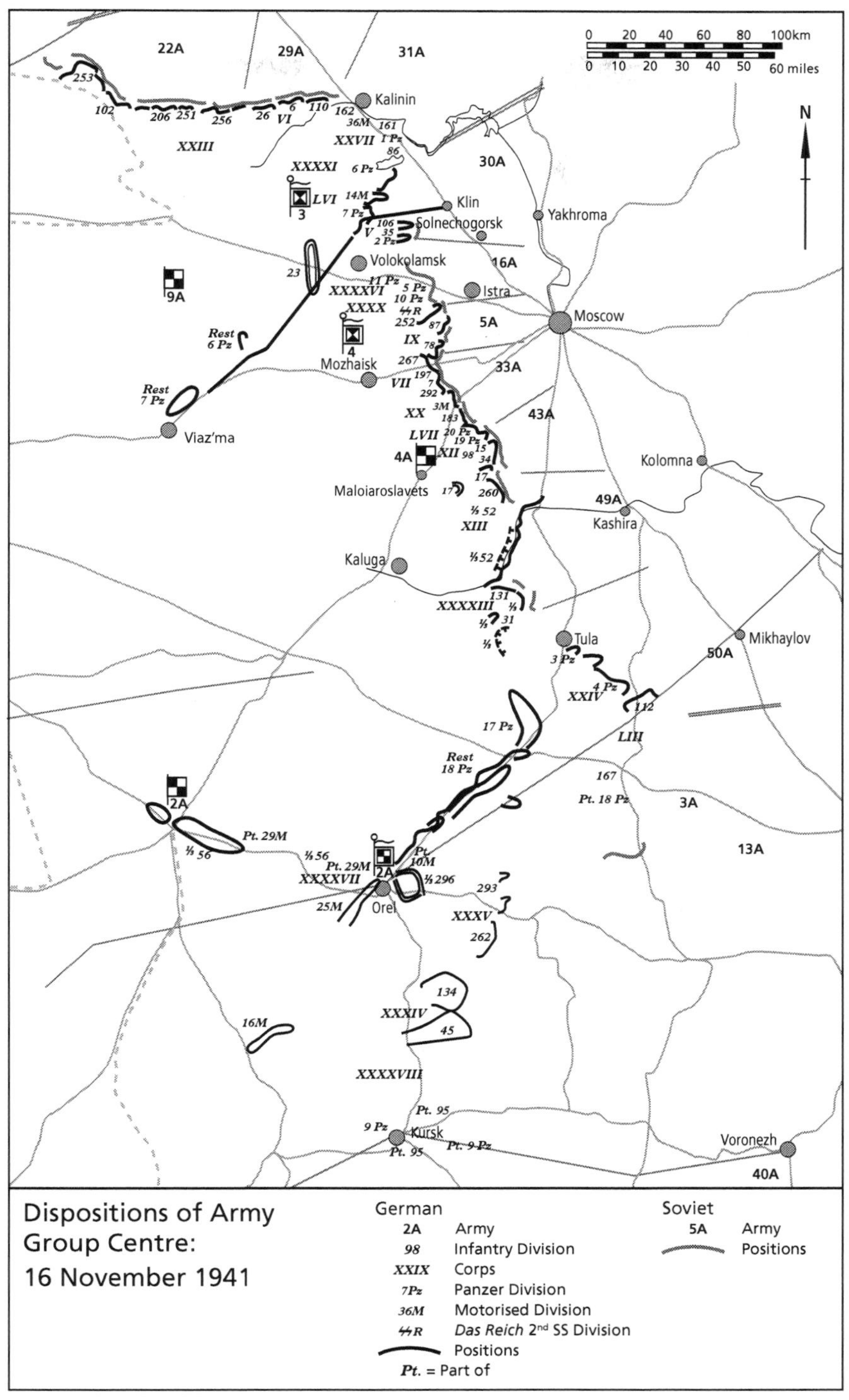

Map 5.1 Dispositions of Army Group Centre, 16 November 1941

way worse than that of other fronts.' Bock also pointed out that Guderian's ratio was 'significantly less favourable' and that the perceived lack of action from the Second Panzer Army was precisely what the Ninth Army now saw from Kluge's forces and was 'not without risk'.[12]

The Fourth Army informed Bock that the attack would commence the next day (18 November), but then changed tack and fifteen minutes later reported that only Ruoff's v Corps and elements of Vietinghoff's xxxxvi Panzer Corps were intended to attack. The attacks of Stumme's xxxx Panzer Corps, Geyer's ix Army Corps and Fahrmbacher's vii Army Corps were now being delayed until 19 November. Bock informed Halder of Kluge's 'wavering intentions' and added that a piecemeal attack was 'a mistake', but it could not be altered on account of amended orders not getting through. Halder wanted Bock to put more pressure on Kluge, and the following day (18 November) contemplated proposing an order to Brauchitsch expressly ordering Kluge to attack. Bock, however, rejected this and accepted Kluge's insistence that the situation on his right wing was 'serious and difficult', requiring the further transfer of reinforcements south to shore-up Felber's and Schroth's vulnerable corps.[13] Indeed, Army Group Centre's war diary includes reports from the Fourth Army stating that at least one infantry regiment had a combat strength of just 400 men and that the divisions 'were at the limit of their physical ability'.[14] Halder, however, was unimpressed and told Bock, 'we must understand that things are going much worse for the enemy than for us and that these battles are less a question of strategic command than a question of energy'.[15]

The initial offensive by Strauss' Ninth Army hit the connection between the Soviet Thirtieth and Sixteenth Armies, which helped to facilitate the German advance north to the Volga River. Yet while Zhukov's forces could fall back to the Volga in the north they had to carry on defending Klin as the gateway to the Moscow–Volga canal and the northern approaches to Moscow. The Western Front commanded some 240,000 men, 1,254 guns, 502 tanks and 600–700 aircraft, which was weaker than it could have been owing to Stalin's insistence on conducting local counteroffensives.[16] Yet the apparent futility of these attacks must be balanced against the psychological and strategic effect on the German commanders (principally Kluge, but also later Guderian), whose reluctance to attack was considerably heightened as a result. Numerically Zhukov's Western Front was substantially inferior to

Army Group Centre, but the inability of Bock's forces to manoeuvre rapidly and concentrate their strength forced the Germans to confront Soviet defences on far more even terms. On 17 November, the 6th Panzer Division's war diary spoke of encountering countless enemy bunkers, unusually heavy mining and the so-called Soviet 'mine dogs'.[17] These were dogs fitted with explosive devices that were triggered by a spring-loaded wooden lever that stood-up from the dog's back. The dogs were trained to find food under armoured vehicles and when they crawled under a tank the lever was compressed leading to detonation.[18] Mine dogs, however, were far less effective than ordinary mines, which accounted for many more German vehicles and proved much harder to counter. As Rokossovsky noted: 'Our engineers were of great help in combating the enemy's "roaming" armoured groups. They travelled in trucks and planted mines and ground bombs on expected routes of advance. I encouraged every display of useful initiative, and the results were excellent.'[19] Rooting entrenched Soviet infantrymen out of bunkers, clearing strong points, villages and minefields was labour-intensive work, and Panzer Group 3 requested urgent infantry reinforcements to offset the current drag in operations.[20] The combat was unavoidably brutal and gritty. The Germans were pushing forward, but it was a staggered advance and without the decisive breakthrough and 'shock' effect of past offensives.

While Panzer Group 3 had struggled to advance alone, it was at last supported on 18 November by the advance of Ruoff's V Army Corps. This corps had been strengthened for the attack by the addition of Veiel's 2nd Panzer Division (in addition to Lieutenant-General Walther Fischer von Weikersthal's 35th and Major-General Ernst Dehner's 106th Infantry Divisions). Success was rapid with the fall of Bujgorod and the capture of some 1,550 Soviet POWs, with many more killed in action.[21] It was also estimated that over the past three days some sixty Soviet tanks had been destroyed.[22] Driving into Soviet defences quickly started to redress the imbalance with one tank battle on 19 November resulting in five Soviet and five German tanks knocked out. Veiel's panzer division, which had only been on the eastern front for six weeks, also noted the alarming problem of hitting a Soviet T-34 many times with no effect.[23] Even worse, Fehn's 5th Panzer Division, also a recent addition to Army Group Centre, reported engaging a Soviet KV-1 heavy tank with three Mark III panzers and one 37-mm anti-tank gun. The fate of the KV-1 was not recorded, but all three German tanks were destroyed.[24] As one German tanker recorded in his diary on 20 November after closing to point-blank range in a battle against a crippled KV-1: 'we fired thirty shots into him. Nothing got through. There weren't 10 cm without a direct hit. We'd never experienced anything like it.'[25] If the panzer divisions were having trouble with the new Soviet medium and heavy tanks, the effect upon the more poorly equipped infantry divisions was far worse.[26] Blumentritt noted that these formations 'felt themselves naked and defenceless' and that a new anti-tank gun of at least 75-mm calibre was urgently needed. However, as Blumentritt noted, the absence of such a weapon 'marked the beginning of what came to be called the "tank terror"'.[27]

Notwithstanding the problem of Soviet tanks, Hoepner's attack was further strengthened on 19 November with five corps committed to the attack from his own panzer group and the Fourth Army. The weight of German forces was more than the defending Soviet armies could bear and forward progress was steady, but not rapid.[28] Unlike the former commanders of the Soviet Western Front facing German offensives in June and October, Zhukov was able to hold his front together, maintaining cohesion between his armies and conducting a stubborn fighting front even while it was being pushed back.[29] As Panzer Group 4's war diary observed on 19 November: 'The [Soviet] defence was again especially strong on the main roads ... A breakthrough has not yet been achieved.'[30]

Pressure was also being exerted by the sustained advance of Reinhardt's Panzer Group 3, which by 18 November was operating east of the Lama River and south of the Volga reservoir.[31] Strauss also took the decision to reinforce the advance with Lieutenant-General Walter Model's XXXXI Panzer Corps[32] at Kalinin (1st Panzer Division, 36th Motorised Infantry Division and *Lehrbrigade* 900).[33] The following day (19 November), however, it was noted that the lack of fuel in Kalinin prevented any movement by Model's corps and that an improvement 'was impossible for many days'. Indeed, on 20 November, Bock noted that fuel supplies would not arrive until 24 and 28 November.[34] Even in normal conditions the XXXXI Panzer Corps estimated the total supply needs (fuel and munitions) of an attacking panzer division at 175 tons a day. Model, however, would have to operate on a fraction of this as the result of shortages at the railhead depots, excessive distances and the lack of wheeled transport.[35] While Model was effectively stranded at Kalinin, Schaal's LVI Panzer Corps was still making progress

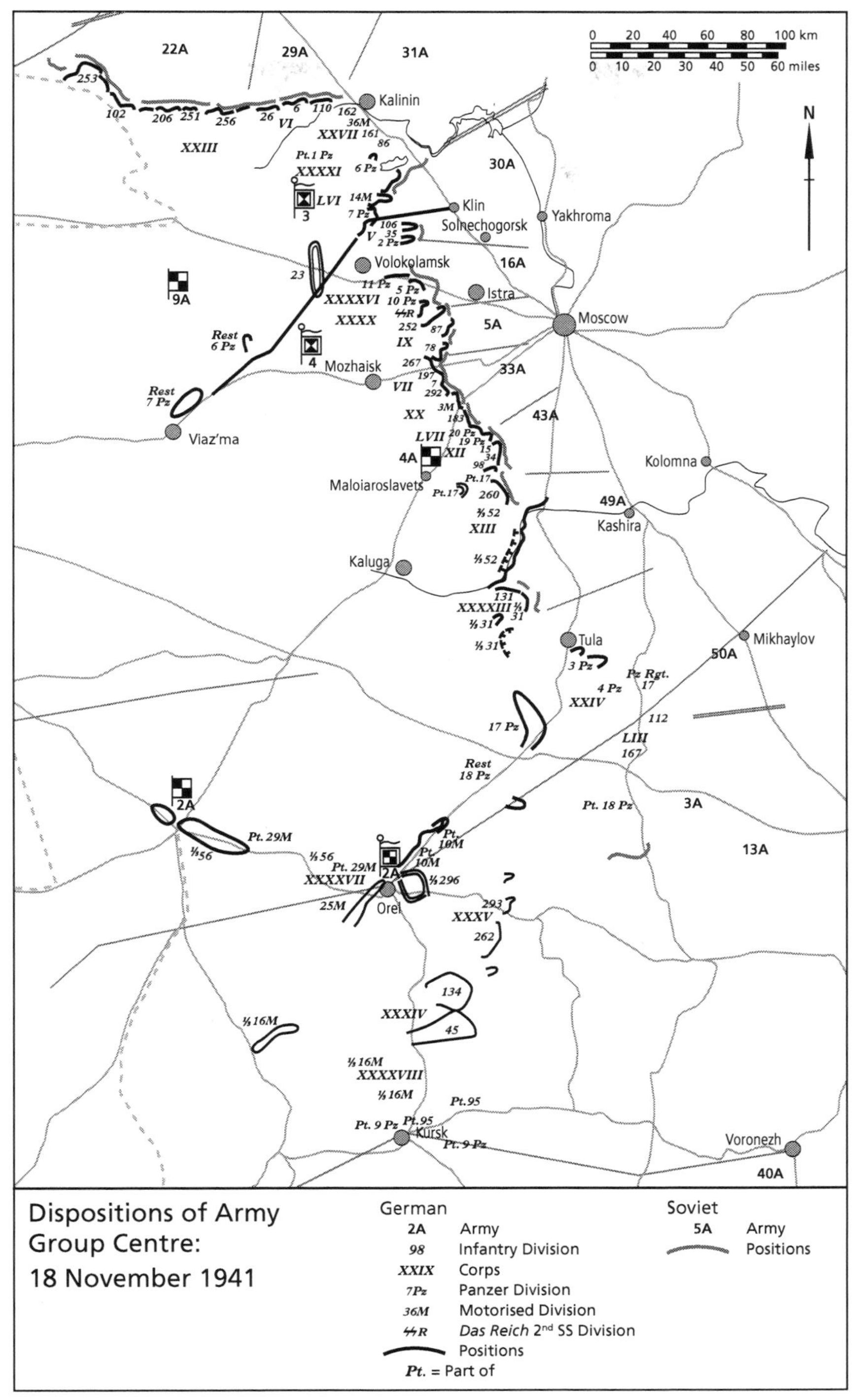

Map 5.2 Dispositions of Army Group Centre, 18 November 1941

towards the east, prompting Bock to remove Panzer Group 3 from the Ninth Army and subordinate it directly to Army Group Centre.[36] Schaal was also experiencing supply difficulties. Funck's 7th Panzer Division reported fuel shortages on 19 November[37] and, on the same day, Bock observed: 'In spite of all our efforts, it may turn out that we are halted in the middle of the attack for reasons of supply. Nevertheless, I have not waited to attack because the present period of good weather, also with regard to the Luftwaffe, has to be exploited.'[38]

Hoepner, too, was hamstrung from the very outset with fuel shortages. Scheller's 11th Panzer Division was sending most of its infantry forward on foot with the intention of sending their trucks after them once fuel arrived.[39] Thoma's 20th Panzer Division was even more indicative of the problem. Having made seventy-five tanks serviceable by 6 November (and potentially more since then), only forty-nine could be committed to the attack (eight Mark IIs, thirty-seven Mark IIIs and four Mark IVs).[40] Such results made a mockery of efforts to raise tank numbers and underlined the fundamental importance of coordinating means with effort. While the lack of fuel proved to be the most immediate impediment to sustained operations north of Moscow, a report received by Panzer Group 4 on 19 November that a single panzer detachment had already lost 50 per cent of its vehicles on account of the cold indicated serious new problems on the horizon.[41] Karl Knoblauch noted in his diary on the same day (19 November): 'In the coming days the weather situation will force us into inactivity.'[42]

Army Group Centre was taking its chances between the mud of the Russian *rasputitsa* and the deep snow of winter. At the same time, it was tempting fate between precariously low supply stockpiles and the still considerable distances to Moscow (even the closest divisions were still some 80 km from the capital). The gamble also involved serious risks; far more than the German command recognised at the time, especially since the Red Army was proving to be far more adept in the worsening conditions and was constantly receiving reinforcements. For now, however, the conditions still favoured Army Group Centre and Bock was determined to exploit every possibility to wring another victory from his tired armies. As Anatoly Shvebig, a Soviet soldier caught in the German offensive recalled: 'The 16 of November was a calamity. Many of our forward units were surrounded by the enemy, and Rokossovsky himself was desperately trying to avoid encirclement. The Germans got onto the road from Volokolamsk to Moscow and we had virtually nothing left to stop them with.'[43] Sensing their opportunity to strike a blow and exploit their initial success, Hoepner issued a general order to all his divisions on 19 November: 'Russian radio transmission suggests withdrawal. Inform troops: Tireless pursuit! Saves losses, shortens the campaign.'[44] However, even in this period the war diaries of both Reinhardt's and Hoepner's panzer groups are replete with examples of stalwart Soviet resistance. On 18 November, Landgraf's 6th Panzer Division reported heavy resistance on its route of advance with very active enemy air activity and no German fighter cover. It also noted intelligence from captured Soviet troops that two new regiments had been equipped with recently delivered American weapons.[45] Even more explicit was a report from *Das Reich* claiming that its current battle with the 78th Siberian Division was the hardest it had experienced in the whole of the eastern campaign. These men were said to fight to the last and that in the recent battle for Gorodischtsche no less than 812 dead enemy soldiers were counted in and around the village.[46] There were even examples of local reverses in which all captured Germans were massacred. After one such incident in which thirty wounded Germans were shot, Hoepner issued a new order to his troops intended to counter such brutality with an even more radicalised response. Hoepner's order stated: 'This behaviour is indicative of the Bolsheviks and is a mockery of any international law. I hope that this incident becomes known to every fighting man in the panzer group. Mercy towards such an enemy has no place. He is to be mercilessly annihilated. Every German soldier is fighting for his life.'[47] Certainly, this would have been a view familiar to many of the men fighting in the *Ostheer*. Even beyond the context of an ideological clash, the harsh conditions of the battlefield radicalised behaviour still further and brought forth what one soldier termed 'the savage instincts'.[48] Indeed, the personal writings of many men evinced a sentiment similar to Hoepner's latest order. One letter read: 'Man becomes an animal. He must destroy, in order to live. There is nothing heroic on this battlefield ... The battle returns here to its most primeval, animal-like form; whoever does not see well, fires too slowly, fails to hear the crawling on the ground in front of him as the enemy approaches, he will be sent under.'[49]

While German soldiers fought, killed and died their efforts were at least creating a rising sense of crisis at the point of main concentration within Western Front. For three days Rokossovsky's Sixteenth Army had been successfully straining to hold the German attacks, but the army's flanks were progressively being enveloped on both sides and there were no reserves left to shore them up. Rokossovsky sent a desperate request to Zhukov asking that his army be allowed to pull back to the line of the Istra River south of the Volga reservoir, the last natural barrier on the road to Moscow, but this was refused. When Rokossovsky then appealed to Marshal Boris Shaposhnikov, the Red Army's Chief of the General Staff, he was taken to task by Zhukov who bluntly informed his subordinate army commander: 'I am the Front Commander! I countermand the order to withdraw to the Istra Reservoir and order you to defend the lines you occupy without retreating one step.' Rokossovsky lamented the decision, but had no option other than to obey. He sent his deputy, Major-General F. D. Zakharov, to organise resistance at Klin, but his concerns were well founded.[50] Hoepner's panzer group had managed about 4–6 km a day since the start of its offensive, but late on 20 November the front was broken and an advance of 18–23 km was achieved.[51] Hopes were buoyed within Army Group Centre, but this was not an operation seeking to cut off another Soviet army or even eliminate the Western Front (which had already been largely achieved twice before). The goal was unambiguously Moscow.

While Soviet commanders debated their defensive strategy similar concerns about the offensive pervaded Army Group Centre. Even at the start of the offensive the hard-nosed Hoepner was clearly aware of his panzer group's limitations and questioned its ability to endure in the cold. Writing to his mother on 17 November Hoepner declared:

> It is really cold, especially for those who have to stay out at night. The cold phenomenon also reveals a weakness in my people. Everything revolves around the villages. One actually only fights just for these. As a result security is often neglected and Russian raids have been successful. It is difficult to enforce one's will because the officers' nerves are quite strained. I noticed this with myself and also with my staff.[52]

The files of the panzer group make this even more explicit and suggest serious problems motivating the troops to resume the attack. In part this was a reaction to the winter conditions, but also, for the first time, a reaction to the lack of decisive success in earlier periods of the campaign. On 18 November, the war diary of Vietinghoff's XXXXVI Panzer Corps stated:

> Generally it has been shown that in these days the strong will of all leaders is necessary to bring the troops back to the attack. One has to surmount the great disappointment that followed the success at the battle of Viaz'ma in which the opponent's defensive strength was in no way broken and every subsequent operation caused heavy losses. There is also a certain reluctance to leave the modified quarters which are suitable for winter.[53]

Such problems were not unknown to the highest ranks of the army, but they were dismissed because, according to Halder on 19 November, the Red Army 'is certainly even worse off than we'. Halder did, however, agree with Bock that both sides were 'at the last of their strength and that the hardest will would win out'.[54] The day before (18 November), Brauchitsch expressed a similar sentiment to Halder. The Commander-in-Chief of the Army appeared to Halder 'very impatient' about the 'dwindling chances of getting to Moscow'. Halder's solution was clear as he wrote in his diary the whole matter was a 'Question of will!'[55] Such pronouncements make it clear that the army leadership independently internalised central tenants of the Nazi ethos. It was not just that they were 'working towards the Führer', as was so often the case in the formulation of Nazi and Wehrmacht policy, but that the army leadership themselves firmly believed in the power of 'will'. The German soldier was not to be stopped by freezing conditions, a lack of fuel and other supplies, or even the tenacious resistance of the Red Army, the German soldier could be stopped only by insufficient determination to achieve the objectives set. Making the soldiers themselves responsible for the many failings of the army high command was as perverse as it was absurd, but avoiding responsibility for the catalogue of mistakes that pervaded the direction of the eastern campaign in 1941 allowed many of these to be repeated in 1942.

With the middle and lower ranks looking to the high command to recognise the limitations of Army Group Centre, and the OKH forcing the issue back onto the troops and their officers by expecting them to surmount all difficulties through sheer force of will, there was no accountability within the German army. Pleas for a more restrained strategy in the light of the advanced season and the state of the army group (what Halder referred as *Erhaltungsgedanken* – the conservation of strength) had fallen on deaf ears, leaving many officers increasingly nervous as the new offensive sapped the last reserves of strength that

Army Group Centre still possessed. Hellmuth Stieff at Fourth Army noted on 19 November:

> I am frightened by what might happen here. We have no more reserves, and fresh reinforcements will not arrive before the spring. We are poorly equipped for winter and have no prepared positions – and the enemy is becoming increasingly active. Hopefully the snow will soon put a stop to the fighting and allow our troops to get some rest, otherwise we are heading for disaster.
>
> We have got ourselves into a fine mess. And it is infuriating to hear the nonsense our propaganda people churn out. It is astonishing how many fairy tales they are making up. They deride the Russians, again and again. It is as if they are deliberately tempting fate.[56]

Nor was such dissent always a well-kept secret from the men, with some officers openly doubting German strategy in front of the troops, which could only have added to the faltering morale and motivation of some units. Franz Frisch recalled: 'even the officers were starting to ask the question, "What stupidity is this?" – to start an attack ... with trucks that wouldn't move, ammunition trucks with cold brakes and no springs. The units were not combat-ready because of the lack of transportation. The faithful and industrious horses fared poorly in the cold, and could not pull half-trucks.'[57] If Typhoon's ultimate success was dependent upon a triumph of the will, then the reports of flagging motivation among the troops should have been cause for pause and reconsideration. Yet such an act on the part of the high command would itself have betrayed the basic principle of an iron will to seek victory at all costs. Without any of the physical hardships of the campaign, setting such an example from the relative comfort of the OKH headquarters was hardly comparable. However, it was altogether in-keeping with the detached and isolated method of command that the generals would later accuse Hitler of practising.

While the generals of the OKH were deeply complicit in the distortion of German strategy in the east, often without any input at all from Hitler, they at least proceeded under the unquestioned assumption that the war against the Soviet Union could still be won. The same cannot be said with certainty of Hitler. Identifying Hitler's own perception of the war in the east has been difficult to ascertain because of his ardent insistence, until the final days of the war, on the *Endsieg* (final victory).

Yet while the German generals pursued operational successes to the detriment of wider strategic factors, Hitler at least had some understanding of economics as a fundament of modern warfare. In this regard, the war in the east was already an outright failure, something that Hitler, if he had not already determined it for himself,[58] was bluntly told by his minister for armaments and munitions, Fritz Todt, at the end of November. Exasperated by the demands of the war in the east, Todt frankly informed Hitler: 'Given the arms and industrial supremacy of the Anglo-Saxon powers, we can no longer militarily win this war.'[59]

Far from a rapid summer campaign to counter the long-term effects of Great Britain's blockade by securing a wealth of raw materials and prosperous lands, Operation Barbarossa's failure added massively to Nazi Germany's economic deficit, while at the same time demanding greatly increased outputs. Hitler's original conception for war against the Soviet Union had thus failed by the end of the summer of 1941, to be replaced by a far more dangerous war of attrition. When in mid-August 1941 the generals were lauding their successful direction of the campaign and bitterly opposing any interference from Hitler, the German dictator resolutely insisted upon recasting German strategy towards economic objectives in Ukraine. It was at this same point that Goebbels noted Hitler's uncharacteristic display of doubt. Hitler suggested that a peace initiative from Stalin would be accepted. Bolshevism without the Red Army, Hitler told Goebbels, would be no danger to Germany. At another point, Hitler told Goebbels of his certainty that Japan would soon invade the Soviet Union.[60] Phantom peace deals and imaginary allies were no doubt soothing remedies to Hitler's troubled state of mind, but in concrete terms Hitler knew he was facing the sum of all his strategic fears: a war of attrition on two fronts.

What was more characteristic of Hitler's personality was not the despair he briefly disclosed, but his return to an outward conviction in victory, which he maintained for much of the rest of the war. Indeed, when, on 22 November, Goebbels confronted Hitler with the question of whether or not he still believed in victory Hitler's answer was characteristic: 'if he had believed in victory in 1918 when he lay without help as a half-blinded corporal in a Pomeranian military hospital, why should he not believe in our victory when he controlled the strongest armed forces in the world and almost the whole of Europe was prostrate at his feet?'[61]

Hitler's outward conviction in victory is not to suggest that he anticipated outright defeat, but it seems very likely he recognised that his blitzkrieg strategy of short wars and large gains was now at an end. The problem was that this was the only real option for Germany to maintain its position, while offsetting the enormous industrial advantage of the allied powers. Ensnarement in a war of high intensity was tantamount to defeat. Hitler may therefore have switched to what John Lukacs has called 'a Friderician strategy', based on the dictator's admiration for the Prussian King Frederick II (1712–86). Throughout the Seven Years War Frederick the Great avoided defeat – and won a number of outstanding victories – against a coalition of powerful adversaries. This enemy coalition, one far more conventional than an alliance of capitalists and communists in the Second World War, eventually collapsed leaving Frederick victorious. Hitler, according to Lukacs, may have hoped for something similar.[62] It was a far less certain strategy, which Hitler, much more than any of his generals in 1941, recognised threatened Germany with the prospect of total defeat. If Hitler had badly miscalculated in his blitzkrieg against the Soviet Union, his judgement was again seriously at fault with the Friderician strategy. Hitler's war of annihilation and the mass murder of Soviet Jews had invalidated any hope of a negotiated settlement with the allied powers. Accordingly, long before Army Group Centre's failure before Moscow, or even Pearl Habor, Hitler's war – the one he had originally planned to wage and win – had failed. The alternative, as Hitler knew, had far less certain prospects for victory, but this was in fact stillborn on account of the radical excesses of the Nazi state. There could be no compromise peace with Hitler's Germany. When Hitler confronted his party faithful on 8 November and told them that the war was now 'a struggle of life and death',[63] he was not exaggerating, but even he did not fully appreciate that the implications of what he was saying already pointed ahead to Nazi Germany's apocalyptic fate.

The stillborn offensive in the south: Guderian's attack flounders

While in the north Reinhardt's and Hoepner's panzer groups began their offensive towards Moscow at somewhat long odds, Guderian's panzer army in the south did not even have an outside chance of reaching the Soviet captial. The Second Panzer Army was terribly weakened and had almost twice the distance to cover, which called into question the most basics tenets of Bock's plan. The strategic concept for the investment of Moscow was predicated upon the success of Army Group Centre's northern and southern arms. The failure of one meant the failure of both and therefore Typhoon's success was only as probable as its weakest offensive arm, which was undeniably Guderian's panzer army. A local attack had succeeded in taking Bogoroditsk on 16 November,[64] but the main offensive towards Kolomna, some 125 km from Tula (and still well short of the final objective in the encirclement of Moscow), was due to begin on 18 November.[65]

While there were many factors counting against Guderian's offensive, the most serious was the shortage of fuel. Indeed, Guderian informed Army Group Centre on 17 November that his army had only enough fuel for about 80 km.[66] Nor was this a sudden revelation. Since the start of November Second Panzer Army had been receiving an average of 317 m^3 of fuel a day, however, for an offensive of the distance planned Guderian needed four times this amount. As a result, days before the attack the three motorised infantry divisions within the panzer army (10th, 25th and 29th) were starved of fuel to provide everything for the panzer divisions.[67] Yet there was still a considerable shortfall and the day before the offensive (17 November) Guderian wrote in a letter: 'We are only nearing our final objective step by step in this icy cold and with all the troops suffering from the appalling supply situation. The difficulties of supplying us by rail are constantly increasing – that is the main cause of all our shortages since without fuel the trucks can't move. If it had not been for this we should by now be much nearer our objective.'[68] On the same day, Bock told Halder that the expected extent of the Second Panzer Army's advance was more dependent on fuel supplies than on Soviet resistance.[69]

Yet the ability of Guderian's panzer army to break Soviet resistance also relied on the strength of his spearhead and, here too, the offensive was in trouble before it even began. Schweppenberg's XXIV Panzer Corps was the most powerful corps in the panzer army with three of the four panzer divisions, as well as Colonel Walter Hörnlein's Infantry Regiment *Grossdeutschland* and the 296th Infantry Division. Its initial task was to cut-off and capture Tula, while also seizing Kashira on the Oka River as a stepping stone to a further advance on Kolomna.[70] Schweppenberg's strength resided in his panzer force, but his three divisions fielded a total of just 100 tanks between them on 17 November. Major-General Hermann Breith's 3rd Panzer Division was the strongest with sixty tanks, followed by Langermann-Erlancamp's 4th Panzer Division with twenty-five tanks and lastly Colonel Rudolf-Eduard

Licht's[71] 17th Panzer Division with just fifteen tanks.[72] While Breith and Langermann-Erlancamp were directed towards Tula, it was Licht's division (organised into an ad hoc battle group) that was charged with the capture of Kashira on the vital road to Moscow. Thus, it is no exaggeration to say that while Reinhardt and Hoepner were attacking north of Moscow with hundreds of tanks, Guderian's advance was spearheaded by just fifteen tanks. Guderian's last panzer division, Nehring's 18th Panzer Division, was operating 120 km south of Tula attacking the industrial town of Efremov as part of Lemelsen's XXXXVII Panzer Corps. The rest of Lemelsen's corps (the 10th, 25th and 29th Motorised Infantry Divisions) was operating further north, and in the forthcoming offensive was charged with attacking towards Mikhaylov (80 km northeast of the recently captured town of Bogoroditsk).[73] On 18 November, the Second Panzer Army, which had started the war with about 1,000 tanks and in the course of the campaign had received a further 150 reinforcements, now counted just 150 tanks in total.[74] Given that even this pitiful sum could be supplied only with a quarter of the fuel required, one wonders just what convinced Bock and Halder that there was any prospect of closing the southern arm of the ring around Moscow.

Guderian's Second Panzer Army also had two army corps attached to it. Weisenberger's LIII Army Corps operated in the gap between Schweppenberg and Lemelsen, and was tasked with driving on Venev. Heinrici's XXXXIII Army Corps was deployed to the west of Tula between Lichvin and Kaluga, and was to advance northwest of Tula both to aid in cutting off the city, while also maintaining contact with Kluge's Fourth Army.[75] An assessment of corps and divisions in mid-November reveals the true strength of the panzer army, with most of the combat formations badly under strength and some even deemed incapable of any offensive action at all. Thus, Bock's dismissal of Soviet resistance simply because fuel shortages constituted a greater problem was wholly unjustified. Even with an abundance of fuel, Guderian's entire army possessed fewer tanks than a single full strength panzer division, and what the army did have was not even concentrated together against one objective. Moreover, on 18 November, Bock noted intelligence reports which claimed that some thirty-four fresh Siberian divisions has been transferred to the west since the battle of Smolensk and no less than twenty-one of these had been directed towards Army Group Centre's front.[76] Indeed, Guderian was to encounter his own share of well-clad Siberian troops in the coming offensive,[77] which made a stark contrast to his own motley collection of men in threadbare uniforms and improvised winter clothing. One soldier noted during his deployment to Tula on 16 November, when the temperature had sunk to -18°C, that: 'On the way we had to freeze miserably; tips of fingers, ears and feet hurt so much at times that one thought second or even third degree frostbite had occurred.'[78] Nor was it just the shortage of winter uniforms that dogged the Second Panzer Army in the prelude to the offensive. As Guderian noted: 'Ice was causing a lot of trouble, since the calks for the tracks had not yet arrived. The cold made the telescopic sights useless; the salve which was supposed to prevent this had also not arrived. In order to start the engines of the tanks fires had to be lit beneath them. Fuel was freezing on occasions and the oil became viscous.'[79] It was an ominous set of circumstances in which to begin an offensive, but, ready or not, on 18 November Guderian's panzer army went over to the offensive.

The first day of the offensive was characterised in Bock's diary as 'an attack to the northeast', which 'moved slowly forward'.[80] Halder also referred to the slow progress of the initial attack,[81] which was understandable given the weakness of the operational spearhead, but also worrying given that an attack generally loses strength as it continues. With limited vehicles and men pressing the attack forward on foot, it is not surprising that Guderian noted that an advance of only between 5 and 10 km was possible. Indeed, while many of the assertions in Guderian's postwar memoir must be viewed with doubt, his conclusion that from the very beginning of the November offensive: 'It seemed to me questionable whether my army was capable of carrying out the task assigned it', is consistent with his private correspondence from the time.[82] Guderian had not yet given up on the offensive, but he was racked by doubts and aware of the many intractable problems that stood between him and Moscow.

At the sharp end of the offensive the divisional war diaries indicate that the Red Army had also been able to prepare itself during the early November pause. Not only had Soviet reserves been brought up, but at the obvious points of main effort (around Tula and on the road to Moscow) defences in-depth had been constructed. On 18 November, the war diary of Breith's 3rd Panzer Division recorded: 'The day required unusually stubborn fighting in unfavourable weather conditions against an enemy in well-developed field positions and villages. Approximately 150 of our men lost.'[83] The following day (19 November), German intelligence revealed that more Soviet reserves, 'ostensibly Siberian',

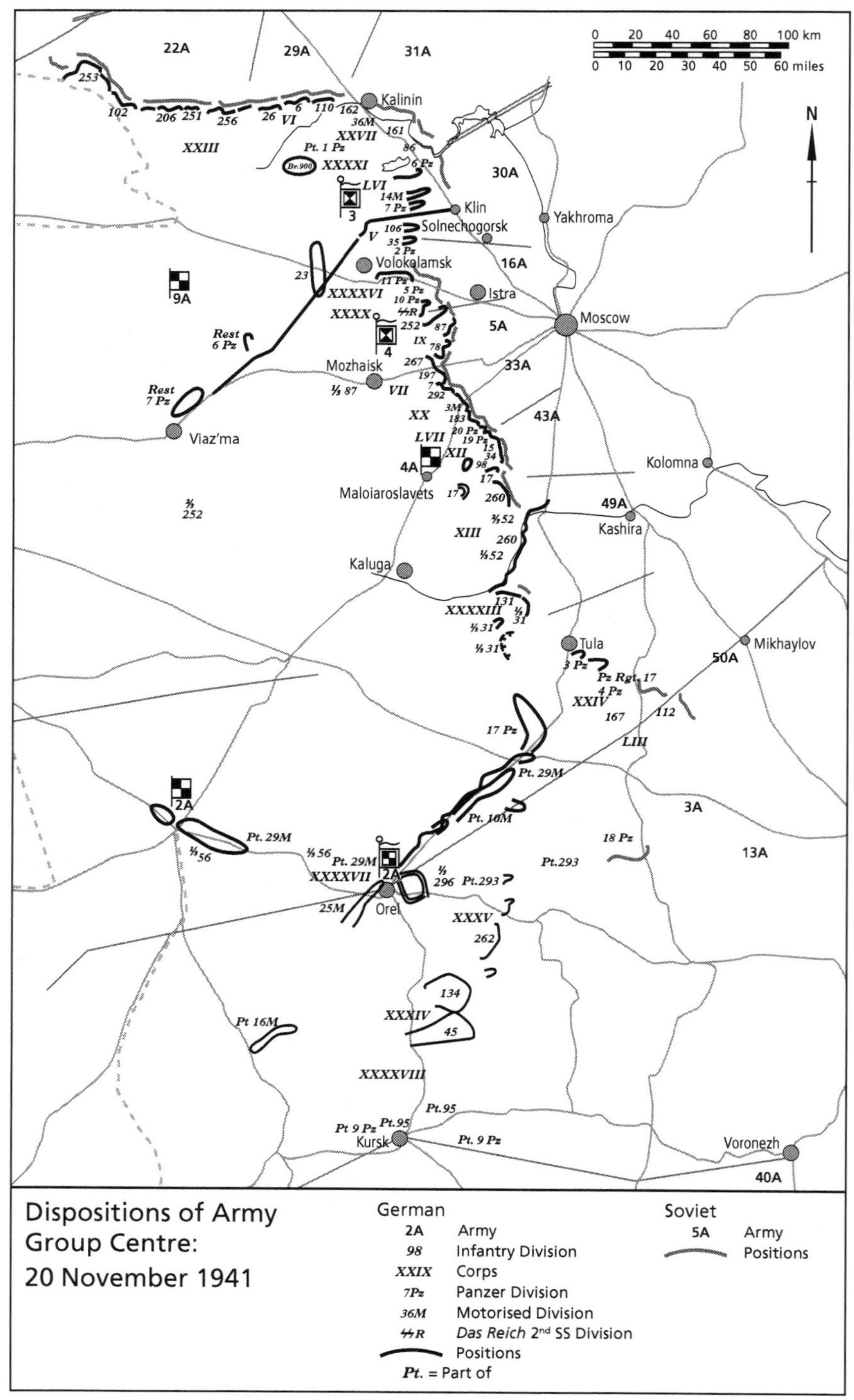

Map 5.3 Dispositions of Army Group Centre, 20 November 1941

were being shifted by train to oppose Schweppenberg's XXIV Panzer Corps and Weisenberger's LIII Army Corps.[84] Even before the arrival of Soviet reserves the attack on Tula was faltering. The war diary of Langermann-Erlancamp's 4th Panzer Division noted on only the second day of the offensive: 'Division does not believe that the deployed strength on 19.11 is sufficient to continue the attack with success ... The division has lost much of its fighting strength.'[85] The report then listed a host of weaknesses, which spanned the full spectrum of its combat readiness. Among the main points was the fact that the division started with only twenty-five tanks, no calks to gain traction on the ice, 'very weak' infantry support, too few officers, not enough quarters for the men in the newly conquered area and limited artillery on account of unserviceable tractors.[86] On the third day of the offensive (20 November), the war diary of the Second Panzer Army reported that the combat strength of the three panzer divisions in Schweppenberg's corps had 'declined heavily'.[87] When one considers their extremely limited starting strengths and the negligible success of their attack to date, the stalling of Guderian's offensive, if it was not already apparent before the attack began, was now unmistakeable.

On the panzer army's southern flank Nehring's 18th Panzer Division was tasked with seizing the town of Efremov, a rather pointless objective, but, given the absence of fuel, a better option than having the division attempt to deploy northwards. After an impressive advance of some 50 km, Nehring's division succeeded in taking Efremov on 20 November.[88] The divisional war diary made clear in just what circumstances this task was achieved: 'Under the worst circumstances the division took the important industrial city of Efremov[89] ... without tank, without anti-aircraft gun, without assault gun, without support from our own planes, with only two engineer companies.'[90] Clearly, the division was operating on a shoestring and it was about to come under even more pressure as Army Group Centre reported on 20 November that Soviet reserves were being moved to counter Nehring's attack at Efremov.[91]

Fears that mobility would suffer in the conditions also proved to be well founded. Lemelsen's XXXXVII Panzer Corps, which contained three motorised infantry divisions, noted sharp fall-out rates on only the first day of the offensive. In one instance a column of vehicles from Dmitrowsk to Kromy reported thirty-three breakdowns with six total losses.[92] The following day (19 November), an attempt by tanks of the 18th Panzer Division to cross a bridge required first ascending a ramp, but, without ice calks for the tracks, the first two tanks slid off and the attempt had to be abandoned.[93] By the third day of the offensive (20 November), the panzer corps was reporting that the combined effects of icy roads, high fuel consumption (because of driving in low gears) and breakdowns was resulting in barely half of all trucks arriving at their destinations.[94] The loss of so many trucks created its own problems, and already on the second day of the offensive the Quartermaster-General of the Second Panzer Army referred to a 'serious supply crisis' should the front extend any further from the railhead, because 'the available transport is no longer enough as a result of the fatigue of the drivers and the high fall-out rates of the trucks'.[95] Even with so many vehicles dropping out of service fuel shortages remained a stubbornly insoluble problem. As an indication of the demand this was placing on the German war economy fuel reserves that had to be built up by the end of December, allocated 12,000 tons for Germany and its occupied regions, 2,000 tons for southeast Europe, 5,000 tons for the North African campaign and a massive 88,000 tons for the *Ostheer*.[96]

The imposing economic demands of the war were starkly underlined when the head of the Main Committee for tank production, Walter Rohland, and his delegation of industrialists arrived at Guderian's headquarters in Orel to gain a first-hand impression of the needs at the front. Guderian met the men on 18 November and left them in no doubt about the superiority of the heavy Soviet tanks. Although the Soviet T-34 was technically a medium tank Guderian does not seem to have differentiated between this and the much heavier KV-1. Not only were the Soviet tanks better, but, Guderian made clear, their numbers were increasing as the campaign continued. He also drew attention to the inadequacy of German anti-tank guns and suggested that a new 75-mm anti-gun was 'urgently necessary for winter equipment'.[97] The delegation was then taken on a tour of the front where the shocking condition of the men and their equipment left a profound impression. When Rohland returned to Germany he reported: 'Our troops were far too lightly dressed, in some cases wrapped in blankets! An assorted picture of frozen-up cars abandoned at the side of the road, with panje carts drawn by Russian ponies doing their best to provide inadequate supplies. The tanks could not be employed; if the motors and gearboxes still worked, the weapons failed due to freezing up.' Nor was Rohland just concerned with the immediate matters at the front. He became convinced that the implications of rebuilding the *Ostheer* and supplying it for a war on such a vast scale was simply beyond Germany's industrial and resource base. As he told Fritz Todt, 'the war against Russia cannot be won!'. It was a conclusion that Todt himself had also reached,[98] and together the two men confronted Hitler with the news. The dictator received the news calmly, perhaps well aware of the economic implications of his failed blitzkrieg. Before dismissing the two men, however, Hitler posed the question: 'How then should I end the war?' To which Todt replied: 'It can only be ended politically.'[99] In a war of attrition there was no military solution to the war in the east.[100]

Figures reporting raw material estimates by the Reich Office for Economic Development make Todt's conclusion abundantly clear. In November 1941, Germany could access 9.7 million tons of oil, while the United States and Britain could access 257.8 million tons and the Soviets 29.8 million tons of oil. Supplies of manganese ore were even less favourable, with the German sphere providing just 56.5 million tons as against 1,343 million tons for the western allies and 1,200 million tons in European Russia. Indeed, across a range of essential raw materials Germany's own figures demonstrated a crushing allied superiority. Nickel ore saw the allies with access to twenty-five times more than the total German amount, copper ore thirteen times more, chrome ore nine times more and tungsten ore almost four times more. Even coal, one of Germany's abundant resources, was still only half the allied total. Only in bauxite/aluminium did Germany hold a slight lead with access to 398.6 million tons as against 356.9 million tons for the allies.[101] Whatever Germany's success on the battlefield the ability to maintain its position in Europe was just as much, if not more so, dependent upon the supply of raw materials to its arms industry.

While economic factors were already forcing the most dire conclusions to be drawn about Hitler's war in the east, this had little impact on the Nazi regime's willingness to go on killing Jews in November. Hinrich Lohse, the Reich Commissar for the Baltic and Belarus, forwarded a request to Alfred Rosenberg's Ministry of the Eastern Territories asking if Jews were to be killed: 'irrespective of age, sex or economic factors'? The reply ignored the first two categories, as if the answer was implicit, and responded only that the demands of the economy 'should be ignored'.[102] As a result thousands of Jewish labourers employed in Riga tailoring millions of captured sheepskins into ear protectors, fur caps, waistcoats and other such vital articles of clothing for the troops were shot at the end of November 'in accordance with the

Führer's orders'.[103] At the same time, Hitler refused to cancel any of the colossal building projects he had commissioned for Berlin and Nuremberg in spite of the fact that the contracts for the granite alone came to some 30 million Reichmarks. Hitler's chief architect, Albert Speer, approached the dictator in November to suggest that the resource-intensive building projects be halted until after the war. However, according to Speer, he was rebuffed with the words: 'I am not going to let the war keep me from accomplishing my [building] plans.'[104]

With such absurdities pervading the organisation of the Nazi empire it was increasingly difficult for men with a clearer sense of priorities, like Todt, Rohland and, to a lesser extent, Speer, to remain silent. Indeed, November was in many ways a tipping point when men (civilian, party and military) finally began to speak their minds about the many deluded policies that the Nazi regime sustained. At Second Panzer Army Guderian could plainly see the hypocrisy of reporting on his 'progress to Moscow' when, within just kilometres from his starting line, the attack was stalling. On 20 November, three days after Typhoon resumed in the south, Guderian contacted Army Group Centre with the shattering news that his army was too weak to fulfil its task.[105] Bock even had to request conformation of what was being reported before passing the news on to the OKH.[106] For the blinkered generals directing the battle for Moscow it should have been plainly apparent that the offensive was doomed. Having ignored all the reports from the divisions and corps they now had Guderian, the formidable panzer army commander, telling them he could no longer carry out his orders. Without the southern arm of the drive on Moscow there could be no encirclement of the city. The whole strategic concept for the offensive was floundering.

Nor was Guderian the only, or even the highest ranking, commander pressing for a drastic change of plans in the east. Field Marshal Rundstedt, the commander of Army Group South, had been unsuccessfully requesting that his army group be allowed to halt its offensive activity throughout most of November.[107] On 21 November, Rostov was taken, but Kleist's First Panzer Army was dangerously over-extended and under attack by the reinforced Soviet Southern Front. Rundstedt pleaded, again unsuccessfully, for permission to abandon Rostov and withdraw to the Mius River 75 km to the rear.[108] At the end of November, with encirclement inevitable, Rundstedt defiantly ordered Kleist to begin his retreat without authorisation.[109] When the shocking news reached Hitler's headquarters he immediately dispatched

Figure 5.1 The commander of the Second Panzer Army, Colonel-General Heinz Guderian during a visit to the 167th Infantry Division (November 1941)

a telegram to Rundstedt stating bluntly: 'Stay where you are. No more retreats.' Rundstedt replied that it was 'insanity to try to hold the position' and offered his resignation.[110] Hitler accepted and replaced him with Field Marshal Walter von Reichenau, who, after quickly assessing the situation, repeated Rundstedt's request for an immediate withdrawal, which was granted at last.

If the events overtaking German plans were not obvious enough, the fact that senior figures within the economics ministry and *Ostheer* were now openly confronting Hitler and the high command over their concerns says much about the realisation that Germany was on a path to ruin. Adding to the chorus of dissent Franz von Papen, the German ambassador to Turkey, was reported on 18 November to have told a foreign news service that owing to Germany's declining military strength in the war against the Soviet Union a peace deal should be sought 'as soon as possible'.[111] Echoing this sentiment was the commander of the German reserve army and director of the army's armaments effort, Colonel-General Fritz Fromm, who, on 24 November, reported to Halder on the declining output in German arms production. As Halder noted: 'He thinks of the necessity to make peace!'[112] If Halder was surprised by the conclusion Fromm was drawing one wonders how he reconciled the relationship between Germany's falling armaments production and the costly war of attrition in the east, which, by Halder's own admission, would continue long into 1942. Even without the United States' direct involvement in the war, Roosevelt's indirect support for the allied war effort was already seeing American (and British) armaments turning up on the eastern front. As one soldier wrote home from Guderian's panzer army on 21 November: 'Even if we capture Moscow, I doubt whether this will finish the war in the east. The Russians are capable of fighting to the very last man, the very last square metre of their vast country. Their stubbornness and resolve is quite astonishing. We are entering a war of attrition – and I only hope in the long run Germany can win it!'[113] If individual soldiers were worried about the implications of a war of attrition, it is hard to fathom the optimism of men like Halder who had access to far more evidence of these problems. Perhaps the power of individual 'will' eclipsed the ability to reason as effectively as the ability to doubt.

With Guderian's offensive already faltering little could be expected of Schmidt's Second Army on the southern wing of Bock's army group. After seizing Kursk the army had launched an abortive attempt to continue the offensive towards Voronezh, but this soon failed on account of sheer exhaustion and a lack of supplies. On 12 November, it was decided that the army would renew its offensive on 16 November,[114] but, as a result of ongoing supply difficulties, on 15 November the army's start date was postponed by two days to 18 November.[115] On the following day (16 November), the offensive was again set back a further two days, to 20 November, again due to shortages in supply.[116] The problem then arose that Schmidt's right wing needed to be supported by the continued advance of Reichenau's Sixth Army (belonging to Army Group South). Yet, on 17 November, the Sixth Army reported that any offensive was out of the question until the start of December.[117] Certainly, Reichenau had the support of his army group commander (Rundstedt), yet, in the event, Schmidt's own logistic weaknesses meant that there was little danger of a deep advance exposing his right wing. When the Second Army's offensive at last resumed on 20 November it encountered little enemy resistance and thus made some minor early gains.[118]

All the formations of Army Group Centre had to contend with the common problem of conducting an offensive in extreme winter conditions. The weather in October had certainly been cold; with some brief spells of freezing temperatures, but nothing like the temperatures from the middle of November. According to the war diary of the 11th Panzer Division, the temperature at the centre of Bock's army group ranged between −12°C on 13 November to −18°C on 21 November.[119] As Helmut Günther noted: 'This morning the thermometer remained stuck at −18°Celsius. Not one square centimetre of my skin was exposed.'[120]

Such temperatures introduced a whole host of new complications, which further hindered the conduct of operations. German tanks had a much narrower track width than the new Soviet model tanks, making the nominal ground pressure ratio much higher, which reduced traction and mobility, especially in snow and ice. What made things even worse was the absence of calks for the tracks, making it almost impossible for the tanks to climb frozen slopes. Optical instruments also suffered from frost, causing distortions that affected tanks as well as the artillery and caused shells to be inaccurately fired, sometimes landing 'short' on German positions.[121] Even the shells themselves were affected because the packing grease had frozen solid forcing them to be individually scraped clean with a knife before they would fit into the breach.[122] The oils in the buffering systems of the German artillery were freezing, which highlighted the lack of low-temperature lubricants and graphite. Similarly affected were the sliding parts of machine guns and bolt-action rifles, which routinely jammed even with constant cleaning.[123] As Leo Mattowitz concluded: 'Everything mechanical came to a dead halt. Nothing worked at all ... We had absolutely nothing, we were totally unprepared for the winter. Totally.'[124]

With the resources at hand Army Group Centre could do little to counter the repaid de-motorisation of its mobile formations. Nor was the cold just taking its toll on the mechanical stand of the army group. The resumption of the offensive exposed hundreds of thousands of men in the army group to the freezing conditions, but many were as ill-prepared for the ordeal as their equipment. As was so often the case, the men of the *Ostheer* had to improvise to survive. Heinrich Haape, a doctor in the Ninth Army, advised his men to wear as much underclothing as possible, always keep their socks dry and never to wear tight-fitting boots that might hinder circulation. However, Haape's 'major weapon against the Russian winter' was newspaper, which proved both simple to use and was surprisingly effective. As Haape explained:

> Newspaper in the boots took up little space and could often be changed. Two sheets of newspaper on a man's back, between vest and shirt, preserved the warmth of the body and were windproof. Newspaper round the belly; newspaper in the trousers; newspaper round the legs; newspaper everywhere that the body required extra warmth ... We found old German papers, Russian newspapers, magazines and journals – and propaganda pamphlets by the thousand. Some of the leaflets were our own propaganda, others bore pictures of Lenin and Stalin ... it amused us to think of Russian propaganda leaflets being used to keep German soldiers warm.[125]

Nor was Haape unique in identifying the insulating properties of paper, and some soldiers took delight in using Soviet propaganda leaflets for the purpose. One soldier recalled: 'I remember trying for a week to keep warm on a proclamation that "Surrender is the only sane and sensible course as the issue has been finally decided."'[126]

Yet with the necessity of keeping warm being a matter of life and death, the direction of German improvisation often took a far more sinister course. Willy Peter Reese wrote: 'Any woollen garments we found become ours. Blankets, scarfs, pullovers, shirts and especially gloves we made off with at any opportunity. We pulled the boots off the old men and women on the street if ours were wanting.'[127] Others

Figure 5.2 A German MG-34 crew in Russian winter hats with improvised camouflage and gloves (November 1941)

were more troubled by the consequences of their actions and wrote candidly of their dilemma. On 21 November, Konrad Jarausch was seeking material to have a warm vest made: 'Should I do as my comrades do and exploit this poverty, by exchanging with the women a piece of bread for their last new towels?'[128] Certainly, many German soldiers did not share such reservations and the process of dispossessing Soviet civilians was both ubiquitous and ruthless. Franz Frisch recalled: 'The winter conditions drove German soldiers to ransack peasant homes looking for anything to supplement their uniform. We used bed covers, tablecloths, curtains, anything at all to provide a layer of warmth.'[129] Equally, Helmut Günther alluded to the nature of such rampant looting: 'The time of the large-scale "procurement" had started. Despite intense endeavours, the logistics elements were no longer coming through, and every unit's main concern was to maintain its own stock of material, even if not by the most ethical means.'[130]

Russian civilians were certainly targets of German expropriation, but even they were not as vulnerable as Soviet prisoners of war. While countless German letters make reference to German soldiers looting enemy soldiers, few say anything about what their defenceless captives were left with to protect themselves against the cold. For many the only limit to such activity was concern for their own well-being, as Siegfried Knappe noted, 'we did not dare wear the heavier quilted jackets for fear of being shot as a Russian'.[131] The less intrusive method of looting the dead was also widespread. After a failed enemy attack Ernst Kern describes crawling out among the Soviet dead to loot the bodies for gloves, wristlets and caps.[132] The results of such practices provided a measure of protection, but there were still clear shortages. Meanwhile, the orderly composition of the Wehrmacht was being transformed. As Helmut Günther noted:

> Boy, had we become a wild bunch! ... Now we were totally indifferent to how we looked! ... It goes without saying that the officers had initially complained about our 'costumes', but they couldn't conjure up warm winter uniform items from out of their sleeves. They soon gave up, only to now look the same as we did. It no longer mattered [in] the slightest. Everyone knew who his superiors were.[133]

Despite their comical appearance there was no disguising the resentment among the troops over the lack of winter uniforms. As one soldier noted:

'The men wrapped their blankets about themselves, over their overcoats and caps, and cursed those responsible for not providing us with winter clothing.'[134]

On the other side of the front, the popular Soviet writer Ilya Ehrenburg gained satirical mileage out of the plight of Bock's men, but ended his article 'Freezing them Out' with a warning that was probably more truthful than the usual hyperbole of his propaganda. Ehrenburg wrote: 'How the German soldiers freezing in the fields of Russia must envy their compatriots in Africa! ... They are rushing towards Moscow like frozen men rushing to the fire ... They are ready to come under fire for a pair of felt boots or a woman's warm jacket. That's why they are now doubly dangerous ... In terror they say to each other: "This is only November."'[135] The same theme was picked up in British newspapers and radio programmes. In one example, on 17 November, a cartoon in the *Daily Mirror* featured shivering German soldiers under the caption 'Another frozen asset'.[136] Only the day before (16 November), Goebbels fumed in his diary about British propaganda, 'representing the situation on the eastern front as especially catastrophic'. He accused them of reporting hundreds of thousands of Germans dying as a result of the winter weather.[137] It was a particularly sensitive point for Goebbels as he was well informed about the condition of the troops (he had daily military briefings) and, as recently as 14 November, had expressed grave concerns about the impact of the freezing conditions on the already ebbing morale of the German population. He knew that the extreme cold and suffering of the men at the front, not to mention the inability of the army to deliver enough winter uniforms, would soon be reported back to the German public in hundreds of thousands of letters. This would give a guise of truth to British radio propaganda and any attempt by his propaganda ministry to counteract the British claims ran the risk of also questioning the veracity of the field post and thereby losing all credibility over the issue.[138] Moreover, the latest SD reports on the public mood (dated 17 November) revealed many people expressing concerns about the coming winter and being of the opinion that winter quarters should now be adopted.[139]

Otto Dietrich, the Reich's Press Chief, was also very concerned about the issue of German field post undercutting his news service in its attempt 'to keep the population calm'. As Dietrich knew, any perceived conflict on the issue of how much winter equipment had been sent to the front 'would shake the public's confidence in the German news service at a crucial time'. Consequently, on 18 November, he opted for a more subtle form of pushing his message: 'In selecting pictures, special care must be taken that no photographs appear that might suggest that troops have not yet received winter clothing. Undesirable, for example, are pictures showing a column of prisoners of war wearing overcoats and their German escorts marching without such coats.'[140] Yet elements of the German population were increasingly able to see through the deception of official news reports and deduce for themselves far harsher truths. Helmuth James von Moltke, an aristocrat and avowed opponent of the Nazi regime, wrote in a letter on 18 November:

> The war looks bad. There is a joke going around here: 'Eastern campaign extended by a month owing to great success.' A bitter remark. I don't think that we can still make significant progress before the new year ... The unfortunate millions of troops who now freeze out there, are wet, and die! A comparison with the World War 14/18 is impossible, for then fewer people were involved, and could therefore be better looked after, and there were houses in which they could stay. The present situation is different in both respects. What will the army that we meet again in March be like? With no leave worth mentioning, insufficient supplies, no quarters, no adequate clothing, no military success?[141]

Moltke's deductions were strikingly informed, but still marginalised from the mainstream. Understanding why this was the case is perhaps best seen in Moltke's ultimate fate. While his opposition group (known as the Kreisau Circle) advocated a non-violent form of resistance and took no direct action against the regime, Moltke was eventually hanged along with his confederates because, as he stated, 'we thought together'.[142] It was an offence many Germans knew better to avoid.

6 THE LONG ROAD TO MOSCOW

Feeding the Bear: British and American aid for the battle of Moscow

While the German armies in the Soviet Union were over-extended, under-resourced and fighting their own exhaustion as much as the Red Army, Rommel's small force in North Africa was about to suffer its most serious reversal to date. With an active strength of less than 40,000 men,[1] (in addition to his Italian allies) Rommel's *Afrikakorps* was taken by surprise when General Claude Auchinleck launched his 'Crusader' offensive on 18 November.[2] Rommel was already at a distinct disadvantage with just 249 tanks (seventy of which were the obsolete Mark IIs) in his two panzer divisions (15th and 21st) against some 770 British and American tanks.[3] Moreover, the British enjoyed vastly better logistical and aerial support (some 550 serviceable aircraft to the Luftwaffe's seventy-six), giving Auchinleck a formidable advantage.[4] As one of Rommel's staff officers wrote on 23 November: 'The question is: "to be or not to be" for the Deutsches Afrika Korps.'[5]

No such questions were being asked on the eastern front, but Rommel's surprise at being caught unawares by an enemy offensive was paralleled by the fact that no one in Army Group Centre's command or the OKH had any idea that Stalin was withholding large numbers of reserves for an offensive of his own. Certainly, the Soviet counteroffensive, which was to hit Army Group Centre in early December, was a long way from the carefully timed counterstroke of Soviet mythology.[6] Zhukov had already been forced into launching local offensives in early and mid-November, which were largely premature and gained little ground, but they did grind down parts of the Fourth Army and deeply impacted upon the confidence of senior German officers, not least Kluge. If regimental- and divisional-sized Soviet attacks could induce such results, then Zhukov was correct to argue for the concentrated use of whole Soviet armies. Since early October, in the strictest secrecy, the *Stavka* had been forming a new strategic echelon of reserve armies.[7] Four new armies were formed in October and another eight in November.[8] There can be no question that the quality of these armies bore little resemblance to the Red Army's prewar standards of training and equipment, but this was also true of the German armies against which they would be called to fight. Some of the newly formed divisions were immediately deployed to bolster the Soviet front, but, together with forces being withdrawn from the Far East, the Soviets were able to gather some fifty-eight new divisions that, as yet, were neither committed to the Soviet front nor detected by the German high command.[9] From 21 November a plan was worked out by the Soviet general staff overseen by Marshal Shaposhnikov. The first task was to eliminate the threat of the panzer spearheads driving on Moscow; secondly, the Soviet offensive had to force the Germans back from Moscow; and, thirdly, they had to deal Bock a decisive defeat, which remained ambiguous but probably meant eliminating a sizeable part of his force.[10] Certainly, Zhukov believed that it could be done and, given the rapidly diminishing strength of Bock's army group, there had never been more favourable circumstances for the Red Army to strike a major blow.

While the British army was doing its best to cope with just ten Axis divisions in North Africa (only three of which were German),[11] Churchill was attempting to support Stalin in any way he could given the enormous load the Soviet Union was having to bear against over 160 Axis and Finnish[12] divisions (136 of which were German).[13] Beyond the sheer disparity in numbers, Churchill's policy towards the Soviet Union was determined by two factors: one was his deep personal loathing of Hitler and Nazism; the other was the pro-Soviet sentiment of British public opinion.[14] In the case of the former, there can be no doubting Churchill's resolve, but he did not share the open-ended commitment to the Soviet cause that public opinion sometimes advocated. In 1941, Soviet requests for British aid fell into three broad categories: military equipment and raw materials; British forces to be sent to fight on the Soviet front; and the opening of a second front in western Europe. Churchill, his military advisers and the War Cabinet (with the exception of Lord Beaverbrook) were united in their rejection of opening a second front in 1941.[15] Action leading to fiascos, Churchill told Stalin in September, 'would be of no help to anyone but Hitler'.[16] Churchill was also reluctant to send British forces to fight on the Soviet front, but this met with much stronger resistance from members of his government, not least of whom was the Secretary of State for Foreign Affairs, Anthony Eden, as well as an increasingly anxious public impatient for tangible action. Unlike the establishment of a second front in western Europe, joining the Soviet front required no minimum force to sustain the commitment and could be organised reasonably quickly by redeploying the forces in Iran that took part in the joint Anglo-Soviet occupation in August and September. As it was, Churchill attempted an unwise compromise by suggesting to Stalin that British forces replace those elements of the Red Army in Iran, allowing them to be used at home. This only reinforced the opinion of the Soviet government that the British were prepared to leave the defeat of Nazi Germany largely to the Red Army. As Stafford Cripps, the British ambassador to the Soviet Union, warned the Prime Minister on 26 October: 'They [the Soviets] are now obsessed with the idea that we are prepared to fight to the last drop of Russian blood ... and they interpret every action either from this point of view or else from the point of view that we are sitting back and resting while they are doing the fighting.'[17] The fact that the North African front had been largely inactive since the failure of the British 'Battleaxe' offensive in mid-June only heightened the perception that Churchill was dragging his feet and unwilling to engage the Germans directly. Attempting to explain this fact to Auchinleck, Churchill wrote at the start of November: 'It is impossible to explain to Parliament and the nation how it is our Middle East armies had to stand for four and a half months without engaging the enemy while all the time Russia is being battered to pieces.'[18]

The start of the 'Crusader' offensive in the second half of November and the Soviet success at Rostov towards the end of the month eased the pressure on Churchill to provide forces for the Soviet Southern Front, but they did not end Stalin's suspicions about the British commitment to the Soviet war effort. Throughout the summer and autumn Churchill had repeatedly resisted declaring war on Finland, Hungary and Romania, all of which were actively engaged in Hitler's war against the Soviet Union. Britain was well known to have supported Finland during the recent Winter War against the Soviet Union, and its reluctance to declare Finland an enemy brought old tensions back to the fore. The Soviet ambassador to Britian, Ivan Maisky, accused the British government of reneging on 'the performance of its allied duty'.[19] Churchill was reluctant in the case of Finland and Romania since both, initially at least, were waging wars of liberation to take back territory aggressively seized by the Soviets only the year before.[20] In his correspondence with Stalin, however, the prime minister took a different tack. On 22 November, Churchill argued in a letter that once war was declared upon these countries they would be forever bound to Hitler, forcing them to 'fight it out to the end'. Churchill, nevertheless, agreed to a declaration of war, but asked Stalin for two more weeks of last-ditch diplomacy to see if he could salvage a withdrawal from hostilities of any of the three countries (although Finland was uppermost in his mind). Stalin reluctantly acquiesced, but held Churchill to his promise. 'Otherwise', Stalin noted, 'the impression might be created that we lack unity in the war against Hitler.'[21] Churchill promptly wrote to Field Marshal Carl Gustaf Emil Mannerheim, with whom he had enjoyed a cordial correspondence during the Winter War, and pleaded with him to withdraw from the war 'before it is too late'.[22] Similar letters were dispatched to the Romanian and Hungarian governments, each with a deadline of 5 December. With the passing of the deadline and no positive responses, Britain dutifully declared war on all three nations.[23]

Another thorn in the side of Anglo-Soviet relations during November was the issue of a postwar settlement. Stalin wanted the issue resolved as soon as possible, whereas Churchill, bound by the war aims of the Atlantic Charter and aware of the complicated issues surrounding the setting of Soviet borders vis-à-vis the Baltic states and Poland, wanted it deferred until the end of the war. This became another reason for the Soviets to question British solidarity because, as Christopher Warner pointed out, it encouraged Stalin's belief that Britain wanted the Soviet Union to be 'crippled in crippling the Germans and be of no account in the peace settlement'.[24] Certainly, there was a quietly held school of thought in the United Kingdom as well as the United States that advocated precisely that point of view. General John Kennedy wrote in his diary in September: 'The fundamental difficulty is that although we want the Germans to be knocked out above all, most of us feel ... that it would not be a bad thing if the Russians were to be finished as a military power too.'[25] In his letter of 22 November, Churchill offered to send Eden to Moscow for consultations and attempted to defuse the issue of a postwar settlement by downplaying the ideological differences between Stalin's communism and that of the western democracies, claiming that their differing worldviews did not present 'any obstacle to our making a good plan for our mutual safety and rightful interests', In addition, Churchill emphasised the one overriding aspect of a postwar settlement that all sides could agree upon: the need to restrain future German power.[26] Stalin was cheered by such commitments and Churchill's letter of 22 November seems to have had a soothing effect, at least temporarily, on the much strained Anglo-Soviet relations. Eden's visit was graciously accepted and Stalin even added the hope that outstanding 'reticence or doubts, if any, will be dispelled by the talks with Mr Eden'.[27] The fact that Stalin was sweeping under the rug the underlying tensions and misgivings that plagued Anglo-Soviet relations by referring to 'reticence or doubts' and then questioning 'if any' might be taken as a new attempt at improving relations. Perhaps Churchill's letter had shattered some of the ice, but the fact that German armies were once again marching on Moscow, and with some success in the north, may have provided its own conciliatory inducement.

While Churchill's policy of refusing the prospect of a second front in the foreseeable future and dodging a commitment to provide combat forces to fight in Russia disappointed the Soviets, the prime minister made supporting the Soviet Union materially the cornerstone of his aid policy. It was a policy that took months to organise and implement with a formal agreement, known as the First Protocol, signed on 1 October 1941. This committed Britain and the United States to providing the Soviet Union with 400 aircraft and 500 tanks a month in addition to vast stocks of other weapons, raw materials, foodstuffs, medical supplies and vehicles.[28] While the net tonnage of convoys reaching the Soviet Union early in the war was rather small, in total only seven convoys with a total of fifty-three merchantmen departed for the Soviet Union in 1941,[29] the psychological impact both in the Soviet Union and Britain was profound. As one Soviet admiral later recalled: 'I can still remember with what close attention we followed the progress of the first convoys in the late autumn of 1941, with what speed and energy they were unloaded in Archangel and Murmansk.'[30] Around the same time Beaverbrook was declaring 'Tanks for Russia' week in British factories, and his programmes proved so popular that the frequently strained labour relations were set aside for any orders labelled 'Goods for Russia'.[31] As the *Daily Express* proclaimed: 'These tanks are going straight out to save lives and to KILL.'[32]

By the time of Operation Typhoon's re-launch in mid-November four convoys of allied arms and equipment had reached the Soviet Union and were showing up in the war diaries of German formations on the eastern front. On 4 November, intelligence from Foreign Armies East reported 100 British tanks being unloaded at Archangel,[33] and nine days later on 13 November a defecting Soviet soldier claimed that seventy-three British and twenty-five American bombers were at an airfield 80 km from Kalinin.[34] The following day (14 November), Panzer Group 3's war diary reported that 136 British and American planes had been identified at an enemy airfield, and even claimed that British radio transmissions were being detected.[35] While a small number of active missions by western fighters with Soviet pilots had been conducted as early as September,[36] it was in the defence of Moscow at the end of November that the first concentrated assembly of Lend-Lease fighters and tanks was seen. On 24 November, British planes were reported to have attacked the railway leading to Orel,[37] and two days later (on 26 November) the 6th Panzer Division recorded attacks by enemy planes, at least one of which was identified as being of British origin.[38] As Ilya Ehrenburg wrote on 6 November: 'we welcome our friends [to the war]. At the table, friends clink glasses. At war, friends fight side by side.'[39]

As for Lend-Lease tanks, Soviet sources indicate that ninety-six had been issued to tank battalions of the Red Army by 20 November. These were to be found at Tula in the south, east of Mozhaisk at the centre of Bock's front and in the north near Kiln and Istra.[40] German files also make mention of encountering British tanks across Army Group Centre's front. On 27 November, Foreign Armies East reported: 'before the front of the army groups multiple reports of English tanks'.[41] Panzer Group 4 noted that after a battle on 25 November three destroyed British tanks were discovered,[42] while on 27 November the 5th Panzer Division noted intelligence from POWs that two of the three opposing Soviet tank battalions consisted of British tanks.[43] If the mere presence of British tanks in the Red Army offered a psychological boost to the Anglo-Soviet cause, it follows that it had the opposite effect on German troops. One letter dated only 1941 by an unidentified German soldier noted: 'The war with Russia will last a long time yet. The enemy is offering tremendous resistance and the fanaticism that lies behind this obstinacy knows no bounds. To this must be added absolutely inexhaustible reserves of manpower and equipment, the latter even being augmented by deliveries from America.'[44] In truth, considerably more British equipment arrived in the Soviet Union in 1941 than American,[45] but the fact remains that the United States, even before direct involvement in the war, was destined to become, as Roosevelt put it, the 'arsenal of democracy'.[46]

While British tanks in the Soviet Union may have had a psychological impact, they were little better suited to the Russian late autumn and winter conditions than German tanks. The fact that German tanks in 1941 had much narrower tracks than the Soviet T-34 and KV-1 was also true of the British Valentine and Matilda tanks. Accordingly, while Soviet tanks could still perform in up to 70 cm of snow the British tanks were only capable of operating in up to 40 cm. There was even a suggestion that British tanks should be held back from service until March 1942 as they were 'apparently African vehicles'.[47] The fact that a number of German tanks originally designated for Rommel had been redirected as replacements to Bock's front, but were still painted in their North African camouflage, must have provided Soviet observers with a sense of irony given the temperatures and conditions.[48] The problems for British tanks extended well beyond poor traction and reduced speeds, they were under-gunned for the eastern front, their mechanical durability in the conditions proved to be poor and Soviet crews had barely fifteen days training in their handling.[49] Indeed, their weaknesses in relation to the eastern front were already being acknowledged back in Britain. Lord Maurice Hankey, the Paymaster-General, took Lord Beaverbrook to task in his role as Minister of Supply for advocating increased efforts on the part of the British workforce for equipment that was fundamentally flawed. As Hankey complained: 'Now I have to bring to light the fact that he is building nothing but dud tanks when he is vociferously appealing to the workers to work all day and all night to produce for Russia innumerable tanks – all dud tanks.'[50] The Valentine and Matilda certainly had their drawbacks, especially in comparison with the newer Soviet tanks, but in the desperate fighting before Moscow an extra 100 British tanks (with many more to come) were by no means immaterial to the Soviet defence.[51] Indeed, if one looks at the respective strengths of the Soviet defence versus the German offence, Bock's slender advantage was tangibly affected by the addition of Lend-Lease support.

By the end of 1941 some 466 British tanks (259 Valentines and 187 Matildas)[52] had been delivered to the Soviet Union along with 699 British and American planes.[53] This was short of the amounts stipulated by the First Protocol; however, the problem was less one of western production than the size of the Soviet merchant navy. The agreement placed primary responsibility for shipping Lend-Lease goods with the Soviets, although it was soon realised that Stalin's merchant navy was too small to handle the capacity, and Beaverbrook and Averell Harriman (acting for Britain and United States, respectively) offered to provide as many ships as possible. This was no small favour given the demands of Britain's own war effort and the critical shortage of merchant vessels. In 1941 alone German U-boots sank about 5 million tons of British shipping – more than twice the combined output of British and American shipyards, at a time when the famous Liberty ship-building programme in the United States was only just getting underway.[54] Another problem was finding enough escorts to safeguard passage for the convoys given the constant threat of U-boats and the Luftwaffe operating from airfields in Norway. Indeed, in early November convoy PQ 3 was delayed nine days due to intelligence that the German battleship *Tirpitz* and heavy cruiser *Scheer* were about to break out into the Atlantic to raid British shipping.[55] Finally, the Arctic Sea itself, as well as the time of year, posed profound problems for the ships and their cargo. Rough seas damaged some of the ships, and Stalin even complained to Churchill that some of the planes were arriving damaged (although he chose to blame bad British packing).[56] An even greater hindrance was the advent of pack ice at the end of the year, closing Archangel's port and diverting all ships to Murmansk, which had far from adequate port facilities.[57]

Notwithstanding the many problems confronting Lend-Lease aid to the Soviet Union, western aid was now arriving and the steady flow by the end of 1941 would soon grow to a flood. If the Nazi regime was only now coming to terms with the remarkable potential of its enemy in the east, they still had little idea of just how dangerous their enemies in the west would become. Writing in mid-November Goebbels noted in his diary: 'The war against Bolshevism demands the last strength of the German people and above all the German Wehrmacht. To defeat the western democracies would by comparison be child's play.'[58] Yet British and American war potential was a tangible reality even in 1941, and Lend-Lease aid meant that the Soviet Union was no longer fighting its war in exclusion. Symbolic of this fact was an incident that took place in mid-November. A German bomber flew over Moscow dropping leaflets declaring: 'Your allies are not helping you and will not help.' The German bomber, however, was shot down as it tried to return to its base – the Soviet pilot was flying a fighter from the United States.[59]

Although for the Germans the quantity of Allied aid to be sent to the Soviet Union was still unknown, it should have been clear that the longer major operations in the east continued the weaker the *Ostheer*'s position would become. This was probably the best argument for continuing with Operation Typhoon in November 1941, but it was fundamentally undercut by the weakness of Army Group Centre. It was a realisation with which Bock was slowly coming to terms as his offensive continued. On 21 November, Bock reviewed the advance north of Moscow from his map room and wrote:

> The whole attack is too thin and has no depth. Based on the number of divisions, as seen from the green table, the ratio of forces is no more unfavourable than before. In practice the reduced combat strengths – some companies have only twenty and thirty men left – the heavy officer losses and the over-extension of the units in conjunction with the cold give a quite different picture.[60]

The disparity between the map room and the events 'in practice' was indeed striking, but if the OKH could claim ignorance on this account, it was Bock's duty to rein in their expectation. On 23 November, Bock seems to have made an attempt to do just this, briefing both Halder and Brauchitsch on the critical situation at the front, especially with regard to Guderian's Second Panzer Army. According to Bock's diary, the field marshal 'made it very clear to them the state of our forces must not, "for heaven's sake", be overestimated in the future and that they must be clear that as far as this attack is concerned it is "the eleventh hour"'.[61] The next sentence in Bock's diary, however, gives little hope that the message had got through. As Bock continued:

> Brauchitsch, like Halder, nevertheless advocated a continuation of the panzer army's attack, even at the risk that it might be pulled back later. Both stressed once again that the important thing was to inflict as much damage as possible on the enemy. When I said to Halder that I am doing what I can, he replied. 'Yes, we are very pleased about that'.[62]

Yet if Bock was dutifully serving the will of his superiors, it came at the expense of his men, for the conditions in the battle of Moscow were harder than anything that preceded them and the worst was yet to come.

North of the city Reinhardt and Hoepner were pushing the advance forward with all the strength they could muster. There was little of the rapid manoeuvre and flanking operations that were the hallmark of the panzer groups in the summer and early autumn, instead the panzer troops encountered one prepared position after another and engaged them, for the most part, frontally. On 21 November, Vietinghoff's XXXXVI Panzer Corps (fielding the 5th and 11th Panzer Divisions) reported fighting its way through dense forest and swamplands, encountering camouflaged T-34s that defied all attempts at destruction.[63] Two days later (23 November), the panzer corps' war diary noted: 'The infantry have to fight their way forward step by step with knives and hand grenades. Tree snipers and well dug-in heavy weapons cause the troops great difficulties.'[64] In another indication of the kind of fighting, Fehn's 5th Panzer Division finally captured the small town of Martjuschino on 24 November to find 500 Soviet dead and only 120 prisoners of war.[65] This kind of fighting took its toll. The sole panzer division in Stumme's XXXX Panzer Corps (Fischer's 10th) was already so weakened by 21 November that the corps' war diary noted: 'The losses by the 10 Pz. Div. after countless battles – especially of late – have weakened the division to such an extent that an operation by itself against a strong opponent has little chance of success.'[66] On 21 November, Veiel's 2nd Panzer Division, assigned to Ruoff's V Army Corps along with the 35th and 106th Infantry Divisions, was having an easier time of it, reporting weak enemy resistance, but fog and difficult terrain slowed the advance. Resistance stiffened on 23 and 24 November when a heavy Soviet counterattack with dozens of tanks resulted in a major defensive battle and ended with a clear tactical success for Veiel. His division reported destroying some thirty-four enemy tanks, five of which were British with the production year stamped 'September 1941'.[67]

While the difficulties at the front and the slow pace of the advance did not appear to concern the generals at the OKH, Hoepner was despairing as early as 21 November that the operation to encircle Moscow would fall short. In a letter to his wife, the panzer general evinced a similar pessimism about the strategic situation of Guderian in the south. 'It is really sad to know', Hoepner wrote, 'that our strength will after all not be enough.'[68] That Panzer Group 4 could, for the time being, continue the advance and even capture a number of Soviet towns was not in dispute, but encircling the great city of Moscow and maintaining it over the winter was a forlorn hope. Such questioning was also taking place at every level of Army Group Centre. At a meeting of staff officers in General of Infantry Albrecht Schubert's XXIII Army Corps (part of Strauss' Ninth Army) the conclusion was drawn on 24 November that: 'The expected operational goal of the *Ostheer* will, at this stage, not be obtained.'[69] Even more revealingly, Lieutenant Gerhardt Linke wrote in his dairy on 24 November:

> The offensive continues. But in attacking concealed fortified positions in forest land our companies are bled white and incur heavy losses in equipment ... We are the frequent target of those confounded Stalin pipe-organs ... Fierce battles all day. Our losses are huge, unfortunately, particularly among those in command. Our men are in an extremely dejected mood. Many of them are unfit for action, both from wounds and from sickness, and there is nobody to fill the gaps. Everyday our fighting strength diminishes. Two weeks ago there were 70 men in the company ... tomorrow there will be only 35. Some are already beginning to reckon when their turn will come ... A few good commanders try to inspire their men by their personal example, go in front and are easily picked off by the enemy. This is confirmed by the heavy casualties among officers and NCOs. Today we lost 40, i.e., 50 per cent of the day's losses. The newly appointed unit commanders are poorly trained and unable to deal with the difficult tasks imposed upon them. Some of the soldiers have lost all mental keenness and have become apathetic. They have no initiative left and hoodwink their superiors. They avail themselves of every opportunity to be in the rear. Their favourite pretext is accompanying the wounded. A call for a stretcher-bearer in the midst of a battle will always meet with a hearty response, whereas calls for machine-guns to advance to the front remain unanswered. It is impossible to conceal all the lamentable facts, which did not exist in our regiment before ... Our regimental commander proved beyond all refutation to the highest authorities in the service that there might be a crisis at any moment ... But in the upper circles they do not want to hear such things. We look into the future with alarm.[70]

Of course, not all soldiers were struck with such a pessimistic, if realistic, view of events. For some the fact that Army Group Centre was again on the offensive was cause for genuine excitement. On 21 November one soldier wrote home: 'We here in the field are curious what in this distant eastern land we can still conquer and occupy in the course of this year!'[71] Despite the propaganda such views were in a distinct minority, and those who cheered the offensive were often those with little first-hand knowledge of it. Indeed, it was only on 22 November that German newspapers first began running the stories of Bock's renewed drive on Moscow – a week after the offensive had commenced. These articles utilised maps to show the extent of the advance, but, in contrast to the week of heavy fighting that it took to make such gains, they now appeared to have been achieved in one dramatic leap.[72] In truth, however, the most dramatic event in Bock's army group over the preceding week was the extraordinary erosion of its strength. An army on the offensive always bleeds strength, a fact that had been well illustrated throughout Operation Barbarossa in the summer and Typhoon in October, yet in November without the ability for operational manoeuvre the panzer forces shed strength at an unprecedented rate. Not only were their numbers in free fall, but relative to the gains made in earlier offensives, either in Soviet POWs or ground seized, the November offensive was faltering within days and at the cost of just tens of kilometres of captured ground (depending on the unit). In short, the November offensive, for an army group already so strained by shortages, was not only untenable for the objectives set, but for the security of the whole German position in the east given the time of year and the remarkable regenerative qualities of the Red Army.

Reinhardt's Panzer Group 3 had made steady progress since the start of the offensive and seized the largest share of land, including the important town of Klin (85 km northwest from Moscow) on 23 November,[73] yet the rate of attrition could neither be justified nor sustained. Schaal's LVI Panzer Corps consisted of Landgraf's 6th and Funck's 7th Panzer Divisions, which began the offensive with 100 and 120 tanks, respectively. By 25 November, Landgraf's 6th Panzer Division had a total of just seventeen tanks still combat-ready (six Mark IIs, nine Mark IIIs and two Mark IVs), and on the following day (26 November) this shrank again to just thirteen (five Mark IIs, six Mark IIIs and two Mark IVs).[74] Funck's 7th Panzer Division reported a total of forty operational tanks on 25 November (no individual classifications are available on what these were), which indicates a combined loss of over 160 tanks in only ten days of operations and left Schaal with just fifty-seven tanks to continue Panzer Group 3's offensive.[75] Establishing the total losses of Panzer Group 4 after the same period of time is not possible because of a lack of figures, but the earlier example of Fischer's 10th Panzer Division suggests that the panzer divisions that had been on the eastern front since June 1941 (10th, 11th, 19th and 20th Panzer Divisions) varied from weak to very weak.[76] One week into the offensive the newer arrivals (2nd and 5th Panzer Divisions) had, in the case of the 2nd Panzer Division, already lost an estimated half of its November starting strength,[77] and the 5th Panzer Division had lost one-third of its starting total.[78] While in mid-November these two panzer divisions had a combined sum of between 270 and 320 tanks between them, their losses represent a reduction of over a hundred tanks in the space of a week. Such losses placed an even greater burden on the remaining tanks, which raised the aggregate risk still higher. It may also be surmised that because the distances covered were only a fraction of those undertaken in previous offensives, and given the frontal nature of the attacks, the overall percentage of total losses (i.e., destroyed tanks as opposed to those simply broken down) was much higher in November.

While tanks were clearly the spearhead of the advance, the paucity of wheeled transport also acted as a clear brake on the advance. Funck's 7th Panzer Division noted that 'most' of its units advanced 'on foot', while a good number of the formations supporting the offensive were themselves infantry corps and thus restricted in movement to foot and hoof.[79] On 24 November, Geyer's IX Army Corps (78th, 87th and 252nd Infantry Divisions) proudly reported to Panzer Group 4 that, against heavy enemy resistance, it had still managed an advance of between 3 and 5 km.[80] This was no doubt an accomplishment, but ground was being won only at great sacrifice. Geyer's corps reported on 21 November that every town and village had to be contested, and that all of these had been modified to act as strong points. Moreover, the forest roads were blocked with fallen trees and vast numbers of mines; indeed, in just two days (since 19 November) the corps had removed some 5,000 mines.[81] In the same time period (19–21 November), Fahrmbacher's VII Army Corps (197th and 267th Infantry Divisions) reported encountering 1,089 bunkers and specially constructed strong-points.[82] As Bock noted of Fahrmbacher after a meeting on 21 November: 'The commanding general has been visibly affected by the heavy fighting and described the pitiful state of his divisions, whose strength is spent.'[83] On the same day (21 November), Albert Neuhaus observed in a letter to his wife the main cause of Army Group Centre's problems: 'Again and again one can, and must, wonder with what toughness the Russians defend themselves.'[84]

Beyond the formidable tactical challenge of sustaining the advance, strategically the attack north of Moscow was also presenting difficulties. As the offensive developed an increasing bulge, the German line required ever more strength to defend. Model's XXXXI Panzer Corps, hampered by severe fuel shortages, was struggling eastward from Kalinin to safeguard the northern flank of the offensive. At the same time, Schaal's LVI Panzer Corps was extending itself to the east to secure positions on the Moscow–Volga canal.[85] If Reinhardt's panzer group could achieve this Hoepner's left flank would be secure. Of course, any hope of seizing a city the size of Moscow would require a corresponding drive from the south, which was nowhere in sight, but Hoepner had troubles enough of his own without worrying about where Guderian was. Dejected by his dwindling chances of success, Hoepner was pushing unsuccessfully for Kluge's right wing to join the attack and provide some kind of a breakthrough to reinvigorate the offensive. His failure to influence Kluge and the inability of Bock to offer any additional resources left Hoepner deeply despondent. Writing to his wife on 25 November, the panzer commander stated: 'The attack goes forward slowly. I have daily telephone conversations with Bock and Kluge to get the latter also moving ... The Russians bring new forces from all sides. I stand alone.'[86]

'Five minutes to midnight': Franz Halder

If north of Moscow Hoepner felt his panzer group stood alone, in spite of Reinhardt's support as well as the none too distant forces of the Ninth and Fourth Armies, Guderian's Second Panzer Army was truly isolated. The Fourth Army's right wing was too weak and too distant to afford any aid, and the same was true of Schmidt's Second Army, especially since it had committed its remaining strength to an offensive towards Voronezh. However, it was not just Guderian's material isolation, his army, even more than Hoepner's, was facing counterattacks by increasingly strong enemy forces. After finally conceding on 20 November that his operational objectives vis-à-vis Moscow were beyond him, any expectation that Army Group Centre would change its plans for the November offensive were soon disappointed. On 21 November, Guderian spoke with Bock on the telephone, the essence of which was recorded, with underlining, in Army Group Centre's war diary: 'After his visit to the front Colonel-General Guderian is of the same opinion today as he reported yesterday evening. He no longer believes a crushing operational success can be achieved ... It is necessary to now make a big decision and go over to the defensive.'[87] Bock's own response is not recorded, but he immediately placed a call to Heusinger at the OKH and passed on Guderian's report.[88] For a man who had been such a dynamic and, if anything, excessively optimistic commander to admit defeat so unreservedly was a crippling blow to the OKH's operations and should have been received as such. Indeed, Guderian's professional statements scarcely betrayed the depths of his melancholy and sense of isolation. Writing to his wife on 21 November, Guderian lamented:

> The icy cold, the lack of shelter, the shortage of clothing, the heavy losses of men and equipment, the wretched state of our fuel supplies, all this makes the duties of a commander a misery and the longer it goes on the more I am crushed by the enormous responsibility which I have to bear, a responsibility which no one, even with the best will in the world, can share.
>
> I have been at the front three days running in order to form a clear picture of the conditions there. If the state of the battle allows I intend to go to Army Group [Centre] on Sunday [23 November] in order to find out what are the intentions for the immediate future, concerning which we have so far heard nothing. What these people are planning I cannot guess, nor how we shall succeed in getting [things] straight again before next spring.[89]

Even with Guderian effectively admitting defeat in the battle for Moscow Halder appears to have remained remarkably impervious to its implications. Writing in his diary on 21 November: 'Guderian called in the afternoon, his troops are at their end ... One would hope, that even against the constantly reinforced enemy (new Siberian divisions) they can still secure a good final position.'[90]

If Guderian felt slighted at not being taken more seriously and not having his offensive curtailed or even called off, he soon undercut whatever authority he may have had by expressing a near complete change of heart. On 21 November, Weisenberger's LIII Army Corps unexpectedly reported seizing Uslovaia and on the following day Langermann-Erlancamp's 4th Panzer Division reported crushing a newly arrived Soviet reserve formation and gaining new ground.[91] Guderian took heart that perhaps something could still be salvaged

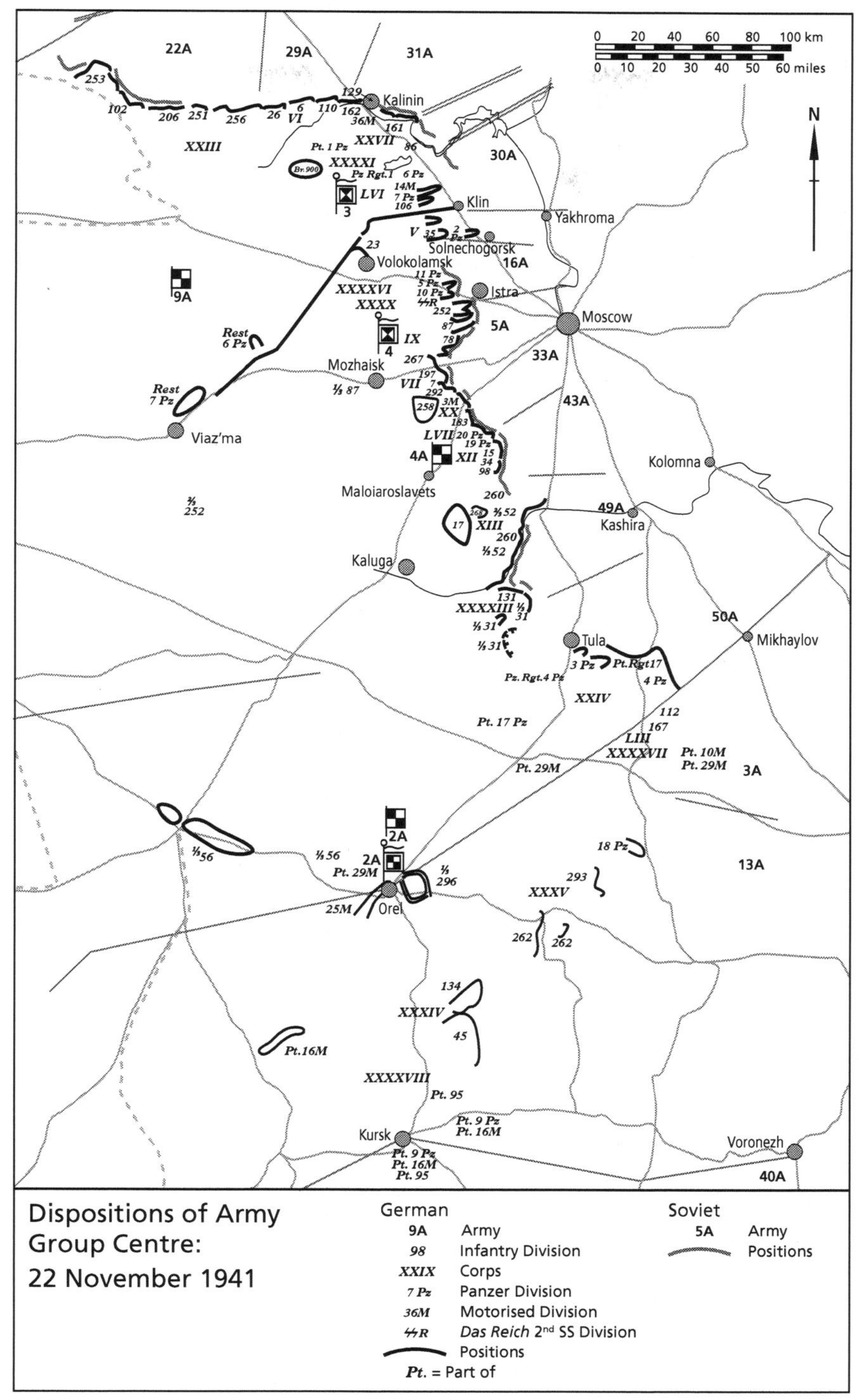

Map 6.1 Dispositions of Army Group Centre, 22 November 1941

from the offensive and added in a letter to his wife: 'Yesterday I was on the brink of despair and my nerves were at an end. Today an unexpected battle success by the brave panzer divisions has given me new hope. Whether it continues remains to be seen.'[92] At Army Group Centre, on 22 November, Guderian's about-face was noted to be 'in complete contrast to the reports from yesterday and the day before'. Guderian now believed he could reach the railway line between Kolomna and Ryazan,[93] which was a significant step towards Moscow, but still over 100 km from the Soviet capital. More to the point, this, if achieved, would greatly endanger the panzer army's southern wing by drawing so much of its remaining strength north. During his meeting with Bock on 23 November Guderian expressed a renewed vigour and 'reported that he can reach his assigned objective, even though the strengths of his panzer and infantry divisions have fallen alarmingly'.[94] As for what to do about the panzer army's southern wing, Bock was adamant that Schmidt's Second Army would simply have to extend itself further north. Outlining the precarious new plan Bock recorded in his diary:

> If the [Second Panzer] army really does reach the Oka [River] between Ryazan and Kolomna, it will be left hanging there in an exposed position – unless this drive also causes the enemy to withdraw in front of Fourth Army. All that is available to cover the Second Panzer Army's southern flank are the forces of the Second Army, meaning seven quite weak divisions manning about 350 km of front – the distance to the immovably fixed northern wing of Army Group South. All this won't work in the long run. But as long as there is a chance that the enemy in front of Fourth Army might give ground in the face of Second Panzer Army's attack, Guderian's drive must be continued, even if the panzer army might be pulled back again after reaching the Oka and after thoroughly destroying the railroad between Ryazan and Kolomna.[95]

Once again everything was to be risked for the sake of maintaining the offensive, yet, while risk is an established part of any military operation, it was the degree of risk that Bock was willing to accept that was extraordinary. While Guderian was still with Bock at Army Group Centre, the two placed a call to Halder at the OKH in order to set out the new plan. Halder was not opposed to the new arrangement, but even he, a consummate risk-taker himself, acknowledged the danger inherent in what was being planned. 'We must now be careful', he warned Bock and

Guderian, 'the state of our strength is precarious. We cannot withstand a counterattack!'[96] It was an ominous statement, which demonstrates that the generals were both aware of the risks they were taking and that they were taking them independently of Hitler. Halder's final comment was equally instructive; referring to the great gamble of the offensive towards Moscow the Chief of the General Staff stated that everyone must be clear it was 'five minutes to midnight'.[97]

After the war Guderian clearly did not want his change of heart on the road to Moscow publicised and so his memoir included an entirely fictional account of his meeting with Bock on 23 November.[98] Guderian claimed to have pleaded the case for his long-suffering soldiers and requested 'that the orders I had received be changed since I could see no way of carrying them out'.[99] In this version of events Guderian blamed not Halder (perhaps because he may have contested the matter), but rather Brauchitsch (who had died in 1948 four years before the memoir was first published).[100] Disguising his flip-flopping commitment to the offensive was no doubt desirable given that Guderian changed his mind yet again on 24 November, and this time dispatched his liaison officer to the OKH, Lieutenant-Colonel Kahlden, 'to tell the Chief of the Army General Staff about our situation. He was at the same time to attempt to arrange that the attack be cancelled.'[101] Kahlden's dispatch to the OKH and his damning depiction of the army's condition can be corroborated by Second Panzer Army's war diary. The picture drawn was a depressing one, which not only supported the view that the offensive should be halted, but warned that 'emerging crises can very quickly become catastrophic because of the shortage of reserves to deal with them'.[102]

By 24 November losses in the Second Panzer Army were staggering. Throughout the army the average combat strength of the companies was thirty-five to forty men and in the worst instances, such as Major-General Gerhard Berthold's 31st Infantry Division, averages were as low as twenty men. In a three-day period (18–20 November), Mieth's 112th Infantry Division sustained 200 dead and 500 wounded, similar casualties were also recorded in Major-General Wolf Trierenberg's 167th Infantry Division. The weather was also taking its toll with 400–500 men a day being admitted to field hospitals for sicknesses related to the cold. Materiel losses were no less remarkable. Only one-third of all artillery guns were operational, one-quarter of prime movers (tractors etc.) and Eberbach's battle group, which contained three of Guderian's four

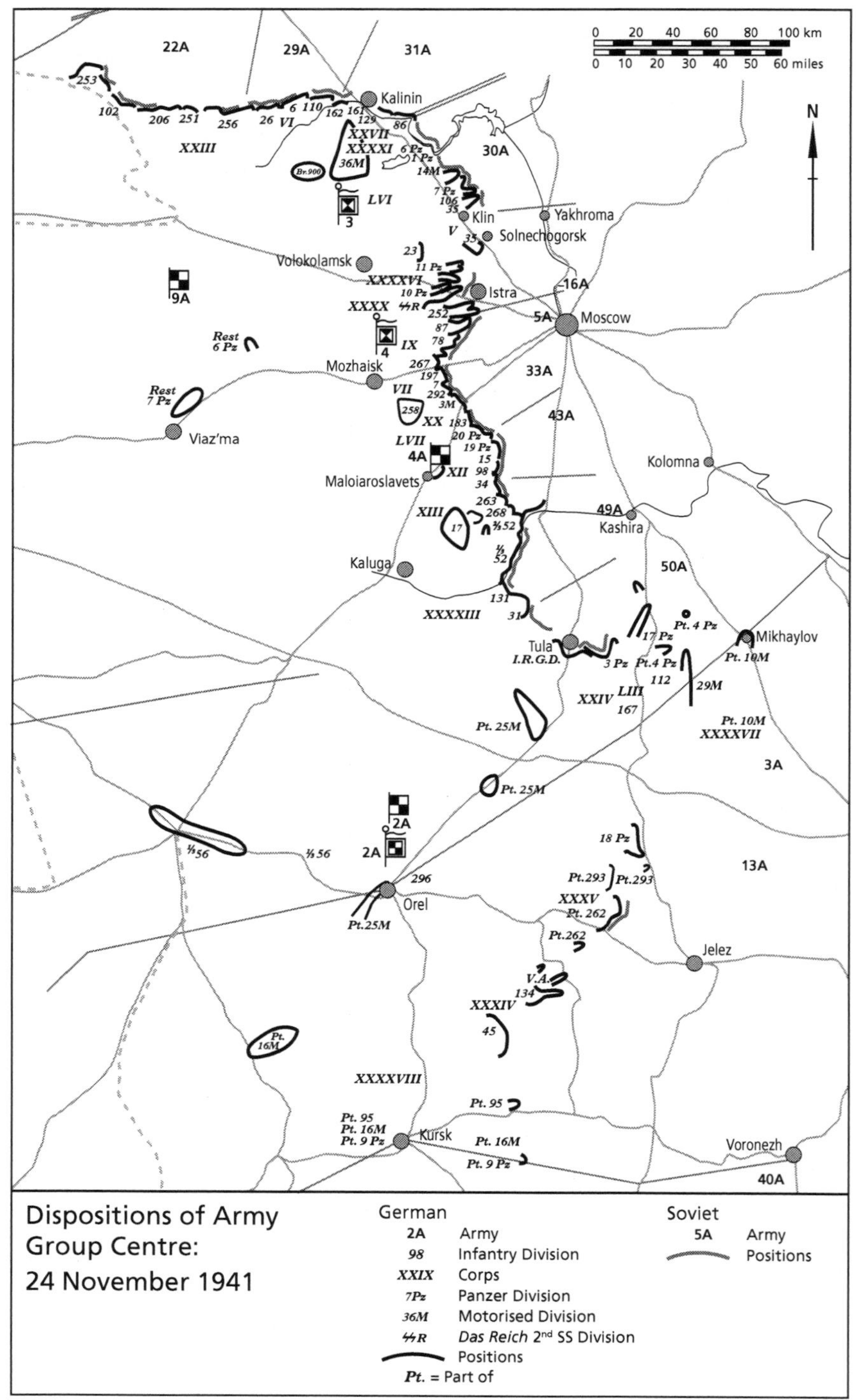

Map 6.2 Dispositions of Army Group Centre, 24 November 1941

panzer divisions, had only thirty-two tanks in total. One of those, Licht's 17th Panzer Division, had only five tanks left.[103] As Erich Hager, one of the few remaining tankers from the division, wrote in his diary after a failed attack on 24 November: 'Flak guns shot a lot of our tanks to pieces. PKWs [cars] and LKWs [trucks] set on fire ... We've been quite disheartened today. What a day!'[104]

Not only were there shortages of men and materiel at the front, but even these could not be properly supplied and the army lived on a hand-to-mouth basis. At the same time, supplementing supplies from the local area was noted to be possible only 'to a very limited extent'.[105] If Guderian hoped that Kahlden's report to Halder might see a change in the panzer army's orders he was again to be disappointed. As Guderian observed, the visit 'achieved nothing' and, having seemingly absolved himself of any responsibility, concluded: 'the military persons in authority now knew of the highly insecure situation in which my army was placed, and at that time I had to assume that Hitler, too, was being kept fully informed'.[106] Precisely what Hitler knew of the state that Army Group Centre was in and how the faltering march on Moscow was affecting him can be gleaned from notes recorded by his army adjutant, Major Gerhard Engel, on 25 November:

> The Führer explains his great anxiety about the Russian winter and weather conditions, says we started one month too late. The ideal solution would have been the surrender of Leningrad and the capture of the south, and then if need be a pincer round Moscow from the south and north, following through in the centre ... Time is his greatest nightmare now.[107]

Apparently Hitler too was starting to doubt the course of operations towards Moscow and was left to reconsider his whole strategic concept against the Soviet Union. The issue of time was also deeply troubling him and one suspects he had a greater sense of the danger Bock was in than the army high command. Nevertheless, Hitler was not about to halt the offensive, he too was willing to stake everything on Bock's eleventh-hour success at Moscow. With such awesome responsibility riding on his shoulders Bock steeled his nerves against doubt by evoking one of the great German myths of his time. As the Germans armies closed in on Paris in September 1914 the unwillingness of the German command to commit their last reserves to battle and press home the attack with an iron will, granted France the reprieve needed to survive Schlieffen's offensive plan. Now in 1941, at five minutes to midnight, Bock conjured up a comparison with the battle on the Marne where, as he told Halder, 'the last battalion that can be thrown in will be decisive'.[108] The fallacy of such thinking was as unsound in 1941 as it had been in 1914, but the consequences of believing it would be the same.[109]

While at the highest levels an understanding of the war in the east was distorted by national myths and Nazi ideas, at the lowest levels the day-to-day experience of the eastern front was dominated by a pitiless struggle for survival and, in that regard, also influenced by Nazi ideas about the enemy. The German war of annihilation cannot be separated from the fighting at the front, each radicalised the other, making it both 'necessary' to kill and 'easier' to perform. Indeed, German soldiers were typically brutalised by their experiences at the front, a process that was hastened by constant combat, physical and emotional exhaustion and heavy losses.[110] To many of the men in the *Ostheer* the violence they perpetrated and experienced quickly became 'normal'. As Helmut Pabst wrote home in a letter: 'you have to accept the basic fact, you're after another man's life. That's war. That's the trade. And it isn't so difficult.'[111] Likewise, Henning Kardell told an interviewer after the war: 'I played my part. I threw hand grenades into trenches. There were many killed on the other side, but there was no time to think about it, there was no time to be afraid, there was no time. You went out, you did your job, you killed.'[112] After having shot seven Russians and then finding a mutilated comrade Hans Rehfeldt wrote nonchalantly in his diary: 'Eye for an eye – tooth for a tooth! "*C'est la guerre*"! That's war!'[113] Nor were these views exceptional or typical only of those more predisposed towards violence. William Lubbeck observed in his memoir that war 'hardens your heart and leads you to do brutal things that you could never have imagined yourself doing in civilian life'.[114] Another soldier ruled out emotions altogether as if the primal instinct to survive dictated all actions: 'There was no bravado left; mercy and compassion were also missing.' He then questioned: 'How cruel could men get?'[115]

German actions on the battlefield sometimes suggested a predominance of emotion, defying any rational impulse to survive. The phenomenon is often alluded to in the writings of soldiers as a kind of crazed battle psychosis arising during the violence of combat and overwhelming all self-restraint. Men became frenzied and acted with murderous rage. Gottlob Bidermann wrote that during one battle:

> suppressed emotions became entangled with every nerve and were strained to the breaking point through the repeated experience of indescribable terror ... The infantrymen became consumed with a remorseless, ever-increasing rage; and the fevered minds could concentrate only on revenging fallen comrades, to kill the enemy, and to destroy. The highest degrees of rage would grow to suicidal levels, so near together lie fear and courage.[116]

The human cost of the fighting and the frequency with which it took place is reflected in the German casualty reports, but to the men at the front the equation was simple; the greater the killing, the lower the value of life. As one soldier explained: 'One becomes totally numb. Human life is so cheap – cheaper than the shovels we use to clear the roads of snow. The state we have reached will seem quite unbelievable to you back home.'[117] Indeed, many letters spoke of a transforming effect of the war, but few summed it up as eloquently as the writer Willy Peter Reese who had arrived on the eastern front in October 1941:

> We stood at the gate of no-man's-land and felt the nearness of danger and pain. The years of darkness were beginning, as the stars had decreed. Like beggars, we left behind the wreckage of our youth, freedom, love, mind, pleasure, and work. We were required to subject our own lives to the will of the age, and our destiny began like a tale of duress, patience, and death. We could not escape the law, there was a breach in our unfinished sense of the world, and like a dream, the march into the other and the unknown began, and all our paths ended in night.[118]

Another German writer, Horst Lange, who was also posted to the eastern front in the autumn of 1941 wrote a similarly vivid depiction of the frightening world he and his comrades were entering: 'Signs of battle are everywhere: charred ruins, broken remnants of weapons and scattered shell fragments ... We are seeing more and more horrendous things, glimpsing terrible images ... Truly, we are entering the underworld.'[119]

There have been a number of theories about how German soldiers coped with the conditions on the eastern front and survived in Lange's so-called 'underworld'. The first was advanced in 1948 by Edward Shils and Morris Janowitz who asserted that German soldiers formed 'primary groups' around which the cohesion of their units was sustained. This pointed to strong social networks built on close personal ties, as opposed to a system of ideas imposed from above, as the core factor in unit solidarity and functionality.[120] Many years later, in 1982, Martin van Creveld released his study on the 'fighting power' of the German army and concluded that its success 'rested almost solely on the excellence of its organization per se'.[121] The conclusions of these earlier works were later contested by Omer Bartov who highlighted ideological factors as the primary feature moulding German soldiers' views and directing their behaviour.[122] More recently, Jeff Rutherford has argued that while shared ideological beliefs and a relatively effective replacement system helped to maintain the troops' staying power, the notion of 'military necessity' proved decisive to the German war effort. This concept led the German army to use all and any means, regardless of their ethical or moral costs, to achieve victory on the battlefield and it resulted in both impressive combat effectiveness and frequent recourse to violent outbursts directed at Soviet civilians.[123]

While the different studies may dispute the primacy of structural, environmental, social and political influences on the men of the *Ostheer*, in fact, as Rutherford's research suggests, these factors would seem to overlap, providing a more complex accounting for the average soldier's behaviour in the east. Another problem with asserting that any one factor predominated over and above the others is that scholars have tended to treat the *Ostheer* as a generic whole, when in fact there were radical differences between various parts of the front at any given time. The destruction of 'primary groups', which Bartov uses to reject Shils' and Janowitz's thesis, might well apply to units attacking Moscow in November 1941, but much less so for those dug-in since mid-September before Leningrad with less fighting and fewer losses. Even in Army Group Centre at this time there were infantry divisions holding largely static positions (in Ninth Army, for example), which saw much more limited combat. We should also be careful to point out that while combat units were in places being decimated by the fighting, other forward units, such as the artillery, tended to suffer much less. Different divisions may also have had different operational cultures based on their past experiences. What is needed are more nuanced studies of the *Ostheer* and an understanding that local conditions, individual command, organisational styles and varying orders from above had a large bearing on motivations and behaviours.

By late November there were a number of factors sustaining morale in the panzer forces driving on Moscow. Fewer and fewer men expressed the hope that the offensive might bring about an end to the war (although the idea persisted), but many more were motivated by the promise that Moscow would offer an end to their exertions as well as a warm bed. Thus, practical necessities, much more than strategic considerations or even orders, were driving the men forward. Helmut Günther recalled: 'We did not care what tactical objective might be the result of capturing a village. Our only concern was a warm room and a roof over our heads.'[124] Thus, Moscow loomed large in discussions throughout Army Group Centre, but the objective served somewhat different ends. While the generals counted down the kilometres for the allure of strategic success and martial prestige, the troops sought shelter, warmth and rest. As Siegfried Knappe noted: 'The cold numbed and deadened the human body from feet up until the whole body was an aching mass of misery. To keep warm, we had to wear every piece of clothing we owned to achieve a layered effect. Each man fought the cold alone, pitting his determination and will against the bitter winter.'[125]

Although the salivation of reaching Moscow beckoned the soldiers forward, it was by no means the only thought sustaining the men through their personal anguish and torment. On the belt buckle of every soldier in the German army were inscribed the words '*Gott mit uns*' ('God is with us'), and for many Christian men in the *Ostheer* this was their most redeeming thought. God transcended the horrors of war, offering a guise of protection and deliverance, while prayer became an emotional sanctuary for personal redemption and spiritual salvation. As Alois Scheuer wrote home in a letter on 15 November: 'There are two things in this world which always sustain me with strength and power to endure in this terrible time. This is my family . . . The second is our Lord God. I pray daily to him for his protection and blessing for me and for you at home.'[126] Even men who had had a more tenuous relationship to their faith relished the solace it offered. Reinhard Goes wrote to his family on 23 November: 'I have come much closer to you, I have seen poverty and death and have learned the exquisite value of prayer and trust in God.'[127] Another soldier wrote: 'Dear Mother, I am happy to write to you even when the fatigue of the march and the thought of our nation's fate dull the mood. But believe me I am nearer to God than usual. The mystery of the light is greater than the darkness.'[128] The writings of Willy Peter Reese illustrate the spiritual journey of one young man from ambivalence and apathy to conviction and faith. In his earliest writings Reese wrote dismissively of those who sought God on the battlefield: 'Nothing beautiful, lofty or pure happened in no-man's-land. God did not dwell on battlefields and the spirit as much as the body died in the trenches. Death held sway in war.'[129] Yet after joining the army he revisited the question of faith and reconsidered his previous refutation:

> At first there was the primordial circling around God. But the idea of God paled against the promise of destiny. I didn't want to be a weakling and lean against his omnipresence in my fear and need, not leave my happiness and sorrow in his fatherly hands, accept my lot as punishment and mercy, and console myself with his sacraments and promises. With rare logic, I didn't want to recognize any commands that, as a soldier, I would be unable to observe, and I told myself even then I wasn't responsible for anything that I lived, thought, or said as a soldier, whether it was wisdom, experience, love, or death. My cosmos was now populated by angels and demons, and Jesus to me became more and more a prophet and less the Son of God.[130]

A devout and long-suppressed devotion to the Orthodox faith was also observed among the Russian and other Soviet peoples, who were at last free to celebrate their religious beliefs openly and reclaim their places of worship.[131] It was the only aspect of liberation under German rule (and a qualified one at that).[132] The 1937 Soviet census revealed that 57 per cent of the population still retained their faith even after almost twenty years of hard-line communism.[133] With the arrival of the Wehrmacht and the reopening of local churches there was an outpouring of joy and enthusiasm, especially in more rural settings, which impacted upon the German soldiers heavily. Hans Meier-Welcker noted that whenever his unit held an outdoor mass the local farmers came, knelt, cried and prayed, in spite of the fact that they understood nothing of what was said and the service was not Orthodox.[134] The first Orthodox mass in the Smolensk cathedral was observed by Hans von Luck, who told of crowds filling the square outside the service because the cathedral was already full. When Luck jostled his way inside he witnessed that the congregation 'fell on their knees and prayed. All had tears in their eyes.' Luck concluded: 'It was an experience I shall never forget.'[135] The gratitude on behalf of the people helped to reinforce the notion that Germany was waging a just war against godless Bolshevism. Some Soviet peasants are understood to have interpreted the black

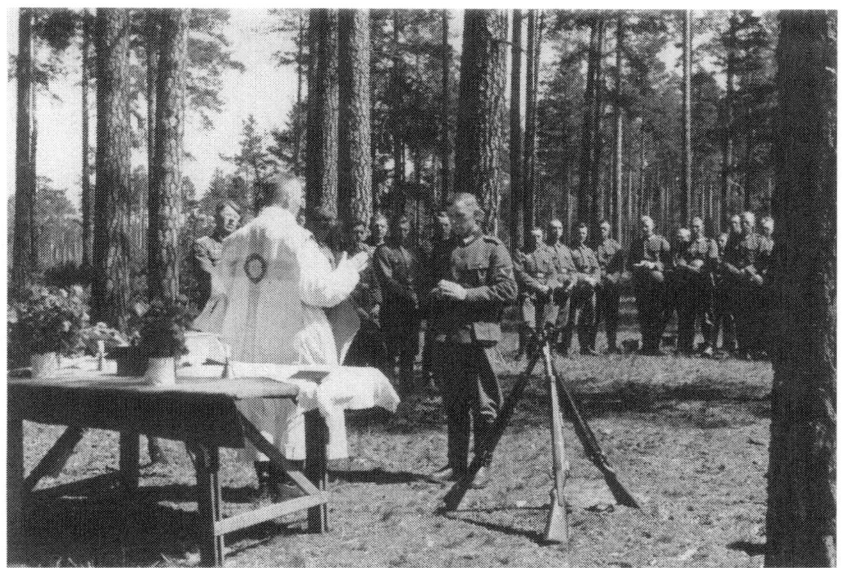

Figure 6.1 A field mass for soldiers in the east (summer 1941)

crosses adorning the vehicles of the German army (the *Balkenkreuz*) as a sign of Christian liberation from Soviet atheism.[136] Indeed, many German soldiers, and especially their accompanying clergy, expressed indignation at the Soviet conversion of Orthodox churches and cathedrals into public halls, market places, grain storage centres, power stations, cinemas and even 'Godless exhibitions'.[137] Field Marshal Bock also took the opportunity to observe an Orthodox ceremony and recounted it in his diary: 'The people – not just the old, but many young as well – streamed into the churches and kissed the holy objects – including the crosses around the necks of the armed forces chaplains – and often remained there praying until evening.' Bock then arrogantly concluded: 'This people would not be difficult to lead!'[138]

While religious beliefs acted to sustain German soldiers spiritually as well as providing an inducement to fight against communism, the delivery of post from Germany was the most popular method of raising morale within a unit. This had been a far more frequent occurrence in the first months of the war when the roads were dry and the front was not as far to the east. However, with the autumn *rasputitsa*, declining motorisation and the renewed advance, there were some units that did not receive post for up to six weeks with serious implications for the morale of the men. On 9 November, the war diary of Krüger's 1st Panzer Division discussed the depressed mood among the troops and the absence of post: 'The connection with the homeland seems to have been severed.'[139] Three days later, it was reported that some 2,000 sacks of post were awaiting delivery to the division in Smolensk.[140] By the end of November the hardening of the road surfaces improved delivery times to about three weeks for a letter.[141]

The occasion of postal distribution was an event of great joy and even celebration among the men. Karl Nünnighoff stated in a letter on 26 November: 'My eyes almost cried with joy when I got my post today.'[142] The occasion would typically be followed by hours of shared exchanges of news as well as packages of edible treats, baked by wives and mothers, being shared out and devoured. Many men then set about replying to the letters they had just received. Beyond the camaraderie such occasions offered, the arrival of post also provided much need emotional support. After a particularly difficult day Werner Adamczyk noted:

> I turned to the several letters from Rosemarie. Thank God, they were more cheerful. She did not mention the war at all – only her feeling of love and her expectations of me coming home on vacation soon. She wrote about many plans of what we would do together. They were lovely letters and they brought me back to a mental balance. Indeed, with much imagination I projected my thoughts and feelings forward to that much-desired time. But would I make it? That was the question I asked myself, with trembling hands and tears in my eyes.[143]

Another soldier referred to post from his wife as 'the nicest and best source of strength', while others dubbed the letters 'little brown darlings' and 'the only gleam of hope'. One soldier wrote of being 'as happy as a small child who had just received a present'. In a letter on 28 November Heinz Heppermann told his wife: 'I often have the symptoms of something, sometimes a cold, then many headaches or stomach upsets, here and there also a torn ligament; but soldiers mostly don't pay attention to such things! All of this disappears when a letter from home arrives for us, with caring words, words of faithfulness and of affiliation.'[144]

While letters to the eastern front typically brought solace and reassurance, the men could also use post to Germany as an emotional valve, confiding their fears and unburdening their hearts.[145] Certainly, by November 1941 there was a great deal of personal suffering and

Figure 6.2 Field post was one of the most important factors sustaining German morale through the battle for Moscow. Here a tired-looking soldier reads a letter from home (November 1941)

organisational shortcomings to report. Goebbels warned of this on 14 November,[146] and then saw it confirmed in the letters arriving in Germany three weeks later. Writing on 12 December, the propaganda minister noted: 'Actually the impact of letters from the front, which had been regarded as extraordinarily important, has to be considered more than harmful today. The soldiers are pretty blunt when they describe the great problems they are fighting under, the lack of winter gear ... insufficient food and ammunition.'[147] There was, of course, censorship in Nazi Germany, but the sheer volume of letters reduced its impact and in many instances offending letters merely had objectionable passages rendered illegible. Soldiers appeared to have expressed themselves with relative frankness, especially when it came to military matters. Criticisms of Hitler or the Nazi party, however, to the extent that such views were held at this time, were far less common. Yet even for those concerned in expressing themselves openly, in-jokes and private codes were soon established (such as a dash at the end of a sentence indicating that the author meant the opposite of what was stated), which kept postal communication open and honest in spite of official regulations.[148]

Another important source of information and diversion was the radio, which most units had access to for military purposes, but the receiver could be tuned to broadcast stations in Germany and other European countries. Contrary to popular perception, radio in Nazi Germany was not overtly politicised, and even in 1943 only some 16 per cent of the content was classed as 'political' (speeches or propaganda).[149] German radio at this time was, as one social historian noted, 'an emotional community-building medium'.[150] There were cultural programmes, poetry recitals, plays, sporting events and 'public information' about new regulations or tips on how housewives could best utilise their rationing allocation. The majority of air-time, however, was taken up with musical programmes, which proved by far the most popular. The highpoint of the week was the *Wunschkonzert für die Wehrmacht* (Request Concert for the Wehrmacht), broadcast every Sunday at 3 pm (prime-time in 1941).[151] This was a live show in which the announcer, Heinz Goedecke, took requests from soldiers and relayed personal messages in return for donations to charity.[152] The selection was usually a mixture of upbeat popular songs, including rousing military tunes like the *Panzerlied* (*Panzer song*), and more sentimental fare like *Glocken der Heimat* (*Bells of the Homeland*).

To the soldiers in the east radio was another tangible connection with Germany, offering escapism into a familiar, if forbidden, world they had once known and grown nostalgic for. Yet, in 1941, a new song appeared, which, more than any other, captured the hearts of the men throughout the *Ostheer* and became a nightly ritual with tremendous resonance. Every night the Wehrmacht radio station *Soldatensender Belgrad*, broadcasting to the Balkans and Mediterranean, played the same final song at 9.57 pm – *Lili Marleen*.[153] As Heinrich Rotard recalled:

> At the end of November 1941, in temporary shelters and dugouts shrouded in snow, our soldiers heard on the radio for the first time the song, '*Lili Marleen*'. The news spread like wildfire. We tuned into the German service on Radio Belgrade, where the song was

> played every evening just before 10.00 p.m. And we listened to Lale Andersen's refrain, for a brief moment we were taken away from the bitter fighting, the cold – and the death that was all around us.[154]

Wilhelm Prüller noted that his one pleasure was the radio: 'Every day is the same, and we have none of civilization's benefits; if we didn't have our marvellous army radio transmitter, we'd be really at sixes and sevens. But at least we can hear the news, music, lectures, and at the end of each day *Lili Marleen*.'[155] Originally written as a poem by a German infantryman during the First World War, it was only published in 1937 and put to music in 1938. The song then fell foul of Goebbels for its melancholy lyrics and somber melody. Consigned to obscurity, it was among a crate of old records found by an employee at the Wehrmacht radio station in Belgrade in August 1941. Josef Bailer recalled first hearing the song on the approaches to Moscow: 'Everyone was talking about it. "You must hear it!" someone said to me. So we tuned our radio transmitter to Radio Belgrade, and listened – completely captivated.'[156]

Lili Marleen's haunting verses adapted the universal themes of longing and absent love to tell the story of a soldier who used to meet his lover under the lantern by the barracks gate. He then goes to war, but cannot forget the fleeting affair and longs to meet his lover again. The song was such a hit that it even transcended national boundaries and as a result the British soon produced a version called *Lilli of the Lamplight*.[157] Meanwhile, on the eastern front, German soldiers toiled and fought their way to Moscow with the one solace at the end of each day being their own rendezvous with *Lili Marleen*. Johann Allmayer-Beck recalled after the war: 'When you consider that millions of German soldiers stood for months at the front without women and with this song were awakened to the memory of the finest moment of peace, even in barracks life, then one can understand that Lili Marleen became a kind of evening prayer, all along the [German] fronts.'[158] The final verse of *Lili Marleen* ran:

> From my quiet existence, from this earthly pale,
> Like a dream you lift me to your loving lips,
> When the night mists swirl and churn
> Then to that lantern I'll return
> As once, Lil Marleen
> As once, Lil Marleen.[159]

7 VICTORY AT ANY PRICE

'More murder than war': the battle against Soviet civilians

As the German advance to Moscow continued one step at a time, the men of Army Group Centre were left exposed to the freezing temperatures, often for days on end. This took its own toll on the fighting units as sickness spread and cases of frostbite became more and more common. By 21 November, Halder had been informed that there were now more German soldiers being treated for illnesses than for wounds. Even this grim statistic was presented with a positive spin in Halder's dairy, when he observed that the current 1:1.4 ratio of wounded to sick was better than previous wars where the ratio had been 1:4.[1] Eric Kern referred to the long nights in Russia as being 'indescribable', and noted that he and his comrades had neither winter coats nor gloves. 'We lay in the Russian trenches, our heads scantily covered with tarpaulins stiff with ice, while outside a howling blizzard drove great waves of powdered snow before it. Many froze to death.'[2] Another German soldier wrote home to his family on 21 November that he was lying outside in his foxhole roughly 80 km north of Moscow with feet that were already half frozen.[3] At the same time, Siegfried Knappe observed: 'The snow blew almost horizontally in blizzards that sometimes lasted all day long, with the wind piercing our faces with a thousand needles ... We reduced sentry duty to one hour, then to thirty minutes, and finally to fifteen minutes. The cold was quite simply a killer; we were all in danger of freezing to death.'[4]

In the Soviet high command recognition that German forces were suffering untold losses on account of the winter conditions convinced

Stalin to expand his already ruthless scorched-earth policy. No longer satisfied with simply burning all structures in the path of Army Group Centre's advance, on 17 November, Stalin sought to maximise the exposure of German troops to the cold by ordering a concentrated effort to destroy anything left behind the German front.[5] This was to be achieved by clearing everything to a depth of 40–60 km behind the front and 20–30 km on either side of all roads. Nothing was to be spared and, characteristic of the Soviet dictator, the military rationale outweighed any consideration for the fate of Soviet civilians caught up in the new policy of destruction.[6] To implement the policy, Soviet aviation and artillery were directed to attack any village or settlement in the prescribed zone, while special ski troops operating behind enemy lines, as well as so-called 'diversion groups' (or partisans), were to destroy buildings by direct attack or by stealth.[7] On 20 November, Lieutenant Gerhardt Linke noted in his diary that a fire, 'most likely sabotage', had destroyed his unit's stable with the loss of eighty-five horses: 'In one night a whole artillery supply column lost its power of locomotion.'[8] Another soldier talked of a fire that he attributed to partisans in which a warehouse housing ninety German vehicles burned to the ground 'lighting up the entire region'.[9] Indeed, in late November it was the attempted burning of a house in a German-occupied village west of Moscow that led to the capture of the famous Soviet partisan heroine Zoya Kosmodemyanskaya.[10] Before she was hanged by the Germans, she reportedly told the assembled gathering: 'You can't hang all 190 million of us.'[11]

While the Germans could at least attempt to guard their captured villages, there was nothing they could do to prevent the destruction of settlements in soon to be occupied areas. Here the Soviet scorched-earth policy was ruthlessly implemented and, by 29 November, Zhukov's Western Front reported that his forces had destroyed some 400 villages.[12] The effects were lamented by the oncoming German troops, who found few quarters and a lot of landmines.[13] Indeed, for all the disparaging remarks the Germans had made towards the peasant homes during their summer advance, there was now a belated recognition of their virtue. As Heinrich Haape wrote: 'We soon learned, too, to appreciate the Russian houses and acknowledged that even the poorest Russian knew how to build a protection against the winter.'[14] Willy Peter Reese described Russian homes as occasionally beautiful, but 'mostly they were squat, ugly huts'.[15] Yet the thick walls, small windows and low, thatched roofs helped to insulate them against the cold, while a great clay stove dominated the single-room constructions providing heat and even a warm bed, because it was large enough for whole families to sleep on. Although German soldiers had once purposely avoided sleeping in the peasant huts for fear of the lice, rodents and bugs that infested them, by November these same dwellings offered desperately sought-after warmth and rest. Indeed, the battles were increasingly centred upon villages for the possession of warm quarters at the end of a day. As one soldier explained: 'operations themselves often centred around groups of houses, the possession of which was the main object of the fight. The winners could move into the shelters against the deadly cold, the losers would have to run back to undisputed shelters'.[16]

The problem the Germans faced as they advanced towards Moscow was not only the scarcity of dwellings, but that these were frequently still occupied by Soviet civilians whose numbers had often been swollen by the destruction of neighbouring houses. After the war German veterans typically skipped over this issue in their memoirs or presented their actions as merely 'borrowing' Russia houses, and justified their actions on the basis of necessity. Franz Frisch wrote: 'It was our best means of surviving the cold, because we could not dig or construct outside shelters in the frozen ground except crudely by dynamiting holes.'[17] It was these aspects of Germany's war in the east that made the war of annihilation one that involved every German soldier. This was not because German soldiers were simply heartless, they too suffered in the sub-zero conditions, but, as a result, they were not opposed to displacing a few civilians in order to avoid the freezing temperatures. Few of the soldiers viewed expelling civilians as a death sentence, and certainly many of the displaced people found refuge in other houses or villages, but, just as surely, many did not. The result was untold numbers of Soviet civilian deaths. As one German pastor observed in his diary on 15 November: 'Last night the last civilians were ordered out of the district. It really grips your heart to see people sent out into such cold with their few belongings. But they don't go far and return at the end of the day. Only today were we able to get rid of them for good.'[18] The ultimate fate of the people was not recorded, and while the pastor expressed concern for their well-being his unit clearly prioritised its own needs above those of the civilians. At the same time, the Germans appeared unable, or unwilling, to find any alternative for them.

Willy Peter Reese spoke of the local people in his area being used almost as German slaves, while he and his comrades occupied their houses: 'Women and children were made to go to the wells for us, water our horses, watch our fires and peel our potatoes. We used their straw for our horses or for bedding for ourselves, or else we drove them out of their beds and stretched out on their stoves.'[19] Later when Reese's company took the village of Kosmomolemyanskoye he wrote:

> We drove the women out of their homes and pushed them into the most wretched of the dwellings. Pregnant or blind, they all had to go. Crippled children we shooed out into the rain and some were left with nothing better than a barn or a shed, where they lay down with our horses. We cleaned the rooms and heated them, and looked after ourselves.[20]

After the Germans occupied half of the houses in the village of Knyaseva, Heinrich Haape's memoir delicately presented the removal of the remaining civilians as 'the desirability of evacuating the entire Russian population, so that we could have the maximum protection against the winter'.[21] Yet an 'evacuation' implies that these civilians were directed somewhere and resettled, an outcome that the front-line troops could probably not have overseen even if they had so desired. More likely 'evacuating' the Russian population was merely a euphemism for more civilian expulsions, and wartime accounts suggest just how brutal the process could be. One captured German sign read in Russian: 'The hamlet Petraninov lies in the battle zone. Therefore the population must leave by 8pm this evening ... Any civilians found later in the hamlet will be shot without warning.'[22] Likewise, Wilhelm Prüller's diary observed:

> You should see the act the civilians put on when we make it clear to them that we intend to use their sties to sleep in. A weeping and yelling begins, as if their throats were being cut, until we chuck them out. Whether young or old, man or wife, they stand in their rags and tatters on the doorstep and can't be persuaded to go ... When we finally threaten them at pistol point, they disappear[23]

No doubt many Soviet peasants knew the fate that awaited them and their families without shelter during the colder months of the year. This, however, did not soften the hearts of the German soldiers performing the expulsions. Willi Kubik observed a group of civilians being thrown out of their homes and wrote: 'It is a terrible scene ... The whole household is packed into two or three sacks. The children, some barefoot, sometimes have only one shirt on. Then they leave on a cart with two cows and an uncertain fate ahead of them.'[24] To gain an impression of the scale of the problem in the winter of 1941/2, it is estimated that some 50,000 German troops were quartered in Smolensk alone. No doubt many former residents of the city had fled, but it was known that there were also at least 20,000 refugees in the city who were forced to live in cellars and attics because German soldiers had taken over many of the best residences.[25]

Soviet families were not always expelled from their homes; sometimes they only had to billet German soldiers, which occasionally brought benefits to the families such as extra food or home repairs. However, it also exposed families to men who often viewed them as 'the enemy' or racially inferior slavs. In these instances, families could be put to work for their guests and were subject to physical and sexual abuse. Robert Rupp wrote in his diary that the seventeen-year-old daughter in the house he was occupying had been raped by three German soldiers who had previously been quartered with the family.[26] In another instance, two German officers from the 20th Panzer Division shot the family they were billeted with after getting drunk.[27]

While the loss of shelter was the most immediate danger to the occupied Soviet population in November 1941, it was by no means the only one. The general shortage of food was radicalising other aspects of German policy with equally deadly results for the civilian population. The looting of Soviet homesteads had been common practice since the first days of the German invasion, but these seldom turned violent unless resistance was offered or the occupants were Jewish. Even the more passive German practice of foraging in forests for mushrooms or digging in the fields for potatoes and onions was no longer possible and, with supplies so far in arrears, the alternative was to extract more from the people with the least. As Franz Frisch noted: 'For a certain time the supply system collapsed completely and we were on our own. Whatever little there was to be taken, we took.'[28] As an example of how far food shortages extended, some units within Guderian's Second Panzer Army were reduced to a daily ration of 30 g of fat for each man along with a loaf of bread shared between five or six men.[29] Soviet peasants naturally sought to protect their precious winter food stocks by hiding them and claiming they had nothing left to give, which in some cases was also the truth, but to the minds of many German soldiers this counted as 'resistance' and led to brutality. Even without the war much of the Soviet peasantry barely maintained a subsistence living, and the implications of the rampant German looting were for many the equivalent of an eventual death sentence. As Willy Peter Reese wrote: 'We saw the hunger and the misery, and under the compulsion of war, we added to it.'[30] He then continued:

> The cooks slaughtered cattle and pigs on the way and requisitioned peas, beans, and cucumbers everywhere. But the midday soup wasn't enough to get us through our exertions. So we started taking the last piece of bread from women and children, had chickens and geese prepared for us, pocketed their small supplies of butter and lard, weighted down our vehicles with flitches of bacon and flour from the larders, drank the over rich milk, and cooked and roasted on their stoves, stole honey from their collective farms, came upon stashes of eggs, and weren't bothered by tears, hand wringing and curses. We were the victors. War excused our thefts, encouraged cruelty, and the need to survive didn't go around getting permission from conscience.[31]

On 22 November, Nina Semonova wrote in her diary how the Germans had stolen the last of her family's grain and potatoes. In desperation her mother took the bold step of complaining to a German officer who told her flatly: 'The German soldier never steals!' Nearby one of the soldiers who had looted the house overheard the conversation and 'struck her a sharp blow'.[32] Another Soviet account stated: 'We had saved a few scraps of food – a little butter, a small amount of meat and some white bread. Naturally, everything has now been stolen from us.'[33] In another instance, a German soldier forced his way into a farmhouse searching for food. The family tried to placate him with offerings of bread and milk, but the man wanted honey, which he soon found, along with flour and lard. The farmer beseeched the soldier not to take their food and then tried to wrest it from him. The account concluded: 'The soldier smashed the farmer's skull, shot the farmer's wife and furiously torched the place.'[34] Many Soviet peasants, especially those in Ukraine, had already seen or experienced the torments of hunger and knew that starvation was only the most direct consequence of their diminished food stocks. Malnutrition greatly increased the danger of life-threatening illnesses and even disease, particularly for the old, weak and very young. Whether death resulted from starvation or indirectly from undernourishment the cause was the same, and the role played by everyday German soldiers, even if at times unwittingly, cannot be ignored.

Mass starvation in November and December 1941 is often discussed in the context of Leningrad's long-suffering population, where, according to Elena Skrjabin's account, people were 'dying like flies'.[35] Indeed, in November alone some 11,000 people died of starvation in the city, and the worst was yet to come.[36] However, while Leningrad remains the most notable example, starvation was in fact widespread throughout the German occupied zone. In Orel alone hundreds were confirmed to have starved to death during the winter of 1941/2,[37] and the situation was worse in towns and villages closer to the front (where the mass of German troops were stationed). Already in October a German doctor observed desperate civilians cutting meat from a dead horse that had been lying by the road for three to four weeks. In another instance, a woman was found to have killed young children aged between three to five in order to sell their flesh as pork at the market.[38] Another German doctor sought to blame Stalin for the lack of food stuffs among the civilian population: 'When the cold weather set in, individual Russians peasants came to ask us what was to become of them during the winter – they had insufficient food to see them through. We could only reply that we ourselves did not have enough and stressed that it was Stalin who ordered the scorched earth policy.'[39] Of course, German requisitions ensured that Bock's troops never suffered the fate of the civilian population. Indeed, many German troops took pride in their ability to find food when there was so little to be had. Franz Weiss wrote to his fiancée: 'All the villagers hide their chickens from me when they see me. But I know how to smell them out. When I locate them a howl goes up, accompanied by a flood of tears, but a threat to use my rifle has a quick soothing effect.'[40]

While many German troops simply did not care what consequences their behaviour held for the impoverished people, others appear to have deluded themselves that their behaviour was just. Horst Lange proudly wrote in his diary at the start of November that he and his comrades were 'thankful and correct' in their treatment of the population, but only three days later he wrote of looting a house and searching it for any valuables while the occupants looked on.[41] To the uninvolved German soldiers who were often beneficiaries of such practices there was even less cause to spare a thought for the people being condemned to hunger and starvation. Wilhelm Prüller wrote in his diary after his comrades returned from a local village: 'Mayer, Pichler and the interpreter reappeared with butter, eggs, cream, potatoes, honey and a pig. Terrific all these treats!'[42] Yet the implications of the army's extortions were never far from view for those willing to accept the consequences of German actions. As Hans Backer wrote: 'In the army there were many who sought only the opportunity to plunder and pillage. They snatched the last shreds of a livelihood from a people for whom existence was a bitter struggle made practically impossible by the additional hardships of war.'[43] If German soldiers believed there were no consequences to their actions against the Soviet populace, Backer drew another conclusion that plausibly illustrates the cycle of violence on the eastern front. After noting that anything was fair game to the German plunderers, Backer concluded: 'From this more than for any other reason the partisans gained their strength.'[44] On 13 November, a report by Lieutenant-General Wilhelm Wetzel's 255th Infantry Division, operating in the rear area of Strauss' Ninth Army, noted that soldiers 'continuously requisition and loot in the villages in a manner which embitters the population and practically drives it into the arms of the partisans'.[45]

Certainly, disaffection within the Soviet population aided the partisan movement in the autumn and winter of 1941, but it did not initially account for it. Unlike Soviet-era histories, which sought to propagate the myth of an immediate, class-engendered insurrection against German occupation, the reality in the early months of the war was that most civilian behaviour in areas under German rule was marked by an ambivalence towards, or even active opposition to, the Soviet war effort. Stalin's annexation of the Baltic states in 1940, as well as his ruthless persecution of Ukrainian peasants in the 1930s, ensured varying degrees of support for the Germans, while in Belarus and Russia, the rear area of Army Group Centre, lack of support for the German cause should not suggest a pro-Soviet sentiment. A majority of civilian households in the occupied parts of the Soviet Union had experienced the rule of the tsar, German occupation in the First World War, White Army rule in the civil war and, ultimately, Soviet communism, making the people first and foremost survivors in times of war and cautious about choosing sides too soon.[46] Even in November 1941 one could not yet speak of a popular movement towards armed resistance in the rear areas of the *Ostheer*, although the wooded regions to the east of Viaz'ma and Briansk were already extremely dangerous for isolated German units guarding strategic objectives like bridges or conveying supplies to the front.[47] The multiple Soviet armies destroyed in the October fighting may have proved a calamity for the Red Army, but it also left countless numbers of Red Army men who had slipped through the German encirclements to carry on the fight in Bock's rear.[48] Whether or not these men were, strictly speaking, 'partisans' is a moot point, but in the eyes of most German soldiers they were referred to and treated as such. Illustrative is the diary of Willi Kubik, who wrote on 30 November: 'Two partisans were shot from 100 metres away. They had Russian uniforms on.'[49]

As German soldiers typically did not distinguish between soldiers and partisans in the rear areas, the option of surrender soon became pointless. Soviet fighters responded in kind, often because they had no way of guarding German captives, but also as a reprisal or simply out of sheer hatred of the enemy. The ruthlessness and barbarity of the war behind the German front was therefore typified by desperate battles to the death, where quarter was neither given nor received and the cycle of violence fed an ever greater thirst for revenge on both sides. Indeed, given that the Soviet partisan movement was still in its nascent phase in November 1941, the real impact of its clandestine operations was probably as much psychological as it was tangible.[50] German fear of the partisans was pervasive and sometimes disproportionate in relation to the extent of the problem. One soldier wrote in a letter written on 28 November: 'New reports arrive daily of German soldiers and officers found dead, they were cut or shot in their vehicles.'[51] Similarly, Helmut Günther wrote: 'As we drew nearer to Moscow the situation became less secure. Already many a "lone traveller" had been found by his comrades with a slashed throat. There were others even less fortunate. Many simply were never seen again, simply listed as "missing!"'[52] Léon Degrelle observed that the partisans, 'were nowhere, yet they were everywhere'.[53] Wild rumours and gruesome stories led many Germans to fear partisans behind every tree, yet this often exaggerated perception, and its resultant paranoia, contributed to the ill-treatment of the civilian population, who were frequently accused of housing and protecting partisans on the flimsiest of evidence.[54]

Even if the Soviet partisan movement in 1941 was only a shadow of what it would become in later years, that is not to suggest that the problem in Army Group Centre's rear was negligible.[55] Indeed, November saw pitched battles taking place far behind the front, with a number of German divisions having to be withheld from the advance on Moscow in order to fight them.[56] Hans Meier-Welcker, a general staff

Figure 7.1 Members of the SS with a tracking dog apprehend suspected partisans (date unknown)

officer in the 251st Infantry Division, wrote on 24 and 26 November about partisan groups in the area around Viaz'ma that fought with artillery.[57] Likewise, Hans Roth wrote in his diary on 18 November of an engagement with a partisan group estimated at being some 2,000 men strong: 'We deploy our men and encounter initial exchanges with these well-armed gangs. They possess machine guns, mortars, Paks [*Panzerabwehrkanone* – anti-tank guns], and even infantry weapons. As these *schweine* are beginning to seriously threaten Lebedyn, we acquire reinforcements from Achtyrka. At one point, we even have to flee, leaving our dead and injured men behind, whom we later find mutilated like animals.'[58] Such encounters not only reflect the extent of the problem in certain areas, but Roth's account also indicates that the Wehrmacht was just as capable of waging merciless anti-partisan warfare as the notorious security divisions, order police and the SS. In the same entry for 18 November, Roth continued: 'During the afternoon, ten hostages were shot dead. We are now acting with an iron fist; the gallows in the town square is always busy. Executions are the daily norm. It has to be this way.'[59] The files of Army Group Centre's panzer forces also support this conclusion. Throughout November the war diary of Guderian's Second Panzer Army details the success of its anti-partisan campaign in the rear by listing the number of partisans shot. Interestingly, at the start of November there are reports of prisoners being taken, but later in the month reports only list how many partisans were shot with no further mention of prisoners. Thus, on 5 November, Lieutenant-General Karl von Oven's 56th Infantry Division reported killing thirty-seven partisans and capturing 136 others. The day before his units had taken another ninety-nine prisoners. Operating in the same area on 4 November elements of Major-General Heinrich Clössner's 25th Motorised Infantry Division took another 227 prisoners.[60] Yet later in the month the same war diary made no further mention of prisoners being taken. Instead, on 18 November, three partisan groups numbering an estimated 200 men were 'annihilated' by Oven's division northwest of Briansk.[61] The next day (19 November), a further sixty partisans were shot,[62] while on 20 November Clössner's division reported shooting forty-five partisans.[63] On 21 November, the two divisions listed a daily total of fifty-six partisans shot.[64] It is not clear whether those shot were as a result of battles or simply individuals arrested on the premise of being partisans; in any case, no prisoners were listed as having been taken and no German losses were recorded.

The Fourth Army reported on 26 November that three types of enemy groups were waging a partisan war in its area of operations. The first were so-called 'special battalions', consisting of two companies of partisans commanded by a staff of officers and used in major attacks against German command centres and 'important objectives'. The second were referred to as 'destruction groups', which were of varying size and used for sabotage and arson attacks. The final group, 'individual people', was said to include boys and girls, and was used for spying and arson attacks.[65] The chief-of-staff at the Fourth Army, Blumentritt, noted after the war that it was during the battle for Moscow that the partisans 'were beginning to make their presence felt'. He then continued: 'We generally lacked the means to combat them. Supply columns were frequently ambushed, and the front-line troops suffered privations in consequence.'[66] The Wehrmacht was neither trained nor equipped for counterinsurgency warfare, and one report from an intelligence officer in Stumme's XXXX Panzer Corps illustrated the extent of the problem. The man was a member of the German *Geheimen Feldpolizei* (secret field police), who dressed himself as a Russian civilian and, together with an older local man, walked around German army positions. They walked past manned guard posts, around the outside of occupied army positions and observed the possibility of passing through them. They also crossed a guarded highway bridge at night. At no time was the officer stopped, questioned or checked. As his report noted, 'none of the soldiers present in the district controlled the non-local civilians'.[67] In another revealing instance an attack on a partisan base by elements of Thoma's 20th Panzer Division killed a number of partisans who were dressed in captured German uniforms.[68]

Not only were the partisans able to move freely among the civilian population, but the German predilection for indiscriminate violence and terror (as established by War Directive 33a in July)[69] steadily eroded the support of anti-communist Russians or nationalist Ukrainians who might otherwise have provided a more robust countermovement to Soviet-controlled partisans. One Soviet agent near Smolensk reported that, in spite of the many willing collaborators in the early weeks of the war, by the autumn 'hatred of the enemy' was 'growing and growing'.[70] The treatment of those suspected of being partisans goes a long way to explaining the resentment of the Soviet population. Paul Kunze wrote home in a letter on 1 December about flogging men he suspected of being partisans to 'within an inch of their lives'. He and his comrades then conducted their interrogation, but could not make them reveal anything so they were hanged: 'What else could we do? They don't deserve any better treatment. That's how days and the weeks go by.'[71]

In November 1941, the partisan movement was ill-equipped, untrained and poorly organised, yet it was also surprisingly innovative and resourceful. In absence of weapons, tactics tended towards sabotage and arson. One simple method was to remove a single log from the corduroy roads used by the Germans so that horses would break their legs or vehicles would suffer spring and axle damage.[72] Another increasingly common method was to affix time-delayed explosives to buildings or houses, a tactic used to great effect after the German occupation of Kiev and again in November at Kursk.[73] Sabotage was also facilitated by infiltrating the new German administrative organisations. Konstantin Zaslonov, a prewar railway engineer, took an administrative position in November supervising a train depot at Orsha and promptly set about hiring dozens of his fellow partisans who used their cover to manufacture mines and set explosives. From mid-November to mid-February 1942 they caused ninety-eight derailments and destroyed or damaged some 200 locomotives.[74] Female spies were also prepared to risk their lives by seducing German soldiers and prostituting themselves for local intelligence. After witnessing the hanging of two young women one German doctor observed: 'With glowing hearts they were ready in the name of communism to sacrifice their bodies to our sex-starved troops and their lives to the hangman's noose. Many a German soldier – and no doubt many an officer – unwittingly gave away information in the warmth of a bunk on top of a Russian oven.'[75]

The Soviet government attempted to stimulate the partisan movement by parachuting supplies, radios and even determined young communists, committed to setting up new cells of resistance, into the German rear.[76] Yet the coordination of partisan actions with centralised objectives was seldom achieved in 1941, as many partisan groups had no form of communication, few weapons and were struggling to survive in the harsh winter conditions.[77] German anti-partisan operations, on the other hand, were similarly hamstrung by a lack of resources and manpower. Wetzel's 255th Infantry Division attempted, with little success, to conduct an anti-partisan sweep between 16 and 30 November. As one report suggested: 'The major operation of the 255th Infantry Division had little success since it never reached the remote villages because of the poor, snow-covered roads; the individual units contented themselves with collecting such booty in the woods as they could use themselves.'[78] In German eyes the inability to combat the partisan menace directly placed all the more emphasis on striking terror into the population. As a result, captured partisans were not just executed, their deaths were made public spectacles, with their bodies left hanging for days and weeks with signs attesting to their guilt. Erich Kern told of one man being paraded around town before his execution with a large sign written in German and Russian: 'I am the man who has been directing the Soviet artillery fire on Kherson and I am responsible for the death of sixty-three Russian women and children together with a number of German soldiers. For this I am to be hanged today.'[79] The partisans, however, were seldom intimidated and were often just as ruthless. In one instance, the Germans left a suspected partisan hanging in a public place only to discover that the next day a German soldier had been hung beside him. Such acts of defiance evoked the full fury of the German approach to pacification in the east and, in this instance, an entire village was massacred.[80]

As Army Group Centre's panzer forces struggled with all their remaining might to press home the attack on Moscow, in November they nevertheless left ample records testifying to their participation in the parallel war of unrestrained terror and cold-blooded murder in the occupied areas. A copy of Reichenau's famous order of 10 October, which called for the killing of all those suspected of partisan involvement, including Soviet soldiers captured behind the lines,[81] was subsequently circulated to all army commanders in the east[82] and appeared in the files of Stumme's XXXX Panzer Corps. On the back of the order was written: 'The fight against the partisans must be pursued with even more draconian means ... Whoever is not with us is against us!'[83] Certainly, Lemelsen's XXXXVII Panzer Corps needed no prodding and, after overrunning a partisan base and capturing fifty men, it promptly had all of them shot.[84] Such individual examples, which are found throughout Army Group Centre's corps and divisional files, illustrate the willingness of the panzer forces to use deadly force, but they only hint at the scale of the killing throughout Army Group Centre. In the course of November records indicate some 14,037 Soviet prisoners were captured in Bock's rear area (not including those taken in the drive on Moscow at the front), which attests, first, to the scale of the problem behind the front and, secondly, to the magnitude of the killing if orders like Reichenau's were being implemented.[85] Of course, even if they were not killed some time after capture, and thousands of Soviet captives were indeed processed as prisoners of war, in November 1941 their fate would scarcely have been much different given the prevailing conditions in German captivity. As Konrad Jarausch observed, 'the whole thing is already more murder than war'.[86]

Figure 7.2 The total war fought by the Soviet Union was reflected in the Red Army with boys and as well as old men pressed into service. Many of the men pictured in this group of Soviet POWs were unlikely to have survived the winter of 1941/2

Hitler's army: the German high command united over Moscow

As the battle for Moscow commanded the attention of the German high command and, erroneously, maintained their hopes for a final decisive success in 1942, on 26 November the war was set on a new path that would have devastating consequences for Germany. On the lonely Japanese island of Iturup, 7,000 km east of Moscow, the powerful Japanese First Air Fleet was setting sail from Hitokappu Bay bound for Pearl Harbor.[87] Hitler had already fatally misjudged the power of his Soviet adversary in the east and, even without forewarning of the impending Japanese attack on Pearl Harbor, he not only foresaw a coming war against the United States, but, when the time came, he initiated it.[88] Already on 22 November he had expressed to Goebbels both his confidence that Japan would soon actively join the war and that Germany would find itself fighting the might of the United States. As Goebbels was assured by Hitler: 'They [the United States] cannot change the situation on the continent [of Europe].'[89] This, of course, was true only in the delusional mind of Adolf Hitler and his devoted followers. In the mind of more objective thinkers, like Ulrich von Hassell, Germany was sliding further and further into the abyss. Writing on 30 November, Hassell noted: 'Every discerning person must see clearly that black clouds are piling up around us, in matters material, moral, and even military. The masses generally still drift along with the stream. They grumble, but are fundamentally without will or judgement. This is also true of the mass of the officer corps.'[90]

Hassell's assessment of the German officer corps, especially at the highest levels, has been borne out by recent research.[91] On 23 November, Halder gave a presentation on the state of the *Ostheer*, which, at least in part, constituted one of his more insightful assessments of the state of Germany's war in the east. Indeed, one may be tempted to concluded that Halder had undergone a change of heart regarding his previously outlandish plans for the late autumn offensive, but his ultimate conclusions pointed yet again to a disconnect between means and ends; reality and fantasy. As Hassell's analogy suggested, it was an ability to see the black clouds and yet to carry on as before. Referring to losses and the wide dispersal of the *Ostheer* throughout the east, Halder acknowledged that: 'An army, like that of June 1941, will henceforth no longer be available to us.'[92] More importantly, he was beginning to grasp that the war he was directing in the east had changed from one of rapid movement and decisive success to a war of attrition and material production. 'We must confront the possibility that neither of the main protagonists have the ability to annihilate or decisively wear down the other. It is possible that the war is shifting from the level of military success to the level of moral and economic endurance.'[93]

While Halder was aware that there was a longer-term economic dimension to victory in the east and that a force comparable to June 1941 could never again be achieved by Germany, he also understood that the Soviet Union's mass and human reserves were more than Germany could hope to conquer: 'In the endless space and inexhaustible manpower of this country it [total victory] is not likely to be 100 per cent achieved. Naturally we knew this from the beginning. In this year we will continue the attack until we have secured favourable positions for the continuation of the attack next year.'[94] What is astounding is that neither Halder nor the majority of the German high command seemed to have come to recognise what the implications of a long-term, exceptionally high-intensity contest against a country they could not hope to occupy might mean.[95] If after five months of unprecedented victories and largely favourable weather this was the outlook, what did Halder imagine his already crippled army might achieve in 1942 after more months of fighting through a Russian winter? Victory against the Soviet Union in 1941 was not just one more war aim of the Nazi state; it was the single most important military objective Nazi Germany had set itself. Germany's inadequate industrial and manpower base made a rapid triumph in a war against the Soviet Union an absolute necessity. Operation Barbarossa's failure started a haemorrhage of men and materiel that Nazi Germany could never stem, never afford and, because of its losses in 1941, never militarily overcome. Halder was correct; the *Ostheer* of June 1941 was a thing of the past and with the war now one of endurance, Germany's fate would be increasingly decided by access to raw materials, factories and manpower. Ultimately, Barbarossa's failure constituted the decisive blow, which turned the tide of the war against Nazi Germany. The recurrent discussions among military historians surrounding questions of German strategy in 1942 and 1943 are important insofar as they prolonged or shortened the war, but they are less important in deciding the ultimate outcome.

At his presentation on 23 November even an incorrigible optimist such as Halder failed to suggest any coherent path to a German victory in the east in 1942, simply making reference to continuing the advance. His one consolation was an assurance that Soviet military power was 'no longer a danger for the development of Europe'. Halder then made clear the depths of delusion with which he fortified his conception of events in the east and no doubt enhanced his appeal to Hitler. 'The enemy has been struck the decisive blow', he told his audience, 'but he is not yet annihilated.'[96] Remarkably, Halder's address had managed to identify the foundation of Germany's ultimate defeat, while concluding the exact opposite. Far from the promised decisive blow that Halder had maintained the November offensive towards Moscow could still achieve, the war would now be longer, more costly and without any clear end, but as a true Nazi officer Halder defiantly maintained an unbending will and resolute faith in victory.

For the current offensive Halder listed the following objectives: Army Group North would have to link up with the Finnish army on Lake Ladoga; Army Group Centre would have to encircle Moscow and secure the Oka and Don regions with the capture of Tula, Ryazan, Yelets and Voronezh; and Army Group South would have to seize Maykop in the Caucasus. In a testament to Halder's woeful strategic direction not one of these objectives would be achieved in 1941. Meanwhile at the front, one general staff officer assessed Germany's prospects at the end of November in the totally contrasting terms: 'There are two possibilities: Either the war will be *very* long or we will lose it before that.'[97]

While the strategic circumstances in which the battle for Moscow was taking place boded extremely ill for Germany, this did not eliminate the prospect of further operational successes. On 26 November, Reinhardt's Panzer Group 3 at last seemed to have broken the back of Soviet resistance, making, according to Bock, 'very good progress'.[98] Schaal's LVI Panzer Corps, spearheaded by Funck's 7th Panzer Division, was at last driving into open country in a headlong dash for the vital Moscow canal (stretching from the Moskva River to the Volga River 128 km to the north).[99] The canal constituted the single most important obstacle to the encirclement of Moscow from the north, but Bock was less concerned with encirclement than he was about using the canal as a shield to secure Reinhardt's left flank as he turned the panzer group due south for a direct charge on the Soviet capital. Bock's thinking seems to have been motivated by the hope of breaking the last resistance before Moscow. With Hoepner's panzer group fully committed and making only slow progress to the west of the city, Bock hoped that the commitment of Reinhardt to an attack on Moscow's northern flank might at last effect a collapse of the remaining resistance. By 27 November, the 7th Panzer Division was just 3 km from the canal,[100] and on 28 November Funck had not only reached it, but he had won a crossing at Yakhroma and immediately formed a small bridgehead on the eastern bank.

Reinhardt was keen to exploit his good fortune and unsuccessfully pressed Bock for a continuation of the advance east of the canal, however, the field marshal remained unconvinced and insisted upon the panzer group's turn southward.[101] As was not uncommon with the panzer generals, Reinhardt privately rejected his orders and simply refused to implement Bock's instructions for an attack towards the south. Yet any hopes Reinhardt may have harboured about continuing his advance to the east of the canal were soon dashed when heavy Soviet counterattacks against the newly formed bridgehead succeeded in forcing the Germans back to the western bank. Two days after issuing his orders, on 30 November, Bock enquired at Panzer Group 3 as to why no ground had been gained south of Yakhroma. It was only when Bock was able to telephone Reinhardt directly that the panzer general could finally be convinced to accept Bock's plan for a turn south. As Bock noted in his

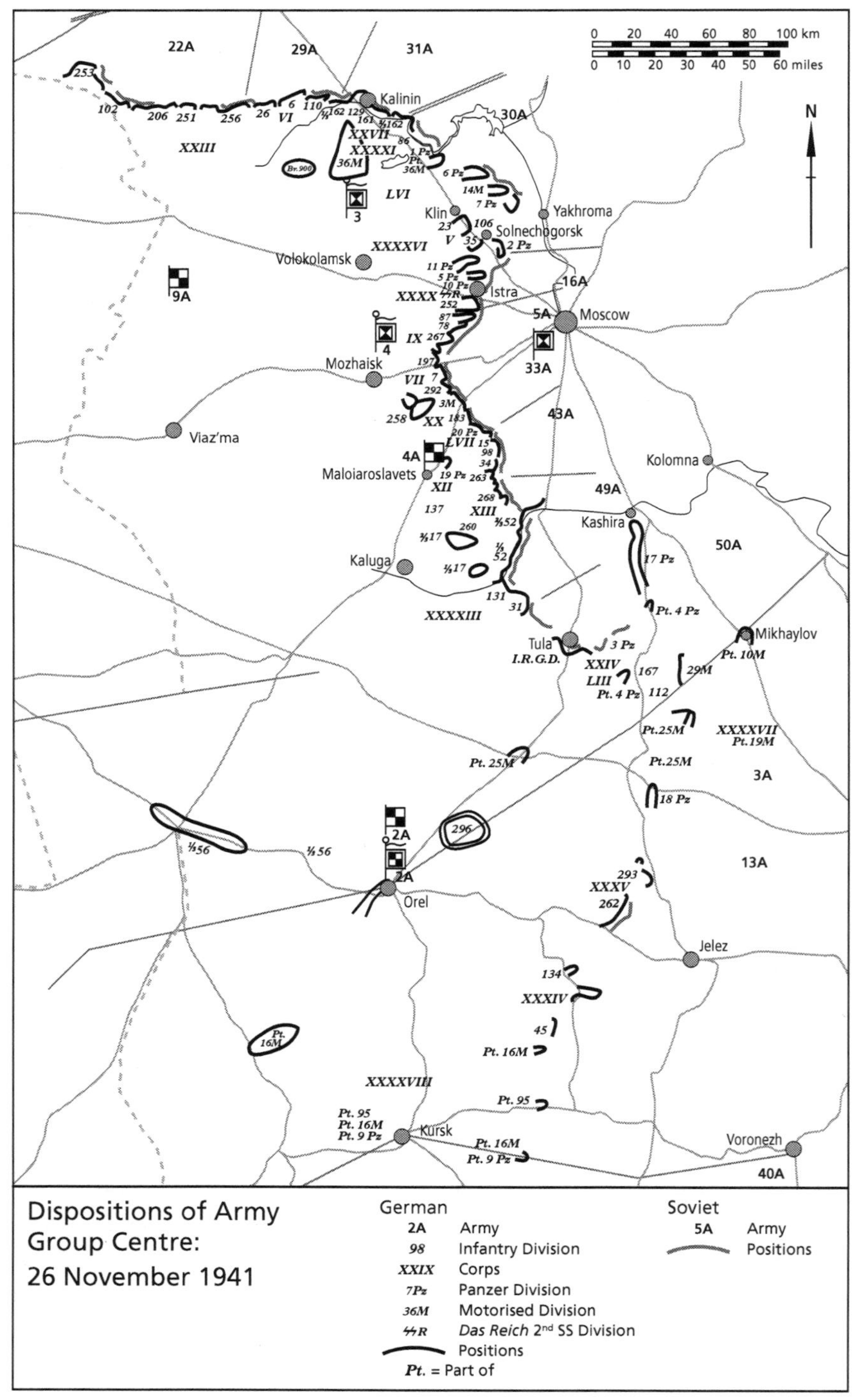

Map 7.1 Dispositions of Army Group Centre, 26 November 1941

diary: 'it was surprisingly difficult to convince him of this necessity'.[102] Yet more than forty-eight hours had now passed since the canal had been reached and the offensive could not get underway until the morning of 1 December. Moreover, the Soviet forces at Yakhroma were now pushing for a bridgehead of their own, tying up Funck's 7th Panzer Division and leaving only Landgraf's weakened 6th Panzer Division to commence the attack.

Just how battered Landgraf's division was is reflected by the fact that on 30 November its total panzer strength amounted to just four Mark II tanks. Funck's panzer division was the only formation of Schaal's LVI Panzer Corps with any real striking power (it still had thirty-six tanks; thirty-three Pz Kpfw 38(t), two Mark IIs and one Mark IV). Yet with Soviet attacks on the canal unrelenting, the only aid for the drive south had to come from Model's more northerly XXXXI Panzer Corps. His only panzer division was Krüger's 1st Panzer Division and this had thirty-seven tanks (six Mark IIs, twenty-eight Mark IIIs and three Mark IVs),[103] but it would require more time to redeploy to the south and would not see action until at least 2 December. Until then, as Reinhardt acknowledged, the combined strength of the two panzer divisions (1st and 6th) was 'only that of a reinforced panzer regiment', although even this analogy would imply many more tanks than the forty-one now committed to the offensive.[104] Indeed, the fact that Panzer Group 3 retained less than eighty serviceable tanks at the end of November speaks for itself about the *Ostheer*'s overblown expectations at the battle for Moscow.[105] Moreover, the knock-on effect of Krüger's redeployment to the south was a massive over-extension of Major-General Hans Gollnick's 36th Motorised Infantry Division, which had already been overstretched and was now a positive danger to Panzer Group 3's whole position.[106]

Illustrative of this danger is the record of Karl Knoblauch, a young non-commissioned officer, who, on 27 November, found himself in the map room of a senior officer. While awaiting his instructions, Knoblauch observed the detailed operational map and the officer on duty there. Studying the map Knoblauch decided to ask the officer how and with what the sections between the roads of advance could be secured. The officer replied that he did not know and then continued: '"Knoblauch that is not your concern. You are a non-commissioned officer not a Marshal. In Führer headquarters they will know what to do!" I agreed. My confidence in the leadership continues unabated.'[107]

While the lower ranks deferred to their high command in the vain hope that their strategic overview would yield some miraculous solution, in reality Hitler was experiencing his own doubts. Heinz Linge, Hitler's personal assistant and valet, observed how in November constant reports of the stubborn Soviet resistance affected the dictator's mood. Hitler was becoming increasingly irritable, and during situation reports vented his frustration on Halder, Brauchitsch and Keitel.[108] Indeed, there is anecdotal evidence of one of Hitler's furious outbursts being directed towards Keitel in which he hurled irate reproaches. The account of this that reached Ulrich von Hassell even suggested: 'Keitel, deeply discouraged, babbled about suicide, and took himself off to Brauchitsch. The break, however, has been healed.'[109]

Perhaps what frustrated Hitler so much was less the details of any one action than the profound implications of the *Ostheer*'s failure before Moscow. As Keitel suggested in an interview after the war: 'When we attacked Moscow we could still maintain that the balance was in our favour. Later on, however, it was realized that unless we could finish the war by winter, a new military power would arise in Russia and would oppose us.'[110] Discussing the same period in his memoir Keitel wrote that it was Hitler's nature to seek scapegoats for failure, 'and even more so if he could hardly fail to see that he himself was to blame for the failure's origins at least'.[111] Certainly, that had been the case with Rundstedt's dismissal after his retreat from Rostov, which even Hitler came to realise had been unjustified, but since he could never allow himself to be seen to have made a mistake the decision had to stand.[112] Hitler's fearsome tirades, coupled with what Rostov demonstrated to be the evident consequences of perceived disloyalty, only reinforced the culture of compliance among his inner circle. As Speer noted after the war: 'The manner in which Hitler and his entourage governed and commanded was bound to stifle gradually every free opinion. Nobody in his surroundings had the courage to put forward his opinions, let alone stand up for them. On the contrary, those who criticized lost their positions, or else fell into disgrace.'[113] Kurt Meyer, a *Brigadeführer* in the *Waffen-SS*, attended a number of conferences at Hitler's headquarters before he realised: 'that Keitel and all the people there said on principle: "Yes, my Führer!" "Yes, my Führer!" "Yes, my Führer!" No matter what he said, they replied: "Yes, my Führer!" The moment a man arrived from the front . . . Keitel and the rest tried to influence the man as to what he should say.'[114]

Thus it was in November 1941, as Germany confronted its first major reversal in the east, that the absurd spectacle of managing Hitler's mood became the priority of his military staff and information was adapted on that basis. As the middle and higher ranks of the *Ostheer* deferred their fears upwards, the OKH under Halder and Brauchitsch remained defiantly impervious to bad news, while the OKW under Keitel and General of Artillery Alfred Jodl actively filtered what they deemed acceptable for Hitler. Indeed, given Hitler's own unwillingness to accept the problems of his army, the sanitising of reports that reached him only reinforced his tendency to issue unrealistic orders. As a result, the faith of the troops in their high command was terribly misplaced and, accordingly, the ability of the men to recognise and prepare for the looming crisis the *Ostheer* confronted was decidedly impaired. As Hans von Luck, an officer with the 7th Panzer Division, recalled: 'Although catastrophe was looming, I couldn't grasp it . . . The men, as well as most of the officers, were unaware of the full extent of what was happening. For them [more immediate] problems took precedence: How can I get my vehicle back in one piece, will enough supplies come up, how can I protect myself against the barbaric cold?'[115]

While in the last days of November Reinhardt's Panzer Group 3 broke through to the Moscow canal, Hoepner's Panzer Group 4 was operating closer to Moscow, but making much slower progress. The costly frontal assaults and grinding combat through one defensive position after another were a far cry from the deep flanking operations of previous advances. Nevertheless, progress was at least still being made, which, given the conditions and state of many units, was no small achievement. On 26 November, Istra, a town only 50 km from Red Square and 35 km to the outskirts of Moscow, was taken by *Das Reich*.[116] Otto Skorzeny, the man who later undertook the Gran Sasso raid to rescue Mussolini in September 1943, wrote of days of bitter fighting to seize Istra.[117] Indeed, what was left of the town was primed with explosives in anticipation of German occupation. Explosives were found in the cellars of larger houses and Molotov cocktails hidden in the ovens of peasant huts. There were also hundreds of mines scattered about the town. In one and a half days a German engineer company in Istra removed some 1,100 mines and 250 kg of high explosives.[118] Although German troops knew to expect such traps and they caused few casualties, the Red Army nevertheless slowed the German occupation of Istra and denied Hoepner's men desperately needed shelter.

Figure 7.3 German Mark IV tanks on the attack towards Istra (25 November 1941)

Hoepner's advance was plagued by the systematic scorched-earth policy of Soviet forces, which left many German units very little shelter against the freezing conditions.[119] Nor was the destruction just taking place in front of the lines. On 27 November, the entire area of Lieutenant-General Friedrich Kirchner's LVII Panzer Corps[120] reported systematic infiltrations by specially trained enemy troops seeking to burn

German-occupied houses and vehicles.[121] Partisans were also reported as being a problem in Kirchner's rear area, but the panzer corps' ability to find them with anti-partisan sweeps met with little success, and only one group of eight people could be found and 'liquidated'.[122] With shelter for the attacking troops at a premium men were almost sleeping on top of one another. Albert Neuhaus wrote in a letter on 29 November that sixteen men were accommodated in a room measuring 6 × 6 m.[123] In another modestly sized house, Theodor Mogge, a non-commissioned artillery officer, noted that sixty men were billeted.[124] The absence of adequate shelter also acted as an incentive, driving the men on towards Moscow where it was believed they would find shelter and rest. The distance to Moscow was therefore followed with great interest among the troops and came to be seen as a kind of deliverance from the war, an end to their toils and suffering.

The allure of Moscow was therefore powerfully reinforced when in the last days of November news spread that the advanced troops could view the outer limits of the city. Otto Skorzeny's account stated that after continuing the advance from Istra, 'we reached a village only fifteen kilometres north-west of Moscow, which we could see from the church tower on clear days. Our batteries actually shelled the suburbs of the city.'[125] At the same time, Blumentritt recalled: 'Moscow was within our grasp. At night we could see the Russian anti-aircraft shells bursting above their capital.'[126] Yet Moscow was an illusion. The same handful of kilometres that separated the German troops from their great prize has been cited again and again in countless histories of the campaign to reflect the supposedly close-run battle that Moscow represents. Yet merely reaching the city is in no way comparable to capturing it, and one does not need the benefit of hindsight to see what a major city battle on the eastern front would mean. Stalingrad may not yet have seen a shot fired in anger, but the *Ostheer* already had the smaller examples of Mogilev in July, Dnepropetrovsk in August, Leningrad in September, Kalinin in October and Tula in November to see how costly urban warfare against a determined defender could be. Thus, German forces were undoubtedly close to Moscow, but still a long way from seriously contesting control of the city, which was a veritable fortress by December 1941 and would have proved harder to seize for the under-strength German divisions than anything, including Stalingrad, that was witnessed during the war. Indeed, the fact that only a handful of German units even reached the outer limits of the city speaks to the difficulty of

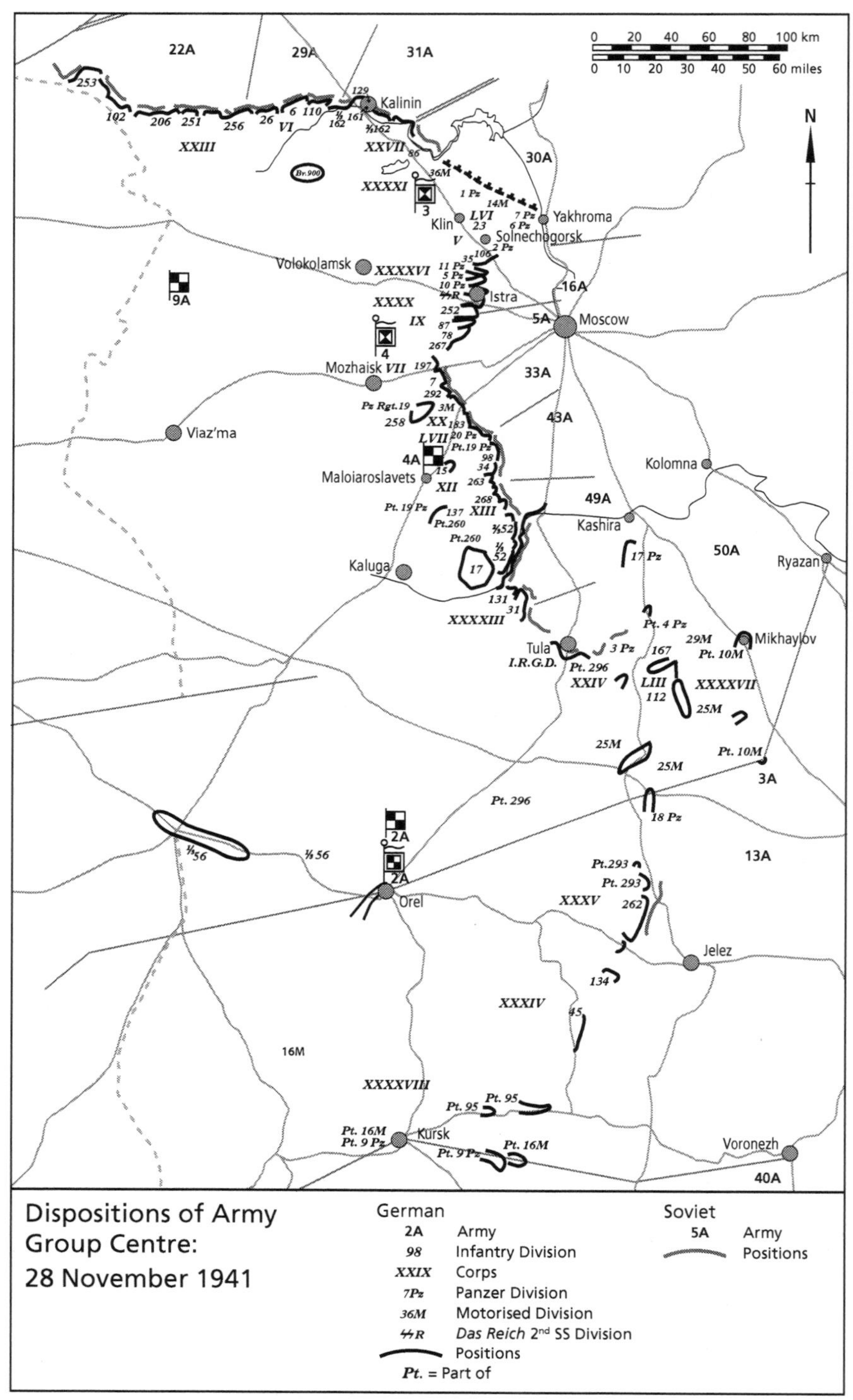

Map 7.2 Dispositions of Army Group Centre, 28 November 1941

Moscow's seizure and the distance Army Group Centre was from ever achieving it. As Skorzeny's memoir observed, after having observed Moscow and shelled its suburbs 'our offensive came to an end at this point. Our neighbour, the 10th Armoured Division, had only a dozen battle-worthy tanks left and most of our guns were without tractors.'[127]

In fact, on 28 November, Fischer's 10th Panzer Division had just twenty serviceable tanks, but that was not even the weakest panzer division in Hoepner's panzer group. Scheller's 11th Panzer Division fielded just fifteen tanks and even Fehn's 5th Panzer Division, which started the November offensive with an estimated 150 tanks (no exact figures are available), was now reduced to seventy.[128] Veiel's 2nd Panzer Division, which fielded 134 tanks in early November (and probably more by the start of the offensive) was now at fifty-four tanks (thirteen Mark IIs, thirty-nine Mark IIIs and two Mark IVs). It was a rate of attrition which was entirely unsustainable, and meant that between both Reinhardt's and Hoepner's panzer groups the German drive on Moscow counted only some 235 tanks by the last days of November; by way of comparison this was weaker than the equivalent strength of any individual panzer division in Panzer Group 3 on 22 June 1941.[129] On 27 November, Wagner, the army's senior Quartermaster-General, who at the start of November Goebbels had praised as 'a man with excellent nerves, who know what he wants and does not let anything get him down',[130] reported to Halder that the army was 'at the end of our personnel and material strength'.[131] This was also the unmistakable conclusion of many of the men at the front. On 29 November, Wilhelm Schröder, fighting in Fischer's 10th Panzer Division noted in a letter: 'The assault continues – but in what conditions! The enemy tanks are inflicting enormous losses. Many of our companies have fewer than ten men left – my own is down to one officer and seven men. And in the fierce cold, we are losing more and more of our comrades to frostbite.'[132]

Tellingly on the same day (29 November) Bock called Halder to express his own mounting doubts about the continuation of the offensive. Bock explained that if the Soviet front northwest of Moscow did not collapse in the next few days the whole attack would have to be called off. Otherwise, according to Bock, this would only lead to a 'soulless frontal clash with an enemy who it seems commands inexhaustible reserves of men and material; it must not come to a second Verdun'.[133] Bock's fear of a second Verdun was entirely justified, although it is hard to see how such a conclusion could for so long have been avoided and even now was only something Bock identified as a future danger. His relentless pursuit of a frontal offensive had already blunted his panzer corps and bled his infantry divisions white, while the freezing conditions were extracting their own toll. Moreover, if the First World War battle earned its bloody reputation for casualties by grinding attacks on and around the fortifications of Verdun, then Bock's analogy would have been dwarfed by what awaited at Moscow. Beyond just the attrition at the front, it must also be remembered that Army Group Centre's drive on Moscow was taking place on a shoestring of supplies, with extremely limited levels of motorisation and significant parts of the army group dangerously over-extended. Thus, if the Red Army indeed possessed the seemingly inexhaustible reserves of men and material that Bock suggested it did, the risk of a Soviet counteroffensive should have been more seriously considered.

As Bock pondered the prospect of a 'second Verdun', Hoepner's Panzer Group 4 was still attacking to the east, but from its starting lines east of Volokolamsk and Mozhaisk the German line had only gained about 60 km in two weeks. In the same period, Reinhardt's Panzer Group 3 had started from a line further north and had advanced about 90 km. This meant an average daily advance of 4 km for Hoepner and 6 km for Reinhardt.[134] By comparison with June, when the November distances were achieved in two or three days and at a far lower cost in men and material, the era of blitzkrieg was clearly over. As were the rapid advances and large enemy encirclements. Between 15 and 28 November Kluge's Fourth Army (to which Hoepner was subordinated) captured a total of 18,187 Soviet POWs, while Reinhardt's panzer group took just 4,750 enemy prisoners. These were a fraction of the totals from previous German offensives, while the figures for captured or destroyed Soviet tanks were now much closer to German losses (about double) with 585 Soviet tanks lost to date during the offensive northwest of Moscow.[135] It was hardly an offensive that promised to deliver any kind of decisive result. On the contrary, it must have heartened the Red Army to see that they were at last coming to grips with a major German offensive even if they were still losing ground.

At the OKH on 30 November Buhle, the chief of the OKH's Organisation Branch, informed Halder that the *Ostheer*, having already absorbed the available reserves of the Replacement Army over the summer, was short 340,000 men. Moreover, he reported that infantry divisions were at half of their established combat strength and that companies averaged between fifty and sixty men. Buhle also reported that plans were afoot to establish three new panzer divisions (to be designated the 22nd, 23rd and 24th) and that new vehicles already existed for all three. There were also plans for two motorised infantry divisions to be transformed into panzer divisions for which 50 per cent of the vehicles could be supplied. Another four infantry divisions were to be rebuilt as motorised divisions, again with 50 per cent of the vehicles at hand. Buhle also reported that 75 per cent of the vehicles were available for the reconstitution of two veteran panzer divisions. However, with outstanding production, training and organisation all these new divisions would require time to assemble. Buhle concluded that the first divisions would, at the earliest, be available by the start of February and that the rest would be available in the middle of May 1942. In a best case scenario, Buhle stated that four panzer divisions could be made ready for the eastern front by the end of March.[136] With everything committed to the battle for Moscow the assembly of a strategic reserve would take months to achieve, but in keeping with the Wehrmacht's high-risk method of warfare, no thought was given to the possibility of a Soviet winter offensive.

One man who was not quite so inclined towards risk as his fellow generals was the commander of the Fourth Army, Kluge, who had from the beginning of the November offensive resisted committing all his forces.[137] His hesitancy has found its fair share of critics both among his fellow generals as well as historians,[138] but beyond the simplistic explanations for his caution (supposedly attributable to him being an 'infantry general'), Kluge's tentativeness was an indication of his contrasting strategic assessment. In short, by the end of November, Kluge saw little chance of his army's commitment making any substantive difference to Army Group Centre's offensive, and he was very worried that even more losses to his under-strength divisions would endanger his lines over the coming winter. Thus, Kesselring's assessment that Kluge was 'more pushed than pushing' to join the offensive is quite accurate.[139] Kluge was, however, hardly an idle observer of the November offensive. Kluge commanded Hoepner's Panzer Group 4 as well as the v Army Corps in the offensive, so the outstanding question was not whether Fourth Army should join the attack – it was already committed with its best forces – but only whether the weak left wing of the army should also now be committed. As Hoepner's attack waned the panzer group commander repeatedly urged this course of action in order to apply maximum pressure to the Soviet front, but in fact very little could be expected from this attack. Indeed, the very notion that Kluge somehow compromised the success of Army Group Centre's drive on Moscow by not committing his left wing earlier largely overstates the strength and importance of the forces involved.

Clearly, no stone was to be left unturned in the commitment of resources to the attack on Moscow, and Kluge's left wing, as the last remaining forces that could conceivably have been committed, was coming under increasing scrutiny from the high command. As pressure mounted on Kluge, he had many conversations with his chief-of-staff, Blumentritt, about the prospect of committing the remainder of his army. As Blumentritt recounted: 'night after night von Kluge and I sat up late discussing whether it would be wise or not ... after five or six days discussion and investigation von Kluge decided to make a final effort'.[140] Ultimately, Kluge's decision may simply have been determined by the inevitability of an order arriving from above as there was increasing impatience, even exasperation, at Kluge's vacillation. On 29 November, Hoepner complained to Bock that the Soviets were concentrating more and more forces against his front and appealed for the Fourth Army's left wing to join the attack in the south. Later in the day Bock noted that: 'Kluge subsequently decided to order the attack for the 1st [of December] "provided that he wasn't forbidden to do so". He is aware of the dangers a failed attack brings with it given our reduced combat strength.'[141] Thus, Kluge opted to throw in his lot with the prevailing wisdom of the German command, as if that was the only sensible solution to the army's reduced combat strength. Indeed, for all the postwar disagreements among the German commanders about who was to blame for which decision at Moscow, one should note that late November 1941 bears few comparisons in the Second World War for the degree of unity found between Hitler, the OKW, the OKH and the field commanders.

With Kluge's agreement the Fourth Army was set to attack on the left on 1 December and, accordingly, Greiffenberg, the chief-of-staff at Army Group Centre, informed Halder: 'I have given my consent, because it is certain that the enemy is shifting forces north from the central and southern fronts of the Fourth Army and because the army group believes that the Supreme Command is very keen that the Russian continues to be attacked even at the risk of the units burning themselves out.' Halder's reply is also recorded: 'This assessment agrees in every point with the Army High Command.'[142] Perhaps the most worrying assessment of all was not the implications of yet another German offensive, but rather the intelligence reports reaching Halder on 29 November suggesting a Soviet offensive was in the offing. Even before his telephone conversation with Greiffenberg, Halder noted in his diary that the enemy was proving livelier in front of Kluge's army. He then continued: 'Enemy offensive preparations are being spoken of.'[143]

8 THE FROZEN OFFENSIVE

Iron crosses and iron resolve: Bock's relentless attack

While there were limited indications to suggest a potential Soviet counter-offensive around Moscow, it was not a prospect that was taken seriously within the German command. After all, if the battle for Moscow was to be decided by the last battalion, it was simply inconceivable to anyone in a position of authority that the *Stavka* could possess the strength both to hold the weight of Army Group Centre at bay, while at the same time marshalling reserves for a substantive offensive of its own. German intelligence compiled by Kinzel's Foreign Armies East also dismissed the prospect of a major Soviet offensive by concluding on 22 November that the movement of Soviet forces from quiet sectors to endangered ones indicated the Western Front 'probably had no more reserves available aside from those that had already been brought from the Far East'.[1] By contrast, Zhukov stated after the war that the 'counteroffensive had been prepared all through the defensive actions', while German forces had been 'bled white' by their constant attacks.[2] In fact in the last week of November the *Stavka* began transporting five of the new reserve armies, formed behind the Volga River, to the front lines.[3] Three of these, the Twenty-Fourth, Twenty-Sixth and Sixtieth, took up positions east of Moscow, while the remaining two were sent south. The Tenth Army was deployed west of the Oka River, downstream from Kashira, to defend both Kolomna and Ryazan from Guderian's panzer army, while the last Soviet army, the Sixty-First, was committed behind the right flank of the South-Western Front.[4] The existence of these armies remained unknown to the German high command[5] and, even without them, Halder predicted in a presentation to Hitler on 19 November that the Red Army would number some 150 divisions along with twenty to thirty tank brigades by 1942. At the same time, the *Ostheer* was predicted to total only about 122 divisions (infantry, motorised, panzer, SS, mountain and security).[6] The resurgence of the Red Army did not begin in late 1942 or even 1943; it was already underway in late 1941 and, what was worse for the German high command, even with the imposing, yet incomplete, figures before them, they continued to dismiss the concept out of hand as well as its implications.

While the deployment of Soviet reserve armies was mainly dictated by Zhukov's plan for the forthcoming winter offensive, there was also an interim need to counter some of the more threatening German spearheads. The defence of Kashira, for example, acquired vital importance once Guderian had recovered his nerve and committed Eberbach's battle group to reach the railway line between Kolomna and Ryazan. Eberbach had forced a hole in the Soviet line and his advance made good progress on 25 and 26 November in spite of retaining only a handful of operational tanks in Licht's 17th Panzer Division.[7] While Eberbach's achievement looked good on the map, there was almost no muscle behind it, and as Bock noted on 26 November 'the Russians are moving in forces from all sides against the Eberbach Brigade driving towards Kashira'.[8] As one may expect from Guderian's panzer troops, the evident danger was no reason to abandon the operation and Eberbach's battle group charged head-long into the battle with numerically superior Soviet forces. The result was recorded in Bock's diary on 27 November: 'Black day for 2nd Panzer Army! ... The enemy pushed very hard from the north through Kashira against the spearhead of Panzer Brigade Eberbach.'[9] The offensive was stopped dead and Licht's panzer division would shortly be fighting a running defensive battle back down the route of his recent advance. Nor was it just the end of the drive on Kashira that caused Bock dismay. An attempted encirclement of the 239th Siberian Rifle Division near Stalinogorsk had been broken with heavy casualties when the Soviets charged the thin lines of Major-General Max Fremerey's 29th Motorised Infantry Division. As Guderian explained following his personal investigation:

> I went by way of the divisional headquarters to the hardest hit of the regiments, Infantry Regiment 71. At first I was of the opinion that a failure of reconnaissance and security arrangements had been the

> cause of the misfortune. Reports by the battalion and company commanders, however, made it quite clear that the troops had done their duty and had been simply overwhelmed by numerical superiority. The great number of dead, all in full uniform and with their weapons in their hand, were grim proof of the truth of what I had heard. I did my best to encourage the badly shaken soldiers and help them get over their misfortune. The Siberians – though without their heavy weapons and vehicles – had slipped away because we had just not had the strength to stop them.[10]

If a lone Soviet division, forsaking its own heavy weapons and vehicles, could not be contained there can be no question of the decline in strength of German units as well as their ability to perform the very encirclements that were the hallmark of their former success. It also placed a large question mark over Guderian's attempts to cut off the Soviet industrial city of Tula, which he now considered his 'most urgent task'.[11] Indeed, the same day that Bock declared Second Panzer Army's 'black day' (27 November), Heinrici's XXXXIII Army Corps opened its attack north of Tula, attempting to drive eastward and help to encircle the city, yet the offensive gained almost no ground. Guderian, like Hoepner, chose to see this failure not as a result of German weakness or Soviet strength, but rather as a result of the inaction of Kluge's right wing. Guderian, away touring the front, had his chief-of-staff, Colonel Kurt Freiherr von Liebenstein, call Bock and instruct him that 'the panzer army would have to call off the operation [towards Tula] if the right wing of the Fourth Army did not attack across the Oka [River] "without delay"'.[12] Liebenstein also requested that Lieutenant-General Wilhelm Stemmermann's 296th Infantry Division be sent to Second Panzer Army as reinforcement for the Tula operation. Bock replied that both requests were 'out of the question', but nevertheless instructed Liebenstein that 'the panzer army is to see through the battle for Tula as well as screen to the east and north'.[13] At all levels the German command was seemingly incapable of recognising or accepting its inherent weakness. According to Hoepner and Guderian, the inaction of Fourth Army's feeble right wing was responsible for both the stalled attack on Moscow as well as on Tula, which grossly overstates the importance of Kluge's forces.[14] Indeed, Bock noted with a measure of exasperation on 30 November: 'Certain qualities seem to be organically linked with the position of commander of a panzer group!'[15] Yet Bock was hardly any better.

Unable to offer his subordinates substantive reinforcements or move Kluge's army into action any faster, he still insisted that the increasingly futile frontal attacks towards Moscow and Tula continue unabated.

As bad as the perception of events at the front was, the OKH outdid even the field commanders in their singular neglect of strategic realities. The information passed on to Hitler's headquarters from the OKH was again filtered through the dictator's own military staff, meaning that Hitler's already over-optimistic outlook was only encouraged. On 30 November, Bock received word from Heusinger at the OKH that Hitler believed Second Panzer Army's attack to be 'too weak' and that at least one corps from Fourth Army's right wing was now to advance as part of the attack so as to facilitate encirclements. Heusinger then made the extraordinary statement 'that the present attack was only supposed to be the prelude to attacks on Voronezh and Yaroslavl!'[16] Voronezh was no less than 150 km to the east of Schmidt's Second Army, and Yaroslavl was 250 km northeast of Strauss' Ninth Army at Kalinin. The same ruinous dispersal that had plagued Army Group Centre's drive on Moscow in October was once again a feature of discussions within the high command – and this at the end of November with the offensive already stalled. Bock resolved to call Brauchitsch and outline just how limited the offensive strength of his army group had become. Recording the conversation in his diary Bock wrote:

> I had already instructed Guderian to concentrate his forces [at Tula] but that I was unsettled by his opinion concerning the Fourth Army's attack. I had pointed out verbally and in writing that the [right wing of Fourth] army was exhausted and that the best that it might do would be to somehow get the attack south of the highway going by exploiting tactically favourable opportunities, in order to relieve the attack north of the highway. An 'encirclement' of the enemy would require forces that I no longer have.[17]

Clearly, local, tactical successes were the best that could be expected from Kluge's right wing, and whether this would have any real impact on Hoepner's drive on Moscow or Guderian's encirclement of Tula was highly questionable. Accordingly, the idea that these operations might only be the prelude to Army Group Centre's resumption of wide-ranging advances over hundreds of kilometres was nothing short of ridiculous, especially since such plans had been proven to be excessively optimistic so

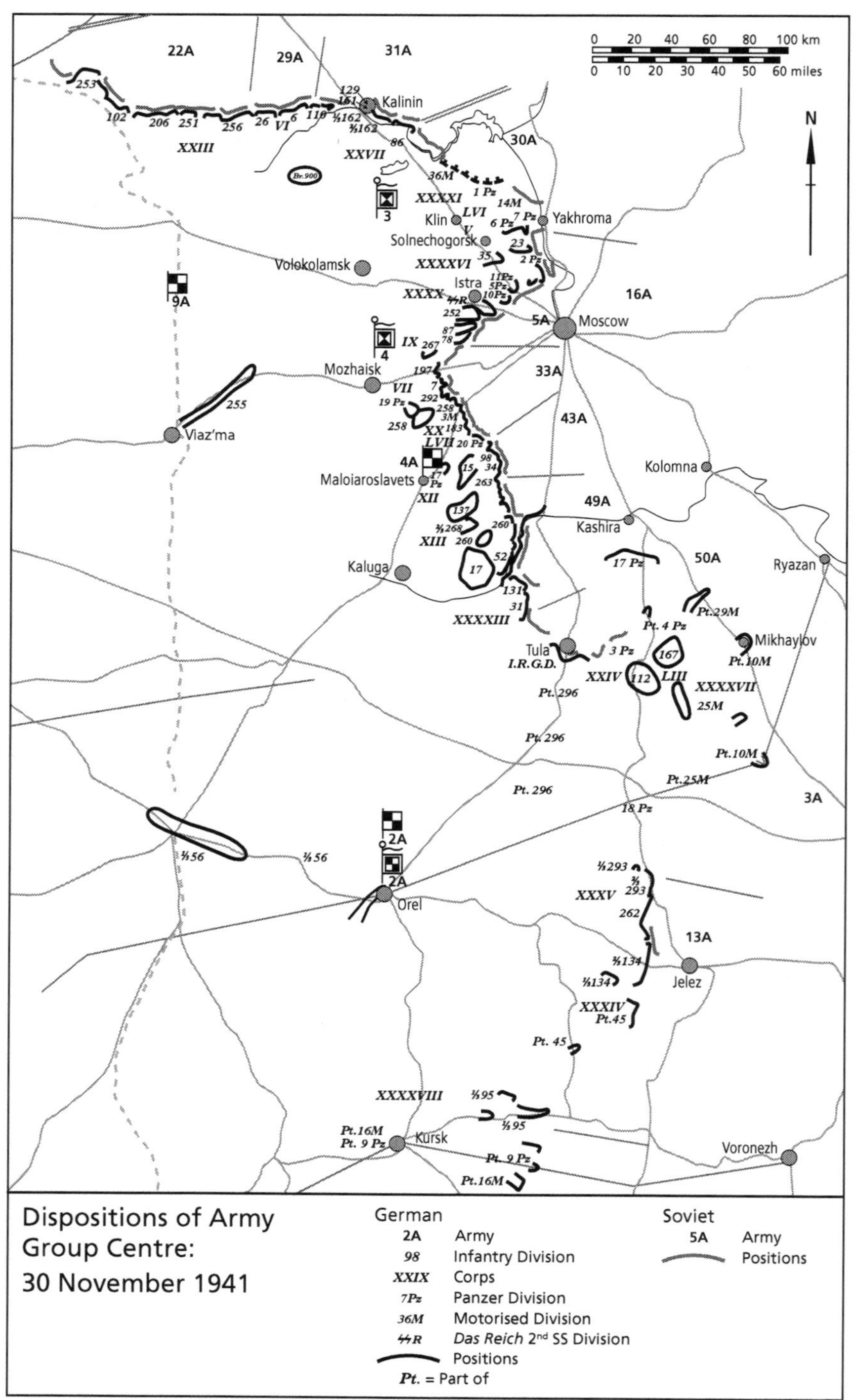

Map 8.1 Dispositions of Army Group Centre, 30 November 1941

often before. As Bock explained to Brauchitsch, 'I repeatedly have the impression of a false assessment of my fighting strength.' He then summed up his conversation with the Commander-in-Chief of the Army by stating: 'Several times I had to ask if Brauchitsch was even still listening and only at the end did he pose the surprising question of whether the attack had been ordered and for when. Something isn't right there.'[18] In fact, there were many things that were not right, and not only at the OKH.

By 30 November, Breith's 3rd Panzer Division fielded twenty-eight operational tanks, Langermann-Erlancamp's 4th Panzer Division had twenty and Licht's 17th Panzer Division retained just ten tanks.[19] All these divisions fell under the command of Schweppenberg's XXIV Panzer Corps and would be directed to attempt a link-up with Heinrici's XXXXIII Army Corps north of Tula.[20] Yet Schweppenberg's artillery could only muster a total of eleven guns,[21] and the combat units had seen no replacements for their losses since October or in other cases since September. In fact, by the end of November the Second Panzer Army had sustained a total of almost 50,000 casualties since the opening of the campaign in the east, and even when there were reserves arriving from the Replacement Army there had never been enough to cover Guderian's losses.[22] Indeed, for all the effort and expenditure of Guderian's November offensive his panzer army had only taken a total of 10,140 Soviet POWs by 28 November.[23] By contrast, the cost to the long-suffering men of the panzer army forced many to the edge of despair. Ernst Guicking wrote home to his wife on 26 November: 'One would think that even the noise of battle would come to an end. But each night the Russians begin again to thunder away, shells burst around us and often wake us from sleep. They give us no rest . . . It is really high time that we get out of here. I do not even want to think about it. It only makes you crazy.'[24]

Between 15 and 28 November Army Group Centre took a total of 44,191 Soviet POWs and captured or destroyed 729 tanks, 202 guns and 150 anti-tank guns.[25] Such figures reflect the changed method in the conduct of German offensive operations, with frontal attacks netting far fewer prisoners. Soviet equipment losses, on the other hand, especially in tanks, reinforce the view that veteran German combat units retained a decisive tactical superiority over the less experienced units of the Red Army. German successes on the battlefield, however, still extracted a high toll, which could in no way be reconciled with the grand objectives being set by the high command. In the two weeks of Bock's offensive Army Group Centre had lost at least 300 tanks as well as some 33,000 men, and yet they had not even reached Moscow to say nothing of encircling or conquering it.[26]

Even as losses mounted at the front, the month of November saw even more men killed behind the German lines as freezing conditions, malnutrition, disease and wanton brutality combined to decimate the Soviet POW populations. Konrad Jarausch, who worked in one of the camps, wrote in a letter on 14 November how the drop in temperature to -12°C affected the prisoners.

> they stagger, fall over, and expire right at our feet. We discovered another case of cannibalism today. Yet the corpses, when they are carried without clothes to the graves, are scrawny like late gothic figures of Christ, frozen stiff. The soldiers look somewhat better because they have their uniforms. There are civilians among the prisoners, many who are just in shirtsleeves – especially the Jews. It would really be the most merciful thing if they would be taken out into the forest and bumped off, as the experts put it.[27]

Understanding the extent of the neglect, Jarausch explained in another letter towards the end of November that his unit was responsible for between 16,000 and 18,000 prisoners and yet had only five Germans in the administration and kitchens. Moreover, there were only eight guards, leading Jarausch to conclude: 'You can imagine that we had to beat and shoot.'[28] The extent of the killing is illustrated by the fact that Jarausch's camp was only one of many in Army Group Centre's rear area and by no means the largest. Indeed, when in early December a new Wehrmacht inspector arrived to visit the site of Jarausch's camp he responded to the request for extra resources with the simple statement: 'We need people in such positions who have robust natures who aren't shaken when a few hundred prisoners die.'[29]

There can be no doubt that such treatment reflected a purposeful German policy rather than circumstances beyond the Wehrmacht's control. On 24 November, Herman Göring bragged that Russian POWs were so hungry that they were eating each other, as well as at least one sentry at a camp. The disgusted Italian foreign minister, Galeazzo Ciano, noted in his diary: 'He [Göring] recounted the incidents with the most absolute indifference ... And we are in the year of grace 1941.'[30] Even at Bock's headquarters in Smolensk the death rate at a nearby POW camp (*Dulag 126*) was well known. On 13 November, Army Group Centre's war diary recorded that out of a population of approximately 15,000 POWs at *Dulag 126* about 100 inmates were dying every day.[31] Even the brave attempts of Soviet civilians to feed or offer water to their countrymen through the camp fences provoked shootings or savage beatings.[32] Conditions were so appalling that some POWs begged their German guards just to shoot them – and their requests were sometimes granted. Indeed, the value of Soviet lives was illustrated by a reprisal action in which some 4,000 POWs were murdered for the killing of six men from Josef 'Sepp' Dietrich's 1st SS Division *Leibstandarte*.[33] In another instance, Albert Neuhaus wrote home to his wife on 9 November about an entire column of Soviet POWs being shot. No explanation for this was given, but Neuhaus concluded: 'As a result of what one sees and experiences here one becomes harder in spirit.'[34]

The treatment of Soviet POWs gave Churchill cause to counter the widespread view that German soldiers acted honourably with regard to their British POWs, which, he believed, encouraged his troops towards being far too amenable to the idea of surrender. Although conditions would generally remain much more humane for non-Slavic soldiers throughout the war, Churchill deplored the popular perception of chivalrous German treatment and railed against newspaper reports to this effect: 'These beastly Huns are murdering people wholesale in Europe and have committed the most frightful atrocities in Russia, and it would be entirely in accordance with their technique to win a reputation for treating British ... soldiers with humanity on exceptional and well-advertised occasions.'[35] Yet, while the British public had to be convinced of the German army's barbarity, no such doubts deluded the minds of Soviet civilians in the occupied areas. Indeed, one German soldier's letter from late November spoke of non-combatant Russian men being seized from the newly occupied zones and press-ganged into labour battalions for the rear. The practice was justified on the grounds that it both prevented their mobilisation by Soviet forces should the Red Army reoccupy a town or a village and that it freed German troops from labour-intensive projects like road building.[36] Dragooning Soviet civilians into forced-work details was only the beginning of their ordeal under the Germans. It was the nature of the work that they were expected to perform that determined just how fortunate they were, and road construction was a relatively benign form of employment. Manually clearing minefields was among the most feared details, but even that was trumped by a number of cases in which Soviet civilians were used as

Figure 8.1 One of the most immediate problems for Army Group Centre in November 1941 was the lack of roads. Such labour-intensive projects often saw Soviet POWs pressed into construction details to build corduroy roads

human shields by advancing German troops. The Soviet attitude to this was entirely predictable and Stalin soon issued orders for the Red Army to ruthlessly gun down any civilians used for this purpose.[37] Clearly, the needs of the *Ostheer* trumped any consideration for the welfare of its POWs or its obligations towards the civilian population. Furthermore, such behaviour, which had been evident since the first days of the German invasion and was frequently publicised by the Soviet state media, was now a powerful motivating force for the Red Army.[38]

Another source of inspiration for the Red Army was the dominance of the Soviet air force throughout the period of Germany's November/December offensive. According to Soviet sources, in the twenty-day period between 15 November and 5 December 1941 Soviet aircraft flew 15,840 sorties against just 3,500 German sorties.[39] Moreover, while Soviet sources typically overstate German figures in 1941 in order to explain their reverses they nevertheless point to a large numerical superiority in aircraft on the Moscow front. While the Soviet capital was defended by some 1,200 Soviet aircraft, German figures are assessed at only 700.[40] More recent scholarship suggests that the numerical gap was even wider. While Bock is said to have possessed some 580 aircraft, Soviet airfields opposite Army Group Centre may have held as many as 1,393 aircraft.[41] Nevertheless, German intelligence maintained that 'the Red Air Force is materially [i.e., the quality of its aircraft] and with regards to its training clearly inferior to the German'.[42] While this may have been true, it took no account of seasonal factors, which affected the Luftwaffe as never before. Importantly, German airfields were, for the most part, extremely primitive. Many had been left ruined by the retreating Red Army in October, and some had been attacked and damaged by German planes during the fighting. As a result, facilities were rudimentary at best and with the severity of the oncoming winter (where temperatures in some areas dropped to -30°C[43]) maintaining the serviceability of aircraft became a losing battle. While many Soviet aircraft had the benefit of Moscow's numerous airports with control towers, floodlights, sealed runways and protective hangers, German airfields were cratered by bombing, exposed to the elements and without running water, heating or electricity. Starting aircraft engines, especially the liquid-cooled engines, became nearly impossible, while ground crews had to work in sub-zero temperatures where skin froze to metal and aircraft tyres became brittle and shredded on the rutted and uneven airfields.[44] As one German pilot noted: 'We have few aircraft. In temperatures like these engines are short-lived.'[45] The absence of airfield lighting and the shortage of daylight hours reduced flying times for the Luftwaffe dramatically, and even when the sun crept above the horizon sorties often had to be cancelled on account of thick fog. In such conditions German intelligence was again proven to be wide of the mark. Soviet aircraft and their crews were far better suited to these conditions and many of their airfields remained operational round the clock.[46] Not surprisingly, the implications for Bock's offensive were profound.

Part of Army Group Centre's problem was the loss of Kesselring's Air Fleet 2 with Loerzer's II Air Corps, all of which had been reassigned to the Mediterranean. This left just Richthofen's VIII Air Corps, which after months of persistent combat was in poor condition and failing to adapt to the winter weather. On 3 December, for example, only sixteen of Richthofen's aircraft could be launched and five days later just three would see service.[47] The rapid decline of the *Ostheer* and the inability of the German war economy to replace its high rate of loss was, in every sense, matched by the weakening of the Luftwaffe. Indeed, on 17 November 1941, Colonel-General Ernst Udet, the Director-General of Equipment for the Luftwaffe, committed suicide because of mounting pressure over his department's inability to balance the alarming disparity between planned and actual aircraft production.[48] The discrepancy was an issue even before Barbarossa began, but the eastern campaign dramatically exacerbated the problem to the point where, by December 1941, the Luftwaffe was at 63 per cent of its authorised strength, down from 94 per cent in March. The German bomber force was the worst hit with just 468 serviceable planes from what should have been 1,950 (24 per cent of authorised strength).[49] Even worse, the production of a new generation of dangerously unstable aircraft, improperly tested and rushed into mass production (notably the Me 210, He 177 and Ju 288) ensured that a great deal of time, resources, factory space and skilled labour were allocated to production that never justified the investment.[50] All of which further underscored the hopeless disadvantage Germany confronted in matching Allied aircraft production.[51]

As aircraft numbers declined throughout the second half of 1941, the attrition among Germany's top fighter aces also continued unabated. Foremost among these was the top-scoring Colonel Werner Mölders with 101 official 'victories'.[52] He was killed in an aircraft crash on route to Udet's funeral. On 4 November, Karl-Heinz Leesmann, a thirty-two victory ace, was badly wounded by Soviet ground fire and never flew again. Nine days later (on 13 November), Edmund Wagner, a fifty-five victory ace, was killed in a dogfight with Soviet Pe-2s and a I-153 fighter.[53] As Kesselring concluded of his last days of service on the eastern front: 'Even a powerful air force could not have helped the frozen and weakened German front decisively against an almost invisible enemy; it was less to be expected of a weak and overtired air force.'[54] By 27 November, the chief of the operations department of the Luftwaffe, Major-General Hoffman von Waldau, commented in his diary that he no longer believed in success at Moscow, 'the troops are quite done', he concluded.[55] The fact that it took Waldau until late November to reach this conclusion (and others in the Luftwaffe were yet to be convinced) only confirms another parallel with the army: that the focus on tactical proficiency came at the expense of strategic competence.[56]

By the end of November the reality of the Luftwaffe's decline was reflected in the combat reports of Army Group Centre's panzer forces. Reinhardt's Panzer Group 3 complained on 25 November about the constant aerial attacks against its forces, resulting in the loss of many vehicles and opposed only by 'very few' German fighters.[57] In a single day (30 November), Funck's 7th Panzer Division reported that its panzer regiment had come under no less that eighteen separate aerial attacks,[58] while on 27 November Landgraf's 6th Panzer Division reported Soviet bombing or strafing attacks every fifteen minutes.[59]

Figure 8.2 Hitler at the state funeral of Germany's top fighter ace, Colonel Werner Mölders, who died on 28 November 1941. (From the right: Field Marshal Erhard Milch, Hitler's accompanying doctor *SS-Sturmbannführer* Dr Karl Brandt, Adolf Hitler, Hitler's Adjutant *SS-Gruppenführer* Julius Schaub and the head of the Party Chancellery *SS-Obergruppenführer* Martin Bormann.)

Similar reports were made by Hoepner's Panzer Group 4 where in places 'heavy losses by the troops resulted, hindering our advance. Our fighter strength is numerically too weak.'[60] Exactly why German fighter cover was so weak is described in the journal of Karl Knoblauch, who wrote on 19 November: 'Heavy snow fall and the resulting bad visibility make flying impossible. In these temperatures between minus 30 and 40 degrees the technical personnel are hardly able to make the machines combat ready.'[61] Geyer's IX Army Corps reported that Soviet bombers had targeted German-held villages leading to 'various losses'. Yet, knowing that the corps' problems would not attract sufficient attention by Richthofen's hard pressed VIII Air Corps, Geyer requested that German planes merely fly over his air space while heading to or from more important sectors.[62] The war diary of Veiel's 2nd Panzer Division included a request from the VIII Air Corps to distinguish its front-line positions better as low cloud and heavy fog made visibility very difficult, especially since German soldiers were adopting the white camouflage, and even captured Soviet winter uniforms, that had until recently helped to denote the Red Army's positions.[63] On the other hand, one may well consider that with the infrequency of the Luftwaffe's operations a degree of confusion between Soviet and German lines might at least help to deflect some Soviet attacks onto their own lines. Indeed, on the following day (28 November) Veiel's panzer division reported: 'Throughout the whole day continuous bombing attacks on all parts of the div[ision]. Absolute Russian air superiority despite Luftwaffe activity. At the spear-heads there were no German fighters observed.'[64] With the dominance of the Soviet air force, it now became apparent that the heavy concentration of German 88-mm anti-aircraft guns to the front to serve in anti-tank roles had further reduced aircraft defences. At the same time, it was noted that the formidable new Soviet Il-2 *Shturmovik* was impervious to the 37-mm German anti-aircraft gun.[65] The Il-2 was a low-flying, heavily armoured ground attack aircraft, which its designer, S. V. Il'yushin, had dubbed the 'flying tank'.[66] While Richthofen's air corps remained seriously outnumbered, for the operations north of Moscow he at least had the token support of the *Escuadrilla Azul* (Spanish Blue Squadron) and two squadrons from the newly formed *Hrvatska Zrakoplovna Legija* (Croatian Air Force Legion).[67]

To the south of Moscow Richthofen's forces were even weaker and the widely dispersed forces of the Fourth Army's right wing, Guderian's Second Panzer Army and Schmidt's Second Army all but guaranteed Soviet aircraft freedom of manoeuvre over wide tracts of the front. Loeper's 10th Motorised Infantry Division reported on 28 November that it could no longer continue its advance 'because of strong Russian aerial activity, which makes every movement impossible and leads to heavy losses (over 150 men)'.[68] Two days later (30 November), Adolf B. wrote home in a letter that his column had been bombed causing 'major damage', with numerous dead and eleven destroyed or damaged vehicles.[69] The war diary of Lemelsen's XXXXVII Panzer Corps told of just how much the air war on the eastern front had changed since June 1941. All movement by day, even by individual vehicles, which it stated Soviet planes were successfully destroying, was deemed impossible. The diary then continued: 'The enemy is, as in past days, sometimes with sixty aircraft in the air. All units report heaviest losses.'[70] Even darkness did not ground Soviet aircraft, although it made them much easier to avoid. The war diary of Nehring's 18th Panzer Division reported the night-time bombing of a town in which part of the division was quartered, and complained that in spite of 'urgent reports and pleas' the division was given neither fighter nor anti-aircraft gun protection.[71] By 29 November the division noted that the Soviet air force would attack even in snow showers or low-hanging cloud, concluding: 'Against this constant danger the division, in the absence of fighters and anti-aircraft guns, is completely helpless'.[72] Schmidt's Second Army was likewise sending desperate messages to Army Group Centre requesting fighter support.[73] The main area of concern was around the town of Tim (65 km east of Kursk) where Hubicki's 9th Panzer Division was under constant aerial attack and, as a result, the drive on Voronezh ground to a halt.[74] Further north, however, Soviet air power could not stop Schmidt's continued advance on the town of Jelez, which he was able to capture in early December.[75]

The collapse of German air power in the east during 1941 has had little impact in shaping judgements about the course of the Nazi–Soviet war as a whole. However, from a modern perspective the idea of conducting a conventional ground attack without aerial supremacy, or, in the *Ostheer*'s case, even a parity of forces, appears, with good reason, to be an already desperate circumstance. The so-called demodernisation of the *Ostheer* in 1941[76] hit the Luftwaffe especially hard owing to its relentless employment at the most critical and hotly contested sectors on the eastern front as well as its dispersal to western Europe and North Africa. As the example of Kesselring's Second Air Fleet reflects, the implication of Germany's failure to end the war in the east could no longer ignore the needs of secondary fronts even at the risk of exacerbating an already mounting crisis for the Luftwaffe in the east. Indeed, even before Hitler's declaration of war on the United States, crisis was the word that now defined the German strategic outlook even if few in the high command recognised it at the time. Nevertheless, the unsettling turn of events in the eastern front's air war was not going unnoticed. As Goebbels noted in his diary on 2 December: 'The panzer units operating there [at Moscow] report heavy enemy aerial activity. Our fighter protection is insufficient and the enemy is absolutely superior. The German losses are high.'[77] Yet Göring's resources, as head of the Luftwaffe, were hopelessly overstretched and Udet did not kill himself because there were any easy solutions. As we have seen, it was at this juncture that, on 29 November, Fritz Todt, the minister for armaments and munitions, bluntly informed Hitler: 'This war can no longer be won by military means.'[78] Evidence for which was nowhere better seen than in the east; and above all in the skies over Russia.

Backs to the Kremlin wall: Zhukov's defiant defence

On 28 November, Hitler learned that the German siege of Tobruk, which had lasted some 241 days, had at last been lifted by the British 'Crusader' offensive that had begun ten days before.[79] The bulk of Rommel's 400 tanks had already been captured, disabled or destroyed, and the combined German and Italian casualties would eventually double those of the British.[80] Moreover, the *Afrikakorps* was now set to follow the example of Kleist's First Panzer Army at Rostov and seek safety in retreat. The idea that another, and even greater, offensive was now being prepared to hit Army Group Centre head-on appeared simply inconceivable.

Since the opening days of Operation Typhoon when Army Group Centre was once again thrusting deep into Soviet territory, the *Stavka* had begun planning for a counteroffensive. As early as 5 October, Stalin ordered the establishment of ten more armies as a strategic reserve. A number of these had to be committed to battle during October and November in order to shore up points of real crisis in the line, but the bulk were withheld and would constitute the backbone of Zhukov's counteroffensive.[81] Planning began at the start of November, once Army Group Centre's offensive had seemingly ground to a halt, it was then renewed at the end of the month when it became apparent that Typhoon was on its last legs and Soviet intelligence indicated that Bock had no reserves. The genius of the *Stavka*'s plan was less in the subtleties of the decision as to where to concentrate its reserve armies than when to employ them. Defending Moscow without committing the full strength of the Red Army and watching as Zhukov's Western Front was slowly rolled back with one town after another falling to the oncoming German panzer forces – Klin, Solnechnogorsk, Yakhroma, Istra – took tremendous nerve.

Indeed, after months of disasters in which German operations had so comprehensively outwitted Soviet countermoves, the *Stavka*'s delicate balancing act, 'allowing' the German offensive to proceed so close to Moscow in the hope of catching them unprepared, exhausted and bled white, reflected an iron resolve as well as a degree of confidence in the outcome that many accounts of the battle of Moscow fail to recognise. The desperate juggling of Soviet forces at the front to defend one sector after another, the frantic pleas of local commanders for more reinforcements, the steady loss of ground and the dwindling number of kilometres to Moscow all feed a dramatic story of desperation and near-run suspense. Nevertheless, without ameliorating the intensity of the fighting or the valour of the Soviet armies shielding Moscow, their struggle was not the final word on the defence of the capital. Whenever a real crisis threatened or the Germans looked to be making a break-through, Stalin was able to drip-feed his hard-pressed army commanders with just enough reinforcements to meet their barest needs.[82] In the first two weeks of November, Zhukov's Western Front was reinforced by some 2,000 guns, 300 tanks and 100,000 fresh troops with many more on route.[83] When Stalin famously questioned Zhukov in mid-November about whether Moscow could be held against the renewed German offensive, the Western Front commander was unequivocal: 'We will, without fail, hold Moscow.'[84] Zhukov's answer was not mere bravado; it was based on strategic factors which he knew greatly favoured Moscow's defence. The heavy concentration of Soviet reserves, the icy conditions that forestalled rapid German movement, the length of German supply lines and their absence of reserves, the transformation of Moscow into a bristling fortress city, and the use of Moscow's infrastructure to move forces and supply the front – all this counted in Zhukov's favour.

Beyond the immediacy of the Western Front's strategic circumstances the bigger picture also played to Zhukov's advantage. Overall at the front on 1 December the Red Army fielded some 4.2 million men, and this figure does not include the *Stavka* reserves.[85] At the same time, the *Ostheer* directed barely 3 million men, maintained a rough parity in tanks, and fielded far fewer aircraft and artillery pieces. What was worse was that Soviet industry, even under the pressure of switching to wartime production as well as managing an unprecedented evacuation of essential industry from threatened regions,[86] still managed to surpass Germany's year-on-year armament production. The Kharkov tractor factory was one shining example, having been evacuated to the Urals in October the factory shipped its first trainload of T-34s on 8 December 1941.[87] Indeed, Soviet tank production rose from 2,794 in 1940 to 6,590 in 1941 and 24,446 in 1942. By contrast, German output was consistently less, and in 1942 German industry was out-produced by some 15,246 Soviet tanks (a total of only 9,200 panzers were built in the course of the year).[88] A similar pattern of figures emerged for Soviet aircraft and artillery production, which, combined with British and American production totals, makes it easy to see why Fritz Todt was drawing the conclusions he was. Of course, there is no straight line to be drawn between the events of 1941 and 1945, but beyond Hitler's 'Fridericitan strategy',[89] which hoped that the alliance against him would eventually fall apart, Germany's military options were anything but encouraging. Nor is this just apparent in retrospect. As early as August 1941 the former Romanian foreign minister, G. Gafenco, told the Swiss envoy: 'From now on the Reich will fight the war of attrition it wanted to avoid.' He then expressed the opinion that this precluded Germany from ever dominating Europe.[90] In October 1941, a Swiss intelligence report from a high-ranking officer (probably Romanian) stated: 'Whatever course the drama may take, in the theatre of war, one thing is certain, and that is that the Axis will collapse.'[91] The following month, on 22 November, another intelligence report reached Berne, which read:

> A leading Swedish figure, presumably very well informed, had expressed the opinion that the Germans can no longer win the war! German officers who served on the Russian front tell me the same thing. The situation is such that they wonder if the time will not soon come when military leaders feel obliged to take over strategic command themselves in order to give themselves another chance to open peace negotiations.[92]

While German fortunes ebbed, sustaining the Soviet cause depended first and foremost upon the morale of its people and the resolve of the Red Army to go on taking immense losses. The Soviet population knew that the German invasion had been unprovoked and by the time Moscow itself was being threatened the reality of life under German occupation, including countless tales of German atrocities, had long since been established by the Soviet media. Indeed, from December 1941 to January 1943 the Leningrad journal *Propaganda and Agitation*, which was often the basis of lecture material for mass rallies, included more articles on German atrocities than any other topic aside from the heroic exploits of the Red Army.[93] Having condemned the Germans for their crimes of aggression, brutality and outright murder, Soviet hate propaganda acted to stiffen the public resolve with fiery rhetoric. Ilya Ehrenburg not only fanned those flames of hatred, but at the same time legitimised them with a kind of moral imperative:

> The idea of vengeance does not satisfy our outraged reason. We do not speak of spite but of hatred; not of revenge but of justice. These

> are not shading of words – these are entirely different feelings. Hatred, as love, is inherent to pure and warm hearts. We hate Fascism because we love people, children, the earth, trees, horses, laughter, books, the warmth of a friend's hand, because we love life. The stronger the love of life is within us, the firmer is our hatred ... To us Hitlerites are not simply enemies; to us the Hitlerites are not people, to us they are murderers, executioners, moral freaks, cruel fanatics, and we therefore hate them.[94]

Demonising the Germans in this way not only helped to remove any objections to killing them, but it recast the war in the Soviet mind-set as an essential struggle between life and death, which, given Nazi postwar plans for the eastern territories, was hardly inappropriate. As Amir Weiner wrote, Soviet citizens had 'something to die for' and, even more to the point, 'a lot to kill for'.[95]

The result may have steeled Soviet resolution, but it also fed a cycle of violence that saw no small amount of Soviet atrocities against German soldiers and later civilians.[96] Boris Baromykin, a Soviet soldier during the battle for Moscow, recalled killing his German captives in a fit of rage: 'We seized five of the German soldiers and literally ripped them apart with our bare hands, our teeth, anything – one man was even using a table leg to smash a skull in. We killed those men in a frenzy of hatred.'[97] Abram Gordon, another Soviet veteran who admitted to executing captured Germans, stated in justification: 'We were soldiers in a war where you had to kill or be killed.'[98] Yet in many instances it was much more than just killing. Soviet violence against German captives was ubiquitous and often gratuitous.[99] One German lieutenant reported seeing six German captives nailed to a table through their tongues, and in another instance he saw twelve to fifteen soldiers who had been thrown down a village well and then stoned to death. As the lieutenant told a comrade: 'These incidents were taken for a reason for repaying it tenfold, twenty and hundredfold.'[100]

As harsh as the Nazi–Soviet war had become, from the *Stavka*'s perspective it at least ensured that the option of surrender for the men in the Red Army was much less likely than it had appeared in the early days and weeks of the war.[101] The troops could therefore be expected to fight and die for their positions, and testaments to this effect are common among Soviet accounts. As Anatoly Shvebig explained in a postwar interview: 'We no longer had anywhere left to retreat to. If we pulled back any further, the Germans would get into Moscow. To stop them, we had to stand and fight where we were – and fight to the death.'[102]

By the same token, Rokossovsky, the commander of the Soviet Sixteenth Army, wrote in his memoirs: 'All of us, from private to army commander, felt that these were decisive days and we had to hold out at all costs. No one needed any prodding. The army as a whole, tried and tested in the crucible of battle, fully realised the measure of its responsibility.'[103] With such determination and resolve Zhukov's confidence that the line at Moscow could be held while Army Group Centre exhausted itself in attack and reserve armies concentrated for their counterattack was justified. Ultimately, the battle for Moscow was not a near-run contest at all. Had the Germans made better progress, more Soviet reserves would simply have been released sooner and, in any case, the real battle for the city itself never eventuated.

Construction of the outer ring of the Moscow defensive zone was at last completed on 25 November, having involved some 100,000 workers (mostly women) and consisting of 1,428 artillery emplacements, 160 km of anti-tank ditches, 120 km of barbed-wire entanglements three rows deep, and numerous other fortifications and obstacles.[104] Moscow's communist brigades, a kind of civilian militia, had increased almost fivefold from their October total and now numbered 48,000.[105] However, the real guarantor of Moscow's defence was the build-up of *Stavka* reserves. In October only four divisions were able to be held in reserve, in November this figure had jumped to twenty-two, and by December some forty-four divisions were in reserve.[106] In total, from October to early December, seventy-five new Soviet divisions had been raised and deployed – some committed directly to the front and others held back. During the same sixty-seven-day period, Army Group Centre did not receive a single division from the OKH as reinforcement. Indeed, as an indication of the remarkable regenerative qualities of the Red Army, the new grouping of Soviet forces deployed for action in early December was numerically at least equivalent to the total Red Army force attacked by Army Group Centre when Operation Typhoon was first launched on 2 October.[107] This by no means lessens the scale of the Soviet disasters at Viaz'ma and Briansk, but it does reflect the extraordinary robustness of the Soviet state, as well as the speed at which the Red Army was able to reconstitute itself.

Unbeknown to Zhukov his offensive was also to be aided by strategic factors he could scarcely have anticipated. Richard Sorge, the

Soviet spy employed at the German embassy in Tokyo, had already provided vital intelligence that convinced Stalin that the Japanese would not attack in the Soviet Far East, thereby freeing him to authorise the transfer of Siberian divisions to the Moscow front. It also pointed to the fact that the Japanese were preparing to strike elsewhere and, with the Hull–Nomura talks having just broken down in Washington, US–Japanese relations had never been more fraught, suggesting a conflict was imminent. What Zhukov could not have known, however, was that on 28 November the Japanese Ambassador to Germany, Ōshima Hiroshi, met with Joachim von Ribbentrop, Hitler's foreign minister, to discuss the international crisis. Although Hitler's policy had previously been to keep the United States out of the war, the dictator now signalled a change of course, which Ribbentrop communicated to his guest: 'Should Japan become engaged in a war with the United States, Germany of course would join the war immediately. There is absolutely no possibility of Germany's entering into a separate peace with the United States under such circumstances. The Führer is determined on that point.'[108] With the Japanese First Air Fleet already on route to Pearl Harbor, the Soviet Union was about to gain a major new ally in the war against Nazi Germany without having to concern themselves about Japan.

On 29 November, Zhukov determined that the time had come to commit Soviet reserve formations to the front and for the commencement of a general Soviet winter offensive against Army Group Centre. Zhukov telephoned Stalin and asked for permission to undertake final preparations. 'Are you sure that the enemy has reached a critical point and is in no position to bring some new large force into action?' Stalin asked. 'The enemy has been bled white', Zhukov replied emphatically before continuing: 'If we don't eliminate them now the enemy can later reinforce his troops in the area of Moscow with large reserves at the expense of his north and south groupings.'[109] In fact, Rundstedt's losses at Rostov as well as his desperate need to contain the current Soviet offensive driving back his army group meant he could scarcely spare anything for Bock.[110] Likewise in the north, Leeb's embattled position at Tikhvin was taking heavy losses and soon would also have to be evacuated, beginning a month-long retreat which David Glantz remarked 'replicated in microcosm Napoleon's dramatic but costly retreat from Moscow in 1812'.[111] Clearly, Bock could expect little, if any, aid from his neighbouring army groups, and with Rommel's *Afrikakorps* now also in crisis, Army Group Centre would have to face Zhukov's offensive alone.

On 30 November, Zhukov submitted his plan for a counteroffensive to the *Stavka*. The main attack would take place north of Moscow using the Western Front's right wing to retake Klin, Solnechnogorsk and Istra. At the same time, a second attack by his left wing would be directed south of Tula towards Uzlovaya and Boroditsk. A third attack was added for the German centre in order to prevent Bock shifting forces to meet the threat on his flanks. When the plan was returned to Zhukov Stalin had scrawled in crayon over the first page: 'Agreed. J. Stalin.'[112] Zhukov's plan had been adopted and the die was now cast for a new phase in the war in the east. The potency of the *Stavka*'s December counteroffensive was less its overall strength of arms (there were few new tanks available) than its sheer numerical (i.e., infantry) superiority,[113] but even more important was the fact that Army Group Centre was nearing total exhaustion. Thus, the fate of Bock's armies would be determined much more by the insistence of the German leadership to continue attacking than by any Soviet aptitude for the offensive. In spite of repeated examples to the contrary throughout the summer and autumn of 1941, the German high command remained stubbornly convinced that it was the Red Army that was at the end of its tether before Moscow. The result of their miscalculation would be decisive.

Even before that storm front arrived the exhaustion of Bock's forces was compounded by the winter conditions, which further 'softened up' Army Group Centre and added to the misery of battle. It also convinced many German soldiers that the very elements themselves were somehow a curse to foreign invaders. Léon Degrelle wrote: 'The old Russian earth, trod upon by foreigners, used its eternal weapons; it defended itself, avenged itself.'[114] Similarly, Wolfgang Paul, who was serving in the 18th Panzer Division, noted: 'The summer had driven us into the eastern flatlands, the fall had held us there with its unyielding, unforgettable mud and the winter wanted to drive us out again. It was as though we had stumbled into a world that we would never really get to know. It seemed everything was cold, inhospitable, and arrayed against us.'[115] Even Greiffenberg, at Army Group Centre, wrote after the war: 'The effect of climate in Russia is to make things impassable in the mud of spring and autumn, unbearable in the heat of summer and impossible in the depths of winter. Climate in Russia is a series of natural disasters.'[116]

By the end of November, the force of the Russian winter had arrived. The Moscow canal was frozen over and Albert Neuhaus noted in a letter on 29 November that it was only 3.15 in the afternoon and already there was hardly enough light to continue writing.[117] Russian records indicate that there had not been a single day since the start of the German offensive when the average daily temperature rose above freezing and the mean temperature was −7°C, but with wind chill it was often much colder.[118] German sentries and defensive positions had the disadvantage of having to face east; staring out into the on-coming easterly winds, biting and sharp with snow flurries obscuring their view.[119] Helmut Günther noted that in snowstorms the view out into the countryside extended barely 10 m,[120] while Franz Frisch wrote that visibility was 'reduced to practically zero from the miserable blowing snow'.[121] At the same time, the deepening snow deadened all noise and made the approach of enemy sappers or raiding parties harder to detect.[122]

The changing conditions altered the tactical environment and helped to deny the panzer divisions their trademark rapid manoeuvre and exploitation. However, while the weather was set to have an inevitable impact on the fighting, its profound role in favouring the Red Army came down to Germany's lack of preparation, especially with regard to winter uniforms. Although the same German officers liked to imagine that the Russians were 'naturally' more accustomed to the extreme conditions than 'cultured' Germans,[123] in reality the cold affected men on both sides equally. The difference was in preparation and in a war of materiel the right clothing became as important as the right weaponry. As Zhukov noted in his memoir: 'Warm clothes and uniforms are also a weapon ... Obviously the Nazi ringleaders grossly miscalculated politically and strategically.'[124] Hellmuth Stieff agreed and wrote in disgust on 19 November that: 'Our winter clothing is only trickling in – a few gloves, woollen vests and hats. God knows when the rest will come! The supply situation should have been resolved weeks ago. It is an extraordinary mess, and we are supposed to be "the best armed forces in the world".'[125] Having already exhausted the supply of winter clothing from the civilian population, German soldiers soon saw the better clad Soviet troops as their only recourse for winter protection.[126] POWs were stripped of their felt boots and greatcoats, but even more desperate measures followed. As one soldier explained: 'We attacked the Russians not only to carry out orders but also to get clothing. It was sort of like old Fritz saying[127]: "What, you have no ammunition? Get it from the enemy men!"'[128] The result was Germans in Soviet uniforms, and while the national insignias were exchanged there were still incidents of friendly fire.[129] Max Kuhnert observed: 'One could hardly distinguish between a

German and a Russian soldier; they all looked filthy, in tatters, with blankets around their shoulders.'[130] Yet with Bock's army group numbering well over a million men no manner of expedients could substitute for such a serious shortfall in winter uniforms. Yet even if supplies in such numbers could be made available there was simply not the rail capacity to transport them to the front. The result was that Bock's soldiers were slowly freezing. Doctor Heinrich Haape noted that the first mild cases of frostbite were reported in mid-November, and he began referring to the icy easterly winds as 'the breath of death'.[131] Nor was this just hyperbole, the freezing easterly gusts combined with a lack of proper clothing soon proved to be a killer combination. As Helmut Günther recalled: 'It was bitterly cold. The temperature? We did not know, but only knew that the cold had greatly intensified in recent days. People talked of -30 to -40 Celsius! No winter clothing had arrived yet. How could it have gotten here?'[132]

As bad as conditions were in Army Group Centre many men found ways to improvise by stuffing newspaper into their uniforms or skinning, tanning and sewing sheepskins for use as coats or waistbands. Some divisions even organised their own local workshops, staffed by Russians, to manufacture old cloth and blankets into all manner of protective clothing.[133] Other men were just lucky to find themselves in areas where shelter was readily available. Leopold Schober wrote to his parents on 27 November that he was in a town 'very near to the capital' and that 'on some days it is already very cold'. Yet Schober knew how lucky he was when he wrote: 'We always sleep in houses thank God.'[134] Just how lucky was already evident on other parts of the front where men were forced to lie down on ground that was frozen to a depth of a metre. Heinrici, in command of the XXXXIII Army Corps, noted in a letter to his family on 29 November how three soldiers had frozen to death because they were pinned down by enemy fire and could not move from their foxholes for ten hours. Under such circumstances he wrote of the desperation his men had for any form of shelter, and noted that a whole battalion was squeezed into just four huts.[135] With even the most passive actions likely to result in death (such as lying too long in a foxhole), soldiers started taking extraordinary risks to stay warm. Ernst Kern wrote that he and his men simply abandoned their positions, took refuge against the cold in a local house and hoped the night would pass quietly.[136] Likewise, Hans-Heinrich Ludwig wrote in a letter on 19–20 November that because of the cold as well as the danger of freezing to death, he and his comrades could not get much sleep. He then added: 'In spite of the Russians we made a fire under the open sky, one could not hold out any longer.'[137] The cold was, in some instances, achieving what the Red Army had not; it was breaking down German discipline and morale. As Siegfried Knappe noted in early December: 'Everyone felt brutalized and defeated by the cold ... Frostbite was taking a very heavy toll now as more and more men were sent back to the field hospitals with frozen fingers and toes.'[138] Hans-Heinrich Ludwig compared losses to cold in his unit with casualty rates of the First World War.[139] Indeed, throughout the *Ostheer* the number of casualties not related to enemy action numbered some 90,000 in December alone.[140]

In spite of such difficulties, the march to Moscow continued with remarkably little concern at the highest levels of the German command for the state of the armies or the condition of the troops. Even if not for compassionate reasons, then a purely military rationale would seem to question the sense of deliberately driving men to the point of utter exhaustion, especially as the worst of the weather was yet to come. As Siegfried Knappe recalled: 'As we approached the suburbs of Moscow a paralysing blast of cold hit us and the temperature dropped far below zero and stayed there.'[141] Hans-Heinrich Ludwig wrote of his rations being issued completely frozen: 'rock-hard bread' and 'sausage like crystal'.[142] At the same time, a number of trains were reported to be arriving with wagons filled not with desperately needed artillery shells or winter clothing, but with red wine from France. The frustration of the troops was all the more in evidence when it was discovered that in the freezing temperatures the bottles in the crates had burst and all that remained were chunks of red ice and glass splinters.[143]

Even more worrying was how the cold was affecting Army Group Centre's ability to maintain operational readiness. As one soldier noted: 'In November 1941 ... the temperature dropped so low that it actually caused the grease in our weapons to freeze unless we fired them regularly or took measures to protect them from the cold. Other soldiers told me that they witnessed entire steam engines that had had been frozen solid down to the grease in their wheels.'[144] The intense cold also made metal more brittle so that the slender firing pins in rifles sometimes snapped.[145] Wheeled vehicles and tanks suffered because the standard engine oil was too thin, there was no anti-freeze and the cooling water froze. As Hans von Luck noted: 'We were soon forced to thaw the water in the morning with blow lamps and procure hot water as soon as we got near a village; or else we had to leave the engines running throughout the night.'[146] Engine repairs were typically undertaken in the open and, according to one soldier, 'often in snowstorms and not infrequently under enemy fire, when lives were in danger and time was short'.[147] As with uniforms, Soviet equipment appeared better suited to the extreme cold, as Siegfried Knappe observed, 'their vehicles were built and conditioned for this kind of weather, but ours were not'.[148]

The same went for horses. Central European breeds were larger and much more powerful than the local panje horses, making them the only choice for the large supply wagons and heavy calibre artillery of the Wehrmacht. Yet from October, when the weather changed and the road conditions worsened, the fallout rate among army horses rose sharply, making the Russian panje ponies a vital replacement even if only for lighter loads. It was the heavy, cold-blooded draft horses that were most susceptible to the winter conditions, especially those already weakened by overwork, insufficient care or lack of fodder.[149] Yet with the offensive still driving forward there was little that could be done to avoid such circumstances. The shortage of mounts meant wranglers could not rest or rotate their horses to avoid overwork, while at night there was often no shelter from the driving easterly winds. As Kurt Gruman wrote in his diary at the beginning of Army Group Centre's November offensive: 'The poor horses were exhausted. The lack of forage and the cold took their toll – all horses stood in the open.'[150] Likewise, Gerhardt Linke noted on 19 November: 'The poor horses are pulling their hardest and are all exhausted. What with the scarcity of fodder and the weather – the animals pass the night out in the open – conditions are really pitiable for them.'[151] Attempts were made to keep horses behind houses at night, while blankets were sometimes strapped to their sides, but even so, as another soldier noted in early December 'our horses started to die from the cold in large numbers for the first time; they would just die in the bitter cold darkness of the night, and we would find them dead the next morning'.[152] Halder noted on 28 November that the lack of availability of horses was now 'very serious',[153] while in early December no less than ten infantry divisions in Kluge's Fourth Army reported an outbreak of the disease mange. In addition, pneumonia and frostbite were noted to be affecting horses in large numbers. Between 16 September and 30 November the veterinary company of the 30th Infantry Division treated 1,072 horses, but only 117 of these were for wounds sustained from enemy fire, the rest were suffering from exhaustion or the effects of the cold.[154]

While all manner of German equipment and machinery, as well as their draft horses, sustained high losses in the freezing conditions, the most pressing issue for Army Group Centre was the suffering of its unprepared and ill-equipped men. One Soviet account speaks of a group of German POWs dressed only in light summer coats and without headgear of any kind. As they stood under guard the only sounds they made were sighs and moans, and one of them shivering uncontrollably repeated again and again, '*O Mein Gott! O Mein Gott!*' ('Oh my God! Oh my God!'). Every now and then one of them would fall down dead.[155] Another German POW was picked up and described by Elena Rzhevskaya, a translator working for the Red Army:

> The German was frozen and had icicles all over his face and on his clothes. He was bundled up in a woman's thick linen shawl and his military hat was perched on top of the shawl. The shawl was big enough to cover his whole body. He was also wearing straw boots – the kind the Germans forced the locals to make for them.[156]

Such scenes did much to reduce the stature of the all-conquering German in the eyes of young Soviet soldiers. Clearly their enemy was in trouble, they knew it and the German soldiers knew it, only in the German high command (including Bock's headquarters) did consideration for the weather and the lack of supplies remain secondary to operational objectives. As one soldier wrote in early December 1941: 'I could not help wondering if our superiors in Berlin had any idea of what they had sent us into. Such thoughts constituted defeatism, I knew, but that threat seemed of little consequence at the moment.'[157] Even the impetuous Guderian claimed in his memoir to have been struck by the state of his men and the dreadful circumstance they now confronted:

> Only he who saw the endless expanse of Russian snow during this winter of our misery, and felt the icy wind that blew across it, burying in snow every object in its path; who drove for hour after hour through that no man's land only at last to find too thin shelter with insufficiently clothed, half-starved men; and who also saw by contrast the well-fed, warmly clad and fresh Siberians, fully equipped for winter fighting; only a man who knew all that can truly judge the events which now occurred.[158]

9 DOWN TO THE WIRE

Victory or death: the Nazi cult of the dead

As of 26 November 1941, the *Ostheer* had sustained 743,112 casualties in the war against the Soviet Union. That equalled 23 per cent of the total German invasion force on 22 June 1941, and even this figure did not include those released from duty due to sickness.[1] Overall, by the end of November more than a quarter of a million men (262,297 German troops) had been killed outright or died of their wounds.[2] With the reserves of the Replacement Army long since exhausted, the *Ostheer* was now some 340,000 men short, which, according to Buhle at the OKH, meant that the combat strength of the infantry divisions was reduced by 50 per cent.[3] Army Group Centre's losses from the beginning of November to 3 December came to 45,735 men.[4] Under such circumstances less and less could be expected of the combat units and yet, as Siegfried Knappe noted, 'Russian resistance became more and more determined now as we neared Moscow, and our casualties were becoming much heavier.'[5] Similarly, Gustav Schrodek recalled: 'Our ranks were getting thinner. A couple got hit every day. When would it be our turn?'[6] Such fatalism was easy to understand among the worst affected companies. One non-commissioned officer, writing a letter home on 21 November, spoke of his company being reduced to just twenty men as early as October: 'We few remaining soldiers of our division crave so badly the forlorn hope of replacement.' Ultimately, the division was forced to provide its own replacements by disbanding one battalion in every regiment and using the men generated to reinforce the remaining formations.[7] Such administrative sleight of hand may have raised the number of active service companies, but it left the same number of men having to achieve the division's objectives. Just how German casualties were impacting upon the long stretches of the eastern front was illustrated by Ernst Kern when he noted on 24 November: 'This time we had to hold a position that, until now, had been defended by a whole battalion. There were five of us in a sector half a kilometre long, with twenty-eight bunkers that we felt were royally built. Each of us could have five bunkers to live in ... We decided to stay together in a centrally located bunker.'[8]

As divisions within the *Ostheer* were now routinely disbanding formations to provide a source of internal reinforcements, the scale of losses by the end of the autumn suggested that this method needed to be adopted at the corps and even army level. Given that the war against the Soviet Union had always been conducted under the pretext of achieving a final victory, which would see the release of numerous divisions, there was a ready-made plan for disbanding German divisions. Accordingly, at the start of November the Army Organisation Department demanded that at least twenty divisions of the *Ostheer* be disbanded to meet the replacement needs of those remaining. A preparatory order was dispatched to the field armies on 17 November, but Hitler opposed the move, citing the negative reaction on the home front if it became known that the *Ostheer* was being forced to take such a radical step.[9] The regime already had to explain the setbacks at Rostov and in North Africa, as well as the less than spectacular progress of Bock's latest offensive towards Moscow, which, after the pronouncements of impending victory from early October, only added to the view that all was not well in the east. Indeed, with men close to the regime predicting military defeat, Hitler and Goebbels were engaged in a damage-control exercise and, fearing the worst, wanted no further action that might unsettle public opinion about the war. Tellingly, on 30 November, Goebbels' thoughts returned to November 1918: 'That Germany collapsed in 1918 was the fault of her leadership not the German people. Whatever the circumstances the leadership of today is determined to use every means to avoid a collapse of the people's morale.'[10] Of course, it was the soldiers at the front who were best placed to judge the veracity of German propaganda about the progress of the war. As one soldier wrote in a letter home after listening to a radio broadcast: 'If I was not in the military and someone said something like that to me, I would flatly reply, I don't believe it.'[11]

With thousands of such letters being written back to Germany, Goebbels soon recognised that the regime could not go on deluding the population about the reality of the war in the east without further harming its credibility.[12]

In some areas of Germany local Nazi party branches were already countering concerns about the cost of the war in the east with warnings of an apocalyptic alternative should the war ever be lost. Interestingly, many of the scenarios German propaganda suggested would result from a defeat mirrored actual Nazi policies currently being enacted in the east. The purpose was to promote unquestioned support for the war effort out of fear for 'Jewish–Bolshevik' atrocities. As one Nazi article from 1941 suggested, Germany's defeat would result in:

> Destruction of all cities and villages, expropriation of each private property, inconceivable blood bath of the population, martyrdom and slaughter of millions, hunger and misery through destruction of the social prosperity, destruction of the supplies and smashing of production, deportation of millions as work slaves to the north Russian and Siberian steppes, forceful re-education of children in reformatory Bolshevik child camps, elimination of the institution of family, razing of all churches and cultural treasures to the ground.[13]

Against such an alternative the demands of the war against the 'Jewish–Bolshevik' enemy were for many inconsequential.

With the army unable to disband divisions within the *Ostheer*, the need for replacements became even more pressing. The solution was to use the German divisions stationed in France as a kind of surrogate Replacement Army. To begin with those divisions had to be made 'ready for the east' (*ostfähig*) through extensive supplies of new material, but what they desperately needed was younger men as they consisted overwhelmingly of older age groups. To provide these a new process began that would continue in varying forms for the rest of the war. Soldiers born after 1908 who were fit for active service, but only serving in administrative jobs or rear units of the Replacement Army, were exchanged with the older men not fully fit for active service. By the end of the autumn this 'combing out' of the rear area had led to the transfer of some 250,000 men, including around 25,000 desperately needed non-commissioned officers. In addition, ten west-based divisions were to hand over one battalion each, which had been made 'ready for the east'.[14]

Another solution to the manpower crisis that was mooted, but just as quickly dismissed, was for the raising of local divisions from among Baltic, Ukrainian and White Russian nationalists or anti-communists. Reichenau, the commander of the Sixth Army, was said to favour the idea, but when word reached Hitler the dictator's response was as blunt as it was dismissive: 'Let Reichenau mind his own military problems and leave the rest to me.'[15] Hitler's view would change as the war progressed, but not before the opportunity to create a substantive anti-Soviet movement had passed.[16] Even so, one should not overstate the extent of such a 'missed opportunity'. Germany, it must be remembered, was a long way from being able to supply and equip the *Ostheer* as well as the needs of its Axis allies in the east, so another major force made up of eastern peoples would have been extremely poorly resourced.[17]

Given that the Wehrmacht had largely dominated the fighting since June 1941, it is significant that, even in this period, Nazi Germany was already scraping the bottom of its manpower barrel. It was not just the fact that the *Ostheer* had shed almost three-quarters of a million men during its supposedly victorious advance to Moscow, but that the war had no obvious end in sight. Indeed, Germany, with just 79.5 million people,[18] together with their often dubious allies, had to maintain Hitler's brutal new order throughout Europe, guard the continent against British raids and conduct active operations across 2,700 km of front against the Soviets. This left far too few able-bodied men to meet the colossal demands of Germany's war industry, and the implications would be decisive.[19] Germany's war in the east was decided as much by the manpower available to the factories as the *Ostheer*.

Beyond the strategic implications, heavy losses on the eastern front were bringing the war home to ordinary Germans. By December 1941, the majority of Germans knew someone who had fallen in the east. The secret SD reports gauging German public opinion revealed on 4 December that the setback at Rostov 'renewed fears about high German casualties' and that many ordinary people were now questioning just how many more lives victory in the east would cost.[20] Victor Klemperer wrote in his diary on 30 November: 'Always new battles in the east, although Russia was supposed to have been annihilated long ago.'[21] In addition to the human cost, the war was placing unprecedented strain on everyday staples. The meat ration, which had remained stable at 500 g a week until the invasion of the Soviet Union, began to be constantly cut. An American journalist on assignment in Berlin later observed: 'I think it is not an exaggeration to say that, for the mass of the German people, five months of war with in Russia had cost them four-fifths of their weekly meat ration!'[22] Furthermore, on 30 November, Victor Klemperer wrote in his diary 'everywhere potato crisis',[23] while Ulrich von Hassell noted on the same day: 'The picture is roughly as follows: the food situation is getting more and more serious, especially as the prospects for the next harvest are very bad. The potato and turnip crops are now badly damaged; the raw-material problem is difficult, and the gasoline and fuel-oil shortage perilous.'[24]

The one consolation was that the SD reports revealed that the great majority of Germans remained convinced Moscow would fall before the end of the year.[25] Such hope sustained the belief that an end to the war in the east, the heavy losses and the shortages was on the horizon. The same sentiment was not, however, shared at the front. Ernst Guicking responded to this apparent optimism in his wife's letter when he questioned: 'Bib, are they already talking at home about an end to the war in Russia? I must say we see none of that here.'[26] Similarly, on 29 November, Pastor Sebacher asked in his diary: 'Oh Russia, what have you in store for us, what cruelties will you still inflict upon on us?' Sebacher's answer would not be long in coming; a week later he would be killed.[27]

In the absence of any official figures, death notices in German newspapers were the tell-tale signs of Germany's losses in the east. The typical format was for a black-bordered notice, headed by an Iron Cross and printed in heavy gothic text. The phrasing also followed a certain ritual formula, which spoke of a 'hero's death' in the service of 'Führer and Fatherland' on the 'field of honour'. Yet, from the summer of 1941, it was the sheer volume of these notices that quickly politicised them. At the time it was not uncommon for a death to be commemorated in separate notices by family, businesses and professional organisations, but this, of course, multiplied the number of death notices and the practice was soon banned by Goebbels, who ordered that each individual could only have one death notice. Another method employed by Goebbels was to limit each newspaper to printing a maximum of just ten death notices per day. Curiously, however, neither of Goebbels' directives appear to have been followed very rigorously.[28] For many soldiers at the front the reverence with which their fallen comrades were eulogised was nothing less than appropriate, but increasingly there were those who questioned the celebration of death and heroism, which, as one soldier described in a letter, was 'all empty posturing' that 'can make me downright furious'.[29]

The mythology of death in the Third Reich was as near as the regime came to a pseudo-state religion. The cult of death even had its very own saints, none of whom was more celebrated than Horst Wessel, the leader of an SA troop who was killed by communists in 1930 after he was implicated in the murder of one of their members. His funeral was a lavish affair in which Goebbels gave the eulogy and a song was played that Wessel had written. 'The Flag on High' (also known as the Horst Wessel song) was then adopted as the official anthem of the Nazi movement. Having been written in 1929 at the height of the Nazi street battles with the Communist Party of Germany (KPD), the lyrics took on special meaning in context of the later Nazi–Soviet war. The first verse includes the refrain: 'Comrades shot by the Red Front and reactionaries, march in spirit within our ranks.' Such a blood sacrifice elevated the victim to the status of national martyrdom and, in accordance, Hitler had the more somber *Volkstrauertag* ('Day of National Mourning') reinvented as *Heldengedenktag* ('Heroes Memorial Day'), with pageantry, national pride and military glorification at the centre of proceedings.[30] Yet it was the onset of war that gave full meaning to the cult of death and bore out sacrifice and conflict as central tenets of Nazism. As Hitler explained in 1936:

> There are individual people who think they can damage National Socialism by saying, 'Ah yes, but everything [you have achieved] requires sacrifices!' Indeed, my worthy petits bourgeois, our struggle has required unceasing sacrifice. It's only you who haven't experienced it. Perhaps you fancy that our present-day Germany has become [what it is] because you made no sacrifices! No! Because we knew how to make sacrifices and because we wanted to make them – that is why this Germany has come [into being]. So if somebody tells us, 'The future too will demand sacrifices', then we say, 'Yes, indeed it will!' National Socialism in not a doctrine of inertia but a doctrine of conflict. Not a doctrine of happiness or good luck, but a doctrine of work and a doctrine of struggle, and thus also a doctrine of sacrifice.[31]

By this account the heavy sacrifice necessitated by the war against the Soviet Union was neither remarkable nor something to be avoided; struggle and loss were simply part of Germany's destiny under

Hitler. Moreover, in the Nazi worldview losses on the eastern front were less a matter for sad reflection, than an heroic passage towards 'eternal models of our epoch'. As Goebbels explained, the military struggle was akin to climbing a towering mountain and it was the dead who marked the way to the summit:

> We bury them along the edges of the steep path ... They fell in the first ranks, and all who march after them must pass by them. Like silent directional markers, they point towards the peak ... In this way, our fallen enter the mythology of our *Volk* for all time: they are no longer what they were among us, but instead the eternal models of our epoch ... They are the fulfilled.[32]

Reaching such fulfilled status required dying for the regime, yet the reality of death on the eastern front looked nothing like Goebbels' heroic description nor held the pageantry of the public funerals given to men like Udet and Mölders. Men in the east frequently died in horrific circumstances with no such desire to join the ranks of their fabled 'eternal models'. Even the award of the Knight's Cross (issued only after being awarded the preceding classes of the Iron Cross)[33] was frequently reserved for high-ranking officers, not predominantly men at the front. In only 7 per cent of cases were Knight's Crosses handed out posthumously, which was very different by comparison with British awards such as the Victoria Cross.[34] What is more, in November/December 1941 martyrdom status could not even afford dead soldiers a proper burial. As Otto Skorzeny wrote:

> With the ground frozen solid it was, of course, impossible to bury the dead. We had to collect the bodies in the church. They made a gruesome sight. Arms and legs, which had been oddly twisted in the course of the death struggle, were held in fast in the same position by the cold. We would have to break the joints to give the dead the posture which is supposed to be natural. Glazed eyes stared up at a frozen sky.[35]

In other instances, the solution to burying the dead involved a crude, but effective means. 'We had our hands full with our dead', Gustav Schrodek recalled, 'as we were barely able to bury them. The ground had frozen as hard as a rock, so much so that we were unable to do anything at all with pickaxes and spades. It was only with hand grenades that we were able to blow out a shallow ditch as a grave.'[36] Indeed, after Zhukov's December counteroffensive began Soviet soldiers reported finding piles of dead Germans stacked like logs awaiting the spring thaw to bury them.[37]

Given the official importance of the hero's death, the wording of the death notices in 1939 and 1940 gave rise to increased criticism by the SD of those that stressed personal bereavement over national sacrifice. The more heartfelt or emotional, the more 'tastelessness' the death notice was deemed to be, and the SD even provided an example:

> Now we stand with a sorry look,
> and know our Otto will never come back.
> Rest, oh dear departed one,
> You have freedom, we have pain.

No hint of a hero's death, no 'Führer and Fatherland', no 'field of honour', just a dead man mourned by his loved ones. Pain and grief are emphasised, not the national mythology and by refusing this there is a veiled suggestion that the man may not, in the minds of the relatives, have given his life for these causes. This was another way in which death notices were becoming increasingly politicised. Enthusiastic National Socialists opted for the most expressive language: '*Er fiel für seinen Führer* ('He died for his Führer').[38] While death notices of faithful National Socialists explained death as a gift to Germany:

> When the final chord is sung one day,
> they will say of the German youth:
> That just like the heroes of our epics
> they rallied to the Führer's flag,
> that Germany revealed itself in us,
> Germany, which we carry deep in our hearts.
> If I die, mother, you must bear it,
> and your pride will conquer your pain,
> because you have the privilege of offering a sacrifice
> that is what we mean, when we say Germany.[39]

In Nazi Germany's *Volksgemeinschaft* (people's community) a death on the battlefield was never senseless or tragic, and any such intimation was seen as a failure to honour such a sacrifice.[40] The *Heldentod* (hero's death) was the highest expression of faith in the Nazi cause, and the more there were the greater that expression of faith was held to be. Yet as the war progressed, especially the war in the east, death as an expression of faith in the Nazi cause was increasingly contested in the limited public space open to such a representation. As Victor Klemperer explained:

> If . . . someone is not at all in agreement with National Socialism, if they want to vent their antipathy or perhaps even their hated without, however, showing any demonstrable signs of opposition, because their courage doesn't quite stretch that far, then the appropriate formulation is 'our only son died for the Fatherland' without any mention of the Führer . . . It appears to me that as the number of victims increased, and the hope of victory diminished, the expressions of devotion to the Führer became correspondingly less frequent.[41]

Klemperer's impression was correct. Reference to Hitler in death notices fell from 82 per cent in 1940 to 40 per cent in 1942 and 25 per cent in 1943. Only in September 1944 did the regime finally insist upon a standard death notice: *'Für Führer, Volk und Reich'* ('For Führer, People and Reich').[42]

Understanding the Nazi cult of death demands a certain insight into the Führer state, as well as the personal mythology embodied by Hitler's own 'struggle' and 'sacrifice' for Germany.[43] Like so many aspects of Nazism, Hitler's 'charismatic authority' functioned in practice to dissolve a framework for 'rational' or contrasting opinion.[44] The adoption of a national socialist *Weltanschauung* (worldview), as defined by Hitler, gave heightened meaning to the notion of national sacrifice. As Sebastian Haffner's insightful account from 1940 explained:

> The Nazi leaders love Germany in the way an inconsiderate racehorse owner 'loves' his horse; he wants it to win the race, nothing more. To this end it has been trained and ridden as hard and as inconsiderately as possible. Whether the horse shares his desire for glory and wants to be a racehorse; whether it comes to grief or is henceforth lamed for life, are questions that do not concern him. The comparison is not apposite insofar as one can say of horses that they are there to race. But certainly nations and the men composing them are not there to be collective athletic teams, the fate that the Nazis have imposed on the German people. The Nazi leaders aim at converting Germany into a gigantic sports club which is always winning 'victories' – and thereby losing its happiness, character and, national identity.[45]

Indeed, in the context of a war like the one being waged in the east, Haffner's sports club analogy saw Germany's 'victories' being won at the expense of its youth.

Death was not the only loss to the *Ostheer*, by October/November the ratio of wounded to sick had risen to 1:1.9, meaning that almost two men were falling ill for every one wounded at the front.[46] The damp and then freezing conditions were taking their toll, and the medical services on the eastern front, already overwhelmed, were being inundated with new cases of severe influenza, pneumonia, hypothermia and frostbite. By the opening of Zhukov's December offensive, the *Ostheer* had suffered some 133,000 cases of frostbite.[47] Moreover, after six months of treatment 30 per cent of frostbite patients were still not, or would never be, returned to active duty.[48] As one soldier noted: 'Everyone feared frostbite and hypothermia as much as Soviet weapons.'[49] Nevertheless, the mortality rate from frostbite was relatively low at only 1.5 per cent of cases.[50] Yet fingers, toes and ears were frequently lost, while in more serious cases whole limbs had to be amputated.[51] Ernst Kern recalled encountering a frostbitten comrade whose feet were so frozen his boots and pants had to be cut off: 'For the first time in my life I saw black-blue frozen extremities. [His feet were] rubbed and kneaded to accelerate the blood circulation. But it was too late. The comrade was carried away, and later I heard that both of his lower legs had to be amputated.'[52] Not surprisingly, when the German high command later developed a special medal for those who had served in the east during the first winter of the war (*Medaille Winterschlacht im Osten 1941/42*) it was colloquially known among the men as the '*Gefrierfleischorden*' ('order of the frozen flesh').[53]

One of the major problems confronting the treatment of men was getting them back to the dressing stations fast enough. By November/December 1941 too few vehicles were available for this purpose and the transport of the wounded largely depended on panje horses.[54] Delays in transport and long journeys sometimes resulted in wounded men acquiring frostbite on route to the field hospitals. Nor was that the only danger. Soviet troops, and especially partisans, often had no respect for the sanctity of transporting wounded. In fact, the large red crosses painted on German ambulances were often seen by drivers as making them even more lucrative targets and, in at least one instance, mud was used to cover it.[55] In another instance, a German doctor remarked to a comrade after removing his red-cross armband: 'That

Figure 9.1 Tending to a wounded German soldier on the approaches to Moscow (November/December 1941)

doesn't go with guns. And in any case it means nothing to the Russians. There's no Geneva Convention here.'[56]

While this may have reflected the prevailing Soviet attitude, it would be incorrect to assume that German behaviour was any different. From the first days of the war German troops disregarded the Geneva Convention. An account from June 1941 by Katschowa Lesnewna, a nurse from the fortress of Brest, told how German soldiers 'took out all the wounded, children, women and soldiers, and shot them all before our eyes. We sisters, wearing our distinctive white hats and smocks marked with red crosses, tried to intervene, thinking they might take notice. But the Fascists shot twenty-eight wounded in my ward alone, and when they didn't immediately die, they tossed in hand-grenades among them.'[57] Even if German soldiers did not always actively kill wounded Soviet troops, evidence suggests their plight was largely ignored. Anna Wendling, who worked as a nurse on the eastern front, believed that most of the Soviet wounded were never brought to her hospital, but rather 'left to die in the field'.[58]

While German medical services struggled to cope with the effect of the cold, there were new problems that were only just emerging. Russian houses as well as looted Russian clothes were typically infested with lice and the human body louse is the only vector of *Rickettsia prowazekii*, a bacterium that causes epidemic typhus. Lice had been a growing problem for the Germans since September when they first started talking over peasant homes, but typhus was only now appearing and would soon reach epidemic proportions, accounting for up to 10,000 German dead, mainly in 1942.[59] Soldiers were often warned of the importance of remaining lice free, but with the cold they had little way of protecting themselves from infection or ridding themselves of the parasites without changes of clothes or adequate delousing agents. As Franz Zebet wrote to his wife: 'I do not know how to escape the lice. There are so many lice and nits in my jacket that I dread to put it on.'[60] Another soldier noted: 'Although we were freezing, we still provided enough warmth for the lice that fed on us. We had become, quite simply tormented by vermin. We felt like livestock rather than human beings.'[61] Some soldiers came to resent the civilian population, calling them 'flea machines' and blaming them for the infestation of their homes.[62] Yet, as Leopold Schober noted, civilian houses were 'at least better than freezing'.[63] The real hope was to find a repellent agent, but with the army unable to supply anything soldiers ended up writing home asking families to send any ointments or lotions that might keep the lice away.[64] In the meantime soldiers improvised solutions. Ernst Jauernick maintained that to combat lice a fire from forest brushwood had to be made and the uniforms held over the smoke.[65] Another soldier's remedy required uniforms to be boiled in a pot for an hour and then placed in ice-cold water before being hung outside in the cold for the night.[66] The problem was that many men had no change of clothes to sustain them while their uniform was being 'cleaned', and even if they could manage the process, the lice remaining on their body would in any case ensure a rapid re-infestation.

The condition of the men in Army Group Centre on their slogging advance to Moscow was truly appalling. Starved of supplies, forced to advance in under-strength units with all manner of hardships, the *Ostheer* had long since ceased to be the great operational juggernaut of five months earlier. Indeed, one of the perverse paradoxes of soldiering under the Nazi regime was that the suffering and deprivation endured by its troops was simply expected with next to no sympathy or consideration for their plight. Their *Kampfgeist* ('fighting spirit') had to be superior to whatever events they encountered. This, then, must be contrasted to the Nazi cult of the dead, which took great care to celebrate and honour its fallen heroes. Thus, dead soldiers assumed near mythical status, as well as a degree of attention and adulation unknown in a soldier's lifetime. It was almost as if the regime thought more highly of the dead than the living, which may be an explanation for why the frightful condition of Army Group Centre elicited no discussion among the German command and played no part in considering the continuation of the attack towards Moscow. As Hitler's maxim stated: 'To the German soldier nothing is impossible!'[67] Yet seizing Moscow in December 1941 was out of the question, and the revered dead of Hitler's war in the east were set to multiply.

Cutting no ice: Guderian's final offensive at Tula

Whatever the difficulties, the road to Moscow at the end of November appeared deceptively short for the men of the Fourth Army and Panzer Group 3. Without any knowledge of just how fortified the Soviet capital was or the extent of Red Army reserves now closing up behind Zhukov's front, many men took heart that their long ordeal was almost over. Vera Kalugina, a Soviet civilian, recalled hearing Germans boasting in late November: 'Moscow kaput, Stalin kaput – the war is nearly over!'[68] Helmut Günther recalled believing that it would all be over in a matter of days with his division standing triumphantly on Red Square: 'We attacked each day. One village after another between Istra and Moscow was taken from the Ivans. We counted the kilometers to the Red Capital ... We had no doubt that we would warm our feet with Little Father Stalin in the Kremlin at Christmas.'[69] Another soldier confidently wrote home that in the spring the German advance would continue all the way to the Urals.[70] Yet as Heinrich Haape recalled with bitterness: 'Press chief Dietrich predicted a calm and hopeful Christmas; by then the campaign in the East would be over – it was almost won, now, apparently. All that would remain was "police actions", for the Red Army had been mortally defeated and would never rise again.' Haape then added, 'we half-believed Dietrich that the war would be won by Christmas, in spite of the evidence before our own eyes'.[71] No doubt the men of Army Group Centre had a powerful incentive to see and hear what they wanted to believe, but such opinion, which demanded a certain suspension of reality, was being exposed for the lie it was. Observing the tenuous state of morale at the front,

Goebbels wrote in his diary on 24 November about the 'great damage' that Dietrich's October forecast had done.[72] Field post from the end of November suggested that a percentage of soldiers were yet to be persuaded that the hard fighting would not soon be ending. A soldier from Trierenberg's 167th Infantry Division near Tula wrote home in a letter on 26 November about two competing rumours circulating within his unit. One rumour suggested that the men would be pulled out of Russia before Christmas and the other that they would take up prepared winter quarters in Riesana 150 km from Tula.[73] The prospect of a hard-fought winter campaign was, it seems, not even up for discussion. Like so many men, Alois Scheuer wrote on 30 November that his thoughts were made up of one question: 'When do I get out of this hell?'[74]

While many men wanted to believe that their ordeal on the eastern front was coming to an end and willingly embraced the propaganda that fed this hope, others were far from sure. Gustav Schrodek suggested that by the start of December 'The trust of the troops in the senior leadership dwindled; the morale had been battered.'[75] Erich Mende noted that after the victories in October hopes had risen that the *Ostheer* would surpass even Napoleon's conquests in Russia, but by December he noted 'we wondered if we might suffer a similar fate'.[76] Ingeborg Ochsenknecht, a nurse at a field hospital behind Army Group Centre, noted that the soldiers told her 'nothing good about the front, not of victorious battles, only of snow, the deadly cold, ... [and] the paralysed German offensive'.[77]

Beyond the physical torments of the campaign and the increasingly obvious mistakes of the German leadership, Soviet propaganda was another factor in Army Group Centre's declining morale. Often dismissed by the German soldiers as crude and ridiculous, there was, however, one subject that no one in the *Ostheer* could deny. The Wehrmacht's losses were its Achilles' heel and Soviet propaganda exploited the topic ruthlessly. Philip Jordan, an American war correspondent in Moscow, noted that no less than four daily papers were produced in the German language and dropped on enemy lines during the night or early morning. As Jordan explained:

> These papers are mainly concerned with drawing attention to the unlikelihood of any German soldier ever seeing his family again, and to the ultimate hopelessness of the German effort. The body of a

> dead soldier is photographed and alongside this reproduction are printed the more intimate contents of his pocket book, such as picture of his wife or of his children, and facsimiles of letters from home. And after that there is little more to be said.[78]

Clearly, the propaganda war was as cut-throat as every other element of the war in the east. Another example was an article written by the famed Soviet writer Ilya Ehrenburg, which first appeared in *Red Star* on 26 November and was then translated into German and dropped over their lines. Here Ehrenburg cited the fiancé of Gustav Reisenberg: 'Send me some pink silk for a little blouse and shirt. I have dreamed of it for a long time.' To which Ehrenburg responded: 'Some of these beggarly women are day-dreamers ... They think that the summer of 1940, the looting of France, will be repeated ... Silly German doll. Her Gustav is

Figure 9.2 A Soviet propaganda leaflet dropped to German soldiers with the title: 'The metamorphosis of the Fritizes'

killed. He lies among the snowdrifts near Volkhov. There are neither any shops selling silk nor even houses around. Only white, indifferent snow. And dead Gustav lies face-down in the snow.'[79] Another Soviet pamphlet dropped on German lines in November 1941 took a different approach and simply included a quote from Clausewitz: 'It is impossible either to hold or conquer Russia.'[80] If the men of the *Ostheer* still believed that nothing was impossible for the German soldier, they at least had to concede that conquering Russia was an extremely costly business. Charlotte Haldane, another western correspondent reporting from the Soviet Union, claimed to have been shown captured German military documents, which suggested: 'Their losses in battle were definitely enormous ... And the prospect of the war lasting for two or three years, when he [Hitler] had assured them that the campaign in the east would be merely a matter of two or three months, would add to their depression.'[81]

Certainly, there was a general decline in morale across the board, but how this affected the men of Army Group Centre depended to a large extent on the individual units; their commanders, their assignments and their ability to pull together. Helmut Günther, serving with the SS *Das Reich* division, wrote how he and his comrades 'became mutually tuned in to each other. Only through such comradeship was it possible to survive all the madness around us.'[82] Clearly, his unit had become a major source of support and emotional encouragement, but this was not always the case. Willy Peter Reese, serving with the 95th Infantry Division, recorded a very different experience:

> The extent of my life and thoughts never got beyond tiredness, fantasies of desertion, need for sleep, hunger and cold ... I had no comrades. Everyone fended for himself, hated anyone who found better booty than himself, wouldn't share, would only trade, and tried to get the better of the other. There was no conversation beyond the day to day. The weaker was exploited, the helpless left in misery. I was deeply disappointed, but then I too had become hard.[83]

Enduring the hardships of the eastern front in such an individualistic environment no doubt compounded the depression many felt and, even for those with much more developed social networks, the demands of the war simply overwhelmed them. 'My mood is so down', one soldier wrote on 30 November, 'What I have to do here, it was and is just too much for me. One slowly hits rock bottom.'[84] Indeed, it was sometimes the very closeness of the bonds between men that left soldiers feeling so helpless and depressed when death suddenly took a comrade. After the loss of his friend Fritz Farmbacher wrote in his diary on 20 November: 'Everything is so empty, so meaningless around me.'[85] Nor did a soldier have to suffer a profound personal loss to reach breaking point, sometimes the conditions alone sufficed. Léon Degrelle wrote of the toll the physical effort demanded: 'Sometime a man fell, his nerves broken by the effort. Gasping, his face against the ice, he was hoisted into the first truck that passed'.[86] Likewise, Ernst Jauernick wrote: 'The cold – and the gruelling forced marches – are pushing us to the edge of insanity.'[87] The effect, as Ernst Kern wrote, was a kind of apathetic depression: 'A thorough pessimism began to paralyse us. We no longer lived but just existed.'[88]

Clearly, Army Group Centre was pushing its men to the limit of their endurance, which had a physical as well as an emotional consequence for the *Ostheer*, but the danger this represented elicited no more of a response from the German high command than any other factor that threatened the continuation of the offensive. One regimental commander in the 87th Infantry Division let it be known that if things continued in their current state for much longer 'we would soon be frayed to the extreme'.[89] His report reached all the way to the commander of the IX Army Corps, Hermann Geyer, who responded with the words of the German romantic poet Ludwig Uhland: 'You must believe and have courage, for God makes no promises.'[90] Such indifference was resented, as one lieutenant who wrote in his diary: 'A warrior is not created from a tired, louse-infected, and numerically small company. A soldier ready for battle is not created from this.'[91] Even some of Germany's most celebrated junior officers remarked on the disparity between the higher command and the state of the troops. Hans-Ulrich Rudel, who would emerge from the war as Germany's most highly decorated combat officer,[92] stated of the early December period: 'Iron determination alone is not enough. We have reached the limit of our strength.'[93] By the same token, Alexander Stahlberg, who was later to be appointed adjutant to Field Marshal Erich von Mainstein, recalled: 'Doubts were beginning to gnaw at us all, from private soldier to commanding officer.'[94]

While doubts and fears for the future may have preoccupied the men of Army Group Centre, there was little tolerance for the actions such feelings gave rise to within the Wehrmacht.[95] Gerhard Bopp wrote on

19 November about seeing a German soldier shot (in line with the explicit orders of Strauß, the commander of the Ninth Army) for desertion. As Bopp looked on the condemned man survived the firing squad until 'the officer gives him the "mercy shot" with his pistol'.[96] According to Goebbels, by September 1941 some 800 German troops had already been shot, the majority for desertion.[97] Self-inflicted wounds was another problem on the rise,[98] yet perhaps the most desperate act on the part of Germans seeking to avoid the torments of the eastern front was to risk an even less certain fate by giving themselves up to the Red Army. In spite of Soviet propaganda, very few took such a radical step in November/December 1941 largely because Germans feared the treatment they would receive. A more innovative Soviet tactic discussed in the war diary of the 6th Panzer Division was to place 'German-speaking Jews with a Frankfurt dialect' in the forward Soviet lines and have them call out to German troops as well as issue orders attempting to confuse them so they could be killed or captured.[99]

Benjamin Iwantjer, a Soviet soldier, wrote in a letter on 17 November of meeting a recently captured German soldier who was 'gloomy, dirty and hungry'. Upon interrogation by a political officer the German proved to be very cooperative until it was mockingly proposed that he would be allowed to return to his lines. As Iwantjer's account continued: 'He did not want to go for anything in the world. For him the war was over. He was happy to be in captivity and still alive. For he had believed he would be shot here.'[100] Zhukov's memoir suggested that German morale 'had sharply deteriorated, and that they no longer believed in the possibility of capturing Moscow'.[101] Of course, some German soldiers did still consider Moscow to be an obtainable objective, but it should be questioned just how many German soldiers were actually motivated by such big strategic questions rather than by their own personal circumstances and level of comfort, which were seldom favourable. Indeed, for a majority of the men in Army Group Centre Moscow was not even their objective. The men of the Ninth Army, Second Army, Second Panzer Army and a large percentage of the Fourth Army would still have to hold the line north and south of the city irrespective of whether the Soviet capital was in German hands or not. To these men strategic questions, while not irrelevant, were at least intangibly connected to their most immediate needs.

In many respects surviving on the eastern front was as much about not losing one's life as it was about not losing one's mind, and many who won the first battle lost the second. The physical hardships, the many deprivations, the loss of comrades, the killing at the front and the murder in the rear – the eastern front was truly an apocalyptic world, but the German *Landser* not only inhabited it, he also propagated it. By late November and early December the melancholy of long distances from Germany was aided by thoughts turning to home as Christmas post needed to be written in order to arrive in time for the celebration. Writing at the beginning of December, Harald Henry's letter held back none of the pain he was feeling:

> This shall be my Christmas letter for you, written from the deepest bitterness of a life that has become abysmal. The last few days were again so terrible, the nights so agonizing that they were like the old days when it was said that people turned grey in a single night . . . I am going to be spending this celebration differently from you all, perhaps in a foxhole shattered and wounded by this terrible cold . . . Maybe [if] I am lucky, at least for a few moments, the happiness to think of you all. So many beloved, wonderful years, so many lovely Christmas celebrations . . . Probably I will just be lethargic and sad and think of something edible. Oh, this Christmas![102]

In the event, Henry would suffer none of these things or think of his family; he was killed northwest of Moscow on 22 December. Helmut Günther recalled: 'I imagined what it was now like at home. Would I ever again be able to sit at my father's table? Or would this land absorb all of us?'[103] As one soldier noted in a letter on 22 November, home was not just a great physical distance from the eastern front, it was also an emotional world away. Addressing his wife he wrote: 'Very seldom have I wept . . . Only when I am with you again rested and safe, shall we have to cry a lot and then you will understand your husband.'[104] In the same vain Peter Bamm recalled:

> We were now so distant from our hearths and homes, had been on our wandering so long a time, knew so little of where our way was leading us; so many had already died, so many had been wounded; so many had disappeared into the *terra incognita* of imprisonment – that we were beginning to forget what the past had been like.[105]

Most, however, embraced their past lives as the salvation to which they hoped to return, with family assuming the greatest, and sometimes only, motivation to struggle on. Home represented the solace of a former life to which soldiers yearned to return and in doing so leaving behind the eastern front forever. Hans Roth suggested in his diary that once home he would never speak of the events he had experienced in the east: 'All of our senses have suffered greatly during the war. We have listened to screams and moans; we have witnessed many who have suffered brutal pain, so many images about which we will be silent forever.'[106] Few who experienced the savage violence of the war in the east would ever put it behind them. Thus, Helmuth James von Moltke was correct when he wrote that the men from the east 'who return will never be the same again'.[107]

Certainly, Harald Henry was concerned that after all the trials he had endured on the eastern front he would not recover from the emotional wounds. In a letter home he wrote: 'It seems more and more doubtful to me whether any healing is still possible.'[108] Those who survived the war and opted to speak about it years after reflected the emotional burden the war had become for them. Leo Mattowitz stated:

> I don't want to know those times any more. I must not be reminded of it. I get high blood pressure at the very mention of it. The trouble is, I remember it all only too well. I can't get it out of my mind. Probably I never will. I lost so many friends. Masses of them! There were twenty boys in my school class when the war began. Only two of us were still alive when it ended ... It is indescribable. When it all began there was so much I didn't know. And I learned in the most terrible way, I can tell you. The worst time for me came right at the start, on the very first day of the invasion [of the Soviet Union], when we drove through the towns and there were dead civilians – men, women, children – lying everywhere. Till then I had never seen a dead body in my life and I couldn't eat anything for days, it affected me so deeply. Afterwards, of course, I got used to it, but it wasn't right. It wasn't right.[109]

In a similar vein Heinz Frauendorf told an interviewer:

> After the war I had nightmares even decades afterwards; one experience that I found really terrible followed me as a nightmare ...

> I was with a mortar unit and one day we all had short spades, because we had to dig our mortars in ... I was looking for a good position for our mortar; there was some loose sand and bushes and scrub and suddenly, without any warning, there's this Russian in front of me in a one-man hole, on his own. He looked at me, I looked at him. Believe me, we both got the shock of our lives ... I killed him with the spade. That followed me for a very long time.[110]

In many respects soldiering in the *Ostheer* would never end for its participants, but that was at least one burden which remained mercifully unknown to the men of 1941. Their brutalisation by warfare made them hardened soldiers, but it was the unique character of the war on the eastern front with its terrible suffering and inhumanity that Willy Peter Reese so vividly captured in his wartime writings: 'The armour of apathy with which I had covered myself against terror, horror, fear, and madness, which saved me from suffering and screaming, crushed any tender stirring within me, snapped off the green shoots of hope, faith, and love of my fellow men, and turned my heart to stone.'[111] One might say that none of the men who entered the *Ostheer* ever truly returned after the war, and November/December 1941 was only the end of an initiation period which would lead to ever greater suffering and acts of horror. Yet the men of the *Ostheer* were not victims any more than their actions were victimless. The demands of the eastern front and Hitler's war of annihilation moulded and radicalised the *Ostheer*, making it much more than just an army; it was the single greatest destructive force of Hitler's Third Reich. As Peter Bamm noted of the men who made up this force: 'They had all forgotten that once they had been workers, farmers, tradesmen. That had been too long ago. They had all become highly qualified close-combat specialists.'[112] And some even became highly efficient mass murderers with many shades of grey in between. By the beginning of December 1941, the *Ostheer*'s destructive mould was cast, its troops were inducted into its culture of violence and its months of initiation into warfare in the east were at an end. As Bamm concluded: 'The war was only now beginning in real earnest.'[113]

Having long since ignored the culminating point (as Clausewitz determined it[114]) of their November offensive, Army Group Centre was now deep into its over-extension. Indeed, it was the *modus operandi* of the panzer forces to drive themselves to the point of exhaustion in the hope of forcing a decision, and while that may have had its merits in geographically smaller theatres, the Soviet Union offered no end point; there was always another town to take, another river to cross. As we have seen, Bock was questioning the extent to which Brauchitsch and the rest of the high command (OKH and OKW) understood the precarious nature of his position and, while he was certainly correct in his suspicions, it would be wrong to assume that Bock was somehow uniquely aware of the dangers confronting his army group. Bock was more aware, but he still had little real sense of the danger into which he was leading his men, for he was determined to continue and even expand the offensive. On 1 December, Kluge's Fourth Army joined the attack and then on 2 December, Guderian's Second Panzer Army renewed its offensive north of Tula to encircle and cut off the city. Army Group Centre was wilfully trading the last of its strength in the hope of forcing a decision that was no longer to be decided.

Beyond German weakness there was a complete inability to comprehend Soviet strength. However badly Army Group Centre was faring, Zhukov's Western Front had to be worse, which necessitated remaining on the offensive to ensure the final blow was administered. In this sense the worse things appeared for Army Group Centre the more such logic dictated staying the course. On 2 December, as Second Panzer Army was preparing its offensive north of Tula, Army Group Centre sent a communiqué stating that the enemy was 'approaching the crisis point of his defence'.[115] The plan was for Schweppenberg's XXIV Panzer Corps to drive westward and link up with Heinrici's eastward attacking XXXXIII Army Corps. The operation made good progress at first (mainly due to Breith's 3rd Panzer Division and Langermann-Erlancamp's 4th Panzer Division driving westward), but as Bock noted in his diary: 'The attacking troops are terribly weak; to bolster the attack we have to make do with weak screening forces on the northern and eastern flanks.'[116] While Schweppenberg was throwing in everything he had, Heinrici had little strength to offer from the beginning. On the day before the attack the commander of the XXXXIII Army Corps wrote in a letter to his wife: 'One thing is clear, that it can't go on like this. The losses are very high, the strains on the people are superhuman.'[117]

On the second day of the attack (3 December) there was a driving snowstorm and the icy conditions further hampered movement, yet Langermann-Erlancamp's 4th Panzer Division still managed to seize the vital Moscow–Tula railway. It was a profound achievement under the circumstances, but it was also the end of Schweppenberg's strength as

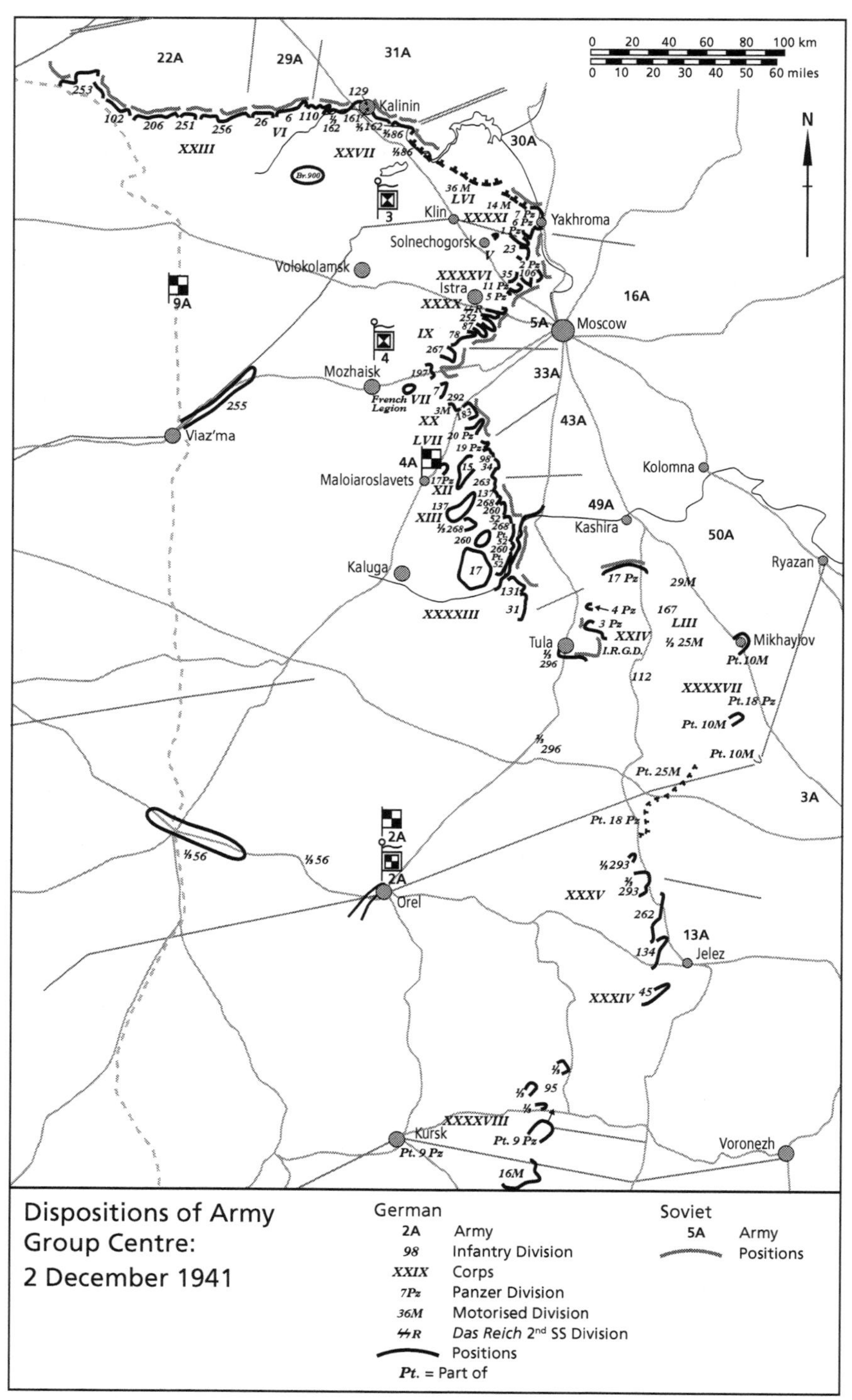

Map 9.1 Dispositions of Army Group Centre, 1 December 1941

well as his fuel. What was worse, on 4 December Soviet reinforcements started to arrive and exploit the weaknesses of XXIV Panzer Corps' exposed flanks.[118] Infantry Regiment *Grossdeutschland* was attacked and its line shattered, but far from making a fighting withdrawal even this elite formation broke and ran. The report in the neighbouring 3rd Panzer Division's war diary stated: 'A panic broke out, the town was lost, a part of Infantry Regiment *Grossdeutschland* was overrun and cut down, at times murdered. Others fled back through the forests to the southeast.'[119] Similar scenes were also unfolding to the north where Licht's 17th Panzer Division, holding the northern flank of Schweppenberg's corps, was also under heavy attack. Erich Hager wrote in his diary on 4 December: 'Our infantry involved in lots of firing in the night. The Russians attacked twice. Infantry made a run for it, lost all vehicles. Officers all dead. Infantry could get back into the village, but not much point in that, the vehicles are all gone . . . They've had enough.'[120]

Bock expressed doubts about whether the operation at Tula could be accomplished, especially since his intelligence had identified a fresh Soviet division moving down towards Tula from Kashira.[121] A last effort to cut off the city was to be made on 5 December when Heinrici's army corps plus Stemmermann's 296th Infantry Division planned a final push from the west, but apart from some local gains the offensive quickly bogged down.[122] Tula had not fallen and the Second Panzer Army was now utterly exhausted by the attempt. What is more, on 5 December aerial intelligence gave an indication of the fearsome scale of Soviet reinforcements. In the area of Ryazan and to its northwest some 2,500 railway wagons were identified along with thirty locomotives. At the same time, another 400 wagons and five locomotives were discovered at Dankowo.[123] It was evidence that the Red Army still retained the strength to punish German hubris. Not only were the Soviets arriving in force just as Guderian's exhausted armies were expending the last of their strength, but the Russian winter was now revealing its true ferocity.

The war diary of the Second Panzer Army recorded that the temperature sank to −35°C on 5 December, meaning that it was taking three to four hours to get frozen tanks started and that the oil in the machine guns had frozen rendering them useless.[124] Trucks were also freezing solid and breaking down in record numbers until the point was reached where food and other supplies could no longer be transported to the front, which meant that the mobility of Guderian's army was largely at an end.[125] The implications, if confronted by a major Soviet offensive, were without precedent for the Wehrmacht and the usual system of expedients was in no way capable of ameliorating such a looming disaster. As one German officer recalled after the war:

> An observer who looks at the Russian campaign in retrospect will come to the conclusion that the multitude of improvisations which were employed far exceeded what Moltke once designated as a 'system of expedients' in the tactical sense. Actually, the Germans were forced to introduce the first improvisations as soon as they crossed the eastern border. The farther they advanced into Russia the more expedients they had to devise. The number rose by leaps and bounds when operations began to be hampered first by mud and swamps and later by snow and ice . . . Improvisations could never be expected to compensate for the lack of vision and the fundamental blunders of the German leadership. It is no exaggeration to state that the entire Russian campaign will go down in history as one gigantic improvisation.[126]

Not surprisingly the size of the requisite improvisation was consummate to the scale of the problem, and the disparity between means and ends in early December 1941 was alarmingly large. Many far-flung German units in the Second Panzer Army were already acting largely independently, and in the coming days and weeks that self-reliance and ability to improvise the most basic requirements would make the difference between life and death. In one of the more extreme instances in early December Lemelsen's XXXXVII Panzer Corps (with Loeper's 10th Motorised Infantry Division and Nehring's 18th Panzer Division) had to somehow screen a front some 180 km long.[127]

Similar problems were plaguing Schmidt's Second Army to the south of Guderian's panzer army. Here planning was in progress for 300 km of front to be held by six infantry divisions of varying strengths. This necessitated an average 50 km of front for each division, which the overall weakness of Schmidt's army made precarious at best. A detailed report from 1 December in Second Army's war diary made clear that the divisions 'quickly and urgently required rest, reconstitution and reinforcement with replacements, trucks, horses, weapons and material'.[128] Wilhelm Prüller, a soldier in the Second Army, lamented in his diary on 2 December: 'It's snowing again, with a sharp wind, and freezing cold. The beards which we've let grow from the time we left Kursk have icicles hanging off them. We learn that we're to stay in this region and make our winter quarters here. It's a situation too disgusting to contemplate. Ah, the Russian campaign!'[129] Yet even with the army in its battered condition Schmidt, who formerly commanded a motorised corps and was a general of panzer troops, brashly insisted upon continuing his offensive towards Jelez. On 3 December, Bock attempted to dissuade him from the idea, and after speaking with him on the telephone wrote in his diary: 'He has to realise that taking and holding Jelez means extending his line far to the east. Schmidt is of the view that it is "impossible" to leave this important junction undestroyed in front of his front. He wants to take it, destroy the railroad and then withdraw.'[130] Nothing could better confirm the German commitment to an offensive doctrine. Even with Schmidt's army in a state of exhaustion, his lines over-extended, his units weakened and with full foreknowledge that Jelez could not be held, he still took the decision to strike out and seize the town.

The idea of taking Jelez for the sole purpose of its destruction must be seen in a wider context for two important reasons. First, if the town of Jelez, before its destruction, did indeed represent a profound military danger to the Second Army, then what did this suggest to Bock about Moscow's position relative to Army Group Centre? Secondly, whatever the military rationale of Schmidt's plan, the harsh reality of seizing Jelez only to destroy it spoke to a new element in the German war of annihilation, one that would become an increasing feature of the German war effort over the coming winter and, indeed, the rest of the war. Jelez fell to the Second Army on 5 December, whereupon one of the first major actions of the *Ostheer*'s ruthless scorched-earth policy was initiated. As the Second Army's war diary noted, all houses within a 15–20-km zone in front of the German winter line had to be burned or blown up with the aim of making the area a 'wasteland'. The report concluded: 'It may be necessary to raze Jelez. The city has 50,000 inhabitants.'[131]

While the Second Army successfully seized Jelez, the achievement further exhausted Schmidt's army and did little to ameliorate the effects of the coming Soviet offensive even though Second Army was far from the main target. Less fortunate was Guderian's Second Panzer Army, which on the same day that Jelez fell (5 December), called off its offensive to cut off Tula. In his memoir Guderian accurately cites the threats to his flanks, the weakness of his forces and the paralysing cold. All of which were valid reasons for halting the Tula offensive; however, Guderian went on to depict the wider German failure in December 1941 less as a result of weather-related circumstances or even Soviet/German strengths and weaknesses, but rather as a result of German command decisions. First, Guderian cited the failure of Kluge's Fourth Army to join the attack, which he absurdly represented as 'limited to an action by a fighting patrol two companies strong which, after completion of its mission, returned to its previous position ... Fourth Army had gone over to the defensive.'[132] As will be made evident in Chapter 10, Fourth Army's attack was far stronger than a mere two companies, and this claim reflects both Guderian's ignorance of the Fourth Army's role in the December fighting as well as his acrimonious relationship with the Fourth Army's commander Kluge.

The second area of blame accorded by Guderian for the failure of German operations (and especially the difficulties of the Second Panzer Army) was the role played by the German high command. Certainly, their culpability in the debacle cannot be denied, but Guderian omitted his own role, which is important to establish. The failure at Tula and, indeed, the whole attack on Moscow was, according to Guderian, 'thanks to the rigidity of our supreme command; despite all our reports those men, far away in East Prussia, could form no true concept of the real conditions of the winter war in which their soldiers were now engaged. This ignorance led to repeatedly exorbitant demands being made on the fighting troops.'[133] While that may have been true, their distance from the front was also an explanation for their exceedingly poor judgement, an explanation which Guderian cannot claim for himself. In fact, he was directly responsible for the operation at Tula, with Schweppenberg's orders coming from Guderian's panzer army not Bock or the OKH. Indeed, the fact that Guderian was able to call off the attack on his own authority demonstrates that he was beholden to no one in continuing with the offensive.[134] The same was true for the direction of operations throughout the Second Panzer Army; for Guderian was not a man who took outside interference in his area of operations lightly, even from his superiors. In his memoir, however, Guderian presents his own role as faultless. According to the panzer general, the desperate situation by 5 December was a product of the aloof command of the desk generals in East Prussia. 'But', as Guderian insisted, 'that was one mistake which no panzer general ever made. I was close enough to the battle and to my

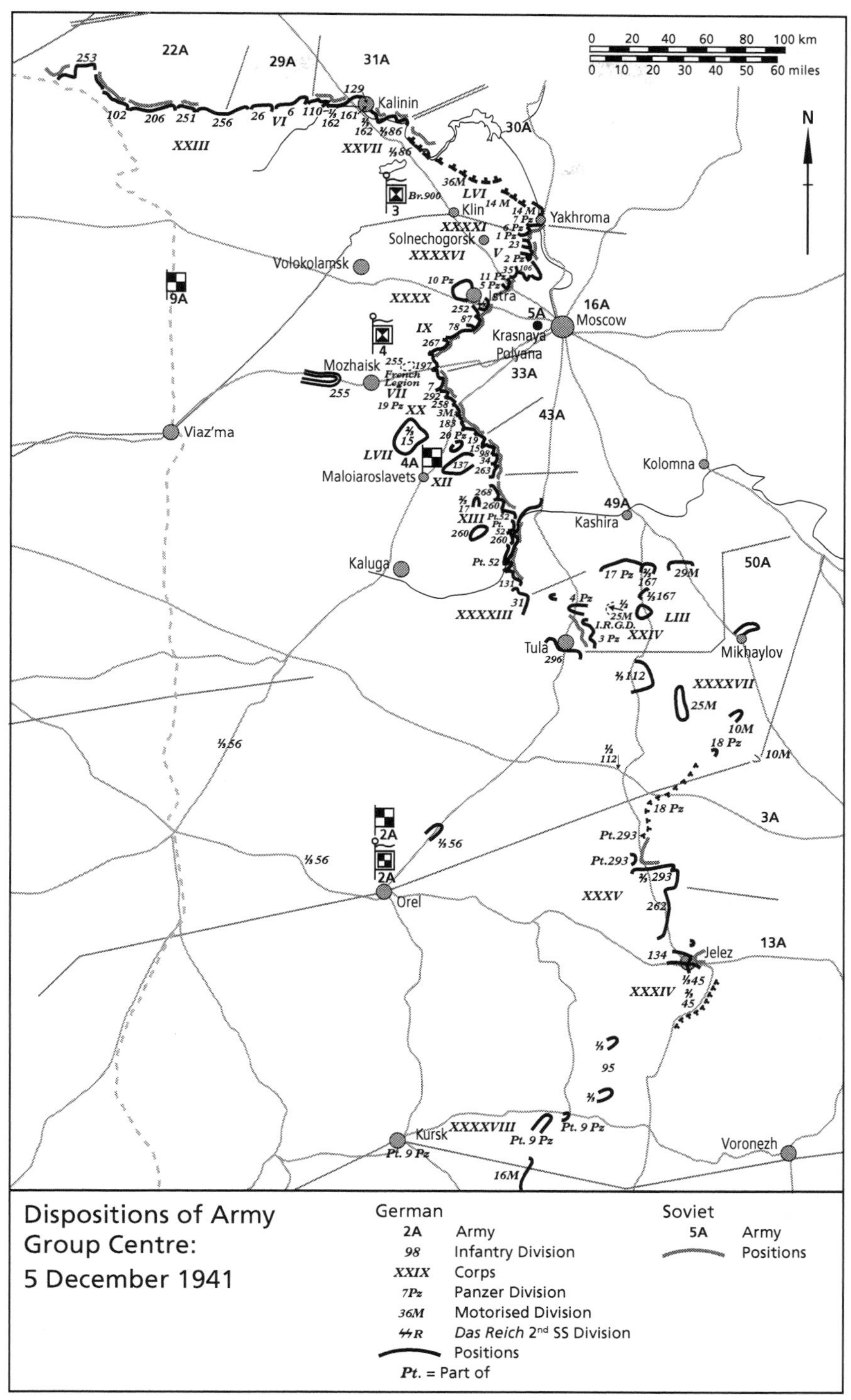

Map 9.2 Dispositions of Army Group Centre, 5 December 1941

soldiers to be able to form a clear judgement of both.'[135] Records tell another story.

When an embittered Guderian finally called Bock to announce the cancellation of his offensive at Tula he also took the time to throw a few barbs at Army Group Centre, probably for the failure to move Kluge's army more robustly towards the attack (the exact complaint is not explained). As Bock wrote in his diary: 'After several digs by Guderian, whose chief of staff only yesterday evening gave a very optimistic assessment of the operation's chances, I concluded the conversation by agreeing to his suggestion that we gradually pull the [Second Panzer] army back behind the Don and the Schat River lines.'[136] Even if we assume Guderian was not as optimistic as his chief-of-staff, it stands to reason that the panzer general continued the offensive at Tula up until 5 December because he still held out some hope for its success, but this was hardly consistent with his supposed 'clear judgement' of either his soldiers or the battle. His subordinate commanders were certainly less convinced. Heinrici wrote in his diary on 4 December: 'Why have we been sent so poorly equipped into a winter battle that makes superhuman demands? Does no one realize what it is like here?'[137] Certainly, Guderian realised less than his memoir suggests. Indeed, assigning blame to Kluge, Bock and the rest of the high command was not only symptomatic of Guderian's indefatigable self-righteousness, but reflects just how limited he was in his understanding of the wider set of problems besetting Army Group Centre. Those problems and their dangers were nowhere as profound as at the focal point of the whole German attack: the battle for Moscow.

10 TO THE GATES OF MOSCOW

'The golden towers of the Kremlin, gleaming in the sunlight': the illusion of Moscow

At the beginning of the month of December the OKH's large-scale maps (1:1 million) of central-western Russia showed two German panzer groups seemingly poised on the very fringes of Moscow, about to deliver the final *coup de grâce*. It was, however, a deceptive impression. The offensive strength of Panzer Groups 3 and 4 had almost reached absolute exhaustion, which not only undercut Germans plans for the capture of Moscow, but took no account of their operational manoeuvrability to meet any potential Soviet winter counteroffensive. Indeed, the little remaining reserve strength within Army Group Centre, principally the inactive forces on the right wing of the Fourth Army, were now to be employed to prop up Bock's stalling attack.

Contrary to a lot of what has been written about the Fourth Army's role in the battle for Moscow, Kluge was by no means responsible for Army Group Centre's failed offensive. The idea that Kluge was the great reluctant commander, whose stubborn refusal to join the attack undermined Bock's whole effort and represents one of the great missed opportunities of Germany's war in 1941, is simply untenable.[1] The Fourth Army's weak right wing never came close to making the difference between victory and defeat at Moscow, but that has not saved Kluge from becoming a scapegoat for much more important German deficiencies and weaknesses.[2]

To begin with Kluge forcefully supported the attack on Moscow from the earliest days of the November offensive with the heavy concentration of his best forces on the Fourth Army's left wing. These were set to combine with Reinhardt's Panzer Group 3 in delivering a powerful blow north of the Soviet capital. Here Kluge committed Hoepner's Panzer Group 4, Fahrmbacher's VII Army Corps, Geyer's IX Army Corps and Ruoff's V Army Corps. These forces were not only the strongest and best resourced in the Fourth Army, but they had, for those same reasons, fared better in the heavy defensive fighting against the Soviet Western Front in early to mid-November. Kluge's right wing, on the other hand, was both markedly weaker in aggregate terms and was starved of resources in order to support his attack on the left. As Kluge's chief-of-staff noted, the decision to commit the right wing of the army to battle when so little could be expected of it was a dangerous proposition that led to hours of deliberation.[3] Kluge – not without justification – doubted the panzer troops' practice of throwing all caution to the wind and staking everything on driving home the attack whatever the cost. This may mean Kluge was by comparison a less aggressive commander, but it is also true that many of his contemporaries were aggressive to a fault. Kluge was at least more aware that the relentless German offensives over the preceding five months had repeatedly failed to deliver on the promise of victory, and he was now more reluctant than ever to exhaust the last of his strength in a further futile attack to seize a few more kilometres of ground.[4]

Denouncing Kluge and placing the blame squarely on his shoulders for not committing the Fourth Army's right wing to battle earlier seems to ignore the fact that the decision was hardly his alone. No order was ever issued to Kluge (or refused by him), and ultimately the decision to join the attack was taken by Kluge himself. Indeed, in the light of the many profound problems plaguing the German advance on Moscow, as well as the highly questionable success that the Fourth Army's right wing might enjoy, Kluge's eventual decision is what should draw criticism. Ironically, for all those who attack him as the reluctant field marshal, throwing in the last of his weak forces in such a desperate gamble to break the Soviet front reflects more on his commitment to the Wehrmacht's cult of the offensive rather than on his attempts to shun it. In any case, on 1 December the strongest elements on Kluge's right wing (Materna's XX Army Corps and Kirchner's LVII Panzer Corps) moved over to the attack.[5] Another two corps (Schroth's XII Army Corps and Felber's XIII Army Corps) were judged to be 'incapable of attacking' and, on Bock's order, would maintain their positions until such time as Guderian's offensive at Tula succeeded as well as those by Kirchner and Materna. Only then would Schroth and Felber be instructed to join the offensive.[6]

The Fourth Army's new offensive began with hard fighting and, in places, heavy losses, particularly around Naro-Fominsk where the Red Army had built a comprehensive system of wooden and stone bunkers protected by countless mines.[7] On this first day, Thoma's 20th Panzer Division lost ten tanks to mines alone, but, together with Lieutenant-General Richard Stempel's 183rd Infantry Division, penetrated deep into the Soviet front line.[8] Further north the left wing of Materna's XX Army Corps also enjoyed some success with tanks provided by Knobelsdorff's 19th Panzer Division (Panzer Regiment 27 was subordinated to Materna). There were also attacks with varying degrees

Figure 10.1 Field Marshal Günther von Kluge (second from right), the commander of the Fourth Army, during a visit to the site of the 1812 battlefield of Borodino (November 1941). The Russian inscription reads: 'On 26 August 1912 the 37th Nezhenskii Infantry Regiment of Her Imperial Highness, the Grand Duchess Mariia Pavlovna, placed this monument to their glorious ancestors of the 37th Nezhenskii Infantry Regiment of Her Imperial Highness the Grand Duchess Mariia Pavlovna who heroically defended the Motherland during the Battle of Borodino. 26 AUGUST 1812'.

of progress by Lieutenant-General Willy Seeger's 292nd, Major-General Karl Pflaum's 258th Infantry Divisions and Lieutenant-General Curt Jahn's 3rd Motorised Infantry Division.[9] Kluge also maintained his attacks on Fourth Army's left wing with the addition of Colonel Roger Henri Labonne's newly arrived LVF.[10] Thus, the charge that Kluge was half-hearted in his commitment to the final German offensive against Moscow (as Guderian suggested in his memoir) is simply untenable.[11] Indeed, without knowing it, elements of Kluge's right wing pressed to within only 3 or 4 km of Zhukov's forward headquarters, causing a brief panic within the Western Front command.[12]

While the progress of Kluge's new offensive was showing signs of promise on the first day, the fresh hint of success sent the German high command into another bout of excited planning. On the evening of 1 December the OKH passed on an inquiry from Hitler questioning the direction of Kluge's new attack towards the northeast (i.e., Moscow). As Bock wrote in his diary: 'the *Führer* thinks it better to first go to the east then turn north later to destroy the enemy'.[13] Bock was incredulous. For days he had been trying to warn Halder and Brauchitsch that his army group was fast approaching the end of its strength and worried that his reports were not being duly passed on to Hitler. Such a suggestion from Hitler, Bock now concluded, was 'fresh confirmation of a completely false appreciation of the Fourth Amy's forces'. Bock confirmed his view with Kluge and then contacted Halder to complain 'that it was astounding how little the highest levels of command were informed of my reports ... We are pleased by any success, whether to the northeast or east. As I have reported a hundred times, I lack the forces to encircle the enemy.'[14] Since the last week of November Bock had certainly been sounding an increasingly desperate tone of restraint, but in reading his comments from early December one should not forget that the exaggerated expectations of his superiors were, at least in part, the result of Bock's former confidence and assurances, which he expressed throughout much of November. Indeed, it was Bock who on numerous occasions disregarded the warnings of his subordinates regarding what might be achieved; just as Halder had done at Orsha when he ordered the November offensive – an offensive Bock wholeheartedly supported.

Whatever role Bock may have played in getting Army Group Centre into its dangerous predicament, the field marshal was now doing his best to extract it. Accordingly, Bock wrote the following memorandum to the OKH:

> In spite of the repeated inquiries and reports sent to the Army High Command by the army group calling attention to the alarming state of its forces, it was decided that the attack should be continued, even at the risk of the units being completely burned out. But the attack currently under way is for the most part being conducted frontally, taking advantage of every tactical opportunity. As reported, I lack the strength for large-scale encirclement movements and now also the opportunity to shift troops to any large degree. The attack will, after further bloody combat, result in modest gains and will also defeat elements of the enemy forces, but it will scarcely have a strategic effect. The fighting of the past fourteen days has shown that the notion that the enemy in front of the army group had 'collapsed' was a fantasy. Halting at the gates of Moscow, where the road and rail net of almost all of eastern Russia converge, is tantamount to heavy defensive fighting against a numerically far superior foe. The forces of the army group are not equal to this, even for a limited time. And even if the improbable should become possible, to gain further territory at first, my forces would not nearly be sufficient to encircle Moscow and seal it off to the southeast, east northeast. The attack thus appears to be without sense or purpose, especially since the time is approaching when the strength of the units will be exhausted. A decision is required now as to what will happen then. At present the army group is extended over 1,000 kilometres with a single weak division in reserve behind the front. In this state, with the heavy losses in officers and the reduced combat strengths, it could not withstand even a relatively well-organised attack. In view of the failure of the railroads there is also no possibility of preparing this extended front for a defensive battle or supplying it during such a battle.[15]

Such an admission reflects the extent to which Bock had been shaken out of his delusions. Army Group Centre may have been closer than ever to Moscow, but its chances of seizing the city had never been further from realisation. Halder, however, epitomised the problem Bock was facing when he wrote in his diary after their telephone conversation that the decline in the army group's strength was a concern: 'But one must try to subdue the enemy with the last available resources.'[16] Clearly, Halder was undeterred by Bock's warning that a continuation of the offensive would 'scarcely have a strategic effect'. Of course, given Halder's consistent disregard for adverse strategic factors, evident throughout Operations Barbarossa and Typhoon, his indifference now to Bock's warning was hardly surprising.[17]

If the improbable was to become possible, as Bock's memorandum postulated, and Army Group Centre was indeed to make further substantive gains at Moscow, hope rested with Reinhardt's and Hoepner's panzer groups rather than with the weak right wing of Kluge's Fourth Army. The advance route being pursued by Reinhardt's tanks was still, in spite of the cold, proving swampy and where the ground was firmer the Soviets had placed thousands of mines, slowing the attack.[18] The war diary of Landgraf's 6th Panzer Division noted the appearance of a small new anti-personnel mine that could be quickly buried and contained enough of a charge to remove a victim's foot, but not kill him outright. Yet it was the density of these new mines that shocked the Germans. On one stretch of 120 m no less than 140 of the small mines were detected.[19] The roads were also mined with high explosives to destroy vehicles and create large craters. Over a 6-km stretch 1,800 kg (almost 2 tons) of explosives were discovered and removed, but such delicate work took time and the Soviets were using it to mine the next stretch of Reinhardt's advance.[20] Delays in the German advance afforded the Soviets the ability to shift their front-line forces from one threatened sector to another,[21] while allowing the newly arrived Soviet reserves to concentrate behind the front in preparation for Zhukov's counteroffensive.

Soviet manoeuvring at the front was, however, interpreted rather differently by German intelligence. According to a report by Foreign Armies East on 2 December:

> The pulling of [Soviet] forces out of the defensive front and their direct employment in particularly endangered places again confirms that the enemy has at present no accessible reserves available and that he is trying, by last-ditch employment of all forces, with the help of particularly strong minefields and by constant counterattacks, to bring the German attack to a halt in various sectors of the front.[22]

Not surprisingly, such reports calmed the nerves of the commanders like Bock and fired the hopes of others like Halder and Brauchitsch, convincing them all to carry on with the offensive secure in the knowledge that, however far their last attacks might reach, utterly exhausting their forces posed little danger because the Soviets would be equally spent. As Halder confidently wrote in his diary on 2 December: 'Defence of the enemy has reached a high-point. No new strength available.'[23] Likewise, Brauchitsch declared that the enemy had 'no large reserve formations'.[24] Bock now felt emboldened to press for a renewed push by all his army group's forces even though he still doubted its overall effect. On the evening of 2 December, messages were sent to all of the corps headquarters 'telling them', as Bock explained in his diary, 'that the undoubtedly serious moment of the crisis that the Russian defenders are facing must be exploited wherever the opportunity presents itself'; however, Bock then concluded, 'I have my doubts whether exhausted units are still capable of doing so.'[25]

Even if the German command believed that there were no more Soviet reserves left for the defence of Moscow, the battles of early December revealed another form of replacement for the Red Army. British tanks were now reported in increasing numbers, particularly in the area of Reinhardt's panzer group. German intelligence from captured Soviet soldiers warned of British tanks being concentrated on the eastern side of the Moscow canal – thirty at Dmitrov and another sixteen nearby.[26] More reports reached the OKH of new Soviet tank brigades comprising two-thirds British tanks and these were in addition to dozens already committed to battle.[27] Gerhard Bopp wrote in his diary on 3 December about seeing many burned and disabled British tanks on the highway from Senesh to Alabuschewo.[28] On the same day (3 December), Karl R., a non-commissioned officer in the 5th Panzer Division, wrote home that: 'We come across a lot of English tanks, but they're not as dangerous as the heavy Russian ones.'[29] Otto Will referred in his diary to seeing 'American tanks', which, given that only a handful of American tanks had reached the Soviet Union in 1941, may have been mistaken for British.[30] Clearly, allied tanks, as well as aircraft and British ships full of war materiels, were now arriving on the Soviet front. What the British would not offer the Soviets were men. In spite of Churchill's letter to Stalin on 22 November, which suggested British troops might be sent via Persia to fight on the southern part of the front,[31] General Sir Alan Brooke, the new Chief of the Imperial General Staff, fervently rejected this idea and on 3 December insisted all British resources be employed to clear the Germans from North Africa. Dispatching forces to Russia, Brooke argued, would be an administrative nightmare, while derailing Auchinleck's Crusader offensive.[32] Churchill did, however, have a consolation for Stalin. In keeping with his promise, on 5 December Britain, Australia, New Zealand, South Africa and Canada all declared war on Germany's eastern front allies Finland, Hungary and Romania.[33]

While Reinhardt's panzer group slowly fought its way south along the west bank of the Moscow canal, the attacks by Hoepner's panzer group made only local gains, prompting Army Group Centre's war diary to note on 2 December that, 'the XXXX, XXXXVI and V Corps have achieved as good as no progress'.[34] The reasons for this were not hard to find. On the same day (2 December) the war diary of Stumme's XXXX Panzer Corps reported that Fischer's 10th Panzer Division was unwilling to attack: 'After reports from the commanders it was no longer possible, even with the harshest measures, to get the troops forward to attack.' As the diary concluded: 'The decisive point is the complete physical and psychological exhaustion of the troops.'[35] Importantly, it was no longer the cold, the lack of supplies or even the enemy resistance that was stunting the German offensive, in places it was now also the opposition of the Germans troops themselves; acts which constituted a dereliction of duty or even revolt. Nor was Fischer's division the exception. Colonel Adolf Raegener, who commanded a regiment in Major-General Heinz Hellmich's 23rd Infantry Division, wrote on 2 December: 'Two of my battalions have refused to advance any further. The losses in officers and men have simply become too high – and there is hardly any ammunition left.'[36] Fighting next to Hellmich's 23rd Infantry Division was Veiel's 2nd Panzer Division, which on the same day (2 December) reported its men to be 'overtired and cold', rendering them 'no longer operational'. What was more, two days later the division had only seventeen operational tanks left, which meant that after arriving on the eastern front at the start of October as a fresh and fully equipped division its combat strength had been largely destroyed in just two months. To compound Veiel's misery, the 2nd Panzer Division's war diary noted that the opposing Soviet forces were receiving fresh reinforcements and were at 'full battle strength and had good morale'.[37]

Not only did the condition of the German troops impair their ability and willingness to attack, but it also made them much less reliable on the defensive against local Soviet counterattacks. Most worrying of all was the effect of the Soviet T-34, which displayed its remarkable ability to maintain its speed in the ice and snow. Holding the line against these formidable machines had always been a challenge for the German infantry, but by the end of the German offensive towards Moscow there were very few anti-tank guns in the forward lines (in part, as a result of losses and, in other instances, because the advance continued at the expense of bringing up heavy equipment). With German morale at an all-time low the result was that 'tank panic' became a major threat to weak and poorly resourced units.[38] The standard German 37-mm anti-tank gun was well known to be ineffective unless it was fortunate enough to hit weak spots such as the mantelet into which the machine gun was fitted.[39] The solutions most commonly discussed were to employ the powerful 88-mm anti-aircraft gun in a ground defence role or to bring up the heavy 100-mm K18 cannon from the artillery section.[40] Yet these were far too few in number (622 88-mm guns and 300 100-mm cannons as of the beginning of Operation Barbarossa) and they both were bulky, heavy and had a high profile.[41] This meant that it took a long time to bring up these guns and dig a prepared position for them, which worked only if the location of a Soviet attack could be anticipated in advance. Committing the 88-mm gun without being able to dig it in first, as was often the case once the ground had frozen, exposed the crew and gun to a much higher risk because the profile (and therefore the target) was so high. A shield was later fitted, but the danger of operating an 88-mm gun at the front was always high as it was a priory target for Soviet tanks. Another drawback of the 88-mm gun was that it was not really designed as an anti-tank gun and therefore the shells, weighing up to 15 kg each, had to be lifted to shoulder height to be loaded in a horizontal breach (a task much easier in the vertical position).[42] The *Ostheer*'s experience with heavily armoured Soviet tanks in 1941 led to a crash programme of producing new and better anti-tank guns, with the first prototype of the 75-mm Pak 40 appearing in November 1941. A brief period of testing followed and industrial production began in April 1942, but it would be too late for the winter battles that Army Group Centre was about to endure.[43]

In spite of the difficulties and minimal progress of Panzer Group 4, on 2 December Hoepner resolutely spurred his men to fight on and even expressed confidence that 'the goal [the close encirclement of Moscow] can still be reached'.[44] Yet on the following day (3 December), with continued poor results, Hoepner seemed to have finally accepted that his confident exhortations would have no effect on the ground. Accordingly, he wrote to Kluge informing him that the offensive strength of his panzer group was largely at an end. Consequently, Hoepner concluded: 'As a result of this situation and that of the neighbours [Panzer Group 3 and Fourth Army's right wing] the high command must decide whether to break-off the attack.' Failure to do so, Hoepner warned, would 'bleed white' his panzer group 'and make defence against Russian counterattacks impossible'.[45]

Kluge was certainly receptive to the news because after the first day's progress on the right wing of the Fourth Army his advance there got into trouble, with elements of Pflaum's spearheading 258th Infantry Division being cut off and encircled by Soviet counterattacks.[46] Desperate fighting ensued to free the trapped German units, and then on 3 December the division had to be withdrawn 'as it was under attack from all sides and found itself in a most difficult situation'.[47] As one soldier in Pflaum's division wrote a few days after the battle:

> On the Russian side there were new, battle-ready Siberian divisions ... In addition, the Russians had established a wide area of defensive positions with mines and fortifications, which first had to be broken through ... The unfavourable weather cancelled a planned strike by the Luftwaffe before we even got underway. An icy snow storm swept across the landscape limiting visibility. The ground was so slippery that our horses had difficulty keeping upright. The machine guns did not work in the cold.
>
> Despite all these disadvantages the attack went ahead and the spearhead of our regiment (the one from Colonel Wolff) came within thirty kilometres of Moscow, which is proof of the heroic courage, preparedness and endurance of our troops. Of course such an operation has its victims ... When in the end the attack could not be capitalized upon ... the effect was that in the night of 3 December we returned to the starting positions. In places there were only small remnants of once strong companies.[48]

Thus, Materna's XX Army Corps had been driven back from its forward position at the village of Troitskoye, while further south Kirchner's LVII Panzer Corps was expelled from its position at Klowa, also with heavy casualties.[49] Kluge commented to Army Group Centre on 3 December: 'The bloody losses are quite colossal.'[50] Not surprisingly therefore Kluge was sympathetic to Hoepner's claim that his panzer group could not attack any further, after all the right wing of Fourth Army was already being driven back by local Soviet counterattacks and there were indications across Kluge's front that Soviet forces were being reinforced.[51]

Part of the confusion in understanding the notion of German 'success' at the battle of Moscow have been some rather famous soldier's accounts, which claim to have seen the very spires of the Kremlin itself.[52] This is, however, a long-standing myth. The only German soldiers who ever saw the Kremlin in the Second World War were being paraded past it as prisoners of war. On 1 December, Karl-Gottfried Vierkorn claimed to have seen 'the golden towers of the Kremlin, gleaming in the sunlight'.[53] Yet Vierkorn was part of Hellmich's 23rd Infantry Division, which was still about 45 km from the centre of Moscow on the day in question (and never came much closer). Claims such as Vierkorn's first appeared in German radio propaganda in which the German soldier was depicted 'waging battles of ever increasing intensity as he came within sight of the spires of Moscow'.[54] The myth then reappeared in fictionalised postwar narratives, particularly the proliferation of German war novels, which, among others, proved very popular among *Ostheer* veterans.[55] Over time these notoriously unreliable accounts contributed towards a new grand narrative of the war in the east, which helped to establish many postwar myths, not least of which was the separation of the Wehrmacht from the crimes of the Nazi state.[56] A further problem is that war veterans, over long periods of time, tend to subconsciously assimilate public and private memories, meaning that the grand narrative as they understand it becomes more and more a part of their own stories and recollections. Thus, the idea that German soldiers came within sight of the Kremlin became an increasingly popular postwar legend, with a guise of 'proof' provided by men like Vierkorn. The problem with this particular claim is that it has become a signature event of the battle of Moscow, creating the impression that the German capture of Moscow was really an incredibly narrow failure.[57]

While no German soldier ever had a view of the Kremlin itself, this is not to say that soldiers from the Fourth Army did not see Moscow in the distance or even buildings on the outskirts of the city. In Heinrich Haape's famous account he claims to have made it to the last stop on the Moscow tram network. Investigating a rubbish bin attached to a small shelter Haape found a handful of tickets: 'We picked out the Cyrillic letters, which by now we knew spelled "Moskva".'[58] Similarly, Gerhard von Bruch's account told of reaching the outermost stops on the city bus service: 'We were only a stone's throw from Moscow's suburbs ... We know we have reached a critical moment. Either the Russian is genuinely at the end of his strength, and we will defeat him, or our advance will peter out.'[59] It certainly was a critical moment in the battle, but not because the Soviets were on the verge of defeat. If Army Group Centre had not already learned it at Minsk, Smolensk, Yel'nya, Kiev, Viaz'ma or Briansk, the Red Army would again demonstrate the remarkable power of Soviet force generation as well as the determination of the *Stavka* to return to the offensive.

Importantly, one must remember that the experiences of Haape and Bruch were very much the exception, not the rule. Most of the soldiers attacking towards Moscow were considerably further away than the capital's outermost tram or bus stops. The closest major settlement in German hands was Krasnaya Polyana some 32 km from Moscow, and only small groups of lightly armed soldiers got much closer. Gustav Schrodek, a non-commissioned officer in Scheller's 11th Panzer Division, stated: 'We were palpably close to the Russian capital. I saw a traffic sign: Moscow – 18.5 kilometres.'[60] Others claimed to have seen Moscow 'through a pair of good field-glasses',[61] but as one artilleryman noted, although they could see the city on the horizon, 'we did not fire any rounds into Moscow. It was too far away.'[62]

'Masses of Russians were suddenly appearing': the reality of Moscow

The German troops themselves may not have known that they now stood at the pinnacle of Army Group Centre's advance towards Moscow, but some in the German command certainly did. On the morning of 3 December, Kluge contacted Bock and stated that maintaining the Fourth Army's right wing in its current position 'would be totally impossible'. Bock, however, resisted the call for their withdrawal, hoping that developments further north might lead to an alleviation of the situation, but by 4 pm Kluge reported that the situation had become untenable and that he, on his own authority, had authorised the withdrawal back behind the Nara River from where the offensive had begun on 1 December. Bock received the news and acquiesced. At the same time, Kluge informed Bock of Hoepner's report stating that Panzer Group 4's offensive strength 'was largely at an end'.[63] It was a bitter moment for Bock, but his resolve was still unbroken and he remained unwilling to concede that his offensive had finally failed. His thoughts now turned to Reinhardt's slow grinding attack in the desperate hope that it might force the Soviet defences to buckle. This was, of course, a long since forlorn hope, but Bock had not earned a reputation as 'the Holy Fire of Küstrin' for his lack of resolve.[64]

As noted earlier, Bock was not the refined and chivalrous Prussian gentleman, seemingly belonging to a bygone era of warfare, he was in fact very much a Nazi-era general compliant in both thought and deed. The war of annihilation in Army Group Centre's rear area progressed with Bock's tacit approval, which included awareness that *Gruppenführer*

Arthur Nebe's *Einsatzgruppe B* was busily murdering tens of thousands of Jews.[65] Indeed, Nebe's headquarters were also located in Smolensk, a short distance from Bock's, where preparations were in hand for new 'actions' (i.e., mass shootings) in Moscow itself. A special *Vorauskommando Moskau* (Advance Commando Moscow) was established to follow the combat troops into the city.[66] Nor is Bock's reputation to be challenged simply on the strength of his passive acceptance of the Nazi state's war of annihilation. In spite of his somewhat more advanced years (Bock turned sixty-one on 3 December 1941), the field marshal was no stickler for older military concepts. He was an overtly offensive-minded commander of the kind frequently attributed to the younger panzer commanders. However, Bock's conception of warfare in 1941, like those of Guderian, Hoepner, Reinhardt and Hoth, was far too operationally focused for his rank and position and, even in operational matters, Bock was aggressively minded to a fault. It was these qualities that kept him from halting the offensive towards Moscow even in the face of so much resistance, as well as the profound danger of utterly exhausting his army group. Not surprisingly, Bock also exhibited elements of the Nazi cult of the 'will', in which material circumstance was secondary to the determination to achieve a desired outcome. The lengths to which Bock was prepared to go to ensure his orders were carried out is revealed by looking ahead to the opening days of the Soviet counteroffensive. On 8 December, Bock answered the desperate pleas of his subordinate commanders with the instruction that 'either one held out or let himself be killed. There were no other choices.' He then concluded: 'Thus the only important thing was to see to it that everyone stubbornly held onto whatever he had to hold.'[67] Such sentiments are more reminiscent of the pitiless orders by well-known 'Nazi' generals from the last year of the war when fanatical, self-sacrificing defence was demanded at all levels. Bock was certainly not sentimental for some bygone age of the kaiser's imperial army where the prosecution of war may be viewed as somewhat less 'total'. From his acceptance of the mass killings in his area of command to his forceful application of new military concepts dominated by panzer operations, Bock was hardly an unusual choice for the stewardship of Hitler's most important army group in the invasion of the Soviet Union. Of course, his strategic grasp of events was woefully lacking, as it was for almost all the senior Wehrmacht commanders, but that was certainly no drawback in a military culture dominated by National Socialist thinking. Bock was no simple participant; he was an active instigator and convinced proponent of Hitler's drive for *Lebensraum*. He was responsible in no small part for both the direction of the war in the east as well as its uncompromising character. That uncompromising character extended to his own men, who would to be driven to the end of their strength, and even beyond, before Bock would surrender his chance to break Moscow's defences.

For all Bock's unbending inflexibility he could not deny the fact that his army group was rapidly nearing the end of its strength, but, with good reason, he still doubted whether Hitler fully appreciated just how far Army Group Centre's combat strength had sunk. Halder claimed that he had been faithfully passing on all Bock's reports to the OKW, but on 3 December Bock confided in his diary his concerns that Hitler was not being given 'the unvarnished truth' and that the thought 'gave me no peace'. Bock therefore took the radical step of bypassing the OKH and contacting Jodl at the OKW directly. As Bock explained: 'Though I don't want to go over the heads of the Army High Command, I am calling you because I don't know if the view of the attack with respect to the state of the forces which I have been putting forward for some time is really clear to the highest level of command.'[68] Bock went on to outline Kluge's failed attack on the Fourth Army's right wing, as well as the fact that Hoepner was capable of only the most minor progress. Bock was, however, forthcoming about his continued hopes for Reinhardt's attack, which may well have undermined the whole purpose of his call. As Bock explained:

> Nevertheless, I am not giving up hope that pressure by Panzer Group 3 will yet result in v Corps' flank being relieved so that this corps can advance south and carry the attack even further. But I cannot promise this. The attack is still ordered for the entire front, but, as I have been doing for days, so today I am pointing out that the hour is in sight when the troops will be exhausted. If the attack is called off then, going over to the defensive will be very difficult. This thought and the possible consequences of going over to the defensive with our weak forces have, save for my mission, contributed to my sticking with this attack so far.[69]

Ironically, Bock may have delivered the unvarnished truth as he understood it, but he also provided an unmistakable argument for continuing with the offensive in spite of all the problems he was so concerned the

OKW did not understand. Indeed, Bock's logic seemed to suggest that the weaker the army group became from its relentless attacking the more dangerous going over to the defensive would be, and thus continuing to attack – without any realisable objective or strategic benefit – was the best course of action.

Smoothing over his bypassing of the OKH, Bock called Halder to report on his conversation with Jodl. Halder emphasised that he had already sent the OKW a detailed report on Army Group Centre's situation that raised, among other things, the question of halting the offensive.[70] It was a prudent, if long overdue, step, but the discussion about bringing Operation Typhoon to a final conclusion still faced significant obstacles. Field Marshal Leeb at Army Group North believed it 'not improbable' that a slackening of the offensive towards Moscow would release Soviet reserves to strengthen attacks against his forces at Tikhvin and Leningrad.[71] There were also implications for the home front. As recently as 25 November the Nazi newspaper the *Völkischer Beobachter* had printed a map on its front page depicting Moscow at the centre of a bull's-eye target. By early December, however, the subject of Moscow's capture had all but disappeared from German newspapers and radio.[72] There could be no denying Moscow's significance to the German people and calling off the offensive would not only represent a major German setback, but clearly signal that the war in the east was far from being decided, as Nazi propaganda had so triumphantly claimed in October.

Another problem in achieving any resolution on the question of halting Typhoon was Hitler's unexpected absence from the 'Wolf's Lair' in East Prussia. Hitler had flown to Mariupol in Ukraine on 2 December to resolve the 'confusion' regarding the First Panzer Army's withdrawal from Rostov, but the weather rapidly deteriorated and Hitler's return flight on 3 December only got as far as Poltava in eastern Ukraine. There he had to spend two more nights (returning to the 'Wolf's Lair' on 5 December).[73] Thus, in the critical days of early December, Hitler, who in any case was more concerned by events in Army Group South than Army Group Centre, was largely outside the loop of discussion concerning Bock's situation. Of much less importance, Brauchitsch's frail health, after suffering a heart attack on 10 November, finally led to discussions about his replacement as Commander-in-Chief of the Army. On 4 December, General of Infantry Bodewin Keitel, head of the Army Personnel Department (and the younger brother of Field

Marshal Keitel at the OKW), met with Halder to sound out the Chief of the Army General Staff. Halder consented to his chief's replacement and the younger Keitel resolved to take the matter to his brother.[74] The post of Commander-in-Chief of the Army, already sidelined by Brauchitsch's ill-health and submissive nature, was soon to be entirely superfluous once Hitler took the title for himself. Probably aware that his days were numbered, on 5 December Brauchitsch informed Halder of his intention to resign his command of the German army.[75]

The difficulties on the eastern front, as well as the increasing nervousness within the Ministry for Armaments and Munitions in the wake of Todt's, and a number of other leading industrialists, doubts about the prospects for Germany's war effort, gave advocates of gas warfare their first real opportunity to promote their ideas. This was not the first time in the war that the use of gas, as either an offensive or defensive agent, had been broached, but Germany's continued rapid success had always pushed the discussion to the margins. Hitler insisted upon a gas capability for Germany should his enemies strike first, but had taken no serious interest in its offensive application. When Barbarossa was first launched there had been fear on all sides that a gas war might result.[76] The British received reports that the Germans intended to use gas in the east and threatened retaliation if they did. At the same time, Goebbels sought to calm fears that the Soviet government planned a gas attack by likewise promising swift retaliation. A pamphlet was also issued to German troops instructing them to expect attacks with poison gas and bacteria in combat with the Red Army. In the event, Germany's string of battlefield successes fed the enduring hope of a final victory against the Soviet Union and left discussions of gas warfare sidelined. With the deepening crisis in German armaments production during in the second half of 1941, lobbyists for gas warfare unsuccessfully attempted to defend their production programmes from cuts. In early December, Hitler received a report on the development of new nerve gases such as Trilon 83 (Tabun) and Trilon 46 (Sarin), which was six times deadlier. The main gas production facility at Dyhernfurth, with a manufacturing capacity of 1,000 tons a month, could be put into full production by spring 1942. The report then concluded: 'Neither captured documents nor other intelligence sources contain any indication that the use of these or similar gases with the same effects is to be expected from the enemy. This means that Germany is clearly superior in the area of gas warfare, and this superiority must be maintained.' Hitler agreed. He was not about to initiate a gas war, but he insisted that German capabilities and superiority be maintained whatever the cost.[77] It was another burden that Germany's overstrained war economy could hardly afford, but it also gave hope to those elements within the chemical industry and armaments agencies who continued to advocate gas as an offensive option, especially for the eastern front. On 7 January 1942, Halder noted in his diary: 'Colonel [Hermann] Ochsner is trying to talk me into a gas war against the Russians.'[78] Such advances were rejected by the German high command, but not out of any timid sensibility towards the use of chemicals as killing agents; rather, there was a genuine fear of Allied reprisals. After all, the experimental killing of Jews with gas was already proceeding apace with 1,200 Jews killed at a clinic in Bernburg on 25 November 1941.[79]

Strategic weapons and German planning were no doubt important components to the development of the wider war, but they had little immediate bearing on the lives of the men in Army Group Centre. Most importantly, no decision had been taken to halt the offensive, so the advance had to continue in spite of its bleak prospects. As Hellmuth Stieff wrote:

> We have launched this attack largely with infantry regiments and can give them little tank protection. Our high command has urged us forward with an almost unreal sense of optimism. I instinctively feel this cannot work. We have assembled everyone we can find, even bringing up security detachments and putting them in the front line. These men are unsuited to intense combat, and when their commanders were killed in the first hour of the offensive, the rest refused to continue. They have been driven forward only because our artillery units threatened to open fire on them.[80]

The reluctance of the men to continue attacking was not just a reflection of their exhaustion or the bitter cold, Soviet defensive positions were often well manned and could be extremely costly to assault. Geyer's IX Army Corps reported between 200 and 300 casualties on 3 and 4 December alone, and there is no reason to believe this was in any way exceptional.[81] Consequently, Bock's offensive was claiming hundreds of men every day, while reports continued to arrive suggesting that the defending Soviet armies were gaining a dangerously large numerical superiority. On 5 December, Ruoff's V Army Corps noted: 'The Russians in front of the corps are far superior in strength (four battle-ready divisions and parts of two further divisions and tank units)'.[82] Likewise, on 4 December, the war diary of Vietinghoff's XXXXVI Panzer Corps noted: 'Intelligence and information from prisoners reveal that the enemy in front of the corps is constantly being reinforced.' The diary went on to speak of three new divisions being added to the enemy's order of battle, at least one of which was from Siberia and said to be 'very powerful'. Yet more worrying was the conclusion of the diary entry, which stated that the enemy were engaging in offensive preparations.[83] Such local reports should not necessarily be understood as the missed opportunity to forewarn Army Group Centre of Zhukov's coming offensive. Foreign Armies East, the army's main intelligence organ, was not reporting any Soviet offensive capability and local Soviet attacks were nothing out of the ordinary. Indeed, some of these could be far from small engagements. One failed Soviet offensive on 4 December against Krüger's 1st Panzer Division resulted in an estimated 1,000 Soviet dead lying in front of the German lines.[84] A more successful Soviet attack against Funck's 7th Panzer Division saw the Germans pushed back, but then, in a counterattack, Funck's men reclaimed their front line. Yet, as Panzer Group 3's war diary noted, the cost of this action was the 'complete exhaustion' of the forces involved, to the point where the observation was made 'some of the people can no longer hold weapons'.[85]

Under such circumstances, Bock decided at midday on 4 December that Reinhardt and Hoepner should pause to gather their strength for a renewed offensive on 6 December.[86] The remainder of Kluge's Fourth Army was now on the defensive, and they would be joined on the following day (5 December) by Guderian's panzer army. Whatever Bock still hoped might result by continuing his offensive now depended upon Panzer Groups 3 and 4 northwest of Moscow. However, in a letter to his wife on 4 December Hoepner revealed that he no longer believed in success: 'I have accomplished very much, but not yet the ultimate goal. The forces are no longer sufficient. The troops are completely finished. One can of course still push them on, but then one day there is nothing left. By contrast the Russian is reinforcing daily, bringing everything available from other fronts against me.'[87] Hoepner was not, however, inclined to conclude that his defeat was a result of Soviet strength; rather, he blamed Kluge, in much the same way Guderian had. Continuing the letter to his wife, Hoepner explained: 'From 18 to 29 November, after heavy fighting, I alone came to within thirty kilometres of Moscow. I demanded that Kluge should also attack so that not all the Russian divisions and tank brigades could be concentrated against me. On 1 December [Kluge] now also attacked, but with grossly inadequate forces and these were withdrawn yesterday.'[88] Hoepner was convinced Kluge had failed to support his attack and yet, as we have seen, the commander of the Fourth Army was hardly the reason behind Army Group Centre's failure at Moscow. Nevertheless, Kluge became a scapegoat for far more complex failings in German strategy. Concluding his letter of 4 December, Hoepner provided a final ignominy: 'It is very bitter when one is convinced that with maximum effort and all available means, to have called for the very last from the troops, to have had success looming and now ... in the deciding moment to be left in the lurch and forced to resignation. Not a pleasant end to the year.'[89]

Even at the point of admitting his defeat one can see how restricted Hoepner's understanding was of what the contributing factors really were. Far beyond Kluge's own role – whatever one may agree that to be – one cannot but wonder how Hoepner conceived of any kind of success in the prevailing conditions. Hoepner, however, was by no means alone in this kind of blinkered thinking. Guderian also sought to blame his defeat at Tula in large part on Kluge; while Bock, who did not blame Kluge for anything, was determinedly pressing on with the offensive supported by his superiors. It was as if the appalling condition of the German troops, the freezing temperatures and the Red Army were all entirely extraneous to German strategic direction; it was as if the generals themselves could lose the battle through blunder or miscalculation, but that it was entirely their battle to win or lose. Deciding not to halt the offensive was therefore a decision not to accept defeat and thus maintain the prospect of victory. Such a conceptual framework almost seems too flimsy to be credible, but one must not forget that the whole German command had for weeks supported an offensive that, even before it began, made little practical sense. Now on 4 December the ambiguous concept of German success can perhaps no longer be understood in any normative sense – if it ever could be in the course of November. Here our understanding requires a transition from the physical to the metaphysical world, something that defies the usual interpretative framework of military histories.

With incontestable evidence linking the Wehrmacht's top leadership to the Nazi cause and its ideals (as research into the war of annihilation has shown), one may well begin to enquire just how far the Nazi worldview informed the generals' judgements in strictly military matters.

In other words, if National Socialist thinking had already convinced the generals to partake in blatantly criminal matters, how far did this same corrupting phenomenon impact their direction of military campaigns? Certainly, there are no easy answers, but already in 1941 one can identify central tenets of the Nazi worldview impacting decisions. Emphasising the primacy of 'will' in the achievement of objectives would be one example, just as the ardent adherence to an *Endsieg* in early December 1941 would be another. In spite of the prevailing circumstances, which seemed to demand a cessation of the attack, the absolute refusal to stop the offensive and concede defeat was an end in itself. It served to avoid defeat and maintain the chance of victory; an objective requiring no more tangible goal or recognisable aim. It certainly did not need to be considered in any other strategic context. Thus, the question of what the German command hoped to achieve on 6 December is moot because they were not focused on a goal that we can measure. The principal aim was to remain on the offensive; that alone promised victory without any further need to consider how that might be obtained. From a contemporary perspective such a viewpoint makes little sense, but in context of National Socialist military thinking there was no discussion about it, unless, like Kluge, one was seen to be opting out of the maximum commitment to victory, which alone allowed defeat.

With orders to renew the attack on 6 December, Hoepner called together the chiefs-of-staff of all the corps in Panzer Group 4 to assess their strengths and capabilities. The meeting took place on 5 December and involved representatives from all five corps (V, VII, IX, XXXX and XXXXVI). Geyer's IX and Fahrmbacher's VII Army Corps were reported to be: 'No longer operational, only conditional defensive capability.' Vietinghoff's XXXXVI Panzer Corps reported that Scheller's 11th Panzer Division was no longer operational (it fielded just fifteen tanks at the end of November), but that Fehn's 5th Panzer Division could resume the attack. Stumme's XXXX Panzer Corps reported that Fischer's 10th Panzer Division was utterly exhausted and required two weeks for complete rest and reorganisation. *Brigadeführer* Wilhelm Bittrich's *Das Reich* was deemed operational, but only with very limited objectives. Ruoff's V Army Corps reported that two of its divisions (Hellmich's 23rd Infantry Division was Veiel's 2nd Panzer Division) could also attack with limited objectives, but that the remainder (Major-General Rudolf Freiherr von Roman's 35th and Dehner's 106th Infantry Divisions)[90] could not attack at all.[91] Thus, out of five German corps just four divisions could be found that still retained an ability to attack, and three of these with only limited objectives.

The situation report in the war diary of Panzer Group 4 on 5 December noted that the troops were 'lacklustre and in alarming masses indifferent'.[92] As Hans-Heinrich Ludwig remarked in a letter home: 'What our men must endure can never be appreciated!'[93] The temperature also reflected the onset of the ferocious Russian winter, with the thermometer on 5 December reaching -30°C and reports being sent from Vietinghoff's XXXXVI Panzer Corps that even the insides of the tanks were now freezing in spite of the motors being kept running.[94] In the first five days of December, Thoma's 20th Panzer Division reported 294 cases of frostbite,[95] while Landgraf's 6th Panzer Division reported 129 cases on 5 December alone.[96] Not surprisingly, Ruoff's V Army Corps concluded: 'As a result of the uninterrupted battle and having to remain out in the open in temperatures of minus twenty-seven degrees the men have reached the limit of their physical endurance.'[97]

On the same day that Hoepner was assessing the strength of his panzer group (5 December), Reinhardt's principal attack formation, Model's XXXXI Panzer Corps, reported that a successful attack 'can no longer be expected of the corps'.[98] On 3 December, Bock's faith in the offensive was largely justified by the hope that Reinhardt might yet unhinge Soviet defences and allow further advances to the southeast,[99] but with Model's corps now also grinding to a halt, Bock's offensive was more an order on paper than a tangible reality. Operation Typhoon was finished whether the German command wanted to acknowledge it formally or not. As Reinhardt wrote after the war: 'Panzer Group 3 saw itself forced on 5.12 to act independently and halt its attack.'[100] Reinhardt's actions may appear a *fait accompli*, brought on by Model's inability to achieve anything more on the attack, but in fact he was also confronting a new and far more serious problem, the extent of which would, in the coming days, astonish the German command.

On 5 December, the Soviet winter offensive opened somewhat modestly with attacks first by the Thirty-First Army of Konev's Kalinin Front against the positions of Strauss' Ninth Army east of Kalinin. This early morning attack was joined at midday by the Twenty-Ninth Army's attack west of Kalinin; in both instances Soviet forces were able to gain shallow crossings over the Volga River.[101] While Konev's Kalinin Front began its attack on 5 December, Zhukov's Western Front did not officially begin its offensive until 6 December, although German records suggest Reinhardt's panzer group was already under heavy attack on 5 December. The front line of Funck's 7th Panzer Division on the Moscow canal was broken through, and further north Major-General Heinrich Wosch's 14th Motorised Infantry Division was also under heavy attack. A single reserve battalion held by Gollnick's 36th Motorised Infantry Division was ordered to Rogachevo to provide support.[102] Gollnick's division held the long, tenuous northern flank of the panzer group and was not yet under attack, but Reinhardt knew he could no longer afford to expend strength on an offensive to the south.[103] No one in the German high command yet knew just how great the danger was, but at the front local intelligence suggested the danger was profound. Heinz Otto Fausten ominously recalled from 5 December: 'The Moscow–Volga canal lay before us, and on the other side, masses of Russians were suddenly appearing. The sheer number of them left us speechless. There were endless marching columns, soldiers on skis, in white coats. And then there were tanks, artillery units and countless motor vehicles. Where had they all come from?'[104] What Fausten witnessed was only the vanguard of Zhukov's counteroffensive. Unbeknown to the German leadership hundreds of thousands of fresh Soviet troops were now moving up from their unidentifited areas of concentration, about to turn the tables on Bock's over-extended army group. The night of 5 December was the eye of the storm between the German typhoon and the Soviet winter offensive.

That evening (5 December) Bock could no longer deny that his great offensive was over. In his diary he noted the worrying new attacks against the Ninth Army and along the Moscow canal, and he admitted that Reinhardt's 'offensive strength is gone' as well as that of Guderian in the south. With Hoepner's handful of remaining operational divisions supposedly set to renew the attack on 6 December, Bock now called Kluge and asked: 'whether, given the situation, the attack by Panzer Group 4 planned for tomorrow should go ahead; he [Kluge] said it should not'.[105] The fact that Bock needed Kluge to confirm this speaks again to his difficulty in accepting Army Group Centre's strategic reality, yet by 5 December even Bock could no longer deny Operation Typhoon's defeat. In the evening he called Halder and gave him the news. As Halder noted in his diary: 'No more strength. Tomorrow's attack by Panzer Group 4 is not possible. Whether a withdrawal is necessary will be reported tomorrow.'[106] A withdrawal would indeed be necessary, but more on Zhukov's terms than on the German high command's.

Even before the Soviet winter offensive began in earnest confirmation that the German attack on Moscow could no longer continue underscored the enormity of Army Group Centre's defeat. As Otto Skorzeny noted: 'The realization that the limit of our advance had been reached was even more depressing than a defeat or the weather. Our goal was within reach and we could not seize it!'[107] Far from seizing Moscow the utter exhaustion to which the German command had subjected Army Group Centre greatly aided what was now to follow. Even before the launch of the Western Front's offensive on 6 December the Red Army had defeated Operation Typhoon and saved Moscow (at least for the winter). Now it was up to Zhukov and Konev to exploit that victory. As the American journalist Cyrus Sulzberger observed, there were columns of Soviet troops passing through Moscow on their way to the front and singing hortatory choruses 'in the remarkable voices common to the Slav peoples':

> The storm breaks over our fields.
> Clouds come down to earth and greet the uninvited guests with rains of fire.
> The hour has struck, Comrade Soldier.
> And not once and not twice we've taught our enemies to keep off the Russian steppe.[108]

CONCLUSION

On 22 November the weekly German magazine *Militär-Wochenblatt* proclaimed the success of the *Ostheer*'s war in the east with a remarkable and, in most instances, roughly accurate tally of achievements:

> November 22nd marks five months since the German Wehrmacht moved against the threat of a Bolshevist attack from the east. In that time, it has occupied 1.7 million square kilometres of the territory of the Soviet Union, containing three quarters of its industry and 75 million of its inhabitants. It has simultaneously taken 3,792,600 prisoners and destroyed 389 divisions; including battle casualties we may estimate total Soviet losses at over eight million soldiers. Materiel losses correspond to human ones: more than 22,000 tanks, 27,452 guns, 16,912 aircraft have been destroyed or captured . . . It is a balance sheet that represents both a proud success for the German Wehrmacht and an annihilating defeat for the enemy.[1]

It was, without question, an extraordinary achievement on paper, but it did not change the basic fact that Germany's war effort was doomed. As Robert Citino concluded, by the end of 1941 Germany had, in a strategic sense, gained nothing: 'In the eastern campaign, the Germans had brought *Bewegungskrieg* [mobile warfare] to a destructive peak that it would never know again . . . But it had achieved precisely nothing.'[2] This is not the impression gained from the figures reported in the

Militär-Wochenblatt, and certainly after the war many cited those statistics – including the surviving German generals – to suggest that it was only after 5 December and the advent of the Soviet winter offensive that Germany suffered its first defeat of the war. Yet suggesting that Operation Barbarossa or Operation Typhoon were anything other than failures is to deny their original intent. Neither operation set out to simply degrade the fighting capability of the Soviet Union; for good reason both operations were tasked with achieving victory in the east. As Field Marshal Friedrich Paulus, one the chief architects of the Barbarossa plan, noted after the war: 'That none of the objectives set for the 1941 campaign had been reached is undeniable. Leningrad had not been captured, Moscow had not fallen and contact with the Finns on the Svir had not been established . . . The operations during the summer and autumn in the south had been held up partly by enemy action and partly by the weather'.[3]

My successive studies of the *Ostheer*'s eastern campaign in 1941 have sought to trace the roots of Germany's defeat in both Barbarossa and Typhoon, while at the same time highlighting the profound ramifications that these failures entailed. From the earliest period the *Ostheer* was not only falling well short of its intended goals, but the cost of these operations made each subsequent phase of the campaign less likely to achieve the ultimate objective. Even before the end of the summer the eastern campaign had transformed from a blitzkrieg to an attritional struggle. In the context of Germany's weak economic base, a war of materiel was precisely what Hitler had hoped to avoid. Accordingly, the end of the *Bewegungskrieg* had one overriding implication: Germany could no longer win the war in the east.

Such a claim does not require one merely to read history backwards. Clear-sighted German contemporaries, especially those unencumbered by a Nazi worldview, were already drawing their own such conclusions about the war in 1941. Ulrich von Hassell and Helmuth James von Moltke evinced the darkest pessimism regarding Germany's future prospects, while even leading Nazis such as Fritz Todt were unable to deny the reality of Germany's situation. Mihail Sebastian, a Romanian Jew, wrote in his diary on 3 December 1941 about reading a copy of Oswald Spengler's *Années decisive* published in 1932. The 'burning topicality' of its 'stunning predictions' about the 'impossibility' of conducting warfare against Russia led Sebastian to copy out whole passages from the book. According to Spengler's prewar view of Russia:

> The population of this vast plain, the largest in the world, cannot be attacked from outside. The spatial expanse is a political and military strength that no one has ever been able to overcome. Napoleon himself had to learn this through experience. Even if the enemy were to occupy the vastest regions, it would still be of no avail ... The whole region to the west of Moscow – Byelorussia, the Ukraine, the whole region between Riga and Odessa that was once the most flourishing in the Empire – is today no more than a huge 'buffer' against Europe that could be abandoned without a collapse of the system. This being so, however, the idea of an offensive by the West makes no sense. It would run up against a void.[4]

Certainly, before Hitler's invasion of the Soviet Union the concept of Spengler's 'void' did not worry anyone in the German high command, and even after months of campaigning there was still a failure to understand that Soviet strength could be sustained from lands well to the east of Moscow. What is more, the tactical and operational advances that had been achieved by the Wehrmacht since the First World War could not in any way offset what Williamson Murray referred to as 'the disastrous results of strategic myopia'.[5] With such profound conceptual limitations, it should not be surprising that, in spite of the back-to-back failures of Barbarossa and Typhoon, not a single general was fired in the German high command (although Brauchitsch was slated for replacement on health grounds). Nor was there even a sense on 5 December that changes needed to be made. Although personalities would soon clash in the wake of the Soviet offensive (and generals would indeed be fired) there can be no question that November and early December 1941 were marked by a remarkably harmonious period of strategic conformity and collaboration (with the one exception being the events in late November in Army Group South). Considering the disastrous predicament into which Army Group Centre, and indeed the entire *Ostheer*, had sunk this relative harmony again suggests the unifying, and yet distorting, presence of a common National Socialist thinking.

Throughout 1941 such thinking fed an insatiable demand for military conquest, which even the unprecedented size and strength of the *Ostheer* could not hope to sustain. As one operation followed another and the panzer groups began to falter, the demands for ever greater conquests did not cease. What is more, the generals responsible for this state of affairs were not simply driven to it by Hitler, nor did they undertake these operations merely in the context of 'working towards the Führer'.[6] The successful indoctrination and Nazification of the Wehrmacht not only led its commanders to perform and comply when instructed, but to think and act independently along National Socialist principles. In this sense they were working without the Führer. The Orsha conference of November 1941 was an entirely army affair, free to determine its own objectives independent of Hitler, yet in the face of almost universal opposition from Army Group Centre's hard-pressed army chiefs-of-staff, Halder dismissively insisted upon a continuation of the offensive towards Moscow.[7] His only concession was that the more distant objectives of Vologda and Gorky, each hundreds of kilometres to the east, could wait until 1942.[8] Nor was Halder the exception in his determination to remain on the offensive. Brauchitsch, Heusinger, Bock, Greiffenberg, Strauss, Kluge, Weichs, Schmidt, Hoepner, Reinhardt, Guderian, Kesselring and Richthofen all backed a continuation of the offensive, albeit with varying degrees of enthusiasm. Undoubtedly, part of their motivation was the so-called 'Marne complex', the myth that the German army could have avoided defeat in the First World War by making one last push towards Paris in 1914.[9] As Heusinger stated after the war: 'By continuing the attack one hoped to seize Moscow before the onset of winter. One did not want to end up looking back and seeing that five minutes before midnight one had given up.'[10] Yet the 'Marne complex' is itself a decidedly self-deceiving concept, investing a greater degree of veracity in the perceived outcome of a battle from 1914 than in the far more relevant and numerous battles of 1941.

In November 1941, two far more instructive conclusions should have framed German strategic thinking. First, that the force generation of the Red Army, which had proven itself consistently equal to the task of patching up the Soviet front even after the calamities at Minsk, Smolensk, Kiev and Viaz'ma, might continue to undermine German plans at Moscow. After all, there were innumerable reports of fresh Siberian divisions arriving at the front throughout November. Was it therefore so hard to believe that even more reserve armies might be forming behind the Soviet front and be poised to threaten any German over-extension just as they had throughout 1941? Secondly, in spite of many failures from June to November, the Red Army had consistently sought the offensive, especially against Army Group Centre.[11] Thus, was it not reasonable to anticipate that the *Stavka* would again seek an offensive stance during the winter months, which were in any case so fabled in the Russian history of 1812? If these were indeed logical conclusions, one must enquire as to the source of their neglect and ask if a dispassionate military rationale was supplanted by a different conception of events, one more in line with National Socialist ideals.

Certainly, after the war it appeared to some former German generals that considerations regarding the Red Army had indeed been mistaken. Field Marshal Gerd von Rundstedt claimed to have unsuccessfully proposed a winter halt for his army group on the Dnieper River line.[12] Likewise, Hoth, the former commander of Panzer Group 3 (before Reinhardt), argued in his postwar writings that the continuation of the offensive after the battles at Viaz'ma and Briansk had been a mistake.[13] Conveniently, Rundstedt could claim his objections had been overruled, while Hoth was no longer in a position to effect a halt when he claimed it made most sense. Their assertions may have seemed entirely reasonable after the war, but, as we have seen, there was no support for them from any of the major figures in Army Group Centre at the time. Indeed, the post-Nazi world did wonders for reforming the views of former generals (not least because many of them found themselves on trial for supporting the more murderous aspects of Nazi policy), as well as filtering their memories for involvement in anything which might have constituted National Socialist thinking. Here the 'Marne complex' in fact allowed a guise of legitimacy for the commanders of Army Group Centre and the OKH, allowing them to convince themselves and their audiences that their decision to remain on the offensive made some kind of rational military sense. However, the 'Marne complex' may also be thought of as the military equivalent to the Nazi party's political 'stab in the back'[14] myth that reportedly undermined Germany's war effort and forced its surrender in the First World War. Thus, timid generalship lacking the iron resolve of National Socialism forestalled German victory on the battlefield in 1914 just as Jews and communists were able to demoralise the home front in 1918.

Nor was the 'Marne complex' unique to November and early December 1941. A cult of the offensive drove the *Ostheer* throughout 1941. Any refusal to seek victory through the most aggressive means possible threatened missing the vital opportunity and allowing the enemy to regain advantage. In this sense, no matter how much had already been achieved or how battle-worn German units were, any failure to commit the last battalion to battle, whenever and wherever the opportunity presented itself, threatened the possibility of defeat. It may have been irrational, and it was certainly illogical, but it did conform to Nazi conceptions about the knife-edge balance between victory and defeat, and therefore the need to devote absolutely everything towards victory. This was the kind of all-or-nothing warfare that Hitler's Germany was committed to in 1941, and its aggressive military culture was openly embraced by the Wehrmacht as setting itself apart from other European armies. Indeed, driving German forces to the point of utter exhaustion had previously sufficed to win campaigns, so why should the Soviet Union be any different? A lack of success only meant driving harder and risking more. Evoking a comparison with the battle of the Marne may appear a harmless enough explanation for German decision making in 1941 (which is why it was openly used after the war), but it betrays the more sinister parameters of a German strategic rationale that can only be described as National Socialist military thinking; the ruinous effects of which are well illustrated in the final stages of the battle for Moscow.

While German strategic direction was the principal cause of failure in November and early December 1941, the use and allocation of Soviet reserves, as well as the resistance offered by the forces already committed, were no doubt critical factors. As Alan Clark phrased it, the *Stavka*'s withholding of reserve armies 'was an operation as delicate and as critical as the *manoletina* of a matador who lets the bull brush his side as he withdraws the cape'.[15] The Soviets were manipulating Army Group Centre's aggressive intent, allowing the Germans to exhaust themselves in preparation for their own winter offensive. Meanwhile, army commanders like Rokossovsky, who commanded the vital Sixteenth Army defending Moscow to the northwest, struggled to hold the line with the barest minimum of forces. As Rokossovsky noted after the war: 'The army's defences were spread so thin that they threatened to burst. It took feats of troop juggling to prevent this from happening.'[16] The same threat of bursting that worried Rokossovsky gave heart to the German commanders, leading them to believe that Soviet defences might collapse at any time. Stalin, however, remained in the Kremlin not simply out of faith in men like Rokossovsky. The Soviet dictator knew something the Germans did not, he knew that there were sizable reserve forces to call upon should the situation deteriorate. Moreover, once the initial period of danger had passed, those same forces could begin to assume an offensive posture, which is what Stalin authorised at the end of November.

The end of the German offensive towards Moscow on 5 December 1941 was not just the end of Operation Typhoon; it was the end of the first phase of the war in the east. The *Ostheer* had sustained some three-quarters of a million casualties, and over a quarter of a million of these (262,297 as of the end of November) had been killed outright or died of their wounds.[17] Of the total German invasion force on 22 June 1941, 24 per cent, almost one in four, was now a casualty – and these were to be remembered as the most successful months of the Germany's war in the east.[18] As Halder acknowledged on 23 November: 'An army, like that of June 1941, will henceforth no longer be available to us.'[19] While the decline of the *Ostheer* proceeded apace, the same was not true of the Red Army. In spite of sustaining over 4.3 million casualties in 1941 alone, the Red Army was in fact growing in size and, although much more slowly, in quality. On 22 June 1941, the *Ostheer* (with Romanian and Finnish allies) outnumbered the Red Army in the western military districts by a factor of roughly 1.4:1. By 1 December 1941, the ratio had swung to favour the Red Army with the *Ostheer* outnumbered 1:1.23. The Soviets may have lost millions of men in the course of Operations Barbarossa and Typhoon, but on 1 December they maintained a front with 4,197,000 men.[20] As Marshal Semen Timoshenko, commanding the Soviet Southwestern Front, stated in November 1941: 'This first phase of the war has been decisively won by *us*, however much a glance at the map may give the public a different impression.'[21]

If events in the east were not cause enough for alarm, then Berlin needed only to note that Rommel was contemplating abandoning all of Cyrenaica, and that Italian shipping had lost fourteen of the twenty-two vessels sent to resupply the *Afrikakorps* in November.[22] Meanwhile, the Royal Air Force had gained priority in British production and its new Stirling and Halifax bombers with their 5-ton bomb bays were coming into squadron service throughout the second half of 1941.[23] Even more to the point, urgent Japanese diplomatic manoeuvring succeeded on 5 December in securing German and Italian agreement to a new protocol, which stipulated in its first article: 'Should a state of war begin between Japan and the United States, Germany and Italy for their part will consider themselves to be in a state of war with the United States, and shall conduct this war with all the forces at their disposal.'[24] Hitler and Mussolini could hardly have doubted that war was looming between Japan and the United States, and yet both were willingly committing their already overstretched forces to a vastly expanded global struggle.[25] What they did not know was that the Japanese First Air Fleet was at that moment just 1,500 km from Pearl Harbor and able to listen to Honolulu's radio stations.[26] A vastly expanded war was but hours away.

Hitler had already fatally misjudged the power of his Soviet adversary in the east, and the addition of the United States to his list of enemies only acted to hasten Germany's downfall. Even if one disputes the inevitability of Germany's defeat in 1941, it is difficult to see how a long-term domination of Europe, given the size of the area and the methods employed, posed anything other than insurmountable military/security challenges. Irregular warfare of increasing scale and sophistication would ultimately have ensured the failure of German plans for the east. Indeed, it might well be said that National Socialist thinking and the hostility it induced in the occupied areas was ultimately as destructive to Hitler's ambitions as it was to the subject peoples. Germany's defeat was not therefore determined simply by Bock's failure at Moscow; it was something that the German high command had actively courted from the very inception of Barbarossa.

Disturbingly, what perhaps stands out most from 5 December 1941 is not the tide of destruction and the extraordinary loss of life that accompanied Germany's invasion of the Soviet Union. It is the fact that all this belonged only to the first phase of the Nazi–Soviet conflict and would be well surpassed by what was still to come. The sheer dimensions of Hitler's war in the east are difficult to appreciate. Even in this first phase, Dshek Altausen was not overstating the matter when he observed in November 1941 that: 'Humanity has never seen a war such as this.'[27] Yet Nazi Germany was not just exporting a war of extermination to foreign lands, it was, by implication of its hubris and behaviour, courting one of its own. As Ilya Ehrenburg's fiery prose predicted in an article published on 18 November 1941 that: 'Millions of widows will say: "Hitler has killed my husband." Millions of orphans will ask: "Hitler, where is our father?" It won't be the fanfares that will sound – it will be the sirens. Germany will know the full measure of woe.'[28] Ehrenburg may have been writing Soviet propaganda, but the veracity of his words was already evident to thousands of mourning German families. Indeed, the day before Ehrenburg's article appeared (17 November) Helmuth James von Moltke wrote to his wife of the widespread 'hunger, disease, and fear' spreading under German rule and then added: 'Nobody knows what the consequences will be or how soon they will set in. But one thing is certain: the Apocalyptic Horsemen are beginners compared with what is ahead of us: *certus an, incertus quando* [it is certain, but uncertain when].'[29]

NOTES

Introduction

1. Andrew Roberts, *The Storm of War. A New History of the Second World War* (London, 2009), p. 175.
2. Siegfried Knappe, with Ted Brusaw, *Soldat. Reflections of a German Soldier, 1936–1949* (New York, 1992), p. 209.
3. Walter Bähr and Hans Bähr (eds), *Kriegsbriefe Gefallener Studenten, 1939–1945* (Tübingen and Stuttgart, 1952), p. 109 (December 1941).
4. 'Dog tags' were a means of personal identification on which information was recorded by indentation on corrosion-resistant metal or an alloy such as aluminium, monel or stainless steel.
5. A full account of these events was filmed as part of the 2013 TV series *Perfect Storms. Disasters that Changed the World*, episode six: 'Hitler's Frozen Army'.
6. As cited in Albert Axell, *Stalin's War. Through the Eyes of his Commanders* (London, 1997), pp. 174–5.
7. James Lucas wrote in 1980 that when Army Group Centre reached Moscow: 'Their goal was only a handful of kilometres distant. One more push and the objective of Army Group Centre would have been attained. But this was not to be.' James Lucas, *War of the Eastern Front 1941–1945. The German Soldier in Russia* (London, 1980), p. 83.
8. Richard Overy, *The Dictators. Hitler's Germany and Stalin's Russia* (London, 2004), p. 495.
9. *Ibid.*
10. As cited in E. Lederrey, *Germany's Defeat in the East. The Soviet Armies at War 1941–1945* (London, 1955), p. 46 fn. 6.
11. John Taylor, 'Hitler and Moscow 1941', *Journal of Slavic Military Studies* 26(3) (2013): 490–527.

12. Evan Mawdsley, *Thunder in the East. The Nazi–Soviet War 1941–1945* (London, 2005), p. 115.
13. G.K. Zhukov, *The Memoirs of Marshal Zhukov* (London, 1971), pp. 347–8.
14. Cyrus Leo Sulzberger, *A Long Row of Candles. Memoirs and Diaries 1934–1954* (Toronto, 1969), p. 157.
15. Franz Halder, *Hitler als Feldherr* (Munich, 1949), p. 43; Erich von Manstein, *Verlorene Siege. Erinnerungen 1939–1944* (Bonn, 1991), pp. 173–4 (English translation, Erich von Manstein, *Lost Victories* (Novato, CA, 1958), pp. 177–8); Walter Warlimont, *Im Hauptquartier der deutschen Wehrmacht 1939 bis 1945, Band 1: September 1939–November 1942* (Koblenz, 1990), p. 221 (English translation: Walter Warlimont, *Inside Hitler's Headquarters, 1939–1945* (New York, 1964), p. 207); Peter Bor, *Gespräche mit Halder* (Wiesbaden, 1950), pp. 207–9.
16. Günther Blumentritt, 'Moscow', in William Richardson and Seymour Freidin (eds), *The Fatal Decisions* (London, 1956), pp. 60–1.
17. David Stahel, *Operation Barbarossa and Germany's Defeat in the East* (Cambridge, 2009); David Stahel, *Kiev 1941. Hitler's Battle for Supremacy in the East* (Cambridge, 2012); David Stahel, *Operation Typhoon. Hitler's March on Moscow, October 1941* (Cambridge, 2013); David Stahel, 'Radicalizing Warfare: The German Command and the Failure of Operation Barbarossa', in Alex J. Kay, Jeff Rutherford and David Stahel (eds), *Nazi Policy on the Eastern Front, 1941. Total War, Genocide and Radicalization* (Rochester, NY, 2012), pp. 19–44.
18. Of an estimated 27 million Soviet deaths in the war only 10 million took place on the battlefield. David M. Glantz and Jonathan House, *When Titans Clashed. How the Red Army Stopped Hitler* (Lawrence, KS, 1995), p. 292.
19. Elke Fröhlich (ed.), *Die Tagebücher von Joseph Goebbels. Teil* II *Diktate 1941–1945, Band 2: Oktober–Dezember 1941* (Munich, 1996), p. 391 (29 November 1941).
20. Sulzberger, *A Long Row of Candles*, p. 165. For other accounts of Sokolovsky's speech, see Henry Cassidy, *Moscow Dateline, 1941–1943* (London, 1943), pp. 85–6; Wallace Carroll, *Inside Warring Russia. An Eye-Witness Report on the Soviet Union's Battle: Compiled from Dispatches, Censored and Uncensored* (New York, 1942). There are no page numbers in this publication, see the dispatch titled 'Nazis in the Soviet Military Grinder'.

1 Parallel wars

1. Tomothy C. Dowling, *The Brusilov Offensive* (Bloomington, IN, 2008), p. xii.
2. Gerhard L. Weinberg, '22 June 1941: The German View', *War in History* 3(2) (1996): 228–9.

3. Laurence Rees, *War of the Century. When Hitler Fought Stalin* (London, 1999), pp. 52–3.
4. Olaf Groehler, 'Goals and Reason: Hitler and the German Military', in Joseph Wieczynski (ed.), *Operation Barbarossa. The German Attack on the Soviet Union June, 1941* (Salt Lake City, UT, 1993), p. 56.
5. A good discussion can be found in Jürgen Förster, 'Zum Russlandbild der Militärs 1941–1945', in Hans-Erich Volkmann (ed.), *Das Russlandbild im Dritten Reich* (Cologne, 1994), pp. 141–63.
6. In fact, the battle of was fought some 30 km east of Tannenberg around the East Prussian villages of Grünfliess, Omulefofen and Kurken, but Tannenberg was selected as the battle's namesake to expunge memories of an earlier defeat in 1410. On this occasion, Germanic knights of the Teutonic Order were defeated by Polish and Lithuanian armies. Christopher Clark, *Iron Kingdom. The Rise and Downfall of Prussia 1600–1947* (London and New York, 2006), p. 608.
7. Hindenburg was only promoted Field Marshal in November 1914.
8. For the best account of the battle, see Dennis E. Showalter, *Tannenberg. Clash of Empires, 1914* (Dulles, VA, 2004).
9. John Keegan, *The First World War* (New York, 2000), p. 149.
10. As Norman Stone wrote, this was not the whole truth: 'In practice, the victory [at Tannenberg] was overrated at the time: the Russians recovered, and invaded East Prussia again a few weeks later. But what was dangerous to the Germans was the myth that Tannenberg launched. Men supposed – and the version produced by Ludendorff, later, buttressed their supposition – that Hindenburg and Ludendorff had made a brilliant strategic manoeuvre, leading to a new Cannae. There was something to this, but it was distorted by exaggeration.' Norman Stone, *The Eastern Front 1914–1917* (London, 1998), p. 66.
11. Max Domarus, *Hitler. Speeches and Proclamations 1932–1945. The Chronicle of a Dictatorship, vol.* IV*: The Years 1941 to 1945* (Wauconda, IL, 2004), pp. 2449–50 (22 June 1941).
12. *Ibid.*, p. 2450 (22 June 1941).
13. There is no debate among serious historians about Stalin's intentions regarding an attack on Germany in 1941. There have, however, been a number of sensationalist publications seeking to give credibility to the preventative war myth. For the best recent surveys of the debate, see Bianka Pietrow-Ennker (ed.) *Präventivkrieg? Der deutsche Angriff auf die Sowjetunion* (Frankfurt am Main, 2011); Gerd R. Ueberschär and Lev A. Bezymenskij (eds), *Der deutsche Angriff auf die Sowjetunion 1941. Die Kontroverse um die Präventivkriegsthese* (Darmstadt, 1998). The most complete guide to the many publications in this debate can be found in the latest edition of Rolf-Dieter Müller and Gerd R. Ueberschär, *Hitler's War in the East 1941–1945. A Critical Assessment* (Oxford, 2009). For some of the main works of revisionist literature, see Stefan Scheil, *Präventivkrieg Barbarossa. Fragen, Fakten, Antworten*

(Frankfurt, 2011); Viktor Suvorov, *Icebreaker. Who Started the Second World War* (London, 1990); Ernst Topitsch, *Stalin's War. A Radical New Theory of the Origins of the Second World War* (New York, 1987); Joachim Hoffmann, 'The Soviet Union's Offensive Preparations in 1941', in Bernd Wegner (ed.), *From Peace to War. Germany, Soviet Russia and the World, 1939–1941* (Oxford, 1997), pp. 361–80.

14. See Peter Hoeres, 'Die Slawen. Perzeptionen des Kriegsgegners bei den Mittelmächten. Selbst und Feindbild', in Gerhard P. Gross (ed.), *Die vergessene Front. Der Osten 1914/15* (Paderborn, 2006), pp. 187–92.
15. As cited in Ben Shepherd, *War in the Wild East. The German Army and Soviet Partisans* (Cambridge, MA, 2004), p. 11.
16. As Peter Fritzsche observed: 'In World War II as in World War I, soldiers classified friends and foes in terms of relative cleanliness, but in this conflict they were much more apt to make sweeping judgements about the population and to rank people according to rigid biological hierarchies. Even the ordinary infantryman adopted a racialized point of view, so that "the Russians" the German fought in 1914–1918 were transformed into an undifferentiated peril, "the Russian," regarded as "dull," "dumb," "stupid," or "depraved" and "barely humanlike."' Peter Fritzsche, *Life and Death in the Third Reich* (Cambridge, MA, 2008), p. 148. See also Niklaus Meier, *Warum Krieg? Die Sinndeutung des Krieges in der deutschen Militärelite 1871–1945* (Paderborn, 2012), pp. 241–2.
17. Such a view was paralled by the German General Staff in the lead up to the First World War. See Hew Strachan, 'Time, Space and Barbarisation: the German Army and the Eastern Front in Two World Wars', in George Kassimeris (ed.), *The Barbarization of Warfare* (New York, 2006), pp. 61–6.
18. This view was not only predominant in Germany at the time, but also in Britain and the United States. See Martin Kahn, '"Russia Will Assuredly be Defeated": Anglo-American Government Assessments of Soviet War Potential before Operation Barbarossa', *Journal of Slavic Military Studies* 25(2) (2012): 220–40; H. F. Hinsley, 'British Intelligence and Barbarossa', in John Erickson and David Dilks (eds), *Barbarossa. The Axis and the Allies* (Edinburgh, 1998), p. 72; Martin Kahn, 'From Assured Defeat to "The Riddle of Soviet Military Success": Anglo-American Government Assessments of Soviet War Potential 1941–1943', *Journal of Slavic Military Studies* 26(3) (2013): 462–89; Robert Cecil, *Hitler's Decision to Invade Russia 1941* (London, 1975), p. 121; Andreas Hillgruber, *Hitlers Strategie. Politik und Kriegführung 1940–1941* (Bonn, 1993), pp. 444, fn. 93 and 558; Gerd R. Ueberschär, 'Das Scheitern des Unternehmens "Barbarossa". Der deutsch-sowjetische Krieg vom Überfall bis zur Wende vor Moskau im Winter 1941/42', in Gerd Ueberschär and Wolfram Wette (eds), *'Unternehmen Barbarossa' Der deutsche Überfall auf die Sowjetunion 1941* (Paderborn, 1984), pp. 150–1.

19. Vejas Gabriel Liulevicius, *War Land on the Eastern Front. Culture, National Identity, and German Occupation in World War I* (Cambridge, 2005), ch. 8; Vejas Gabriel Liulevicius, 'German Military Occupation and Culture on the Eastern Front in World War I', in Charles Ingrao and Franz A. J. Szabo (eds), *The Germans and the East* (West Lafayette, IN, 2008), pp. 201–8. For a longer-term perspective on German views towards the east, see Vejas Gabriel Liulevicius, *The German Myth of the East. 1800 to the Present* (Oxford, 2011).
20. Michael Burleigh, *Germany Turns Eastwards. A Study of 'Ostforschung' in the Third Reich* (Cambridge, 1988).
21. Andreas Hillgruber, 'The German Military Leaders' View of Russia Prior to the Attack on the Soviet Union', in Bernd Wegner (ed.), *From Peace to War. Germany, Soviet Russia and the World, 1939–1941* (Oxford, 1997), pp. 169–70.
22. Earl F. Ziemke, 'Rundstedt', in Correlli Barnett (ed.), *Hitler's Generals* (London, 1989), pp. 177–8.
23. Michael Burleigh, *The Third Reich. A New History* (London, 2001) p. 491.
24. Holger H. Herwig, *The First World War. Germany and Austria-Hungary 1914–1918* (London, 1997), p. 87.
25. Keegan, *The First World War*, pp. 160–1, see also pp. 90–6.
26. In the initial encounters at Kraśnik (23–26 August) the Russian Fourth Army was put to flight, while at Komarów (26–31 August) the Russian Fifth Army was almost encircled, suffering 40 per cent casualties and 20,000 POWs. Lawrence Sondhaus, *Franz Conrad von Hötzendorf. Architect of the Apocalypse* (Boston, MA, 2000).
27. As an American war correspondent reviewing the battlefields in Galicia noted in 1914: 'The theory that Austria was a web of factions that would dissolve at the first impact, and the belief that her troops would not fight, has been absolutely disproved; and it serves to magnify the achievements of the soldiers of the Czar, when we accord to the Austro-Hungarian Army the credit which is due to its courageous defence and the stubborn resistance put up at every favourable opportunity.' Stanley Washburn, *Field Notes from the Russian Front* (London, 1915), p. 119.
28. Ernst Klink, 'The Military Concept of the War Against the Soviet Union', in Militärgeschichtlichen Forschungsamt (ed.), *Germany and the Second World War, vol.* IV*: The Attack on the Soviet Union* (Oxford, 1998), p. 265.
29. Franz Halder, *Kriegstagebuch: Tägliche Aufzeichnungen des Chefs des Generalstabes des Heeres 1939–1942, Band* III*: Der Russlandfeldzug bis zum Marsch auf Stalingrad (22.6.1941–24.9.1942)*, eds Hans-Adolf Jacobsen and Alfred Philippi, Arbeitskreis für Wehrforschung (Stuttgart, 1964), pp. 7–8 (23 June 1941). Hereafter cited as Halder, *KTB* III.
30. As cited in Gerd Niepold, 'Plan Barbarossa', in David M. Glantz (ed.), *The Initial Period of War on the Eastern Front 22 June–August 1941* (London, 1997), p. 70.

31. Hugh Trevor-Roper (ed.), *Hitler's War Directives 1939–1945* (London, 1964), pp. 139–41. Already on 16 July, Hitler had hosted a meeting of top officials to make selections for the posts of Reich and General Commissar (senior civil administrators) in the occupied Soviet territories. See Alex J. Kay, *Exploitation, Resettlement, Mass Murder. Political and Economic Planning for German Occupation Policy in the Soviet Union, 1940–1941* (Oxford, 2006), pp. 180–5.
32. For the most detailed accounts of this battle from the German and Soviet perspectives, see Stahel, *Operation Barbarossa and Germany's Defeat in the East*; David M. Glantz, *Barbarossa Derailed. The Battle for Smolensk 10 July–10 September 1941, vol. 1: The German Advance, the Encirclement Battle, and the First and Second Soviet Counteroffensives, 10 July–24 August 1941* (Solihull, 2010); David M. Glantz, *Barbarossa Derailed. The Battle for Smolensk 10 July–10 September 1941, vol. 2: The German Offensives on the Flanks and the Third Soviet Counteroffensive, 25 August–10 September 1941* (Solihull, 2012); David M. Glantz, *Barbarossa Derailed. The Battle for Smolensk 10 July–10 September 1941, vol. 3: The Documentary Companion. Tables, Orders and Reports Prepared by Participating Red Army Forces* (Solihull, 2014).
33. Keegan, *The First World War*, p. 165; Stone, *The Eastern Front 1914–1917*, p. 66.
34. For a detailed discussion of Smolensk as a German victory, see Stahel, *Operation Barbarossa and Germany's Defeat in the East*, pp. 344–60.
35. Halder, *KTB* III, p. 180 (15 August 1941).
36. 'Kriegstagebuch Nr.1 (Band August 1941) des Oberkommandos der Heeresgruppe Mitte', BA-MA RH 19-II/386, p. 381 (25 August 1941).
37. Hermann Geyer, *Das* IX. *Armeekorps im Ostfeldzug 1941* (Neckargemünd, 1969), p. 122.
38. 'Kriegstagebuch Nr. 1 (Band August 1941) des Oberkommandos der Heeresgruppe Mitte', BA-MA RH 19-II/386, pp. 380, 393–4 (25 and 28 August 1941).
39. *Ibid.*, pp. 393 and 395 (28 August 1941).
40. David M. Glantz, *Barbarossa. Hitler's Invasion of Russia 1941* (Stroud, 2001), p. 95.
41. Halder's title was the 1941 incarnation of the previous Chief of the Great General Staff. For the most detailed record of this strategic dispute, see the relevant sections in my book *Operation Barbarossa and Germany's Defeat in the East.*
42. For a more complete account of the battle of Kiev, see Stahel, *Kiev 1941*.
43. 'KTB 3rd Pz. Div. vom 16.8.40 bis 18.9.41', BA-MA RH 27-3/14, p. 228 (13 September 1941).
44. Johannes Hürter, *Hitlers Heerführer. Die deutschen Oberbefehlshaber im Krieg gegen die Sowjetunion 1941/42* (Munich, 2006), p. 295, fn. 81.

45. Trevor-Roper (ed.), *Hitler's War Directives 1939–1945*, p. 152 (6 September 1941).
46. Herwig, *The First World War*, p. 107.
47. Stone, *The Eastern Front 1914–1917*, pp. 97–8.
48. Hindenburg had been transferred to lead the Ninth Army from his aforementioned command of the Eighth Army.
49. '9. Armee Kriegstagebuch 19.9.1914–31.12.1914', BA-MA PH 511/279, pp. 51–8 (16–18 October 1914).
50. Erich von Falkenhayn, *General Headquarters 1914–1916 and its Critical Decisions* (London, 1919), p. 26.
51. As cited in Michael S. Neiberg and David Jordan, *The Eastern Front 1914–1920. From Tannenberg to the Russo-Polish War* (London, 2008), p. 67.
52. Keegan, *The First World War*, pp. 165–6.
53. See my discussion of past Russian strategy in Stahel, *Operation Typhoon*, ch. 1. See also the comments in Keegan, *The First World War*, p. 164.
54. Hew Strachan, *The First World War, vol. 1: To Arms* (Oxford, 2003), p. 366.
55. Otto Dietrich, *The Hitler I Knew. Memoirs of the Third Reich's Press Chief* (New York, 2010), p. 70.
56. Domarus, *Hitler*, p. 2497 (9 October 1941). Marshal Semen Timoshenko had in fact been transferred to the command of the Soviet Southwestern Front in mid-September.
57. As cited in Janusz Piekalkiewicz, *Moscow 1941. The Frozen Offensive* (London, 1981), p. 113.
58. For the most detailed examination of this battle, see Lev Lopukhovsky, *The Viaz'ma Catastrophe, 1941. The Red Army's Disastrous Stand Against Operation Typhoon* (Solihull, 2013).
59. For a full account of the German campaign in October 1941, see Stahel, *Operation Typhoon.*
60. For the best survey of German military culture or 'way of war', see Robert M. Citino, *The German Way of War. From the Thirty Years' War to the Third Reich* (Lawrence, KS, 2005).
61. James S. Corum, *The Roots of Blitzkrieg. Hans von Seecht and German Military Reform* (Lawrence, KS, 1992); Mary Habeck, *Storm of Steel. The Development of Armor Doctrine in Germany and the Soviet Union, 1919–1939* (New York, 2003).
62. J. P. Stern, *Hitler. The Führer and the People* (Berkeley, CA, 1992), ch. 7 Even after the war Halder wrote in the preface to a study by Colonel-General Erhard Raus: 'It becomes very clear that a strong military leader with great powers of motivation is the most important factor for success.' As cited in Peter Tsouras (ed.), *Panzers on the Eastern Front. General Erhard Raus and his Panzer Divisions in Russia 1941–1945* (London, 2002), p. 9.
63. As cited in Michael Jones, *The Retreat. Hitler's First Defeat* (London, 2009), p. 86.

64. Burleigh, *The Third Reich*, p. 490.
65. Wolfram Wette, 'Juden, Bolschewisten, Slawen. Rassenideologische Rußland-Feindbilder Hitlers und der Wehrmachtgeneräle', in Bianka Pietrow-Ennker (ed.), *Präventivkrieg? Der deutsche Angriff auf die Sowjetunion* (Frankfurt am Main, 2011), pp. 43–4.
66. Stefan Karner and Wolfram Dornik (eds), *Die Besatzung der Ukraine 1918. Historischer Kontext – Forschungsstand – wirtschaftliche und soziale Folgen* (Graz, 2008); Winfried Baumgart, *Deutsche Ostpolitik 1918. Von Brest-Litowsk bis zum Ende des Ersten Weltkreges* (Munich, 1966). See examples in Alfred Knox, *With the Russian Army 1914–1917. Being Chiefly Extracts from the Diary of a Military Attaché* (London, 1921), pp. 164, 166, 169 (29, 30 and 31 October 1914).
67. Joachim Fest, *Hitler* (Orlando, FL, 1974). p. 649.
68. Franz Halder, *Kriegstagebuch. Tägliche Aufzeichnungen des Chefs des Generalstabes des Heeres 1939–1942, Band* II: *Von der geplanten Landung in England bis zum Beginn des Ostfeldzuges (1.7.1940–21.6.1941)*, ed. Hans-Adolf Jacobsen (Stuttgart, 1963), pp. 336–7 (30 March 1941). Hereafter cited as Halder, *KTB* II.
69. Felix Römer, 'The Wehrmacht in the War of Ideologies: the Army and Hitler's Criminal Orders on the Eastern Front', in Alex J. Kay, Jeff Rutherford and David Stahel (eds), *Nazi Policy on the Eastern Front, 1941. Total War, Genocide and Radicalization* (Rochester, NY, 2012), pp. 74–6.
70. As cited in Jürgen Förster, 'Operation Barbarossa as a War of Conquest and Annihilation', in Militärgeschichtliches Forschungsamt (eds), *Germany and the Second World War. vol.* IV: *The Attack on the Soviet Union* (Oxford, 1998), p. 485.
71. The order is reproduced in Erhard Moritz (ed.), *Fall Barbarossa. Dokumente zur Vorbereitung der faschistischen Wehrmacht auf die Aggression gegen die Sowjetunion (1940/41)* (Berlin, 1970). Document 97: 'Erlaß Hitlers über Gewaltmaßnahmen gegen die sowjetische Bevölkerung und über die Einschränkung der Bestrafung von Wehrmachtangehörigen für Kriegsverbrechen in der Sowjetunion (Kriegsgerichtsbarkeitsbefehl), 13. Mai 1941', pp. 316–18.
72. In spite of this, according to new research by Regina Mühlhäuser, sexual violence by German soldiers within the occupied Soviet Union was by no means an exception. See Regina Mühlhäuser, *Eroberungen. Sexuelle Gewalttaten und intime Beziehungen deutscher Soldaten in der Sowjetunion 1941–1945* (Hamburg, 2010). See also Sönke Neitzel and Harald Welzer, *Soldaten. On Fighting, Killing and Dying* (London, 2012), ch. 5.
73. The order is reproduced in Moritz (ed.), *Fall Barbarossa*, document 100: 'Richtlinien des Chefs des OKW für die Verfolgung und Ermordung der Politischen Funktionäre der Sowjetunion (Kommissarbefehl), 6. Juni 1941',

pp. 321–3; Gerd R. Ueberschär and Wolfram Wette (eds), *'Unternehmen Barbarossa' Der deutsche Überfall auf die Sowjetunion 1941* (Paderborn, 1984), pp. 313–14.

74. Römer, 'The Wehrmacht in the War of Ideologies', p. 75. See also Felix Römer, '"Kein Problem für die Truppe"', *Die Zeit Geschichte – Hitlers Krieg im Osten* No. 2 (2011): 42–5.
75. Warlimont, *Im Hauptquartier der deutschen Wehrmacht 1939 bis 1945*, p. 177. (English translation, Warlimont, *Inside Hitler's Headquarters, 1939–1945*, p. 162.)
76. As cited in Jürgen Förster, 'New Wine in Old Skins? The Wehrmacht and the War of "Weltanschauungen", 1941', in Wilhelm Deist (ed.), *The German Military in the Age of Total War* (Leamington Spa, 1985), pp. 309–10.
77. Römer, 'The Wehrmacht in the War of Ideologies', p. 79.
78. One major exception was the murder of French colonial troops. See Raffael Scheck, *Hitler's African Victims. The German Army Massacres of Black French Soldiers in 1940* (New York, 2006).
79. Geoffrey P. Megargee, 'A Blind Eye and Dirty Hands: the Sources of Wehrmacht Criminality in the Campaign against the Soviet Union', in Charles Ingrao and Franz A. J. Szabo (eds), *The Germans and the East* (West Lafayette, IN, 2008), p. 322.
80. Fedor von Bock, *Generalfeldmarschall Fedor von Bock. The War Diary 1939–1945*, ed. Klaus Gerbet (Munich, 1996), pp. 217–18 (4 June 1941). Hereafter references for Bock's diary will be cited as von Bock, *War Diary*.
81. *Ibid.*, p. 219 (7 June 1941).
82. As cited in Martin Gilbert, *The Second World War. A Complete History* (London, 2009), pp. 200–1.
83. Römer, 'The Wehrmacht in the War of Ideologies', p. 80.
84. As Guderian wrote: 'Shortly before the opening of hostilities the OKW sent an order direct to all corps and divisions concerning the treatment that was to be given to the civilian population and to prisoners of war in Russia ... This order, which was to play an important part in the post-war trials of German generals by our former enemies, was consequently never carried out in my Panzer Group. At the time I dutifully informed the Commander-in-Chief of the Army Group [Bock] that I was not publishing or obeying this order. The equally notorious, so-called "Commissar Order" never even reached my Panzer Group. No doubt Army Group Centre had already decided not to forward it. Therefore the "Commissar Order" was never carried out by my troops either.'
Heinz Guderian, *Panzer Leader* (New York, 1996), p. 152. According to Manstein: 'A few days before the offensive started we received an order from the Supreme Command of the Armed Forces (OKW) which has since become known as the "Commissar Order". The gist of it was that all political commissars of the Red Army whom we captured were to be shot out of hand as

exponents of Bolshevik ideology ... An order like the *Kommissarbefehl* was utterly unsoldierly. To have carried it out would have threatened not only the honour of our fighting troops but also their morale. Consequently I had no alternative but to inform my superiors that the Commissars Order would not be implemented by anyone under my command. My subordinate commanders were entirely at one with me in this, and everyone in the corps area acted accordingly. I hardly need add that my military superiors endorsed my attitude.' von Manstein, *Lost Victories*, pp. 179–80; von Manstein, *Verlorene Siege*, pp. 176–7.

85. Mungo Melvin, *Manstein. Hitler's Greatest General* (New York, 2010), pp. 481–4; Marcel Stein, *Field Marshal von Manstein. The Janus Head: A Portrait* (Solihull, 2007), p. 251.
86. Jürgen Förster, 'The German Army and the Ideological War against the Soviet Union', in Gerhard Hirschfeld (ed.), *The Policies of Genocide. Jews and Soviet Prisoners of War in Nazi Germany* (London, 1986), p. 23.
87. Hermann Hoth, *Panzer-Operationen. Die Panzergruppe 3 und der operative Gedanke der deutschen Führung Sommer 1941* (Heidelberg, 1956).
88. As cited in Förster, 'New Wine in Old Skins?', p. 316.
89. Förster, 'The German Army and the Ideological War against the Soviet Union', p. 23.
90. Felix Römer, *Der Kommissarbefehl. Wehrmacht und NS-Verbrechen an der Ostfront 1941/42* (Paderborn, 2008), pp. 398–400.
91. For a recent survey of the literature in German anti-partisan warfare, particularly studies that have appeared in German, see Ben Shepherd, 'The Clean Wehrmacht, the War of Extermination, and Beyond', *Historical Journal* 52(2) (2009): 455–73.
92. As cited in Jürgen Förster, 'Securing "Living-space"', in Militärgeschichtliches Forschungsamt (eds), *Germany and the Second World War, vol.* IV: *The Attack on the Soviet Union* (Oxford, 1998), p. 1197.
93. Trevor-Roper (ed.), *Hitler's War Directives 1939–1945*, p. 144 (23 July 1941).
94. Shepherd, *War in the Wild East*, pp. 84–5.
95. Bob Carruthers (ed.), *The Wehrmacht Last Witnesses. First-hand Accounts from the Survivors of Hitler's Armed Forces* (London, 2010), p. 51.
96. Located in Czechoslovakia to the northwest of Prague, Lidice was the village selected to avenge the assassination of *SS-Obergruppenführer* and Chief of the Reich Security Main Office Reinhard Heydrich, who was mortally wounded by two Czech partisans in an attack on 27 May 1942.
97. Hans Becker, *Devil on my Shoulder* (London, 1957), p. 40.
98. As cited in Stephen G. Fritz, *Frontsoldaten. The German Soldier in World War* II (Lexington, KY, 1995), p. 58.
99. Helmut Pabst, *The Outermost Frontier. A German Soldier in the Russian Campaign* (London, 1957), p. 22.

100. *True To Type. A Selection From Letters and Diaries of German Soldiers and Civilians Collected on the Soviet–German Front* (London, n.d.), pp. 30–1 (23 September 1941).
101. Himmler's SS had a different ranking system from the army. An *Obergruppenführer* had the equivalent rank to an army Lieutenant-General.
102. In addition to Bach-Zelewski's murderous anti-partisan operations in the east, he was also responsible for the suppression of the Warsaw uprising in August and September 1944 where an estimated 150,000 Polish non-combatants were killed, many in cold blood. Timothy Snyder, *Bloodlands. Europe between Hitler and Stalin* (New York, 2010), p. 308.
103. The only available biography on Bach-Zelewski is Wladyslaw Bartoszewski, *Erich von dem Bach* (Warsaw, 1961).
104. Schenkendorf was the commander of Army Group Centre's rear area, which included command of the aforementioned security divisions. For a biographical sketch of Schenkendorf, see Ekkehard Meyer-Düttingdorf, 'Gereral der Inanterie Max von Schenkendorf', in Gerd R. Ueberschär (ed.), *Hitlers militärische Elite* (Darmstadt, 1998), pp. 210–17. For more detailed information, see Jörn Hasenclever, *Wehrmacht und Besatzungspolitik. Die Befehlshaber der rückwärtigen Heeresgebiete 1941–1943* (Paderborn, 2010).
105. In 1941 Weichs and Küchler were not yet Field Marshals, but rather Colonel-Generals.
106. In 1941 Reinhardt was not yet a Colonel-General, but rather General of Panzer Troops.
107. As cited in Matthew Cooper, *The Phantom War. The German Struggle Against Soviet Partisans 1941–1944* (London, 1979), p. 57.
108. Timothy Mulligan, 'Reckoning the Cost of the People's War: the German Experience in the Central USSR', *Russian History* 9(1) (1982): 32.
109. Theo Schulte, *The German Army and Nazi Policies in Occupied Russia* (Oxford, 1989), pp. 135–6.
110. Omer Bartov, *The Eastern Front, 1941–45, German Troops and the Barbarisation of Warfare* (London, 1985), p. 122.
111. Neitzel and Welzer, *Soldaten*, p. 143.
112. Erich Kern, *Dance of Death* (New York, 1951), p. 75.
113. As cited in Fritz, *Frontsoldaten*, p. 57.
114. Heinrich Haape, with Dennis Henshaw, *Moscow Tram Stop. A Doctor's Experiences with the German Spearhead in Russia* (London, 1957), p. 143.
115. As cited in Omer Bartov, *Hitler's Army. Soldiers, Nazis, and War in the Third Reich* (Oxford, 1992), p. 93.
116. As cited in Alan Clark, *Barbarossa. The Russian–German Conflict 1941–1945* (London, 1996), pp. 153–4.
117. Wolfram Wette, '"Rassenfeind". Antisemitismus und Antislawismus in der Wehrmachtspropaganda', in Walter Manoschek (ed.), *Die Wehrmacht im*

Rassenkrieg. Der Vernichtungskrieg hinter der Front (Vienna, 1996), pp. 55–73; Wolfram Wette, 'Die Krieg gegen die Sowjetunion: ein Rassen-ideologische begründeter Vernichtungskrieg', in Wolf Kaiser (ed.), *Täter im Vernichtungskrieg. Der Überfall auf die Sowjetunion und der Völkermord an den Juden* (Berlin, 2002), pp. 15–38.

118. *True To Type*, p. 10 (29 August 1941).
119. *Ibid.*, p. 11 (26 June 1941).
120. Solomon Perel, *Europa Europa* (New York, 1997), p. 44.
121. Nikolai I. Obryn'ba, *Red Partisan. The Memoir of a Soviet Resistance Fighter on the Eastern Front* (Washington, DC, 2007), p. 60.
122. Thanks to the Mordukhovich family who shared this story with me.
123. Guido Knopp, *Die Wehrmacht. Eine Bilanz* (Munich, 2007), p. 233. See also Drossel's comments in Guido Knopp's 2007 documentary *Die Wehrmacht – Eine Bilanz*, episode four: 'Widerstand in Uniform'.
124. Some of the most important participants and conclusions in this debate can be found in Christian Hartmann, Johannes Hürter and Ulrike Jureit (eds), *Verbrechen der Wehrmacht. Bilanz einer Debatte* (Munich, 2005); Hannes Heer and Klaus Naumann (eds), *War of Extermination. The German Military in World War II 1941–1944* (New York and Oxford, 2006).
125. For more on this, see Wolfram Wette, *Retter in Uniform. Handlungsspielräume im Vernichtungskrieg der Wehrmacht* (Frankfurt am Main, 2003).
126. In Germany over the past fifteen years the exhibition of photos by the Hamburg Institute of Social Research, entitled *Vernichtungskrieg. Verbrechen der Wehrmacht 1941 bis 1944* (*War of Annihilation, Crimes of the Wehrmacht 1941 to 1944*) has focused much of the public debate on this question. When the exhibition opened in March 1995, it showcased much of what scholarly publications over the preceding fifteen years had come to accept. Yet right-wing circles protested outside the exhibition and attempted to counter its evidence with publications, which in some instances cast the Wehrmacht in the contrasting role of victim, see Franz W. Seidler, *Verbrechen an der Wehrmacht* (Selent, 1997). The criticism, however, gained some credibility when historians Bogdan Musial and Krisztian Ungvary each published evidence showing that inaccuracies in the identification of a few of the photos did in fact exist. With widespread media attention, the exhibition was closed pending review by an international commission of scholars. Their findings confirmed a handful of inaccuracies and suggested improvements to the presentation of the material, but confirmed the wider claims of the exhibition concerning the role of the Wehrmacht in war crimes. The exhibition reopened in November 2001 under the title *Verbrechen der Wehrmacht. Dimensionen des Vernichtungskrieges 1941–1944* (*Crimes of the Wehrmacht. Dimensions of the War of Annihilation 1941–1944*). For an interesting discussion of the exhibit and its context in

contemporary German historical and cultural consciousness, see K. Michael Prince, *War and German Memory. Excavating the Significance of the Second World War in German Cultural Consciousness* (Lanham, MD, 2009), pp. 54–60. See also Michael Verhoeven's documentary about the exhibition *Der unbekannte Soldat* (available in English as *The Unknown Soldier*).

127. Hannes Heer, 'How Amorality Became Normality: Reflections on the Mentality of German Soldiers on the Eastern Front', in Hannes Heer and Klaus Naumann (eds), *War of Extermination. The German Military in World War II 1941–1944* (New York and Oxford, 2006), pp. 329–44.
128. Neitzel and Welzer, *Soldaten*, pp. 129 and 137–42.
129. The *francs-tireurs* originated in France from private rifle clubs and military societies in the nineteenth century. During the Franco-Prussian war (1870–1) they were used as irregular troops and often operated in the German rear areas, provoking brutal reprisals against civilian targets.
130. Hannes Heer, 'Bittere Pflicht: der Rassenkrieg der Wehrmacht und seine Voraussetzungen', in Walter Manoschek (ed.), *Die Wehrmacht im Rassenkrieg. Der Vernichtungskrieg hinter der Front* (Vienna, 1996), pp. 116–41.
131. Timm C. Richter, 'Die Wehrmacht und der Partisanenkrieg in den besetzten Gebiezen der Sowjetunion', in Rolf-Dieter Müller and Hans-Erich Volkmann (eds), *Die Wehrmacht. Mythos und Realität* (Munich, 1999), p. 845.
132. Waitman W. Beorn, 'A Calculus of Complicity: the Wehrmacht, the Anti-Partisan War, and the Final Solution in White Russia, 1941–42', *Central European History* 44 (2011): 308–37.
133. As cited in Richter, 'Die Wehrmacht und der Partisanenkrieg in den besetzten Gebiezen der Sowjetunion', p. 846.
134. As cited in Peter Longerich, *The Unwritten Order. Hitler's Role in the Final Solution* (Stroud, 2005), p. 113.
135. As cited in Hannes Heer, 'The Logic of the War of Extermination: the Wehrmacht and the Anti-Partisan War', in Hannes Heer and Klaus Naumann (eds), *War of Extermination. The German Military in World War II 1941–1944* (New York and Oxford, 2006), p. 104.
136. *Ibid.*
137. See the insightful essay by Alex J. Kay, 'Transition to Genocide, July 1941: Einsatzkommando 9 and the Annihilation of Soviet Jewry', *Holocaust and Genocide Studies* 27(3) (2013): 411–42.
138. Halder, *KTB* II, p. 320 (17 March 1941).
139. Longerich, *The Unwritten Order*, p. 110.
140. An SS *Reichsführer* had the equivalent rank to an army Field Marshal.
141. For the best recent studies of the *Einsatzgruppen*, see Peter Klein (ed.), *Die Einsatzgruppen in der besetzten Sowjetunion 1941/42. Die Tätigkeits- und Lageberichte des Chefs der Sicherheitspolizei und des SD* (Berlin, 1997);

Andrej Angrick, *Besatzungspolitik und Massenmord. Die Einsatzgrtuppe D in der südlichen Sowjetunion 1941–1943* (Hamburg, 2003); Richard Rhodes, *Masters of Death. The SS Einsatzgruppen and the Invention of the Holocaust* (New York, 2003).

142. Fore the most detailed publication of *Einsatzgruppen* records, see Klaus M. Mallmann, Andrej Angrick, Jürgen Matthäus and Martin Cüppers (eds), *Die 'Ereignismeldung UdSSR' 1941. Dokumente der Einsatzgruppen in der Sowjetunion*. Darmstadt, 2011.
143. Raul Hilberg, *The Destruction of the European Jews* (New York, 1985), pp. 104–6.
144. As cited in Rhodes, *Masters of Death*, p. 39.
145. An SS *Brigadeführer* had the equivalent rank to an army Major-General.
146. Hasenclever, *Wehrmacht und Besatzungspolitik*, pp. 168–72. For a more succinct overview of the Wehrmacht's reaction to the killing of the Jews in 1941 and 1942, see Raul Hilberg, 'Wehrmacht und Judenvernichtung', in Walter Manoschek (ed.), *Die Wehrmacht im Rassenkrieg. Der Vernichtungskrieg hinter der Front* (Vienna, 1996), pp. 23–38.
147. Ernst Klee, Willi Dressen and Volker Riess (eds), *'The Good Old Days'. The Holocaust as Seen by its Perpetrators and Bystanders* (Old Saybrook, 1991), pp. 24 and 27. On Hoepner, see Peter Steinkamp, 'Die Haltung der Hitlergegner Generalfeldmarschall Wilhelm Ritter von Leeb und Generaloberst Erich Hoepner zur verbrecherischen Kriegführung bei der Heeresgruppe Nord in der Sowjetunion 1941', in Gerd R. Ueberschär (ed.), *NS-Verbrechen und der militärische Widerstand gegen Hitler* (Darmstadt, 2000), pp. 47–61.
148. See Dieter Pohl, *Die Herrschaft der Wehrmacht. Deutsche Militärbesatzung und einheimische Bevölkerung in der Sowjetunion 1941–1944* (Munich, 2008), pp. 265, 340 and 342; Hasenclever, *Wehrmacht und Besatzungspolitik*, pp. 496–7, 501–2, 506–7, 519 and 553–4.
149. As cited in Fritz, *Frontsoldaten*, p. 59. For more first-hand accounts on the Wehrmacht's role in the Holocaust, see Joshua Rubenstein and Ilya Altman (eds), *The Unknown Black Book. The Holocaust in the German-Occupied Soviet Territories* (Bloomington, IN, 2008).
150. Even the small of group of anti-Nazi officers who were later to plot Hitler's assassination have been shown to have operated far more closely with the regime's murderous practices than many accounts of their later actions might suggest. Christian Gerlach, 'Men of 20 July and the War in the Soviet Union', in Hannes Heer and Klaus Naumann (eds), *War of Extermination. The German Military in World War II 1941–1944* (New York and Oxford, 2006), pp. 127–45; Christian Gerlach, 'Hitlergegner bei der Heeresgruppe Mitte und die "verbrecherischen Befehle"', in Gerd R. Ueberschär (ed.), *NS-Verbrechen und der militärische Widerstand gegen Hitler* (Darmstadt, 2000), pp. 62–76.

Nevertheless, revisionist views seeking to preserve the myth of an anti-Nazi officer corps continue to surface. See Klaus J. Arnold, 'Verbrecher aus eigener Intiative? Der 20. Juli und die Thesen Christian Gerlachs', *Geschichte in Wissenschaft und Unterricht* 53 (2002): 20–31.

151. Helmut Krausnick and Hans-Heinrich Wilhelm, *Die Truppe des Weltanschauungskrieges. Die Einsatzgruppen der Sicherheitspolizei und des SD 1938–1942* (Stuttgart, 1981), p. 184.
152. As cited in Christopher R. Browning, with contributions by Jürgen Matthäus, *The Origins of the Final Solution. The Evolution of Nazi Jewish Policy, September 1939–March 1942* (London, 2005), p. 273.
153. Walter Manoschek (ed.), *'Es gibt nur eines für das Judentum: Vernichtung'. Das Judenbild in deutschen Soldatenbriefen 1939–1944* (Hamburg, 1995), p. 29 (24 June 1941).
154. Christian Hartmann, *Wehrmacht im Ostkrieg. Front und militärisches Hinterland 1941/42* (Munich, 2010), pp. 272–6; Martin Gilbert, *The Holocaust. The Jewish Tragedy* (London, 1986), p. 160; Longerich, *The Unwritten Order*, pp. 111–12.
155. Geoffrey P. Megargee, *War of Annihilation. Combat and Genocide on the Eastern Front 1941* (Lanham, MD, 2006), p. 69.
156. For the role of the police in the east, see Edward B. Westermann, *Hitler's Police Battalions. Enforcing Racial Warfare in the East* (Lawrence, KS, 2005); Wolfgang Curilla, *Die deutsche Ordnungspolizei und der Holocaust im Baltikum und in Weissrussland 1941–1944* (Paderborn, 2006); Ruth-Bettina Birn, *Die Höheren SS- und Polizeiführer. Himmlers Vertreter im Reich und in den besetzten Gebieten* (Düsseldorf, 1986); Jürgen Matthaus, 'Die Beteiligung der Ordnungspolizei am Holocaust', in Wolf Kaiser (ed.), *Täter im Vernichtungskrieg. Der Überfall auf die Sowjetunion und der Völkermord an den Juden* (Berlin, 2002), pp. 166–85.
157. Martin Dean, *Collaboration in the Holocaust. Crimes of the Local Police in Belorussia and Ukraine 1941–1944* (London, 1999); Antonio Munoz and Oleg V. Romanko, *Hitler's White Russians. Collaboration, Extermination and Anti-Partisan Warfare in Byelorussia 1941–1944. A Study of White Russian Collaboration and German Occupation Policies* (New York, 2003).
158. As cited in Rhodes, *Masters of Death*, pp. 111–12.
159. Megargee, *War of Annihilation*, p. 93.
160. Tobias Jersak, 'Die Interaktion von Kriegsverlauf und Judenvernichtung: ein Blick auf Hitlers Strategie im Spätsommer 1941', *Historische Zeitschrift* 268 (1999): 311–74. See also my discussion in Stahel, *Operation Barbarossa and Germany's Defeat in the East*, pp. 400–22.
161. Elke Fröhlich (ed.), *Die Tagebücher von Joseph Goebbels. Teil II Diktate 1941–1945, Band 1: Juli–September 1941* (Munich, 1996), p. 269 (19 August 1941).

162. Burleigh, *The Third Reich*, p. 613; Hilberg, *The Destruction of the European Jews*, p. 111.
163. An SS *Standartenführer* had the equivalent rank to an army Colonel.
164. Lucy Dawidowicz, *The War Against the Jews 1933–45* (London, 1987).
165. Rhodes, *Masters of Death*, ch. 11.
166. For a short overview, see Jürgen Förster, 'Hitlers Verbündete gegen die Sowjetunion 1941 und der Judenmord', in Christian Hartmann, Johannes Hürter and Ulrike Jureit (eds), *Verbrechen der Wehrmacht. Bilanz einer Debatte* (Munich, 2005), pp. 91–7.
167. In June 1940, Stalin had seized these two Romanian territories as part of his plan to secure areas afforded to the Soviet Union under the secret clause of the Molotov–Ribbentrop Pact.
168. An SS *Gruppenführer* had the equivalent rank to an army lieutenant-general.
169. Dennis Deletant, *Hitler's Forgotten Ally. Ion Antonescu and His Regime, Romania 1940–1944* (London, 2006), p. 127.
170. Alexander Dallin, *Odessa, 1941–1944. A Case Study of Soviet Territory under Foreign Rule* (Oxford, 1998), p. 74.
171. Wendy Lower, 'Axis Collaboration, Operation Barbarossa, and the Holocaust in Ukraine', in Alex J. Kay, Jeff Rutherford and David Stahel (eds), *Nazi Policy on the Eastern Front, 1941. Total War, Genocide and Radicalization* (Rochester, NY, 2012), pp. 208 and 210.
172. There was relatively little variation in the method of killing in 1941, although the deployment of specially developed gas vans sent to Minsk murdered Jews by pumping carbon monoxide into a sealed compartment. See Christian Gerlach, *Kalkulierte Morde. Die deutsche Wirtschafts- und Vernichtungspolitik in Weißrussland 1941 bis 1944* (Hamburg, 2000), pp. 764–7.
173. Sönke Neitzel, *Tapping Hitler's Generals. Transcripts of Secret Conversations, 1942–45* (St Paul, MN, 2007), pp. 204–5, document 119 (28 December 1944).
174. *Ibid.*, p. 205, document 119 (28 December 1944).
175. Christian Streit, 'Soviet Prisoners of War in the Hands of the Wehrmacht', in Hannes Heer and Klaus Naumann (eds), *War of Extermination. The German Military in World War* II *1941–1944* (New York and Oxford, 2006), p. 81. By comparison, 232,000 British and Americans were captured by the Germans during the course of the Second World War. Of these, only 3.5 per cent (some 8,348) died during captivity. Christian Streit, 'Die sowjetischen Kriegsgefangenen in der Hand der Wehrmacht', in Walter Manoschek (ed.), *Die Wehrmacht im Rassenkrieg. Der Vernichtungskrieg hinter der Front* (Vienna, 1996), p. 75.
176. As cited in Karel C. Berkhoff, *Motherland in Danger. Soviet Propaganda During World War* II (Cambridge, MA, 2012), p. 124.

177. Christian Streit, *Keine Kameraden. Die Wehrmacht und die sowjetischen Kriegsgefangenen 1941–1945* (Bonn, 1997), p. 106. David Glantz claims that, during the course of the whole war, anywhere between 250,000 and 1 million Soviet POWs died en route to the camps. David M. Glantz, *Colossus Reborn. The Red Army at War, 1941–1943* (Lawrence, KS, 2005), p. 622. See also G. F. Krivosheev (ed.), *Soviet Casualties and Combat Losses in the Twentieth Century* (London, 1997), p. 236.
178. Hugh Trevor-Roper (ed.), *Hitler's Table Talk, 1941–1944. His Private Conversations* (London, 2000), p. 30 (17–18 September 1941).
179. Alfred Streim, 'International Law and Soviet Prisoners of War', in Bernd Wegner (ed.), *From Peace to War. Germany, Soviet Russia and the World, 1939–1941* (Oxford, 1997), pp. 293–308.
180. Christian Streit, 'Partisans – Resistance – Prisoners of War', in Joseph Wieczynski (ed.), *Operation Barbarossa. The German Attack on the Soviet Union June 22, 1941* (Salt Lake City, UT, 1993), p. 272.
181. As cited in Schulte, *The German Army and Nazi Policies in Occupied Russia*, p. 195.
182. Bartov, *The Eastern Front, 1941–45*, p. 112.
183. As Gerald Reitlinger noted: 'In not one single case could the scale of rations, as laid down by the Quartermaster General of the armed forces, be honoured.' Gerald Reitlinger, *The House Built on Sand. The Conflicts of German Policy in Russia 1939–45* (London, 1960), p. 106. See also Christian Streit, 'Die Behandlung der sowjetischen Kriesgefangenen und völkerrechtliche Probleme des Krieges gegen die Sowjetunion', in Gerd R. Ueberschär and Wolfram Wette (eds), *'Unternehmen Barbarossa' Der deutsche Überfall auf die Sowjetunion 1941* (Paderborn, 1984), pp. 206–7.
184. Gilbert, *The Second World War*, p. 282.
185. Becker, *Devil on my Shoulder*, pp. 23–4.
186. *Ibid.*, p. 24.
187. Christian Hartmann, 'Massensterben oder Massenvernichtung? Sowjetische Kriegsgefangene im "Unternehmen Barbarossa". Aus dem Tagebuch eines deutschen Lagerkommandanten', *Vierteljahrshefte für Zeitgeschichte* 1 (2001): 97–158; Rüdiger Overmans, Andreas Hilger and Paval Polian (eds), *Rotarmmisten in deutscher Hand. Dokumente zu Gefangenschaft, Repatriierung und Rehabilitierung sowjetischer Soldaten des Zweiten Weltkrieges* (Paderborn, 2012), pp. 15–41.
188. As cited in Streit, *Keine Kameraden*, pp. 157–8.
189. *True To Type*, p. 91 (17 September 1941).
190. *Ibid.*, p. 89 (undated).
191. Horst Fuchs Richardson (ed.), *Sieg Heil! War Letters of Tank Gunner Karl Fuchs 1937–1941* (Hamden, CT, 1987), p. 117 (1 July 1941).

192. Perel, *Europa Europa*, p. 30.
193. Obryn'ba, *Red Partisan*, p. 30.
194. Christian Streit, 'The German Army and the Policies of Genocide', in Gerhard Hirschfeld (ed.), *The Policies of Genocide. Jews and Soviet Prisoners of War in Nazi Germany* (London, 1986), p. 12.
195. For many of the command appointments used in this study, see Andris J. Kursietis, *The Wehrmacht at War 1939–1945. The Units and Commanders of the German Ground Forces during World War* II (Soesterberg, 1999), p. 167.
196. Neitzel, *Tapping Hitler's Generals*, p. 231, document 139 (6 May 1945). (Italics in the original.)
197. Snyder, *Bloodlands*, p. 251.
198. See Mechthild Rössler and Sabine Schleiermacher (eds), *Der 'Generalplan Ost'. Hauptlinien der nationalsozialistischen Planungs und Vernichtungspolitik* (Berlin, 1993).
199. Adolf Hitler, *Mein Kampf* (New York, 1999), p. 654. See also Hitler's second book, which dates from 1928, but was not in fact published until after the war. Gerhard Weinberg (ed.), *Hitler's Second Book* (New York, 2003), p. 152.
200. Moritz (ed.), *Fall Barbarossa*, document 1: 'Niederschrift der Rede Hitlers vor den Befehlshabern des Heeres und der Marine über sein Regierungsprogramm, 3. Februar 1933', p. 51.
201. Kay, *Exploitation, Resettlement, Mass Murder*, pp. 100–2. For a recent overview, see Wigbert Benz, *Der Hungerplan im 'Unternehmen Barbarossa' 1941* (Berlin, 2011).
202. Rolf-Dieter Müller, 'Das "Unternehmen Barbarossa" als wirtschaftlicher Raubkrieg', in Gerd R. Ueberschär and Wolfram Wette (eds), *'Unternehmen Barbarossa' Der deutsche Überfall auf die Sowjetunion 1941* (Paderborn, 1984), pp. 180–3.
203. Adam Tooze, *The Wages of Destruction. The Making and Breaking of the Nazi Economy* (London, 2006), pp. 478–9.
204. Snyder, *Bloodlands*, pp. 161–3.
205. The dimensions of the Hunger Plan and the 2 May meeting have recently come under attack from historians seeking to expunge the Wehrmacht's deep-seated involvement. The controversy can be followed in the *Journal of Contemporary History*, see Alex J. Kay, 'Germany's Staatssekretäre, Mass Starvation and the Meeting of 2 May 1941', *Journal of Contemporary History* 41(4) (2006): 685–700; Klaus Jochen Arnold and Gerd C. Lübbers, 'The Meeting of the Staatssekretäre on 2 May 1941 and the Wehrmacht: A Document up for Discussion', *Journal of Contemporary History* 42(4) (2007): 613–26; Alex J. Kay, 'Revisiting the Meeting of the Staatssekretäre on 2 May 1941: A Response to Klaus Jochen Arnold and Gert C. Lübbers', *Journal of Contemporary History* 43(1) (2008): 93–104. Thanks to Alex J. Kay for passing on these references.

206. As cited in Alex J. Kay, '"The Purpose of the Russian Campaign is the Decimation of the Slavic Population by Thirty Million": The Radicalisation of German Food Policy in early 1941', in Alex J. Kay, Jeff Rutherford and David Stahel (eds), *Nazi Policy on the Eastern Front, 1941. Total War, Genocide and Radicalization* (Rochester, NY, 2012), pp. 107–8. The German text is reproduced in Norbert Müller, *Wehrmacht und Okkupation 1941–1944* (Berlin, 1971), p. 59.
207. As cited in Mark Mazower, *Hitler's Empire. Nazi Rule in Occupied Europe* (London, 2009), p. 282.
208. Kay, *Exploitation, Resettlement, Mass Murder*, p. 148.
209. As cited in Steven M. Miner, *Stalin's Holy War. Religion, Nationalism, and Alliance Politics, 1941–1945* (Chapel Hill, NC, 2003), p. 54.
210. For first-rate case studies reflecting the impact of these policies in 1941, see Jeff Rutherford, 'The Radicalization of German Occupation Policies: *Wirtschaftsstab Ost* and the 121st Infantry Division in Pavlovsk, 1941', in Alex J. Kay, Jeff Rutherford and David Stahel (eds), *Nazi Policy on the Eastern Front, 1941. Total War, Genocide and Radicalization* (Rochester, NY, 2012), pp. 130–54; Norbert Kunz, 'Das Beispiel Charkow: Eine Stadtbevölkerung als Opfer der deutschen Hungerstrategie 1941/42', in Christian Hartmann, Johannes Hürter and Ulrike Jureit (eds), *Verbrechen der Wehrmacht. Bilanz einer Debatte* (Munich, 2005), pp. 136–44.
211. As cited in Bartov, *The Eastern Front, 1941–45*, pp. 130 and 135.
212. As cited in Alexander Dallin, *German Rule in Russia 1941–1945. A Study of Occupation Policies* (London, 1981), p. 215. In some regions, such as the Ukraine and the Baltic states, the Germans were initially viewed as liberators from communist rule.
213. *True To Type*, p. 22 (5 July 1941).
214. Pabst, *The Outermost Frontier*, pp. 18–19 and 39.
215. *True To Type*, p. 93 (6 January 1942).
216. As cited in Hürter, *Hitlers Heerführer*, p. 492.
217. Henry Metelmann, *Through Hell For Hitler* (Havertown, PA, 2005), p. 30.
218. Dieter Beese, 'Kirche im Krieg. Evangelische Wehrmachtpfarrer und die Kriegführung der deutschen Wehrmacht', in Rolf-Dieter Müller and Hans-Erich Volkmann (eds), *Die Wehrmacht. Mythos und Realität* (Munich, 1999), p. 492.
219. Klee, Dressen and Riess (eds), *'The Good Old Days'*, p. 43.
220. Konrad H. Jarausch and Klaus J. Arnold (eds), *'Das stille Sterben ...' Feldpostbriefe von Konrad Jarausch aus Polen und Russland 1939–1942* (Munich, 2008), p. 309 (13 September 1941). This book now appears in English translation, see Konrad H. Jarausch (ed.), *Reluctant Accomplice. A Wehrmacht Soldier's Letters from the Eastern Front* (Princeton, NJ, 2011), p. 283 (13 September 1941).

221. Jarausch and Arnold (eds), *'Das stille Sterben . . .'*, p. 312 (16 September 1941).
222. As cited in Leon Goldensohn (ed.), *Nuremberg Interviews. An American Psychiatrist's Conversations with the Defendants and Witnesses* (New York, 2004), p. 322 (4 February 1946). On Kesselring, see also Kerstin von Lingen, *Kesselring's Last Battle. War Crimes Trials and Cold War Politics, 1945–1960* (Lawrence, KS, 2009).
223. Kesselring was only stationed on the eastern front until November 1941 and later served in Italy where, in the final eighteen months of the war, he was implicated in numerous war crimes while combating local partisans.
224. Neitzel, *Tapping Hitler's Generals*, p. 112, document 44 (14–17 October 1944).
225. *Ibid.*, p. 211, document 120 (28 December 1944).
226. For more on this and its lasting effects, see Ronald Smelser and Edward J. Davies II, *The Myth of the Eastern Front. The Nazi–Soviet War in American Popular Culture* (Cambridge, 2008). See also Hew Strachan, 'Die Vorstellungen der Anglo-Amerikaner von der Wehrmacht', in Rolf-Dieter Müller and Hans-Erich Volkmann (eds), *Die Wehrmacht. Mythos und Realität* (Munich, 1999), pp. 92–104.
227. For more on this, see Valerie Geneviève Hébert, *Hitler's Generals on Trial. The Last War Crimes Tribunal at Nuremberg* (Lawrence, KS, 2010).
228. Wolfram Wette, *The Wehrmacht. History, Myth, Reality* (Cambridge, 2006), ch. 5.
229. The first attempt to comprehensively deal with both sides of the Wehrmacht's history came in volume VI of the Militärgeschichtliches Forschungsamt (ed.), *Das Deutsche Reich und der Zweite Weltkrieg. Der Angriff auf die Sowjetunion* (Stuttgart, 1983). Unfortunately, the one outstanding omission from this otherwise excellent volume is the absence of any serious discussion of the Holocaust in the Soviet Union during 1941. The most complete treatment of Germany's war in the east is the study by Stephen Fritz, *Ostkrieg. Hitler's War of Extermination in the East* (Lexington, KY, 2011). For the 1941 period, see Megargee, *War of Annihilation.*
230. Krivosheev (ed.), *Soviet Casualties and Combat Losses in the Twentieth Century*, p. 83. See also John Erickson, 'Soviet War Losses: Calculations and Controversies', in John Erickson and David Dilks (eds), *Barbarossa. The Axis and the Allies* (Edinburgh, 1998), pp. 255–77.
231. Glantz and House, *When Titans Clashed*, p. 292.
232. For some of the best studies of the German occupation, see Pohl, *Die Herrschaft der Wehrmacht*; Bernhard Chiari, *Alltag hinter der Front. Besatzung, Kollaboration und Widerstand in Weißrußland 1941–1944* (Düsseldorf, 1998); Wendy Lower, *Nazi Empire-Building and the Holocaust in Ukraine* (Chapel Hill, NC, 2005); Ray Brandon and Wendy Lower (eds), *The Shoah in Ukraine. History, Testimony, Memorialization* (Bloomington, IN,

2008); Karel C. Berkhoff, *Harvest of Despair. Life and Death in Ukraine Under Nazi Rule* (Cambridge, MA, 2004).

233. Rüdiger Overmans, *Deutsche militärische Verluste im Zweiten Weltkrieg* (Munich, 2000), p. 208.

234. While there can be no doubt about the criminal nature of German rule in the east, the question has recently been asked whether this resulted from radicalising external factors encountered by the Germans in the east (as argued by Jörg Baberowski and Klaus J. Arnold), or whether the radicalising factors were something imbued in Nazi ideology and German plans for the east (as far more convincingly argued by Alex J. Kay). See Jörg Baberowski, 'Kriege in staatsfernen Räumen: Rußland und die Sowjetunion 1905–1950', in Dietrich Beyrau, Michael Hochgeschwender and Dieter Langewiesche (eds), *Formen des Krieges. Von der Antike bis zur Gegenwart* (Paderborn, 2007), pp. 291–309; Klaus J. Arnold, *Die Wehrmacht und die Besatzungspolitik in den besetzten Gebieten der Sowjetunion. Kriegführung und Radikalisierung im 'Unternehmen Barbarossa'* (Berlin, 2005); Alex J. Kay, 'A "War in a Region beyond State Control"? The German–Soviet War, 1941–1944', *War in History* 18(1) (2011): 109–22.

235. Berkhoff, *Motherland in Danger*, p. 123.

2 The idle Typhoon

1. Hermann Hoth, the aforementioned commander of Panzer Group 3, was replaced by Reinhardt in early October.
2. For an informative new study of the fighting around Kalinin, see Jack Radey and Charles Sharp, *The Defense of Moscow. The Northern Flank* (Barnsley, 2012).
3. As cited in M. Jones, *The Retreat*, pp. 83–4.
4. Helmut Günther, *Hot Motors, Cold Feet. A Memoir of Service with the Motorcycle Battalion of SS-Division 'Reich' 1940–1941* (Winnipeg, 2004), p. 208.
5. 'Kriegstagebuch Nr.1 2.Panzerarmee Band III vom 1.11.1941 bis 26.12.41', BA-MA RH 21-2/244, fol. 1 (1 November 1941).
6. von Bock, *War Diary*, p. 348 (2 November 1941).
7. Peter Bamm, *The Invisible Flag* (New York, 1958), p. 47.
8. 'Anlagen zum Kriegstagebuch Tagesmeldungen Bd.1 1.11-31.12.41', BA-MA RH 21-3/71, fol. 8 (1 November 1941).
9. In the wake of Reinhardt's promotion to command Panzer Group 3 the XXXXI Panzer Corps was eventually handed to General of Panzer Troops Walter Model on 26 October 1941. Model, however, would not be able to leave his command of the 3rd Panzer Division and take up his new appointment until 15 November, and in the interim the panzer corps was commanded by Lieutenant-General Friedrich Kirchner. Marcel Stein, *A Flawed Genius. Field*

Marshal Walter Model. A Critical Biography* (Solihull, 2010), p. 73. For the suggestion that Model's appointment to XXXXI Panzer Corps may have been at act of favouritism by Brauchitsch, see Steven H. Newton, *Hitler's Commander. Field Marshal Walter Model: Hitler's Favorite General* (Cambridge MA, 2006), pp. 149–50.

10. 'Anlagenband zum KTB XXXXI A.K. Ia 3.Verteidigung von Kalinin 15.10.41–20.11.41', BA-MA RH 24-41/15 (4 November 1941). The diary has no folio stamped page numbers so references must be located using the date. The XXXXI Panzer Corps also commanded a small number of tanks under Colonel Walther Krause's motorised infantry regiment *Lehrbrigade* 900.
11. 'Kriegstagebuch Nr.3 der 7.Panzer-Division Führungsabteilung 1.6.1941–9.5.1942', BA-MA RH 27-7/46, fol. 165 (4 November 1941).
12. 'Anlagen zum Kriegstagebuch Tagesmeldungen Bd.I 1.11-31.12.41', BA-MA RH 21-3/71, fol. 39 (5 November 1941).
13. Erhard Raus, *Panzer Operations. The Eastern Front Memoir of General Raus, 1941–1945*, comp. and trans. Steven H. Newton (Cambridge, MA, 2005), p. 88.
14. Hans Reinhardt, 'Panzer-Gruppe 3 in der Schlacht von Moskau und ihre Erfahrungen im Rückzug', *Wehrkunde* 9 (1953): 1.
15. 'Gen.Kdo.LVII.Pz.Korps KTB Nr.2 vom 1.11.41–31.12.41', BA-MA RH 24-57-3, fols 4 and 7 (1 and 3 November 1941).
16. 'Kriegstagebuch Nr.3. der Führungsabteilung (Ia) des Gen. Kdo. (mot.) XXXX.Pz. Korps vom 31.05.1941–26.12.1941', BA-MA RH 24-40/18 (2 November 1941). The diary has no folio stamped page numbers so references must be located using the date.
17. 'Anlage zum KTB Panzer Gruppe 4: 15.10.41–10.11.41', BA-MA RH 21-4/35, fol. 164 (1 November 1941).
18. 'Kriegstagebuch Nr.3. des XXXXVI.Pz.Korps vom 24.08.41–31.12.41', BA-MA RH 24-46/21, fol. 106 (2 November 1941).
19. 'Anlage zum KTB Panzer Gruppe 4: 15.10.41–10.11.41', BA-MA RH 21-4/35, fol. 162 (1 November 1941).
20. On urban warfare in the east in 1941, including at Dnepropetrovsk, see Adrian Wettstein, 'Operation "Barbarossa" und Stadtkampf', *Militärgeschichtliche Zeitschrift* 66 (2007): 21–44; Adrian Wettstein, 'Urban Warfare Doctrine on the Eastern Front', in Alex J. Kay, Jeff Rutherford and David Stahel (eds), *Nazi Policy on the Eastern Front, 1941. Total War, Genocide and Radicalization* (Rochester, NY, 2012), pp. 45–72.
21. Guderian, *Panzer Leader*, p. 245.
22. 'Kriegstagebuch Nr.1 2.Panzerarmee Band III vom 1.11.1941 bis 26.12.41', BA-MA RH 21-2/244, fol. 18 (4 November 1941).
23. Guderian, *Panzer Leader*, p. 245.
24. 'Kriegstagebuch Nr.1 2.Panzerarmee Band III vom 1.11.1941 bis 26.12.41', BA-MA RH 21-2/244, fol. 18 (4 November 1941).

25. Guderian, *Panzer Leader*, p. 245.
26. 'Kriegstagebuch Nr.1 2.Panzerarmee Band III vom 1.11.1941 bis 26.12.41', BA-MA RH 21-2/244, fols 8 and 18 (2 and 4 November 1941).
27. 'Kriegstagebuch 4.Panzer-Divison Führungsabtl. 26.5.41–31.3.42', BA-MA RH 27-4/10, p. 228 (1 November 1941).
28. Rudolf Steiger, *Armour Tactics in the Second World War. Panzer Army Campaigns of 1939–41 in German War Diaries* (Oxford, 1991), p. 127.
29. 'Kriegstagebuch Nr.1 2.Panzerarmee Band III vom 1.11.1941 bis 26.12.41', BA-MA RH 21-2/244, fol. 20 (4 November 1941).
30. Steiger, *Armour Tactics in the Second World War*, p. 107.
31. 'Kriegstagebuch Nr.1 2.Panzerarmee Band III vom 1.11.1941 bis 26.12.41', BA-MA RH 21-2/244, fols 19–21 (4 November 1941).
32. 'Armeeoberkommando 2. I.a KTB Teil.2 19.9.41–16.12.41', BA-MA RH 20-2/207, p. 91 (1 November 1941).
33. H. C. Robbins Landon and Sebastian Leitner (eds), *Diary of a German Soldier* (London, 1963), pp. 119–20 (1 November 1941).
34. *Ibid.*, pp. 121–3 (2 November 1941).
35. '9.Pz.Div. KTB Ia vom 19.5.1941 bis 22.1.1942', BA-MA RH 27-9/4, p. 153 (4 November 1941).
36. Robbins Landon and Leitner (eds), *Diary of a German Soldier*, p. 123 (11 November 1941).
37. As cited in Catherine Merridale, *Ivan's War. Life and Death in the Red Army, 1939–1945* (New York, 2006), p. 133.
38. Kempf's XXXXVIII Panzer Corps formally belonged to Guderian's Panzer Group 2, which launched its autumn offensive two days before Operation Typhoon began.
39. Halder, *KTB* III, p. 278 (3 November 1941).
40. 'Kriegstagebuch Nr.1 (Band November 1941) des Oberkommandos der Heeresgruppe Mitte', BA-MA RH 19-II/387, fols 13–14 (3 November 1941).
41. *Ibid.*
42. Robbins Landon and Leitner (eds), *Diary of a German Soldier*, pp. 123–4 (18 November 1941). (Italics in the original.)
43. Fröhlich (ed.), *Die Tagebücher von Joseph Goebbels. Teil* II, *Band* 2, p. 215 (1 November 1941).
44. *Ibid.*, p. 218 (1 November 1941).
45. *Ibid.*, p. 213 (1 November 1941).
46. von Bock, *War Diary*, p. 349 (3 November 1941).
47. 'Kriegstagebuch Nr.1 (Band November 1941) des Oberkommandos der Heeresgruppe Mitte' BA-MA RH 19-II/387, fol. 7 (1 November 1941).
48. *Ibid.*, fol. 19 (1 November 1941).
49. David Garden and Kenneth Andrew (eds), *The War Diaries of a Panzer Soldier. Erich Hager with the 17th Panzer Division on the Russian Front 1941–1945* (Atglen, PA, 2010), p. 55 (2 November 1941).

50. Otto Will, *Tagebuch eines Ostfront-Kämpfers. Mit der 5. Panzerdivision im Einsatz 1941–1945* (Selent, 2010), p. 27 (3 November 1941).
51. Pabst, *The Outermost Frontier*, p. 39.
52. Elisabeth Wagner (ed.), *Der Generalquartiermeister. Briefe und Tagebuchaufzeichnungen des Generalquartiermeisters des Heeres General der Artillerie Eduard Wagner* (Munich, 1963), p. 212 (2 November 1941).
53. Nicolaus von Below, *Als Hitlers Adjutant 1937–45* (Mainz, 1999), p. 294.
54. E. Wagner (ed.), *Der Generalquartiermeister*, p. 317.
55. Rolf-Dieter Müller, 'The Failure of the Economic "Blitzkrieg Strategy"', in Militärgeschichtliches Forschungsamt (ed.), *Germany and the Second World War, vol. IV: The Attack on the Soviet Union* (Oxford, 1998), p. 1136.
56. As cited in Klaus Reinhardt, *Moscow: The Turning Point. The Failure of Hitler's Strategy in the Winter of 1941–42* (Oxford, 1992), p. 181, fn. 41.
57. Albrecht Kesselring, *The Memoirs of Field-Marshal Kesselring* (London, 1988), p. 96.
58. Blumentritt, 'Moscow', p. 54.
59. Martin Gareis, *Kampf und Ende der Fränkisch-Sudetendeutschen 98. Infanterie-Division* (Eggolsheim, 1956), p. 163.
60. *Ibid.*, p. 161.
61. 'Kriegstagebuch Nr.1 (Band November 1941) des Oberkommandos der Heeresgruppe Mitte', BA-MA RH 19-II/387, fol. 25 (5 November 1941).
62. 'Anlage zum KTB Pz.Gruppe 4 Meldungen von unten 15.10.41–15.11.41', BA-MA RH 21-4/39, fol. 155 (1 November 1941).
63. 'Anlage zum KTB Panzer Gruppe 4: 15.10.41–10.11.41', BA-MA RH 21-4/35, fols 34, 38 and 155 (2, 3 and 4 November 1941); von Bock, *War Diary*, pp. 348–9 (2 and 3 November 1941).
64. At the end of the war Vietinghoff would once again reveal his independent streak by engaging in unauthorised surrender negotiations with the Allies in Italy. This led to his dismissal by Kesselring. Samuel W. Mitcham Jr, *The Panzer Legions. A Guide to the German Army Tank Divisions of WWII and their Commanders* (Mechanicsburg, PA, 2007), p. 67.
65. 'Anlage zum KTB Panzer Gruppe 4: 15.10.41–10.11.41', BA-MA RH 21-4/35, fols 164–165 (1 November 1941). (Underlining in the original.)
66. *Ibid.*, fol. 165 (1 November 1941). (Underlining in the original.)
67. *Ibid.*, fol. 162 (3 November 1941).
68. As cited in M. Jones, *The Retreat*, p. 78.
69. As cited in Heinrich Bücheler, *Hoepner. Ein deutsches Soldatenschicksal des Zwantigsten Jahrhunderts* (Herford, 1980), p. 156.
70. 'Kriegstagebuch Nr.3. des XXXXVI.Pz.Korps vom 24.08.41–31.12.41', BA-MA RH 24-46/21, fol. 109 (5 November 1941).
71. 'Anlage zum KTB Panzer Gruppe 4: 15.10.41–10.11.41', BA-MA RH 21-4/35, fol. 157 (4 November 1941).

72. *Ibid.*, fol. 160 (4 November 1941).
73. '5. Panzer Division KTB Nur.8 vom 11.9.41–11.12.41', BA-MA RH 27-5/29, fol. 67 (3 November 1941).
74. '11.Pz.Div. KTB Abt.Ia vom 22.10.41–24.1.42', BA-MA RH 27-11/24, fol. 10 (3 November 1941).
75. Franz A. P. Frisch, in association with Wilbur D. Jones, Jr, *Condemned to Live. A Panzer Artilleryman's Five-Front War* (Shippensburg, 2000), p. 85.
76. Fuchs Richardson (ed.), *Sieg Heil!*, pp. 154–5 (6 November 1941).
77. Ingo Stader (ed.), *Ihr daheim und wir hier draußen. Ein Briefwechsel zwischen Ostfront und Heimat Juni 1941–März 1943* (Cologne, 2006), p. 49 (11 November 1941).
78. As cited in Georg Meyer, *Adolf Heusinger. Dienst eines deutschen Soldaten 1915 bis 1964* (Berlin, 2001), p. 162 (5 November 1941).
79. Halder, *KTB* III, pp. 278–9 (3 November 1941).
80. Hans Meier-Welcker, *Aufzeichnungen eines Generalstabsoffiziers 1939–1942* (Freiburg, 1982), pp. 136–7 (6 November 1941).
81. Gareis, *Kampf und Ende der Fränkisch-Sudetendeutschen 98. Infanterie-Division*, p. 162.
82. Halder, *KTB* III, p. 283 (7 November 1941).
83. See my discussion in Stahel, *Operation Barbarossa and Germany's Defeat in the East*, p. 437.
84. Geoffrey P. Megargee, *Inside Hitler's High Command* (Lawrence, KS, 2000), p. 135.
85. Today Gorky is known as Nizhny Novgorod.
86. Megargee, *Inside Hitler's High Command*, pp. 135–6.
87. von Bock, *War Diary*, p. 354 (11 November 1941).
88. For Bock's reaction to German war crimes committed in Poland, see Burleigh, *The Third Reich*, p. 439.
89. Richard Brett-Smith, *Hitler's Generals* (London, 1976), p. 84.
90. von Bock, *War Diary*, pp. 13–15.
91. See Stahel, *Operation Barbarossa and Germany's Defeat in the East*; Glantz, *Barbarossa Derailed. The Battle for Smolensk 10 July–10 September 1941, vol. 1.*
92. See Stahel, *Kiev 1941*; Glantz, *Barbarossa Derailed. The Battle for Smolensk 10 July–10 September 1941*, vol. 2, chs 8 and 9.
93. Charles Messenger, *The Last Prussian. A Biography of Field Marshal Gerd von Rundstedt 1875–1953* (London, 1991), p. 154.
94. As cited in K. Reinhardt, *Moscow: The Turning Point*, p. 175.
95. Bähr and Bähr (eds), *Kriegsbriefe Gefallener Studenten, 1939–1945*, p. 331 (4 November 1941).
96. As cited in K. Reinhardt, *Moscow: The Turning Point*, p. 189, fn. 10.
97. Robert Forczyk, *Leningrad 1941–44. The Epic Siege* (Oxford, 2009), p. 40.

98. Alexander Stahlberg, *Bounden Duty. The Memoirs of a German Officer 1932–45* (London, 1990), p. 178.
99. David M. Glantz, *The Siege of Leningrad 1941–1944. 900 Days of Terror* (Osceola, WI, 2001), pp. 49 and 53.
100. von Bock, *War Diary*, pp. 346–7 (31 October 1941); '3rd Pz. Gr. KTB Nr.2 1.9.41–31.10.41', BA-MA Microfilm 59060 (29 October 1941); Stahel, *Operation Typhoon*, pp. 288–9.
101. As cited in Bücheler, *Hoepner*, p. 155.
102. In Roman mythology this is the 'sender of rain'.
103. Kesselring, *The Memoirs of Field-Marshal Kesselring*, p. 96.

3 Preparing the final showdown

1. As cited in Rodric Braithwaite, *Moscow 1941. A City and its People at War* (New York, 2006), pp. 252–4.
2. Alexander Hill, *The Great Patriotic War of the Soviet Union, 1941–45. A Documentary Reader* (Abingdon and New York, 2010), p. 75, document 54 (6 November 1941).
3. *Ibid.*
4. *Ibid.*, p. 76.
5. For Goebbels' reaction to the speech, see Fröhlich (ed.), *Die Tagebücher von Joseph Goebbels. Teil* II, *Band* 2, p. 248 (8 November 1941).
6. Braithwaite, *Moscow 1941*, p. 252.
7. Interestingly, the German high command was anticipating a Soviet ground offensive to mark the occasion of the October Revolution. See Halder, *KTB* III, p. 282 (6 November 1941).
8. Zhukov, *The Memoirs of Marshal Zhukov*, p. 336.
9. Thanks to Jack Radey and Charles Sharp for sharing their research with me. This information comes from the *Journal of Military Activities of the Forces of the Front during November 1941*, 'TsAMO RF fond 208 opis' 2511 delo 218'.
10. On Soviet intelligence, see David M. Glantz, *Soviet Military Intelligence in War* (Abingdon, 1990). See also the text and footnotes in Stahel, *Operation Typhoon*, pp. 273–4.
11. As cited in Andrew Nagorski, *The Greatest Battle. Stalin, Hitler, and the Desperate Struggle for Moscow that Changed the Course of World War* II (New York, 2007), p. 223.
12. Stalin instructed that a parallel parade be held at Kuybyshev, 800 km east of Moscow, where the Soviets had established a reserve capital. See Marius Broekmeyer, *Stalin, the Russians, and Their War 1941–1945* (London, 2004), p. 68. As Quentin Reynolds observed: 'They paraded by with their tanks and their artillery, and you didn't have to be Russian to feel a pride in these

grim-faced fighting men. They did not look like men who had been beaten. They did not look like men who would ever be beaten.' Quentin Reynolds, *Only the Stars are Neutral* (London, 1944), p. 149.

13. Braithwaite, *Moscow 1941*, pp. 252 and 258.
14. Zhukov, *The Memoirs of Marshal Zhukov*, p. 336; Yevgeny Vorobyov, 'Sanctum Sanctorum', in S. Krasilshchik (ed.) *World War* II. *Dispatches from the Soviet Front* (New York, 1985), pp. 38–43.
15. As cited in Nagorski, *The Greatest Battle*, p. 223.
16. As cited in Otto Preston Chaney, *Zhukov* (Norman, OK, 1996), p. 174.
17. Mikhail M. Gorinov, 'Muscovites' Moods, 22 June 1941 to May 1942', in Robert Thurston and Bernd Bonwetsch (eds), *The People's War. Responses to World War* II *in the Soviet Union* (Chicago, IL, 2000), p. 126. See also Alexander Werth, *Russia at War 1941–1945* (New York, 1964), p. 250.
18. My thanks to Mark Edele for allowing me early access to his research. Mark Edele, '"What Are We Fighting For?" Loyalty in the Soviet War Effort, 1941–1945', *International Labor and Working-Class History* 84 (2013): 1–21.
19. John Erickson, *The Road to Stalingrad. Stalin's War with Germany* (London, 1975), vol. 1, pp. 218–19.
20. A 'hedgehog' was a static anti-tank obstacle usually made of thick, angled iron.
21. Braithwaite, *Moscow 1941*, pp. 205 and 251.
22. As cited in Nagorski, *The Greatest Battle*, p. 186.
23. Ralph Ingersoll, *Action on All Fronts* (New York, 1942), p. 86.
24. Braithwaite, *Moscow 1941*, p. 252.
25. As cited in Cathy Porter and Mark Jones, *Moscow in World War* II (London, 1987), pp. 129–30.
26. von Bock, *War Diary*, p. 349 (3 November 1941).
27. As cited in K. Reinhardt, *Moscow: The Turning Point*, p. 174.
28. Guderian, *Panzer Leader*, pp. 246–7.
29. K. Reinhardt, *Moscow:The Turning Point*, p. 174.
30. von Bock, *War Diary*, p. 352 (7 November 1941).
31. Hans Dollinger (eds.), *Kain, wo ist dein Bruder? Was der Mensch im Zweiten Weltkrieg erleiden mußte: dokumentiert in Tagebüchern und Briefen* (Munich, 1983), pp. 108–9 (6 November 1941).
32. Kurt Miethke, Museumsstiftung Post und Telekommunikation, Berlin, 3.2002.0912 (9 November 1941). Hereafter cited as MPT.
33. Richard Overy, *Russia's War* (London, 1997), p. 33.
34. Otherwise referred to as 'deep battle', this concept arose in the 1920s and 1930s from reforms to the Soviet operational art as emphasised by Mikhail Frunze, Vladimir Triandafillov and Mikhail Tukhachevsky. The emphasis was first on breaking through the enemy front (tactical deep battle) and then using uncommitted reserves to achieve wide-ranging strategic depth in the enemy's rear (deep-battle operations).

35. For a first-rate work on the Red Army in this period, see Roger R. Reese, *Stalin's Reluctant Soldiers. A Social History of the Red Army 1925–1941* (Lawrence, KS, 1996).
36. Glantz, *Barbarossa*, p. 167.
37. As cited in Braithwaite, *Moscow 1941*, pp. 263–4. See also Overy, *Russia's War*, p. 114.
38. As cited in James Lucas, *War of the Eastern Front 1941–1945*, p. 33. See also Nagorski, *The Greatest Battle*, p. 226; Overy, *Russia's War*, pp. 87–8.
39. As cited in Rhodes, *Masters of Death*, p. 123.
40. This figure includes the 2nd and 5th Panzer Divisions not previously counted among panzer strengths (because they were not present on 22 June), as well as three infantry regiments.
41. Hans-Adolf Jacobsen (ed.), *Kriegstagebuch des Oberkommandos der Wehrmacht (Wehrmachtfürungsstab), Band I/2: 1. August 1940–31. Dezember 1941* (Munich, 1982), pp. 1074–5, document 106 (6 November 1941) (hereafter cited as KTB OKW, vol. II). Albert Seaton claims that the OKH figures 'if anything understated the seriousness of the position of the troops of the Eastern Front'. Albert Seaton, *The Battle for Moscow* (New York, 1971), p. 111. See also discussions in Hürter, *Hitlers Heerführer*, p. 303, fn. 119; Burkhart Müller-Hillebrand, *Das Heer 1933–1945, Band* III: *Der Zweifrontenkrieg. Das Heer vom Beginn des Feldzuges gegen die Sowjetunion bis zum Kriegsende* (Frankfurt am Main, 1969), p. 23; Megargee, *Inside Hitler's High Command*, p. 136.
42. Goebbels even commented in his diary that losses were 'not even eight percent of the World War'. Fröhlich (ed.), *Die Tagebücher von Joseph Goebbels. Teil* II, *Band* 2, p. 263 (10 November 1941).
43. Halder, *KTB* III, p. 286 (10 November 1941).
44. Ortwin Buchbender and Reinhold Sterz (eds), *Das andere Gesicht des Krieges. Deutsche Feldpostbriefe 1939–1945* (Munich, 1982), pp. 85–6 (5 November 1941).
45. Karl Knoblauch, *Zwischen Metz und Moskau. Als Soldat der 95. Infanteriedivision in Frankreich und als Fernaufklärer mit der 4.(4)/14 in Russland* (Würzburg, 2007), p. 188 (6 November 1941).
46. K. Reinhardt, *Moscow: The Turning Point*, p. 201, fn. 19.
47. Hans Pichler, *Truppenarzt und Zeitzeuge. Mit der 4. SS-Polizei-Division an vorderster Front* (Dresden, 2006), p. 114 (6 November 1941).
48. As cited in Piekalkiewicz, *Moscow 1941*, p. 58.
49. Bähr and Bähr (eds), *Kriegsbriefe Gefallener Studenten, 1939–1945*, p. 112 (6 November 1941).
50. Alois Scheuer, *Briefe aus Russland. Feldpostbriefe des Gefreiten Alois Scheuer 1941–1942* (St Ingbert, 2000), p. 48 (6 November 1941).
51. The German Replacement Army had 385,000 men to send as replacements for the eastern campaign. Halder, *KTB* II, p. 222 (20 May 1941).

52. '6. Panzer Division KTB 16.9.1941–30.11.1941', BA-MA RH 27-6/19, pp. 200–16 and 260–4 (6 November 1941).
53. 'Kriegstagebuch Nr.1 (Band November 1941) des Oberkommandos der Heeresgruppe Mitte', BA-MA RH 19-II/387, fol. 4 (1 November 1941).
54. 'Kriegstagebuch Nr.3. der Führungsabteilung (Ia) des Gen. Kdo. (mot.) XXXX.Pz. Korps vom 31.05.1941–26.12.1941', BA-MA RH 24-40/18 (5 November 1941).
55. '2. Panzer Division KTB Nr.6 Teil I. Vom 15.6.41–3.4.42', BA-MA RH 27-2/21 (29 October 1941). The diary has no folio stamped page numbers so references must be located using the date.
56. 'Kriegstagebuch 4.Panzer-Divison Führungsabtl. 26.5.41–31.3.42', BA-MA RH 27-4/10, p. 237 (7 November 1941).
57. Heinz Boberach (ed.), *Meldungen aus dem Reich. Die geheimen Lageberichte des Sicherheitsdienstes der SS 1938–1945*, 17 vols (Berlin, 1984), vol. 8, p. 2938, document 234 (3 November 1941).
58. *Ibid.*, p. 2948, document 235 (6 November 1941).
59. Marlis G. Steinert, *Hitler's War and the Germans. Public Mood and Attitude during the Second World War*, ed. and trans Thomas E. J. de Witt (Athens, OH, 1977), pp. 131–2.
60. Fröhlich (ed.), *Die Tagebücher von Joseph Goebbels. Teil II, Band 2*, p. 230 (4 November 1941). See also Goebbels' comments on p. 357 (24 November 1941).
61. Dietrich, *The Hitler I Knew*, p. 70.
62. Domarus, *Hitler*, pp. 2508–9 (8 November 1941).
63. *Ibid.*, p. 2509 (8 November 1941).
64. The speech in Munich was not broadcast publicly on German radio and was only printed later in the newspapers, which was cause for considerable disappointment. As the SD report of 13 November stated: 'In the cities the focal point of public interest is the Führer's speech on the eve of 9 November [it should read 8 November]. According to reports from all parts of the Reich, the fact that it was not broadcast on the radio is a source of great disappointment. Many fellow citizens felt a need to hear the Führer's voice again and derive new strength from his words since their expectations regarding the course of the eastern campaign during the recent weeks have not been met.' Boberach (ed.), *Meldungen aus dem Reich*, vol. 8, p. 2970, document 237 (13 November 1941).
65. Halder, *KTB* III, p. 283 (8 November 1941).
66. In December 1940, during his convalescence from a serious stomach ailment, Bock read a series of articles in the *Neuen Zürichen Zeitung* entitled 'How France Lost the War', here he noted: 'I found Maurois' [the journalist] view of the fall of Paris especially interesting.' Bock then copied into his diary the following passage from the article; 'After the loss of Paris France became a body without a head. The war was lost!' von Bock, *War Diary*, p. 195 (14 December 1940).

67. As cited in K. Reinhardt, *Moscow: The Turning Point*, pp. 182–3, fn. 54.
68. As cited in Mazower, *Hitler's Empire*, p. 323.
69. Halder, *KTB* III, p. 281 (5 November 1941).
70. *Ibid.* See also the discussion in Earl F. Ziemke and Magna E. Bauer, *Moscow to Stalingrad. Decision in the East* (New York, 1988), p. 43; Victor Madeja, *Russo-German War. Autumn 1941: Defeat of Barbarossa* (Allentown, PA, 1988), p. 39.
71. Barry Leach, 'Halder', in Correlli Barnett (ed.), *Hitler's Generals* (London, 1989), pp. 119–20.
72. Ian Kershaw, *Hitler 1936–1945. Nemesis* (London, 2001), p. 438.
73. Earl F. Ziemke, 'Franz Halder at Orsha: the German General Staff Seeks a Consensus', *Military Affairs* 39(4) (1975): 174.
74. 'Kriegstagebuch Nr.1 (Band November 1941) des Oberkommandos der Heeresgruppe Mitte', BA-MA RH 19-II/387, fol. 4 (1 November 1941).
75. H. Reinhardt, 'Panzer-Gruppe 3 in der Schlacht von Moskau und ihre Erfahrungen im Rückzug', p. 2.
76. 'Anlagenband zum KTB XXXXI A.K. Ia 3.Verteidigung von Kalinin 15.10.41–20.11.41', BA-MA RH 24-41/15 (6 November 1941); 'Anlagen zum Kriegstagebuch Tagesmeldungen Bd.I 1.11–31.12.41', BA-MA RH 21-3/71, fol. 51 (6 November 1941).
77. The correct designation was Second Panzer Army.
78. von Bock, *War Diary*, p. 351 (7 November 1941).
79. As cited in M. Jones, *The Retreat*, p. 81.
80. *Ibid.*, p. 88.
81. 'Anlagenband zum KTB XXXXI A.K. Ia 3.Verteidigung von Kalinin 15.10.41–20.11.41', BA-MA RH 24-41/15 (8 November 1941).
82. *Ibid.* (12 November 1941).
83. *Ibid.* (8 November 1941).
84. 'Anlagen zum Kriegstagebuch Tagesmeldungen Bd.I 1.11–31.12.41', BA-MA RH 21-3/71, fol. 57 (7 November 1941).
85. H. Reinhardt, 'Panzer-Gruppe 3 in der Schlacht von Moskau und ihre Erfahrungen im Rückzug', p. 2.
86. Raus, *Panzer Operations*, p. 88.
87. '3rd Pz. Gr. KTB Nr.2 1.9.41–31.10.41', BA-MA Microfilm 59060 (21 October 1941).
88. 'Anlagen zum Kriegstagebuch Tagesmeldungen Bd.I 1.11–31.12.41', BA-MA RH 21-3/71, fol. 34 (4 November 1941).
89. 'Anlagenband zum KTB XXXXI A.K. Ia 3.Verteidigung von Kalinin 15.10.41–20.11.41', BA-MA RH 24-41/15 (8 November 1941).
90. 'Oberkommando des Heeres Generalstab des Heeres O.Qu.IV-Abt.Fr.H.Ost (II)', BA-MA RH/2-2670, fol. 14 (4 November 1941).
91. '20.Pz.Div. KTB vom 15.8.41 bis 20.10.41 Band Ia.', BA-MA RH 27-20/25, fol. 133 (16 October 1941).

92. '20.Pz.Div. KTB vom 21.10.41 bis 30.12.41 Band Ia2.', BA-MA RH 27-20/26, fol. 28 (6 November 1941).
93. 'Kriegstagebuch Nr.3. des XXXXVI.Pz.Korps vom 24.08.41–31.12.41', BA-MA RH 24-46/21, fol. 108 (4 November 1941).
94. 'Kriegstagebuch 19.Panzer-Division Abt.Ib für die Zeit vom 1.6.1941–31.12.1942', BA-MA RH 27-19/23, fol. 69 (9 November 1941).
95. *Ibid.*, fol. 68 (6 November 1941).
96. Klink, 'The Military Concept of the War against the Soviet Union', p. 318.
97. K. Reinhardt, *Moscow: The Turning Point*, p. 148; Richard Overy, *Why the Allies Won* (New York, 1996), pp. 215–16. See also R-D. Müller, 'The Failure of the Economic "Blitzkrieg Strategy"', p. 1137.
98. Rolf-Dieter Müller, 'Beginnings of a Reorganization of the War Economy at the Turn of 1941/1942', in Militärgeschichtliches Forschungsamt (ed.), *Germany and the Second World War, vol.* V/I*: Organization and Mobilization of the German Sphere of Power* (Oxford, 2000), p. 744.
99. 'Kriegstagebuch 19.Panzer-Division Abt.Ib für die Zeit vom 1.6.1941–31.12.1942', BA-MA RH 27-19/23, fol. 68 (6 November 1941).
100. For a good discussion of German fuel shortages in the east during 1941, see Joel Hayward, *Stopped at Stalingrad. The Luftwaffe and Hitler's Defeat in the East, 1942–1943* (Lawrence, KS, 1998), pp. 5–12. See also Gerhard Schreiber, 'Mussolini's "Non-Belligerence"', in Militärgeschichtlichen Forschungsamt (ed.), *Germany and the Second World War, vol.* III*: The Mediterranean, South-east Europe and North Africa 1939–1941* (Oxford, 1995), pp. 25–7. On the role of oil in German strategy, see Dietrich Eichholtz, *War for Oil. The Nazi Quest for an Oil Empire* (Dulles, VA, 2012), pp. 59–74.
101. 'Kriegstagebuch Nr.1 (Band November 1941) des Oberkommandos der Heeresgruppe Mitte', BA-MA RH 19-II/387, fol. 6 (1 November 1941). See citations from Blumentritt and related discussion in A. Clark, *Barbarossa*, pp. 176–7.
102. As cited in M. Jones, *The Retreat*, p. 81.
103. As cited in Piekalkiewicz, *Moscow 1941*, p. 158.
104. Bähr and Bähr (eds), *Kriegsbriefe Gefallener Studenten, 1939–1945*, p. 67 (10–12 November 1941). (Italics in the original.)
105. *Ibid.*, pp. 85–6 (9 November 1941); Hans Bähr and Walter Bähr (eds.), *Die Stimme des Menschen. Briefe und Aufzeichnungen aus der ganzen Welt. 1939–1945* (Munich, 1961), p. 117 (9 November 1941).
106. 'Kriegstagebuch Nr.3. der Führungsabteilung (Ia) des Gen. Kdo. (mot.) XXXX. Pz.Korps vom 31.05.1941–26.12.1941', BA-MA RH 24-40/18 (5 November 1941).
107. Pabst, *The Outermost Frontier*, p. 40.

108. Glantz, *Barbarossa*, p. 167.
109. 'Anlage zum KTB Panzer Gruppe 4: 15.10.41–10.11.41', BA-MA RH 21-4/35, fols 14 and 20 (6 and 7 November 1941).
110. 'Kriegstagebuch Nr.1 (Band November 1941) des Oberkommandos der Heeresgruppe Mitte', BA-MA RH 19-II/387, fol. 56 (12 November 1941).
111. For Soviet losses, see *ibid*. For German losses, see 'Anlage zum KTB Pz. Gruppe 4 Meldungen von unten 15.10.41–15.11.41', BA-MA RH 21-4/39, fol. 20 (13 November 1941). Rokossovsky's memoir claimed the number of German tanks was much higher, 'some 50 damaged and gutted tanks'. K. Rokossovsky, *A Soldier's Duty* (Moscow, 1985), p. 69.
112. von Bock, *War Diary*, p. 358 (14 November 1941).
113. *Ibid.*, pp. 358–9 (15 November 1941).
114. Guderian, *Panzer Leader*, p. 246.
115. *Ibid.*
116. von Bock, *War Diary*, p. 352 (9 November 1941).
117. 'Kriegstagebuch Nr.1 2.Panzerarmee Band III vom 1.11.1941 bis 26.12.41', BA-MA RH 21-2/244, fol. 80 (14 November 1941).
118. Guderian, *Panzer Leader*, p. 249.
119. 'Kriegstagebuch Nr.1 2.Panzerarmee Band III vom 1.11.1941 bis 26.12.41', BA-MA RH 21-2/244, fol. 45 (14 November 1941).
120. Bartov, *Hitler's Army*, p. 22.
121. 'Kriegstagebuch Nr.1 2.Panzerarmee Band III vom 1.11.1941 bis 26.12.41', BA-MA RH 21-2/244, fol. 70 (12 November 1941).
122. Guderian, *Panzer Leader*, p. 248.
123. 'Kriegstagebuch Nr.1 2.Panzerarmee Band III vom 1.11.1941 bis 26.12.41', BA-MA RH 21-2/244, fol. 64 (11 November 1941).
124. *Ibid.* See also fol. 38 (8 November 1941).
125. *Ibid.*, fol. 56 (10 November 1941).
126. 'Kriegstagebuch Nr.2 XXXXVII.Pz.Korps. Ia 23.9.1941–31.12.1941', BA-MA RH 24-47/258, fol. 79 (8 November 1941).
127. '18. Panzer-Div- Ia Kriegstagebuch vom 20.10.41–13.12.41', BA-MA RH 27-18/69 (4 November 1941). The diary has no folio stamped page numbers so references must be located using the date.
128. 'K.T.B. der 10.Inf.Div. (mot) 11.6.1941–29.12.1941', BA-MA RH 26-10/9, fol. 250 (8 November 1941).
129. Steiger, *Armour Tactics in the Second World War*, p. 117.
130. Frisch, *Condemned to Live*, p. 84.
131. Jürgen Kleindienst (ed.), *Sei tausendmal gegrüßt. Briefwechsel Irene und Ernst Guicking 1937–1945* (Berlin, 2001). Accompanying this book is a CD Rom with some 1,600 letters mostly unpublished in the book. The quoted letter appears only on the CD Rom and can be located by its date (5 November 1941).

132. Ulrich von Hassell, *Vom Andern Deutschland* (Freiburg, 1946), p. 224 (20 September 1941). For the English translation, see Ulrich von Hassell, *The von Hassell Diaries 1938–1944* (London, 1948), p. 194 (20 September 1941).

4 The Orsha conference

1. Halder, *KTB* III, p. 281 (5 November 1941).
2. There were no participants from the Second, First Panzer or Eleventh Armies. Halder, *KTB* III, p. 288 (13 November 1941).
3. As cited in Ziemke, 'Franz Halder at Orsha', pp. 174–5.
4. Magnus Pahl, *Fremde Heere Ost. Hitlers militärische Feindaufklärung* (Berlin, 2012), p. 87.
5. *Ibid*., p. 174. See also 'Kriegstagebuch Nr.1 (Band November 1941) des Oberkommandos der Heeresgruppe Mitte', BA-MA RH 19-II/387, fols 67–68 (15 November 1941).
6. KTB OKW, vol. II, pp. 1074–5, document 106 (6 November 1941).
7. It is instructive here to note Jeremy Black's assessment: 'The prime killer of men in the Second World War was neither aircraft nor tanks, but, as in the First World War, artillery.' Jeremy Black, *War and the Cultural Turn* (Cambridge, 2012), p. 94.
8. Ziemke, 'Franz Halder at Orsha', pp. 174–5.
9. *Ibid*., p. 175.
10. Directive 32a formalised the pre-eminence of the air force and navy in armament production by ordering all 'non-essential' army production cancelled. The new directive stated in relation to the army: 'The extension of arms and equipment and the production of new weapons, munitions, and equipment will be related, with immediate effect, to the smaller forces which are contemplated for the future.' Trevor-Roper (ed.), *Hitler's War Directives 1939–1945*, p. 137 (14 July 1941).
11. For an overview of Germany's muddled economic priorities in 1941, see Stahel, *Kiev 1941*, ch. 2.
12. Ziemke, 'Franz Halder at Orsha', p. 175.
13. *Ibid.*
14. See Blumentritt's observations in Basil Liddell Hart, *The Other Side of the Hill* (London, 1999,) p. 285.
15. As cited in K. Reinhardt, *Moscow: The Turning Point*, p. 193.
16. Ziemke, 'Franz Halder at Orsha', p. 175.
17. Guderian, *Panzer Leader*, p. 247; 'Kriegstagebuch Nr.1 2.Panzerarmee Band III vom 1.11.1941 bis 26.12.41', BA-MA RH 21-2/244, fols 83–84 (15 November 1941).
18. Ziemke, 'Franz Halder at Orsha', p. 175.

19. Walter Chales de Beaulieu, *Generaloberst Erich Hoepner. Militärisches Porträt eines Panzer-Führers* (Neckargemünd, 1969), p. 210.
20. Ziemke, 'Franz Halder at Orsha', pp. 175–6.
21. See discussions in Stahel, *Operation Barbarossa and Germany's Defeat in the East*; Barry Leach, *German Strategy against Russia 1939–1941* (Oxford, 1973).
22. Halder, *KTB* III, p. 285 (10 November 1941).
23. Warlimont, *Inside Hitler's Headquarters, 1939–1945*, p. 194.
24. Kesselring, *The Memoirs of Field-Marshal Kesselring*, p. 96.
25. Meier-Welcker, *Aufzeichnungen eines Generalstabsoffiziers 1939–1942*, p. 139 (14 November 1941). (Italics in the original.)
26. As cited in K. Reinhardt, *Moscow: The Turning Point*, pp. 186–7.
27. Ziemke, 'Franz Halder at Orsha', p. 175.
28. As cited in M. Jones, *The Retreat*, p. 78.
29. 'Kriegstagebuch Nr.1 2.Panzerarmee Band III vom 1.11.1941 bis 26.12.41', BA-MA RH 21-2/244, fol. 33 (7 November 1941).
30. *Ibid.*
31. *Ibid.*, fol. 34 (7 November 1941).
32. Léon Degrelle, *Campaign in Russia. The Waffen SS on the Eastern Front* (Torrance, CA, 1985), p. 19.
33. Halder, *KTB* III, p. 287 (11 November 1941).
34. von Bock, *War Diary*, p. 355 (11 November 1941).
35. '11.Pz.Div. KTB Abt. Ia vom 22.10.41–24.1.42', BA-MA RH 27-11/24 (10, 11 and 13 November 1941).
36. Garden and Andrew (eds), *The War Diaries of a Panzer Soldier*, p. 57 (13 November 1941).
37. Kleindienst (ed.), *Sei tausendmal gegrüßt*, CD Rom (12 November 1941).
38. As cited in M. Jones, *The Retreat*, p. 81.
39. Knappe, *Soldat*, p. 229.
40. Ernst Kern, *War Diary 1941–45. A Report* (New York, 1993), p. 20.
41. Haape, *Moscow Tram Stop*, p. 181.
42. 'Anlagen zum Kriegstagebuch Tagesmeldungen Bd.I 1.11–31.12.41', BA-MA RH 21-3/71, fol. 95 (13 November 1941).
43. 'Anlagenband zum KTB XXXXI A.K. Ia 3.Verteidigung von Kalinin 15.10.41–20.11.41', BA-MA RH 24-41/15 (13 November 1941). (Underlining in the original.)
44. 'Anlagen zum Kriegstagebuch Tagesmeldungen Bd.I 1.11–31.12.41', BA-MA RH 21-3/71, fol. 88 (12 November 1941).
45. Martin Humburg, *Das Gesicht des Krieges. Feldpostbriefe von Wehrmachtssoldaten aus der Sowjetunion 1941–1944* (Wiesbaden, 1998), p. 249 (10 August 1941).
46. 'Anlagen zum Kriegstagebuch Tagesmeldungen Bd.I 1.11–31.12.41', BA-MA RH 21-3/71, fol. 88 (12 November 1941).

47. 'Kriegstagebuch Nr.7 des Kdos. Der 1.Panzer-Div. 20.9.41–12.4.42', BA-MA 27-1/58, fol. 47 (13 November 1941).
48. Johannes Hamm, MPT, 3.2002.7184 (16 November 1941).
49. 'Gen.Kdo.LVII.Pz.Korps KTB Nr.2 vom 1.11.41–31.12.41', BA-MA RH 24-57-3, fol. 16 (13 November 1941).
50. As cited in A. Clark, *Barbarossa*, p. 166.
51. For a postwar overview of German tactics and operations during winter, see Erhard Rauss, 'Effects of Climate on Combat in European Russia', in Peter G. Tsouras (ed.), *Fighting in Hell. The German Ordeal on the Eastern Front* (New York, 1997), pp. 147–67. Note that Raus' name is spelled incorrectly in the aforementioned title.
52. 'Gen.Kdo.LVII.Pz.Korps KTB Nr.2 vom 1.11.41–31.12.41', BA-MA RH 24-57-3, fol. 20 (15 November 1941).
53. Gottlob Herbert Bidermann, *In Deadly Combat. A German Soldier's Memoir of the Eastern Front* (Lawrence, KS, 2000) p. 62.
54. 'Kriegstagebuch Nr.1 2.Panzerarmee Band III vom 1.11.1941 bis 26.12.41', BA-MA RH 21-2/244, fols 63–64 (11 November 1941).
55. von Bock, *War Diary*, p. 357 (13 November 1941). See also 'Kriegstagebuch Nr.1 (Band November 1941) des Oberkommandos der Heeresgruppe Mitte', BA-MA RH 19-II/387, fols 59–60 (13 November 1941).
56. Trevor-Roper (ed.), *Hitler's Table Talk, 1941–1944*, p. 125 (12 November 1941).
57. Klaus Schüler, 'The Eastern Campaign as a Transportation and Supply Problem', in Bernd Wegner (ed.), *From Peace to War. Germany, Soviet Russia and the World, 1939–1941* (Oxford, 1997), p. 213.
58. Humburg, *Das Gesicht des Krieges*, p. 235 (14 November 1941).
59. As cited in Megargee, *Inside Hitler's High Command*, p. 137. See also R-D. Müller, 'The Failure of the Economic "Blitzkrieg Strategy"', p. 1137.
60. von Bock, *War Diary*, p. 354 (11 November 1941).
61. 'Kriegstagebuch Nr.1 (Band November 1941) des Oberkommandos der Heeresgruppe Mitte', BA-MA RH 19-II/387, fol. 48 (11 November 1941).
62. von Bock, *War Diary*, p. 355 (11 November 1941).
63. *Ibid.*
64. 'Kriegstagebuch Nr.1 (Band November 1941) des Oberkommandos der Heeresgruppe Mitte', BA-MA RH 19-II/387, fol. 51 (11 November 1941).
65. von Bock, *War Diary*, p. 356 (11 November 1941).
66. 'Kriegstagebuch Nr.1 (Band November 1941) des Oberkommandos der Heeresgruppe Mitte', BA-MA RH 19-II/387, fol. 55 (12 November 1941).
67. von Bock, *War Diary*, p. 357 (14 November 1941).
68. 'Kriegstagebuch Nr.1 (Band November 1941) des Oberkommandos der Heeresgruppe Mitte', BA-MA RH 19-II/387, fol. 71 (15 November 1941).
69. K. Reinhardt, *Moscow: The Turning Point*, p. 180, fn. 32.

70. R-D. Müller, 'The Failure of the Economic "Blitzkrieg Strategy"', p. 1137.
71. Martin van Creveld, *Supplying War. Logistics from Wallenstein to Patton* (Cambridge, 1984), p. 173.
72. 'Kriegstagebuch Nr.1 2.Panzerarmee Band III vom 1.11.1941 bis 26.12.41', BA-MA RH 21-2/244, fol. 56 (10 November 1941).
73. Halder, *KTB* III, p. 299 (19 November 1941).
74. R-D. Müller, 'The Failure of the Economic "Blitzkrieg Strategy"', p. 1137.
75. van Creveld, *Supplying War*, p. 173.
76. At Orsha, Halder stated that only 500 serviceable Soviet locomotives had been captured during the course of the war, which was just one-tenth of the anticipated number. Ziemke, 'Franz Halder at Orsha', p. 175.
77. Schüler, 'The Eastern Campaign as a Transportation and Supply Problem', pp. 209–10.
78. van Creveld, *Supplying War*, pp. 153 and 178. On the problem of trains in occupied Poland, see 'Kriegstagebuch Nr.1 (Band November 1941) des Oberkommandos der Heeresgruppe Mitte', BA-MA RH 19-II/387, fol. 90 (18 November 1941).
79. Ziemke, 'Franz Halder at Orsha', p. 175.
80. van Creveld, *Supplying War*, p. 179. See also the discussion in David Downing, *Sealing their Fate. Twenty-Two Days that Decided the Second World War* (London, 2009), pp. 114–15.
81. Gilbert, *The Second World War*, p. 259; A. Clark, *Barbarossa*, p. 173.
82. Knappe, *Soldat*, p. 229.
83. Günther, *Hot Motors, Cold Feet*, pp. 195–6.
84. Pabst, *The Outermost Frontier*, p. 39.
85. A. Roberts, *The Storm of War*, p. 177.
86. As cited in Mawdsley, *Thunder in the East*, pp. 107–8.
87. As Dominic Lieven observed: 'Subsequently Napoleon himself and some of his admirers were much inclined to blame the unusually cold winter for the destruction of his army. This is mostly nonsense.' Dominic Lieven, *Russia Against Napoleon. The Battle for Europe, 1807 to 1814* (London, 2010), p. 265.
88. See the first-rate discussion in Ueberschär, 'Das Scheitern des Unternehmens "Barbarossa"', pp. 165–66. Ironically, Goebbels wrote in his diary on 15 November: 'This campaign will surely not go down as a war between Hitler and Stalin, but rather as a war between Hitler and the weather.' Fröhlich (ed.), *Die Tagebücher von Joseph Goebbels. Teil* II, *Band* 2, p. 288 (15 November 1941).
89. Ferdinand Prinz von der Leyen, *Rückblick zum Mauerwald. Vier Kriegsjahre im OKH* (Munich, 1965), p. 37.
90. Haape, *Moscow Tram Stop*, p. 188.
91. Günther, *Hot Motors, Cold Feet*, p. 210.

92. E. Wagner (ed.), *Der Generalquartiermeister*, p. 317.
93. Fröhlich (ed.), *Die Tagebücher von Joseph Goebbels. Teil* II, *Band* 2, p. 269 (11 November 1941).
94. As cited in Messenger, *The Last Prussian*, p. 154.
95. van Creveld, *Supplying War*, p. 174.
96. 'Kriegstagebuch der O.Qu.-Abt. Pz. A.O.K.2 von 21.6.41 bis 31.3.42', BA-MA RH 21-2/819, fol. 147 (7 November 1941).
97. Buchbender and Sterz (eds), *Das andere Gesicht des Krieges*, p. 86 (11 November 1941).
98. Elmar Lieb, MPT, 3.2002.7255 (8 November 1941).
99. Garden and Andrew (eds), *The War Diaries of a Panzer Soldier*, p. 56 (7 November 1941).
100. Walter Görlitz, *Paulus and Stalingrad* (London, 1963), pp. 141–2.
101. Blumentritt, 'Moscow', p. 55.
102. Jürgen Förster, 'Volunteers for the European Crusade against Bolshevism', in Militärgeschichtliches Forschungsamt (ed.), *Germany and the Second World War, vol.* IV*: The Attack on the Soviet Union* (Oxford, 1998), pp. 1058–63; Chris Bishop, *Hitler's Foreign Divisions. Foreign Volunteers in the Waffen-SS 1940–1945* (London, 2005), pp. 40–1. For references to the French unit in the diaries of Bock and Army Group Centre, see von Bock, *War Diary*, pp. 349–51 and 359 (4, 6 and 15 November 1941); 'Kriegstagebuch Nr.1 (Band November 1941) des Oberkommandos der Heeresgruppe Mitte', BA-MA RH 19-II/387, fol. 75 (16 November 1941). For a recent study of Frenchmen who fought in the Wehrmacht or SS, see Philippe Carrard, *The French Who Fought for Hitler. Memories from the Outcasts* (Cambridge, 2010).
103. James S. Corum, *Wolfram von Richthofen. Master of the German Air War* (Lawrence, KS, 2008), p. 276; von Bock, *War Diary*, p. 350 (5 November 1941).
104. In the first half of November there are countless reports in the German divisional and corps diaries of Soviet aerial attacks. See also 'Kriegstagebuch Nr.1 (Band November 1941) des Oberkommandos der Heeresgruppe Mitte', BA-MA RH 19-II/387, fol. 72 (15 November 1941).
105. Degrelle, *Campaign in Russia*, p. 24.
106. Horst Lange, *Tagebücher aus dem Zweiten Weltkrieg* (Mainz, 1979), p. 90 (12 November 1941).
107. 'Kriegstagebuch Nr.1 (Band November 1941) des Oberkommandos der Heeresgruppe Mitte', BA-MA RH 19-II/387, fol. 71 (15 November 1941).
108. Max Kuhnert, *Will We See Tomorrow? A German Cavalryman at War, 1939–1942* (London, 1993), p. 109.
109. Blumentritt, 'Moscow', p. 59.
110. Ernst Kern, *War Diary 1941–45*, p. 16.
111. *Ibid.*

112. Robbins Landon and Leitner (eds), *Diary of a German Soldier*, p. 115 (20 October 1941).
113. Kleindienst (ed.), *Sei tausendmal gegrüßt*, CD Rom (5 November 1941).
114. As cited in M. Jones, *The Retreat*, p. 98.
115. *Ibid.*, p. 90.
116. 'Kriegstagebuch Nr.1 (Band November 1941) des Oberkommandos der Heeresgruppe Mitte', BA-MA RH 19-II/387, fol. 70 (15 November 1941).
117. 'Armeeoberkommando 2. I.a KTB Teil.2 19.9.41–16.12.41', BA-MA RH 20-2/207, p. 110 (11 November 1941).
118. As cited in Friedrich-Christian Stahl, 'Generaloberst Rudolf Schmidt', in Gerd R. Ueberschär (ed.), *Hitlers militärische Elite* (Darmstadt, 1998), p. 221.
119. 'Armeeoberkommando 2. I.a KTB Teil.2 19.9.41–16.12.41', BA-MA RH 20-2/207, p. 91 (1 November 1941).
120. 'Kriegstagebuch XXXXVIII.Pz.Kps. Abt.Ia November 1941', BA-MA RH 24-48/35, fol. 4 (6 November 1941).
121. '9.Pz.Div. KTB Ia vom 19.5.1941 bis 22.1.1942', BA-MA RH 27-9/4, p. 157 (11 November 1941).
122. K. Reinhardt, *Moscow: The Turning Point*, pp. 199–200.
123. As cited in M. Jones, *The Retreat*, pp. 89–90.
124. K. Reinhardt, *Moscow: The Turning Point*, p. 200.
125. Blumentritt, 'Moscow', pp. 54–5.
126. 'Oberkommando des Heeres Generalstab des Heeres O.Qu.IV-Abt.Fr.H.Ost (II)', BA-MA RH/2-2670, fols 20 and 31 (5 and 7 November 1941).
127. Karl Reddemann (ed.), *Zwischen Front und Heimat. Der Briefwechsel des münsterischen Ehepaares Agnes und Albert Neuhaus 1940–1944* (Münster, 1996), p. 348 (11 November 1941).
128. As cited in David W. Wildermuth, 'Widening the Circle: General Weikersthal and the War of Annihilation, 1941–42', *Central European History* 45 (2012): 318.
129. Stader (ed.), *Ihr daheim und wir hier draußen*, p. 49 (11 November 1941).
130. Scheuer, *Briefe aus Russland*, p. 50 (15 November 1941).
131. Christine Alexander and Mark Kunze (eds), *Eastern Inferno. The Journals of a German Panzerjäger on the Eastern Front, 1941–43* (Philadelphia, PA and Newbury, 2010), p. 123 (15 November 1941).

5 Typhoon re-launched

1. von Bock, *War Diary*, p. 358 (15 November 1941). The diary incorrectly states that this corps belonged to the Second Army.
2. Halder, *KTB* III, p. 290 (15 November 1941).
3. H. Reinhardt, 'Panzer-Gruppe 3 in der Schlacht von Moskau und ihre Erfahrungen im Rückzug', p. 2. For a general day-by-day account of the fighting

in the east, see Brian Taylor, *Barbarossa to Berlin. A Chronology of the Campaigns on the Eastern Front 1941 to 1945, vol. 1: The Long Drive East 22 June 1941 to 18 November 1942* (Staplehurst, 2003).

4. 'Kriegstagebuch Nr.3 der 7.Panzer-Division Führungsabteilung 1.6.1941–9.5.1942', BA-MA RH 27-7/46, fol. 178 (16 November 1941).
5. 'Anlagen zum Kriegstagebuch Tagesmeldungen Bd.I 1.11–31.12.41', BA-MA RH 21-3/71, fols 112–13 (16 November 1941).
6. Alexander Statiev, '"La Garde meurt mais ne se rend pas!" Once Again on the 28 Panfilov Heroes', *Kritika: Explorations in Russian and Eurasian History* 13(4) (2012): 773.
7. *Ibid.*, pp. 769–98. See also Chris Bellamy, *Absolute War. Soviet Russia in the Second World War* (New York, 2007), pp. 306–8; Braithwaite, *Moscow 1941*, pp. 267–8. For the Soviet account of the legend, see Vladimir Sevruk (ed.) *Moscow Stalingrad 1941–1942. Recollections, Stories, Reports* (Moscow, 1970), pp. 141–6.
8. Overy, *Russia's War*, p. 116; Werth, *Russia at War 1941–1945*, p. 255.
9. As cited in M. Jones, *The Retreat*, p. 93.
10. Rokossovsky, *A Soldier's Duty*, p. 74.
11. von Bock, *War Diary*, p. 360 (16 November 1941).
12. *Ibid.*, pp. 360–1 (17 November 1941); 'Kriegstagebuch Nr.1 (Band November 1941) des Oberkommandos der Heeresgruppe Mitte', BA-MA RH 19-II/387, fol. 80 (17 November 1941); Halder, *KTB* III, p. 292 (17 November 1941).
13. von Bock, *War Diary*, pp. 361–2 (17 and 18 November 1941); Halder, *KTB* III, p. 292 (17 November 1941).
14. 'Kriegstagebuch Nr.1 (Band November 1941) des Oberkommandos der Heeresgruppe Mitte', BA-MA RH 19-II/387, fol. 78 (16 November 1941).
15. von Bock, *War Diary*, p. 362 (18 November 1941); *ibid.*, fol. 87 (18 November 1941).
16. Glantz, *Barbarossa*, pp. 169–70.
17. '6. Panzer Division KTB 16.9.1941–30.11.1941', BA-MA RH 27-6/19, p. 277 (17 November 1941).
18. For a diagram, see C. G. Sweeting, *Blood and Iron. The German Conquest of Sevastopol* (Washington, DC, 2004), p. 143. For individual encounters, see Hans von Luck, *Panzer Commander. The Memoirs of Colonel Hans von Luck* (New York, 1989), pp. 57–8; Paul Carell (aka Paul Karl Schmidt), *Hitler's War on Russia. The Story of the German Defeat in the East* (London, 1964), pp. 133–4; William Lubbeck, with David B. Hurt, *At Leningrad's Gates. The Story of a Soldier with Army Group North* (Philadelphia, PA, 2006), p. 112. Another source claimed that the dogs trained on Soviet tanks sometimes destroyed vehicles belonging to the Red Army. See Raus, *Panzer Operations*, p. 87.
19. Rokossovsky, *A Soldier's Duty*, p. 75.

20. 'Anlagen zum Kriegstagebuch Tagesmeldungen Bd.I 1.11–31.12.41', BA-MA RH 21-3/71, fol. 129 (18 November 1941).
21. 'Anlage zum KTB Panzer Gruppe 4: 11.11.41–5.12.41', BA-MA RH 21-4/36, fol. 93 (18 November 1941).
22. 'Anlage zum KTB Pz.Gruppe 4 Meldungen von unten 16.11.41–5.12.41', BA-MA RH 21-4/40, fol. 192 (18 November 1941).
23. '2. Panzer Division KTB Nr.6 Teil I. Vom 15.6.41–3.4.42', BA-MA RH 27-2/21 (19 November 1941).
24. '5. Panzer Division KTB Nur.8 vom 11.9.41–11.12.41', BA-MA RH 27-5/29, fol. 83 (20 November 1941).
25. Garden and Andrew (eds), *The War Diaries of a Panzer Soldier*, p. 58 (20 November 1941).
26. For an excellent source on the Soviet tanks of 1941, see Steven J. Zaloga and James Grandsen, *Soviet Tanks and Combat Vehicles of World War Two* (London, 1984), pp. 129–46.
27. Blumentritt, 'Moscow', p. 56.
28. von Bock, *War Diary*, p. 363 (19 November 1941).
29. For Zhukov's own somewhat embellished account, see *The Memoirs of Marshal Zhukov*, pp. 338–9.
30. 'Anlage zum KTB Panzer Gruppe 4: 11.11.41–5.12.41', BA-MA RH 21-4/36, fol. 89 (19 November 1941).
31. H. Reinhardt, 'Panzer-Gruppe 3 in der Schlacht von Moskau und ihre Erfahrungen im Rückzug', p. 2.
32. Model replaced the aforementioned Lieutenant-General Friedrich Kirchner in command of the corps on 15 November 1941. On 17 November, Kirchner took over command of the LVII Panzer Corps.
33. von Bock, *War Diary*, p. 363 (18 November 1941).
34. *Ibid.*, pp. 363–4 (19 and 20 November 1941).
35. 'Anlagenband zum KTB XXXXI A.K. Ia 3.Verteidigung von Kalinin 15.10.41–20.11.41', BA-MA RH 24-41/15 (18 November 1941).
36. von Bock, *War Diary*, p. 363 (19 November 1941).
37. 'Kriegstagebuch Nr.3 der 7.Panzer-Division Führungsabteilung 1.6.1941–9.5.1942', BA-MA RH 27-7/46, fol. 188 (19 November 1941).
38. von Bock, *War Diary*, p. 363 (19 November 1941).
39. '11.Pz.Div. KTB Abt.Ia vom 22.10.41–24.1.42', BA-MA RH 27-11/24, fol. 16 (16 November 1941).
40. '20.Pz.Div. KTB vom 21.10.41 bis 30.12.41 Band Ia2.', BA-MA RH 27-20/26, fol. 51 (16 November 1941).
41. 'Anlage zum KTB Pz.Gruppe 4 Meldungen von unten 16.11.41–5.12.41', BA-MA RH 21-4/40, fol. 187 (19 November 1941).
42. Knoblauch, *Zwischen Metz und Moskau*, p. 194 (19 November 1941).
43. As cited in M. Jones, *The Retreat*, p. 92.

44. 'Kriegstagebuch Nr.3. der Führungsabteilung (Ia) des Gen. Kdo. (mot.) XXXX.Pz. Korps vom 31.05.1941–26.12.1941', BA-MA RH 24-40/18 (19 November 1941).
45. '6. Panzer Division KTB 16.9.1941–30.11.1941', BA-MA RH 27-6/19, p. 280 (18 November 1941).
46. 'Anlage zum KTB Pz.Gruppe 4 Meldungen von unten 16.11.41–5.12.41', BA-MA RH 21-4/40, fol. 169 (20 November 1941).
47. 'Kriegstagebuch Nr.3. der Führungsabteilung (Ia) des Gen. Kdo. (mot.) XXXX.Pz. Korps vom 31.05.1941–26.12.1941', BA-MA RH 24-40/18 (20 November 1941).
48. As cited in M. Jones, *The Retreat*, p. 108.
49. As cited in Bartov, *Hitler's Army*, p. 26.
50. Rokossovsky, *A Soldier's Duty*, pp. 78–9.
51. Glantz, *Barbarossa*, p. 170.
52. As cited in Bücheler, *Hoepner*, pp. 157–8.
53. 'Kriegstagebuch Nr.3. des XXXXVI.Pz.Korps vom 24.08.41–31.12.41', BA-MA RH 24-46/21, fol. 128 (18 November 1941).
54. Halder, *KTB* III, p. 294 (19 November 1941).
55. *Ibid.*, p. 293 (18 November 1941).
56. As cited in M. Jones, *The Retreat*, p. 95.
57. Frisch, *Condemned to Live*, p. 85.
58. See my discussion of economic factors in the Nazi state in Stahel, *Kiev 1941*, pp. 48–65.
59. As cited in Gilbert, *The Second World War*, p. 265.
60. Fröhlich (ed.), *Die Tagebücher von Joseph Goebbels. Teil* II, *Band 1*, pp. 262–3 (19 August 1941).
61. Fröhlich (ed.), *Die Tagebücher von Joseph Goebbels. Teil* II, *Band 2*, p. 338 (22 November 1941).
62. John Lukacs, *The Hitler of History* (New York, 1998), pp. 156–8.
63. Domarus, *Hitler*, p. 2507 (8 November 1941).
64. von Bock, *War Diary*, p. 360 (16 November 1941).
65. K. Reinhardt, *Moscow: The Turning Point*, p. 200.
66. 'Kriegstagebuch Nr.1 (Band November 1941) des Oberkommandos der Heeresgruppe Mitte', BA-MA RH 19-II/387, fol. 82 (17 November 1941).
67. 'Kriegstagebuch Nr.1 2.Panzerarmee Band III vom 1.11.1941 bis 26.12.41', BA-MA RH 21-2/244, fol. 92 (16 November 1941). The war diary of Army Group Centre includes a similar report from the Second Panzer Army on 14 November, but this suggests that the amount of fuel received was only one-sixth of the daily requirement. *Ibid.*, fol. 63 (14 November 1941). Another report from war diary of Second Panzer Army's quartermaster stated that an average of 400 m^3 of fuel was arriving a day, but that this only covered operating needs while the army was at a standstill. For a resumption of the offensive a minimum

of 1,000–1,200 m^3 of fuel a day were necessary. 'Kriegstagebuch der O.Qu.-Abt. Pz. A.O.K.2 von 21.6.41 bis 31.3.42', BA-MA RH 21-2/819, fol. 142 (11 November 1941).

68. Guderian, *Panzer Leader*, p. 249.
69. 'Kriegstagebuch Nr.1 2.Panzerarmee Band III vom 1.11.1941 bis 26.12.41', BA-MA RH 21-2/244, fol. 84 (17 November 1941).
70. Guderian, *Panzer Leader*, p. 250.
71. The aforementioned commander of the 17th Panzer Division, Lieutenant-General Hans-Jürgen von Arnim, was replaced by Licht on 11 November.
72. 'Kriegstagebuch Nr.1 2.Panzerarmee Band III vom 1.11.1941 bis 26.12.41', BA-MA RH 21-2/244 (17 November 1941).
73. Guderian, *Panzer Leader*, p. 250.
74. 'Kriegstagebuch Nr.1 2.Panzerarmee Band III vom 1.11.1941 bis 26.12.41', BA-MA RH 21-2/244, fol. 100 (18 November 1941).
75. Guderian, *Panzer Leader*, pp. 250–1.
76. von Bock, *War Diary*, p. 362 (18 November 1941).
77. Seaton, *The Battle for Moscow*, pp. 158–60.
78. Stader (ed.), *Ihr daheim und wir hier draußen*, p. 52 (16 November 1941).
79. Guderian, *Panzer Leader*, p. 248.
80. von Bock, *War Diary*, p. 362 (18 November 1941).
81. Halder, *KTB* III, p. 293 (18 November 1941).
82. Guderian, *Panzer Leader*, p. 251.
83. 'KTB 3rd Pz. Div. vom 19.9.41 bis 6.2.42', BA-MA RH 27-3/15, p. 338 (18 November 1941).
84. 'Kriegstagebuch Nr.1 2.Panzerarmee Band III vom 1.11.1941 bis 26.12.41', BA-MA RH 21-2/244, fol. 107 (19 November 1941).
85. 'Kriegstagebuch 4.Panzer-Divison Führungsabtl. 26.5.41–31.3.42', BA-MA RH 27-4/10, pp. 252–3 (19 November 1941).
86. *Ibid.*, p. 253 (19 November 1941).
87. 'Kriegstagebuch Nr.1 2.Panzerarmee Band III vom 1.11.1941 bis 26.12.41', BA-MA RH 21-2/244, fol. 115 (20 November 1941). (Underlining in the original.)
88. 'Kriegstagebuch Nr.1 (Band November 1941) des Oberkommandos der Heeresgruppe Mitte', BA-MA RH 19-II/387, fol. 101 (20 November 1941).
89. Efremov was founded as a simple fortress of Muscovy in 1637 and served to keep marauding Tatar raiders at bay. It had a small amount of industry in 1941, but its importance to Operation Typhoon was doubtful. It was granted town status in 1777, but was certainly not a city. One source even referred to it as a 'straggling village'. Seaton, *The Battle for Moscow*, p. 158.
90. '18. Panzer-Div- Ia Kriegstagebuch vom 20.10.41–13.12.41', BA-MA RH 27-18/69 (20 November 1941). (Underlining in the original.)

91. 'Kriegstagebuch Nr.1 (Band November 1941) des Oberkommandos der Heeresgruppe Mitte', BA-MA RH 19-II/387, fol. 101 (20 November 1941).
92. 'Kriegstagebuch Nr.2 XXXXVII.Pz.Korps. Ia 23.9.1941–31.12.1941', BA-MA RH 24-47/258, fol. 92 (18 November 1941).
93. *Ibid.*, fol. 94 (19 November 1941).
94. *Ibid.*, fol. 98 (20 November 1941).
95. 'Kriegstagebuch der O.Qu.-Abt. Pz. A.O.K.2 von 21.6.41 bis 31.3.42', BA-MA RH 21-2/819, fol. 134 (19 November 1941).
96. Halder, *KTB* III, p. 295 (19 November 1941).
97. 'Kriegstagebuch Nr.1 2.Panzerarmee Band III vom 1.11.1941 bis 26.12.41', BA-MA RH 21-2/244, fols 100–101 (18 November 1941). (Underlining in original.)
98. Albert Speer described Todt in autumn 1941 as 'close to despair'. Albert Speer, *Inside the Third Reich* (London, 1971) p. 262.
99. As cited in Tooze, *The Wages of Destruction*, p. 507. See also Eleanor Hancock, *The National Socialist Leadership and Total War 1941–45* (New York, 1991), p. 31.
100. See also the dated, but useful, dissertation by William J. Fanning Jr, 'The German War Economy 1941. A Study of Germany's Material and Manpower Problems in Relation to the Overall Military Effort', PhD dissertation, Texas Christian University, 1983.
101. Fritz, *Ostkrieg*, p. 492.
102. As cited in Gilbert, *The Second World War*, p. 256.
103. Neitzel, *Tapping Hitler's Generals*, pp. 226–7, document 135 (25 April 1945).
104. Speer, *Inside the Third Reich*, p. 259. For more on Hitler's building plans, see Mazower, *Hitler's Empire*, pp. 124–6.
105. 'Kriegstagebuch Nr.1 (Band November 1941) des Oberkommandos der Heeresgruppe Mitte', BA-MA RH 19-II/387, fol. 101 (20 November 1941).
106. von Bock, *War Diary*, p. 365 (20 November 1941).
107. Keith Cumins, *Cataclysm. The War on the Eastern Front 1941–1945* (Solihull, 2011), p. 57.
108. Glantz, *Barbarossa*, p. 180.
109. Messenger, *The Last Prussian*, pp. 154–5.
110. Domarus, *Hitler*, pp. 2519 and 2521 (30 November 1941). See also Walter Görlitz (ed.), *The Memoirs of Field-Marshal Keitel. Chief of the German High Command, 1938–1945* (New York, 1966), pp. 160–1; Günther Blumentritt, *Von Rundstedt. The Soldier and the Man* (London, 1952), pp. 112–14.
111. Fröhlich (ed.), *Die Tagebücher von Joseph Goebbels. Teil* II, *Band 2*, p. 309 (18 November 1941).

112. Halder, *KTB* III, p. 309 (24 November 1941).
113. As cited in M. Jones, *The Retreat*, p. 98. See also Meier-Welcker, *Aufzeichnungen eines Generalstabsoffiziers 1939–1942*, p. 142 (1 December 1941).
114. 'Kriegstagebuch Nr.1 (Band November 1941) des Oberkommandos der Heeresgruppe Mitte', BA-MA RH 19-II/387, fol. 55 (12 November 1941).
115. *Ibid.*, fol. 71 (15 November 1941).
116. *Ibid.*, fol. 75 (16 November 1941).
117. *Ibid.*, fol. 81 (17 November 1941). For more on the condition of the Sixth Army, see Görlitz, *Paulus and Stalingrad*, p. 133.
118. Halder, *KTB* III, p. 300 (20 November 1941).
119. '11.Pz.Div. KTB Abt.Ia vom 22.10.41–24.1.42', BA-MA RH 27-11/24 (13–21 November 1941).
120. Günther, *Hot Motors, Cold Feet*, p. 189.
121. Seaton, *The Battle for Moscow*, p. 142.
122. A. Clark, *Barbarossa*, p. 174.
123. Seaton, *The Battle for Moscow*, p. 142.
124. Carruthers (ed.), *The Wehrmacht Last Witnesses*, p. 53.
125. Haape, *Moscow Tram Stop*, pp. 182–3.
126. As cited in A. Clark, *Barbarossa*, p. 173.
127. Willy Peter Reese, *A Stranger to Myself. The Inhumanity of War: Russia, 1941–1944* (New York, 2005), pp. 36–7.
128. Jarausch (ed.), *Reluctant Accomplice*, p. 328 (21 November 1941).
129. Frisch, *Condemned to Live*, p. 94.
130. Günther, *Hot Motors, Cold Feet*, p. 189.
131. Knappe, *Soldat*, p. 230.
132. Ernst Kern, *War Diary 1941–45*, p. 22.
133. Günther, *Hot Motors, Cold Feet*, p. 192.
134. Knappe, *Soldat*, p. 230.
135. Ilya Ehrenburg, *Russia at War* (London, 1943), pp. 82–3 (30 November 1941).
136. As cited in Downing, *Sealing their Fate*, p. 22.
137. Fröhlich (ed.), *Die Tagebücher von Joseph Goebbels. Teil* II, *Band* 2, p. 298 (16 November 1941).
138. *Ibid.*, p. 284 (14 November 1941).
139. Boberach (ed.), *Meldungen aus dem Reich*, vol. 8, p. 2995, document 238 (17 November 1941).
140. As cited in Piekalkiewicz, *Moscow 1941*, pp. 175–6.
141. Helmuth James von Moltke, *Letters to Freya. 1939–1945* (New York, 1990), pp. 187–8 (18 November 1941).
142. As cited in Roger Moorhouse, *Berlin at War. Life and Death in Hitler's Capital, 1939–45* (London, 2010), p. 276.

6 The long road to Moscow

1. The *Afrikakorps* officially numbered some 48,500 men, but in November 1941 some 11,066 of these were listed as sick. Martin Kitchen, *Rommel's Desert War. Waging World War* II *in North Africa, 1941–1943* (Cambridge, 2009), p. 146.
2. As one officer on Rommel's staff noted in a letter on 23 November: 'The fact is that we didn't know, didn't hear anything about the fact, that the English would suddenly appear in such enormous strength!' Hans-Albrecht Max Schraepler (ed.), *At Rommel's Side. The Lost Letters of Hans-Joachim Schraepler* (London, 2007), p. 178 (23 November 1941).
3. Kitchen, *Rommel's Desert War*, pp. 146 and 149. There were some 300 American Stuart light tanks delivered to the British through the Lend-Lease programme.
4. Antony Beevor, *The Second World War* (New York, 2012), p. 225.
5. Schraepler (ed.), *At Rommel's Side*, p. 178 (23 November 1941).
6. Mawdsley, *Thunder in the East*, p. 115.
7. Bellamy, *Absolute War*, p. 318.
8. Glantz and House, *When Titans Clashed*, pp. 67–70.
9. Overy, *Russia's War*, p. 118.
10. Bellamy, *Absolute War*, p. 321.
11. In his postwar testimony General of Artillery Alfred Jodl disparagingly referred to the fighting in North Africa as 'Rommel's little shooting expedition in North Africa'. As cited in Robert M. Citino, *The Wehrmacht Retreats. Fighting a Lost War, 1943* (Lawrence, KS, 2012) p. 313, fn. 63.
12. Finland, which contributed fourteen divisions to the war against the Soviet Union, was not a part of the Axis.
13. On the number of German divisions in the east in November 1941, see KTB OKW, vol. II, pp. 1074–5, document 106 (6 November 1941).
14. Max Hastings, *Winston's War. Churchill, 1940–1945* (New York, 2010), p. 138.
15. David Carlton, *Churchill and the Soviet Union* (New York, 2000), p. 88.
16. Ministry of Foreign Affairs of the USSR (ed.), *Stalin's Correspondence with Churchill, Attlee, Roosevelt and Truman 1941–1945* (New York, 1958), p. 22, document 11 (6 September 1941).
17. Gabriel Gorodetsky (ed.), *Stafford Cripps in Moscow 1940–1942. Diaries and Papers* (London, 2007), p. 192 (26 October 1941).
18. Martin Kitchen, *A World in Flames. A Short History of the Second World War in Europe and Asia 1939–1945* (London, 1990), p. 94.
19. Ivan Maisky, *Memoirs of a Soviet Ambassador. The War 1939–43* (London, 1967), p. 199.

20. Carlton, *Churchill and the Soviet Union*, pp. 87–8.
21. Ministry of Foreign Affairs of the USSR (ed.), *Stalin's Correspondence*, pp. 34–6, documents 21 and 22 (22 and 23 November 1941).
22. Carl Gustaf Emil Mannerheim, *The Memoirs of Marshal Mannerheim* (London, 1953), p. 436. See also Jonathan Clements, *Mannerheim. President, Soldier, Spy* (London, 2009), pp. 263–4; Henrik O. Lunde, *Finland's War of Choice. The Troubled German–Finnish Coalition in World War* II (Havertown, PA, 2011), p. 185.
23. Martin Kitchen, *British Policy towards the Soviet Union during the Second World War* (London, 1986), p. 106.
24. As cited in *ibid.*
25. As cited in Hastings, *Winston's War*, p. 145.
26. Ministry of Foreign Affairs of the USSR (ed.), *Stalin's Correspondence*, p. 35, document 21 (22 November 1941). The US government was also unnerved by the thought of the British making promises on a postwar settlement and advised Churchill not 'to enter into commitments regarding specific terms of the post-war settlement. Above all, there must be no secret accords.' As cited in Robert Huhn Jones, *The Roads to Russia. United States Lend-Lease to the Soviet Union* (Norman, 1969), p. 75.
27. Ministry of Foreign Affairs of the USSR (ed.), *Stalin's Correspondence*, p. 36, document 22 (23 November 1941).
28. A detailed list of the supplies is provided in Joan Beaumont, *Comrades in Arms. British Aid to Russia 1941–1945* (London, 1980), pp. 58–60; Gilbert, *The Second World War*, pp. 240–2.
29. B. B. Schofield, *The Arctic Convoys* (London, 1977), p. 14. For a complete listing of all the convoys and the ships that sailed in them, see Bob Ruegg and Arnold Hague, *Convoys to Russia 1941–1945. Allied Convoys and Naval Surface Operations in Arctic Waters 1941–1945* (Kendal, 1993), pp. 20–4.
30. As cited in Hastings, *Winston's War*, p. 143.
31. Paul Kemp, *Convoy! Drama in Arctic Waters* (London, 1993), pp. 16–17.
32. P. M. H. Bell, *John Bull and the Bear. British Public Opinion, Foreign Policy and the Soviet Union 1941–1945* (London, 1990), p. 54.
33. 'Oberkommando des Heeres Generalstab des Heeres O.Qu.IV-Abt.Fr.H.Ost (II)', BA-MA RH/2-2670, fol. 14 (4 November 1941). See also Fröhlich (ed.), *Die Tagebücher von Joseph Goebbels. Teil* II, *Band* 2, p. 237 (6 November 1941).
34. 'Oberkommando des Heeres Generalstab des Heeres O.Qu.IV-Abt.Fr.H.Ost (II)', BA-MA RH/2-2670, fol. 45 (13 November 1941); 'Kriegstagebuch Nr.1 (Band November 1941) des Oberkommandos der Heeresgruppe Mitte', BA-MA RH 19-II/387, fol. 65 (14 November 1941). See also Fröhlich (ed.), *Die Tagebücher von Joseph Goebbels. Teil* II, *Band* 2, p. 296 (16 November 1941).

35. 'Anlagen zum Kriegstagebuch Tagesmeldungen Bd.1 1.11–31.12.41', BA-MA RH 21-3/71, fol. 102 (14 November 1941).
36. See individual reports in Willi Kubik, *Erinnerungen eines Panzerschützen 1941–1945. Tagebuchaufzeichnung eines Panzerschützen der Pz.Aufkl.Abt. 13 im Russlandfeldzug* (Würzburg, 2004), pp. 95, 97 and 104 (2, 6 and 17 October 1941); Alexander and Kunze (eds), *Eastern Inferno*, p. 117 (6 October 1941). For more on the shipment of western aircraft to the Soviet Union in 1941 and the training of Soviet pilots by the British 151st Fighter Wing, see Christer Bergström, *Barbarossa. The Air Battle: July-December 1941* (Hersham, 2007), pp. 79–80; Geoffrey W. Raebel, *The RAAF in Russia. 455 RAAF Squadron: 1942* (Loftus, NSW, 1997), ch. 4; John Erickson and Ljubica Erickson, *Hitler versus Stalin. The Second World War on the Eastern Front in Photographs* (London, 2004), p. 54.
37. 'Oberkommando des Heeres Generalstab des Heeres O.Qu.IV-Abt.Fr.H.Ost (II)', BA-MA RH/2-2670, fol. 86 (24 November 1941).
38. '6. Panzer Division KTB 16.9.1941–30.11.1941', BA-MA RH 27-6/19, p. 299 (26 November 1941). For one Soviet account, see Artem Drabkin (ed.), *The Red Air Force at War. Barbarossa and the Retreat to Moscow. Recollections of Fighter Pilots on the Eastern Front* (Barnsley, 2007), p. 11.
39. Ilya Ehrenburg and Konstantin Simonov, *In One Newspaper. A Chronicle of Unforgettable Years* (New York, 1985), pp. 83–4.
40. Alexander Hill, 'British Lend-Lease Tanks and the Battle for Moscow, November–December 1941: Revisited', *Journal of Slavic Military Studies* 22(4) (2009): 575–6. See also Alexander Hill, 'British "Lend-Lease" Tanks and the Battle for Moscow, November–December 1941: A Research Note', *Journal of Slavic Military Studies* 19(2) (2006): 289–94.
41. 'Oberkommando des Heeres Generalstab des Heeres O.Qu.IV-Abt.Fr.H.Ost (II)', BA-MA RH/2–2670, fol. 101 (27 November 1941).
42. 'Anlage zum KTB Pz.Gruppe 4 Meldungen von unten 16.11.41–5.12.41', BA-MA RH 21-4/40, fol. 113 (26 November 1941). See also Downing, *Sealing their Fate*, p. 142.
43. '5. Panzer Division KTB Nur.8 vom 11.9.41–11.12.41', BA-MA RH 27-5/29, fol. 118 (27 November 1941).
44. *True To Type*, p. 107 (1941). See also Walter Tilemann, *Ich, das Soldatenkind* (Munich, 2005), p. 145.
45. For a good overview, see Alexander Hill, 'British Lend-Lease Aid and the Soviet War Effort, June 1941–June 1942', *Journal of Military History* 71(3) (2007): 773–808.
46. Albert L. Weeks, *Russia's Life-Saver. Lend-Lease Aid to the U.S.S.R. in World War II* (Lanham, MD, 2004), p. 11.
47. Hill, 'British Lend-Lease Tanks and the Battle for Moscow', pp. 581–2.

48. On German tanks painted in African camouflage, see Rokossovsky, *A Soldier's Duty*, p. 75.
49. Hill, 'British Lend-Lease Tanks and the Battle for Moscow', pp. 581–2.
50. As cited in Hastings, *Winston's War*, p. 143.
51. See also the table of comparison for tanks in Hill, 'British Lend-Lease Aid and the Soviet War Effort, June 1941–June 1942', p. 784.
52. Hill, *The Great Patriotic War of the Soviet Union, 1941–45*, p. 84. Only a handful of American tanks were delivered to the Soviet Union in 1941. See Hubert P. van Tuyll, *Feeding the Bear. American Aid to the Soviet Union, 1941–1945* (Westport, CT, 1989), pp. 53 and 167, table 22.
53. Hill, 'British Lend-Lease Aid and the Soviet War Effort, June 1941–June 1942', p. 792.
54. George C. Herring Jr, *Aid to Russia 1941–1946: Strategy, Diplomacy. The Origins of the Cold War* (New York, 1973), pp. 42–3.
55. Schofield, *The Arctic Convoys*, p. 15.
56. Ministry of Foreign Affairs of the USSR (ed.), *Stalin's Correspondence*, p. 34, document 20 (8 November 1941).
57. Kemp, *Convoy!*, pp. 23–4.
58. Fröhlich (ed.), *Die Tagebücher von Joseph Goebbels. Teil* II, *Band* 2, p. 289 (15 November 1941).
59. Ilya Ehrenburg, *The Tempering of Russia* (New York, 1944), p. 85 (17 November 1941).
60. von Bock, *War Diary*, p. 366 (21 November 1941).
61. *Ibid.*, p. 368 (23 November 1941).
62. *Ibid.*
63. 'Kriegstagebuch Nr.3. des XXXXVI.Pz.Korps vom 24.08.41–31.12.41', BA-MA RH 24-46/21, fols 132–133 (21 November 1941).
64. *Ibid.*, fol. 136 (23 November 1941).
65. '5. Panzer Division KTB Nur.8 vom 11.9.41–11.12.41', BA-MA RH 27-5/29, fol. 99 (24 November 1941).
66. 'Kriegstagebuch Nr.3. der Führungsabteilung (Ia) des Gen. Kdo. (mot.) XXXX.Pz. Korps vom 31.05.1941–26.12.1941', BA-MA RH 24-40/18 (21 November 1941). See also the letter from the operations officer of the division to Paulus, written on 17 November 1941, Walter Görlitz (ed.), *Paulus und Stalingrad. Lebensweg des Generalfeldmarschalls Friedrich Paulus* (Frankfurt am Main, 1960). p. 146; Görlitz, *Paulus and Stalingrad*, p. 143.
67. '2. Panzer Division KTB Nr.6 Teil I. Vom 15.6.41–3.4.42', BA-MA RH 27-2/21 (24 November 1941).
68. As cited in Bücheler, *Hoepner*, p. 159.
69. Meier-Welcker, *Aufzeichnungen eines Generalstabsoffiziers 1939–1942*, p. 140 (24 November 1941).
70. *True To Type*, p. 35 (24 November 1941).

71. Stader (ed.), *Ihr daheim und wir hier draußen*, p. 60 (21 November 1941).
72. Downing, *Sealing their Fate*, p. 101.
73. von Bock, *War Diary*, p. 367 (23 November 1941).
74. 'Anlagen zum Kriegstagebuch Tagesmeldungen Bd.1 1.11–31.12.41', BA-MA RH 21-3/71, fols 171 and 179 (25 and 26 November 1941); 'A.O.K.4 Ia Anlagen B 19 zum Kriegstagebuch Nr.9. 23.11.–27.11.41', BA-MA RH 20-4, fol. 113 (25 November 1941).
75. 'Anlagen zum Kriegstagebuch Tagesmeldungen Bd.1 1.11–31.12.41', BA-MA RH 21-3/71, fol. 171 (25 November 1941); 'A.O.K.4 Ia Anlagen B 19 zum Kriegstagebuch Nr.9. 23.11.–27.11.41', BA-MA RH 20-4, fol. 113 (25 November 1941).
76. Only the war diary of Thoma's 20th Panzer Division offers a figure. The division had fifty-six operational tanks as of 24 November. '20.Pz.Div. KTB vom 21.10.41 bis 30.12.41 Band Ia2.', BA-MA RH 27-20/26, fol. 69 (24 November 1941).
77. '2. Panzer Division KTB Nr.6 Teil I. Vom 15.6.41–3.4.42', BA-MA RH 27-2/21 (28 November 1941).
78. '5. Panzer Division KTB Nur.8 vom 11.9.41–11.12.41', BA-MA RH 27-5/29, fol. 126 (28 November 1941).
79. 'Anlagen zum Kriegstagebuch Tagesmeldungen Bd.1 1.11–31.12.41', BA-MA RH 21-3/71, fol. 171 (25 November 1941).
80. 'Anlage zum KTB Pz.Gruppe 4 Meldungen von unten 16.11.41–5.12.41', BA-MA RH 21-4/40, fol. 133 (24 November 1941).
81. *Ibid.*, fol. 156 (22 November 1941).
82. *Ibid.*, fol. 145 (23 November 1941).
83. von Bock, *War Diary*, p. 365 (21 November 1941).
84. Reddemann (ed.), *Zwischen Front und Heimat*, pp. 356–7 (21 November 1941).
85. H. Reinhardt, 'Panzer-Gruppe 3 in der Schlacht von Moskau und ihre Erfahrungen im Rückzug', p. 3.
86. As cited in Bücheler, *Hoepner*, p. 159.
87. 'Kriegstagebuch Nr.1 (Band November 1941) des Oberkommandos der Heeresgruppe Mitte', BA-MA RH 19-II/387, fol. 107 (21 November 1941). (Underlining in the original.)
88. *Ibid.*
89. Guderian, *Panzer Leader*, pp. 251–2.
90. Halder, *KTB* III, p. 302 (21 November 1941).
91. 'Kriegstagebuch 4.Panzer-Divison Führungsabtl. 26.5.41–31.3.42', BA-MA RH 27-4/10, p. 259 (22 November 1941).
92. As cited in Kenneth Macksey, *Guderian. Panzer General* (London, 1975), p. 156.
93. 'Kriegstagebuch Nr.1 (Band November 1941) des Oberkommandos der Heeresgruppe Mitte', BA-MA RH 19-II/387, fol. 111 (22 November 1941). (Underlining in the original.) See also Halder, *KTB* III, p. 303 (22 November 1941).

94. von Bock, *War Diary*, p. 368 (23 November 1941). See also Halder, *KTB* III, p. 308 (23 November 1941).
95. von Bock, *War Diary*, p. 368 (23 November 1941).
96. Halder's remarks were recorded in speech marks in the war diary. 'Kriegstagebuch Nr.1 (Band November 1941) des Oberkommandos der Heeresgruppe Mitte', BA-MA RH 19-II/387, fol. 117 (23 November 1941).
97. *Ibid.*
98. As seen above, Guderian's postwar account is disproved by the wartime diaries of Bock, Halder and Army Group Centre.
99. Guderian, *Panzer Leader*, p. 252.
100. According to the memoir, Brauchitsch 'ignored the actual difficulties, refused to agree to my proposals and ordered that the attack continue. After repeated requests that at least I be assigned an objective that I could hope to reach and that I could transform into a defensible line, he finally gave me the line Michailov–Zaraisk and declared that the thorough destruction of the railroad Ryazan–Kolomna was essential.' Guderian, *Panzer Leader*, p. 252.
101. *Ibid.*
102. 'Kriegstagebuch Nr.1 2.Panzerarmee Band III vom 1.11.1941 bis 26.12.41', BA-MA RH 21-2/244, fol. 137 (24 November 1941).
103. *Ibid.*, fols 135–137 (24 November 1941).
104. Garden and Andrew (eds), *The War Diaries of a Panzer Soldier*, p. 59 (24 November 1941).
105. 'Kriegstagebuch Nr.1 2.Panzerarmee Band III vom 1.11.1941 bis 26.12.41', BA-MA RH 21-2/244, fol. 136 (24 November 1941).
106. Guderian, *Panzer Leader*, p. 252.
107. Hildegard von Kotze (ed.), *Heeresadjutant bei Hitler 1938–1943. Aufzeichnungen des Majors Engel* (Stuttgart, 1974), p. 116 (25 November 1941). Engel's book, although presented in the form of a diary, was in fact written after the war from his personal notes.
108. Halder, *KTB* III, p. 303 (22 November 1941).
109. See also the discusson in Gerhard P. Gross, *Mythos und Wirklichkeit. Geschichte des operativen Denkens im deutschen Heer von Moltke d.Ä. bis Heusinger* (Paderborn, 2012), pp. 235–6.
110. See, for example, Christoph Rass, *'Menschenmaterial'. Deutsche Soldaten an der Ostfront: Innenansichten einer Infanteriedivision 1939–1945* (Paderborn, 2003).
111. Pabst, *The Outermost Frontier*, p. 27.
112. Carruthers (ed.), *The Wehrmacht Last Witnesses*, p. 56.
113. Hans Heinz Rehfeldt, *Mit dem Eliteverband des Heeres 'Grossdeutschland' tief in den Weiten Russlands. Erinnerungen eines Angehörigen des Granatwerferzuges 8. Infanterierregiment (mot.) 'Grossdeutschland' 1941–1943* (Würzburg, 2008), p. 32.

114. Lubbeck, *At Leningrad's Gates*, p. 112.
115. Kuhnert, *Will We See Tomorrow?*, p. 113.
116. Bidermann, *In Deadly Combat*, p. 52.
117. As cited in M. Jones, *The Retreat*, p. 82.
118. W. P. Reese, *A Stranger to Myself*, p. 7.
119. As cited in M. Jones, *The Retreat*, p. 111.
120. Edward A. Shils, and Morris Janowitz, 'Cohesion and Disintegration in the Wehrmacht in World War II', *Public Opinion Quarterly* 12(2) (1948): 280–315. Although this thesis was later challenged by Omer Bartov's claim that the primary groups were largely destroyed in 1941, support for the endurance of the primary groups can be seen in Christoph Rass' study of the 253rd Infantray Division. Rass, *'Menschenmaterial'*.
121. Martin van Creveld, *Fighting Power. German and US Army Performance, 1939–1945* (Westport, CT, 1982), p. 166.
122. Bartov, *The Eastern Front, 1941–45*; Bartov, *Hitler's Army*. See also Omer Bartov, 'A View from Below. Survival, Cohesion and Brutality on the Eastern Front', in Bernd Wegner (ed.), *From Peace to War. Germany, Soviet Russia and the World, 1939–1941* (Oxford, 1997), pp. 325–40.
123. Thanks to Jeff Rutherford for giving me early access to his research. See Jeff Rutherford, *Combat and Genocide on the Eastern Front. The German Infantry's War, 1941–1944* (Cambridge, 2014).
124. Günther, *Hot Motors, Cold Feet*, p. 210.
125. Knappe, *Soldat*, pp. 230–1.
126. Scheuer, *Briefe aus Russland*, p. 50 (15 November 1941).
127. Bähr and Bähr (eds), *Kriegsbriefe Gefallener Studenten, 1939–1945*, p. 457 (23 November 1941).
128. Bähr and Bähr (eds), *Die Stimme des Menschen*, p. 156 (6 November 1941).
129. W. P. Reese, *A Stranger to Myself*, p. 10.
130. *Ibid.*, p. 26.
131. For more on the relationship between the Orthodox Church and the Soviet state during the war, see Miner, *Stalin's Holy War*. On German policy, see Dallin, *German Rule in Russia 1941–1945*, ch. XXII.
132. Yet as Hitler and Goebbels made clear the power of the Orthodox Church would not be aided or advanced in any way under German rule. Fröhlich (ed.), *Die Tagebücher von Joseph Goebbels. Teil II, Band 2*, p. 414 (2 December 1941). For more on policy, see Alex Alexiev, 'Soviet Nationals in German Wartime Service, 1941–1945', in Antonio Munoz (ed.), *Soviet Nationals in German Wartime Service 1941–1945* (n.p., 2007), pp. 19–20.
133. Overy, *The Dictators*, p. 276.
134. Meier-Welcker, *Aufzeichnungen eines Generalstabsoffiziers 1939–1942*, pp. 135–6 (1 November 1941).

135. von Luck, *Panzer Commander*, p. 59.
136. Antony Beevor and Luba Vinogradova (eds), *A Writer at War. Vasily Grossman with the Red Army 1941–1945* (New York, 2005), p. 38.
137. Josef Perau, *Priester im Heers Hitler. Erinnerungen 1940–1945* (Essen, 1962), p. 42 (20 November 1941); Degrelle, *Campaign in Russia*, p. 25.
138. von Bock, *War Diary*, pp. 272–3 (4 August 1941).
139. 'Kriegstagebuch Nr.7 des Kdos. Der 1.Panzer-Div. 20.9.41–12.4.42', BA-MA 27-1/58, fol. 45 (9 November 1941).
140. *Ibid.*, fol. 47 (12 November 1941).
141. Halder, *KTB* III, p. 312 (27 November 1941).
142. Karl Nünnighoff, MPT, 3.2008.1388 (26 November 1941).
143. Werner Adamczyk, *Feuer! An Artilleryman's Life on the Eastern Front* (Wilmington, NC, 1992), p. 159.
144. All examples as cited in Hester Vaizey, *Surviving Hitler's War. Family Life in Germany, 1939–48* (London, 2010), p. 57. For further examples, see Bähr and Bähr (eds), *Kriegsbriefe Gefallener Studenten, 1939–1945*, pp. 85–6 (9 November 1941); Bähr and Bähr (eds.), *Die Stimme des Menschen*, p. 117 (9 November 1941).
145. For a contrasting insight into the importance of field post on the Finnish front, see Sonja Hagelstam, 'Families, Separation and Emotional Coping in War Bridging Letters Between Home and Front, 1941–44', in Tiina Kinnunen and Ville Kivimäki (eds), *Finland in World War II. History, Memory, Interpretations* (Boston, MA, 2012), pp. 277–312.
146. Fröhlich (ed.), *Die Tagebücher von Joseph Goebbels. Teil II, Band 2*, p. 284 (14 November 1941).
147. *Ibid.*, p. 483 (12 December 1941). See also Fritzsche, *Life and Death in the Third Reich*, p. 149.
148. Vaizey, *Surviving Hitler's War*, p. 55. On the importance of field post, see discussions in Humburg, *Das Gesicht des Krieges*; Klaus Latzel, 'Feldpostbriefe: Überlegungen für Aussagekraft einer Quelle', in Christian Hartmann, Johannes Hürter and Ulrike Jureit (eds), *Verbrechen der Wehrmacht. Bilanz einer Debatte* (Munich, 2005), pp. 171–81.
149. Moorhouse, *Berlin at War*, p. 214.
150. Vaizey, *Surviving Hitler's War*, p. 60.
151. Moorhouse, *Berlin at War*, pp. 214–17.
152. Vaizey, *Surviving Hitler's War*, p. 60.
153. Moorhouse, *Berlin at War*, pp. 216–17.
154. As cited in M. Jones, *The Retreat*, p. 112.
155. Robbins Landon and Leitner (eds), *Diary of a German Soldier*, p. 114 (13 October 1941). See also the entries at p. 104, fn. 2 (11 September 1941) and p. 109 (28 September 1941).

156. As cited in M. Jones, *The Retreat*, pp. 112–13. For more examples, see Karl Nünnighoff, MPT, 3.2008.1388 (11 November 1941); Bamm, *The Invisible Flag*, p. 43.
157. Moorhouse, *Berlin at War*, p. 216.
158. Johann Christoph Allmayer-Beck, *'Herr Oberleitnant, det lohnt doch nicht!' Kriegserinnerinnerungen an die Jahre 1938 bis 1945* (Vienna, 2013), p. 287.
159. Adapted from M. Jones, *The Retreat*, p. 113.

7 Victory at any price

1. Halder, *KTB* III, p. 303 (21 November 1941).
2. Erich Kern, *Dance of Death*, p. 99.
3. Buchbender and Sterz (eds), *Das andere Gesicht des Krieges*, p. 87 (21 November 1941).
4. Knappe, *Soldat*, pp. 230–1.
5. A Soviet general staff study compiled from the lessions learned during the 1941/2 winter fighting concluded that it was desirable to 'deny the enemy the possibility of finding warm places for his troops to rest and get warm in villages, woods, or folds in the terrain by destroying populated places and other sorts of cover and by the use of obstacles and air strikes', See Michael Parrish (ed.), *Battle for Moscow. The 1942 Soviet General Staff Study* (London, 1989), p. 21.
6. For more on this, see Alexander Brakel, 'The Relationship between Soviet Partisans and the Civilian Population in Belorussia under German Occupation, 1941–4', in Ben Shepherd and Juliette Pattinson (eds), *War in a Twilight World. Partisans and Anti-Partisan Warfare in Eastern Europe, 1939–45* (New York, 2010), pp. 80–101.
7. Hill, *The Great Patriotic War of the Soviet Union, 1941–45*, p. 77, document 55 (17 November 1941).
8. *True To Type*, p. 35 (20 November 1941).
9. Degrelle, *Campaign in Russia*, p. 19.
10. For a short biography of her life and the Soviet legend she became in death, see Albert Axell, *Russia's Heroes 1941–45* (New York, 2001) ch. 6. See also Roger D. Markwick and Euridice Charon Cardona, *Soviet Women on the Frontline in the Second World War* (London, 2012), pp. 120–5. Maurice Hindus, *Mother Russia* (London, 1944), pp. 33–56; James von Geldern and Richard Stites (eds), *Mass Culture in Soviet Russia. Tales, Poems, Songs, Movies, Plays, and Folklore 1917–1953* (Bloomington, IN, 1995), pp. 341–4.
11. As cited in Gilbert, *The Second World War*, p. 265.
12. Mawdsley, *Thunder in the East*, p. 112.
13. Stader (ed.), *Ihr daheim und wir hier draußen*, p. 60 (23 November 1941). See also Tilemann, *Ich, das Soldatenkind*, p. 144.
14. Haape, *Moscow Tram Stop*, p. 183.

15. W. P. Reese, *A Stranger to Myself*, p. 33.
16. Roy Mark-Alan, *White Coats under Fire. With the Italian Expedition Corps in Russia: 1941* (New York, 1972), p. 68.
17. Frisch, *Condemned to Live*, pp. 92 and 94.
18. *True To Type*, p. 14 (15 November 1941).
19. W. P. Reese, *A Stranger to Myself*, p. 35.
20. *Ibid.*, p. 36.
21. Haape, *Moscow Tram Stop*, p. 185.
22. Charlotte Haldane, *Russian Newsreel. An Eye-Witness Account of the Soviet Union at War* (New York, 1943), p. 91. (Underlining in original.)
23. Robbins Landon and Leitner (eds), *Diary of a German Soldier*, p. 108 (26 September 1941).
24. Kubik, *Erinnerungen eines Panzerschützen 1941–1945*, p. 125 (3 December 1941).
25. Theo J. Schulte, 'Die Wehrmacht und die nationalsozialistische Besatzungspolitik in der Sowjetunion', in Roland G. Foerster (ed.), *'Unternehmen Barbarossa'. Zum historischen Ort der deutsch-sowjetischen Beziehungen von 1933 bis Herbst 1941* (Munich, 1993), p. 168.
26. Dollinger (ed.), *Kain, wo ist dein Bruder?*, p. 107 (early November 1941).
27. Neitzel, *Tapping Hitler's Generals*, pp. 192–3, document 107 (16–17 September 1944).
28. Frisch, *Condemned to Live*, p. 95.
29. Carl Wagener, *Moskau 1941. Der Angriff auf die russische Hauptstadt* (Dorheim, 1985), p. 98.
30. W. P. Reese, *A Stranger to Myself*, p. 32.
31. *Ibid.*, p. 35.
32. As cited in M. Jones, *The Retreat*, p. 100.
33. As cited in *ibid.*, pp. 76–7.
34. W. P. Reese, *A Stranger to Myself*, p. 41.
35. Dollinger (ed.), *Kain, wo ist dein Bruder?*, p. 109 (15 November 1941).
36. A. Roberts, *The Storm of War*, p. 172.
37. Nicholas Ganson, 'Food Supply, Rationing and Living Standards', in David Stone (ed.), *The Soviet Union at War* (Barnsley, 2010), p. 73. See also Werth, *Russia at War 1941–1945*, pp. 690–1.
38. Pichler, *Truppenarzt und Zeitzeuge*, pp. 106 and 109–10 (14 and 20 October 1941).
39. Haape, *Moscow Tram Stop*, p. 185.
40. *True To Type*, p. 91 (3 October 1941).
41. Lange, *Tagebücher aus dem Zweiten Weltkrieg*, pp. 84–5 (1 and 4 November 1941).
42. Robbins Landon and Leitner (eds), *Diary of a German Soldier*, p. 116 (21 October 1941).

43. Becker, *Devil on my Shoulder*, p. 30.
44. *Ibid.*
45. As cited in Cooper, *The Phantom War*, p. 24.
46. See also the discussion in Alexander Hill, *The War Behind the Eastern Front. The Soviet Partisan Movement in North-West Russia 1941–1944* (New York, 2006), pp. 62–4.
47. For a useful map depicting Soviet partisan regions throughout the German occupied east in the winter of 1941/2, see Kenneth Slepyan, *Stalin's Guerrillas. Soviet Partisans in World War II* (Lawerence, KS, 2006), p. 29.
48. Referring to the vast number of Soviet POWs taken in the aftermath of Army Group Centre's October encirclements, one German account spoke of another problem that was feeding the rise of the partisan problem in Bock's rear: 'There could be no question of guarding them [the Soviet POWs]. I should imagine that there was one German to every five hundred Russians, and am sure that thousands of prisoners took advantage of the situation and escaped.' See Otto Skorzeny, *Skorzeny's Special Missions. The Memoir of Hitler's Most Daring Commando* (London, 2006), p. 23.
49. Kubik, *Erinnerungen eines Panzerschützen 1941–1945*, p. 123 (30 November 1941).
50. Kurt DeWitt and Wilhelm Koll, 'The Bryansk Area', in John A. Armstrong (ed.), *Soviet Partisans in World War II* (Madison, WI, 1964), p. 467.
51. Buchbender and Sterz (eds), *Das andere Gesicht des Krieges*, p. 88 (28 November 1941).
52. Günther, *Hot Motors, Cold Feet*, p. 195.
53. Degrelle, *Campaign in Russia*, p. 23.
54. For a detailed German account of how such villages could be 'punished', see Ingrid Hammer and Susanne zur Nieden (eds), *Sehr selten habe ich geweint. Briefe und Tagebücher aus dem Zweiten Weltkrieg von Menschen aus Berlin* (Zürich, 1992), pp. 255–7 (27 October 1941).
55. Edgar M. Howell, *The Soviet Partisan Movement 1941–1944* (Washington, DC, 1956), p. 73.
56. See the excellent maps in Munoz and Romanko, *Hitler's White Russians*, pp. 140–7.
57. Meier-Welcker, *Aufzeichnungen eines Generalstabsoffiziers 1939–1942*, p. 141 (24 and 26 November 1941).
58. Alexander and Kunze (eds), *Eastern Inferno*, p. 125 (18 November 1941).
59. *Ibid.*
60. 'Kriegstagebuch Nr.1 2.Panzerarmee Band III vom 1.11.1941 bis 26.12.41', BA-MA RH 21-2/244, fols 22 and 25 (4 and 5 November 1941).
61. *Ibid.*, fol. 104 (18 November 1941).
62. *Ibid.*, fol. 108 (19 November 1941).
63. *Ibid.*, fol. 112 (20 November 1941).

64. *Ibid.*, fols 119–120 (21 November 1941).
65. 'A.O.K.4 Ia Anlagen B 19 zum Kriegstagebuch Nr.9. 23.11.–27.11.41', BA-MA RH 20-4, fol. 138 (26 November 1941).
66. Blumentritt, 'Moscow', p. 55.
67. 'KTB SS 2nd Div. "*Das Reich*"', BA-MA RS 3-2/6, fol. 31 (13 November 1941).
68. '20.Pz.Div. KTB vom 21.10.41 bis 30.12.41 Band Ia2.', BA-MA RH 27-20/26, fol. 30 (7 November 1941).
69. Trevor-Roper (ed.), *Hitler's War Directives 1939–1945*, p. 144 (23 July 1941).
70. As cited in Merridale, *Ivan's War*, p. 133.
71. *True To Type*, p. 119 (1 December 1941).
72. Lange, *Tagebücher aus dem Zweiten Weltkrieg*, p. 87 (9 November 1941).
73. Robbins Landon and Leitner (eds), *Diary of a German Soldier*, p. 123 (11 November 1941).
74. Downing, *Sealing their Fate*, pp. 84–5.
75. Haape, *Moscow Tram Stop*, p. 191.
76. Walter Schwabedissen, *The Russian Air Force in the Eyes of the German Commanders* (New York, 1960), p. 147; Haape, *Moscow Tram Stop*, p. 189.
77. Leonid Grenkevich, *The Soviet Partisan Movement 1941–1944* (London, 1999), pp. 173 and 199.
78. Gerhard L. Weinberg, 'The Yelnya–Dorogobuzh area of Smolensk Oblast', in John A. Armstrong (ed.), *Soviet Partisans in World War* II (Madison, WI, 1964), p. 407.
79. Erich Kern, *Dance of Death*, p. 70.
80. Lange, *Tagebücher aus dem Zweiten Weltkrieg*, p. 87 (9 November 1941).
81. For a copy of the order, see Gerd R. Ueberschär (ed.), 'Armeebefehl des Oberbefehlshabers der 6. Armee, Generalfeldmarschall von Reichenau, vom 10.10.1941', in Gerd R. Ueberschär and Wolfram Wette (eds), *'Unternehmen Barbarossa' Der deutsche Überfall auf die Sowjetunion 1941* (Paderborn, 1984), pp. 339–40, document collection 20; Knopp, *Die Wehrmacht*, p. 171.
82. Förster, 'Securing "Living-space"', pp. 1212–13.
83. 'KTB SS 2nd Div. "*Das Reich*"', BA-MA RS 3-2/6, fol. 32 (13 November 1941).
84. 'Kriegstagebuch Nr.2 XXXXVII.Pz.Korps. Ia 23.9.1941–31.12.1941', BA-MA RH 24-47/258, fol. 75 (6 November 1941).
85. 'A.O.K.4 Ia Anlagen B 20 zum Kriegstagebuch Nr.9. 28.11.–3.12.41', BA-MA RH 20-4, fol. 156 (2 December 1941).
86. Jarausch (ed.), *Reluctant Accomplice*, p. 325 (14 November 1941).
87. Downing, *Sealing their Fate*, pp. 155–61.
88. To understand Hitler's decision, see Ian Kershaw, *Fateful Choices. Ten Decisions that Changed the World, 1940–1941* (New York, 2007) ch. 9; Norman Rich, *Hitler's War Aims. Ideology, the Nazi State, and the Course of Expansion* (New York, 1972), ch. 20.

89. Fröhlich (ed.), *Die Tagebücher von Joseph Goebbels. Teil* II, *Band* 2, p. 339 (22 November 1941).
90. von Hassell, *Vom Andern Deutschland*, p. 234 (30 November 1941) (von Hassell, *The von Hassell Diaries 1938–1944*, p. 203 (30 November 1941)).
91. See, in particular, Hürter, *Hitlers Heerführer*.
92. Halder, *KTB* III, p. 306 (23 November 1941).
93. *Ibid.*
94. *Ibid.*
95. Halder's adjutant suggested that the Chief of the General Staff was influenced by an 'old school belief' that if only Moscow could be seized the war would reach 'a positive turning point'. He also expressed the view that Halder underestimated the fanaticism of Soviet resistance. See Christian Hartmann, *Halder Generalstabschef Hitlers 1938–1942* (Munich, 1991), p. 295. Yet Halder's letters to his wife from the first weeks of the war make clear that he expected 'that this campaign will not be ended by a capitulation or something similar'. See Heidemarie Gräfin Schall-Riaucour, *Aufstand und Gehorsam. Offizierstum und Generalstab im Umbruch. Leben und Wirken von Generalobberst Franz Halder Generalstabchef 1938–1942* (Wiesbaden, 1972), p. 172.
96. Halder, *KTB* III, p. 306 (23 November 1941).
97. Meier-Welcker, *Aufzeichnungen eines Generalstabsoffiziers 1939–1942*, p. 141 (29 November 1941). (Italics in the original.)
98. von Bock, *War Diary*, p. 370 (26 November 1941).
99. According to the war diary of Panzer Group 3, the success of the advance was largely aided by Soviet withdrawals. 'Anlagen zum Kriegstagebuch Tagesmeldungen Bd.I 1.11–31.12.41', BA-MA RH 21-3/71, fol. 177 (26 November 1941).
100. von Bock, *War Diary*, p. 371 (27 November 1941).
101. *Ibid.*, p. 372 (28 November 1941).
102. *Ibid.*, p. 374 (30 November 1941). See also 'Kriegstagebuch Nr.I (Band November 1941) des Oberkommandos der Heeresgruppe Mitte', BA-MA RH 19-II/387, fols 152–153 (30 November 1941).
103. 'Anlagen zum Kriegstagebuch Tagesmeldungen Bd.I 1.11–31.12.41', BA-MA RH 21-3/71, fol. 211 (30 November 1941).
104. H. Reinhardt, 'Panzer-Gruppe 3 in der Schlacht von Moskau und ihre Erfahrungen im Rückzug', p. 3.
105. On the weaknesses of the panzer group, see 'Kriegstagebuch Nr.I (Band November 1941) des Oberkommandos der Heeresgruppe Mitte', BA-MA RH 19-II/387, fol. 152 (30 November 1941).
106. Hans Röttiger, 'XXXXI Panzer Corps during the Battle of Moscow in 1941 as a Component of Panzer Group 3', in Steven H. Newton (ed.), *German Battle Tactics in the Russian Front 1941–1945* (Atglen, PA, 1994), p. 36.

107. Knoblauch, *Zwischen Metz und Moskau*, p. 195 (27 November 1941).
108. Henrik Eberle and Matthias Uhl (eds), *The Hitler Book. The Secret Dossier Prepared for Stalin from the Interrogations of Hitler's Personal Aides* (New York, 2005), p. 78.
109. Hassell, *Vom Andern Deutschland*, p. 236 (30 November 1941) (Hassell, *The von Hassell Diaries 1938–1944*, p. 206 (30 November 1941)). See also I. Kershaw, *Hitler 1936–1945*, p. 441.
110. Richard Overy, *Interrogations. The Nazi Elite in Allied Hands, 1945* (London, 2001), p. 344.
111. Görlitz (ed.), *The Memoirs of Field-Marshal Keitel*, p. 160.
112. Messenger, *The Last Prussian*, pp. 155–6.
113. Overy, *Interrogations*, p. 248.
114. Neitzel, *Tapping Hitler's Generals*, p. 124, document 54 (21–22 December 1944).
115. von Luck, *Panzer Commander*, p. 64.
116. 'Kriegstagebuch Nr.3. der Führungsabteilung (Ia) des Gen. Kdo. (mot.) XXXX. Pz.Korps vom 31.05.1941–26.12.1941', BA-MA RH 24-40/18 (26 November 1941).
117. Skorzeny, *Skorzeny's Special Missions*, p. 24.
118. 'Kriegstagebuch Nr.3. des XXXXVI.Pz.Korps vom 24.08.41–31.12.41', BA-MA RH 24-46/21, fol. 145 (27 November 1941).
119. *Ibid*., fol. 144 (26 November 1941).
120. The aforementioned General of Panzer Troops, Adolf Kuntzen, gave up command of the corps on 14 November and was replaced by Lieutenant-General Friedrich Kirchner on 15 November.
121. 'Gen.Kdo.LVII.Pz.Korps KTB Nr.2 vom 1.11.41–31.12.41', BA-MA RH 24-57-3, fol. 37 (27 November 1941).
122. *Ibid*., fol. 38 (29 November 1941).
123. Reddemann (ed.), *Zwischen Front und Heimat*, p. 362 (29 November 1941).
124. Theodor Mogge's unpublished personal account of his experiences on the eastern front were recorded in 1978 and kindly provided to me by his son Klaus Mogge.
125. Skorzeny, *Skorzeny's Special Missions*, p. 24.
126. Blumentritt, 'Moscow', p. 57.
127. Skorzeny, *Skorzeny's Special Missions*, p. 24.
128. 'A.O.K.4 Ia Entwurf zum Kriegstagebuch Nr.9. 10.10.–3.12.41', BA-MA RH 20-4 (28 November 1941). The diary has no folio stamped page numbers, so references must be located using the date. An entry from two days earlier (26 November) in the war diary of the 5th Panzer Division listed 108 serviceable tanks. '5. Panzer Division KTB Nur.8 vom 11.9.41–11.12.41', BA-MA RH 27-5/29, fol. 113 (26 November 1941).
129. For German tank strengths on 22 June 1941, see Müller-Hillebrand, *Das Heer 1933–1945, Band* III, p. 205. Reproduced in Bryan I. Fugate, *Operation*

Barbarossa. Strategy and Tactics on the Eastern Front, 1941 (Novato, CA, 1984), p. 349.

130. Fröhlich (ed.), *Die Tagebücher von Joseph Goebbels. Teil* II, *Band* 2, p. 218 (1 November 1941).
131. Halder, *KTB* III, p. 311 (27 November 1941).
132. As cited in M. Jones, *The Retreat*, p. 107.
133. 'Kriegstagebuch Nr.1 (Band November 1941) des Oberkommandos der Heeresgruppe Mitte', BA-MA RH 19-II/387, fol. 143 (29 November 1941). See also von Bock, *War Diary*, p. 373 (29 November 1941); Halder, *KTB* III, p. 316 (29 November 1941).
134. See graph in T. N. Dupuy and Paul Martell, *Great Battles on the Eastern Front. The Soviet–German War, 1941–1945* (Indianapolis, IN, 1982), p. 45.
135. 'Kriegstagebuch Nr.1 (Band November 1941) des Oberkommandos der Heeresgruppe Mitte', BA-MA RH 19-II/387, fol. 142 (28 November 1941).
136. Halder, *KTB* III, pp. 319–20 (30 November 1941).
137. Ernst Klink, 'The Conduct of Operations', in Militärgeschichtlichen Forschungsamt (ed.), *Germany and the Second World War, vol.* IV*: The Attack on the Soviet Union* (Oxford, 1998), p. 698.
138. Beaulieu, *Generaloberst Erich Hoepner*, pp. 211–12; K. Reinhardt, *Moscow: The Turning Point*, p. 218; Robert Kirchubel, *Hitler's Panzer's Armies on the Eastern Front* (Barnsley, 2009), p. 147.
139. Kesselring, *The Memoirs of Field-Marshal Kesselring*, p. 96.
140. As cited in A. Clark, *Barbarossa*, p. 176.
141. von Bock, *War Diary*, p. 373 (29 November 1941). See also 'Kriegstagebuch Nr.1 (Band November 1941) des Oberkommandos der Heeresgruppe Mitte', BA-MA RH 19-II/387, fol. 146 (29 November 1941).
142. von Bock, *War Diary*, p. 373 (29 November 1941). See also Halder, *KTB* III, p. 318 (29 November 1941).
143. Halder, *KTB* III, p. 315 (29 November 1941).

8 The frozen offensive

1. 'Oberkommando des Heeres Generalstab des Heeres O.Qu.IV-Abt.Fr.H.Ost (II)', BA-MA RH/2–2670, fol. 75 (22 November 1941). See also Erickson, *The Road to Stalingrad*, pp. 270–1.
2. Zhukov, *The Memoirs of Marshal Zhukov*, pp. 347–8.
3. David M. Glantz, *Soviet Military Deception in the Second World War* (London, 1989), pp. 47–56.
4. Earl F. Ziemke, *The Red Army 1918–1941. From Vanguard of World Revolution to US Ally* (London, 2004), p. 307. See also Bellamy, *Absolute War*, p. 310.
5. As Kesselring wrote after the war: 'It is still a puzzle to me, even today, that our long-distance reconnaissance, although reporting lively movement on the roads,

never to my knowledge gave warning of the strategic concentration of the Russian armies' Kesselring, *The Memoirs of Field-Marshal Kesselring*, p. 96.

6. Halder, *KTB* III, p. 299 (19 November 1941).
7. Ibid., p. 310 (25 November 1941).
8. von Bock, *War Diary*, p. 370 (26 November 1941).
9. *Ibid.* (27 November 1941).
10. Guderian, *Panzer Leader*, p. 254. See also 'Kriegstagebuch Nr.2 XXXXVII.Pz. Korps. Ia 23.9.1941–31.12.1941', BA-MA RH 24-47/258, fol. 108 (25 November 1941). In the end the encirclement netted just 1,530 Soviet POWs and forty-four guns.
11. Guderian, *Panzer Leader*, p. 255.
12. von Bock, *War Diary*, p. 371 (27 November 1941).
13. *Ibid.*
14. As Dennis Showalter observed in his history of the German panzer forces: 'The operational environment, in short, was anything but conducive to balanced judgement and cold reason in the pattern of the elder Moltke.' Dennis Showalter, *Hitler's Panzers. The Lightning Attacks that Revolutionized Warfare* (New York, 2009), p. 188.
15. von Bock, *War Diary*, p. 374 (30 November 1941).
16. *Ibid.*
17. *Ibid.*
18. *Ibid.* See also 'Kriegstagebuch Nr.1 (Band November 1941) des Oberkommandos der Heeresgruppe Mitte', BA-MA RH 19-II/387, fol. 154 (30 November 1941).
19. For figures for the 3rd and 17th Panzer Divisions, see 'Kriegstagebuch Nr.1 2. Panzerarmee Band III vom 1.11.1941 bis 26.12.41', BA-MA RH 21-2/244, fol. 172 (30 November 1941). See also Traditionverband der Division (ed.), *Geschichte der 3.Panzer-Division. Berlin-Brandenburg 1935–1945* (Berlin, 1967), p. 216. The figure for the 4th Panzer Division is taken from 'Kriegstagebuch 4.Panzer-Divison Führungsabtl. 26.5.41–31.3.42', BA-MA RH 27-4/10, p. 269 (30 November 1941). See also Hans Schäufler (ed.), *Knight's Cross Panzers. The German 35th Panzer Regiment in WWII* (Mechanicsburg, PA, 2010), p. 161.
20. Johannes Hürter (ed.), *Ein deutscher General an der Ostfront. Die Briefe und Tagebücher des Gotthard Heinrici 1941/42* (Erfurt, 2001), pp. 114–15.
21. Guderian, *Panzer Leader*, p. 255.
22. 'Verlustmeldungen 5.7.1941–25.3.1942', BA-MA RH 21-2/757, fols 25 (4 December 1941).
23. 'Kriegstagebuch Nr.1 (Band November 1941) des Oberkommandos der Heeresgruppe Mitte', BA-MA RH 19-II/387, fol. 142 (28 November 1941).
24. Kleindienst (ed.), *Sei tausendmal gegrüßt*, CD Rom (26 November 1941).

25. 'Kriegstagebuch Nr.1 (Band November 1941) des Oberkommandos der Heeresgruppe Mitte', BA-MA RH 19-II/387, fol. 142 (28 November 1941).
26. Downing, *Sealing their Fate*, p. 228.
27. Jarausch (ed.), *Reluctant Accomplice*, p. 325 (14 November 1941).
28. *Ibid.*, p. 331 (25 November 1941).
29. *Ibid.*, p. 337 (2 December 1941).
30. Malcolm Muggeridge (ed.), *Ciano's Diary 1939–1943* (London, 1948), pp. 402–3 (24 November 1941).
31. 'Kriegstagebuch Nr.1 (Band November 1941) des Oberkommandos der Heeresgruppe Mitte', BA-MA RH 19-II/387, fol. 58 (12 November 1941).
32. Dollinger (ed.), *Kain, wo ist dein Bruder?*, p. 108 (early November 1941).
33. George H. Stein, *The Waffen SS. Hitler's Elite Guard at War 1939–1945* (New York, 1984), p. 133.
34. Reddemann (ed.), *Zwischen Front und Heimat*, p. 347 (9 November 1941).
35. As cited in Hastings, *Winston's War*, p. 226.
36. Humburg, *Das Gesicht des Krieges*, p. 143 (22 November 1941).
37. Overy, *Russia's War*, p. 90.
38. Roger R. Reese, *Why Stalin's Soldiers Fought. The Red Army's Military Effectiveness in World War* II (Lawrence, KS, 2011), pp. 177–86; Richard Bidlack, 'Propaganda and Public Opinion', in David R. Stone (ed.), *The Soviet Union at War 1941–1945* (Barnsley, 2010), pp. 62–4.
39. Ray Wagner, *The Soviet Air Force in World War* II. *The Offical History, Originally Published by the Ministry of Defence of the USSR* (Melbourne, 1974), pp. 78–9.
40. M. N. Kozhevnikov, *The Command and Staff of the Soviet Army Air Force in the Great Patriotic War 1941–1945. A Soviet View* (Moscow, 1977), pp. 60–1.
41. Von Hardesty and Ilya Grinberg, *Red Phoenix Rising. The Soviet Air Force in World War* II (Lawrence, KS, 2012), p. 87.
42. Richard Muller, *The German Air War in Russia* (Baltimore, MD, 1992), p. 43.
43. Horst Boog, 'The Luftwaffe', in Militärgeschichtliches Forschungsamt (ed.), *Germany and the Second World War, vol.* IV: *The Attack on the Soviet Union* (Oxford, 1998), p. 795.
44. Von Hardesty, *Red Phoenix. The Rise of Soviet Air Power 1941–1945* (Washington, DC, 1982), pp. 70–1.
45. Hans-Ulrich Rudel, *Stuka Pilot* (New York, 1979), p. 49.
46. Hermann Plocher, *The German Air Force versus Russia, 1941* (New York, 1965), p. 239.
47. Muller, *The German Air War in Russia*, p. 61.
48. For an excellent overview of the crisis in the Luftwaffe's aircraft production, see Tooze, *The Wages of Destruction*, pp. 576–84; Richard Overy, *The Air War 1939–1945* (London, 1980), pp. 50–2.

49. Williamson Murray, *The Luftwaffe 1933–45. Strategy for Defeat* (Washington, DC, 1996), pp. 101–2.
50. Overy, *Why the Allies Won*, pp. 219–20.
51. In spite of heavy losses throughout the preceding six months, at the end of 1941 the Soviet air force alone operated some 12,000 planes. Hill, 'British Lend-Lease Aid and the Soviet War Effort, June 1941–June 1942', p. 792.
52. After reaching 101 'kills' Mölders was forbidden from flying combat missions, but is known to have continued in this role for some time and unofficially shot down an even higher number of enemy aircraft.
53. Bergström, *Barbarossa. The Air Battle*, pp. 108–9; John Weal, *More Bf 109 Aces of the Russian Front* (Oxford, 2007), p. 22.
54. Kesselring, *The Memoirs of Field-Marshal Kesselring*, p. 97.
55. 'Gen.v.Waldau, Chef Fü St Lw Persönl. Tagebuch, Auszugeweise', BA-MA RL 200/17, p. 86 (27 November 1941).
56. Williamson Murray, *Military Adaptation in War. With Fear of Change* (Cambridge, 2011), ch. 4.
57. 'Anlagen zum Kriegstagebuch Tagesmeldungen Bd.I 1.11–31.12.41', BA-MA RH 21-3/71, fol. 172 (25 November 1941).
58. 'Kriegstagebuch Nr.3 der 7.Panzer-Division Führungsabteilung 1.6.1941–9.5.1942', BA-MA RH 27-7/46, fol. 220 (30 November 1941).
59. '6. Panzer Division KTB 16.9.1941–30.11.1941', BA-MA RH 27-6/19, p. 300 (27 November 1941).
60. 'Anlage zum KTB Panzer Gruppe 4: 11.11.41–5.12.41', BA-MA RH 21-4/36, fol. 38 (29 November 1941).
61. Knoblauch, *Zwischen Metz und Moskau*, pp. 194–5 (19 November 1941).
62. 'Anlage zum KTB Pz.Gruppe 4 Meldungen von unten 16.11.41–5.12.41', BA-MA RH 21-4/40, fol. 102 (27 November 1941).
63. '2. Panzer Division KTB Nr.6 Teil I. Vom 15.6.41–3.4.42', BA-MA RH 27-2/21 (27 November 1941).
64. *Ibid.* (28 November 1941).
65. 'Kriegstagebuch Nr.3. der Führungsabteilung (Ia) des Gen. Kdo. (mot.) XXXX.Pz. Korps vom 31.05.1941–26.12.1941', BA-MA RH 24-40/18 (28 November 1941).
66. Hardesty, *Red Phoenix*, p. 170.
67. Hans Werner Neulen, *In the Skies of Europe. Air Forces Allied to the Luftwaffe 1939–1945* (Marlborough, 2000), pp. 172 and 277–9.
68. 'Kriegstagebuch Nr.1 2.Panzerarmee Band III vom 1.11.1941 bis 26.12.41', BA-MA RH 21-2/244, fol. 161 (28 November 1941).
69. Stader (ed.), *Ihr daheim und wir hier draußen*, p. 63 (30 November 1941).
70. 'Kriegstagebuch Nr.2 XXXXVII.Pz.Korps. Ia 23.9.1941–31.12.1941', BA-MA RH 24-47/258, fol. 113 (27 November 1941).

71. '18. Panzer-Div-Ia Kriegstagebuch vom 20.10.41–13.12.41', BA-MA RH 27-18/69 (16 November 1941).
72. *Ibid.* (29 November 1941).
73. 'Armeeoberkommando 2. I.a KTB Teil.2 19.9.41–16.12.41' BA-MA RH 20-2/207, p. 131 (23 November 1941).
74. '9.Pz.Div. KTB Ia vom 19.5.1941 bis 22.1.1942', BA-MA RH 27-9/4, pp. 161 and 165 (21 and 23 November 1941); 'Kriegstagebuch XXXXVIII.Pz.Kps. Abt. Ia November 1941', BA-MA RH 24-48/35, fols 8–9 (22 and 23 November 1941). For Second Army's orders, see von Bock, *War Diary*, pp. 368 and 374 (23 and 30 November 1941).
75. Stahl, 'Generaloberst Rudolf Schmidt', p. 221.
76. For the demodernisation concept, see Bartov, *Hitler's Army*, ch. 1.
77. Fröhlich (ed.), *Die Tagebücher von Joseph Goebbels. Teil* II, *Band* 2, p. 412 (2 December 1941).
78. Tooze, *The Wages of Destruction*, p. 507.
79. Gilbert, *The Second World War*, p. 265.
80. Gerhard L. Weinberg, *A World at Arms. A Global History of World War* II (Cambridge, 1994), pp. 232–3; Kitchen, *A World in Flames*, p. 96.
81. Geoffrey Roberts, *Stalin's General. The Life of Georgy Zhukov* (New York, 2012), p. 143.
82. From 1 November to 15 November the *Stavka* authorised 100,000 men, 300 planes and 2,000 guns to reinforce Zhukov's Western Front. K. Reinhardt, *Moscow: The Turning Point*, p. 210, fn. 9.
83. Albert Seaton, *The Russo-German War 1941–45* (Novato, CA, 1971), p. 203.
84. As cited in Mawdsley, *Thunder in the East*, p. 115.
85. Ziemke, *The Red Army 1918–1941*, p. 299; Glantz and House, *When Titans Clashed*, p. 292.
86. On the evacuation process, see Mark Harrison, *Soviet Planning in Peace and War 1938–1945* (Cambridge, 2002), pp. 63–79; G. A. Kumanev, 'The Soviet Economy and the 1941 Evacuation', in Joseph Wieczynski (ed.), *Operation Barbarossa. The German Attack on the Soviet Union June 22, 1941* (Salt Lake City, UT, 1993), pp. 163–93; John Barber and Mark Harrison, *The Soviet Home Front 1941–1945. A Social and Economic History of the USSR in World War* II (London, 1991), pp. 127–32.
87. Mark Harrison, 'Industry and the Economy', in David R. Stone (ed.), *The Soviet Union at War 1941–1945* (Barnsley, 2010), p. 30; Harrison, *Soviet Planning in Peace and War 1938–1945*, p. 77.
88. See table of production in Stahel, *Operation Typhoon*, p. 29; Richard Overy, 'Statistics', in I. C. B. Dear and M. R. D. Foot (eds), *The Oxford Companion to the Second World War* (Oxford, 1995), p. 1060, table 2.
89. See Lukacs, *The Hitler of History*, pp. 156–8.

90. Daniel Bourgeois, 'Operation "Barbarossa" and Switzerland', in Bernd Wegner (ed.), *From Peace to War. Germany, Soviet Russia and the World, 1939–1941* (Oxford, 1997), pp. 606–7.
91. *Ibid.*, p. 607.
92. *Ibid.*
93. Bidlack, 'Propaganda and Public Opinion', p. 61.
94. Ehrenburg and Simonov, *In One Newspaper*, p. 147. See also R. R. Reese, *Why Stalin's Soldiers Fought*, p. 178.
95. Amir Weiner, 'Something to Die For, a Lot to Kill For: the Soviet System and the Barbarisation of Warfare, 1939–1945', in George Kassimeris (ed.), *The Barbarization of Warfare* (New York, 2006), pp. 101–25.
96. See the detailed discussions in Craig W. H. Luther, *Barbarossa Unleashed. The German Blitzkrieg through Central Russia to the Gates of Moscow* (Atglen, PA, 2013), pp. 458–472; Christian Hartmann, *Operation Barbarossa. Nazi Germany's War in the East, 1941–1945* (Oxford, 2013), pp. 122–30.
97. As cited in M. Jones, *The Retreat*, p. 74.
98. As cited in Nagorski, *The Greatest Battle*, p. 248.
99. For examples captured on film, see R. C. Raack, 'Nazi Film Propaganda and the Horrors of War', *Historical Journal of Film, Radio and Television* 6(2) (1986): 192–3.
100. Neitzel and Welzer, *Soldaten*, pp. 90–1.
101. Robert Thurston, 'Cauldrons of Loyalty and Betrayal: Soviet Soldiers' Behavior, 1941 and 1945', in Robert Thurston and Bernd Bonwetsch (eds), *The People's War. Responses to World War* II *in the Soviet Union* (Chicago, IL, 2000), pp. 235–57.
102. As cited in M. Jones, *The Retreat*, p. 93.
103. Rokossovsky, *A Soldier's Duty*, p. 84.
104. Harrison E. Salisbury (ed.), *Marshal Zhukov's Greatest Battles* (London, 1971), p. 61.
105. Nagorski, *The Greatest Battle*, pp. 234–5.
106. Walter S. Dunn Jr, *Stalin's Keys to Victory. The Rebirth of the Red Army in WW*II (Mechanicsburg, PA 2006), p. 90.
107. Glantz, *Barbarossa*, pp. 177–9.
108. As cited in Evan Mawdsley, *December 1941. Twelve Days that Began a World War* (New Haven, CT, 2011), p. 20. See also Gerhard Krebs, 'Japan and the German–Soviet War, 1941', in Bernd Wegner (ed.), *From Peace to War. Germany, Soviet Russia and the World, 1939–1941* (Oxford, 1997), pp. 541–60.
109. Zhukov, *The Memoirs of Marshal Zhukov*, pp. 347–448. See also Mawdsley, *December 1941*, p. 46.
110. On conditions inside the First Panzer Army, see Kubik, *Erinnerungen eines Panzerschützen 1941–1945*, pp. 122–3 (29 and 30 November 1941).

111. Glantz, *Barbarossa*, pp. 179–80.
112. Roberts, *Stalin's General*, p. 143 (underlining in the original); Mawdsley, *December 1941*, p. 47; G. K. Zhukov, *Marshal of the Soviet Union G. Zhukov. Reminiscences and Reflections*, vol. 2 (Moscow, 1985), pp. 45–6. For discussion of offensive plans in Konev's Kalinin Front, see Albert Seaton, *Stalin as Warlord* (London, 1976), p. 134.
113. Dunn, *Stalin's Keys to Victory*, p. 90.
114. Degrelle, *Campaign in Russia*, p. 19.
115. Hans Schäufler, *Panzer Warfare on the Eastern Front* (Mechanicsburg, PA, 2012), p. 43.
116. As cited in Lucas, *War of the Eastern Front 1941–1945*, p. 78.
117. Reddemann (ed.), *Zwischen Front und Heimat*, p. 362 (29 November 1941).
118. Taken from a chart displayed at the Museum of the Great Patriotic War in Moscow (September 2012).
119. Lucas, *War of the Eastern Front 1941–1945*, p. 80.
120. Günther, *Hot Motors, Cold Feet*, p. 210.
121. Frisch, *Condemned to Live*, p. 92.
122. Pabst, *The Outermost Frontier*, p. 39.
123. Erhard Rauss, 'The Russian Soldier and the Russian Conduct of Battle', in Peter G. Tsouras (ed.), *Fighting in Hell. The German Ordeal on the Eastern Front* (New York, 1997), pp. 16–21.
124. Zhukov, *The Memoirs of Marshal Zhukov*, p. 344.
125. As cited in M. Jones, *The Retreat*, p. 94.
126. Knappe, *Soldat*, p. 230.
127. The term 'old Fritz' refers to the Prussian king Frederick II (otherwise known as Frederick the Great).
128. Günther, *Hot Motors, Cold Feet*, p. 210.
129. Department of the US Army (ed.), *Effects of Climate on Combat in European Russia* (Washington, DC, 1952), p. 18.
130. Kuhnert, *Will We See Tomorrow?*, p. 113.
131. Haape, *Moscow Tram Stop*, p. 181.
132. Günther, *Hot Motors, Cold Feet*, p. 209.
133. Department of the US Army (ed.), *Military Improvisations during the Russian Campaign* (Washington, DC, 1951), p. 65.
134. Franz and Leopold Schober, *Briefe von der Front. Feldpostbriefe 1939–1945*, ed. Michael Hans Salvesberger (Gösing am Wagram, 1997), p. 134 (27 November 1941).
135. Hürter (ed.), *Ein deutscher General an der Ostfront*, p. 115 (29 November 1941).
136. Ernst Kern, *War Diary 1941–45*, p. 17.
137. Bähr and Bähr (eds), *Kriegsbriefe Gefallener Studenten, 1939–1945*, p. 68 (19–20 November 1941).

138. Knappe, *Soldat*, p. 234.
139. Bähr and Bähr (eds), *Kriegsbriefe Gefallener Studenten, 1939–1945*, p. 68 (19–20 November 1941).
140. Bernhard R. Kroener, 'The Winter Crisis of 1941–1942: the Distribution of Scarcity or Steps Towards a More Rational Management of Personnel', in Militärgeschichtliches Forschungsamt (ed.), *Germany and the Second World War, vol.* V/I: *Organization and Mobilization of the German Sphere of Power* (Oxford, 2000), p. 1018.
141. Knappe, *Soldat*, p. 233.
142. Bähr and Bähr (eds), *Kriegsbriefe Gefallener Studenten, 1939–1945*, p. 68 (19–20 November 1941).
143. Blumentritt, 'Moscow', pp. 62–3. See also Carell, *Hitler's War on Russia*, pp. 162–3. Maybe not all of the bottles described in Blumentritt's account were in fact lost. One of Ernst Guicking's letters from this period speaks of his unit receiving bottles of wine from Reims in France. Kleindienst (ed.), *Sei tausendmal gegrüßt*, CD Rom (25 November 1941).
144. Mark-Alan, *White Coats under Fire*, p. 106.
145. Lucas, *War of the Eastern Front 1941–1945*, p. 81.
146. von Luck, *Panzer Commander*, p. 63.
147. Stahlberg, *Bounden Duty*, p. 181.
148. Knappe, *Soldat*, p. 234.
149. Department of the US Army (ed.), *Effects of Climate on Combat in European Russia*, pp. 21–2. See also Niklas Zetterling and Anders Frankson, *The Drive on Moscow, 1941. Operation Taifun and Germany's First Great Crisis in World War* II (Havertown, PA, 2012), pp. 183–4.
150. Elena Rzhevskaia, 'Roads and Days: the Memoirs of a Red Army Translator', *Journal of Slavic Military Studies* 14(1) (2001): 61.
151. *True To Type*, p. 34 (19 November 1941).
152. Knappe, *Soldat*, pp. 229 and 233.
153. Halder, *KTB* III, p. 312 (28 November 1941). See also Blumentritt, 'Moscow', p. 55.
154. Richard L. DiNardo, *Mechanized Juggernaut or Military Anachronism. Horses and the German Army in World War* II (London, 1991), pp. 47–9.
155. As cited in Nagorski, *The Greatest Battle*, pp. 239–40.
156. *Ibid.*, p. 251.
157. Knappe, *Soldat*, p. 234.
158. Guderian, *Panzer Leader*, pp. 254–5.

9 Down to the wire

1. Halder, *KTB* III, p. 318 (30 November 1941). See also KTB OKW, vol. II, pp. 1120–1 (5 January 1942). The total losses for the *Waffen SS* as of 19

November 1941 were: 407 officers and 7,930 men were killed; 816 officers and 26,299 men had been wounded; 13 officers and 923 men were listed as missing; 4 officers and 125 men had been killed in accidents. G. H. Stein, *The Waffen SS*, p. 134.

2. Overmans, *Deutsche militärische Verluste im Zweiten Weltkrieg*, p. 278.
3. Halder, *KTB* III, p. 319 (30 November 1941).
4. Zetterling and Frankson, *The Drive on Moscow, 1941*, p. 248.
5. Knappe, *Soldat*, p. 231.
6. Schäufler, *Panzer Warfare on the Eastern Front*, p. 46.
7. Buchbender and Sterz (eds), *Das andere Gesicht des Krieges*, p. 87 (21 November 1941).
8. Ernst Kern, *War Diary 1941–45*, p. 21.
9. Kroener, 'The Winter Crisis of 1941–1942', p. 1023.
10. Fröhlich (ed.), *Die Tagebücher von Joseph Goebbels. Teil* II, *Band* 2, p. 401 (30 November 1941).
11. Buchbender and Sterz (eds), *Das andere Gesicht des Krieges*, p. 86 (11 November 1941).
12. Fröhlich (ed.), *Die Tagebücher von Joseph Goebbels. Teil* II, *Band* 2, p. 361 (25 November 1941).
13. As cited in Aristotle A. Kallis, *Nazi Propaganda and the Second World War* (New York, 2005), p. 116.
14. Kroener, 'The Winter Crisis of 1941–1942', p. 1022.
15. Kesselring, *The Memoirs of Field-Marshal Kesselring*, p. 100.
16. For some key works on the raising of these forces, see Dallin, *German Rule in Russia 1941–1945*, ch. XXIV; Antonio Munoz (ed.), *Soviet Nationals in German Wartime Service 1941–1945* (n.p., 2007); Rolf-Dieter Müller, *An der Seite der Wehrmacht. Hitlers ausländische Helfer beim 'Kreuzzug gegen den Bolschewismus' 1941–1945* (Berlin, 2007). For the role of writer Edwin Erich Dwinger and his support for the raising of a Russian liberation army, see Jay W. Baird, *Hitler's War Poets. Literature and Politics in the Third Reich* (Cambridge, 2008), pp. 154–9.
17. See also my discussion in Stahel, *Kiev 1941*, pp. 81–3.
18. Officially in the summer of 1941 the Greater German Reich had a much larger population, but this included the annexation of large parts of Poland, small ones in Belgium and the city of Danzig. It also included the extension of German civilian administration over Alsace and Lorraine, Luxembourg, Bialstok, northern Slovenia and the Protectorate of Bohemia and Moravia. In total, this Greater Germany numbered some 116 million people, but not all were loyal to their new state. See Jürgen Förster, 'Germany', in I. C. B. Dear and M. R. D. Foot (eds), *The Oxford Companion to the Second World War* (Oxford, 1995), pp. 455–557.
19. Bernhard R. Kroener, 'The "Frozen Blitzkrieg": German Strategic Planning against the Soviet Union and the Causes of its Failure', in Bernd Wegner (ed.),

From Peace to War. Germany, Soviet Russia and the World, 1939–1941 (Oxford, 1997), pp. 142–3.

20. Boberach (ed.), *Meldungen aus dem Reich*, vol. 8, pp. 3059–60, document 243 (4 December 1941).
21. Victor Klemperer, *Ich will Zeugnis ablegen bis zum letztem. Tagebücher 1933–1941* (Berlin, 1997), p. 691 (30 November 1941).
22. Howard K. Smith, *Last Train from Berlin* (New York, 1943), p. 123.
23. Klemperer, *Ich will Zeugnis ablegen bis zum letztem*, p. 691 (30 November 1941).
24. Hassell, *Vom Andern Deutschland*, p. 234 (30 November 1941) (Hassell, *The von Hassell Diaries 1938–1944*, p. 202 (30 November 1941)).
25. Boberach (ed.), *Meldungen aus dem Reich*, vol. 8, p. 3060, document 243 (4 December 1941).
26. Kleindienst (ed.), *Sei tausendmal gegrüßt*, CD Rom (22 November 1941).
27. *True To Type*, p. 14 (29 November 1941).
28. Moorhouse, *Berlin at War*, pp. 253 and 255.
29. Bähr and Bähr (eds), *Kriegsbriefe Gefallener Studenten, 1939–1945*, p. 98 (21 November 1941).
30. Moorhouse, *Berlin at War*, pp. 258–9.
31. As cited in Stern, *Hitler*, p. 23.
32. As cited in Moorhouse, *Berlin at War*, p. 260.
33. The Iron Cross Second Class and the Iron Cross First Class preceded the Knight's Cross. The Knight's Cross had numerous sub-categories and was followed by the Order of the Grand Cross (issued only to Hermann Göring).
Norman Davies, *No Simple Victory. World War* II *in Europe, 1939–1945* (London, 2006), p. 267.
34. Neitzel and Welzer, *Soldaten*, p. 40. For a contrasting insight into death and sacrifice in the Finnish war experience, see Ville Kivimäki and Tuomas Tepora, 'Meaningless Death or Regenerating Sacrifice? Violence and Social Cohesion in Wartime Finland', in Tiina Kinnunen and Ville Kivimäki (eds), *Finland in World War* II. *History, Memory, Interpretations* (Boston, MA, 2012), pp. 233–75.
35. Skorzeny, *Skorzeny's Special Missions*, p. 24.
36. Schäufler, *Panzer Warfare on the Eastern Front*, p. 46.
37. Nagorski, *The Greatest Battle*, p. 240. Indeed, largely owing to the rapid Soviet operations from 1943 onwards, as well as the Red Army's frequent desecration of German graves, of the official 3.1 million German soldiers who died fighting the Soviet Union in the Second World War only 200,000 have marked graves. Moorhouse, *Berlin at War*, p. 257.
38. As cited in Moorhouse, *Berlin at War*, p. 256.
39. Jay W. Baird, *To Die For Germany. Heroes in the Nazi Pantheon* (Bloomington, IN, 1990), pp. 232–3.

40. Jörg Echternkamp, 'Violence Given Free Rein', in Militärgeschichtlichtlichen Forschungsamt (ed.), *Germany and the Second World War, vol.* IX/1: *German Wartime Society 1939–1945: Politicization, Disintegration, and the Struggle for Survival* (Oxford, 2008), p. 50.
41. Victor Klemperer, *Language of the Third Reich* (London, 2006), p. 114.
42. As cited in Moorhouse, *Berlin at War*, pp. 256–7.
43. Jörg Echternkamp, 'Hitler's Charismatic Rule, and the Führer Myth', in Militärgeschichtlichtlichen Forschungsamt (ed.), *Germany and the Second World War, volume* IX/1: *German Wartime Society 1939–1945: Politicization, Disintegration, and the Struggle for Survival* (Oxford, 2008), pp. 25–31.
44. For more on the concept of Hitler's 'charismatic authority', see Ian Kershaw, '"Working Towards the Führer": Reflections on the Nature of the Hitler Dictatorship', in Ian Kershaw and Moshe Lewin (eds), *Stalinism and Nazism. Dictatorships in Comparison* (Cambridge, 2003), pp. 100–1.
45. Sebastian Haffner, *Germany Jekyll and Hyde. A Contemporary Account of Nazi Germany* (London, 2008), p. 48.
46. Kroener, 'The Winter Crisis of 1941–1942', p. 1016. See also Gareis, *Kampf und Ende der Fränkisch-Sudetendeutschen 98. Infanterie-Division*, p. 166.
47. Overy, *Russia's War*, p. 119.
48. Kroener, 'The Winter Crisis of 1941–1942', p. 1018.
49. Mark-Alan, *White Coats under Fire*, p. 108.
50. Kroener, 'The Winter Crisis of 1941–1942', p. 1018.
51. Knappe, *Soldat*, p. 232.
52. Ernst Kern, *War Diary 1941–45*, p. 21.
53. The medal was awarded to soldiers who fought in the east for at least fourteen days between 15 November 1941 and 15 April 1942. Agustin Sáiz, *Deutsche Soldaten. Uniforms, Equipment and Personal Items of the German Soldier 1939–45* (Madrid, 2008), p. 242; Showalter, *Hitler's Panzers*, p. 189.
54. Gareis, *Kampf und Ende der Fränkisch-Sudetendeutschen 98. Infanterie-Division*, p. 150.
55. Bamm, *The Invisible Flag*, pp. 53–4.
56. Haape, *Moscow Tram Stop*, p. 28.
57. As cited in Robert Kershaw, *War Without Garlands. Operation Barbarossa 1941/42* (New York, 2000), p. 78.
58. Edmund Blandford (ed.), *Under Hitler's Banner. Serving the Third Reich* (Edison, NJ, 2001), p. 89.
59. Davies, *No Simple Victory*, p. 260.
60. Ehrenburg, *The Tempering of Russia*, p. 89.
61. Knappe, *Soldat*, p. 232.
62. Robbins Landon and Leitner (eds), *Diary of a German Soldier*, p. 114 (13 October 1941).
63. F. and L. Schober, *Briefe von der Front*, p. 132 (14 November 1941).

64. Humburg, *Das Gesicht des Krieges*, p. 152 (16 November 1941).
65. M. Jones, *The Retreat*, p. 96.
66. Will, *Tagebuch eines Ostfront-Kämpfers*, p. 28 (8 November 1941).
67. Cecil, *Hitler's Decision to Invade Russia 1941*, p. 134. See also Fest, *Hitler*, p. 647.
68. As cited in M. Jones, *The Retreat*, p. 77.
69. Günther, *Hot Motors, Cold Feet*, pp. 207–8.
70. Buchbender and Sterz (eds), *Das andere Gesicht des Krieges*, p. 87 (17 November 1941).
71. Haape, *Moscow Tram Stop*, p. 187.
72. Fröhlich (ed.), *Die Tagebücher von Joseph Goebbels. Teil* II, *Band* 2, p. 357 (24 November 1941). For more on Dietrich's announcement, see Stahel, *Operation Typhoon*, pp. 98–106. For Goebbels' own role in eliciting unrealistic expectations about the progress of the war in November, see the comments by Kleist cited in A. Clark, *Barbarossa*, p. 178.
73. Buchbender and Sterz (eds), *Das andere Gesicht des Krieges*, p. 87 (26 November 1941).
74. Scheuer, *Briefe aus Russland*, p. 51 (30 November 1941).
75. Schäufler, *Panzer Warfare on the Eastern Front*, p. 46.
76. As cited in M. Jones, *The Retreat*, p. 102.
77. Ingeborg Ochsenknecht, *'Als ob der Schnee alles zudeckte'. Eine Krankenschwester erinnert sich an ihren Kriegseinsatz an der Ostfront* (Berlin, 2005), p. 89.
78. Philip Jordan, *Russian Glory* (London, 1942), pp. 115–16.
79. Ehrenburg, *The Tempering of Russia*, pp. 88–9.
80. Neitzel, *Tapping Hitler's Generals*, p. 214, document 124 (14–15 Feburary 1945).
81. Haldane, *Russian Newsreel*, pp. 113–14.
82. Günther, *Hot Motors, Cold Feet*, p. 207.
83. W. P. Reese, *A Stranger to Myself*, p. 36.
84. Scheuer, *Briefe aus Russland*, p. 51 (30 November 1941).
85. As cited in Thomas Kühne, *Kameradschaft. Die Soldaten des nationalsozialistischen Krieges und das 20. Jahrhundert* (Konstanz, 2006), p. 168.
86. Degrelle, *Campaign in Russia*, p. 25.
87. As cited in M. Jones, *The Retreat*, p. 96.
88. Ernst Kern, *War Diary 1941–45*, p. 22.
89. Rzhevskaia, 'Roads and Days', p. 63.
90. *Ibid.*
91. *Ibid.*
92. He flew his Ju-87 on 2,530 sorties and was credited with the destruction of 519 enemy tanks and 800 vehicles. By the end of the war, he had won the

Knight's Cross of the Iron Cross with Golden Oak Leaves, Swords and Diamonds as well as numerous other awards. Friedemann Bedürftig, *Drittes Reich und Zweiter Weltkrieg. Das Lexikon* (Munich, 2002), p. 433.

93. Rudel, *Stuka Pilot*, p. 49.
94. Stahlberg, *Bounden Duty*, p. 181.
95. Indeed, as Sönke Neitzel and Harald Welzer wrote of German POW conversations: 'Stories about "nerves being shot" needed to be told via a surrogate in order to be deemed acceptable. Communicatively, showing any sort of weakness seems to have been perceived as dangerous ... Today, we talk about soldiers' suffering post-traumatic stress disorder, but this diagnosis did not exist during World War II. The military frame of reference left no room for physical weakness – to say nothing of psychological vulnerability. In this respect, no matter how thoroughly they were integrated into the total group of their commando or unit, soldiers were psychologically alone.' Neitzel and Welzer, *Soldaten*, p. 161.
96. Gerhard Bopp, *Kriegstagebuch. Aufzeichnungen Während des* II. *Weltkrieges 1940–1943* (Hamburg, 2005), p. 139 (19 November 1941).
97. Fröhlich (ed.), *Die Tagebücher von Joseph Goebbels. Teil* II, *Band 1*, p. 444 (18 September 1941). See also Magnus Koch, *Fahnenfluchten. Deserteure der Wehrmacht in Zweiten Weltkrieg: Lebenswege und Entscheidungen* (Paderborn, 2008).
98. Stahel, *Operation Typhoon*, p. 203; Gilbert, *The Second World War*, p. 257.
99. '6. Panzer Division Ia KTB 1.12.1941–31.3.1942', BA-MA RH 27-6/20, p. 311 (1 December 1941).
100. Bähr and Bähr (eds), *Die Stimme des Menschen*, p. 125 (17 November 1941).
101. Zhukov, *The Memoirs of Marshal Zhukov*, p. 343.
102. Bähr and Bähr (eds), *Kriegsbriefe Gefallener Studenten, 1939–1945*, pp. 88–9 (1–3 December 1941)
103. Günther, *Hot Motors, Cold Feet*, p. 190.
104. Dollinger (ed.), *Kain, wo ist dein Bruder?*, p. 110 (22 November 1941).
105. Bamm, *The Invisible Flag*, p. 51.
106. Alexander and Kunze (eds), *Eastern Inferno*, p. 121 (28 October 1941).
107. von Moltke, *Letters to Freya*, p. 177 (5 November 1941).
108. Bähr and Bähr (eds), *Kriegsbriefe Gefallener Studenten, 1939–1945*, pp. 86–7 (1–3 December 1941)
109. Carruthers (ed.), *The Wehrmacht Last Witnesses*, pp. 50–1.
110. *Ibid.*, pp. 49–50.
111. W. P. Reese, *A Stranger to Myself*, p. 137.
112. Bamm, *The Invisible Flag*, p. 53.

113. *Ibid.*
114. See Carl von Clausewitz, *On War*, eds and trans. Michael Howard and Peter Paret (New York, 1993) p. 639.
115. 'Kriegstagebuch Nr.1 2.Panzerarmee Band III vom 1.11.1941 bis 26.12.41', BA-MA RH 21-2/244, fol. 189 (2 December 1941).
116. von Bock, *War Diary*, p. 377 (2 December 1941).
117. Hürter (ed.), *Ein deutscher General an der Ostfront*, p. 116 (1 December 1941).
118. Guderian, *Panzer Leader*, p. 257.
119. 'KTB 3rd Pz. Div. vom 19.9.41 bis 6.2.42', BA-MA RH 27-3/15, p. 356 (4 December 1941).
120. Garden and Andrew (eds), *The War Diaries of a Panzer Soldier*, p. 60 (4 December 1941).
121. von Bock, *War Diary*, p. 380 (4 December 1941).
122. Guderian, *Panzer Leader*, p. 258.
123. Dankowo may have been mis-identified or spelled incorrectly in the German record because there is no record of a Russian town by this name in the area. 'Kriegstagebuch Nr.1 2.Panzerarmee Band III vom 1.11.1941 bis 26.12.41', BA-MA RH 21-2/244, fol. 212 (5 December 1941).
124. *Ibid.*, fols 212–214.
125. 'KTB 3rd Pz. Div. I.b 19.5.41–6.2.42', BA-MA RH 27-3/218 (5 December 1941). This war diary has no folio stamped page numbers so references must be located using the date.
126. Department of the US Army (ed.), *Military Improvisations during the Russian Campaign*, pp. 103–4.
127. 'Kriegstagebuch Nr.2 XXXXVII.Pz.Korps. Ia 23.9.1941–31.12.1941', BA-MA RH 24-47/258 (1 December 1941).
128. 'Armeeoberkommando 2. I.a KTB Teil.2 19.9.41–16.12.41', BA-MA RH 20-2/207, pp. 147 and 150 (1 December 1941).
129. Robbins Landon and Leitner (eds), *Diary of a German Soldier*, p. 125 (2 December 1941).
130. von Bock, *War Diary*, p. 380 (3 December 1941). See also Stahl, 'Generaloberst Rudolf Schmidt', p. 221.
131. 'Armeeoberkommando 2. I.a KTB Teil.2 19.9.41–16.12.41', BA-MA RH 20-2/207, p. 162 (5 December 1941).
132. Guderian, *Panzer Leader*, pp. 258–9.
133. *Ibid.*, p. 259.
134. Halder, *KTB* III, p. 302 (5 December 1941).
135. Guderian, *Panzer Leader*, p. 259.
136. von Bock, *War Diary*, p. 381 (5 December 1941).
137. Hürter (ed.), *Ein deutscher General an der Ostfront*, pp. 116–17 (4 December 1941).

10 To the gates of Moscow

1. Alan Clark concluded: 'it was essential that Kluge attack with all his strength against the Russian centre, or the whole offensive was in danger of withering away'. A. Clark, *Barbarossa*, p. 176. Similarly, Robert Forczyk suggested that Kluge's actions 'robbed Typhoon's final phase of any chance of success'. Robert Forczyk, *Moscow 1941. Hitler's First Defeat* (Oxford, 2006), p. 79.
2. Portraying Kluge as doddering and indecisive, Albert Seaton wrote: 'In vain did Hoepner telephone von Kluge day after day asking him to start his attack to the west of Moscow from the area of the Nara. For some unknown reason von Kluge was slow to act, as he repeatedly talked the matter over with Blumentritt and von Bock.' Seaton, *The Russo-German War 1941–45*, pp. 206–7.
3. Blumentritt, 'Moscow', p. 58.
4. Richard Lamb wrote of Kluge: 'The more intelligent Kluge had been opposed to an unsupported armoured advance on Moscow, realizing better than Hitler and his superiors the inherent dangers, and perhaps mindful of the critical moments the year before around Arras when Rommel's tanks had advanced too far without infantry support.' Richard Lamb, 'Kluge', in Correlli Barnett (ed.), *Hitler's Generals* (London, 1989), pp. 402–3.
5. Glantz, *Barbarossa*, pp. 175–6.
6. von Bock, *War Diary*, p. 377 (1 December 1941).
7. 'A.O.K.4 Ia Anlagen B 20 zum Kriegstagebuch Nr.9. 28.11.–3.12.41', BA-MA RH 20-4, fol. 155 (1 December 1941).
8. 'Gen.Kdo.LVII.Pz.Korps KTB Nr.2 vom 1.11.41–31.12.41', BA-MA RH 24-57-3, Fol. 40 (1 December 1941).
9. 'Kriegstagebuch 19.Panzer-Division Abt.Ib für die Zeit vom 1.6.1941–31.12.1942', BA-MA RH 27-19/23, fol. 82 (1 December 1941).
10. Förster, 'Volunteers for the European Crusade against Bolshevism', pp. 1058–63.
11. Guderian, *Panzer Leader*, pp. 258–9.
12. Mawdsley, *December 1941*, p. 87, fn. 18.
13. von Bock, *War Diary*, p. 377 (1 December 1941).
14. *Ibid.* See also 'Kriegstagebuch Nr.1 (Band December 1941) des Oberkommandos der Heeresgruppe Mitte', BA-MA RH 19-II/122, fols 7–8 (1 December 1941).
15. von Bock, *War Diary*, pp. 375–6 (1 December 1941).
16. Halder, *KTB* III, p. 322 (1 December 1941).
17. See my discussion of Halder in Stahel, *Operation Barbarossa and Germany's Defeat in the East.*
18. von Bock, *War Diary*, p. 378 (2 December 1941).

19. '6. Panzer Division Ia KTB 1.12.1941–31.3.1942', BA-MA RH 27-6/20, p. 312 (1 December 1941).
20. 'Anlagen zum Kriegstagebuch Tagesmeldungen Bd.I 1.11–31.12.41', BA-MA RH 21-3/71, fol. 216 (1 December 1941).
21. von Bock, *War Diary*, p. 378 (2 December 1941).
22. As cited in Mawdsley, *December 1941*, p. 88.
23. Halder, *KTB* III, p. 323 (2 December 1941).
24. As cited in Overy, *Russia's War*, p. 117.
25. von Bock, *War Diary*, p. 378 (2 December 1941).
26. 'Anlagen zum Kriegstagebuch Tagesmeldungen Bd.I 1.11–31.12.41', BA-MA RH 21-3/71, fol. 235 (4 December 1941). See also reports in 'Kriegstagebuch Nr.3 der 7.Panzer-Division Führungsabteilung 1.6.1941–9.5.1942', BA-MA RH 27-7/46, fol. 227 (3 December 1941).
27. Halder, *KTB* III, p. 326 (4 December 1941).
28. Bopp, *Kriegstagebuch*, p. 140 (3 December 1941). Bopp's published diary also includes a rare picture he took of one of the disabled British tanks (p. 140). For another soldier's report of seeing a British tank in early December 1941, see Lange, *Tagebücher aus dem Zweiten Weltkrieg*, p. 100 (2 December 1941).
29. As cited in Luther, *Barbarossa Unleashed*, p. 647.
30. Will, *Tagebuch eines Ostfront-Kämpfers*, p. 32 (29 November 1941). On American tank deliveries to the Soviet Union in 1941, see van Tuyll, *Feeding the Bear*, pp. 53 and 167, table 22.
31. Ministry of Foreign Affairs of the USSR (ed.), *Stalin's Correspondence*, pp. 34–5, document 21 (22 November 1941).
32. Downing, *Sealing their Fate*, pp. 269–70; Beaumont, *Comrades in Arms*, pp. 70–1.
33. Gilbert, *The Second World War*, p. 270.
34. 'Kriegstagebuch Nr.1 (Band December 1941) des Oberkommandos der Heeresgruppe Mitte', BA-MA RH 19-II/122, fol. 13 (2 December 1941).
35. 'Kriegstagebuch Nr.3. der Führungsabteilung (Ia) des Gen. Kdo. (mot.) XXXX.Pz. Korps vom 31.05.1941–26.12.1941', BA-MA RH 24-40/18 (2 December 1941).
36. As cited in M. Jones, *The Retreat*, pp. 126–7.
37. '2. Panzer Division KTB Nr.6 Teil I. Vom 15.6.41–3.4.42', BA-MA RH 27-2/21 (2 and 4 December 1941).
38. 'Kriegstagebuch Nr.3. der Führungsabteilung (Ia) des Gen. Kdo. (mot.) XXXX.Pz. Korps vom 31.05.1941–26.12.1941', BA-MA RH 24-40/18 (1 December 1941).
39. Zetterling and Frankson, *The Drive on Moscow, 1941*, p. 206.
40. Anatoly Golovchansky, Valentin Osipov, Anatoly Prokopenko, Ute Daniel and Jürgen Reulecke (eds), *'Ich will raus aus diesem Wahnsinn'. Deutsche Briefe von*

der Ostfront 1941–1945 Aus sowjetischen Archiven (Hamburg, 1993), p. 47 (4 December 1941).

41. Robert Forczyk, *Panzerjäger vs KV-1. Eastern Front 1941–43* (Oxford, 2012), p. 28.
42. Terry Gander, *The German 88. The Most Famous Gun of the Second World War* (Barnsley, 2012), p. 146.
43. Forczyk, *Panzerjäger vs KV-1*, p. 34.
44. 'Anlage zum KTB Panzer Gruppe 4: 11.11.41–5.12.41', BA-MA RH 21-4/36, fols 143–144 (2 December 1941).
45. *Ibid.*, fol. 134 (3 December 1941). Hoepner's communication is reproduced at length in Bellamy, *Absolute War*, pp. 317–18. The English translation here, however, appears to have come from a Russian source rather than direct from a German source.
46. von Bock, *War Diary*, p. 378 (2 December 1941); Halder, *KTB* III, p. 324 (3 December 1941).
47. von Bock, *War Diary*, pp. 378–9 (3 December 1941).
48. Buchbender and Sterz (eds), *Das andere Gesicht des Krieges*, p. 90 (7 December 1941).
49. 'Kriegstagebuch Nr.1 (Band December 1941) des Oberkommandos der Heeresgruppe Mitte', BA-MA RH 19-II/122, fol. 15 (3 December 1941); 'Gen. Kdo.LVII.Pz.Korps KTB Nr.2 vom 1.11.41–31.12.41', BA-MA RH 24-57-3, fol. 46 (3 December 1941).
50. 'Kriegstagebuch Nr.1 (Band December 1941) des Oberkommandos der Heeresgruppe Mitte', BA-MA RH 19-II/122, fol. 19 (3 December 1941).
51. *Ibid.*, p. 12 (2 December 1941).
52. According to John Keegan: 'Legend has it that German troops were to approach close enough in the days following [the capture of Krasnaya Polyana] to see the towers of the Kremlin gleaming in a burst of evening sunshine'. John Keegan, *Barbarossa. Invasion of Russia 1941* (New York, 1971), p. 151.
53. As cited in M. Jones, *The Retreat*, p. 117. See also A. Clark, *Barbarossa*, p. 180.
54. Ernst Kris and Hans Speier, *German Radio Propaganda. Report on Home Broadcasts During the War* (London, 1944), p. 160.
55. About 350 of these novels were published in the 1950s alone.
56. Helmut Peitsch, 'Towards a History of "Vergangenheitsbewältigung": East and West German War Novels of the 1950s', *Monatshefte* 87(3) (1995): 287–308.
57. According to Heinz Magenheimer: 'It can also be argued that the attempts by several senior commanders to seize the ultimate chance and force a decision against an exhausted opponent with the "last battalion" were not completely hopeless.' Heinz Magenheimer, *Hitler's War. Germany's Key Strategic Decisions 1940–1945* (London, 1999), p. 114.
58. Haape, *Moscow Tram Stop*, p. 206.
59. As cited in M. Jones, *The Retreat*, p. 116.

60. Schäufler, *Panzer Warfare on the Eastern Front*, p. 46.
61. Werth, *Russia at War 1941–1945*, p. 254.
62. Frisch, *Condemned to Live*, p. 84.
63. von Bock, *War Diary*, pp. 378–9 (3 December 1941).
64. Samuel W. Mitcham Jr, *The Men of Barbarossa. Commanders of the German Invasion of Russia, 1941* (Newbury, 2009), p. 38; Alfred W. Turney, *Disaster at Moscow. Von Bock's Campaigns 1941–1942* (Albuquerque, NM, 1970), p. 6.
65. Nebe reported that cooperation with Army Group Centre was 'excellent'. Browning, *The Origins of the Final Solution*, p. 260. Even before the invasion of Poland, Bock learned from Hitler himself of the special role of the SS in wartime. As Bock told Fabian von Schlabrendorff: 'At the same time Hitler informed the generals that he would proceed against the Poles after the end of the campaign with relentless vigour ... He required of the army that the generals should not interfere in these matters but restrict themselves to their military duties.' Gerald Reitlinger, *The SS. Alibi of a Nation 1922–1945* (London, 1981), pp. 124–5. For more on the activites of *Einsatzgruppe B*, see Christian Gerlach, 'Die Einsatzgruppe B 1941/42', in Peter Klein (ed.), *Die Einsatzgruppen in der besetzten Sowjetunion 1941/42. Die Tätigkeits- und Lageberichte des Chefs der Sicherheitspolizei und des SD* (Berlin, 1997), pp. 52–70.
66. Martin Holler, 'Extending the Genocidal Program: Did Otto Ohlendorf Initiate the Systematic Extermination of Soviet "Gypsies"?' in Alex J. Kay, Jeff Rutherford and David Stahel (eds), *Nazi Policy on the Eastern Front, 1941. Total War, Genocide and Radicalization* (Rochester, NY, 2012), p. 276.
67. von Bock, *War Diary*, pp. 385–6 (8 December 1941).
68. *Ibid.*, p. 378 (3 December 1941).
69. *Ibid.*, p. 379 (3 December 1941). For a detailed account of Bock's converation with Jodl, see 'Kriegstagebuch Nr.1 (Band December 1941) des Oberkommandos der Heeresgruppe Mitte', BA-MA RH 19-II/122, fols 17–18 (3 December 1941).
70. 'Kriegstagebuch Nr.1 (Band December 1941) des Oberkommandos der Heeresgruppe Mitte', BA-MA RH 19-II/122, fol. 18 (3 December 1941). See also Halder, *KTB* III, p. 324 (3 December 1941).
71. Georg Meyer (ed.), *Generalfeldmarschall Wilhelm Ritter von Leeb. Tagebuchaufzeichnungen und Lagebeurteilungen aus zwei Weltkriegen* (Stuttgart, 1976), p. 403 (3 December 1941).
72. Jay W. Baird, *The Mythical World of Nazi War Propaganda, 1939–1945* (Ann Arbor, MI, 1974), p. 169.
73. Mawdsley, *December 1941*, pp. 85–6.
74. Halder, *KTB* III, p. 327 (4 December 1941).
75. *Ibid.*, p. 328 (5 December 1941).
76. For German expectations, see Luther, *Barbarossa Unleashed*, p. 97.

77. Rolf-Dieter Müller, 'World Power Status through the Use of Poison Gas? German Preparations for Chemical Warfare, 1919–1945', in Wilhelm Deist (ed.), *The German Military in the Age of Total War* (Leamington Spa, 1985), pp. 192–5.
78. Halder, *KTB* III, p. 376 (7 January 1942).
79. Gilbert, *The Second World War*, p. 263.
80. As cited in M. Jones, *The Retreat*, p. 120.
81. 'Anlage zum KTB Pz.Gruppe 4 Meldungen von unten 16.11.41–5.12.41', BA-MA RH 21-4/40, fol. 20 (4 December 1941).
82. *Ibid.*, fol. 15 (5 December 1941).
83. 'Kriegstagebuch Nr.3. des XXXXVI.Pz.Korps vom 24.08.41–31.12.41', BA-MA RH 24-46/21, fol. 160 (4 December 1941).
84. 'Kriegstagebuch Nr.7 des Kdos. Der 1.Panzer-Div. 20.9.41–12.4.42', BA-MA 27-1/58, fol. 66 (4 December 1941).
85. 'Anlagen zum Kriegstagebuch Tagesmeldungen Bd.I 1.11–31.12.41', BA-MA RH 21-3/71, fol. 246 (5 December 1941).
86. Halder, *KTB* III, p. 326 (4 December 1941).
87. As cited in Bücheler, *Hoepner*, p. 160.
88. *Ibid.*
89. *Ibid.*
90. Walther Fischer von Weikersthal, the aforementioned commander of the 35th Infantry Division, was replaced by Roman on 1 December 1941.
91. 'Kriegstagebuch Nr.3. der Führungsabteilung (Ia) des Gen. Kdo. (mot.) XXXX.Pz. Korps vom 31.05.1941-26.12.1941', BA-MA RH 24-40/18 (5 December 1941).
92. 'Anlage zum KTB Panzer Gruppe 4: 11.11.41–5.12.41', BA-MA RH 21-4/36, fol. 132 (5 December 1941).
93. Bähr and Bähr (eds), *Kriegsbriefe Gefallener Studenten, 1939–1945*, p. 68 (1 December 1941).
94. 'Kriegstagebuch Nr.3. des XXXXVI.Pz.Korps vom 24.08.41–31.12.41', BA-MA RH 24-46/21, fol. 162 (5 December 1941).
95. '20.Pz.Div. KTB vom 21.10.41 bis 30.12.41 Band Ia2.', BA-MA RH 27-20/26, fol. 90 (5 December 1941).
96. 'Anlagen zum Kriegstagebuch Tagesmeldungen Bd.I 1.11–31.12.41', BA-MA RH 21-3/71, fol. 252 (5 December 1941); Steiger, *Armour Tactics in the Second World War*, p. 104.
97. 'Anlage zum KTB Pz.Gruppe 4 Meldungen von unten 16.11.41–5.12.41', BA-MA RH 21-4/40, fol. 15 (5 December 1941).
98. 'Anlagen zum Kriegstagebuch Tagesmeldungen Bd.I 1.11–31.12.41', BA-MA RH 21-3/71, fol. 247 (5 December 1941).
99. von Bock, *War Diary*, p. 379 (3 December 1941).
100. H. Reinhardt, 'Panzer-Gruppe 3 in der Schlacht von Moskau und ihre Erfahrungen im Rückzug', p. 3.

101. Mawdsley, *December 1941*, p. 125.
102. 'Kriegstagebuch No.2 der 36. Inf. Div. (mot) 22.9.41–5.12.41', BA-MA RH 26-36/9 (5 December 1941). The diary has no folio stamped page numbers so references must be located using the date.
103. 'Kriegstagebuch Nr.1 (Band December 1941) des Oberkommandos der Heeresgruppe Mitte', BA-MA RH 19-II/122, fol. 31 (5 December 1941); H. Reinhardt, 'Panzer-Gruppe 3 in der Schlacht von Moskau und ihre Erfahrungen im Rückzug', p. 3.
104. As cited in M. Jones, *The Retreat*, p. 135.
105. von Bock, *War Diary*, p. 381 (5 December 1941).
106. Halder, *KTB* III, p. 328 (5 December 1941).
107. Skorzeny, *Skorzeny's Special Missions*, p. 24.
108. Sulzberger, *A Long Row of Candles*, p. 157.

Conclusion

1. As cited in Robert M. Citino, *Death of the Wehrmacht. The German Campaigns of 1942* (Lawrence, KS, 2007) p. 48.
2. *Ibid.*
3. Görlitz, *Paulus and Stalingrad*, p. 133.
4. Mihail Sebastian, *Journal, 1935–1944* (London, 2003), p. 448 (3 December 1941).
5. Murray, *Military Adaptation in War*, p. 257.
6. This is the famous thesis espoused by the renowned British historian Ian Kershaw, see Kershaw, 'Working Towards the Führer'.
7. Alan Clark, not unjustifiably, referred to the Orsha conference as 'one of the decisive moments in the history of the German Army'. A. Clark, *Barbarossa*, p. 168.
8. Ziemke, 'Franz Halder at Orsha', pp. 175–6.
9. Mawdsley, *Thunder in the East*, p. 111.
10. As cited in Bücheler, *Hoepner*, p. 157.
11. Many of these offensives belong to what David Glantz refers to as the 'forgotten battles'. See David M. Glantz, *Forgotten Battles of the German–Soviet War (1941–1945). vol. 1: The Summer–Fall Campaign (22 June–4 December 1941)* (privately published study by David M. Glantz, 1999); David M. Glantz, 'Forgotten Battles', in The Military Book Club (ed.), *Slaughterhouse. The Encyclopedia of the Eastern Front* (New York, 2002), pp. 471–96.
12. Liddell Hart, *The Other Side of the Hill*, pp. 279–80.
13. Hoth, *Panzer-Operationen*, p. 137.
14. After the First World War, German right-wing politicians, including Hitler, propagated the so-called *Dolchstoßlegende* (the 'stab in the back myth'), which explained Germany's defeat in the war not as a military failing, but rather as a

result of Jews, communists and fifth columnists who successfully conspired to bring Germany down on the home front.

15. A. Clark, *Barbarossa*, p. 172.
16. Rokossovsky, *A Soldier's Duty*, p. 87.
17. Overmans, *Deutsche militärische Verluste im Zweiten Weltkrieg*, p. 278.
18. Halder, *KTB* III, p. 345 (14 December 1941).
19. *Ibid.*, p. 306 (23 November 1941).
20. Glantz and House, *When Titans Clashed*, pp. 292 and 301.
21. As cited in David Irving, *Hitler's War*. vol. I (New York, 1977), p. 380.
22. Downing, *Sealing their Fate*, pp. 287–8.
23. Max Hastings, *Bomber Command* (London, 1993), p. 117.
24. As cited in Mawdsley, *December 1941*, p. 124.
25. Already on 22 November, Hitler had expressed to Goebbels both his confidence that Japan would soon actively join the war and that Germany would find itself fighting the United States. Fröhlich (ed.), *Die Tagebücher von Joseph Goebbels. Teil* II, *Band* 2, p. 339 (22 November 1941).
26. Downing, *Sealing their Fate*, p. 289.
27. Bähr and Bähr (eds), *Die Stimme des Menschen*, p. 177 (21 November 1941).
28. Ehrenburg, *Russia at War*, p. 78 (18 November 1941).
29. von Moltke, *Letters to Freya*, p. 187 (17 November 1941).

BIBLIOGRAPHY

Archival references

Bundesarchiv-Militärarchiv, Freiburg im Breisgau (BA-MA)

High Command of the Army

BA-MA RH/2-2670, 'Oberkommando des Heeres Generalstab des Heeres O.Qu.IV-Abt.Fr.H.Ost (II)'.

Army Group Centre

BA-MA RH 19-II/386, 'Kriegstagebuch Nr.1 (Band August 1941) des Oberkommandos der Heeresgruppe Mitte'.

BA-MA RH 19-II/387, 'Kriegstagebuch Nr.1 (Band November 1941) des Oberkommandos der Heeresgruppe Mitte'.

BA-MA RH 19-II/122, 'Kriegstagebuch Nr.1 (Band December 1941) des Oberkommandos der Heeresgruppe Mitte'.

Second Army

BA-MA RH 20-2/207, 'Armeeoberkommando 2. I.a KTB Teil.2 19.9.41–16.12.41'.

BA-MA RH 24-48/35, 'Kriegstagebuch XXXXVIII.Pz.Kps. Abt.Ia November 1941'.

BA-MA RH 27-9/4, '9.Pz.Div. KTB Ia vom 19.5.1941 bis 22.1.1942'.

Second Panzer Army

BA-MA RH 21-2/244, 'Kriegstagebuch Nr.1 2.Panzerarmee Band III vom 1.11.1941 bis 26.12.41'.

BA-MA RH 21-2/819, 'Kriegstagebuch der O.Qu.-Abt. Pz. A.O.K.2 von 21.6.41 bis 31.3.42'.

BA-MA RH 21-2/757, 'Verlustmeldungen 5.7.1941–25.3.1942'.

BA-MA RH 24-47/258, 'Kriegstagebuch Nr.2 XXXXVII.Pz.Korps. Ia 23.9.1941–31.12.1941'.

BA-MA RH 26-10/9, 'K.T.B. der 10.Inf.Div. (mot) 11.6.1941–29.12.1941'.

BA-MA RH 27-3/14, 'KTB 3rd Pz. Div. vom 16.8.40 bis 18.9.41'.

BA-MA RH 27-3/15, 'KTB 3rd Pz. Div. vom 19.9.41 bis 6.2.42'.

BA-MA RH 27-3/218, 'KTB 3rd Pz. Div. I.b 19.5.41–6.2.42'.

BA-MA RH 27-4/10, 'Kriegstagebuch 4.Panzer-Divison Führungsabtl. 26.5.41–31.3.42'.

BA-MA RH 27-18/69, '18. Panzer-Div- Ia Kriegstagebuch vom 20.10.41–13.12.41'.

Fourth Army

BA-MA RH 20-4, 'A.O.K.4 Ia Anlagen B 19 zum Kriegstagebuch Nr.9. 23.11.–27.11.41'.

BA-MA RH 20-4, 'A.O.K.4 Ia Anlagen B 20 zum Kriegstagebuch Nr.9. 28.11.–3.12.41'.

BA-MA RH 20-4, 'A.O.K.4 Ia Entwurf zum Kriegstagebuch Nr.9. 10.10.–3.12.41'.

Panzer Group 3

BA-MA Microfilm 59060, '3rd Pz. Gr. KTB Nr.2 1.9.41–31.10.41'.

BA-MA RH 21-3/71, 'Anlagen zum Kriegstagebuch Tagesmeldungen Bd.I 1.11-31.12.41'.

BA-MA RH 24-41/15, 'Anlagenband zum KTB XXXXI A.K. Ia 3.Verteidigung von Kalinin 15.10.41–20.11.41'.

BA-MA 27-1/58, 'Kriegstagebuch Nr.7 des Kdos. Der 1.Panzer-Div. 20.9.41–12.4.42'.

BA-MA RH 27-6/19, '6. Panzer Division KTB 16.9.1941–30.11.1941'.

BA-MA RH 27-6/20, '6. Panzer Division Ia KTB 1.12.1941–31.3.1942'.

BA-MA RH 27-7/46, 'Kriegstagebuch Nr.3 der 7.Panzer-Division Führungsabteilung 1.6.1941–9.5.1942'.

BA-MA RH 26-36/9, 'Kriegstagebuch No.2 der 36. Inf. Div. (mot) 22.9.41–5.12.41'.

Panzer Group 4

BA-MA RH 21-4/35, 'Anlage zum KTB Panzer Gruppe 4: 15.10.41–10.11.41'.

BA-MA RH 21-4/36, 'Anlage zum KTB Panzer Gruppe 4: 11.11.41–5.12.41'.

BA-MA RH 21-4/39, 'Anlage zum KTB Pz.Gruppe 4 Meldungen von unten 15.10.41–15.11.41'.
BA-MA RH 21-4/40, 'Anlage zum KTB Pz.Gruppe 4 Meldungen von unten 16.11.41–5.12.41'.
BA-MA RH 24-40/18, 'Kriegstagebuch Nr.3. der Führungsabteilung (Ia) des Gen. Kdo. (mot.) XXXX.Pz.Korps vom 31.05.1941–26.12.1941'.
BA-MA RH 24-46/21, 'Kriegstagebuch Nr.3. des XXXXVI.Pz.Korps vom 24.08.41–31.12.41'.
BA-MA RH 24-57-3, 'Gen.Kdo.LVII.Pz.Korps KTB Nr.2 vom 1.11.41–31.12.41'.
BA-MA RS 3-2/6, 'KTB SS 2nd Div. "*Das Reich*"'.
BA-MA RH 27-2/21, '2. Panzer Division KTB Nr.6 Teil I. Vom 15.6.41–3.4.42'.
BA-MA RH 27-5/29, '5. Panzer Division KTB Nur.8 vom 11.9.41–11.12.41'.
BA-MA RH 27-11/24, '11.Pz.Div. KTB Abt. Ia vom 22.10.41–24.1.42'.
BA-MA RH 27-19/23, 'Kriegstagebuch 19.Panzer-Division Abt. Ib für die Zeit vom 1.6.1941–31.12.1942'.
BA-MA RH 27-20/25, '20.Pz.Div. KTB vom 15.8.41 bis 20.10.41 Band Ia.'.
BA-MA RH 27-20/26, '20.Pz.Div. KTB vom 21.10.41 bis 30.12.41 Band Ia2.'.

Luftwaffe

BA-MA RL 200/17, 'Gen.v.Waldau, Chef Fü St Lw Persönl. Tagebuch, Auszugeweise'.

Ninth Army (1914)

BA-MA PH 5II/279, '9. Armee Kriegstagebuch 19.9.1914–31.12.1914'.

Museumsstiftung Post und Telekommunikation (MPT) Berlin

3.2002.7255: Elmar Lieb (8 November 1941).
3.2002.0912: Kurt Miethke (9 November 1941).
3.2008.1388: Karl Nünnighoff (11 and 26 November 1941).
3.2002.7184: Johannes Hamm (16 November 1941).

Primary and secondary sources

Adamczyk, Werner, *Feuer! An Artilleryman's Life on the Eastern Front.* Wilmington, NC, 1992.
Alexander, Christine and Mark Kunze (eds), *Eastern Inferno. The Journals of a German Panzerjäger on the Eastern Front, 1941–43*. Philadelphia, PA and Newbury, 2010.

Alexiev, Alex, 'Soviet Nationals in German Wartime Service, 1941–1945', Antonio Munoz (ed.), *Soviet Nationals in German Wartime Service 1941–1945*. n.p., 2007, pp. 5–44.

Allmayer-Beck, Johann Christoph, *'Herr Oberleitnant, det lohnt doch nicht!' Kriegserinnerinnerungen an die Jahre 1938 bis 1945*. Vienna, 2013.

Angrick, Andrej, *Besatzungspolitik und Massenmord. Die Einsatzgrtuppe D in der südlichen Sowjetunion 1941–1943*. Hamburg, 2003.

Arnold, Klaus J., *Die Wehrmacht und die Besatzungspolitik in den besetzten Gebieten der Sowjetunion. Kriegführung und Radikalisierung im 'Unternehmen Barbarossa'*. Berlin, 2005.

'Verbrecher aus eigener Intiative? Der 20. Juli und die Thesen Christians Gerlachs', *Geschichte in Wissenschaft und Unterricht* 53 (2002): 20–31.

Arnold, Klaus Jochen and Gerd C. Lübbers, 'The Meeting of the Staatssekretäre on 2 May 1941 and the Wehrmacht: A Document up for Discussion', *Journal of Contemporary History* 42(4) (2007): 613–26.

Axell, Albert, *Russia's Heroes 1941–45*. New York, 2001.

Stalin's War. Through the Eyes of his Commanders. London, 1997.

Baberowski, Jörg, 'Kriege in staatsfernen Räumen: Rußland und die Sowjetunion 1905–1950', in Dietrich Beyrau, Michael Hochgeschwender and Dieter Langewiesche (eds), *Formen des Krieges. Von der Antike bis zur Gegenwart*. Paderborn, 2007, pp. 291–309.

Bähr, Hans and Walter Bähr (eds), *Die Stimme des Menschen. Briefe und Aufzeichnungen aus der ganzen Welt. 1939–1945*. Munich, 1961.

(eds), *Kriegsbriefe Gefallener Studenten, 1939–1945*. Tübingen and Stuttgart, 1952.

Baird, Jay W., *Hitler's War Poets. Literature and Politics in the Third Reich*. Cambridge, 2008.

The Mythical World of Nazi War Propaganda, 1939–1945. Ann Arbor, MI, 1974.

To Die For Germany. Heroes in the Nazi Pantheon. Bloomington, IN, 1990.

Bamm, Peter, *The Invisible Flag*. New York, 1958.

Barber, John and Mark Harrison, *The Soviet Home Front 1941–1945. A Social and Economic History of the USSR in World War* II. London, 1991.

Bartoszewski, Wladyslaw, *Erich von dem Bach*. Warsaw, 1961.

Bartov, Omer, 'A View from Below. Survival, Cohesion and Brutality on the Eastern Front', in Bernd Wegner (ed.), *From Peace to War. Germany, Soviet Russia and the World, 1939–1941*. Oxford, 1997, pp. 325–40.

Hitler's Army. Soldiers, Nazis, and War in the Third Reich. Oxford, 1992.

The Eastern Front, 1941–45, German Troops and the Barbarisation of Warfare. London, 1985.

Baumgart, Winfried, *Deutsche Ostpolitik 1918. Von Brest-Litowsk bis zum Ende des Ersten Weltkreges*. Munich, 1966.

Beaulieu, Walter Chales de, *Generaloberst Erich Hoepner. Militärisches Porträt eines Panzer-Führers*. Neckargemünd, 1969.

Beaumont, Joan, *Comrades in Arms. British Aid to Russia 1941–1945*. London, 1980.

Becker, Hans, *Devil on my Shoulder*. London, 1957.

Bedürftig, Friedemann, *Drittes Reich und Zweiter Weltkrieg. Das Lexikon*. Munich, 2002.

Beese, Dieter, 'Kirche im Krieg. Evangelische Wehrmachtpfarrer und die Kriegführung der deutschen Wehrmacht', in Rolf-Dieter Müller and Hans-Erich Volkmann (eds), *Die Wehrmacht. Mythos und Realität*. Munich, 1999, pp. 486–502.

Beevor, Antony, *The Second World War*. New York, 2012.

Beevor, Antony and Luba Vinogradova (eds), *A Writer at War. Vasily Grossman with the Red Army 1941–1945*. New York, 2005.

Bell, P. M. H., *John Bull and the Bear. British Public Opinion, Foreign Policy and the Soviet Union 1941–1945*. London, 1990.

Bellamy, Chris, *Absolute War. Soviet Russia in the Second World War*. New York, 2007.

Below, Nicolaus von, *Als Hitlers Adjutant 1937–45*. Mainz, 1999.

Benz, Wigbert, *Der Hungerplan im 'Unternehmen Barbarossa'* 1941. Berlin, 2011.

Beorn, Waitman W., 'A Calculus of Complicity: the Wehrmacht, the Anti-Partisan War, and the Final Solution in White Russia, 1941–42', *Central European History* 44 (2011): 308–37.

Bergström, Christer, *Barbarossa. The Air Battle: July–December 1941*. Hersham, 2007.

Berkhoff, Karel C., *Harvest of Despair. Life and Death in Ukraine Under Nazi Rule*. Cambridge, MA, 2004.

Motherland in Danger. Soviet Propaganda During World War II. Cambridge, MA, 2012.

Bidermann, Gottlob Herbert, *In Deadly Combat. A German Solder's Memoir of the Eastern Front*. Lawrence, KS, 2000.

Bidlack, Richard, 'Propaganda and Public Opinion', in David R. Stone (ed.), *The Soviet Union at War 1941–1945*. Barnsley, 2010, pp. 45–68.

Birn, Ruth-Bettina, *Die Höheren SS- und Polizeiführer: Himmlers Vertreter im Reich und in den besetzten Gebieten*. Düsseldorf, 1986.

Bishop, Chris, *Hitler's Foreign Divisions. Foreign Volunteers in the Waffen-SS 1940–1945*. London, 2005.

Black, Jeremy, *War and the Cultural Turn*. Cambridge, 2012.

Blandford, Edmund (ed.), *Under Hitler's Banner. Serving the Third Reich*. Edison, NJ, 2001.

Blumentritt, Günther, 'Moscow', in William Richardson and Seymour Freidin (eds), *The Fatal Decisions*. London, 1956, pp. 29–75.

Von Rundstedt. The Soldier and the Man. London, 1952.

Boberach, Heinz (ed.), *Meldungen aus dem Reich. Die geheimen Lageberichte des Sicherheitsdienstes der SS 1938–1945*, 17 vols. Berlin, 1984.

Bock, Fedor von, *Generalfeldmarschall Fedor von Bock. The War Diary 1939–1945*, ed. Klaus Gerbet. Munich, 1996.

Boog, Horst, 'The Luftwaffe', in Militärgeschichtliches Forschungsamt (ed.), *Germany and the Second World War, vol.* IV*: The Attack on the Soviet Union*. Oxford, 1998, pp. 763–832.

Bopp, Gerhard, *Kriegstagebuch. Aufzeichnungen Während des* II. *Weltkrieges 1940–1943*. Hamburg, 2005.

Bor, Peter, *Gespräche mit Halder*. Wiesbaden, 1950.

Bourgeois, Daniel, 'Operation "Barbarossa" and Switzerland', in Bernd Wegner (ed.), *From Peace to War. Germany, Soviet Russia and the World, 1939–1941*. Oxford, 1997, pp. 593–610.

Braithwaite, Rodric, *Moscow 1941. A City and its People at War*. New York, 2006.

Brakel, Alexander, 'The Relationship between Soviet Partisans and the Civilian Population in Belorussia under German Occupation, 1941–4', in Ben Shepherd and Juliette Pattinson (eds), *War in a Twilight World. Partisans and Anti-Partisan Warfare in Eastern Europe, 1939–45*. New York, 2010, pp. 80–101.

Brandon, Ray and Wendy Lower (eds), *The Shoah in Ukraine. History, Testimony, Memorialization*. Bloomington, IN, 2008.

Broekmeyer, Marius, *Stalin, the Russians, and Their War 1941–1945*. London, 2004.

Brett-Smith, Richard, *Hitler's Generals*. London, 1976.

Browning, Christopher R., with contributions by Jürgen Matthäus, *The Origins of the Final Solution. The Evolution of Nazi Jewish Policy, September 1939–March 1942*. London, 2005.

Buchbender, Ortwin and Reinhold Sterz (eds), *Das andere Gesicht des Krieges. Deutsche Feldpostbriefe 1939–1945*. Munich, 1982.

Bücheler, Heinrich, *Hoepner. Ein deutsches Soldatenschicksal des 20. Jahrhunderts*. Herford, 1980.

Burleigh, Michael, *Germany Turns Eastwards. A Study of 'Ostforschung' in the Third Reich*. Cambridge, 1988.

The Third Reich. A New History. London, 2001.

Carell, Paul (aka Paul Karl Schmidt), *Hitler's War on Russia. The Story of the German Defeat in the East*. London, 1964.

Carlton, David, *Churchill and the Soviet Union*. New York, 2000.

Carrard, Philippe, *The French Who Fought for Hitler. Memories from the Outcasts*. Cambridge, 2010.

Carroll, Wallace, *Inside Warring Russia. An Eye-Witness Report on the Soviet Union's Battle: Compiled from Dispatches, Censored and Uncensored.* New York, 1942.

Carruthers, Bob (ed.), *The Wehrmacht Last Witnesses. First-hand Accounts from the Survivors of Hitler's Armed Forces.* London, 2010.

Cassidy, Henry, *Moscow Dateline, 1941–1943.* London, 1943.

Cecil, Robert, *Hitler's Decision to Invade Russia 1941.* London, 1975.

Chaney, Otto Preston, *Zhukov.* Norman, OK, 1996.

Chiari, Bernhard, *Alltag hinter der Front. Besatzung, Kollaboration und Widerstand in Weißrußland 1941–1944.* Düsseldorf, 1998.

Citino, Robert M., *Death of the Wehrmacht. The German Campaigns of 1942.* Lawrence, KS, 2007.

The German Way of War. From the Thirty Years' War to the Third Reich. Lawrence, KS, 2005.

The Wehrmacht Retreats. Fighting a Lost War, 1943. Lawrence, KS, 2012.

Clark, Alan, *Barbarossa. The Russian–German Conflict 1941–1945.* London, 1996.

Clark, Christopher, *Iron Kingdom. The Rise and Downfall of Prussia 1600–1947.* London and New York, 2006.

Clausewitz, Carl, von, *On War*, eds and trans. Michael Howard and Peter Paret. New York, 1993.

Clements, Jonathan, *Mannerheim. President, Soldier, Spy.* London, 2009.

Cooper, Matthew, *The Phantom War. The German Struggle Against Soviet Partisans 1941–1944.* London, 1979.

Corum, James S., *The Roots of Blitzkrieg. Hans von Seecht and German Military Reform.* Lawrence, KS, 1992.

Wolfram von Richthofen. Master of the German Air War. Lawrence, KS, 2008.

Creveld, Martin van, *Fighting Power. German and US Army Performance, 1939–1945.* Westport, CT, 1982.

Supplying War. Logistics from Wallenstein to Patton. Cambridge, 1984.

Cumins, Keith, *Cataclysm. The War on the Eastern Front 1941–1945.* Solihull, 2011.

Curilla, Wolfgang, *Die deutsche Ordnungspolizei und der Holocaust im Baltikum und in Weissrussland 1941–1944.* Paderborn, 2006.

Dallin, Alexander, *German Rule in Russia 1941–1945. A Study of Occupation Policies.* London, 1981.

Odessa, 1941–1944. A Case Study of Soviet Territory under Foreign Rule. Oxford, 1998.

Davies, Norman, *No Simple Victory. World War II in Europe, 1939–1945.* London, 2006.

Dawidowicz, Lucy, *The War Against the Jews 1933–45.* London, 1987.

Dean, Martin, *Collaboration in the Holocaust. Crimes of the Local Police in Belorussia and Ukraine 1941–1944*. London, 1999.

Degrelle, Léon, *Campaign in Russia. The Waffen SS on the Eastern Front*. Torrance, CA, 1985.

Deletant, Dennis, *Hitler's Forgotten Ally. Ion Antonescu and His Regime, Romania 1940–1944*. London, 2006.

Department of the US Army (ed.), *Effects of Climate on Combat in European Russia*. Washington, DC, 1952.

(ed.), *Military Improvisations during the Russian Campaign*. Washington, DC, 1951.

DeWitt, Kurt and Wilhelm Koll, 'The Bryansk Area', in John A. Armstrong (ed.), *Soviet Partisans in World War* II. Madison, WI, 1964, pp. 458–516.

Dietrich, Otto, *The Hitler I Knew. Memoirs of the Third Reich's Press Chief*. New York, 2010.

DiNardo, Richard L., *Mechanized Juggernaut or Military Anachronism. Horses and the German Army in World War* II. London, 1991.

Dollinger, Hans (ed.), *Kain, wo ist dein Burder? Was der Mensch im Zweiten Weltkrieg erleiden mußte: dokumentiert in Tagebüchern und Briefen*. Munich, 1983.

Domarus, Max, *Hitler. Speeches and Proclamations 1932–1945. The Chronicle of a Dictatorship, vol.* IV*: The Years 1941 to 1945*. Wauconda, IL, 2004.

Dowling, Tomothy C., *The Brusilov Offensive*. Bloomington, IN, 2008.

Downing, David, *Sealing their Fate. Twenty-Two Days that Decided the Second World War*. London, 2009.

Drabkin, Artem (ed.), *The Red Air Force at War. Barbarossa and the Retreat to Moscow. Recollections of Fighter Pilots on the Eastern Front*. Barnsley, 2007.

Dunn Jr, Walter S., *Stalin's Keys to Victory. The Rebirth of the Red Army in WW*II. Mechanicsburg, PA, 2006.

Dupuy, T. N. and Paul Martell, *Great Battles on the Eastern Front. The Soviet–German War, 1941–1945*. Indianapolis, IN, 1982.

Eberle, Henrik and Matthias Uhl (eds), *The Hitler Book. The Secret Dossier Prepared for Stalin from the Interrogations of Hitler's Personal Aides*. New York, 2005.

Echternkamp, Jörg, 'Hitler's Charismatic Rule, and the Führer Myth', in Militärgeschichtlichtlichen Forschungsamt (ed.), *Germany and the Second World War, vol.* IX/I*: German Wartime Society 1939–1945: Politicization, Disintegration, and the Struggle for Survival*. Oxford, 2008, pp. 25–31.

'Violence Given Free Rein', in Militärgeschichtlichtlichen Forschungsamt (ed.), *Germany and the Second World War, vol.* IX/I*: German Wartime Society 1939–1945: Politicization, Disintegration, and the Struggle for Survival*. Oxford, 2008, pp. 41–83.

Edele, Mark, '"What Are We Fighting For?" Loyalty in the Soviet War Effort, 1941–1945', *International Labor and Working-Class History* 84 (2013): 1–21.

Ehrenburg, Ilya, *Russia at War*. London, 1943.

The Tempering of Russia. New York, 1944.

Ehrenburg, Ilya and Konstantin Simonov, *In One Newspaper. A Chronicle of Unforgettable Years*. New York, 1985.

Eichholtz, Dietrich, *War for Oil. The Nazi Quest for an Oil Empire*. Dulles, VA, 2012.

Erickson, John, 'Soviet War Losses. Calculations and Controversies', in John Erickson and David Dilks (eds), *Barbarossa. The Axis and the Allies*. Edinburgh, 1998, pp. 255–77.

The Road to Stalingrad. Stalin's War with Germany, 2 vols. London, 1975.

Erickson, John and Ljubica Erickson, *Hitler versus Stalin. The Second World War on the Eastern Front in Photographs*. London, 2004.

Falkenhayn, Erich von, *General Headquarters 1914–1916 and its Critical Decisions*. London, 1919.

Fanning Jr, William J., 'The German War Economy 1941. A Study of Germany's Material and Manpower Problems in Relation to the Overall Military Effort', PhD dissertation, Texas Christian University, 1983.

Fest, Joachim, *Hitler*. Orlando, FL, 1974.

Forczyk, Robert, *Leningrad 1941–44. The Epic Siege*. Oxford, 2009.

Moscow 1941. Hitler's First Defeat. Oxford, 2006.

Panzerjäger vs KV-1. Eastern Front 1941–43. Oxford, 2012.

Förster, Jürgen, 'Germany', in I. C. B. Dear and M. R. D. Foot (eds), *The Oxford Companion to the Second World War*. Oxford, 1995, pp. 455–557.

'Hitlers Verbündete gegen die Sowjetunion 1941 und der Judenmord', in Christian Hartmann, Johannes Hürter and Ulrike Jureit (eds), *Verbrechen der Wehrmacht. Bilanz einer Debatte*. Munich, 2005, pp. 91–7.

'New Wine in Old Skins? The Wehrmacht and the War of "Weltanschauungen", 1941', in Wilhelm Deist (ed.), *The German Military in the Age of Total War*. Leamington Spa, 1985. pp. 304–22.

'Operation Barbarossa as a War of Conquest and Annihilation', in Militärgeschichtliches Forschungsamt (eds), *Germany and the Second World War, vol. IV: The Attack on the Soviet Union*. Oxford, 1998, pp. 481–521.

'Securing "Living-space"', in Militärgeschichtliches Forschungsamt (eds), *Germany and the Second World War, vol. IV: The Attack on the Soviet Union*. Oxford, 1998, pp. 1189–244.

'The German Army and the Ideological War against the Soviet Union', in Gerhard Hirschfeld (ed.), *The Policies of Genocide. Jews and Soviet Prisoners of War in Nazi Germany*. London, 1986, pp. 15–29.

'Volunteers for the European Crusade against Bolshevism', in Militärgeschichtliches Forschungsamt (ed.), *Germany and the Second World War, vol. IV: The Attack on the Soviet Union*. Oxford, 1998, pp. 1049–80.

'Zum Russlandbild der Militärs 1941–1945', in Hans-Erich Volkmann (ed.), *Das Russlandbild im Dritten Reich*. Cologne, 1994, pp. 141–63.

Frieser, Karl-Heinz, *The Blitzkrieg Legend. The 1940 Campaign in the West*. Annapolis, MD, 2005.

Frisch, Franz A. P., in association with Wilbur D. Jones, Jr, *Condemned to Live. A Panzer Artilleryman's Five-Front War*. Shippensburg, PA, 2000.

Fritzsche, Peter, *Life and Death in the Third Reich*. Cambridge, MA, 2008.

Fritz, Stephen G., *Frontsoldaten. The German Soldier in World War II*. Lexington, KY, 1995.

Ostkrieg. Hitler's War of Extermination in the East. Lexington, KY, 2011.

Fröhlich, Elke (ed.), *Die Tagebücher von Joseph Goebbels. Teil II Diktate 1941–1945, Band 1: Juli–September 1941*. Munich, 1996.

(ed.), *Die Tagebücher von Joseph Goebbels. Teil II Diktate 1941–1945, Band 2: Oktober–Dezember 1941*. Munich, 1996.

Fuchs Richardson, Horst (ed.), *Sieg Heil! War Letters of Tank Gunner Karl Fuchs 1937–1941*. Hamden, CT, 1987.

Fugate, Bryan I., *Operation Barbarossa. Strategy and Tactics on the Eastern Front, 1941*. Novato, CA, 1984.

Gander, Terry, *The German 88. The Most Famous Gun of the Second World War*. Barnsley, 2012.

Ganson, Nicholas, 'Food Supply, Rationing and Living Standards', in David Stone (ed.), *The Soviet Union at War*. Barnsley, 2010, pp. 69–92.

Garden, David and Kenneth Andrew (eds), *The War Diaries of a Panzer Soldier. Erich Hager with the 17th Panzer Division on the Russian Front 1941–1945*. Atglen, PA, 2010.

Gareis, Martin, *Kampf und Ende der Fränkisch-Sudetendeutschen 98. Infanterie-Division*. Eggolsheim, 1956.

Goldensohn, Leon (ed.), *Nuremberg Interviews. An American Psychiatrist's Conversations with the Defendants and Witnesses*. New York, 2004.

Golovchansky, Anatoly, Valentin Osipov, Anatoly Prokopenko, Ute Daniel and Jürgen Reulecke (eds), *'Ich will raus aus diesem Wahnsinn'. Deutsche Briefe von der Ostfront 1941–1945 Aus sowjetischen Archiven*. Hamburg, 1993.

Gorodetsky, Gabriel (ed.), *Stafford Cripps in Moscow 1940–1942. Diaries and Papers*. London, 2007.

Geldern, James von and Richard Stites (eds), *Mass Culture in Soviet Russia. Tales, Poems, Songs, Movies, Plays, and Folklore 1917–1953*. Bloomington, IN, 1995.

Gerlach, Christian, 'Die Einsatzgruppe B 1941/42', in Peter Klein (ed.), *Die Einsatzgruppen in der besetzten Sowjetunion 1941/42. Die Tätigkeits- und*

Lageberichte des Chefs der Sicherheitspolizei und des SD. Berlin, 1997, pp. 52–70.

'Hitlergegner bei der Heeresgruppe Mitte und die "verbrecherischen Befehle"', in Gerd R. Ueberschär (ed.), *NS-Verbrechen und der militärische Widerstand gegen Hitler*. Darmstadt, 2000, pp. 62–76.

Kalkulierte Morde. Die deutsche Wirtschafts- und Vernichtungspolitik in Weißrussland 1941 bis 1944. Hamburg, 2000.

'Men of 20 July and the War in the Soviet Union', in Hannes Heer and Klaus Naumann (eds), *War of Extermination. The German Military in World War* II *1941–1944*. New York and Oxford, 2006, pp. 127–45.

Geyer, Hermann, *Das* IX. *Armeekorps im Ostfeldzug 1941*. Neckargemünd, 1969.

Gilbert, Martin, *The Holocaust. The Jewish Tragedy*. London, 1986.

The Second World War. A Complete History. London, 2009.

Glantz, David M., *Barbarossa. Hitler's Invasion of Russia 1941*. Stroud, 2001.

Barbarossa Derailed. The Battle for Smolensk 10 July–10 September 1941, vol. 1: The German Advance, the Encirclement Battle, and the First and Second Soviet Counteroffensives, 10 July–24 August 1941. Solihull, 2010.

Barbarossa Derailed. The Battle for Smolensk 10 July–10 September 1941, vol. 2: The German Offensives on the Flanks and the Third Soviet Counteroffensive, 25 August–10 September 1941. Solihull, 2012.

Barbarossa Derailed. The Battle for Smolensk 10 July–10 September 1941, vol. 3: The Documentary Companion. Tables, Orders and Reports Prepared by Participating Red Army Forces. Solihull, 2014.

Colossus Reborn. The Red Army at War, 1941–1943. Lawrence, KS, 2005.

'Forgotten Battles', in The Military Book Club (ed.), *Slaughterhouse. The Encyclopedia of the Eastern Front*. New York, 2002, pp. 471–96.

Forgotten Battles of the German–Soviet War (1941–1945), vol. 1: The Summer–Fall Campaign (22 June–4 December 1941). Privately published study by David M. Glantz, 1999.

Soviet Military Deception in the Second World War. London, 1989.

Soviet Military Intelligence in War. Abingdon, 1990.

The Siege of Leningrad 1941–1944. 900 Days of Terror. Osceola, WI, 2001.

Glantz, David M. and Jonathan House, *When Titans Clashed. How the Red Army Stopped Hitler*, Lawrence, KS, 1995.

Gorinov, Mikhail M., 'Muscovites' Moods, 22 June 1941 to May 1942', in Robert Thurston and Bernd Bonwetsch (eds), *The People's War. Responses to World War* II *in the Soviet Union*. Chicago, IL, 2000, pp. 108–34.

Görlitz, Walter, *Paulus and Stalingrad*. London, 1963.

(ed.), *Paulus und Stalingrad. Lebensweg des Generalfeldmarschalls Friedrich Paulus*. Frankfurt am Main, 1960.

(ed.), *The Memoirs of Field-Marshal Keitel. Chief of the German High Command, 1938–1945*. New York, 1966.

Grenkevich, Leonid, *The Soviet Partisan Movement 1941–1944*. London, 1999.

Groehler, Olaf, 'Goals and Reason: Hitler and the German Military', in Joseph Wieczynski (ed.), *Operation Barbarossa. The German Attack on the Soviet Union June, 1941*. Salt Lake City, UT, 1993), pp. 48–61.

Gross, Gerhard P., *Mythos und Wirklichkeit. Geschichte des operativen Denkens im deutschen Heer von Moltke d.Ä. bis Heusinger*. Paderborn, 2012.

Guderian, Heinz, *Panzer Leader*. New York, 1996.

Günther, Helmut, *Hot Motors, Cold Feet. A Memoir of Service with the Motorcycle Battalion of SS-Division 'Reich' 1940–1941*. Winnipeg, 2004.

Haape, Heinrich, with Dennis Henshaw, *Moscow Tram Stop. A Doctor's Experiences with the German Spearhead in Russia*. London, 1957.

Habeck, Mary, *Storm of Steel. The Development of Armor Doctrine in Germany and the Soviet Union, 1919–1939*. New York, 2003.

Haffner, Sebastian, *Germany Jekyll and Hyde. A Contemporary Account of Nazi Germany*. London, 2008.

Hagelstam, Sonja, 'Families, Separation and Emotional Coping in War Bridging Letters Between Home and Front, 1941–44', in Tiina Kinnunen and Ville Kivimäki (eds), *Finland in World War II. History, Memory, Interpretations*. Boston, MA, 2012, pp. 277–312.

Haldane, Charlotte, *Russian Newsreel. An Eye-Witness Account of the Soviet Union at War*. New York, 1943.

Halder, Franz, *Hitler als Feldherr*. Munich, 1949.

Kriegstagebuch. Tägliche Aufzeichnungen des Chefs des Generalstabes des Heeres 1939–1942, Band II: Von der geplanten Landung in England bis zum Beginn des Ostfeldzuges (1.7.1940–21.6.1941), ed. Hans-Adolf Jacobsen. Stuttgart, 1963.

Kriegstagebuch. Tägliche Aufzeichnungen des Chefs des Generalstabes des Heeres 1939–1942, Band III: Der Russlandfeldzug bis zum Marsch auf Stalingrad (22.6.1941–24.9.1942), eds Hans-Adolf Jacobsen and Alfred Philippi. Stuttgart, 1964.

Hammer, Ingrid and Susanne zur Nieden (eds), *Sehr selten habe ich geweint. Briefe und Tagebücher aus dem Zweiten Weltkrieg von Menschen aus Berlin*. Zürich, 1992.

Hancock, Eleanor, *The National Socialist Leadership and Total War 1941–45*. New York, 1991.

Hardesty, Von, *Red Phoenix. The Rise of Soviet Air Power 1941–1945*. Washington, DC, 1982.

Hardesty, Von and Ilya Grinberg, *Red Phoenix Rising. The Soviet Air Force in World War II*. Lawrence, KS, 2012.

Harrison, Mark, 'Industry and the Economy', in David R. Stone (ed.), *The Soviet Union at War 1941–1945*. Barnsley, 2010, pp. 15–44.

Soviet Planning in Peace and War 1938–1945. Cambridge, 2002.

Hartmann, Christian, *Halder Generalstabschef Hitlers 1938–1942*. Munich, 1991.

'Massensterben oder Massenvernichtung? Sowjetische Kriegsgefangene im "Unternehmen Barbarossa". Aus dem Tagebuch eines deutschen Lagerkommandanten', *Vierteljahrshefte für Zeitgeschichte* 1 (2001): 97–158.

Operation Barbarossa. Nazi Germany's War in the East, 1941–1945. Oxford, 2013.

Wehrmacht im Ostkrieg. Front und militärisches Hinterland 1941/42. Munich, 2010.

Hartmann, Christian, Johannes Hürter and Ulrike Jureit (eds), *Verbrechen der Wehrmacht. Bilanz einer Debatte*. Munich, 2005.

Hasenclever, Jörn, *Wehrmacht und Besatzungspolitik. Die Befehlshaber der rückwärtigen Heeresgebiete 1941–1943*. Paderborn, 2010.

Hassell, Ulrich von, *The von Hassell Diaries 1938–1944*. London, 1948.

Vom Andern Deutschland. Freiburg, 1946.

Hastings, Max, *Bomber Command*. London, 1993.

Winston's War. Churchill, 1940–1945. New York, 2010.

Hayward, Joel, *Stopped at Stalingrad. The Luftwaffe and Hitler's Defeat in the East, 1942–1943*. Lawrence, KS, 1998.

Hébert, Valerie Geneviève, *Hitler's Generals on Trial. The Last War Crimes Tribunal at Nuremberg*. Lawrence, KS, 2010.

Heer, Hannes, 'Bittere Pflicht: der Rassenkrieg der Wehrmacht und seine Voraussetzungen', in Walter Manoschek (ed.), *Die Wehrmacht im Rassenkrieg. Der Vernichtungskrieg hinter der Front*. Vienna, 1996, pp. 116–41.

'How Amorality Became Normality: Reflections on the Mentality of German Soldiers on the Eastern Front', in Hannes Heer and Klaus Naumann (eds), *War of Extermination. The German Military in World War* II *1941–1944*. New York and Oxford, 2006, pp. 329–44.

'The Logic of the War of Extermination: the Wehrmacht and the Anti-Partisan War', in Hannes Heer and Klaus Naumann (eds), *War of Extermination. The German Military in World War* II *1941–1944*. New York and Oxford, 2006, pp. 92–126.

Heer, Hannes and Klaus Naumann (eds), *War of Extermination. The German Military in World War* II *1941–1944*. New York and Oxford, 2006.

Herring Jr, George C., *Aid to Russia 1941–1946: Strategy, Diplomacy. The Origins of the Cold War*. New York, 1973.

Herwig, Holger H., *The First World War. Germany and Austria-Hungary 1914–1918*. London, 1997.

Hilberg, Raul, *The Destruction of the European Jews*. New York, 1985.

'Wehrmacht und Judenvernichtung', in Walter Manoschek (ed.), *Die Wehrmacht im Rassenkrieg. Der Vernichtungskrieg hinter der Front.* Vienna, 1996. pp. 23–38.

Hill, Alexander, 'British Lend-Lease Aid and the Soviet War Effort, June 1941–June 1942', *Journal of Military History* 71(3) (2007): 773–808.

'British "Lend-Lease" Tanks and the Battle for Moscow, November–December 1941: A Research Note', *Journal of Slavic Military Studies* 19(2) (2006): 289–94.

'British Lend-Lease Tanks and the Battle for Moscow, November–December 1941: Revisited', *Journal of Slavic Military Studies* 22(4) (2009): 574–87.

The Great Patriotic War of the Soviet Union, 1941–45. A Documentary Reader. Abingdon and New York, 2010.

The War Behind the Eastern Front. The Soviet Partisan Movement in North-West Russia 1941–1944. New York, 2006.

Hillgruber, Andreas, *Hitlers Strategie. Politik und Kriegführung 1940–1941*. Bonn, 1993.

'The German Military Leaders' View of Russia Prior to the Attack on the Soviet Union', in Bernd Wegner (ed.), *From Peace to War. Germany, Soviet Russia and the World, 1939–1941*. Oxford, 1997, pp. 169–85.

Hindus, Maurice, *Mother Russia*. London, 1944.

Hinsley, H. F., 'British Intelligence and Barbarossa', in John Erickson and David Dilks (eds), *Barbarossa. The Axis and the Allies*. Edinburgh, 1998, pp. 43–75.

Hitler, Adolf, *Mein Kampf*. New York, 1999.

Hoeres, Peter, 'Die Slawen. Perzeptionen des Kriegsgegners bei den Mittelmächten. Selbst und Feindbild', in Gerhard P. Gross (ed.), *Die vergessene Front. Der Osten 1914/15*. Paderborn, 2006, pp. 179–200.

Hoffmann, Joachim, 'The Soviet Union's Offensive Preparations in 1941', in Bernd Wegner (ed.), *From Peace to War. Germany, Soviet Russia and the World, 1939–1941*. Oxford, 1997, pp. 361–80.

Holler, Martin, 'Extending the Genocidal Program: Did Otto Ohlendorf Initiate the Systematic Extermination of Soviet "Gypsies"?' in Alex J. Kay, Jeff Rutherford and David Stahel (eds), *Nazi Policy on the Eastern Front, 1941. Total War, Genocide and Radicalization*. Rochester, NY, 2012, pp. 267–88.

Hoth, Hermann, *Panzer-Operationen. Die Panzergruppe 3 und der operative Gedanke der deutschen Führung Sommer 1941*. Heidelberg, 1956.

Howell, Edgar M., *The Soviet Partisan Movement 1941–1944*. Washington, DC, 1956.

Humburg, Martin, *Das Gesicht des Krieges. Feldpostbriefe von Wehrmachtssoldaten aus der Sowjetunion 1941–1944*. Wiesbaden, 1998.

Hürter, Johannes (ed.), *Ein deutscher General an der Ostfront. Die Briefe und Tagebücher des Gotthard Heinrici 1941/42*. Erfurt, 2001.

Hitlers Heerführer. Die deutschen Oberbefehlshaber im Krieg gegen die Sowjetunion 1941/42. Munich, 2006.

Ingersoll, Ralph, *Action on All Fronts*. New York, 1942.

Irving, David, *Hitler's War*, vol. 1. New York, 1977.

Jacobsen, Hans-Adolf (ed.), *Kriegstagebuch des Oberkommandos der Wehrmacht (Wehrmachtfürungsstab), Band I/2: 1. August 1940–31. Dezember 1941*. Munich, 1982.

Jarausch, Konrad H. (ed.), *Reluctant Accomplice. A Wehrmacht Soldier's Letters from the Eastern Front*. Princeton, NJ, 2011.

Jarausch, Konrad H. and Klaus J. Arnold (eds), *'Das stille Sterben ...' Feldpostbriefe von Konrad Jarausch aus Polen und Russland 1939–1942*. Munich, 2008.

Jersak, Tobias, 'Die Interaktion von Kriegsverlauf und Judenvernichtung: ein Blick auf Hitlers Strategie im Spätsommer 1941', *Historische Zeitschrift* 268 (1999): 311–74.

Jones, Michael, *The Retreat. Hitler's First Defeat*. London, 2009.

Jones, Robert Huhn, *The Roads to Russia. United States Lend-Lease to the Soviet Union*. Norman, OK, 1969.

Jordan, Philip, *Russian Glory*. London, 1942.

Kahn, Martin, 'From Assured Defeat to "The Riddle of Soviet Military Success": Anglo-American Government Assessments of Soviet War Potential 1941–1943', *Journal of Slavic Military Studies* 26(3) (2013): 462–89.

'"Russia Will Assuredly be Defeated": Anglo-American Government Assessments of Soviet War Potential before Operation Barbarossa', *Journal of Slavic Military Studies* 25(2) (2012): 220–40.

Kallis, Aristotle A., *Nazi Propaganda and the Second World War*. New York, 2005.

Karner, Stefan and Wolfram Dornik (eds), *Die Besatzung der Ukraine 1918. Historischer Kontext – Forschungsstand – wirtschaftliche und soziale Folgen*. Graz, 2008.

Kay, Alex J., 'A "War in a Region beyond State Control"? The German–Soviet War, 1941–1944', *War in History* 18(1) (2011): 109–22.

Exploitation, Resettlement, Mass Murder. Political and Economic Planning for German Occupation Policy in the Soviet Union, 1940–1941. Oxford, 2006.

'Germany's Staatssekretäre, Mass Starvation and the Meeting of 2 May 1941', *Journal of Contemporary History* 41(4) (2006): 685–700.

'Revisiting the Meeting of the Staatssekretäre on 2 May 1941: A Response to Klaus Jochen Arnold and Gert C. Lübbers', *Journal of Contemporary History* 43(1) (2008): 93–104.

'"The Purpose of the Russian Campaign is the Decimation of the Slavic Population by Thirty Million": The Radicalisation of German Food

Policy in early 1941', in Alex J. Kay, Jeff Rutherford and David Stahel (eds), *Nazi Policy on the Eastern Front, 1941. Total War, Genocide and Radicalization*. Rochester, NY, 2012, pp. 101–29.

Kay, Alex J., 'Transition to Genocide, July 1941: Einsatzkommando 9 and the Annihilation of Soviet Jewry', *Holocaust and Genocide Studies* 27(3) (2013): 411–42.

Keegan, John, *Barbarossa. Invasion of Russia 1941*. New York, 1971.

The First World War. New York, 2000.

Kemp, Paul, *Convoy! Drama in Arctic Waters*. London, 1993.

Kern, Erich, *Dance of Death*, New York, 1951.

Kern, Ernst, *War Diary 1941–45. A Report*. New York, 1993.

Kershaw, Ian, *Fateful Choices. Ten Decisions that Changed the World, 1940–1941*. New York, 2007.

Hitler 1936–1945. Nemesis. London, 2001.

'"Working Towards the Führer": Reflections on the Nature of the Hitler Dictatorship', in Ian Kershaw and Moshe Lewin (eds), *Stalinism and Nazism. Dictatorships in Comparison*. Cambridge, 2003, pp. 88–106.

Kershaw, Robert, *War Without Garlands. Operation Barbarossa 1941/42*. New York, 2000.

Kesselring, Albrecht, *The Memoirs of Field-Marshal Kesselring*. London, 1988.

Kirchubel, Robert, *Hitler's Panzer Armies on the Eastern Front*. Barnsley, 2009.

Kitchen, Martin, *A World in Flames. A Short History of the Second World War in Europe and Asia 1939–1945*. London, 1990.

British Policy towards the Soviet Union during the Second World War. London, 1986.

Rommel's Desert War. Waging World War II *in North Africa, 1941–1943*. Cambridge, 2009.

Kivimäki, Ville and Tuomas Tepora, 'Meaningless Death or Regenerating Sacrifice? Violence and Social Cohesion in Wartime Finland', in Tiina Kinnunen and Ville Kivimäki (eds), *Finland in World War* II. *History, Memory, Interpretations*. Boston, MA, 2012, pp. 233–75.

Klee, Ernst, Willi Dressen and Volker Riess (eds), *'The Good Old Days'. The Holocaust as Seen by Its Perpetrators and Bystanders*. Old Saybrook, CT, 1991.

Klein, Peter (ed.), *Die Einsatzgruppen in der besetzten Sowjetunion 1941/42. Die Tätigkeits- und Lageberichte des Chefs der Sicherheitspolizei und des SD*. Berlin, 1997.

Kleindienst, Jürgen (ed.), *Sei tausendmal gegrüßt. Briefwechsel Irene und Ernst Guicking 1937–1945*. Berlin, 2001.

Klemperer, Victor, *Ich will Zeugnis ablegen bis zum letztem. Tagebücher 1933–1941*. Berlin, 1997.

Language of the Third Reich. London, 2006.

Klink, Ernst, 'The Conduct of Operations', in Militärgeschichtlichen Forschungsamt (ed.), *Germany and the Second World War, vol. IV: The Attack on the Soviet Union*. Oxford, 1998, pp. 525–763.

'The Military Concept of the War Against the Soviet Union', in Militärgeschichtlichen Forschungsamt (ed.), *Germany and the Second World War, vol. IV: The Attack on the Soviet Union*. Oxford, 1998, pp. 225–385.

Knappe, Siegfried, with Ted Brusaw, *Soldat. Reflections of a German Soldier, 1936–1949*. New York, 1992.

Knoblauch, Karl, *Zwischen Metz und Moskau. Als Soldat der 95. Infanteriedivision in Frankreich und als Fernaufklärer mit der 4.(4)/14 in Russland*.Würzburg, 2007.

Knopp, Guido, *Die Wehrmacht. Eine Bilanz*. Munich, 2007.

Knox, Alfred, *With the Russian Army 1914–1917. Being Chiefly Extracts from the Diary of a Military Attaché*. London, 1921.

Koch, Magnus, *Fahnenfluchten. Deserteure der Wehrmacht in Zweiten Weltkrieg: Lebenswege und Entscheidungen*. Paderborn, 2008.

Kotze, Hildegard von (ed.), *Heeresadjutant bei Hitler 1938–1943. Aufzeichnungen des Majors Engel*. Stuttgart, 1974.

Kozhevnikov, M. N., *The Command and Staff of the Soviet Army Air Force in the Great Patriotic War 1941–1945. A Soviet View*. Moscow, 1977.

Krausnick, Helmut and Hans-Heinrich Wilhelm, *Die Truppe des Weltanschauungskrieges. Die Einsatzgruppen der Sicherheitspolizei und des SD 1938–1942*. Stuttgart, 1981.

Krebs, Gerhard, 'Japan and the German–Soviet War, 1941', in Bernd Wegner (ed.), *From Peace to War. Germany, Soviet Russia and the World, 1939–1941*. Oxford, 1997, pp. 541–60.

Kris, Ernst and Hans Speier, *German Radio Propaganda. Report on Home Broadcasts During the War*. London, 1944.

Krivosheev, G. F. (ed.), *Soviet Casualties and Combat Losses in the Twentieth Century*. London, 1997.

Kroener, Bernhard R., 'The "Frozen *Blitzkrieg*": German Strategic Planning against the Soviet Union and the Causes of its Failure', in Bernd Wegner (ed.), *From Peace to War. Germany, Soviet Russia and the World, 1939–1941*. Oxford, 1997, pp. 135–49.

'The Winter Crisis of 1941–1942: the Distribution of Scarcity or Steps Towards a More Rational Management of Personnel', in Militärgeschichtliches Forschungsamt (ed.), *Germany and the Second World War, vol. V/I: Organization and Mobilization of the German Sphere of Power*. Oxford, 2000, pp. 1001–127.

Kubik, Willi, *Erinnerungen eines Panzerschützen 1941–1945. Tagebuchaufzeichnung eines Panzerschützen der Pz.Aufkl.Abt. 13 im Russlandfeldzug*. Würzburg, 2004.

Kühne, Thomas, *Kameradschaft. Die Soldaten des nationalsozialistischen Krieges und das 20. Jahrhundert*. Konstanz, 2006.

Kuhnert, Max, *Will We See Tomorrow? A German Cavalryman at War, 1939–1942*. London, 1993.

Kumanev, G. A., 'The Soviet Economy and the 1941 Evacuation', in Joseph Wieczynski (ed.), *Operation Barbarossa. The German Attack on the Soviet Union June 22, 1941*. Salt Lake City, UT, 1993, pp. 163–93.

Kunz, Norbert, 'Das Beispiel Charkow: Eine Stadtbevölkerung als Opfer der deutschen Hungerstrategie 1941/42', in Christian Hartmann, Johannes Hürter and Ulrike Jureit (eds), *Verbrechen der Wehrmacht. Bilanz einer Debatte*. Munich, 2005, pp. 136–44.

Kursietis, Andris J., *The Wehrmacht at War 1939–1945. The Units and Commanders of the German Ground Forces during World War II*. Soesterberg, 1999.

Lamb, Richard, 'Kluge', in Correlli Barnett (ed.), *Hitler's Generals*. London, 1989, pp. 395–409.

Lange, Horst, *Tagebücher aus dem Zweiten Weltkrieg*. Mainz, 1979.

Latzel, Klaus, 'Feldpostbriefe: Überlegungen für Aussagekraft einer Quelle', in Christian Hartmann, Johannes Hürter and Ulrike Jureit (eds), *Verbrechen der Wehrmacht. Bilanz einer Debatte*. Munich, 2005, pp. 171–81.

Leach, Barry, *German Strategy against Russia 1939–1941*. Oxford, 1973.

'Halder', in Correlli Barnett (ed.), *Hitler's Generals*. London, 1989, pp. 101–26.

Lederrey, E., *Germany's Defeat in the East. The Soviet Armies at War 1941–1945*. London, 1955.

Leyen, Ferdinand Prinz von der, *Rückblick zum Mauerwald. Vier Kriegsjahre im OKH*. Munich, 1965.

Liddell Hart, Basil, *The Other Side of the Hill*. London, 1999.

Lieven, Dominic, *Russia Against Napoleon. The Battle for Europe, 1807 to 1814*. London 2010.

Lingen, Kerstin von, *Kesselring's Last Battle. War Crimes Trials and Cold War Politics, 1945–1960*. Lawrence, KS, 2009.

Liulevicius, Vejas Gabriel, 'German Military Occupation and Culture on the Eastern Front in World War I', in Charles Ingrao and Franz A. J. Szabo (eds), *The Germans and the East*. West Lafayette, IN, 2008, pp. 201–8.

The German Myth of the East. 1800 to the Present. Oxford, 2011.

War Land on the Eastern Front. Culture, National Identity, and German Occupation in World War I. Cambridge, 2005.

Longerich, Peter, *The Unwritten Order. Hitler's Role in the Final Solution*. Stroud, 2005.

Lopukhovsky, Lev, *The Viaz'ma Catastrophe, 1941. The Red Army's Disastrous Stand Against Operation Typhoon*. Solihull, 2013.

Lower, Wendy, 'Axis Collaboration, Operation Barbarossa, and the Holocaust in Ukraine', in Alex J. Kay, Jeff Rutherford and David Stahel (eds), *Nazi Policy on the Eastern Front, 1941. Total War, Genocide and Radicalization*. Rochester, NY, 2012, pp. 186–219.

Nazi Empire-Building and the Holocaust in Ukraine. Chapel Hill, NC, 2005.

Lubbeck, William, with David B. Hurt, *At Leningrad's Gates. The Story of a Soldier with Army Group North*. Philadelphia, PA, 2006.

Lucas, James, *War of the Eastern Front 1941–1945. The German Soldier in Russia*. London, 1980.

Luck, Hans von, *Panzer Commander. The Memoirs of Colonel Hans von Luck*. New York, 1989.

Lukacs, John, *The Hitler of History*. New York, 1998.

Lunde, Henrik O., *Finland's War of Choice. The Troubled German–Finnish Coalition in World War II*. Havertown, PA, 2011.

Luther, Craig W. H., *Barbarossa Unleashed. The German Blitzkrieg through Central Russia to the Gates of Moscow*. Atglen, PA, 2013.

Macksey, Kenneth, *Guderian. Panzer General*. London, 1975.

Madeja, Victor, *Russo-German War. Autumn 1941: Defeat of Barbarossa*. Allentown, PA, 1988.

Magenheimer, Heinz, *Hitler's War. Germany's Key Strategic Decisions 1940–1945*. London, 1999.

Maisky, Ivan, *Memoirs of a Soviet Ambassador. The War 1939–43*. London, 1967.

Mallmann, Klaus M., Andrej Angrick, Jürgen Matthäus and Martin Cüppers (eds), *Die 'Ereignismeldung UdSSR' 1941. Dokumente der Einsatzgruppen in der Sowjetunion*. Darmstadt, 2011.

Mannerheim, Carl Gustaf Emil, *The Memoirs of Marshal Mannerheim*. London, 1953.

Manoschek, Walter (ed.), *'Es gibt nur eines für das Judentum: Vernichtung'. Das Judenbild in deutschen Soldatenbriefen 1939–1944*. Hamburg, 1995.

Manstein, Erich von, *Lost Victories*. Novato, 1958.

Verlorene Siege. Erinnerungen 1939–1944. Bonn, 1991.

Mark-Alan, Roy, *White Coats under Fire. With the Italian Expedition Corps in Russia: 1941*. New York, 1972.

Markwick, Roger D. and Euridice Charon Cardona, *Soviet Women on the Frontline in the Second World War*. London, 2012.

Matthaus, Jürgen, 'Die Beteiligung der Ordnungspolizei am Holocaust', in Wolf Kaiser (ed.), *Täter im Vernichtungskrieg. Der Überfall auf die Sowjetunion und der Völkermord an den Juden*. Berlin, 2002, pp. 166–85.

Mawdsley, Evan, *December 1941. Twelve Days that Began a World War*. New Haven, CT, 2011.

Thunder in the East. The Nazi-Soviet War 1941–1945. London, 2005.

Mazower, Mark, *Hitler's Empire. Nazi Rule in Occupied Europe*. London, 2009.

Megargee, Geoffrey P., 'A Blind Eye and Dirty Hands: the Sources of Wehrmacht Criminality in the Campaign against the Soviet Union', in Charles Ingrao and Franz A. J. Szabo (eds), *The Germans and the East*. West Lafayette, IN, 2008, pp. 310–27.

Inside Hitler's High Command. Lawrence, KS, 2000.

War of Annihilation. Combat and Genocide on the Eastern Front 1941. Lanham, MD, 2006.

Meier, Niklaus, *Warum Krieg? Die Sinndeutung des Krieges in der deutschen Militärelite 1871–1945*. Paderborn, 2012.

Meier-Welcker, Hans, *Aufzeichnungen eines Generalstabsoffiziers 1939–1942*. Freiburg, 1982.

Melvin, Mungo, *Manstein. Hitler's Greatest General*. New York, 2010.

Merridale, Catherine, *Ivan's War. Life and Death in the Red Army, 1939–1945*. New York, 2006.

Messenger, Charles, *The Last Prussian. A Biography of Field Marshal Gerd von Rundstedt 1875–1953*. London, 1991.

Metelmann, Henry, *Through Hell For Hitler*. Havertown, PA, 2005.

Meyer, Georg, *Adolf Heusinger. Dienst eines deutschen Soldaten 1915 bis 1964*. Berlin, 2001.

(ed.), *Generalfeldmarschall Wilhelm Ritter von Leeb. Tagebuchaufzeichnungen und Lagebeurteilungen aus zwei Weltkriegen*. Stuttgart, 1976.

Meyer-Düttingdorf, Ekkehard, 'Gereral der Inanterie Max von Schenkendorf', in Gerd R. Ueberschär (ed.), *Hitlers militärische Elite*. Darmstadt, 1998, pp. 210–17.

Militärgeschichtliches Forschungsamt (ed.), *Das Deutsche Reich und der Zweite Weltkrieg. Der Angriff auf die Sowjetunion*. Stuttgart, 1983.

Miner, Steven M., *Stalin's Holy War. Religion, Nationalism, and Alliance Politics, 1941–1945*. Chapel Hill, NC, 2003.

Ministry of Foreign Affairs of the USSR (ed.), *Stalin's Correspondence with Churchill, Attlee, Roosevelt and Truman 1941–1945*. New York, 1958.

Mitcham Jr, Samuel W., *The Men of Barbarossa. Commanders of the German Invasion of Russia, 1941*. Newbury, 2009.

The Panzer Legions. A Guide to the German Army Tank Divisions of WWII and their Commanders. Mechanicsburg, PA, 2007.

Moltke, Helmuth James von, *Letters to Freya. 1939–1945*. New York, 1990.

Moorhouse, Roger, *Berlin at War. Life and Death in Hitler's Capital, 1939–45*. London, 2010.

Moritz, Erhard (ed.), *Fall Barbarossa. Dokumente zur Vorbereitung der faschistischen Wehrmacht auf die Aggression gegen die Sowjetunion (1940/41)*. Berlin, 1970.

Muggeridge, Malcolm (ed.), *Ciano's Diary 1939–1943*. London, 1948.

Mühlhäuser, Regina, *Eroberungen. Sexuelle Gewalttaten und intime Beziehungen deutscher Soldaten in der Sowjetunion 1941–1945*. Hamburg, 2010.

Muller, Richard, *The German Air War in Russia*. Baltimore, MD, 1992.

Müller, Norbert, *Wehrmacht und Okkupation 1941–1944*. Berlin, 1971.

Müller, Rolf-Dieter, *An der Seite der Wehrmacht. Hitlers ausländische Helfer beim 'Kreuzzug gegen den Bolschewismus' 1941–1945*. Berlin, 2007.

'Beginnings of a Reorganization of the War Economy at the Turn of 1941/1942', in Militärgeschichtliches Forschungsamt (ed.), *Germany and the Second World War, vol.* V/I: *Organization and Mobilization of the German Sphere of Power*. Oxford, 2000, pp. 722–86.

'Das "Unternehmen Barbarossa" als wirtschaftlicher Raubkrieg', in Gerd R. Ueberschär and Wolfram Wette (eds), *'Unternehmen Barbarossa' Der deutsche Überfall auf die Sowjetunion 1941*. Paderborn, 1984, pp. 173–96.

'The Failure of the Economic "Blitzkrieg Strategy"', in Militärgeschichtliches Forschungsamt (ed.), *Germany and the Second World War, vol.* IV: *The Attack on the Soviet Union*. Oxford, 1998, pp. 1081–188.

'World Power Status through the Use of Poison Gas? German Preparations for Chemical Warfare, 1919–1945', in Wilhelm Deist (ed.), *The German Military in the Age of Total War*. Leamington Spa, 1985, pp. 171–209.

Müller, Rolf-Dieter and Gerd R. Ueberschär, *Hitler's War in the East 1941–1945. A Critical Assessment*. Oxford, 2009.

Müller-Hillebrand, Burkhart, *Das Heer 1933–1945, Band* III: *Der Zweifrontenkrieg. Das Heer vom Beginn des Feldzuges gegen die Sowjetunion bis zum Kriegsende*. Frankfurt am Main, 1969.

Mulligan, Timothy, 'Reckoning the Cost of the People's War: the German Experience in the Central USSR', *Russian History* 9(1) (1982): 27–48.

Munoz, Antonio (ed.), *Soviet Nationals in German Wartime Service 1941–1945*. n.p., 2007.

Munoz, Antonio and Oleg V. Romanko, *Hitler's White Russians. Collaboration, Extermination and Anti-Partisan Warfare in Byelorussia 1941–1944. A Study of White Russian Collaboration and German Occupation Policies*. New York, 2003.

Murray, Williamson, *Military Adaptation in War. With Fear of Change*. Cambridge, 2011.

The Luftwaffe 1933–45. Strategy for Defeat. Washington, 1996.

Nagorski, Andrew, *The Greatest Battle. Stalin, Hitler, and the Desperate Struggle for Moscow that Changed the Course of World War* II. New York, 2007.

Neiberg, Michael S. and David Jordan, *The Eastern Front 1914–1920. From Tannenberg to the Russo-Polish War*. London, 2008.

Neitzel, Sönke, *Tapping Hitler's Generals. Transcripts of Secret Conversations, 1942–45*. St. Paul, MN, 2007.

Neitzel, Sönke and Harald Welzer, *Soldaten. On Fighting, Killing and Dying*. London, 2012.

Neulen, Hans Werner, *In the Skies of Europe. Air Forces Allied to the Luftwaffe 1939–1945*. Marlborough, 2000.

Newton, Steven H., *Hitler's Commander. Field Marshal Walter Model: Hitler's Favorite General*. Cambridge, MA, 2006.

Niepold, Gerd, 'Plan Barbarossa', in David M. Glantz (ed.), *The Initial Period of War on the Eastern Front 22 June–August 1941*. London, 1997, pp. 66–77.

Obryn'ba, Nikolai I., *Red Partisan. The Memoir of a Soviet Resistance Fighter on the Eastern Front*. Washington, DC, 2007.

Ochsenknecht, Ingeborg, *'Als ob der Schnee alles zudeckte'. Eine Krankenschwester erinnert sich an ihren Kriegseinsatz an der Ostfront*. Berlin, 2005.

Overmans, Rüdiger, *Deutsche militärische Verluste im Zweiten Weltkrieg*. Munich, 2000.

Overmans, Rüdiger, Andreas Hilger and Paval Polian (eds), *Rotarmmisten in deutscher Hand. Dokumente zu Gefangenschaft, Repatriierung und Rehabilitierung sowjetischer Soldaten des Zweiten Weltkrieges*. Paderborn, 2012.

Overy, Richard, *Interrogations. The Nazi Elite in Allied Hands, 1945*. London, 2001.

Russia's War. London, 1997.

'Statistics', in I. C. B. Dear and M. R. D. Foot (eds), *The Oxford Companion to the Second World War*. Oxford, 1995, p. 1060.

The Air War 1939–1945. London, 1980.

The Dictators. Hitler's Germany and Stalin's Russia. London, 2004.

Why the Allies Won. New York, 1996.

Pabst, Helmut, *The Outermost Frontier. A German Soldier in the Russian Campaign*. London, 1957.

Pahl, Magnus, *Fremde Heere Ost. Hitlers militärische Feindaufklärung*. Berlin, 2012.

Parrish, Michael (ed.), *Battle for Moscow. The 1942 Soviet General Staff Study*. London, 1989.

Peitsch, Helmut, 'Towards a History of "Vergangenheitsbewältigung": East and West German War Novels of the 1950s', *Monatshefte* 87(3) (1995): 287–308.

Perau, Josef, *Priester im Heers Hitler. Erinnerungen 1940–1945*. Essen, 1962.

Perel, Solomon, *Europa Europa*. New York, 1997.

Pichler, Hans, *Truppenarzt und Zeitzeuge. Mit der 4. SS-Polizei-Division an vorderster Front*. Dresden, 2006.

Piekalkiewicz, Janusz, *Moscow 1941. The Frozen Offensive*. London, 1981.

Pietrow-Ennker, Bianka (ed.), *Präventivkrieg? Der deutsche Angriff auf die Sowjetunion*. Frankfurt am Main, 2011.

Plocher, Hermann, *The German Air Force versus Russia, 1941*. New York, 1965.

Pohl, Dieter, *Die Herrschaft der Wehrmacht. Deutsche Militärbesatzung und einheimische Bevölkerung in der Sowjetunion 1941–1944*. Munich, 2008.

Porter, Cathy and Mark Jones, *Moscow in World War* II. London, 1987.

Prince, K. Michael, *War and German Memory. Excavating the Significance of the Second World War in German Cultural Consciousness*. Lanham, MD, 2009.

Raack, R. C., 'Nazi Film Propaganda and the Horrors of War', *Historical Journal of Film, Radio and Television* 6(2) (1986): 189–95.

Radey, Jack and Charles Sharp, *The Defense of Moscow. The Northern Flank*. Barnsley, 2012.

Raebel, Geoffrey W., *The RAAF in Russia. 455 RAAF Squadron: 1942*. Loftus, NSW, 1997.

Rass, Christoph, *'Menschenmaterial':. Deutsche Soldaten an der Ostfront: Innenansichten einer Infanteriedivision 1939–1945*. Paderborn, 2003.

Raus, Erhard, *Panzer Operations. The Eastern Front Memoir of General Raus, 1941–1945*, comp. and trans. Steven H. Newton. Cambridge, MA, 2005.

Rauss, Erhard, 'Effects of Climate on Combat in European Russia', in Peter G. Tsouras (ed.) *Fighting in Hell. The German Ordeal on the Eastern Front*. New York, 1997, pp. 145–224.

'The Russian Soldier and the Russian Conduct of Battle', in Peter G. Tsouras (ed.), *Fighting in Hell. The German Ordeal on the Eastern Front*. New York, 1997, pp. 16–51.

Reddemann, Karl (ed.), *Zwischen Front und Heimat. Der Briefwechsel des münsterischen Ehepaares Agnes und Albert Neuhaus 1940–1944*. Münster, 1996.

Rees, Laurence, *War of the Century. When Hitler Fought Stalin*. London, 1999.

Reese, Roger R., *Stalin's Reluctant Soldiers. A Social History of the Red Army 1925–1941*. Lawrence, KS, 1996.

Why Stalin's Soldiers Fought. The Red Army's Military Effectiveness in World War II. Lawrence, KS, 2011.

Reese, Willy Peter, *A Stranger to Myself. The Inhumanity of War: Russia, 1941–1944*. New York, 2005.

Rehfeldt, Hans Heinz, *Mit dem Eliteverband des Heeres 'Grossdeutschland' tief in den Weiten Russlands. Erinnerungen eines Angehörigen des Granatwerferzuges 8. Infanterierregiment (mot.) 'Grossdeutschland' 1941–1943*. Würzburg, 2008.

Reinhardt, Hans, 'Panzer-Gruppe 3 in der Schlacht von Moskau und ihre Erfahrungen im Rückzug', *Wehrkunde* 9 (1953): 1–11.

Reinhardt, Klaus, *Moscow: The Turning Point. The Failure of Hitler's Strategy in the Winter of 1941–42*. Oxford 1992.

Reitlinger, Gerald, *The House Built on Sand. The Conflicts of German Policy in Russia 1939–45*. London, 1960.

The SS. Alibi of a Nation 1922–1945. London, 1981.

Reynolds, Quentin, *Only the Stars are Neutral*. London, 1944.

Rhodes, Richard, *Masters of Death. The SS Einsatzgruppen and the Invention of the Holocaust*. New York, 2003.

Rich, Norman, *Hitler's War Aims. Ideology, the Nazi State, and the Course of Expansion*. New York, 1972.

Richter, Timm C., 'Die Wehrmacht und der Partisanenkrieg in den besetzten Gebiezen der Sowjetunion', in Rolf-Dieter Müller and Hans-Erich Volkmann (eds), *Die Wehrmacht. Mythos und Realität*. Munich, 1999, pp. 837–57.

Robbins Landon, H. C. and Sebastian Leitner (eds), *Diary of a German Soldier*. London, 1963.

Roberts, Andrew, *The Storm of War. A New History of the Second World War*. London, 2009.

Roberts, Geoffrey, *Stalin's General. The Life of Georgy Zhukov*. New York, 2012.

Rokossovsky, K., *A Soldier's Duty*. Moscow, 1985.

Römer, Felix, *Der Kommissarbefehl. Wehrmacht und NS-Verbrechen an der Ostfront 1941/42*. Paderborn, 2008.

'"Kein Problem für die Truppe"', *Die Zeit Geschichte – Hitlers Krieg im Osten* 2 (2011): 42–5.

'The Wehrmacht in the War of Ideologies: the Army and Hitler's Criminal Orders on the Eastern Front', in Alex J. Kay, Jeff Rutherford and David Stahel (eds), *1941 and Nazi Policy on the Eastern Front. Total War, Genocide and Radicalization*. Rochester, NY, 2012, pp. 73–100.

Rössler, Mechthild and Sabine Schleiermacher (eds), *Der "Generalplan Ost". Hauptlinien der nationalsozialistischen Planungs und Vernichtungspolitik*. Berlin, 1993.

Röttiger, Hans, 'XXXXI Panzer Corps during the Battle of Moscow in 1941 as a Component of Panzer Group 3', in Steven H. Newton (ed.), *German Battle Tactics in the Russian Front 1941–1945*. Atglen, PA, 1994, pp. 13–54.

Rubenstein, Joshua and Ilya Altman (eds), *The Unknown Black Book. The Holocaust in the German-Occupied Soviet Territories*. Bloomington, IN, 2008.

Rudel, Hans-Ulrich, *Stuka Pilot*. New York, 1979.

Ruegg, Bob and Arnold Hague, *Convoys to Russia 1941–1945. Allied Convoys and Naval Surface Operations in Arctic Waters 1941–1945*. Kendal, 1993.

Rutherford, Jeff, *Combat and Genocide on the Eastern Front. The German Infantry's War, 1941–1944*. Cambridge, 2014.

'The Radicalization of German Occupation Policies: *Wirtschaftsstab Ost* and the 121st Infantry Division in Pavlovsk, 1941', in Alex J. Kay, Jeff Rutherford and David Stahel (eds), *Nazi Policy on the Eastern Front, 1941. Total War, Genocide and Radicalization*. Rochester, NY, 2012, pp. 130–54.

Rzhevskaia, Elena, 'Roads and Days: the Memoirs of a Red Army Translator', *Journal of Slavic Military Studies* 14(1) (2001): 53–106.

Sáiz, Agustin, *Deutsche Soldaten. Uniforms, Equipment & Personal Items of the German Soldier 1939–45*. Madrid, 2008.

Salisbury, Harrison E. (ed.), *Marshal Zhukov's Greatest Battles*. London, 1971.

Schall-Riaucour, Heidemarie Gräfin, *Aufstand und Gehorsam. Offizierstum und Generalstab im Umbruch. Leben und Wirken von Generalobberst Franz Halder Generalstabchef 1938–1942*. Wiesbaden, 1972.

Schäufler, Hans (ed.), *Knight's Cross Panzers. The German 35th Panzer Regiment in WWII*. Mechanicsburg, PA, 2010.

Panzer Warfare on the Eastern Front. Mechanicsburg, PA, 2012.

Scheck, Raffael, *Hitler's African Victims. The German Army Massacres of Black French Soldiers in 1940*. New York, 2006.

Scheil, Stefan, *Präventivkrieg Barbarossa. Fragen, Fakten, Antworten*. Frankfurt, 2011.

Scheuer, Alois, *Briefe aus Russland. Feldpostbriefe des Gefreiten Alois Scheuer 1941–1942*. St Ingbert, 2000.

Schober, Franz and Leopold, *Briefe von der Front. Feldpostbriefe 1939–1945*, ed. Michael Hans Salvesberger. Gösing am Wagram, 1997.

Schofield, B. B., *The Arctic Convoys*. London, 1977.

Schraepler, Hans-Albrecht Max (ed.), *At Rommel's Side. The Lost Letters of Hans-Joachim Schraepler*. London, 2007.

Schreiber, Gerhard, 'Mussolini's "Non-Belligerence"', in Militärgeschichtlichen Forschungsamt (ed.), *Germany and the Second World War, vol. III: The Mediterranean, South-east Europe and North Africa 1939–1941*. Oxford, 1995, pp. 8–98.

Schüler, Klaus, 'The Eastern Campaign as a Transportation and Supply Problem', in Bernd Wegner (ed.), *From Peace to War. Germany, Soviet Russia and the World, 1939–1941*. Oxford, 1997, pp. 205–22.

Schulte, Theo J., 'Die Wehrmacht und die nationalsozialistische Besatzungspolitik in der Sowjetunion', in Roland G. Foerster (ed.), *'Unternehmen Barbarossa'. Zum historischen Ort der deutsch-sowjetischen Beziehungen von 1933 bis Herbst 1941*. Munich, 1993, pp. 163–76.

The German Army and Nazi Policies in Occupied Russia. Oxford, 1989.

Schwabedissen, Walter, *The Russian Air Force in the Eyes of the German Commanders*. New York, 1960.

Seaton, Albert, *Stalin as Warlord*. London, 1976.
The Battle for Moscow. New York, 1971.
The Russo-German War 1941–45. Novato, CA, 1971.
Sebastian, Mihail, *Journal, 1935–1944*. London, 2003.
Seidler, Franz W., *Verbrechen an der Wehrmacht*. Selent, 1997.
Sevruk, Vladimir (ed.), *Moscow Stalingrad 1941–1942. Recollections, Stories, Reports*. Moscow, 1970.
Shepherd, Ben, 'The Clean Wehrmacht, the War of Extermination, and Beyond', *Historical Journal* 52(2) (2009): 455–73.
War in the Wild East. The German Army and Soviet Partisans. Cambridge, MA, 2004.
Shils, Edward A. and Morris Janowitz, 'Cohesion and Disintegration in the Wehrmacht in World War II', *Public Opinion Quarterly* 12(2) (1948): 280–315.
Showalter, Dennis E., *Hitler's Panzers. The Lightning Attacks that Revolutionized Warfare*. New York, 2009.
Tannenberg. Clash of Empires, 1914. Dulles, VA, 2004.
Skorzeny, Otto, *Skorzeny's Special Missions. The Memoir of Hitler's Most Daring Commando*. London, 2006.
Slepyan, Kenneth, *Stalin's Guerrillas. Soviet Partisans in World War II*. Lawrence, KS, 2006.
Smelser, Ronald and Edward J. Davies II, *The Myth of the Eastern Front. The Nazi–Soviet War in American Popular Culture*. Cambridge, 2008.
Smith, Howard K., *Last Train from Berlin*. New York, 1943.
Snyder, Timothy, *Bloodlands. Europe between Hitler and Stalin*. New York, 2010.
Sondhaus, Lawrence, *Franz Conrad von Hötzendorf. Architect of the Apocalypse*. Boston, MA, 2000.
Speer, Albert, *Inside the Third Reich*. London, 1971.
Stader, Ingo (ed.), *Ihr daheim und wir hier draußen. Ein Briefwechsel zwischen Ostfront und Heimat Juni 1941–März 1943*. Cologne, 2006.
Stahel, David, *Kiev 1941. Hitler's Battle for Supremacy in the East*. Cambridge, 2012.
Operation Barbarossa and Germany's Defeat in the East. Cambridge, 2009.
Operation Typhoon. Hitler's March on Moscow, October 1941. Cambridge, 2013.
'Radicalizing Warfare: The German Command and the Failure of Operation Barbarossa', in Alex J. Kay, Jeff Rutherford and David Stahel (eds), *Nazi Policy on the Eastern Front, 1941. Total War, Genocide and Radicalization*. Rochester, NY, 2012, pp. 19–44.
Stahl, Friedrich-Christian, 'Generaloberst Rudolf Schmidt', in Gerd R. Ueberschär (ed.), *Hitlers militärische Elite*. Darmstadt, 1998, pp. 218–25.

Stahlberg, Alexander, *Bounden Duty. The Memoirs of a German Officer 1932–45*. London, 1990.

Statiev, Alexander, '"La Garde meurt mais ne se rend pas!" Once Again on the 28 Panfilov Heroes', *Kritika: Explorations in Russian and Eurasian History* 13(4) (2012): 769–98.

Steiger, Rudolf, *Armour Tactics in the Second World War. Panzer Army Campaigns of 1939–41 in German War Diaries*. Oxford, 1991.

Stein, George H., *The Waffen SS. Hitler's Elite Guard at War 1939–1945*. New York, 1984.

Stein, Marcel, *A Flawed Genius. Field Marshal Walter Model. A Critical Biography*. Solihull, 2010.

Field Marshal von Manstein. The Janus Head: A Portrait. Solihull, 2007.

Steinert, Marlis G., *Hitler's War and the Germans. Public Mood and Attitude during the Second World War*, ed. and trans. Thomas E. J. de Witt. Athens, OH, 1977.

Steinkamp, Peter, 'Die Haltung der Hitlergegner Generalfeldmarschall Wilhelm Ritter von Leeb und Generaloberst Erich Hoepner zur verbrecherischen Kriegführung bei der Heeresgruppe Nord in der Sowjetunion 1941', in Gerd R. Ueberschär (ed.), *NS-Verbrechen und der militärische Widerstand gegen Hitler*. Darmstadt, 2000, pp. 47–61.

Stern, J. P., *Hitler. The Führer and the People*. Berkeley, CA, 1992.

Stone, Norman, *The Eastern Front 1914–1917*. London, 1998.

Strachan, Hew, 'Die Vorstellungen der Anglo-Amerikaner von der Wehrmacht', in Rolf-Dieter Müller and Hans-Erich Volkmann (eds), *Die Wehrmacht. Mythos und Realität*. Munich, 1999, pp. 92–104.

The First World War, vol. I: To Arms. Oxford, 2003.

'Time, Space and Barbarisation: the German Army and the Eastern Front in Two World Wars', in George Kassimeris (ed.), *The Barbarization of Warfare*. New York, 2006, pp. 58–82.

Streim, Alfred, 'International Law and Soviet Prisoners of War', in Bernd Wegner (ed.), *From Peace to War. Germany, Soviet Russia and the World, 1939–1941*. Oxford, 1997, pp. 293–308.

Streit, Christian, 'Die Behandlung der sowjetischen Kriesgefangenen und völkerrechtliche Probleme des Krieges gegen die Sowjetunion', in Gerd R. Ueberschär and Wolfram Wette (eds), *'Unternehmen Barbarossa' Der deutsche Überfall auf die Sowjetunion 1941*. Paderborn, 1984, pp. 197–218.

'Die sowjetischen Kriegsgefangenen in der Hand der Wehrmacht', in Walter Manoschek (ed.), *Die Wehrmacht im Rassenkrieg. Der Vernichtungskrieg hinter der Front*. Vienna, 1996, pp. 74–89.

Keine Kameraden. Die Wehrmacht und die sowjetischen Kriegsgefangenen 1941–1945. Bonn, 1997.

'Partisans – Resistance – Prisoners of War', in Joseph Wieczynski (ed.), *Operation Barbarossa. The German Attack on the Soviet Union June 22, 1941*. Salt Lake City, UT, 1993, pp. 260–75.

'Soviet Prisoners of War in the Hands of the Wehrmacht', in Hannes Heer and Klaus Naumann (eds), *War of Extermination. The German Military in World War* II *1941–1944*. New York and Oxford, 2006, pp. 80–91.

'The German Army and the Policies of Genocide', in Gerhard Hirschfeld (ed.), *The Policies of Genocide. Jews and Soviet Prisoners of War in Nazi Germany*. London, 1986, pp. 1–14.

Sulzberger, Cyrus Leo, *A Long Row of Candles. Memoirs and Diaries 1934–1954*, Toronto, 1969.

Suvorov, Viktor, *Icebreaker. Who Started the Second World War?* London, 1990.

Sweeting, C. G., *Blood and Iron. The German Conquest of Sevastopol*. Washington, DC, 2004.

Taylor, Brian, *Barbarossa to Berlin. A Chronology of the Campaigns on the Eastern Front 1941 to 1945, vol. 1: The Long Drive East 22 June 1941 to 18 November 1942*. Staplehurst, 2003.

Taylor, John, 'Hitler and Moscow 1941', *Journal of Slavic Military Studies* 26(3) (2013): 490–527.

Thurston, Robert, 'Cauldrons of Loyalty and Betrayal: Soviet Soldiers' Behavior, 1941 and 1945', in Robert Thurston and Bernd Bonwetsch (eds), *The People's War. Responses to World War* II *in the Soviet Union*. Chicago, IL, 2000, pp. 235–57.

Tilemann, Walter, *Ich, das Soldatenkind*. Munich, 2005.

Tooze, Adam, *The Wages of Destruction. The Making and Breaking of the Nazi Economy*. London, 2006.

Topitsch, Ernst, *Stalin's War. A Radical New Theory of the Origins of the Second World War*. New York, 1987.

Traditionverband der Division (ed.), *Geschichte der 3. Panzer-Division. Berlin-Brandenburg 1935–1945*. Berlin, 1967.

Trevor-Roper, Hugh (ed.), *Hitler's Table Talk, 1941–1944. His Private Conversations*. London, 2000.

(ed.), *Hitler's War Directives 1939–1945*. London, 1964.

True To Type. A Selection From Letters and Diaries of German Soldiers and Civilians Collected on the Soviet–German Front (London, n.d.). (This book makes no reference to its editor or date of publication.)

Tsouras, Peter (ed.), *Panzers on the Eastern Front. General Erhard Raus and his Panzer Divisions in Russia 1941–1945*. London, 2002.

Turney, Alfred W., *Disaster At Moscow. Von Bock's Campaigns 1941–1942*. Albuquerque, NM, 1970.

Tuyll, Hubert P. van, *Feeding the Bear. American Aid to the Soviet Union, 1941–1945*. Westport, CT, 1989.

Ueberschär, Gerd R., 'Armeebefehl des Oberbefehlshabers der 6. Armee, Generalfeldmarschall von Reichenau, vom 10.10.1941', in Gerd R. Ueberschär and Wolfram Wette (eds), *'Unternehmen Barbarossa' Der deutsche Überfall auf die Sowjetunion 1941*. Paderborn, 1984, pp. 339–40.

'Das Scheitern des Unternehmens "Barbarossa". Der deutsch-sowjetische Krieg vom Überfall bis zur Wende vor Moskau im Winter 1941/42', in Gerd Ueberschär and Wolfram Wette (eds), *"Unternehmen Barbarossa" Der deutsche Überfall auf die Sowjetunion 1941*. Paderborn, 1984, pp. 140–72.

Ueberschär, Gerd R. and Lev A. Bezymenskij (eds), *Der deutsche Angriff auf die Sowjetunion 1941. Die Kontroverse um die Präventivkriegsthese*. Darmstadt, 1998.

Ueberschär, Gerd R. and Wolfram Wette (eds), *"Unternehmen Barbarossa" Der deutsche Überfall auf die Sowjetunion 1941*. Paderborn, 1984.

Vaizey, Hester, *Surviving Hitler's War. Family Life in Germany, 1939–48*. London, 2010.

Vorobyov, Yevgeny, 'Sanctum Sanctorum', in S. Krasilshchik (ed.) *World War II. Dispatches from the Soviet Front*. New York, 1985, pp. 38–43.

Wagener, Carl, *Moskau 1941. Der Angriff auf die russische Hauptstadt*. Dorheim, 1985.

Wagner, Elisabeth (ed.), *Der Generalquartiermeister. Briefe und Tagebuchaufzeichnungen des Generalquartiermeisters des Heeres General der Artillerie Eduard Wagner*. Munich, 1963.

Wagner, Ray, *The Soviet Air Force in World War II. The Official History, Originally Published by the Ministry of Defense of the USSR*. Melbourne, 1974.

Warlimont, Walter, *Im Hauptquartier der deutschen Wehrmacht 1939 bis 1945, Band 1: September 1939–November 1942*. Koblenz, 1990.

Inside Hitler's Headquarters, 1939–1945. New York, 1964.

Washburn, Stanley, *Field Notes from the Russian Front*. London, 1915.

Weal, John, *More Bf 109 Aces of the Russian Front*. Oxford, 2007.

Weeks, Albert L., *Russia's Life-Saver. Lend-Lease Aid to the U.S.S.R. in World War II*. Lanham, MD, 2004.

Weinberg, Gerhard L., '22 June 1941: The German View', *War in History* 3(2) (1996): 225–33.

A World at Arms. A Global History of World War II. Cambridge, 1994.

(ed.), *Hitler's Second Book*. New York, 2003.

'The Yelnya–Dorogobuzh area of Smolensk Oblast', in John A. Armstrong (ed.), *Soviet Partisans in World War II*. Madison, WI, 1964, pp. 389–457.

Weiner, Amir, 'Something to Die For, a Lot to Kill For: the Soviet System and the Barbarisation of Warfare, 1939–1945', in George Kassimeris (ed.), *The Barbarization of Warfare*. New York, 2006, pp. 101–25.

Werth, Alexander, *Russia At War 1941–1945*. New York, 1964.

Westermann, Edward B., *Hitler's Police Battalions. Enforcing Racial Warfare in the East*. Lawrence, KS, 2005.

Wette, Wolfram, 'Die Krieg gegen die Sowjetunion: ein Rassen-ideologische begründeter Vernichtungskrieg', in Wolf Kaiser (ed.), *Täter im Vernichtungskrieg. Der Überfall auf die Sowjetunion und der Völkermord an den Juden*. Berlin, 2002, pp. 15–38.

'Juden, Bolschewisten, Slawen. Rassenideologische Rußland-Feindbilder Hitlers und der Wehrmachtgeneräle', in Bianka Pietrow-Ennker (ed.), *Präventivkrieg? Der deutsche Angriff auf die Sowjetunion*. Frankfurt am Main, 2011, pp. 40–58.

'"Rassenfeind". Antisemitismus und Antislawismus in der Wehrmachtspropaganda', in Walter Manoschek (ed.), *Die Wehrmacht im Rassenkrieg. Der Vernichtungskrieg hinter der Front*. Vienna, 1996, pp. 55–73.

Retter in Uniform. Handlungsspielräume im Vernichtungskrieg der Wehrmacht. Frankfurt am Main, 2003.

The Wehrmacht. History, Myth, Reality. Cambridge, 2006.

Wettstein, Adrian, 'Operation "Barbarossa" und Stadtkampf', *Militärgeschichtliche Zeitschrift* 66 (2007): 21–44.

'Urban Warfare Doctrine on the Eastern Front', in Alex J. Kay, Jeff Rutherford and David Stahel (eds), *Nazi Policy on the Eastern Front, 1941. Total War, Genocide and Radicalization*. Rochester, NY, 2012, pp. 45–72.

Wildermuth, David W., 'Widening the Circle: General Weikersthal and the War of Annihilation, 1941–42', *Central European History* 45 (2012): 306–24.

Will, Otto, *Tagebuch eines Ostfront-Kämpfers. Mit der 5. Panzerdivision im Einsatz 1941–1945*. Selent, 2010.

Zaloga, Steven J. and James Grandsen, *Soviet Tanks and Combat Vehicles of World War Two*. London, 1984.

Zetterling, Niklas and Anders Frankson, *The Drive on Moscow, 1941. Operation Taifun and Germany's First Great Crisis in World War* II. Havertown, PA, 2012.

Zhukov, G. K., *Marshal of the Soviet Union G. Zhukov. Reminiscences and Reflections*, 2 vols. Moscow, 1985.

The Memoirs of Marshal Zhukov. London, 1971.

Ziemke, Earl F., 'Franz Halder at Orsha: the German General Staff Seeks a Consensus', *Military Affairs* 39(4) (1975): 173–6.

'Rundstedt', in Correlli Barnett (ed.), *Hitler's Generals*. London, 1989, pp. 175–207.

The Red Army 1918–1941. From Vanguard of World Revolution to US Ally. London, 2004.

Ziemke, Earl F. and Magna E. Bauer, *Moscow to Stalingrad. Decision in the East*. New York, 1988.

Documentaries

Knopp, Guido, *Die Wehrmacht. Eine Bilanz*, episode 4: 'Widerstand in Uniform', 2007.

Kot, Michael and Margaret O'Brien, *Perfect Storms. Disasters that Changed the World*, episode six: 'Hitler's Frozen Army', 2013.

Verhoeven, Michael, *Der unbekannte Soldat*, 2007.

INDEX

Maps, photographs and illustrations are denoted in bold typeface.